W9-DAW-584

ENCYCLOPEDIA
OF EDUCATION
AND HUMAN
DEVELOPMENT

VOLUME THREE

ENCYCLOPEDIA OF EDUCATION AND HUMAN DEVELOPMENT

STEPHEN J. FARENGA
AND DANIEL NESS
EDITORS

VOLUME THREE

FOREWORD BY JAMES H. BORLAND

M.E.Sharpe
Armonk, New York
London, England

Library of Congress Cataloging-in-Publication Data

Encyclopedia of education and human development / Stephen J. Farenga and Daniel Ness, editors.
     p. cm.
Includes bibliographical references and index.
ISBN 0-7656-1268-2 (hardcover : alk. paper)
  1. Education—Encyclopedias. 2. Educational psychology—Encyclopedias. I. Farenga, Stephen J., 1958–
II. Ness, Daniel, 1966–

LB15.E473 2005
370'.3—dc22   004030349

Printed in the United States of America

The paper used in this publication meets the minimum requirements of
American National Standard for Information Sciences
Permanence of Paper for Printed Library Materials,
ANSI Z 39.48-1984.

MV (c)   10   9   8   7   6   5   4   3   2   1

Publisher: Myron E. Sharpe
Vice President and Editorial Director: Patricia Kolb
Vice President and Production Director: Carmen Chetti
Executive Editor and Manager of Reference: Todd Hallman
Production Editor: Jennifer Morettini
Program Coordinator: Cathleen Prisco
Compositor: Zeph Ernest
Text Design: Carmen Chetti
Cover Design: Jesse Sanchez

Contents

Tables and Figures

Tables

Figures

ENCYCLOPEDIA
OF EDUCATION
AND HUMAN
DEVELOPMENT

VOLUME THREE

23

LANGUAGE DEVELOPMENT

The field of linguistics, which is concerned with understanding and describing language, and the field of psycholinguistics, which undertakes the study of how language is comprehended and produced, have contributed to what we know about child language development. Psycholinguistics is a branch of cognitive psychology. Cognitive psychologists conduct research to understand how the human mind represents the real world. Psycholinguists have developed theories and research processes to untangle the mysteries of language development. A major concern of some psycholinguists is how children acquire language with the ease and relative speed that has been observed.

Scholars have attempted to clarify the relationships between thought and language for generations. Does language control the way we think and observe the world, or do our cognitive abilities regulate our development of language? Can humans think without language? Are language and thinking identical? Perhaps they are not. Artists sometimes think in colors and shapes, and musicians think about pitch, rhythm, timbre, and other musical elements without using language. Rudolf Arnheim, a psychologist of art and proponent of visual thinking, acknowledged that, although language might not be essential for thought, it can aid thought.

Linguists and anthropologists Edward Sapir and Benjamin Lee Whorf developed a widely influential theory in the early 1900s. The Sapir-Whorf hypothesis claimed that language determines the way humans think and that distinctions about the world vary according to one's native language. An example of the theory compares English and Hopi words. In Hopi, only one word is used for everything that flies with the exception of birds, but in English, there are separate words for insects, airplanes, balloons, and other flying objects. The theory suggested that individuals categorize and label things according to

what is available in their language. This theory has been criticized because it might not follow that a speaker of a language is unable to grasp a concept simply because a language lacks a word for that concept.

An opposing view of language and thought was offered by Swiss psychologist Jean Piaget, who argued that it is one's conceptual and cognitive development that enables language to develop—not the other way around. That is, humans must be able to think and form concepts for language to develop.

American linguist Noam Chomsky proposed a somewhat different theory. He regarded cognitive development as a necessary but insufficient condition for language development, and he believed that humans also must draw upon an innate language-acquisition device. It is this innate ability that makes language learning possible. An innate capacity for language learning has yet to be verified, but the presence of a language instinct makes intuitive sense to many scholars.

Like Sapir and Whorf, Russian psychologist Lev Vygotsky (1962) viewed concept development as a type of social constructivism wherein important concepts are learned through the medium of language. Such learning, however, develops from social interactions between language users. In time, researchers might definitively sort out the relationships between thought and language.

From the time of their birth until they enter first grade, children develop a degree of facility with the many complexities of language. For example, a six-month-old child may only babble, but a six-year-old is able to describe in detail the series of actions of a parent or friend, although the actions may have been unpredictable (e.g., *Dad stood on his hands. He tipped over.*). Learning continues throughout one's lifetime, and it is likely that language never is completely learned. A six-year-old, however, has developed a considerable amount of control over a complex system of communication.

It has been theorized that children are born with a natural instinct for language but not for any particular language. Children learn whichever language is used by parents and caregivers as they adapt to the particular culture into which they are born. Thousands of languages are spoken across the globe. Some are spoken by only a handful of people, such as Busa-Boko, spoken in parts of Nigeria and Benin, while other languages, such as Russian and French, are spoken by millions. Children born to families of one language and culture develop language in much the same way as those of others. Language is not learned separately, as is walking or riding a bicycle. Language develops as part of nearly everything that a child experiences. Being dressed, being fed, and, later, getting dressed and eating are occasions for language learning. Language penetrates nearly every waking activity. Children do more than echo what they hear. In preparation for language, infants coo and babble in self-directed activity. Imitation is a part of language acquisition, but imitation often is experimental and creative. Children often say *mouses* for *mice*, for example, and *goed* or *goned* for *went*. These are not imitations of what they have heard. Such errors represent overextensions of syntactic rules that have been internalized—adding *s* for plurals and *ed* for past tense.

Language development does not follow any tight sequence. Children do not first learn every speech sound of a language, and then the words, and then the sentence patterns. Language is a highly complicated system of interrelated codes used to understand and convey meaning. For children with no hearing problems, language is initially oral. They develop oral language years before they begin to understand the functions of written language and learn to read and write. Children with hearing impairments develop language through signing, finger spelling, and lip reading.

In English, the oral code consists of forty-four distinct speech sounds that can be combined and recombined to represent all the words one learns and uses. Words may be thought of as labels for concepts, and in the preschool years, most words are learned orally. By learning to discriminate among speech sounds, children recognize that combinations of sounds represent specific concepts. As they learn to understand and articulate words, children develop the earliest stages of language. From that point on, language development escalates as children learn to understand and utter sentences and experiment with intonation patterns.

Swiss semiotician Ferdinand de Saussure believed that understanding anything in the world around us is dependent on the interpretation of signs (Crystal 1997). Thunder and lightning on a cloudy day are a sign that a storm is near. Removing one's hat when a flag bearer marches past is a sign of respect. Words are signs for concepts. For children to learn a word, they must have a mental representation or concept, and they must learn that a certain word form represents that concept. Children learn to comprehend some words months before their first birthday, and they learn to produce words orally by the time of their first birthday or shortly thereafter. By age two, many are able to produce hundreds of different words and comprehend many more. British linguist David Crystal (1997) described research conducted in Germany that, using microphones and tape recorders, documented considerable growth in daily word production by young subjects. In language research, the word *type* refers to particular words, and the word *tokens* refers to all words in a language sample. For example, in the sentence *The judge entered and all the people stood*, there are eight tokens but only seven types because the word *the* occurs twice. The German researchers recorded an average daily output of about 20,000 word tokens produced by two-year-olds and 37,000 word tokens produced by children under age four as they engaged in normal activities.

Without words, language could not exist, but language also is dependent on an established system of combining words to convey meaning. The syntax or grammar of a language is a set of conventions used to signal specific patterns of meaning. Syntactic rules enable speakers to understand that *The boy chased the dog* has quite a different meaning from *The dog chased the boy*. Through the rules of syntax, statements can be transformed into questions. For example, *This is her new car* can become *Is this her new car?* Passive sentences can be formed from active sentences: *He was comforted by her words* means about the same as *Her words comforted him*. The syntax of a language specifies acceptable, conventional sequences of words that "make sense" to native speakers of the language. When a non-native is speaking a foreign language, the spoken syntax sometimes becomes disordered, and it will sound incorrect to a native speaker.

As children develop language, they progress from one-word utterances such as *Mine* to two-word sentences such as *Mama gone*, *Tommy kick*, and *See puppy?* By age two, children can produce three- and four-word sentences such as *Tommy kick ball*. By age four, their syntactic complexity advances rapidly, and this skill continues to develop in the early school years.

Language development involves more than learning the patterns of sound and syntax and the development of vocabulary. Children begin to use language patterns and intonations appropriate to an increasing variety of social situations. Sometime between the ages of two and four, children acquire the skills to participate in conversation. They learn ways to initiate a conversation, hold a listener's attention, and listen to another person, and they develop an understanding of taking turns. Children come to understand that certain words they have heard some adults use are taboo when spoken by children. They learn to use language to request, to persuade, and to comply. By the time they enter school, many young children have developed surprisingly adultlike conversational skills. Language development continues in the early and late school years as pupils acquire the ability to read and write and to comprehend and use language in more polished and mature ways.

Every child is a unique individual, and not all children develop language with the same degree of ease. Some reasons for delayed language acquisition are physiological or cognitive, and others are environmental. The amount and quality of language interaction between a child and parent or caregiver from birth onward are of major significance in language growth. Children who have others to spend time talking to them, listening to them, and reading to them regularly have an advantage in language development.

This chapter on language development has seven entries. In the first entry, the nature of language is described and exemplified. The origins and elements of language are addressed, and semiotics is introduced briefly. Language processes and children's acquisition of the processes are the topics of the second entry, in which theories of language learning are compared.

Vocabulary development is the topic of entry three, where attention is given to the ways in which children learn words. Continuation of language growth in the early years in school is described in entry four. Its focus is the acquisition of reading and writing ability and the further development of oral language. Entry five addresses and exemplifies four purposes for language development in the intermediate and upper grades: using language for information and understanding, for literary response and expression, for critical analysis and evaluation, and for social interaction. Entry six discusses major factors that inhibit language development, including child-, home-, and school-based factors. The final entry of the chapter presents aspects of language that are often overlooked though widely used: onomastics, expressions, and abbreviations.

Dale Johnson and Bonnie Johnson

THE NATURE OF LANGUAGE

All humans use some form of language. Linguists, psychologists, and psycholinguists—scholars who study language—have examined each aspect of language and its development. A great deal now is known about this marvelous mechanism through which humans communicate. Language is defined as a formal system of sounds and symbols and the rules that govern them for the formation, expression, and comprehension of meanings, thoughts, and feelings.

There are about 6,000 distinct languages spoken on our planet, although most of them are spoken by only a few people. Some languages with few speakers include Kankanaey, spoken in the Philippines; Marka, spoken in Burkina Faso; and Simeulue, spoken in Indonesia. About one in ten languages has a writing system to represent its oral code. Over two hundred languages are spoken by more than one million people each: they include Pwo, spoken in Thailand; Yiddish, spoken in the United States, Israel, and Russia; Welsh, spoken in Wales; and Swahili, spoken in eastern Africa. The languages that are in most widespread use are Mandarin (Chinese), English, Hindi, and Spanish. Nearly half of the world's population speaks one of these four languages as their native language. The expansion in use of the major languages may bring about the elimination of many of the rarer languages within a century.

Languages differ, but every language has certain characteristics. Each language is systematic; that is, it is orderly, regular, uniform, and largely consistent. Without consistency and uniformity, speakers of a particular language would not be able to understand one another. Each language is arbitrary in the connection between its sounds, symbols, words, and the objects and ideas they represent. For example, the word *bad* in English means about the same thing as *schlecht* in German. In English, twenty-six letters are used to represent about forty-four speech sounds, but Russian uses thirty-two symbols, and Chinese has up to 4,000 basic characters and as many as 50,000 characters for literary use. English is read from left to right and top to bottom, but Hebrew and Arabic are read from right to left. Japanese is read from right to left. There are fourteen different patterns of directionality of script used in different languages.

Each language is flexible in that new words are added and old words change meaning or fall out of use. For example, the verb *google* (to seek information using an Internet search engine of that name) entered the language in recent years, and its longevity is not yet determined. Slang words such as *fliv* (a car) and *bazoo* (mouth) have fallen from use. *Bully* originally meant *a kind, upstanding person*; the meaning gradually changed to the opposite. Most major languages are variable in that the languages have words with more than one meaning and meanings represented by more than one word. Some languages have more than one dialect used in different locations, by different social groups, or by individuals with different ethnic backgrounds. The dialects may vary in pronunciation, word choice, and sentence structure but remain recognizable to other native speakers of the language. Every language is initially oral in terms of human development and language acquisition.

Children begin to express themselves orally and comprehend oral language years before they learn to use the written system of the language. Many languages are only oral and do not have a writing system, but no language has only a writing system without an oral language. For some written languages, including Old Akkadian and Latin, the spoken language has become extinct. Spoken language, in one form or another, has been in use for 50,000 years or more, but alphabetic (not pictorial) writing systems are much more recent inventions, dating back to about 3500 B.C.E. Pictographic symbols, such as ideographs (shapes that represent concepts), cuneiforms (wedge-shaped symbols that represent sounds and meanings), hieroglyphics (pictures that denote objects, concepts, and sounds), and logograms such as Chinese and Japanese characters that represent whole words or phrases, were precursors to alphabetic writing.

ORIGIN OF LANGUAGE

A subject of interest to scholars for centuries has been the origin of human language. Danish linguist Otto Jespersen identified and grouped a number of theories that had been postulated and later discredited. These included the *bow-wow* theory, wherein early people were thought to imitate the sounds of animals as the initial stage of speech. The *pooh-pooh* theory posited that speech arose from instinctive sounds attributed to human emotions. The *ding-dong* theory asserted that early people responded to the sounds of the world around them by producing oral sounds. The *yo-he-ho* theory stipulated that language arose from rhythmical communal grunts caused by the physical efforts of the ancients working together. Finally, the *la-la* theory suggested that the factors that initiated language were the romantic sounds associated with love, play, and song (Crystal 1997).

More recently, scientific evidence from the fields of archaeology, genetics, and human behavioral ecology has shed light on the origin of language. Research on the brain sizes of Neanderthals and Cro-Magnons, with an analysis of the shape of the jaws and oral cavities preserved as fossils, has provided information. There is general support for considering the period 100,000–20,000 B.C.E. as the time during which speech developed. Some researchers have suggested that the first human language began about 50,000 years ago in Africa among the Hadza of eastern Africa and the Khosian of southern Africa. The language used click sounds to serve the role of consonants. Between 50,000 and 10,000 years ago, humans dispersed from the African homeland, and one language became many because of distance and ethnic differentiation. Oral language seems to have emerged many thousands of years before the first evidence of any type of written language.

Scholars who study the history of language have identified a range of nineteen to thirty-two different language families. Included among them are Afro-Asiatic, Eskimo-Aleut, Indo-European, and Sino-Tibetan. Each language family shares some commonalities in terms of speech sounds, vocabulary, and sentence structures. Attempting to classify languages is complex and usually is done in one of two ways. Genetic classification assumes that languages in a family developed from a common ancestor language. Typological classification is based on the similarities and differences among languages. For example, some languages include different tones to signify meaning and use sounds not found in other languages. English descended from the Indo-European family of languages. There are fifty-five different varieties in the Indo-European family, including Celtic, Germanic, and Italic. Whether or not all major language families stem from one or several original languages is still unclear. The origin of language remains of intense interest to researchers from a number of disciplines.

COMPONENTS OF LANGUAGE

Human language exists to convey, expand, and comprehend meaning, that is, to communicate. Languages have a number of components or systems, including the phonological (sounds), orthographical (written symbols), morphological (words and word parts), syntactic (sentences), and semantic (meanings) systems. These systems help us access the prior knowledge, experiences, and beliefs stored in our minds and help us expand and modify such knowledge.

The sound system is called the phonology. Phonemes are the smallest distinctive speech sounds used in a language. For example, the phonemes /b/ and /d/ are used to distinguish such words as *bill* and *dill*, *bark* and *dark*. Approximately forty-four phonemes are used in English, depending on a person's dialect (e.g., *Don* and *Dawn* are pronounced the same way in some dialects but not in others). Everything that we say or hear in language uses these forty-four distinct sounds combined in different ways to represent

different words. When we listen to each other in conversation, we hear a steady stream of spoken sound, and we seem oblivious to the individual phonemes of the language.

In addition to phonemes, the sound system of a language involves melodic and rhythmic patterns of speech. These patterns, called prosodic features of language, include variations of stress, juncture, and intonation. Stress is the relative loudness given to syllables or words. In *sofa*, the first syllable is stressed. In the word *conversation*, the third syllable is stressed. Juncture refers to the location of a pause within a word or sentence (e.g., we buy flowers at a *greenhouse*, and we might live in a *green house*). Intonation is the rise and fall of the voice. Intonation is used to signal questions, in contrast to statements: *Is that a monkey? That is a monkey.* It also can convey feelings or attitudes such as boredom, excitement, sarcasm, and frustration.

Related to the phonological system is the written system of a language, called the orthography. In English, the twenty-six letters of the alphabet are used with punctuation marks, certain typographical features or logograms (e.g., $, &, %), and spacing to represent oral language. English lacks uniformity in letter-sound correspondence. Some letters represent many sounds (e.g., the letter *a* in *at*, *able*, *call*, *father*, and *away*). Some phonemes can be represented by more than one combination of letters. For example, the long *a* sound heard in the word *able* can be represented in words such as *play*, *pain*, *stake*, *steak*, *neighbor*, and *they*. Due to these variations, there are hundreds of letter/sound correspondences in English words. Variations can be seen by contrasting the pronunciations of pairs of words such as: *break-speak*, *paid-said*, *five-give*, *low-how*, *though-enough*.

Other language elements are the morphology, syntax, and semantics of the language. Morphology involves the structure of words and how they are formed. The smallest distinctive units of meanings in a language are called morphemes, of which there are two types. Free morphemes are units of meaning that need not be attached to other morphemes. Words are considered free morphemes. The word *happy* carries one unit of a meaning. Bound morphemes also carry meaning, but they cannot stand alone. The morpheme *un-* can mean *not*, but it must be attached to a free morpheme (a word). When *un-* is attached to *happy*, a new word, *unhappy,* is created. *Unhappy,* therefore, consists of the free morpheme *happy* and the bound morpheme *un-.* Thousands of English words are created through the use of morphological rules that give us compound words (e.g., *roadblock*), words with prefixes (e.g., *rewrite*), words with suffixes (e.g., stubborn*ness*), conversions in which a noun (e.g., *paper*) becomes a verb (e.g., *to paper*) and other modifications discussed in the final entry of this chapter.

The syntactic system comprises of the rules of language that determine permissible word order and function. The sentence *The dog ran down the hill* makes sense, but *Hill dog down the ran the* makes no sense because it does not follow syntactic rules. These rules also allow us to know that *The baby smiles a lot* means about the same thing as *She is a smiley baby.* It is the syntax that enables us to generate sentences that we never have spoken before but will be understood by the listener. Syntactic rules enable us to understand what others say. Although all languages differ, they do share some commonalities in syntactic structure. For example, all languages have two types of modifiers corresponding to adjectives and adverbs. All languages enable the conversion of sentences (e.g., *That is a school*) into questions (e.g., *Is that a school?*), negatives (e.g., *That is not a school*), and commands (e.g., *Show me the school*). There are a number of other syntactic similarities across languages, and there are some differences. In English, for example, the past, present, or future tense is indicated by the verb (e.g., *He walks. He walked. He will walk.*). In Japanese, adjectives can indicate the tense (e.g., *shiroi* means *white*, but *shirokatta* means *was white*). In English sentences, place occurs before time as in the example, *I am coming home at two o'clock.* In German sentences, time is referred to before place. For example, *Ich komme um zwei Uhr nach Hause* would be translated literally as *I am coming at two o'clock home.*

Semantics refers to the meaning system of the language. It consists of the vocabulary of a language, also called its lexicon. Morphemes contribute to this meaning system. Semantics refers to the nuances and variations of meanings of words as they are used in particular situations. English has many words that carry multiple meanings. For example, the word *down* has different meanings in the following sentences: *My computer is down, The sun is down, We went down South, I tied it down, I wrote it down, Today I feel down.* Similarly, our language has many synonyms, or words that mean about—but not exactly—the same thing. Synonyms for the word *excellent* include *superior, first-rate, top-notch, superlative, outstanding, magnificent, sensational, unsurpassed, superb, stellar,* and more. Semantics also refers to other meaningful elements such as idioms (e.g., *in a pickle*), proverbs (e.g., *Waste not, want not*), and slang (e.g., *a greasy spoon*).

An important aspect of the semantic system of language is the concept of pragmatics, concerns the different meanings of a sentence in a particular situation. These differences may be in terms of the intent of the communication (e.g., persuading, demanding), the conversational interaction (e.g., opening or closing a conversation, taking turns, changing the topic), and speech style (e.g., the tone and vocabulary used in addressing a small child or an adult). For example, *Here comes the bus* takes on one meaning if a person is simply waiting for a bus but a different meaning when used as a warning to someone standing in the street, and a third meaning when uttered by a vendor upon seeing a tourist bus arrive. In the two sentences *I saw her come into the theater* and *I saw her go into the theater*, we are able to discern whether the speaker was inside or outside the theater. Pragmatic factors influence our selection of words, syntactic structures, and prosodic features.

Humans also engage in nonverbal communication, that is, communication external to or in addition to language. There are three categories of such communication. Paralanguage refers to aspects of vocal behavior. Speakers use tone of voice, volume, stress, tempo, and hesitation to convey different feelings or meanings, such as suspicion, surprise, anger, doubt, or enthusiasm. In the sentence *Mary Anna spent the dollar*, different words are emphasized in response to the questions *What did Mary Anna spend? Who spent the dollar? What did Mary Anna do with the dollar?* A second type of nonverbal communication is kinesics or body language. This involves the use of posture, facial expressions, gestures, eye contact, nodding, toe tapping, and other physical movements to convey feelings of disappointment, joy, impatience, and more. Third, nonlinguistic utterances also are used to express feelings. The sound *nnnnhhhh* by a class when the teacher announces a pop quiz is an example of a nonlinguistic utterance.

These language systems—the phonology, orthography, morphology, syntax, and semantics—enable us to communicate and be understood. In addition, there is a visual language used primarily by people with hearing impairments. Various systems of sign language have been devised to represent the spoken elements of language. Sign languages are as complex as spoken and written language, and they perform the same functions. Sign languages were created in different parts of the world, and they are not mutually intelligible. Although the spoken and written English of North America and Great Britain are quite similar, their sign languages are not. American sign language employs about 4,000 different signs that can convey a vast range of meanings. The term *cherology* refers to the different signs and is analogous to the phonology of spoken language. A somewhat different type of sign language is dactylology, or finger spelling, in which each letter of the alphabet has its own sign. Finger spelling has scope and flexibility, but it is a very slow system of language. It often serves as a bridge between spoken and sign language.

There are other gestural systems of communication. These simple gestural systems are used in a wide range of situations and by a variety of professions. A finger to the lips indicates a desire for silence, and a motioning gesture toward the body can mean *Come here*. Theater, film, and television directors use hand signals to indicate available remaining time and degrees of loudness desired. Sports officials use hand signals to indicate infractions and time-outs. Auctioneers use gestures to regulate bidding. Bicyclists sometimes use hand signals to indicate intentions. These are not true sign language in the sense of those used by the hearing impaired. They lack structural complexity and communicative range, but they are a form of communication. New Zealand psychologist Michael Corvallis suggested that gestures preceded oral language and came into use when early humans started to walk on two legs, freeing the hands for signals. To this day, gesturing continues to be an expressive part of human communication (Wade 2003).

SEMIOTICS

Semiotics is the study of the properties of signs and

signaling systems found in all forms of human communication. Plato and Aristotle speculated about the differences between natural signs (e.g., the sounds of birds) and conventional signs, such as those used in human speech. Flushed skin could be seen as a natural sign that someone has a fever or has been in the sun too long. Ferdinand de Saussure, considered the father of semiotics, defined linguistic signs as two-sided entities: the signifier (the oral or written word) and the signified (the mental concept identified by the signifier). Stated simply, signifiers and the signified refer respectively to words and their meanings (Crystal 1997). American philosopher Charles Sanders Peirce conceptualized signs as having three elements. He used the terms *Representamen*, *Object*, and *Interpretant* to indicate the word, the thing, and the concept respectively (Crystal 1997). Consider a schoolhouse on a street. The schoolhouse is Peirce's Object. The mental concept of a schoolhouse is his Interpretant. The spoken or written word *schoolhouse* is Peirce's Representamen. In contrast, Saussure would have referred simply to the signifier (i.e., the word *schoolhouse*) and the signified (i.e., the mental concept of a schoolhouse).

This is a major simplification of a complex body of theory on the nature and elements of signs. Semiotics concerns the sign systems in all modes of human communication (i.e., sight, sound, taste, touch, and smell) and in all contexts (e.g., politics, film, clothing, dance). Volumes of scholarship have been devoted to the study of semiotics. For the purpose of this chapter, communication signs consist of the phonological, orthographical, morphological, syntactic, semantic, and paralanguage elements described previously.

Dale Johnson and Bonnie Johnson

CHILDREN'S ACQUISITION OF LANGUAGE PROCESSES

LANGUAGE PROCESSES

The four principal language processes are listening, speaking, reading, and writing. The first two, listening and speaking, are processes of *oracy*. Reading and writing comprise the processes of *literacy*. The processes of listening and reading are the comprehension processes through which we attain meaning by decoding the oral or written messages to which we are exposed. Speaking and writing are the productive processes of language through which we encode the meanings, experiences, or feelings that we want to express to others. We use listening and reading to learn, and we use speaking and writing to express something.

None of this is as simple as it seems. Using language is a human endeavor that we often take for granted and to which we usually give no more thought than breathing. Consider the information that we have stored in our minds for each of the tens of thousands of different words that we know as adults: the meaning of the word, its pronunciation, its spelling, how to move the lips and vocal cords to form the word, and how and when to use the word. British linguist Jean Aitchison used the term *mental lexicon* to describe each human's storehouse of words (1994). A lexicon can be considered a collection of words such as those found in a dictionary. Most good dictionaries contain definitions, spellings, pronunciations, grammatical functions, some illustrations, word histories, and sample usage. Our mental lexicons hold most of this information for each word, but they also hold our negative or positive personal experiences with the word, that is, associated words (e.g., salt, pepper), aversions (e.g., snake, spider), biases (e.g., conservative, liberal), and other special word and world knowledge.

Words in our mental lexicons are organized not alphabetically but, rather, by sound and meaning. Consider the speed with which we access words when we engage in speaking or writing and the speed with which we usually comprehend the speech or writing of others. Eevery human has at least two vocabularies in the mental lexicon: the phonological words used in listening and speaking and, if we are not illiterate, the orthographic words used when we read and write. We comprehend input through phonological (listening) and orthographic (reading) information, and we produce output phonologically (speaking) and orthographically (writing). If we are fluent in second or third languages, the number of vocabularies is multiplied. How did we learn all of this? How did we develop the automaticity in language production and comprehension that we exhibit so effortlessly?

ACQUISITION OF LANGUAGE

Children do not wake up on the morning of their first birthday and begin speaking. The groundwork for language skills starts to be laid practically from birth. Think of the monumental tasks that confront children from the time of their birth until they enter school. They need to recognize and later produce all the sounds of their first language. Young children must learn hundreds of ways of combining these sounds to form the words that they utter and to comprehend the words that they hear.

Most children learn several thousand words by the time they are six years old. They hear and utter hundreds of grammatical constructions, and they internalize the rules that permit these constructions, although they are not aware of those rules. Numerous ways to use the prosodic features of pitch, juncture, and stress to convey different meanings, feelings, and intentions will be learned. Youngsters will understand that certain words and expressions are unacceptable to some people. In other words, they will begin to learn the many nuances of language use. Upon entering school, most children will face the added demands of learning to read and write the language. This involves learning the skills and strategies of letter recognition and formation, letter/sound relationships, spellings, reading comprehension, writing techniques, figurative expressions, and more.

Researchers use a variety of processes to study how children acquire language and in what sequence language develops. Most of what we have learned has come through tracking individual children. Youngsters have been observed and recorded in naturalistic settings at home and at play. Researchers use the diaries kept by parents that document the words and sentences spoken by their child to understand language development. Systematic investigation of language acquisition was made possible in the mid-1900s when the tape recorder came into routine use. Later, video recorders, microphones, and special observational facilities enabled researchers to accumulate reliable data on the stages of language development. Naturalistic settings such as home or a room equipped with toys, and with other children or adults present, are best for sampling children's spontaneous language. Much of this research is conducted with individual children.

In contrast, cross-sectional studies look at particular variables in groups of children. Youngsters at age four, for example, may be asked in groups to engage in a conversation with a toy stuffed animal. The types of constructions the children use are tallied and analyzed. Psychologist Roger Brown and British psycholinguist Gordon Wells have conducted this type of research using sampling intervals to gather information on several children over time (Crystal 1997). Researchers have observed that individual differences form a range of language acquisition. Factors such as societal background, intelligence, and personality characteristics contribute to these differences. Most children follow the same general path as they acquire speech, but they do so with large variations in rate of acquisition.

Some researchers have argued that humans have a critical period or "window of opportunity" for first language learning, which begins to close between ages six and twelve. There have been accounts of children raised with no linguistic interaction with other humans for several years after their birth. Children who have been isolated from language input during those critical years have rarely developed language facility beyond that of a preschool child. Psycholinguist Eric Lenneberg studied brain maturation and argued that the critical window for language learning ended at puberty, when the brain was fully developed (Bolinger 1968). This view has been disputed. Some researchers believe that the language-learning window begins to close much earlier for children who are deprived of language interactions.

During their first year, most children learn to recognize auditory differences in the speech they hear, and they begin to produce sounds that are used in their native language. Hearing the native language influences speech perception in very young children. They are born with the ability to perceive all of the differences in sounds used in any and all languages. As they continue to hear and imitate the dominant or native language around them, they experiment and begin to focus only on the speech sounds pertinent to that language; they eliminate phonemic features unimportant to it. By age two, children articulate several vowel sounds and such consonant sounds as /b/, /d/, /t/, /m/, /n/, and /p/. Most of the rest of the consonant and vowel phonemes are in use by age four. The last consonant phonemes to be learned are those heard in the words *thin*, *this*, *judge*,

and *measure*. Some children do not learn these latter phonemes until the early school grades.

After children begin to discriminate the differences among sounds, they start to use those sound differences to distinguish particular words. By about the age of two months, children begin to coo; that is, to make vowel-like sounds. By the time babies are five to six months old, they can produce sequences of vowel- and consonant-like sounds that mark the difference between cooing and babbling. Initial babbling typically makes the sounds of repeated syllables such as *buh buh buh*, *da da da*, and others. When babies are nine or ten months old, they begin to use consistent sounds in different situations or in accompaniment to specific behaviors. They use certain sounds such as /u/ (heard in *food*) to show pleasure and others such as /ae/ (heard in *hat*) or /o/ (heard in *bowl*) when cranky. Between the ages of nine and eighteen months, infants' babbles become more complex and show differences in stress and intonation to the point of sounding more like speech.

Most children produce their first recognizable words by the end of their first year. With their first steps in learning single words, they are embarking on a word-learning journey that will continue throughout life. This is not surprising because most languages have hundreds, thousands, or even millions of words. No one could ever learn them all. Children engage in three separate but related word-learning tasks. The first is naming. Youngsters begin to recognize that certain combinations of speech sounds they hear and later produce serve as the names of people or things. More than 60 percent of their initial words serve a naming function, and about 20 percent express an action. The sounds heard as *muh-muh* become understood as the name *mama*. This is called the *holophrastic* stage of language development. A child may use the word *shoe* to mean *I want my shoe* or *Where is my shoe?* The second task in word learning involves grouping words that fall together in a category. The initial word *kitty* may label the family pet, and later the child may use the word *kitty* to refer to other cats, pictures of cats, and toy cats. The third vocabulary-learning task requires that children figure out how different words relate to or are different from words within and across categories. They come to understand that kitties have fur, a tail, and purr, but birdies have feathers, a beak, and chirp.

Each of these tasks, naming, categorizing, and relating, are significant, individual language discoveries. Learning new words involves first comprehension and later production. Children with no neurological problems, and who are raised by caring adults who communicate with them, acquire new words and the other systems of language quite effortlessly. Young children require human interaction to attach meanings to words. Their vocabularies, with adult input, can grow remarkably quickly. Psycholinguist Eve Clark reported research studies indicating that children from age two on acquire about ten new words a day on average or about 3,500 words a year for an average total of about 14,000 words in their mental lexicons by age six (1993).

Before they are three years old, most children combine words to produce sentences. Linguists call these short, simple word combinations telegraphic sentences. They are the first indication that children are beginning to learn something about syntax. The telegraphic stage looks more like real grammar. A sentence such as *Doggie bark* seems to indicate an awareness of a subject and verb sentence, and a sentence such as *Want milk* indicates a verb plus object construction. Later, these simple patterns are expanded into three-word sentences (e.g., *Mama read book*) and four-word constructions (e.g., *Me go bed now*). By age three, sentences become longer as children string clauses together to tell little stories and express more complex thoughts. Sophistication increases so that the sentence *He give milks to kitty* by a three-year-old becomes *He gave milk to the kitty* by age four. A child's syntax continues to develop through the early school years and into the teens.

As children learn to construct two-, three-, and four-word sentences, they also develop the ability to use language for different purposes or with different intentions. British psycholinguist M. A. K. Halliday described seven functions of language used by infants and young children: instrumental, regulatory, interactional, personal, heuristic, imaginative, and informative. The instrumental function is used to satisfy basic needs, such as when a baby holds up a cup and says, "More." The regulatory function is used to influence the behavior of someone. The toddler who says "Tie shoe" is using language to influence behavior. The interactional function is used to establish contact with someone (e.g., "Daddy"). The personal function is used to express feelings or attitudes. The child who finishes her pudding and says "Yum

yum" is showing her feelings about the dessert. Exploration or questioning is the heuristic function of language. The child who points at a vase and say "What at?" is using heuristic language. Imaginative language is used when the child is at play. A young boy who seems to be talking with his toy figure is using language for imaginative purposes. When a child wants to communicate information (e.g., *Me cold*), the child is using language to inform.

Children show tremendous growth in syntactic production and comprehension during the preschool years. From ages two to four, their sentences grow longer and their communication intentions expand. Three- and four-year-olds are able to make requests (*Let's go home*), give responses (*O.K. I go bed now*), provide descriptions (*Doggy got big teeth*), make statements (*Billy being good today*), regulate conversation (*I done now*), and use language to tease or joke (*There bug on you*). By age five, children have learned to express themselves using the same syntactic type for different purposes. For example, they can use questions to obtain information (*Where are you going?*) or to initiate a conversation (*Can you tell me?*) or as a request (*Can I have some?*). Between ages two and five, children learn that there are several skills involved in carrying on conversations. They learn when to speak and when to listen. They learn to make comments appropriate to the topic, how to take turns, and how to terminate a conversation or change topics.

Learning to speak and listen with all of the above nuances is a process that develops spontaneously and naturally through interactions between parent or caregiver and child. If there are no physical problems, no language specialist is needed for the child to achieve success. Learning literacy, however, almost always requires instruction and support from teachers and others, such as older siblings and relatives. Nonetheless, some developmental accomplishments pave the way for preschoolers to achieve later literacy acquisition.

The following emergent literacy accomplishments are typical of preschool children who later learn to read and write with ease. Some time before age three, these children recognize specific books by their covers. They learn how to handle a book and turn pages, and they pretend to read books. They enjoy listening to stories and looking at accompanying pictures and are able to name objects and talk about characters in books. Children may begin to notice letters in words, and they may produce letter-like forms in scribbles. Not all children accomplish these tasks, but those who do are often successful when learning to read.

Accomplishments by three- and four-year-olds that lead to later success in reading include knowing that it is the print, not the pictures, that is read in stories, learning to recognize local environmental print (e.g., popular fast-food restaurant names), understanding that spaces delineate words, and realizing that alphabet letters have names. These children enjoy hearing repeated sounds in language and rhyming elements (e.g., *cat/hat*). They show an interest in books and reading, become aware of sequences of events in stories, and begin to connect stories to life experiences. Children try out new vocabulary in syntactic constructions in their own speech, and they can understand and follow oral directions.

Children are born with biological traits passed along in the genes of their forbears; among these traits is the capacity to acquire natural language. Psycholinguists, psychologists, and linguists study the developmental processes children use over their first five or six years to become competent speakers of one of the world's 6,000 languages. These processes are complex and require the use of children's perceptual, cognitive, communicative, and learning skills as they interact with parents, caregivers, and other mature language users. How this enormous amount of learning is possible has been a subject of continuing interest, and a number of language-learning theories have been proposed. These are discussed next.

THEORIES OF LANGUAGE DEVELOPMENT

Philosopher John Locke, in the seventeenth century, postulated that at birth, a child's mind is a blank slate and knowledge accumulates through experience. Locke's position has contributed to the long-standing debate over the role of nature (innate processes) versus nurture (the environment) in how children learn anything, including their natural language. This debate continues between adherents of various learning theories.

The acquisition of language has been viewed as a process of imitation and reinforcement. Psychologist B. F. Skinner proposed a behaviorist theory of learning based on a process called operant conditioning. The theory stipulated that changes occur in behavior based on events or actions that follow the behavior. Positive reinforcement increases the possibility that a behavior will recur, and punishment decreases the probability of recurrence. In terms of language development, the child who looks at her father and says "Dada" may be rewarded with positive comments and perhaps a hug. The same child, however, who looks at her father and says "Mama" might be corrected or possibly reprimanded, "No, no, no, I'm Dada." In behaviorist theory, imitation is thought to play an important role in children's language acquisition. Thus, the views of behaviorists tend to fall on the nurture end of the nature versus nurture scale. This theory has been criticized because it does not explain some facts about language development, such as children's ability to utter or comprehend unique sentences that they have never heard before.

Noam Chomsky's nativist theory of learning argued that the ability to learn language is an innate behavior in humans, and, barring any neurological or physiological deficiencies, children are automatically born ready to learn language (Pinker 1994). Children are presumed to have an internal language acquisition device (LAD) that enables them to process language and produce sentences that will correspond to adult language. This theory rests on the argument that because language is unique to the human species, it must be genetically or biologically determined. The theory further argues that because of the inordinate complexity of language, it would not be possible for five-year-old children to develop the language facility they do unless they brought innate knowledge to the process. In other words, children are "wired" to learn language, and they develop facility in the particular language to which they are exposed. Nativist theory recognizes that environment is important in language acquisition but primarily to activate the innate language mechanism. Compared to behaviorism, the nativist theory is on the opposite end of the nature versus nurture scale, weighing in on the side of nature. It has proved difficult to detail the properties of the LAD, and this has led to additional theories of language development.

A third theory, the cognitive theory, seems to fall between behaviorism and nativism. Cognitive theorists, such as Jerome Bruner (1960), recognize the role of innate knowledge in language acquisition, but they believe that innate knowledge is more generally cognitive rather than just linguistic. Cognitive theorists believe that language development is but one ability dependent on cognitive development. Cognitive proponents view environment as a critical element in children's language acquisition, but they do not see children as passive recipients, that is, blank slates. Instead, they believe that there is an essential interaction between children's innate cognitive structures and their linguistic and nonlinguistic environments. It has been difficult to distinguish precisely the interrelationships between cognitive and linguistic development as children become more advanced.

There are additional theories of language development that are modifications of one or more of the three theories described. For example, Lev Vygotsky proposed one slightly different version of cognitive theory (1962). It postulates that although children have innate cognitive bases for language acquisition, the actual learning begins with functions that children want to express. Thus, they develop language to express the functions (e.g., *Where mama?* or *More milk!*). The purpose drives what they learn. British evolutionary psychologist Robin Dunbar asserted that language originally developed because of the social needs that bind individuals into communities (Wade 2003). Similarly, the social/communicative theorists believe that children's early social and communicative interactions are of major importance in language acquisition. Youngsters' acquisition of linguistic forms and rules grows out of their interactions with parents or caregivers. Under this theory, the caregiver and the child play highly active roles in the development of language.

Finally, the connectionist theory of language development proposed by David Rumelhart suggested that language knowledge consists of connections and networks of connections, rather than rules (Tomasello and Bates 2001). His theory developed from research in artificial intelligence. The theory contends that children acquire language without ever figuring out the rules or even that there are rules. Connectionist theory is in its developmental stage and has yet to gain widespread acceptance.

Theories are not facts, and although a great deal of research has been conducted, it still is not known exactly how children are able to succeed in the remarkable feat of language acquisition. Some attempts to relate cognitive and linguistic development using the Piagetian stages, described in an earlier chapter, have not been successful. Major advances have occurred in understanding both linguistic and cognitive development, but as of this writing, these advances have not been shown to have a close relationship. Numerous scholars continue to engage in research in cognitive development and the interplay between cognitive development and language learning. In the meantime, children continue to develop language practically from birth, and that development expands well into the school years. It is not possible with the present state of knowledge to choose definitively from the different theories. It seems logical that a combination of imitative skills, an innate language acquisition device, cognitive development, and social communication interactions contribute to language development. How these factors interact will continue to be of interest to child language researchers. The next entry describes the one aspect of language development that begins at about age one and continues throughout the remainder of our lives: vocabulary development.

Dale Johnson and Bonnie Johnson

VOCABULARY DEVELOPMENT

Few things in life seem more ordinary than words. We take words for granted and rarely think about the words we use in our speech and writing or the words we hear in everyday conversation. How do we choose the words we use so automatically? How do we understand the meanings of the words we hear? How did we learn all of the words that we use so readily?

Words have been defined as "labels for concepts," "combinations of sounds that are meaningful," and "units of meaning." One major dictionary requires four dense columns of type to define *word*. Words can be thought of in three major categories: lexical words, grammatical words, and onomastic words. Lexical words have meanings that can be described. They usually are common nouns (e.g., campus, door, lasagna), verbs (e.g., dash, consider, stretch), or modifiers (e.g., recently, huge, always). Some words can be classified in different lexical ways. For example, the word *round* can serve as an adjective (a *round* ball), a verb (*round* the bend), or a noun (to sing a *round*). Grammatical words are the structure or function words that link lexical words in sentences. Conjunctions (e.g., but, although, therefore), determiners (e.g., few, that, every), pronouns (e.g., they, she, it), auxiliary verbs (e.g., is, are, have), prepositions (e.g., from, of, over), and interjections (e.g., oh! hooray! wow!) are examples of grammatical words. Onomastic words are the names of particular persons (e.g., Steve), places (e.g., Penn Station), and things (e.g., Long Island Railroad). Each word has a phonological form used in speech and an orthographic form used in writing. Some words are derived using morphological rules (e.g., teach, teaches, teacher, teaching, teachable, reteach), but others are pure units of meaning to which morphemes may be attached (e.g., prairie, odd, watch). British linguist David Crystal used the term *lexical item* or *lexeme* in place of *word* because lexemes could accommodate units of meaning longer than a word (1995, 1997). In English, some units of meaning that are longer than a word but learned as though they were single words include idioms (e.g., to be in the driver's seat) and slang (e.g., a basket case). The meanings are not literal combinations of the words; instead, they have unique meanings.

It is impossible to know precisely how many words are in a language, but for English, the estimates run to more than two million with new words added every year. Some words are taken from other languages. For example, *kayak* is an Inuit word, *noodle* is German, and *charisma* is Greek. New words are coined from contemporary concepts. In recent years, *blog, Frankenfood, morph,* and *soccer mom* have entered the language. Multiple-meaning words also lead to imprecision in word counts; consider the different meanings of *line* in a *line of type, a line at the box office, a fishing line, to drop a line,* and *to hand someone a line.* Thousands of words have more than one meaning, and some words have more than one hundred meanings (e.g., set, run). Although we cannot be certain about the number of words in English, we can be certain that vocabulary is the one aspect of language that no one ever completely masters. No one knows every word, but every word is known by someone.

It also is impossible to know how many words any individual actually knows, and there are degrees or shades of knowing a word. We can know the meaning of a word, its sound, its spelling, when to use the word, and other words to which it is related. Preschool children, for example, learn several thousand words orally, but they can recognize only a few of them in their printed forms. As mentioned earlier, humans have an astounding penchant for expanding their vocabularies. Children utter their first words at about age one and have learned approximately 14,000 words by age six. High school graduates know about 45,000 words, and college graduates know 100,000 words or more. From our earliest years until adulthood, we comprehend more words that we hear or read than we produce in our own speaking or writing. In other words, we know many more words than we actually use. Shakespeare used only 18,000 different words in all of the works he produced—many fewer than most of us had stored in our mental lexicons when we were in high school and certainly fewer words than Shakespeare could comprehend.

In recent decades, a number of computer analyses of large bodies of words have been undertaken to determine the frequency of use of individual words. Some words (e.g., the, of, and, to, a, in, that, is, was) are used far more often than other words (e.g., accordion, ferrule, splice). Linguists Henry Kucera and W. Nelson Francis analyzed a body of one million words (i.e., word tokens) of printed text and determined that 50,000 different words (i.e., word types) occurred, but that a mere one hundred of those words accounted for about half the occurrences of all 50,000 different words (1967). English-language scholar E. D. Hirsch compiled a list of more than 5,000 names (e.g., Buffalo Bill), words (e.g., guru), proverbs (e.g., Half a loaf is better than none), and dates (e.g., 1776) that he believed to be essential for intelligent communication (Hirsch 1988). He argued that a national vocabulary of cultural literacy should be indispensable in any society. Swedish linguist Morris Swadesh identified one hundred concepts that he considered so basic that each of the world's 6,000 languages had words for them (Miller 1991). He included among the fifty-four nouns *woman, man, fish, bird, skin, sun, moon, earth,* and *fire.* Words other than nouns on his list of universal concepts included *we, this, that, drink, eat, sleep, stand, give, hot,* and *cold.* Word lists have been compiled for decades for every imaginable purpose (e.g., survival words, sight words, comic book words).

LEARNING WORDS

Before learning words, infants begin to discern and analyze the world around them. They especially attend to shapes and mentally create object categories. As they hear words used by others, they begin to map the words onto some of the concepts they have observed. Assume children have observed a dog, a ball, a clock, a bed, and a teddy bear. The children recognize the shapes of the objects and this allows them to attach words they hear (e.g., dog, ball, clock, bed, teddy bear) to this prior knowledge. Sometimes this mapping process leads to overextension, such that all four-legged animals are referred to as dogs, and apples and other small round objects are referred to as balls. Later, children learn to sort out the relationships. The same process applies with actions, sounds, and smells. After children begin to absorb and produce their first words at about age one, the pace picks up rapidly, and they may produce up to two hundred different words by eighteen months and five hundred different words by age two, but this pace varies from child to child. Some infants produce only one word at a time for several months, but others seem to use two-word utterances shortly after their first words.

In a research study conducted by psycholinguist Eve Clark, a two-year-old child was able to produce 477 words, of which two-thirds were labels for objects. The array of words learned by this child included eighteen words for people (e.g., baby, boy), twenty-five words for animals (e.g., duck, mouse), eighteen words for vehicles (e.g., bike, sled), fourteen words for body parts (e.g., toe, nose), thirty-five words for toys (e.g., block, doll), fourteen words for clothing (e.g., sock, button), twelve words for furniture (e.g., rug, bed), eighteen words for utensils (e.g., spoon, bowl), thirty-one words for food (e.g., egg, carrot), twenty-four words for attributes (e.g., big, wet), and seventy-four words for activities (e.g., go, fall). The child also used words for locations, routines, and responses. Children gradually progress from naming and categorizing to differentiating words within and across categories (e.g., dogs and horses have a tail and four legs, but dogs bark and horses neigh). Learning new words involves first the comprehension of words heard and subsequently the production of words orally.

The vocabulary of a language is complex. In learning about words, children must develop an understanding of their pronunciation and meaning and how to create new words through compounding and adding prefixes and suffixes. They must learn how some words are alike in some ways but different in other ways (e.g., hurricane, tornado). Children must learn that many words have more than one meaning and some meanings are expressed with synonyms. They must understand that word choice reflects the intentions of the speaker. Young people eventually must learn that many words may denote the same general meaning but have different connotations. For example, *funny*, *silly*, *hilarious*, *witty*, *goofy*, and *zany* refer to the same general quality, but each has a different shade of meaning. A *silly* person may be immature, and a *hilarious* person is extremely funny. A *witty* person is more likely to be bright and quick, but a *goofy* person is humorous by acting unintelligent. A *zany* person is entertainingly unusual.

The important roles of parents, caregivers, siblings, and others in word learning by preschool children cannot be overstated. The size of toddlers' vocabularies and their rates of vocabulary growth depend, in large part, on human interaction. These interactions allow children to attach meanings to words. Engaging in frequent interactive conversation enables preschoolers to learn not only words but also how to talk, use syntax, and develop expanding meanings. With communicative interaction, children appear to learn casually, and this may be attributed to the language instinct with which children are born. One way to account for children's rapid acquisition of language is that there is a human predisposition to language learning, although this predisposition must be nurtured by ample oral interaction. Large differences in vocabulary development can be noted between children who have such interactions regularly from about age two and those who do not. These differences carry into the school years, and children who begin school with limited vocabulary and limited language development are at a significant disadvantage compared to more fortunate children. In a later entry, what schools do to further language development is discussed.

Linguist Jean Aitchison (1994) has theorized about the ways words are stored in the mental lexicon. She uses the analogy of each word's having two sides like a coin. On one side is the sound of the word, which enables us to orally recognize and comprehend a word we hear. On the other side is the word's meaning, which enables us to retrieve the word from memory and use it when we speak. When children acquire literacy, both sides of the coin—sound and meaning—they must also learn the word's spelling to enable their reading and writing the word.

The term *word webs* or *semantic fields* is used to describe ways in which words are related to one another in the mental lexicon. Semantic networks of interconnected words (i.e., word webs or semantic fields) are within our internal storage systems. The words are acquired through listening and reading and are retrieved from memory for speaking and writing. Storage and retrieval are accomplished rapidly because of the semantic interconnectedness of the words. Words relate to one another in at least ten types of association:

1. *Synonyms* are words with nearly the same meaning (e.g., skinny, thin, trim, scrawny, slender).
2. *Antonyms* are words with opposite meanings (e.g., birth-death, hot-cold, in-out).
3. *Collocations* are words that often occur together in language usage (e.g., green grass, torrential downpour, unruly behavior).
4. *Hypernyms-hyponyms* are the superordinate and subordinate words in a category. The hypernym is the category name (e.g., schools). Hyponyms are the subordinate members of the category (e.g., colleges, universities, high schools).
5. *Hypernyms-meronyms* are terms for wholes and parts. The hypernym is the whole (e.g., tree), and meronyms are the parts (e.g., trunk, branches, roots).
6. *Hypernyms-attributes* are words and the semantic features that describe them (e.g., hypernym: desert; attributes: dry, barren, hot).
7. *Hypernyms-functions* are words and descriptions of how they function (e.g., hypernym: refrigerator; functions: freezes ice, preserves food, holds decorative magnets).
8. *Coordinates* are words that share some semantic element but are not superordinate or subordinate to one another (e.g., carousel, Ferris wheel, roller coaster).
9. *Homophones* are words that sound alike but have different spellings and meanings (e.g., great-grate, plain-plane, here-hear).
10. *Homographs* are words with identical spellings but different meanings and sometimes different pronunciations (e.g., bank, coast, record).

Categories of semantic fields, as shown above, reveal some of the details of how words relate to and differ from one another within a broad domain.

Psychologist George A. Miller (1991) has described some of the most overarching or generic concepts or *superhypernyms* in language (which he calls *unique beginners*) under which all words are in some ways interrelated. He identifies twenty-five unique beginners that are nouns (e.g., activity, attribute, event, feeling, location) and fourteen that are verbs (e.g., motion, consumption, creation). These two sets of overarching unique beginners form the foundation of the semantic fields to which children add new words as they acquire them for oral and written language. Consider the following example using one of the unique beginners, *plant*. One type of plant is a flower. One type of flower is a lily. Using lily as a hypernym, some hyponyms are stargazer, snow queen, and mondeo. Some meronyms of lily are petals, stem, and leaves. Some attributes are beautiful, fragrant, and colorful. Some functions are wedding bouquets, table decorations, and funeral sprays. Some coordinates of lily are zinnias, roses, and marigolds. It is these networks or semantic fields that enable humans to comprehend and produce words seemingly without effort.

When children develop literacy, in most instances upon entering school, the new tools of reading and writing help with their refinement of vocabulary. Words serve different purposes when one reads and when one writes. Readers must recognize words and map them to meanings. Writers must choose words to convey ideas. Readers can get the sense of a word from the context in which it is found. Writers have the obligation to be more precise and use the best words to convey the intended sense. In the next two sections the continuation of language development in school is discussed.

Dale Johnson and Bonnie Johnson

LANGUAGE DEVELOPMENT IN THE EARLY GRADES

The skills of speaking and listening, called oracy, are inextricably intertwined with skills of reading and writing, called literacy, but they are not the same. In school the four processes are referred to as the language arts. Although oracy and literacy co-mingle and support each other, they are treated separately in this entry to help the reader understand the developmental processes.

THE DEVELOPMENT OF ORACY IN THE EARLY GRADES

Most daily communication is conducted in spoken language. The abilities to speak and listen effectively can make substantial differences in what humans can accomplish. Children, as noted above, enter school at age five or six quite capable in their understanding and production of oral language, but that development does not stop at the schoolhouse door. Oral communication is defined as the process of interacting through spoken and heard messages in a variety of situations. The two processes, listening and speaking, are interrelated and involve transactions between at least two people.

Communicative competence is a term used to describe an array of language strategies appropriately used for different purposes in different situations. The emphasis on functional language development stems from research that modifies the views of psychologist Jean Piaget. He considered children younger than seven or eight egocentric, that is, unable to consider their listeners' wishes and viewpoints. Evidence by other researchers, such as psychologist Lev Vygotsky, has shown children to be sociocentric in that they seek social interaction with other children and adults. It is believed that function precedes form in language development. Before school, children use language for a range of social functions (instrumental, regulatory, imaginative, and others), and this type of usage increases during the early school years.

Oracy is a major tool for learning in elementary, middle, and secondary education. Prior to 1980, it was estimated that children in the early grades spent as much as 60 percent of classroom time involved in listening. Teachers did most of the talking and asked 90 percent of the questions. The teacher primarily controlled school language, and children had fewer communicative opportunities in school than they most had had in the home. Children were passive, asked few questions, and spoke less in school than they had at home before they entered school. Instead of building on the interest and curiosity about language that many children bring with them to school, pupils were told to listen respectfully without interrupting, to stay on topic, and to respond with appropriate expressions of understanding messages. As speakers, they were encouraged to use appropriate vocabulary, correct pronunciations, and to speak in complete sentences.

Beginning in the 1980s, this imbalance changed, and there was a greater emphasis on involving children in speaking activities as well as listening. Listening and speaking often develop through children's engagement in language activities that are designed to enhance reading and writing ability as well as oral language. Greater amounts of classroom time were allocated to conversation and discussion. Attention was given to helping children learn to adjust their language to be more sensitive to their audiences. Children practiced conversational rules, turn taking, and topic shifting. A focus on using language in naturalistic settings became widespread. Among the listening and speaking activities were role playing, group discussion, and conversation in circles.

Children were given opportunities to use oral language to ask for information and make requests. They were given opportunities to share facts, opinions, and ideas in oral reports, in show-and-tell sessions, and in small and large group discussions. Pupils learned to follow directions requiring a sequence of steps and how to identify and respond to informational environmental sounds, such as fire alarms and school announcements. Asking questions to clarify topics or routines and retelling information sequentially were encouraged. Children used oral language to connect personal experiences to information heard as well as to share observations from school, home, or elsewhere.

Classroom time also was devoted to engaging pupils' imagination. When children engage in dramatic play, they use oral language to convey thoughts and feelings and to further develop their imaginations. They use different vocabulary and different speech patterns when they act out various roles. Pupils were encouraged to speak audibly and with expression as they shared rhymes, riddles, and stories with their classmates. They engaged in individual and group singing, storytelling, and finger plays. Through choral speaking, role playing, creative dramatics, and puppet shows, children developed a number of oral language competencies. They compared stories they heard in class with stories from their own experiences and used a variety of words to express emotions or moods. Pupils told or retold imaginative stories and described familiar persons, places, or objects. Children discussed songs, tales, and legends from different cultures.

Children also were given opportunities to use personal criteria to express opinions and attitudes and to try to persuade their listeners to agree with them. They used oral language to resolve conflicts or problems. Through these kinds of in-school oral language activities, children expanded the variety of syntactic structures they used as well as increased their listening and speaking vocabularies. New words and new meanings for old words were learned through oral activities in the early elementary grades.

By the late 1990s, however, the attention given to oral language development began to wane in many schools as more states instituted rigid accountability systems with standardized tests, primarily of reading, writing, and mathematics. As a result of these tests and accompanying pressures, teachers were compelled to spend more time on literacy and mathematics to the detriment of oral language and other school subjects such as science, social studies, art, and music. Perhaps the pendulum one day will swing away from school curriculum controlled by testing mandates and return to techniques for developing oral language within a more rounded curriculum.

THE DEVELOPMENT OF LITERACY IN THE EARLY GRADES

Literacy is concerned with the written system of language. Earlier it was noted that spoken language can be traced back at least 50,000 years, but that writing systems are a relatively new achievement in human development. The Roman alphabet was developed in the sixth and seventh century B.C.E. It was derived from the older Greek alphabet, and it is the basis of the alphabet used in English today. The evolution of written language enabled communication to exist without the face-to-face requirements of oral language. At the start of the twentieth century, psychologist Edmund Burke Huey (1908) wrote that the greatest achievement any psychologist could attain would be to analyze completely what humans do when they read. To do that, he believed, would be to describe the human mind and its most intricate workings, and to unravel the story of what he considered the most remarkable individual accomplishment of anyone's lifetime: learning how to read and write.

Most preschool children do not learn to comprehend or produce the written forms of words, so for most children, the development of literacy is left to the schools. Emergent literacy, nonetheless, begins to develop in children before they enter school. Through becoming familiar with books, having stories read to them, attempting to "read" by telling a story from its pictures, and attempting to "write" by scribbling and drawing, the processes of literacy emerge. For most children, literacy begins to develop from emergent literacy when they start school.

There they are faced with new challenges. Children find themselves in a social, emotional, and intellectual environment different from home. They become members of a group—a class of twenty or more children mostly like themselves. New routines must be learned. The attention of one adult must be divided among all the students. Pupils are compared to one another. It is during the first year or two of school, in kindergarten and first grade, when most children begin to read and write. As young children adjust to the culture of school and spend less time with parents or caregivers, they engage in a variety of literacy activities, and there are expectations that they will learn along with other children. Each child comes to school with a different level of language development, different words in the mental lexicon, and a different set of prior experiences. Some have been read to frequently, and others rarely. Nonetheless, by the end of the first grade, most of these individual, unique children have developed some degree of reading and writing ability.

Learning to read begins when children learn to identify and comprehend words in print; that is, they learn to recognize the printed forms of words they already know. Part of this initial ability includes learning the connections between print and speech—the letter/sound correspondences that are part of the code of the language. Along with learning letter/sound relationships, children learn new words, word parts, and new meanings for known words. Their command of syntax expands, they learn to spell, and they develop systems of comprehension.

Learning to read requires the development of a number of understandings and the acquisition of a number of skills. Among them are the ability to distinguish between phonemes, to use letter/sound correspondences to identify the meanings of words, to use the context of what is being read, to understand and define unfamiliar words in a text, to develop strategies for comprehending what is read, and to become aware that reading provides the same kind of information as listening but through the medium of print. Reading development also includes understanding story elements such as settings, characters, problems, events, and solutions. It includes learning literary devices such as dialogue and figurative language, and learning about expository text structures such as causes and effects, main ideas and details, and chronological order. Learning to read means learning to use a text's punctuation, capitalization, and spacing as guides to comprehension. Reading involves not only understanding explicitly stated information but also making inferences from implied information. Reading well requires making judgments about what is read.

Learning to write includes learning to form letters, learning the spelling of speech sounds, developing legible handwriting, and learning to select the best ways to convey meaning. Learning to write necessitates developing an understanding of the conventions of sentence and paragraph structure, punctuation, capitalization, and organization of longer pieces of writing. As writers develop, they learn a number of purposes for writing and the special requirements of each, and they experience the processes of writing (e.g., planning, drafting, revising).

Reading and writing development requires a number of steps, but the steps are not innate or automatic. Children require instruction and practice. Not everyone learns to read and write in the same way or by following the same sequence. Teachers vary the procedures they use to develop literacy in their pupils depending on the teachers' experience, knowledge, pedagogical philosophies, the availability of materials and time, and the dictates of those outside the classroom. Regardless of the approach the teacher takes, the following accomplishments are achieved by most children at the following grade levels:

1. Kindergarten children follow a line of print when being read to, notice when pages have been skipped by the reader, listen attentively when the teacher reads to the class, retell stories in some detail, make predictions while listening to stories, recognize and name some letters of the alphabet, use unconventional writing and invented spellings to express meaning, write their own names, answer questions about stories correctly, identify differences in speech sounds (i.e., phonemic awareness), and know some books by their titles.

2. First graders read age-appropriate text aloud, have a reading vocabulary of three hundred or more words, understand simple written instructions, spell some short words correctly, use some punctuation and capitalization, answer questions about material read by themselves, and write readable short sentences and short paragraphs.

3. Second graders comprehend age-appropriate fiction and nonfiction, read voluntarily, re-read sentences to clarify meaning, contrast characters and events in stories read by others, attend to spelling and punctuation when revising their writing, compare information from different sources, read irregularly spelled words, and pose answers to *why*, *how*, and *what if* questions.

4. Third graders correctly spell previously misspelled words, point out words or phrases causing difficulties in comprehension, read aloud with fluency from grade-appropriate books, distinguish between facts and opinions, write paragraphs with clarity after revision, share writing with others, infer word meanings from

context, make inferences about unstated information in text, and read books divided into chapters and extended nonfiction works.

It must be emphasized that reading materials should be age-appropriate and that some children will not attain these accomplishments at these grade levels. The initial steps in children's literacy development continue throughout their schooling and take on greater sophistication in the upper grades.

Dale Johnson and Bonnie Johnson

LANGUAGE DEVELOPMENT IN THE INTERMEDIATE AND UPPER GRADES

By the time children enter the fourth grade, most of them have developed basic literacy skills. Periodic assessments undertaken by the federal government show that although less than 10 percent of fourth graders have achieved advanced literacy skills, about 25 percent are proficient in their development of literacy and another 30 or 40 percent may be characterized as having basic literacy skills. The remaining 25–35 percent of fourth graders have not achieved basic levels of literacy, and as a result, have a difficult time with schoolwork. The next section of this chapter discusses reasons why some learners make slow progress toward achieving desired levels of literacy in school.

In the intermediate and upper grades, the four language arts (listening, speaking, reading, writing) become more intertwined and mutually reinforcing. Older children expand their productive language abilities (speaking and writing) and receptive language abilities (listening and reading). Language learning in the intermediate and upper grades becomes more integrated. Students engage in fewer activities that are distinctly listening, speaking, reading, or writing. Instead, they develop sophistication in their comprehension of language, whether listening or reading, and in their production of language, whether writing or speaking. Students progress in their language development to fulfill four broad purposes. They use language for information and understanding, for literary response and expression, for critical analysis and evaluation, and for social interaction.

When using language for information and understanding, learners develop listening and reading skills through gathering and interpreting information from reference works, electronic sources, oral interviews, and pictorial sources. Students develop skill in notetaking, summarizing, categorizing, and organizing information. They make greater use of their prior knowledge as well as the structural and contextual cues in oral or printed language to develop meaning. Learners distinguish between relevant and irrelevant information, and they compare and contrast information from different sources.

Speaking and writing abilities develop in a variety of ways. Students acquire facility with the writing processes of prewriting, drafting, revising, and proofreading. They prepare oral and written reports on a range of topics, and they learn to develop information by using supporting materials, such as examples, anecdotes, and details. Students use appropriate vocabulary and sentence structures in their presentations of oral or written information, and they become more considerate and understanding of the audiences they are addressing and their purposes for providing information.

Intermediate and upper-grade students develop their use of language for literary response and expression through listening and reading. They learn to identify important literary elements such as foreshadowing, symbolism, metaphor, irony, and climax. Learners hear, read, and view materials in a wide range of genres on a variety of topics from a variety of authors. They improve their abilities to read aloud with expression to convey the meaning and mood of a work. Students develop skills in evaluating the literary merits of what they hear and read, and they recognize different levels of meaning of a literary work.

When speaking and writing for literary response and expression, students write poems, stories, essays, and plays that show increasing understanding of the conventions and genres. They develop ways to make their writing more distinctive. They become adept at presenting personal interpretations of literature as they speak and write about stories and books. Students continue to gain skill in drawing upon their own knowledge and experiences as they connect with an audience when writing or speaking. They learn to create sequels to stories and reviews of literature.

The development of language for critical evaluation and analysis includes understanding that individuals have different points of view and recognizing those differences in text they read or hear. Students learn to analyze and evaluate information, ideas, and language usage in different types of text, such as advertisements, editorials, documents, and reviews. They learn to assess the credibility of an author or a speaker and to develop sophistication in evaluating their own work and the work of others on a variety of criteria including originality, clarity, completeness, and reasoning. Students come to understand bias and certain propaganda techniques used in speeches and writings. They learn to compare different interpretations of the same event.

When speaking and writing for critical analysis and evaluation, students develop written and oral arguments for persuasive purposes through the use of details and evidence. They present, in papers and speeches, clear analyses of ideas, events, and issues, and support their positions through reasoning. Learners continue to refine their use of spoken and written language, including precise vocabulary to make effective presentations that can influence their intended audience. They present oral and written reviews of books, films, television programs, and performances, and they support their evaluations with references to elements of the work. Students learn to generate persuasive advertisements for products or ideas. They realize that they need to monitor and adjust their own presentations according to the conventions of the genre they use. In the intermediate and upper grades, students learn to view their own writing through the eyes of a reader and their own speaking through the ears of a listener, and they begin to experiment with ways to improve the language they produce.

Intermediate and upper-grade learners continue their development of the use of language for social interaction. In listening and speaking, they refine their verbal and nonverbal skills to improve communication. They become more attuned to listening attentively to build on the ideas of others with whom they are engaged in conversation. Students learn to express themselves clearly and convincingly in group discussions and conversations, and they understand more thoroughly the different roles of speakers and listeners in various types of oral communication. They learn to use language and style of expression that is appropriate to the situation and audience, and they consider the interests and backgrounds of their audience.

When reading or writing for social interaction, students develop skills in writing personal letters, invitations, greetings, and electronic messages to acquaintances, relatives, and friends. The students read and discuss social communications of other writers, and they adapt some of these techniques in their own writings.

Although we have generally considered listening and reading, on the one hand, and speaking and writing, on the other hand, it must be reiterated that reading and writing are related processes of literacy, and they have many commonalities. Reading and writing may be thought of as an interplay between mind and text that brings about new learning. The two processes are dependent upon exposure to and use of written language. We use our reading abilities to construct meaning from written text by relating the text to our prior knowledge, experience, and beliefs. We use writing to construct meaning by producing written language based on our prior knowledge, experience, and beliefs. Through writing and revision, we clarify our understandings of what we already know.

Literacy is not a case of "either/or." It exists along a continuum with illiteracy at one end and advanced literacy at the other. Words such as semiliteracy, marginal literacy, survival literacy, and functional literacy are used to describe points along the continuum. Extensions of the use of the term *literacy* to imply competence are found in such expressions as computer literacy, economic literacy, and cultural literacy. The term *aliteracy* is used to describe the condition of individuals who can read and write but do not.

An additional goal of literacy development in school is the development of *critical literacy*. This is the ability not only to read and write but also to understand the power relationships in society through assessment of written materials that underlie or advance these relationships. Critical literacy proponents argue that literacy is not neutral and that reading and writing are shaped by social processes and patterns of power within social settings. For example, the work of Paulo Freire (1970) in teaching Cuban illiterates to read was based on the realization that, without literacy, some would remain on the bottom rung of the power structure ladder. Plantation owners in the antebellum United States did not allow their slaves to learn to read or write. The punishment often was severe if a slave even was caught with a book. Critics of high-stakes tests see these instruments as a way to ensure a permanent underclass of mostly minority, minimum-wage workers, because schools must pay greater attention to the memorization of facts than to the development of critical literacy.

Most humans develop proficiency in oral language before entering school, and that development continues to be refined and expanded throughout the school years. This is not the case, however, with literacy. A sizable number of children enter school with detriments that lower their likelihood of developing literacy with ease. The factors that inhibit the development of literacy and the further development of oracy are discussed in the next entry.

Dale Johnson and Bonnie Johnson

FACTORS THAT INHIBIT LANGUAGE DEVELOPMENT

The language development patterns described thus far are characteristic of the majority of but not all, language learners. Factors that inhibit language development are present in the child, the home, and the school.

Severe cognitive deficiencies are among the child-based inhibitors of language development. Some of the deficiencies stem from neurological sources, some from low birth weight, and others from prenatal drug or alcohol abuse by the mother. Psychological or physiological conditions that develop during childhood also can lead to cognitive deficiencies.

Early language impairment may result in delayed language development in children. Hearing impairment is one cause of this delay. Language initially is oral; therefore, children with hearing impairments may acquire oracy and literacy slowly. Language delay may be noticeable to parents, relatives, preschool teachers, or others who are in a position to compare children. Language-delayed two-year-olds may not use two-word sentences such as *All gone* and *Go bye-bye,* as most children that age do. They may not yet have fifty words that they can produce, as most two-year-olds have. Three-year-olds with delayed language may not be understood by their parents more than half the time. The delayed development may be an early indicator of a more general developmental disability or a neurological condition. There is variation in the rate at which children develop language. When there is a significant developmental delay, however, the children are likely to enter school far behind their peers, and it may become difficult for them to maintain the academic pace set by the curriculum—especially the development of literacy.

Children with uncorrected visual impairment may develop language quite normally up to the point of literacy acquisition. Much of what happens in school requires that children have the ability to read and write; therefore, it is imperative that any visual impairment be corrected. Schools usually provide visual screening tests for children who are entering kindergarten.

Another child-based factor that can delay language development is attention deficit hyperactivity disorder (ADHD). Symptoms of ADHD include an inability to pay attention and an inability to follow instructions. Children with ADHD often do not complete tasks, and they misplace things. They frequently are in motion or talk when it is not appropriate. They appear to daydream, and they interrupt other people's conversations. These characteristics contribute to a lack of attention to language learning and a delay in language development. ADHD typically is noticed when children are very young, but it may last into adult life. Children with ADHD often have difficulty developing their literacy skills throughout the school years—even though they may have normal or above-normal intelligence.

Dyslexia is a term for a congenital or hereditary condition that interferes with the acquisition of reading skills and often is a part of a broader language problem. Dyslexic children have difficulties with verbal coding, particularly phonological coding. Researcher Sally E. Shaywitz tracked dyslexics from elementary school through adulthood (Morris 2003). Based on the use of brain scans, she identified two groups. In one group, learners had a predominantly genetic type of dyslexia caused by gaps in their neural circuitry. A second group showed a more environmentally influenced type of dyslexia. There were no difficulties with the second group's language processing systems, but they relied heavily on memory rather than using other linguistic centers of the brain. Shaywitz asserted that dyslexics of the latter type were more likely to attend disadvantaged schools.

Family-based factors that can delay language development are many, among them a family history of difficulty with literacy. Children whose older siblings or parents have had problems with reading and writing often have those same problems. If children are diagnosed with a reading disability, there is a higher than average chance that other family members have had similar disabilities.

The literacy environment of the home contributes to language development and, in particular, the development of literacy skills. The most important factor in the home is the quantity and quality of verbal interactions between parents or caregivers and children. It is through these interactions that vocabulary and oral language facilities develop. Shared conversations and reading to and with children make a large difference. Children reared in homes without such verbal interactions and without a value placed on literacy (e.g., reading materials in the home, parents or caregivers who are readers), therefore, are at a disadvantage throughout their elementary school years.

Related to home environment is the language or dialect spoken at home. If most of the language used at home is a language other than the one used in school, or if the dialect spoken at home is a nonstandard dialect, children will have to learn a second language or nearly the equivalent of another language when they enter school, in addition to developing literacy.

A final home-based factor that influences language development of children is the socioeconomic status of the family. Children whose families have low incomes are more likely to lack proper medical care, dental care, and nutrition. Youngsters from low-income families frequently live in homes with only one parent—usually the mother. Due to the demands of outside employment and the stresses of coping with poverty, these parents have less time for verbal interaction with the children. Low-income families also are likely to have limited resources for such items as books, children's magazine subscriptions, computers, and other advantages that contribute to language and literacy development. Low-income families, therefore, often are unable to provide the same level of support to their children as that enjoyed by children from families of higher income.

Research has shown that children from low-income families likely have learned fewer words and conventions of language than children from middle- or high-income families. In addition to vocabulary deficits, spelling, reading, and composition skills among these children may lag behind those of the more affluent children. These deficits are hurdles for the children and their teachers to overcome. Research on reading and writing achievement conducted over the past thirty years shows a significant language gap based on socioeconomic status, and this gap has widened rather than narrowed. Low-income children are more likely to attend substandard, underfunded schools. These schools often lack basic supplies, such as sufficient literacy materials, school and classroom libraries, funds for field trips, and specialists to teach art and music.

Family-based factors that contribute to delayed language development are difficult to separate from factors that stem from the school children attend and from the neighborhood and community in which they reside. In recent years, language development activities in school have been dramatically altered. The imposition of high-stakes testing demands has had serious negative effects by narrowing the curriculum, placing unwarranted pressures on children and teachers, and restricting what goes on in schools. Valuable school time is spent in test-preparation activities, and this situation is especially the case in underfunded schools that serve children who are economically disadvantaged. Pressures have been placed on school administrators and teachers to increase test scores or face punitive actions—even school closure. Teachers, in turn, devote too much instructional time to drilling students for tests, because students in some states face the consequence of grade repetition if they fail the tests. Children from more affluent homes are spared the test-preparation anxieties, because they are more likely to enter school with well-developed language abilities and, as a result, have little difficulty with high-stakes tests. Their background experiences and literacy resources in the home have better equipped them for test language and content.

When schools are in need of repair, have inadequate resources, and are located in dangerous neighborhoods, there tend to be more classroom interruptions and disciplinary problems and more negative rather than positive reinforcement from school personnel. As a result, language development suffers. Too often the least experienced and least qualified teachers are assigned to the schools with the greatest needs. The demands of high-stakes testing isolate teachers from one another. The mood becomes competitive, and there is less discussion and sharing of ideas and resources. Parental or caregiver communication with teachers in underfunded schools may not be as prevalent as it is in more affluent areas. Single parents or caregivers often must work long hours to provide for their children. Sometimes the parent cannot leave work, for fear of job loss, to attend school meetings or conferences. In some cases, the parent or caregiver has no telephone or has lost phone service due to unpaid bills. Transportation to and from the school also can present major problems for the person who has no car or access to public transportation. It is well documented that children whose parents are involved in school affairs usually do better in school.

Language development does not proceed in an orderly fashion for all children. There are child-based, family-based, school-based, and societal factors that play important roles in how rapidly and how well language develops. Some deficits never may be overcome because the window of learning one's native language with ease begins to close at least by the time of early adolescence.

Several aspects of language have not received the instructional attention that is warranted by their prevalence in spoken and written language. Among them are onomastics; expressions such as idioms, proverbs, and catchphrases; slang; special sayings such as slogans and mottoes; and abbreviations. The next section examines these colorful but often overlooked aspects of language.

Dale Johnson and Bonnie Johnson

Other Aspects of Language Development

Onomastics

Onomastics is the study of names. Names are so commonplace that they often are ignored as a source of material to enrich language learning. Humans seem to have a propensity to attach a name to everything. This eliminates confusion when referring to particular persons, places, and things, but humans go beyond this practical type of naming to include names for things such as boats (e.g., Bev's Barge) and cars (e.g., The Clunk). Single-family homes with names usually are expensive real estate (e.g., Southwind Manor, Murmuring Pines). There are many categories of names, including *eponyms, toponyms, pseudonyms,* and *demonyms.*

Eponyms are words named after people, and they are numerous in English. The medical profession lists at least 15,000 eponyms. Among them are *Down syndrome* named for British physician John Down (1828–1896), *Parkinson's disease* named after British surgeon James Parkinson (1755–1824), and *Alzheimer's disease* named for German neurologist Alios Alzheimer (1864–1915). Eponyms can be found in nearly every category of words. Under the category *plants,* eponyms include *bibb lettuce* (Jack Bibb, 1789–1884), *boysenberry* (Rudolph Boysen, 1895–1950), and *douglas fir* (Scotsman David Douglas, 1798–1834). *Guppy* (after Trinidadian R. J. Lechmere Guppy, 1836–1916) is an example of a fish eponym, and *graham crackers* (after Sylvester Graham, 1795–1851) is an example of a food eponym. Some other eponyms in common use are: *blanket* (noun), *blurb, boycott, cardigan, diesel, Frisbee, maverick, Reuben sandwich* (double eponym), *salmonella,* and *watt.*

Toponyms are words named after places. *Paisley* takes its name from the Scottish town of Paisley where the pattern originated. *Tuxedo* comes from Tuxedo Park, New York, where the formal wear became popular in the 1880s. *Canaries,* the tiny yellow birds, are named after the Canary Islands. Other common toponyms include *mayonnaise, tangerine, denim,* and *rhinestone.*

Pseudonyms are names that people use that are different from their birth names. People use pseudonyms for a variety of reasons: to avoid gender or ethnic discrimination, to hide one's real identity, and to simplify a birth name, among others. Authors sometimes use pseudonyms that are called pen names. Table 23.1 shows well-known authors' pen names and their birth names.

Demonyms are names for people who live in specific places. For example, a person from New York State is called a New Yorker. A person from Florida is a Floridian. Attempts have been made to identify rules for

Table 23.1

Pen Names

Pen Name	Birth Name
Mark Twain	Samuel Langhorne Clemens
George Eliot	Mary Ann Evans
Agatha Christie	Agatha Mary Clarissa Miller
Lewis Carroll	Charles Lutwidge Dodgson
Dr. Seuss	Theodore Seuss Geisel

Source: Bonnie von Hoff Johnson, *Wordworks: Exploring Language Play.* Golden, CO: Fulcrum Resources, 1999.

Table 23.2

Demonyms

City, State	City Demonym	State Demonym
Baraboo, Wisconsin	Barabooian	Wisconsinite
Council Bluffs, Iowa	Council Bluffsian	Iowan
Long Beach, California	Long Beacher	Californian
Lubbock, Texas	Lubbockite	Texan
Montpelier, Vermont	Montpelierite	Vermonter
New Orleans, Louisiana	New Orleanian	Louisianian
Portland, Maine	Portlander	Mainer

Source: Paul Dickson, *Labels for Locals: What to Call People from Abilene to Zimbabwe.* Springfield, MA: Merriam-Webster, 1997.

forming demonyms; however, constructing demonyms usually is a result of what the local denizens prefer to call themselves. Table 23.2 illustrates the variety of demonyms within the United States.

There are other areas of onomastic study such as *odonyms* (street names), *anemonyms* (storm names, such as Hurricane Andrew), *nicknames* (e.g., The Big Easy, The Cornhusker State), *aptronyms* (names that seem to fit one's profession, such as Sara Bones, M.D., and Marvin Dime, coin dealer), and unusual town and city names (e.g., Two Egg, Florida; Peculiar, Missouri).

PROVERBS

Proverbs are concise statements that give advice (e.g., Haste makes waste) or make an observation about living (e.g., They know most who know they know little). Most proverbs are quite old and can be found in all cultures. Proverbs from long ago include *You can lead*

a horse to water, but you can't make it drink (1100s); *Out of sight, out of mind* (1200s); *Time heals all wounds* (1300s); *Still waters run deep* (1400s); *Feed a cold, starve a fever* (1500s); *Don't cry over spilled milk* (1600s).

Proverbs often use rhyming words (e.g., Two in distress makes sorrow less) or alliteration (e.g., Never trouble trouble till trouble troubles you). Sometimes proverbs are metaphors (e.g., Don't judge a book by its cover). There are several proverbs that contradict one another. Among them are:

A heavy purse makes a light heart; and *Money isn't everything.*
The early bird catches the worm; and *Late is often lucky.*
The squeaky wheel gets the grease; and *Silence catches a mouse.*
Slow and steady wins the race; and *Slow help is no help.*
Nothing ventured, nothing gained; and *Better safe than sorry.*
Look before you leap; and *Those who hesitate are lost.*
Too many cooks spoil the broth; and *Many hands make light work.*

Although many proverbs date back centuries, some are of more recent vintage and have American origins. A few of these are: *Money doesn't grow on trees* (1750); *If the shoe fits, wear it* (1773); *An apple never falls far from the tree* (1839); *There's always room at the top* (1900); *You can't unscramble eggs* (1928); *One who slings mud loses ground* (1940); and *The best things in life are free* (1940). Children in the intermediate and upper grades begin to develop an awareness and understanding of proverbs.

IDIOMS

An idiom is an expression whose meaning is different from the usual meanings of the words that comprise the idiom; the expression cannot be taken literally. For example, the idiom *to get cold feet* does not mean that one's feet are chilly. It means that one is reluctant to do something. There are so many idioms in the English language that entire dictionaries of idioms have been compiled. For those whose first language is not English, or for young

Table 23.3

Idioms

Animals

a wild goose chase	to call off the dogs	to take the bull by the horns
living high on the hog	a white elephant	to get on one's high horse
monkey business	a sitting duck	a cash cow

Colors

to paint the town red	to have a green thumb	to talk a blue streak
to get a pink slip	rose-colored glasses	not to have a red cent
to be true blue	to see red	to look green around the gills

Food

to spill the beans	sour grapes	to dangle a carrot
to bring home the bacon	to have egg on one's face	one's bread and butter
pie-in-the-sky	icing on the cake	a piece of cake

The Body

a sight for sore eyes	at your fingertips	to put one's foot in one's mouth
sticky fingers	head in the clouds	two left feet
to have a big head	hand over fist	to have one's nose in the air

Numbers

to put two and two together	on cloud nine	to zero in on
in seventh heaven	to dress to the nines	to put in one's two cents
to two-time someone	behind the eight ball	a three-ring circus

Source: Bonnie von Hoff Johnson, *Wordworks: Exploring Language Play.* Golden, CO: Fulcrum Resources, 1999.

children who are developing language, learning idioms can be challenging.

Many idioms have staying power, as the following idioms and the dates they entered English reveal: *at a snail's pace* (1400), *to keep one's nose to the grindstone* (1532), *too many irons in the fire* (1549), *to smell a rat* (1550), *to walk on eggs* (1621), *not to hold a candle to* (1640), *to have bigger fish to fry* (1660), *with flying colors* (1692). William Shakespeare is credited with coining several idioms that still are in use today, including *it's Greek to me, salad days, green-eyed monster, something is rotten in [the state of] Denmark,* and *to go against the grain.* Other well-known writers used idioms to make their writing more colorful. Examples include Edgar Allan Poe (*to go by the book*), Charles Dickens (*before you can say Jack Robinson*), Bret Harte (*to cost a pretty penny*), and Arthur Conan Doyle (*crystal clear*).

Part of the richness of language learning is knowing the story behind the origin of some idioms. Although idioms are figurative expressions, many originally had literal meanings. The idiom *to give someone the cold shoulder* comes from a practice popular during the 1800s. When an unexpected, unwanted visitor appeared on one's doorstep around meal time, that visitor might be fed a piece of cold meat—often a cheap shoulder portion instead of something more elegant or substantial. *To strike while the iron is hot* can be traced to a tale by Chaucer in 1386. It originally referred to the work of blacksmiths who had to shape iron before it cooled. Grade school children often enjoy using idioms in their speech and writing and find them amusing.

Idioms can be found in most languages. Some foreign language idioms are comparable to idioms in common use in English. For example, German speakers might say, *Es liegt mir auf der Zunge,* and English speakers would say, *It's on the tip of my tongue.* Americans say that someone is *rolling in money,* and Germans say, *im Geld schwimmen* (swimming in money).

Some idioms fall into categories, as illustrated in Table 23.3.

SLANG

Slang refers to words and expressions created by subcultures for known concepts. *Plastic* is slang for credit cards. Slang is not jargon, which is words and expressions created by members of a particular occupation. Jargon usually is more technical than slang. Although some slang might be offensive to certain individuals, much slang has been around so long that it eventually became a part of Standard English. Words such as cranky, groggy, and dull (i.e., boring) are words that originally were considered slang. Some slang, like some idioms, has been in use for a long time. For example, *broke* (i.e., lacking money) entered English in 1661, *lowlife* in 1766, *flunk* in 1837, and *mouthpiece* (i.e., a lawyer) in 1857. Slang from the early 1900s included *gooey* (1903), *dud* (i.e., a failure, 1904), and *cushy* (1915). For a slang term to earn longevity, it must be picked up by more than just members of the group that coined the term. With today's mass media, a slang term that finds its way to a medium with a large audience will have a better chance of becoming part of our everyday language than will those that do not receive media coverage. Some concepts seem to generate a wealth of slang. These include money (e.g., greenbacks, bread, lettuce, moola, do-re-mi), cars in poor condition (e.g., crate, beater, junk heap, rust bucket), and important people (e.g., big cheese, high mucky-muck, big enchilada). Slang is a part of everyday language, and its use is especially appealing to youth who want to demonstrate that they are members of a subgroup.

CATCHPHRASES

Catchphrases are sayings that have been popular with a large group of people during a particular time. *Chalk that up to experience* is a catchphrase from the 1800s. As with slang, idioms, and other types of colorful words and expressions, many catchphrases have become so commonplace that they have worked their way into Standard English. Familiar catchphrases include *all dressed up with no place to go* (1914); *last of the big spenders* (1920s); *famous last words* (1930s); *back to the drawing board* (1940s); *Is it bigger than a breadbox?* (1950); *Don't call us, we'll call you* (1961); *on a scale of one to ten* (1970s); *been there, done that* (1980s); and *Get a life* (1990s).

SLOGANS

Slogans are sayings that try to persuade readers or listeners to support a particular person, product, or position. Slogans usually are brief and often rhyme. Examples of campaign slogans that supported certain candidates include *Tippecanoe and Tyler too* (1840, William Henry Harrison), *Phooey on Dewey* (1948, Harry S Truman), *I Like Ike* and *We're Madly for Adlai* (1952, Dwight D. Eisenhower and Adlai Stevenson), and *The Nation Needs Fixin' with Nixon* (1972, Richard M. Nixon).

MOTTOES

Mottoes are sayings that often inspire readers and listeners. They can be used as tools of persuasion, but they are not commercial. Some mottoes have only one word. For example, *Forward* is the motto of the State of Wisconsin. One of inventor Thomas Edison's mottoes was *There is no substitute for hard work.* Theodore Roosevelt's motto was *Speak softly and carry a big stick; you will go far.*

ABBREVIATIONS

Abbreviations, which are shortened forms of words or phrases, can be traced back to ancient Egyptian, Greek, and Roman written languages. Dictionaries containing hundreds of thousands of abbreviations in English have been compiled, but they all fall into five major categories: initialisms, acronyms, clipped words, blends, and words that are abbreviated in writing only. They are learned in the same ways as words and idioms.

Initialisms are abbreviations that can be spoken only as letters. Common initialisms include *AI* (artificial intelligence), *CPR* (cardiopulmonary resuscitation), *ER* (emergency room), *FBI* (Federal Bureau of Investigation), *RDA* (recommended daily allowance), and *TBA* (to be announced).

Acronyms are abbreviations that are pronounceable words and are made from the first letter or letters of a group of words. The number of acronyms has exploded since World War II. Some well-known acronyms include *FEMA* (Federal Emergency Management Agency), *NATO* (North Atlantic Treaty Organization), and *UNICEF* (originally, United Nations International Children's Emergency Fund). Some acronyms have become so familiar that it is easy to forget that they are not single words. Examples include *scuba* (self-contained underwater breathing apparatus), *radar* (radio detecting and ranging), and *laser* (light amplification by stimulated emission of radiation).

Clipped words are abbreviations in which parts of words stand for entire words. Words can be clipped from the front (e.g., *burger* from hamburger), the back (e.g., *chimp* for chimpanzee), or both front and back (e.g., *flu* for influenza). Some familiar clipped words include *auto* (automobile), *demo* (demonstration), *lab* (laboratory), *phone* (telephone), and *pro* (professional).

Blends are abbreviations that consist of two or more other words. Blends also are called *portmanteau* words. Common blends include *brunch* (from breakfast and lunch), *flurry* (from flutter and hurry), *glimmer* (from gleam and shimmer), *infomercial* (from information and commercial), and *splatter* (from splash and spatter).

Some words are abbreviated for writing only. Examples of these words include *adj.* (adjective), *attn.* (attention), *bldg.* (building), *blvd.* (boulevard), *co.* (company), *dept.* (department), *Dr.* (doctor), *hr.* (hour), *Mr.* (mister), and *tbsp.* (tablespoon).

Most children have a fascination for words and language practically from birth, and many exhibit natural talents for language manipulation. Children develop language abilities through playing with words and expressions. There are two benefits to children when schools incorporate activities with the aspects of language described in this section: children's interest in language is enhanced, and they learn to comprehend and produce these frequently occurring language elements.

A newborn child faces a long journey in language development that begins with the first cooing sounds and continues to the level of sophistication in comprehension and usage that they achieve by the time they enter high school. For some the journey is smooth, but for others it is bumpy. The acquisition of spoken and written language just may be the greatest intellectual feat of anyone's lifetime.

Dale Johnson and Bonnie Johnson

GLOSSARY

ADHD. Attention deficit hyperactivity disorder, characterized by impulsivity, inattentiveness, and lack of motivation.

Blend. A word consisting of abbreviated forms of two or more other words. *Caplet* is a blend formed from *capsule* and *tablet*.

Catchphrase. A phrase or sentence popular with a large group of people. "On a scale of one to ten" is a catchphrase from the 1970s.

Cherology. The study of signs and gestures and their functions in sign language.

Clipped word. A type of abbreviation in which a part of a word stands for the word. "Burbs" is a clipped word for suburbs.

Conversion. A word whose part of speech has changed without adding a prefix or a suffix. In the sentence "Dan passed the final," the word "final" has been converted from an adjective to a noun.

Dactylology. The study of finger movements that correspond to letters or letter combinations used in finger spelling by some hearing-impaired people.

Dyslexia. Reading disability characterized by delayed phonological coding in persons with adequate vision and hearing and normal intelligence and language development.

Emergent literacy. Development of the association of print with meaning and the awareness of reading and writing concepts.

Eponym. A word named after a person. "Boycott" is an eponym named after Captain Charles Boycott (1832–1897).

High-stakes test. A test with serious consequences (e.g., repeat the grade, receive no diploma) for failure.

Holophrase. A single word used to express the meanings of a phrase or a sentence (e.g., a baby says, "puppy," but means, "Where is the puppy?").

Idiom. An expression whose meaning is different from the meanings of the individual words. "To paint the town red" means to celebrate in a big way.

Initialism. A type of abbreviation that can be spoken only as letters. FDA (Food and Drug Administration) is an initialism.

Jargon. Words or phrases that are common to a specific occupation or hobby. "Rubric" is an example of education jargon.

LAD (Language Acquisition Device). A theorized innate cognitive characteristic that enables an infant to acquire language naturally.

Lexeme. A lexical item of meaning that may be a word or a nonliteral expression such as an idiom.

Lexicon. A work of reference (e.g., a dictionary, glossary, word list) that lists and explains words.

Literacy. Fluency in reading and writing.

Literary response. A cognitive or emotional reaction to what is read.

Mental lexicon. All the words, meanings, and related information about the words in a person's mind.

Morpheme. A minimal unit of form and meaning including words, prefixes, suffixes, and inflected endings (e.g., walk*s*, walk*ing*).

Morphology. The study of the structure of words and their meaningful units.

Motto. A word, phrase, or sentence that is particular to a person or group of people and is intended to inspire others. The motto of the state of New Hampshire is "Live free or die."

Onomastics. The study of names.

Oracy. Fluency in speaking and listening.

Orthography. The study of written symbols and their functions in language.

Paralanguage. Voice variation, gestures, and facial expressions that affect meaning.

Phoneme. A minimal unit of speech sound used in combinations to form words.

Phonology. The study of speech sounds and their functions in language.

Pragmatics. Language choices and their effects in social interactions.

Proverb. A saying that makes an observation or offers advice. Proverbs often are metaphorical; for example, "Make hay while the sun shines."

Semantics. The study of the meanings of words, sentences, denotations, connotations, implications, and ambiguities.

Semiotics. The theory of signs, their meanings, and relations in language and life.

Slogans. A word, phrase, or sentence that is intended to be influential or persuasive. A 1948 Truman campaign slogan was "Don't tarry—vote Harry."

Syntax. The study of the structural patterns of acceptable word order in phrases and sentences.

Telegraphic speech. An early stage in language development in which all but essential words are omitted.

Toponym. A word named after a place. "Limousine" is a toponym from Limousin, France.

Unique beginners. Overarching categories of concepts (e.g., event, feeling) from which all subordinate concepts stem.

Word webs. Networks of interrelated words.

REFERENCES

Aitchison, Jean. (1994) *Words in the Mind: An Introduction to the Mental Lexicon.* 2nd ed. Oxford, UK: Blackwell.

———. (1997) *The Language Web: The Power and Problem of Words.* Cambridge, UK: Cambridge University Press.

Altmann, Gerry T.M. (1997) *The Ascent of Babel: An Exploration of Language, Mind, and Understanding.* Oxford, UK: Oxford University Press.

Arnheim, Rudolf. (1969) *Visual Thinking.* Berkeley: University of California Press.

Bloom, Paul. (2000) *How Children Learn the Meanings of Words.* Cambridge, MA: MIT Press.

Bolinger, Dwight. (1968) *Aspects of Language.* New York: Harcourt, Brace and World.

Bowerman, Melissa, and Stephen C. Levinson, eds. (2001) *Language Acquisition and Conceptual Development.* Cambridge, UK: Cambridge University Press.

Bruner, Jerome S. (1960) *The Process of Education.* New York: Vintage Books.

Clark, Eve V. (1993) *The Lexicon in Acquisition.* Cambridge, UK: Cambridge University Press.

Crystal, David. (1997) *The Cambridge Encyclopedia of Language.* 2nd ed. Cambridge, UK: Cambridge University Press.

Dickson, Paul. (1997) *Labels for Locals: What to Call People from Abilene to Zimbabwe.* Springfield, MA: Merriam-Webster.

Fellbaum, Christiane, ed. (1998) *Wordnet: An Electronic Lexical Database.* Cambridge, MA: MIT Press.

Flood, James, Diane Lapp, James R. Squire, and Julie M. Jensen, eds. (2003) *Handbook of Research on Teaching the English Language Arts.* 2nd ed. Mahwah, NJ: Lawrence Erlbaum.

Freire, Paulo. (1970) *Pedagogy of the Oppressed.* New York: Continuum.

Gaur, Albertine. (1984) *A History of Writing.* Rev. ed. New York: Cross River Press.

Harris, Theodore I., and Richard F. Hodges, eds. (1995) *The Literacy Dictionary.* Newark, DE: International Reading Association.

Hirsch, E.D., Jr. (1988) *The Dictionary of Cultural Literacy: What Every American Needs to Know.* Boston: Houghton Mifflin.

Huey, Edmund Burke. (1908) *The Psychology and Pedagogy of Reading.* New York: Macmillan.

James, Sharon L. (1990) *Normal Language Acquisition.* Boston: Allyn & Bacon.

Johnson, Bonnie von Hoff. (1999) *Wordworks: Exploring Language Play.* Golden, CO: Fulcrum Resources.

Johnson, Dale D. (2001) *Vocabulary in the Elementary and Middle School.* Boston: Allyn & Bacon.

Johnson, Dale D., and Bonnie Johnson. (2002) *High Stakes: Children, Testing, and Failure in American Schools.* Lanham, MD: Rowman & Littlefield.

Kucera, Henry, and W. Nelson Francis. (1967) *Computational Analysis of Present-Day American English.* Providence, RI: Brown University Press.

Lighter, J.E., ed. (1994) *Random House Historical Dictionary of American Slang, Volume I.* New York: Random House.

———. (1997) *Random House Historical Dictionary of American Slang, Volume II.* New York: Random House.

Mayo Foundation for Medical Education and Research. (2002) *Understanding Attention-Deficit Hyperactivity Disorder (ADHD).* Rochester, MN: Mayo Clinic.

Miller, George A. (1991) *The Success of Words.* New York: Scientific American Library.

Morris, Bonnie Rothman. (2003) "Two Types of Brain Problems Are Found to Cause Dyslexia." *The New York Times,* 8 July, D5.

Pinker, Steven. (1994) *The Language Instinct: How the Mind Creates Language.* New York: HarperPerennial.

Snow, Catherine E., M. Susan Burns, and Peg Griffin, eds. (1998) *Preventing Reading Difficulties in Young Children.* Washington, DC: National Academy Press.

Tomasello, Michael, and Elizabeth Bates, eds. (2001) *Language Development: The Essential Readings.* Oxford, UK: Blackwell.

Vygotsky, Lev S. (1962) *Thought and Language.* Cambridge, MA: MIT Press.

Wade, Nicholas. (2003) "Early Voices: The Leap to Language." *The New York Times,* 15 July, F1, F4.

24

Semiotic Principles and Human Communication

Semiotics is the study of how meaning is made both consciously and unintentionally through the activity of signals, signs, symbols, and systems of signs and their interactions. As an example, the sun has been used by humans to indicate a variety of information. Louis XIV of France was known as the Sun King, an indicator of his power and glory. People may use the phrase "her sunny smile" to indicate the warmth of a person. The dashboard of an automobile utilizes the iconic marker of a sun to show where to turn on the lights of the car. People indicate happiness through phrases such as, "You are my sunshine." Each of these instances employs a sign, symbol, or system of signs used in communication acts. Semiotics is the study of how signs connect to other signs and become communication. This process is called semiosis, and is the study of the actual processes and effects of action and the making of meaning by humans, other animals, and nonhumans in culture and nature. Therefore, semioticians study the processes and exchanges of the interactions that occur between people, other animals, and events that transpire as cultural, biological, and chemical exchanges.

Semiosis is seen as a dynamic and constant process. Whenever people ask how or what happened, or what led from step one to step two of an exchange or interaction, they are engaging in a semiotic hunt for the signals and signs of activity. As examples, people and other animals interpret and act upon the noise and smoke of a developing forest fire, a child is pulled away from a growling dog by an adult, and a teacher decides that a student who didn't turn in her mathematics homework receives a zero. In each of these events, there is a process of interactions and exchanges between animals, people, and nature, or

a deliberate setting where activity creates other activity. In the example of the forest fire, usually smoke and flame represent, or act as signals of, danger to all living beings. However, signs and signals can also be misinterpreted. To a forester, the forest fire could represent nature's ability to self-regulate and rejuvenate the forest; the growling dog was perhaps actually being friendly and trying to get attention, or the child did not turn in her homework because there had been a family emergency and she had been expected to take care of her brother and sister. Semiotics is the study of the process of how signs, symbols, and systems of signs evolve and can be interpreted.

Semioticians view language as a component of a range of communicative processes that help in the awareness about what is known and how things are known. Semiotics extends the study of human language as it expands the concept of language to the deliberate and unintentional communicative interactions of culture and nature. It makes a difference where someone lives, such as in a city or a rural area, just as it makes a difference whether someone grows up as a male or female in a particular society, in how one uses language to communicate. For example, in Australia, if one wants a portable light source, he/she asks for a torch. In the United States, someone asking for a torch in a dark situation would elicit a different response from an American. Context also makes a difference in reference to a species of animals, such as cows, where they are born and if they are in a culture where humans regard them as a food source or as special creatures. Semiotics investigates the diverse and inverse relationships between people, cultures, and natural phenomena; semiotics can be seen at the heart of every experience and event. Any social reality or culture is a community of meaning making, and language in any community is more than shared words or sentences. A shared cultural base means that there is an "exchange of meanings in interpersonal contexts" where people act out the social structure in their daily lives, "affirming their own statuses and roles, and establishing and transmitting the shared systems of value and of knowledge" (Halliday 1978, 2). Those shared values exist as semiotic pathways where people use and interpret signals, symptoms, signs, indices, symbols, and names to communicate information about society. A U.S. flag flying at half mast from a public building indicates that someone important to the nation has died or that there has been a publicly acknowledged disaster, such as 9/11, which in itself has become a sign that represents the destruction of the World Trade Center, the attack on the Pentagon, the airplane crash in Pennsylvania, and the erosion of feelings of immunity from terrorism for Americans on September 11, 2001.

Linda J. Rogers

SEMIOTIC PRINCIPLES

There are many discussions on using signs to engage in understanding how humans communicate, either effectively or ineffectively, and how signs have been used specifically in human meaning making (Deely 1990). Three influential twentieth-century semioticians with specific theories concerning semiotics were the Swiss linguist Ferdinand de Saussure (1857–1913); the American Charles Sanders Peirce (1839–1914); and Thomas Sebeok (1920–2001), a Hungarian who did much of his work in the United States but extended his work to engage semioticians working internationally.

FERDINAND DE SAUSSURE

Ferdinand de Saussure's theory on semiotics grew from "his lecture notes from 1907 to 1911 on general linguistics" (Smith 2001, 54), and focused on the study of language. Saussure discussed language comprising two aspects, the signified and a signifier. The signifier is the sign/word that society has agreed upon to represent a specific thing and the aspect of

the sign that is the "signified" is the concept, or set of concepts about that sign that evolves or emerges from social usage. There is, according to Saussure, an arbitrary relationship in language between a sign of a word and how society uses the word/sign. Saussure used the word *tree* as his illustration. The word tree, in English, is an arbitrary word, but it is the word used as the sign for tree. The use of the word tree for a speaker of English will bring an image or concept of a tree to the signifier, so that a treelike image, the signified, comes to mind. If the word tree is used when a very young child points to a flower or a log, the child will be "corrected" and be given the word tree as the signifier for the tree object. Therefore, the child will form a series of communicative relationships making distinctions between things and people and will know the difference between a tree and a flower, and a tree and a pole, and a tree and a tall man. People share a general concept of "trees" so that if the word tree occurs or a sentence pattern is used with the word tree, such as, "a chestnut tree" or "that group of trees," a speaker of English does not expect to see a clump of flowers or a stretch of grass. The sign of tree is not representational—tree is an agreed-upon sign. Tree is the signifier that means tree.

The word tree, however, can be a signified concept, such as, "He is as unbending as that tree." The signification of the word tree in society has cultural implications and agreements and it is the signification of tree that becomes the point of engagement and discussion. For example, a friend of mine went to a Chinese restaurant with a boy he mentors as a Big Brother. The boy could not remember the word for the dish he wanted but said, "those things that look like little trees." My friend was able to understand that the boy was referring to broccoli because of how the notion of little trees was being used in that context. Different cultures or subgroups within a culture could have varying perspectives on trees, such as the use and value of trees, the use or value of places that trees grow, or who makes decisions about trees. Although the word tree is the signifier of the thing that is a tree, culture, through societal discussion, determines the signification of what meaning and value is given to a tree, or a group of trees, at any given time. Given that meaning is constantly undergoing change, semiotics is not just language or an ascribed term, rather it is the cornerstone of agreements and understandings at the core of social life (Blonsky 1985).

CHARLES SANDERS PEIRCE

Charles Sanders Peirce's work on signs (in Merrell 1995; Smith 2001) evolves from his extensive discussion on signs as being universal phenomena and basic to human experience. He accords signs the primary medium of human communication. He stated, "We think only in signs . . . in use and experience meaning grows" (Peirce 1931–58, 53). His discussion of signs catalogs the process, or the semiosis of how thought forms into signs through features that he described as firstness, secondness, and thirdness as a streaming effect. Firstness would be that aspect of the sign as a "quality, sensation, sentiment . . . the mere possibility of some consciousness of something" (Merrell 1995, 38). For the purpose of this discussion imagine a person noticing a small, black, furry creature on four legs with a tail in his backyard, assuming that it must be a cat. The initial recognition is the firstness of the concept.

Secondness is considered what something is in relation to something else. For example, that same person, when observing the small, black, furry, creature then begins to make a distinction between a cat and a skunk. The person would observe, "That is not a cat," while taking in information that what he was looking at was a small, furry, black *and white* creature, with four legs and a tail, but not quite knowing what the creature is.

Thirdness would be the mediation or the negotiation between points of evolving information: (1) that it is a small, black, furry creature (firstness); (2) it is not a cat (secondness); and (3) that it is other than a cat; it has a white stripe upon its back and tail and then the signification, or consciousness, along with having the convention or knowledge of other not-cat creatures, forming the category of skunk (thirdness).

Each act ties into one another and requires a flow of knowing or translation of knowing between perception and consciousness of what something is and what is known about it. It is not a question of a person's intelligence as much as having a perception of a concept, a framework or convention of knowledge, as well as an experiential base for that concept. As an example, although there are still many places in the world where computer access is limited, no one expects a school in the United States to be newly stocked with typewriters. The entire set of expectations, language, behavior skills, and even products having to do with how schools prepare students for writing acts has changed since the mid-1980s and the ubiquity of personal computers. Many ten-year-old children would not know what they were looking at if they were given a box of carbon copy paper suitable for making multiple copies of a document on a typewriter, although they would understand current computer-related concepts and terminology such as being "online" and getting "email."

Peirce's work in semiotics is a complex system of organizing communicative processes. Once the concept of a sign having firstness, secondness, and thirdness is comprehended, Peirce presents ten classes of signs (Merrell 2001) to help a semiotician discuss art, mathematics, time, the sciences, and philosophy. Peircian semiotics creates a process of semiosis as flowing from sign to sign, of being linked to extending and multiple sign systems so that each sign is inevitably connected and related to other signs. For example, the sign "child" can be related to youth, issues on parents, health, and an evolving myriad of signs depending upon the context and the sign user. Peirce did not believe in meaning as a stable or given entity, but as a continually changing process depending upon how a sign was linked to another sign. For example, the concept of spam used to refer to a canned and processed meat product, but now spam, as a term, has been linked to unwanted email and evolved in meaning. Signs are always going to change according to the user and how the signs are contextually linked.

THOMAS SEBEOK

Thomas Sebeok (1920–2001) began his academic career as a linguist (Deely 2001) but his work in semiotics, which encompasses both Saussurian semiotics and Peirce's semiotic schema, extended from a science of signs to a doctrine of signs and he viewed semiotics "as the umbrella term for the doctrine of signs in its full extent" (p. xxv). Sebeok invited scholars in diverse fields of study to apply semiotic analysis to other animals (zoosemiosis), plants (phytosemiotics), and to open the study of signs as biosemiotics (Hoffmeyer and Emmeche 1999). Sebeok's vision of semiotics as a general doctrine extends the study of signs to incorporate the biological, or all living things, as well as microorganisms. Therefore, as Saussure posited, semiosis is not just what happens as a product of the interactions between language and philosophical or cognitive factors; instead, semiotic study encompasses evolving interactions of the natural, cultural, and even imagined world. A child who grows up learning to be aware of the impeding smell of snow adjusts to weather, food, terrain, the types of animals, and hears different stories or sagas of goodness and courage than the child who grows up in a desert. Semiotics, according to Sebeok (1994), includes how any being or thing creates or reacts to messages in a given context. People who utilize semiotic analysis are able to examine in detail messages, their frameworks, and receivers or receptors as an ongoing and changing process. Sebeok's response to the question, "What is semiotics?" was that it is "'the exchange of any messages whatsoever—in a word, *communication*.'" (Nuessel 2001, 13) A goose honks as a warning of danger to goslings, human pulse rates increase at times of excitement or illness, and a teacher uses grades of A, B, C, D, or F to symbolize a student's effort in a class. Sebeok saw semiotics as the process of the exchange of signs and sign systems that humans use in any type of communication.

Linda J. Rogers

USING SEMIOTICS

There are extensive discussions on the variety of signs and their descriptions, as well as what signs do, and who or what uses signs (Eco 1979; Deely 1990; Noth 1990; Sebeok 1994; Merrell 1995; Smith 2001), but for the purpose of this discussion I will focus upon humans using signs. As Eugen Baer stated, "While the whole universe may be perfused with signs, and while innumerable species may be using signs, only humans actually make signs the object of systematic studies, only we humans practice semiotics" (2001, 8). The basic premise of Many semioticians is that semiosis consists of a three-way relationship. That is, in any given sign vehicle, there is the sign itself that stands for something else, a referent (what the

sign represents), and the user or interpreter, who makes distinctions between the referent and the sign. The word school can be a sign for a place, as in a building or center, where learning happens; it is also a referent in that different people and different cultures have a variety of understandings of what school is, who has access to schooling, and what is appropriate in teaching/learning situations. Both the sign and referent change in relation to whom and for what purpose they are being interpreted. A teacher may have a different understanding or interpretation of school than a student, parent, or a community. Each aspect of the three-way process is interdependent upon the others.

To illustrate that, consider using the concept of school as the referent of a sign. The referent of a sign brings with it a constantly evolving set of ideas, expectations, and impressions depending on who is discussing the concept of school. So, although a semiotic relationship can be drawn between the sign, the referent, and the interpreter, that relationship is always in motion and continuous. Each sign is dependent upon the other signs with which it is connected. Therefore, the sign, "school," needs to be seen in relation to other signs, such as: child, teacher, a person with disabilities, a school event (testing, retention, graduation), or the history of schooling, and those signs are dependent upon the innumerable signs and interpretations that are present in that particular discussion.

There are basic semiotic tools that semioticians use to investigate their various fields and disciplines to help them refine and/or make distinctions in delineating the functioning of signs: referents, and interpreters. Sebeok (1994), Danesi (1994), and Danesi and Perron (1999) list six types of signs: signals, symptoms, icons, indices, symbols, and names. Frank Nuessel's article in Simpkin and Deely's *Semiotics 2000: "Sebeok's Century"* (2001) gives another very useful summary of these definitions:

1. Signal: This is a sign that naturally or artificially triggers a reaction in or to a receiver. A dog loudly barking and baring its teeth signals aggression to the person confronting the dog. The poisonous Australian red-back spider has a bright red mark on its back, a signal of danger to someone overturning a lump of wood.

2. Symptom: Symptoms are natural outcomes or links to signs. They are automatically linked to one another. For example, swelling and redness of the skin indicates the possibility of having been exposed to poison ivy; or coughing and eyes stinging are symptoms of having been exposed to heavy smoke from a fire.

3. Icon: Icons are signs that represent a similarity between what is signified and what it is. A typical icon would be a road sign representing dangerous turns in the road about to be approached, or a right arrow with a cross through it indicating no right turn is allowed. Another typical icon is a capital *H* indicating that a hospital is nearby.

4. Index: Sebeok (1994) writes that the index is contiguous, or closely related to the sign that it represents. Footprints in snow are indexical markers that someone has been walking in winter.

5. Symbol: Symbols have a more arbitrary relationship between what they are and what they represent. They evolve through conventional use. For example, someone in a hospital may be considered a medical doctor when wearing a long white coat and stethoscope around her neck. Or, the use of fencing to symbolize, even in vast unpopulated areas, spaces that the general public is not invited to use. Symbols, however, have evolved through convention, culture, and as a part of communicative usage, and do not mean the same thing to all people. The word "organic" when used as a sign of a particular aspect of food production is a positive sign to some people while to others it is a sign of unnecessary expense.

6. Names: These are signs that give or create a class or grouping, such as people with disabilities, veterans, the unemployed, college graduates, Native American Indians, seniors, bacteria, and flowers. Groupings also indicate professional membership and behaviors. Lawyers study law and deal with people only on legal issues. Medical doctors treat people for health issues. Medical doctors in the United States usually use the sign "Dr." in front of their names, but that sign does not always indicate that someone is a medical doctor. Names of people are frequently used for their symbolic value, such as Faith or Angel.

SEMIOTIC ANALYSIS

These six sign functions allow a researcher/philosopher to analyze communicative acts in any given situation from diverse perspectives. The actual properties or conventions of a sign undergo change as society changes. In the recent past, a restaurant might have displayed a sign indicating that a public phone is available inside, but many restaurants now display signs that have the shape of a cell phone with a large X covering the image, indicating that cell phones are not permitted. As a further example, the evolution of terms and concepts dealing with disability studies are rich in semiotic interpretation. A person with disabilities could be seen as undergoing communicative and interpretive processes within a culture. Linda Rogers and Beth Swadener (2001) used applied semiotic analysis to discuss the effects of labeling (naming) people into categories such as learning disabled, or deaf, or hard of hearing. Who participates in the creation of these categories? Does the creation of these categories lead to more open systems of access and communication (Noth 1990) or do these labels create a categorical system that socially stigmatizes an individual (closed systems), making it more difficult to be known for what the person can do rather than what a person cannot do? A meta-analysis of what is considered disability in a given culture would examine how a person is assigned wholeness and is seen as being able to fully participate in social and educational events compared to those who are considered disabled and for whom facilities for social participation are not provided. Or, what physical, social, or psychological differences determine whether or not a person is considered able or disabled considering everyone differs in ability and expertise? "Is someone who is deaf going to be framed only and continually by that deafness or by their complete range and style of interactions?" (Rogers and Swadener 2001, 5) Semiotic analysis allows a researcher to investigate the referents of signs and their inherent links, as in able persons compared to people with disabilities and the cultural messages that are intended and unintended (e.g., when only stairs are available for access to a sports arena), as well as how an individual or culture responds and interprets available signs.

Linda J. Rogers

APPLIED SEMIOTICS

An applied semiotic analysis means that a researcher will examine in detail the signals, symptoms, icons, indexes, symbols, and names of a particular area of study. As semiotics seeks connections that link sign to sign, it also looks at the nature of the links and meanings that humans use to make or communicate other connections. Humans make knowledge, take knowledge, and use knowledge. Applied semiotic methodology traces the semiosis of linking information to make more knowledge, or different categories of knowledge, and examines how knowledge becomes both personal and generalized to different frameworks. Donald Cunningham (1995) adapted Gilles Deleuze's rhizome metaphor to illustrate that point (see Patton 1996). A rhizome, a specialized underground plant stem, has no fixed points of connection, and its tangled roots mean that there are no hierarchies in its connection process and its structure is constantly changing. One structure could break away or be broken away from the main group and reform, making an entirely new grouping and system of connections. Similarly, therefore, using a semiotic lens to examine a particular field allows an examination of how culture interplays with human considerations.

A sign can overrepresent, or overdetermine, how a person is acknowledged. If an observer saw a man sitting in a wheelchair, the observer would automatically think that the man was unable to walk on his own. However, many even raise their voices to someone in a wheelchair as if that person also had problems with hearing. For some people, the prevailing concept of disability overrepresents the person in the wheelchair so that he or she is considered as having multiple disabilities.

John Rausch, Rhonda VanMeter, and Cheryl Lovett (2002) utilized semiotic analysis to examine the phrase "think things over" (p. 35) as it applied to the twenty-five adolescents with whom they worked. These teenagers came from backgrounds that had been categorized as at-risk, meaning that common features of their lives included poverty, low academic achievement, and social and emotional problems. Adult social workers had further characterized these at-risk youth as making poor or unfortunate decisions, and the teenagers were judged to be impulsive, failing to consider the consequences of their actions. The teenagers were told often to "think things over" but these young people had difficulty expressing their emotions and had lived through "traumatic experiences, such as physical and/or sexual abuse" (p. 37) as well as losing people they loved. One of the reasons the teenagers were in trouble was because they had difficulty finding ways, or frameworks, to think about, or understand how to think about, their traumatic experiences. Furthermore, since the teenagers did not verbalize or put their experiences into language they could not render them into thought. These thoughts, then, were nonexistent and unavailable for the teenager to "think over."

Using semiotic analysis meant the researchers could examine how all the participants connected to the sign of the word *thought*. It was important to understand the differences in how the teenagers and the social workers perceived the referent of thought and its relationship to language as a necessary step to "thinking things over." It is a feature of semiotics that all the participants in the dynamic could examine their expectations and presumptions and reinterpret those to make other communicative links that were more helpful for all. The social workers needed to examine their ideas and sign pathways concerning how they linked thought to experience, to developmental processes, and their subsequent expectation of behavior modification.

The teenagers needed sign pathways to form communicative links between feelings, language, and experience. The researchers suggested that expressive frames, or other sign systems—painting, drawing, creating a short story, using music, or drama—be attempted so that the teenagers could find a means to translate or to communicate, to themselves and others, their deeply troubling experiences; then, those experiences could be available for reflection. The researchers were able to provide the teenagers with artistic sign systems so that they could explore their feelings.

Once the teenagers shaped their feelings into an

art form, that art form could be discussed as symbolic representation and the young people could, through the artistic sign pathways, begin to recognize signals or triggers of anger and exert control or channel their feelings more appropriately. Igor Klyukanov (2002, 27) believes that language behavior has a two-way relationship "between communicative needs and available tools." The adolescents' range of communication strategies grew as they were introduced to another way of representing their thinking. It was paradoxical that the social workers, who had expertise in age-appropriate strategies for teenagers and were communicating their ideas in non-complex terminology ("thinking things over"), were nevertheless asking the teenagers to do the very activity that was unavailable to them.

Using semiotics as a methodology does not simplify a field of observation. It is a communicative strategy that in effect re-complicates or brings into detail all of the processes, implications, expectations, and nuances of a situation. It is a deliberate and painstaking investigation of what is present in a communication act and who are the interpreters. Semiotic analysis in this situation highlighted paradoxes and double binds in the scenario of the social workers and the teenagers. The teenagers had "lost" people they trusted and did not have access to language structures that would help them recognize situations or feelings that initiated feelings of hostility, depression, or rejection. They had used the thought processes that were available to them and as one boy stated, "I think I can trust animals more because I can talk to animals and I know they won't tell anybody. If they leave, or die, there is always another one that is exactly like it" (Rausch, VanMeter, and Lovett 2002, 35). The teenagers had engaged in thought processes but that semiosis, or connective processing of thinking did not bring them into control of their feelings or more communication. For them, thinking, was a sign pathway that related to adults they did not trust and who had proved emotionally dangerous to them in the past. Those sign pathways then related to communicative links that meant "telling" and telling connected to links of psychological or physical pain.

The social workers' expertise in development meant that they had an expectation of cognitive strategies, or analytic thinking skills that typical teenagers should be able to use. According to Piagetian theory (Piaget 1959), between the ages of eleven or twelve and beyond, the onset of adolescents engage in Formal Operational Thought, where they can think hypothetically, logically, and abstractly. By this time, adolescents have developed thinking strategies that allow them to imagine or explore situations for their outcomes and consequences. A typical teenager is able to "grasp" situations in terms of "imagined or deduced events" (p. 149). The adolescent can also explore notions of interpersonal and social possibilities.

Through deductive thought processes the teenager can reason what is appropriate behavior, what are social norms, what is wanted, and what it would mean—or what would be the probable outcome of engaging in non-socially accepted behavior. Those steps are the "thinking it over" processes that the social workers expected the adolescents to use. However, although an adolescent is capable of forming theories, the theories formed by teenagers are interdependent with experience and social interactions. For the at-risk teenagers in this study, the directive statement "thinking things over" did not have contextual value. They had practiced suppressing their experiences and their feelings about them. Their schema for thinking linked to their distrust of people and into the schema of "not telling." The process of using semiotics analysis meant that each party in the discussion had to examine their sign referents and understand what thought meant to each interpreter in the situation as well as what links were being made by each interpreter as connective bases to other concepts.

To utilize the rhizome metaphor and the process of semiosis, there were multiple and diverse connections surrounding the sign-word, *thought*. Those schemas needed to be traced, disembedded, and decoded, and then recoded so that a general understanding of the concepts of thought and action related to the teenagers. The at-risk teenagers were enabled, through the use of artistic sign pathways, to conceptualize their feelings and begin to recognize their own signs and patterns of behavior. The social workers also had to reconceptualize their understanding of what they knew as developmentally appropriate thinking and action in terms of these particular teenagers.

Linda J. Rogers

Semiotics Principles and Human Development Issues

Formal developmental theories (Piaget 1959; Thomas 2000) begin with sign pathways that present the process of the semiosis of human growth and development as an individual acquiring increasingly complex attainments. The infant moves into childhood, then adolescence, and finally adulthood on a hierarchical grading of development, a linear movement upward into complex thinking strategies and elaborated skill development. Although Piaget clearly states that his theories only apply to those children who experience typical development, nevertheless he believed that all children moved through sequential, hierarchical, transformational, and universal patterns. However, when actually examining the schematic world of young children, it is obvious that they are able to make cognitively complex distinctions in their thinking. For instance, almost all children at a very early age are expected to demonstrate differentiating behavior between a parent and an uncle or an aunt, between a sister and a female cousin, or between a family friend and a teacher.

Children are also required to recognize themselves as symbolic representations of a social order, e.g., "My family is Italian American," even though their family has lived in the United States for three or more generations. Children also recognize the difference between public and private behaviors. They learn quickly that there are family patterns of behavior, such as what words parents use and what words they can use.

Children also learn what is expected on a broader social range, such as whether or not a boy or girl can cry in public and to whom they can tell secrets. A semiotic reading of childhood situates cognition (Kirshner and Whitson 1997) as a process that evolves between children, communities, available experience, social customs and practices, and even historical time periods. Alan Prout and Allison James (1997) state that rather than theorists discussing childhood as representing a "culture of childhood" with specific tasks and organizing patterns, there are many experiences of childhood. Children are not just the representation of "biological immaturity" (p. 8). Children's experiences will differ according to their gender, social expectations, available role models, economic status, health, and their own active involvement in the given social context they act within. A semiotic reading of the sign "child" means that a child is also understood to be an active participant, a "giver and receiver of messages" (Rastier 1997, p.5) in an evolving set of conditions that includes social practices and expectations. Semiotic readings of signs, such as child, teenager, and adult, would examine the semiosis or connections between the society and individual(s) being discussed and attempt to detail the communication schema and processes that contribute to each sign.

Using semiotics as an analytic tool is an attempt to gain an understanding of the diverse meanings held in communicative situations, and the responses that are made, intentionally or unintentionally, by message makers. Signs are part of the informal world of communicative exchange in the form of smiles and frowns or a raised voice. Signs are an essential part of every culture's formal and deliberate organization into social order in terms of teaching the representational nature of letters and numbers, historical context, artistic representations, and scientific information. Signs also convey available role models for men and women that give information on how people are expected to interact as well as what is not socially sanctioned behavior or activities. Signs are used by everyone and everything in communicative processes. The field of semiotics and human communication examines the processes, or the semiosis, through which signs—through the process of interpretation—become understood, and the overt and covert meanings society has attached to signs, symbols, and sign systems.

Linda J. Rogers

REFERENCES

Baer, Eugen. (2001) Ecce Homo: How semiotics becomes what it is. *The American Journal of Semiotics* 17, no. 2 (Spring): 7–18.

Blonsky, Marshall, ed. (1985) *On Signs.* Baltimore: Johns Hopkins University Press.

Bohm, David. (1988) *Wholeness and the Implicate Order.* London: Ark Paperbacks.

Cunningham, D. (1995) "Timeless Ideas." Paper presented at the Annual Meeting of the American Educational Research Association, San Francisco (March).

Danesi, Marcel. (1994) *Signs: An Introduction to Semiotics.* Toronto: University of Toronto Press.

Danesi, Marcel, and Paul Perron. (1999) *Analyzing Cultures: An Introduction and Handbook.* Bloomington: Indiana University Press.

Deely, John. (1990) *Basics of Semiotics.* Bloomington: Indiana University Press.

———. (1994) *The Human Use of Signs or Elements of Anthroposemiois.* Lanham, MD: Rowman & Littlefield.

———. (2001) "Sebeok's Century." In *Semiotics 2000: "Sebeok's Century,"* ed. S. Simpkins and J. Deely, xvii–xxxiv. New York: Legas.

Eco, Umberto. (1979) *A Theory of Semiotics.* Bloomington: Indiana University Press.

Elam, Keir. (1980) *The Semiotics of Theatre and Drama.* London: Methuen.

Halliday, M.A.K. (1978) *Language as Social Semiotic: The Social Interpretation of Language and Meaning.* London: Edward Arnold.

Hoffmeyer, Jesper, and Claus Emmeche. (1999) "Code-Duality and the Semiotics of Nature." In *On Semiotic Modeling,* ed. Myrdene Anderson and Floyd Merrell, 117–66. Berlin: Mouton de Gryter.

James, Allison, Chris Jenks, and Alan Prout. (1998) *Theorizing Childhood.* New York: Teachers College Press.

Kirshner, David, and James A. Whitson. (1997) *Situated Cognition: Social, Semiotic and Psychological Perspectives.* Mahwah, NJ: Lawrence Erlbaum.

Klyukanov, Igor. (2002) Language behavior as semiosis. *International Journal of Applied Semiotics* 3, no. 1 (Spring): 23–32.

Merrell, Floyd. (1995) *Peirce's Semiotics Now: A Primer.* Toronto: Canadian Scholar's Press.

Noth, W. (1990) *Handbook of Semiotics.* Bloomington: Indiana Press University.

Nuessel, Frank. (2001) "Thomas A. Sebeok: A Review of His Contributions to Semiotics." In *Semiotics 2000: "Sebeok's Century,"* ed. Scott Simpkins and John Deely, 1–17. New York: Legas Press.

Patton, P., ed. (1996) *Deluze: A Critical Reader.* London: Blackwell.

Peirce, Charles Sanders. (1931–58) *The Collected Papers.* Vol. 2. Cambridge, MA: Harvard University Press.

Piaget, Jean. (1959) *The Language and Thought of the Child.* New York: Meridian.

Piaget, Jean, and Barbel Inhelder. (1969) *The Psychology of the Child.* New York: Basic Books.

Prout, Alan, and Allison James. (1997) "A New Paradigm for the Sociology of Childhood? Provenance, Promise and Problems." In *Constructing and Reconstructing Childhood: Contempory Issues in the Sociological Study of Childhood,* ed. Allison James and Alan Prout, 7–33. London: Falmer Press.

Rastier, Francois. (1997) *Meaning and Textuality.* Toronto: University of Toronto Press.

Rausch, L. John; Rhonda VanMeter, Cheryl R. Lovett. (2002) The artistic expression of emotion. *International Journal of Applied Semiotics* 3, no. 1 (Spring): 33–44.

Rogers, Linda J., and Beth Blue Swadener, eds. (2001) *Semiotics and Disability: Interrogating Categories of Difference.* Albany: State University of New York Press.

Sebeok, Thomas. (1994) *Signs: An Introduction to Semiotics.* Toronto: University of Toronto Press.

Smith, Howard A. (2001) *Psychosemiotics.* New York: Peter Lang.

Thomas, Murray R. (2000) *Comparing Theories of Child Development.* Belmont, CA: Wadsworth Thompson Learning.

25

DEVELOPMENT OF QUANTITATIVE AND SPATIAL THINKING

The study of mathematics content and pedagogy requires an in-depth understanding of the cognitive and intellectual processes in the course of human development. Accordingly, this chapter deals with the course of an individual's most basic cognitive forms of mathematical knowledge—quantitative development and spatial development.

Research in mathematics development and cognition suggests that young children are active learners. In fact, experts in the fields of mathematics development and cognition since the mid-1990s have obtained astonishing results from numerous experiments suggesting that quantitative awareness begins at birth—even from the first days following birth. Infants show interest in the external world shortly after birth and this interest unfolds in a variety of forms into adolescence and adulthood. The concepts of magnitude and comparison are two of the earliest forms of quantitative—that is, early mathematical—thought. However, this position regarding young children's mathematical development was by no means dominant among psychologists and early childhood specialists in the past. We need only hark back to the pre-behaviorist models of learning advocated by Edward L. Thorndike (1905) and subsequently by William Kilpatrick (1951) during the first few decades of the twentieth century.

PHILOSOPHICAL-PSYCHOLOGICAL UNDERPINNINGS AND PERSPECTIVES

We can place the psychological roots of quantitative and spatial thinking and learning in perspective from two closely interrelated models. The first model (Figure 25.1) has to do with the philosophical bases of how we as human beings know not only mathematics, but also any field of study. Historians of the discipline of psychology have generally—and often crudely—categorized these views under the headings of empiricism, rationalism, and materialism. Since the essential question has to do with how we know anything, one can examine various perspectives of knowledge acquisition based on the philosophical underpinnings of each of these terms.

For the empiricist, the identification of knowledge acquisition is based on three significant components. The first component has to do with the idea that anything we know is an outcome of the senses (e.g., what we see or hear). The second component deals with the number of times that something occurs through the senses, that is, the probability that something takes place. The higher the probability that something occurs, and the greater the number of people who perceive that situation through the senses, the greater the validity of the existence of that occurrence—hence, knowledge of something. The third component is founded on causal properties, or the association between an external element and one's learning of something based on that element.

In another psychological perspective, knowledge acquisition deals with the individual's physiological endowments; that is, one's level of knowledge acquisition has little to do with association and everything to do with the individual's brain composition—the individual's neurological system. The materialists and nativists would most often favor this view.

In a third perspective, we find the rationalist view, which argues that if knowledge is the result of one's experiences (the empiricist view), then these experiences are founded on core, a *priori*, precepts that govern any form of experience. A number of mathematicians, mathematics educators, philosophers of mathematics, and developmental psychologists, particularly in the area of mathematical thinking and de-

Figure 25.1 Philosophical/Psychological Bases for Mathematics Thinking and Learning
(Arrows indicate more than one philosophical position.)

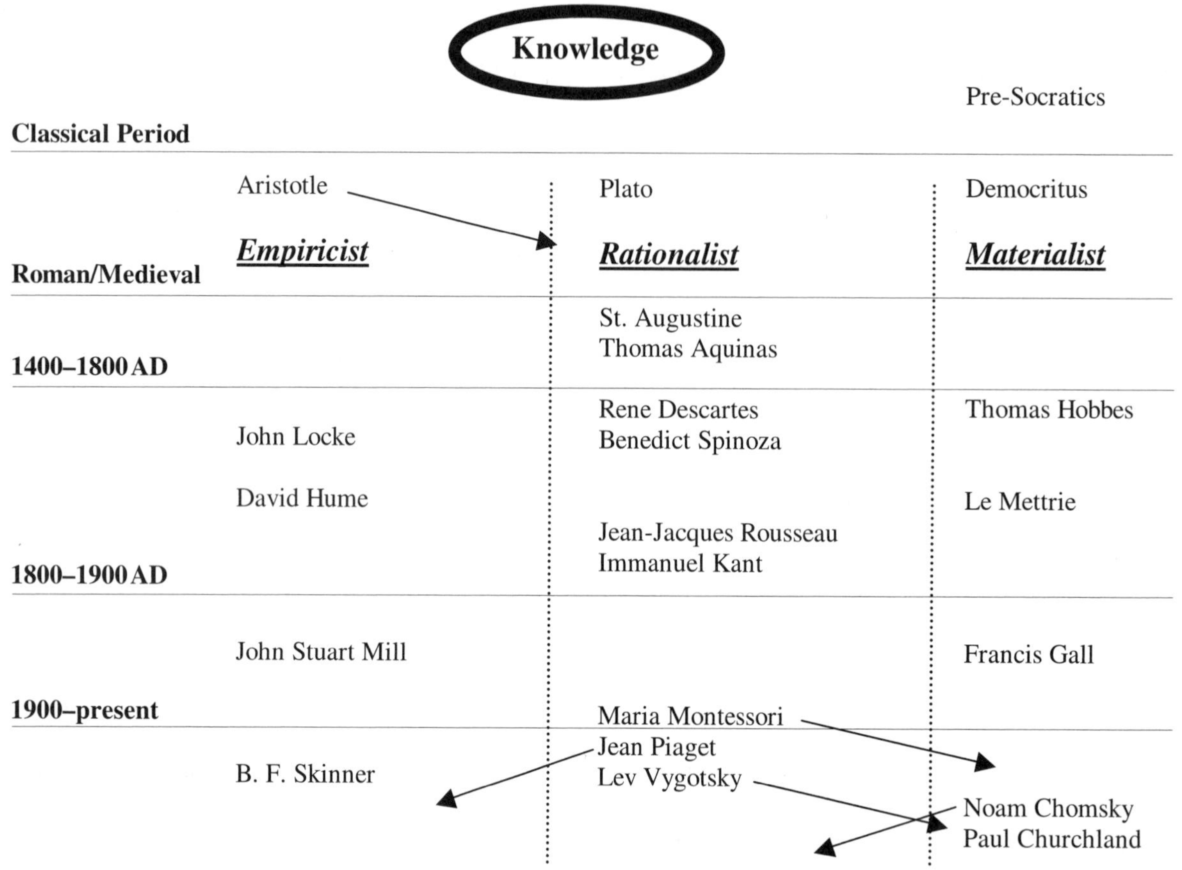

	Knowledge	
		Pre-Socratics
Classical Period		
Aristotle	Plato	Democritus
Empiricist	**_Rationalist_**	**_Materialist_**
Roman/Medieval		
	St. Augustine Thomas Aquinas	
1400–1800 AD		
John Locke	Rene Descartes Benedict Spinoza	Thomas Hobbes
David Hume		Le Mettrie
	Jean-Jacques Rousseau Immanuel Kant	
1800–1900 AD		
John Stuart Mill		Francis Gall
1900–present		
	Maria Montessori	
B. F. Skinner	Jean Piaget Lev Vygotsky	Noam Chomsky Paul Churchland

Researchers in the Acquisition of
Mathematical Concepts and Procedures

Although the individuals listed below may not be categorized in any single philosophical-psychological tradition (Empiricist, Rationalist, Materialist), their work may lean toward at least one of the three philosophical-psychological strands.

Learning Theoretical Experimental Psychological	**Developmental Psychological Schema-Based**	**Nativist Neurocognitive-Scientific**
Elizabeth Fennema	Robert Davis	Catherine Sophian
David Geary	Herbert Ginsburg	Rochelle Gelman
Robert Siegler	Arthur Baroody	Karen Wynn

Source: Adapted from Arthur Baroody, "The Development of Adaptive Expertise and Flexibility: The Integration of Conceptual and Procedural Knowledge." In *The Development of Arithmetic Concepts and Skills: Constructing Adaptive Expertise*, ed. Arthur Baroody and Ann Dowker. Mahwah, NJ: Lawrence Erlbaum Associates, 2003.

velopment, would favor the philosophical underpinnings of the rationalist view because their belief is that certain mathematical principles are not created, but are discovered. This view of mathematical thinking dates back at least as far as Pythagoras in the sixth century BC, and later to Descartes of the sixteenth and seventeenth centuries AD. In short, the belief that the bisection of a rectangle produces two equal right triangles, or, that the square of the length of the longest side of a right triangle is equal to the sum of the squares of the lengths of the two shorter sides is a commonly held rationalist argument in that this idea (the so-called Pythagorean Theorem) was present prior to our own existence and will be present well beyond human existence. That is, these mathematical principles have always existed apart from experience and disconnected from physiological or material components.

THE MEANING OF MATHEMATICS AND MATHEMATICAL THINKING

In addition to the significance of philosophical and psychological perspectives, definitions for the term "mathematics" abound. Individuals who espouse the "mathematics standards" movement define mathematics as "the identification and appreciation of patterns and relationships" (National Council of Teachers of Mathematics [NCTM] 2000).

The twentieth-century German-born philosopher Ludwig Wittgenstein (1967) defines "mathematics" as "a motley of techniques and proof." Later, he says that "mathematics . . . is always measure, not [the] thing measured. . . ." That is, mathematics is not the measurement of distinct objects; rather, it is the concept of measure.

Mathematical thinking, however, cannot be defined in the same manner as mathematics because mathematical thinking is a dynamic process that spans a period of time. Mathematics, on the other hand, is a system of rules using a set of symbols (grammar or semiotic relationships) and structure and order of those symbols (syntax) that govern the process of solving both pure and practical problems.

CHAPTER COMPONENTS

Important aspects of quantitative development and spatial development—the foundational components of mathematical thinking and cognition—will be discussed in this chapter. Discussion of these two seminal areas of study will be divided into ten entries. The first entry discusses the origins of these foundational components of mathematical thinking and cognition, in particular, the development of quantitative and spatial abilities of infants, toddlers, and preschool-aged children. The following two entries will deal with the acquaintance and familiarity with mathematical symbolism among young children and the learning of operative mechanisms of the quantitative concepts that are referred to by those symbols, respectively. In the fourth entry, spatial development is discussed in a broad context. This is followed by a general, and related, discussion on the topic of mapping and location concepts.

A general discussion follows—comparing, contrasting, and synthesizing procedural knowledge and conceptual knowledge. The seventh entry discusses mathematical process skills associated with cognitive development of mathematical thinking with an emphasis on problem solving. The eighth entry deals with mathematical errors and misunderstandings of both procedures and concepts. The following entry has to do with mathematical thinking in older children, adolescents, and young adults, and their strengths and possible misconceptions that are based on the analyses of errors discussed in the previous entry. The tenth and last entry discusses mathematical learning disabilities and the strengths and weaknesses of students who have been diagnosed with any one of these disabilities. A fairly exhaustive glossary of important terms associated with mathematics and quantitative and spatial thinking can be found at the end of the chapter. Contemporary cognitive research, primarily research based on the contributions of the Swiss psychologist Jean Piaget, as well as post-Piagetian research and its integration with neurocognitive psychology, permeates the chapter.

Daniel Ness

SPONTANEOUS/EVERYDAY MATHEMATICS AND THE DEVELOPMENT OF NUMBERS

This entry begins with a general overview of mathematical thinking from birth, and how infants con-

strue quantities. The entry then continues with definitions of spontaneous mathematics and everyday
mathematics and summarizes the role of mathematical thinking during the preschool years.

A number of cognitive research scientists within
the past decade have suggested that mathematical
thinking begins only a few days after birth. Mathematical thinking in this case refers to evidence that
demonstrates the infant's reaction to quantity,
whether it be discrete numbers or amount. Research
on the cognitive development of infants with regard to quantitative reasoning has been undertaken
by a number of experts in the fields of cognitive
psychology. The work of two individuals—namely,
Rene Baillargeon and Karen Wynn—will be discussed in detail.

Rene Baillargeon's interest in infant cognition is
broader in scope than Karen Wynn's work—the
former investigating general cognitive abilities (1995)
and the latter focusing on mathematical cognition
(see Wynn 1998). Nevertheless, Baillargeon has conducted a number of studies to tap whether infants
may have much more cognitive appreciation of the
physical world and reality than Piaget would have
contended, based on his writing on the sensory motor stage. One study that illustrates Baillargeon's
approach is the following:

> An infant is able to look at a platform that has a
> box on it. And there are several scenes presented.
> In one scene, the box is quite firmly sitting on the
> middle of the platform. In the next scene, the box
> has been moved very close to the edge of the plat-
> form. In the third scene, the box has been moved
> right off the platform. (see Figure 25.2)

The technique that Baillargeon and many other
infant cognition specialists (like Karen Wynn with
number cognition) use is a method known as inspection time (sometimes referred to in the literature as "looking time")—the amount of time a child
actually looks at something as evidence of recognition or interest.

An infant of three months old will spend very little
time looking at the depiction of the box on a platform. The same infant will spend a little bit more
time but not a significantly greater time looking at a
box that is at the edge of that platform. The movement of a box from the center of the platform to the

Figure 25.2 **Baillargeon's Platform Task**

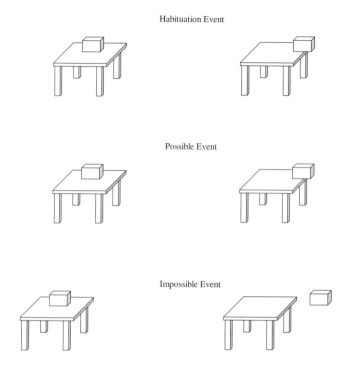

Habituation Event

Possible Event

Impossible Event

edge of the platform is referred to as the habituation
event. Now, if you have the box off the platform,
suspended in midair without any supports whatsoever, this three-month-old infant will gape at the
scene. The evidence of manifest uncertainty, namely,
"What is going on here?" is evident when you observe videotaped excerpts of infants who are subjected to these and similar scenarios. Any adult
looking at the scenes of the box would say: "This
box is suspended in thin air, and there is absolutely
nothing holding it." Baillargeon's findings suggest
that the infant already has a conception of how objects in the external world are supposed to behave.
When an object in the external world even as the
form of a depiction violates what might be referred
to as the laws of physics as understood within the
experiential context of infant life, it may be necessary to reconsider when cognition in general and
spatial sense in particular really begin.

Baillargeon then takes infants who are six-and-one-
half months old. This is a long time in development
from three to six-and-one-half months. Now the box
is either in the middle of the platform, or at the edge
of the platform—half on and half off, or it is a little
bit more than half off the platform. This arrests the
attention of the six-and-one-half-month-old because

this young child is having a "surprise" perception: "This object is very close to going off the edge."

Research of this kind is part of a large realm of findings challenging Piaget's stage theory: The more we learn about infants, the more we learn that they are more intelligent than we have ever thought. Individuals are able to do things at much earlier points than Piaget's theory would suggest. It is not even quite clear whether the stage concept is the most valid concept. Different infants differ in abilities related to perception of spatial structures. Some have argued that cognitive development is a rising and falling of certain waves of ability and prowess. The story is not complete about this since the data are still not all in. But what can be said is that the more one learns about infants, the more intelligent they get.

Similarly, Wynn's (1998) research, involved the use of a display of a small number of objects. She, too, uses a method involving infants' inspection time as a means of tapping into infant cognitive development. The sequence of events in Wynn's experiments adheres to the following procedure:

1. A hand is shown moving into the left side of a large open box and placing an object in the infant's view.
2. A screen is then used to cover the box so that the object is hidden from the infant's view.
3. The hand leaves the scene empty.
4. The hand re-enters the box with a second object. The screen is still covering the box. So, either two objects are present, or one object is present, and the second object that was considered is placed out of sight behind the screen.
5. The hand leaves the scene empty or with one object.

Two situations may occur. In the first situation, the screen drops, and two objects are revealed. In the second case, the screen drops, and only one object is revealed. Wynn's results demonstrate that infants showed surprise and longer periods of inspection when the number of objects remaining (one object in the above case) did not match the number of items in the change that had occurred, namely, the addition of another object. So, the infant expected more than one item. In general, Wynn's research is groundbreaking in that it was the first time a researcher found evidence showing the ability for an infant of perhaps a few days or

weeks old to be able to distinguish between one object and more than one object (Wynn 1998).

Wynn's research has shed a great deal of light on the origins of mathematical development. However, a good deal of Wynn's results led many cognitive specialists to conclude that quantitative ability is part of our innate endowment. In other words, Wynn takes a nativist position with respect to the origins of quantitative development. Another current view, namely that based on the research of Mix, Huttenlocher, and Levine (2002), considers the role of mathematical thinking of infants to be founded on the role of overall amount—that is, infants do not yet possess the cognitive wherewithal to distinguish between discrete numerical values (i.e., natural numbers); instead, they think in terms of amount (i.e., more versus less). This position is less nativistic in that it does not support the notion of full endowment of quantitative abilities—one's natural tendency to identify one-to-one correspondence—from birth.

EVERYDAY MATHEMATICS/ SPONTANEOUS MATHEMATICS

Spontaneous mathematics is a term commonly associated with the development of mathematical thinking in early childhood, particularly with the everyday mathematical concepts learned before one enters formal schooling. This term is frequently used by educators and psychologists who embrace the constructivist position of learning because their position on the development of knowledge is strongly situated within the belief that learning unfolds as a result of schema (for example, sucking one's thumb to satisfy the sucking reflex) that develop shortly after birth. This process of unfolding, then, allows children to invent new strategies for solving problems from prior situations. A large number of these problems involve quantitative and spatial thinking processes.

Other common terms that have been used by individuals in the developmental psychology and mathematics education communities in place of "spontaneous mathematics" are "informal mathematics," "everyday mathematics," and sometimes "practical arithmetic." The term informal mathematics is a general term mostly associated with nonwritten mathematical activity. Everyday mathematics is often used to describe children who are engaged in both written and non-written mathematical activity outside of the school context. Given their casual use in research and in practice, these meanings are not entirely definitive.

RELEVANT RESEARCH

The idea of spontaneous mathematics—a topic rich in both quantitative and qualitative educational research—was developed as a means of challenging the commonplace belief in popular culture that young children cannot do mathematics, and that the subject is initially encountered upon entering formal schooling. Empirical evidence suggests that mathematical thinking begins shortly after birth. In order to identify the significance of spontaneous procedures in solving mathematical problems, researchers have developed assessment techniques that are suitable for identifying such behavior. Standardized assessments are not suitable for measuring such activity because they do not allow the investigator to tap into children's thinking procedures. Instead, developmental psychologists and mathematics educators rely on observational techniques for the most part to identify children's spontaneous cognitive behavior. One of the most conducive environments for observing children in their "natural" setting is in the preschool during free-play hours. This is because children in this setting are more interested in their involvement in a play activity than wondering why a grownup is observing them.

Spontaneous mathematics occurs well beyond birth. Although the amount of time spent on mathematical activity actually increases with age, preschoolers in general are engaged in spontaneous mathematical activity nearly 50 percent of the time during free play. There seems to be an increase in spontaneous mathematical activity during free play and other informal contexts as children increase in age. At the same time, there is a lack of social class (SES) differences when considering frequency of children's spontaneous mathematical activity (Ginsburg, Pappas, and Seo 2001). Despite the apparent lack of SES difference, spontaneous mathematical activity seems to be more frequent among children of certain nationalities, for example, Chinese preschoolers (Ginsburg, Lin, Ness and Seo 2003).

SPONTANEOUS ACTIVITY INVOLVING COUNTING AND NUMBERS

As early as three years and six months of age, young children develop informal strategies for counting objects. Since counting, a generally accepted informal mathematical activity, is considered by many in educational and cognitive research to be the basis for formal mathematical instruction, educators and psychologists have developed assessment techniques, like the clinical interview or contextualized observation, as a means of identifying young children's spontaneous strategies in determining cardinality of sets and one-to-one correspondence—two indispensable criteria for counting objects properly.

By counting objects and ideas in a one-by-one manner, children work hard at attempting to master the counting procedure. Nevertheless, their accuracy improves greatly with time. However, counting itself is only one part of spontaneous mathematical activity. The strategies for counting provide even more evidence that spontaneous mathematics occurs. The following are some of these spontaneous strategies:

1. *Pushing aside.* One important strategy that children use to develop more efficient counting using spontaneous techniques is the process of pushing aside. Children spontaneously discover a simple and elegant procedure for counting one by one. After a child counts an object, she simply moves it to the side, away from those that remain to be counted. This strategy is extremely powerful because it minimizes strain on the child's memory. At this point, it is not necessary to remember which individual objects in a random collection have and have not been counted. Having pushed to the side each object counted, the child need only remember to count all remaining items. Invention of this simple strategy results in a tremendous increase in accuracy.

2. *Tagging.* Pushing aside demonstrates a spontaneous action on the part of the child to facilitate counting in an efficient manner. However, one step above this action is the process of tagging, which does not account for the time spent pushing objects aside from the ones that are not yet counted. Instead, tagging involves making a one-to-one correspondence between a child's finger, which points to, or touches, an object of a set, and the objects themselves. This procedure allows the child to arrive at answers and conclusions about sets slightly more quickly than pushing aside alone.

3. *Subitizing.* There is an obstacle to pushing aside, however; as time progresses, children develop ways

to become more efficient in their problem solving. And this problem solving is associated with mathematical thinking. After using more primitive strategies, like pushing aside or tagging, children learn to "see" small numbers directly so that they do not need to count small collections—that is, those consisting of two, three, four, or five—to know their number. They can perceive ♦♦♦♦♦ as "five," just as they can directly convert the letter "w" into the sound "double you." This kind of spontaneous recognition of number is called subitizing, which comes from the Italian "subito," often found in musical notation, and means "immediate." Children practice subitizing when they repeatedly count sets and remember the results. If a child counts to a number enough times, they learn to "see" that number without actually counting each object of the set.

4. *Grouping.* After mastery of immediate recognition of number with regard to objects, children develop grouping strategies that allow them to determine numbers in increasingly efficient ways. Often they begin by grouping objects by twos. Instead of counting one by one, a child may count "two, four, six. . . ." to yield a result. As seen in Figure 25.3, a child in the third grade might determine the number of dots in the set below by identifying five groups of three dots and an additional two dots—17 dots altogether.

5. *Arithmetic Procedures.* Older children use relatively advanced forms of arithmetic in basically the same strategy. In solving the "dot" problem above, another third grader might solve this situation by saying: "I know that five times three is 15, plus two is 17." Indeed, this strategy is easier than counting; if developed properly, it is just as accurate. As seen from the above spontaneous strategies, children proceed from counting one by one to applying operations to groups of objects of a set.

PRACTICE OF SPONTANEOUS MATHEMATICAL ACTIVITY

Spontaneous mathematical activity need not solely be associated with numbers and the operations connected with them. This form of activity is also evident in children's involvement with spatial and geometric activities. Two preschool children, Les and

Figure 25.3 **Arrangement of Seventeen Dots**

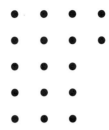

Samantha, both approximately three years six months, decide to walk over to the block area. Both children insist upon building a "big square" that they will use as a hurdle as soon as it is complete. Les and Samantha demonstrate their understanding of spontaneous geometric concepts as they are constructing their big square, using different sizes of blocks. Their big square, however, looks more like a rectangle with unequal adjacent sides than a square.

What, if any, mathematical ideas stem from this account? First, although their rendition of the big square appears more like a rectangle than a square (given that the opposite sides of their figure are equal and the adjacent sides are not), they do know that the term "square" is also associated with a four-sided figure and four right angles. A second aspect of their construction is their desire to be meticulous and precise in making certain that the big square is enclosed and resembles a four-sided figure with four right angles. In working together to construct their big square, both children used four types of blocks for their structure: the half-unit, unit, double-unit, and the quadruple-unit block. These are typical block sizes in the standard block set. Les initially places one quadruple-unit block parallel to the wall at a distance equal to approximately five unit blocks. The children do not begin to build the perpendicular sides; instead, they place another quadruple-unit block next to and parallel with the wall and also parallel with the initial quadruple-unit block.

The children then construct the left perpendicular side, using a double unit block and two unit blocks. Next, knowing that they need to close the gap, they use two half-unit blocks to do so. The right perpendicular side was the last to be constructed. At this point, they were running out of double-unit and single-unit blocks. In order to complete the "square," Les and Samantha knew that they needed four half-unit blocks to finish the shape (see Figure 25.4). Both children possess spontaneous strategies for producing a legitimate geometric shape. Constructivist educators would posit that this idea demonstrates the children's considerable potential for doing mathematics in school. Further, Les and Samantha's thinking goes beyond identification of shape alone; they are able to recognize shape properties as well.

GENERAL FINDINGS ON THE ORIGINS AND DEVELOPMENT OF QUANTITATIVE AND SPATIAL THINKING

In sum, there is widespread agreement in the research communities in both education and psychology that quantitative and spatial thinking occur well before the beginning of formal schooling; however, just precisely how much before is a subject of debate among many experts in the field of the development of mathematical thinking. Wynn (1998) argues that infants as young as only a few days after birth are able to recognize discrete numerical quantities, indeed a remarkable finding when it had been published in 1992. In contrast, Mix, Huttenlocher, and Levine (2002) argue that no clear empirical evidence exists that demonstrates infants' abilities to represent the exact number of discrete entities. Their research demonstrates that quantification begins with the concept of amount, and that infants can discriminate between different sets based on size, not on number.

The literature is also very clear with respect to young children's quantitative and spatial abilities. Numerous studies on young children's mathematical thinking conclude that young children, well before formal education, engage in mathematical thinking, even in the everyday environment. Educational and psychological research have demonstrated that children build ideas about quantity and ideas about space through active performance, not merely through passive viewing. They engage in a considerable amount of mathematical activity during free play; contrary to popular belief, they do not engage simply in rote, mechanical versions of mathematics that one finds in most "convenience store" mathematics workbooks. To be sure, there is a great deal of mathematical activity of several types in the everyday free play of young children of all socioeconomic backgrounds. In fact, there is no significant difference in terms of the amount of time

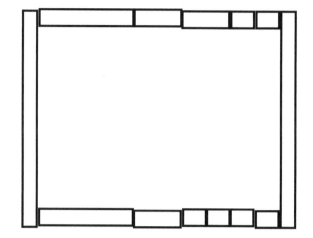

Figure 25.4   **Les and Samantha's "Square"**

children spend on mathematical activities and socioeconomic background. The data presented in these studies give all the more reason for schools and organizations to support mathematics education at the preschool and kindergarten level.

Daniel Ness

MATHEMATICAL SYMBOLISM AND QUANTITATIVE THINKING

There is a great deal of controversy with regard to when young children (post-infancy) develop an understanding of number concepts. This controversy, for the most part, was a result of Piaget's discovery that young children are unable to conserve equivalence relations—often referred to as conservation of number. A child who understands that the quantities of both of the sets appearing on the opposite page (see Figure 25.5) are equal can appreciate the irrelevance of physical arrangement, and therefore conserve equivalence relations—that is, conserve number.

The main idea here is that one's inability to conserve assumes that individual's inability to distinguish between distinct number and amount. A number of researchers have argued against Piaget's discovery positing that young children can conserve when different experimental procedures are implemented. This entry discusses how number is learned and the process in which children develop number concepts. It will be necessary for children to distinguish between a countable set (containing a cardinal number) of objects and the physical arrangement of those objects in order to master the number concept.

HOW THE NUMBER CONCEPT IS LEARNED

Perhaps the most difficult mathematically related task for the young child is for that child to associate a mathematical symbol with a mathematical concept to which the symbol refers. That is to say, young children have a great deal of difficulty grappling with the meaning of mathematical symbols when first encountering them. A mathematical symbol is any idea—verbal or written—that represents a concept having to do with quantity or spatial relations. Children often begin their formal mathematics journey by attempting to associate the numeral—that is, the symbol whose referent is a number (e.g., the numeral "7" whose meaning is the idea or concept of seven things or objects)—to the number of objects that are represented by that numeral: "3" for three cats; "4" for four chairs; "5" for five cars, and so forth.

Learning the numbers, for example, 1 through 10 or 1 through 12, is perhaps one of the most prevalent topics of quantitative reasoning up to five or six years of age. Traditionally, the teaching and learning of number skills and concepts has been at the core of mathematics curricula in the United States, Canada, and in most countries throughout the world (Reys, Nohda, and Shimizu 1994).

Number concepts refer to the relationship between a number and other numbers in a complex system called whole numbers. Number sense refers to number concepts based on one's intuitions and understanding of all numbers. A young child's use of numbers manifests itself in at least four different ways: Cardinally, ordinally, by measurement, and nominally. Children demonstrate the cardinal meaning of number when they quantify a collection of objects. We say, then, that five books, five nickels, and five candlesticks belong to the same number class—"five"—because each one of these sets demonstrates a classified collection of five objects. Further, we often use numbers in an ordinal manner. That is, we might refer to the third house on the block, or the sixth parking space from the left. Next, number can be used in measurement, for example,

Figure 25.5 **Diagram of a Conservation Task**

Set 1:   ●   ●   ●   ●   ●

Set 2:   ● ● ● ● ●

when we say that someone is four feet tall, or a small bookcase weighs eight kilograms. Children also learn that numbers can be used nominally, that is, as labels for certain things. For example, the "2 train" does not refer to two trains, nor does it refer to the second train or even two units. Instead, it is a designation of a transportation route used as a means to differentiate one particular route from other routes.

Mathematics curricula in the early grades, particularly in the preschool and kindergarten levels, emphasize the numbers 0 through 12 for a couple of reasons. First, these numbers (with the exception of zero) clearly exist in our everyday environment. Young children see and hear these numbers on a daily basis when listening to their parents or teachers observing a clock or a watch, looking at a calendar, identifying one dozen eggs in a carton, or counting the number of inches on a ruler. Next, as research on the development of mathematical cognition indicates, each number from 0 through 12 is unique in that there is a lack of pattern based on the way each number is verbalized. When children begin to learn the counting of numbers beyond 12, they are initially acquainted with an underlying base-10 pattern ("thir*teen,* four*teen,* fif*teen,* and so on). In the English language, children generally do not identify patterns in decade transition until they begin counting with the number 20. As a result, many, but certainly not all, children, especially in preschool and kindergarten, learn the sounds of the first twelve numbers and usually do not continue counting beyond the number 12. This, however, does not conclude that a child is performing below the developmentally appropriate level.

Still, much research within the past two decades has shown that children learn a great deal about numbers outside of school, without instruction or special help, and sometimes in adverse situations. In fact, recent evidence suggests that even infants are sensitive to change in numerical value.

IDENTIFICATION OF NUMBER CONCEPT KNOWLEDGE

With proper instruction, schooling can greatly influence and enhance children's knowledge of number concepts. Given a great deal of research supporting the existence of young children's everyday mathematics, adults' awareness of students' competencies and weaknesses in enumeration is a necessary component of mathematical development. The term "enumeration" refers to one's understanding of the concept of number. What, then, underlies one's ability to enumerate? That is, how do we know when a student understands number sense or the meaning of number? First, when a child counts, she or he needs to know the counting words. But knowing the counting words alone does not necessarily mean that a child understands the concept of number. Second, the child also needs to say the number words in their accurate sequence ("one, two, three, four, etc.," that is, the stable-order principle). Again, this does not demonstrate a child's mastery of number sense. Third, the child must count each member of a collection of items once and only once (i.e., one-to-one principle). Young children often count objects of a set more than once, or may "combine" two objects that are close in proximity as one item.

Fourth, the child must also recognize that the counting words do not have to be assigned to particular objects (i.e., order relevance principle). For example, if we see a row of nine checkers, whether we start counting from the left, the right, or from the middle, we still should end up with nine checkers. This may pose a major obstacle for many young children. Fifth, the child also has to learn that the physical arrangement of these objects is irrelevant to the total number of objects. Piaget's conservation of number task, mentioned above, is an illustrative example. Still, the recognition of the equivalence of two sets does not indicate one's understanding of the concept of number. Sixth, counting objects should tell us the total number of objects in a relevant collection (i.e., cardinality principle). For example, the number "5" is not the name of the fifth object or sixth one. Rather, it tells us something about the total number of objects in the set—the cardinal number. Mastery of cardinality is strong evidence that a child's conceptual knowledge of number is forming and taking shape.

Finally, the child needs to know that the last number in a sequence relates to other numbers in unique ways. That is, 5 is one more than 4, 5 is one less than 6, 10 is double 5, and so forth. This knowledge of a number in relation to other numbers in a complex system provides the definitive role of number concepts. In addition, at this point, the child understands that anything can be counted, even if the objects counted are not of the same kind (i.e., the abstraction principle).

Research in mathematics instruction suggests that teachers should represent numbers using different concrete models in the early grades so that students will be able to appreciate the different ways to represent equal quantities in the later grades. At the same time, teachers who use materials or models in a rote manner run the risk of failing to bridge the gap between students' everyday mathematical knowledge and formal mathematical concepts.

In fact, many teachers, especially in the early grades, have often likened the concepts of number and operations with the teaching and learning of mathematics in general. Nevertheless, despite this association, children's mastery of number concepts provides a strong foundation for learning more complex and challenging mathematical concepts in the later grades.

Understanding the concept of numbers 0 through 12 has an additional benefit: If developed appropriately, children will be able to sharpen their number fact knowledge—operations on numbers between 0 and 12—in the following grade levels. This is a crucial next step, which will prepare students for more challenging topics in the years ahead.

Subsequent stages of symbol development occur when young children are initially acquainted with operator symbols ($+$, $-$, $\times$, $\div$). To date, research studies in mathematics education have not confirmed whether children's understanding of operator meanings are gradual through the learning of arithmetic operations, or whether it is a question of transition from one developmental stage to another. Nevertheless, the research is clear with respect to the level of difficulty in understanding each of the operation symbols. The "$+$" symbol for addition, for example, is less difficult for most young children than the "$-$" symbol for subtraction.

Chia-ling Lin

MATHEMATICAL OPERATIONS AND FUNCTIONS

The theme of this entry deals with the development of operative knowledge; that is, the child's informal knowledge of arithmetic operations and the presentation of formal arithmetic operations in school.

CONNECTING EVERYDAY NUMBER CONCEPTS WITH FORMAL NUMBER CONCEPTS

By six or seven years of age, children begin to greatly expand their number repertoire. Their knowledge that there are 10 fingers on both hands, most animals have 2 or 4 legs, and that there are 12 months in the year will seem obvious for many children at this age. At this point, they learn that some months have as many as 31 days, that there are 60 seconds in a minute, or perhaps they will race each other to see who could recite the number words to 100 the fastest. Although these tasks do not necessarily demonstrate mastery of number concepts to 100, students at this age seem to learn numbers based on the spoken words that represent them, or use numbers as a measurement tool.

Mathematics curriculum developers for the first grade have commonly used several benchmark numbers along the counting route to the common target number of 100. As mentioned above, some of these numbers are 10 (for ten fingers), 12 (for twelve months), 25 (as in a quarter of a dollar), 30 (for the approximate average number of days a month), 50 (as in half of 100), 60 (for the number of seconds in a minute, or the number of minutes in an hour), and possibly 75 (or, three-fourths of the way up to 100).

In the elementary school, children learn the numbers above 10 or 12 in order to achieve mastery in more complex mathematical topics learned at later points. The reason has to do with the concept of place value. The base-10 classification of our number system is one that is prevalent in most countries worldwide. Although the United States has not adopted the metric system for measurement, the base-10 classification system is practically embedded in nearly all aspects of human endeavor here and elsewhere.

RESEARCH AND EFFECTIVE PRACTICE

By the time they enter formal schooling, children are faced with a number of difficulties when dealing with mathematics. First, they will only recently be acquainted with formal terms—for example, written expression and basic operations of addition and subtraction. Also, when they begin to count above 12, they often make mistakes because they are unable to identify patterns and relationships. Some studies have argued that the English language is not always conducive to pattern detection. For example, decade transition is not consistent: after "ten"; we don't have "ten-one," and instead, we have a unique-sounding number called "eleven." "Twelve-two" is also unique—we call it "twelve." Further, the "teen" numbers are spoken as if the one's come before the tens—unlike the "twenties," "thirties," and above, where the first spoken number is the tens digit followed by the ones digit. Children begin to notice a pattern when reaching the "twenties"—the "tens" sound comes first and the "one's" sound comes next (as in "thirty-one" and "forty-two"). When listening to students count to "100," there is usually a pause before each decade transition ("sixty-eight, sixty-nine . . . seventy"). Students often have difficulty determining what number comes after "eighty-nine" (as opposed to the numbers coming after, say, "sixty-nine" or "seventy-nine"; this is because they hear the "eight . . . nine" sounds and therefore might follow the "eight-nine-ten" pattern and say unreal sounding numbers like "eighty-ten" (Ginsburg 1989).

Other students may have difficulty in counting by twos above twelve because they simply do not have the experience with the patterns that exist beyond that number. Only when students identify many patterns in double-digit counting will they be able to make a smooth transition into counting beyond 100. Finally, children will run into numerous difficulties in mathematics if they do not master place value. This problem can be resolved if teachers make every attempt to connect students' invented strategies and informal knowledge with the formal mathematics skills and concepts. Success in number concepts depends on children making the connections between various mathematical ideas through the identification of patterns and relationships.

ADDITION AND SUBTRACTION

There are four basic arithmetic operations—addition, subtraction, multiplication, and division. Children are often confronted with real-life problems that involve addition and subtraction of numbers, particularly the numbers 0 through 12. Prior to formal schooling, children are involved in numerous activities in which adding and subtracting single and even some double-digits are used. In the most basic case, very young children, even as early as one year old, ask for "more" of something, clearly suggesting a sense of knowledge for quantity or amount. Children become more aware and precise when dealing with situations in which they need to determine "how many" of something.

Since the early days of formal schooling, mathematics curricula in the early grades focused on early number concepts involving the addition and subtraction operations with single-digit numbers. However, over the years, teachers have carried out different approaches to teaching addition and subtraction facts. Mathematics curricula have emphasized memorization of number facts at the expense of fostering conceptual knowledge of numbers. These curricula have overlooked a great deal of the research which supports the finding that young children are capable of adding and subtracting using their own invented strategies.

On the other side of the continuum, if we examine young children's informal mathematical activities, research suggests that they are not only involved in mathematical activities during everyday activities, but have a good deal of potential if only teachers attempt to recognize it. Further, overemphasis on memorizing number facts in a rote manner usually thwarts conceptual understanding because children's understanding of written symbolism usually lags behind their informal arithmetic competencies. By having students explain their verbal and written work, teachers create a more conducive environment for understanding their students' thinking processes in mathematics.

The concept of addition stems from children's informal counting methods. Based on the examples above, two major strategies that children often use as a means of adding items in two or more sets are: "counting all" and "counting on." When children become adept at counting objects in one set success-fully, they then move on to count objects in two or more sets. This procedure, counting all, demonstrates young children's mastery of the basic addition concept, namely, combining two or more sets. Children then develop more efficient strategies, that is, counting on, whereby the child identifies the total number of one set, usually the larger one, and then continues counting each member of the second, smaller set. This process can be seen as the foundation of formal addition.

Teachers' failure to appreciate and understand mathematical development runs the risk of the inability to prevent mathematics anxiety and may provide an environment of indifference or frustration, thus producing a large student population with a possible aversion toward arithmetic and mathematics in general.

Young children's knowledge of addition and subtraction is determined through specific questions that will allow for the identification of their strengths and weaknesses of the subject. For example, a teacher attempts to tap into what a six-year-old child is thinking and how the child thinks about a particular mathematics problem. Karen, a first grader, is asked to solve a couple of mathematical problems involving single-digit addition and subtraction. The problem asks: "Jimmy has 3 marbles and Amanda has 5 marbles. How many marbles are there altogether? Karen responded with the answer "seven" and was asked how she figured it out. Her explanation was: "I was thinking 5 and 3. There were 5. Then I moved one of the marbles (thinking in her head) from Jimmy to the 5, and it was 6. Then I moved another marble over to the 6 and it was 7" (clinical interview conducted by author, April 25, 2003).

In general, Karen was moving mental images of the marbles as she was thinking about the number of marbles there are in all. It is clear, however, that Karen invented her own strategies to solve this problem. Young children's invented strategies for addition and subtraction are generally not grounded in the standard algorithms for these operations.

Karen is asked the following question: "Jimmy has 8 marbles and he gives 2 of them to Amanda. How many marbles does Jimmy have now?" Karen responded: "Five marbles." When asked to explain her rationale, she answered: "I know that 5 and 2 is 8. And if Jimmy has 8 marbles, and he wants to give 2 of them to Amanda, then he must have 5 left."

On a superficial level, Karen provided incorrect answers to the two problems. Many adults (parents, teachers, administrators, etc.) might exaggerate the situation and erroneously conclude that Karen is less mathematically able than other students her age, that she is possibly learning disabled, or that she simply lacks intelligence or an average IQ score. However, based on her rationale, one can identify logical thinking processes of a child who might otherwise be considered "less able" than her peers.

First, Karen's thought processes were mathematically logical and precise. In the second example, when asked how she knew that "Jimmy had 5 marbles left," Karen responded in a way that clearly revealed her understanding of subtraction as being the reverse process of addition. Furthermore, in the first example, Karen used the strategy of "counting on" to arrive at her answer. Counting on is a procedure that young children develop outside of the school context, and serves as an invaluable tool for adding two or more sets. This procedure is an extension of "counting all," in which a child counts all the objects or images in two or more sets starting from the number "1." Karen demonstrated her understanding of an additional mathematical concept as well; in attempting to find the answer to 3 + 5, Karen argued that the answer would be the same as the one for 5 + 3, hence revealing her informal understanding of commutativity in the process of addition; that is, Karen recognizes the fact that no matter how you add the two numbers, namely 5 and 3, the result is the same.

MULTIPLICATION AND DIVISION

The operation of multiplication, too, has its origins in the everyday environment of the child, that is, prior to formal education. The concept of multiplication generally unfolds as children develop strategies for counting by numbers greater than one, for example, 2, 4, 6, 8, 10, 12, and so on, or 5, 10, 15, 20, 25, 30, and so forth. Children eventually learn in their everyday activities that these sequences can also refer to several groups of the same number of objects—4 bags with 3 sandwiches in each (12 sandwiches), 5 pockets with 6 coins in each (30 coins), 3 streets with 7 houses on each (21 houses). So, the overarching concept of multiplication, initially involving the natural numbers (i.e., 1, 2, 3, etc.), is the idea of repeated addition. As in the above examples,

Figure 25.6 **Showing Fraction Multiplication through Visual Aids**

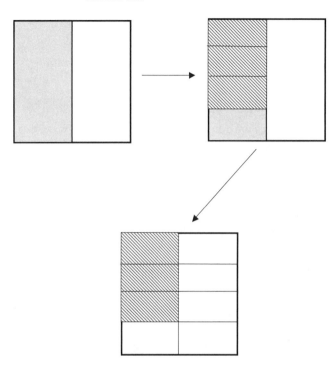

we have 3 + 3 + 3 + 3 (four 3s), 6 + 6 + 6 + 6 + 6 (five 6s), and 7 + 7 + 7 (three 7s). But repeated addition is only one conceptual perspective on multiplication. Another multiplication concept is multiplication by 1, which refers to an arithmetic property, namely the identity property. A third multiplication concept is multiplication by zero, another arithmetic property in which the product will always be zero.

Yet another multiplication concept that does not adhere to repeated addition has to do with the multiplication of fractions. The conceptual meaning of multiplication by fractions is the following: What is the relationship of the first factor to the second factor with respect to the whole? For example, take the problem $\frac{3}{4} \times \frac{1}{2}$. The procedural knowledge here is straightforward: Simply multiply the numerators to obtain a new numerator and multiply the denominators to obtain the new denominator. We thus have $\frac{3}{8}$. But, what does this mean conceptually? To answer this question, examine the corresponding diagram (Figure 25.6).

Draw a diagram of the second factor in a pie chart. Shade in $\frac{3}{4}$ of the $\frac{1}{2}$ in the diagram. Now the question is: What is the fractional part of the shaded region with respect to the whole? To do this, we divide the other half into fourths. As you can see, the number of partitions at this point is 8, and the number of shaded regions of the 8 is 3; hence $\frac{3}{8}$ of the whole pie is shaded.

The operation of division works in a similar manner as multiplication but in reverse: Rather than repeated addition, the concept of division with natural numbers deals with repeated subtractions. For example, take the problem $18 \div 3$. Rather than asking for the total number of elements of groups with n elements in each group, in terms of division, one is asking how many groups (m) that can be made with a total number of elements when considering n elements in each group. So, in the above example, 18 is the total number of elements. If 3 of the 18 elements constitute each group, how many groups are there?

Similar to the operation of multiplication, the identity property still holds with division—namely $a \div 1 = a$. However, not so with the zero property; $\frac{0}{a} = 0$, but $\frac{a}{0}$ is undefined. We can interpret this concept as the following: Zero parts of an entity yield no pieces (or zero pieces). But we cannot take a countable number (a) of pieces of zero. This is both a physical and an abstract impossibility. Moreover, this concept can be expressed graphically through the topic of slope. A horizontal line has a slope equal to zero because there is no gradient (rise or run). A vertical line, however, does not have a slope (undefined) because rise and run do not exist.

In the intermediate elementary school grades (from grades three to five typically), students usually become adept when learning the procedure for fraction division. However, their knowledge of the concept of fraction division is lacking. Much of this has to do with the teacher's lack of knowledge with respect to this concept. Take the following example: $2\frac{1}{2} \div \frac{1}{4}$. Again, the procedure is straightforward—take the reciprocal of the divisor (the second number) and multiply the divisor by the dividend as an improper fraction. Hence, $\frac{5}{2} \times \frac{4}{1} = \frac{20}{2} = 10$. The concept, too, is straightforward. In this example, we ask: How many fourths ($\frac{1}{4}$ ths) are there in $2\frac{1}{2}$ (see Figure 25.7)? Or in general terms, how many of the divisor are there in the dividend? This is the same idea when we consider the division of whole numbers (other than zero) and integers in general.

Extensive research has shown that before entering school, young children know basic concepts like greater than, less than, and basic addition (put together), and subtraction (take away). However, upon

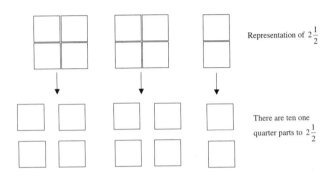

Figure 25.7 Showing Fraction Division through Visual Aids

Representation of $2\frac{1}{2}$

There are ten one quarter parts to $2\frac{1}{2}$

entering school, children are required to learn mathematics formally using numerals and symbols that might be foreign to them. That is, the interpretation of mathematical symbols is entirely different from the language children are exposed to from infancy, like English, Spanish, and Chinese. The following criteria are foundational characteristics for the transition from everyday mathematics before school to formal mathematical learning in school.

First, children should have a strong conceptual base of addition and subtraction concepts before they are introduced to formal symbols and procedures and well before they learn their number facts. This will help in preventing children from thinking of addition and subtraction as meaningless operations and series of procedures that have no bearing on their everyday activity. Adults' recognition of informal knowledge will enable students to identify and appreciate the concepts and properties of each operation. For example, when teaching addition and subtraction, problems in which the students are able to identify patterns as a way of building their experiences with early formal concepts (e.g., $4 + 3 = 7$; $3 + 4 = 7$; $7 - 4 = 3$; $7 - 3 = 4$) should be utilized. These patterns should also suggest to the student that subtraction is a complement to addition and that addition is commutative.

Second, when introducing formal symbolism, teachers should be sensitive to the methods in which they organize the mathematical problems. In the example above, Karen's teacher should provide her with groups of objects like coins or small blocks so that she can verify her answer. So, if Karen had started with eight blocks and took two blocks away by pushing them aside, she would have seen that six blocks would be left, not five. Repeated practice in this manner will help students like Karen to connect informal strategies with formal mathematical speech and symbolism.

Last, addition and subtraction curricula in the first grade should emphasize both external (formal mathematical structure) and internal factors (children's informal mathematics) in children's understanding. For example, children seem to understand the meaning of equivalence. But when confronted with the subject in school, the equals sign (=) takes on entirely different meanings for students.

Chia-ling Lin

THE BASE-10 SYSTEM AND PLACE VALUE

This entry has to do with the significance of the base-10 system in learning arithmetic and mathematics in general, and how the base-10 system affects student performance in arithmetic using place value when involved with calculation.

PLACE VALUE IN TERMS OF NUMBER

Several patterns emerge when children begin to count numbers higher than 12. First, they begin to notice something known as decade transition—that is, after a number with a nine, there is a new sounding number (for example, "twenty-nine, thirty; forty-nine, fifty; seventy-nine, eighty"). Second, they know that after the number "12," each number ends in "teen" (e.g., thirteen, fourteen, fifteen). Also children can use different ways to count to 100. In other words, children do not always count by ones; they often count by twos, fives, tens, and even threes. This experience with decade transition in counting, then, provides an important switch to the formal knowledge of multiplication and place value.

Place value is perhaps one of the most challenging concepts in mathematical development learned after the concept of number. Moreover, this does not account for the different skills students need to learn, especially those involving mathematical symbolism.

Many children between five and eight have difficulty with the knowledge of place value. For example,

when asked what the number 15 means with regard to place value, many children provide the following response: "The 1 in fifteen is in the tens column and the five is the number in the ones column." However, when asked the meaning of "tens" and the meaning of "ones," they often do not develop a cogent explanation, let alone a correct one: "Tens is tens [pointing to the tens column] and ones is ones [pointing to the ones column]." However, when asked the meaning of the 1 in the tens column, Albert replied: "It's 1, the number 1." Many childen reply in a similar way (Ginsburg 1989).

When using manipulatives to identify the number 15 as well as the place values for the 1 and the 5, young children do not yet understand place value symbolism. When asked to represent the 5 in the ones column, they often count five blocks accurately and push the rest of the blocks aside. But when asked to represent the 1 in the tens column, they erroneously take one block.

This development of mathematical thinking presents some important points that teachers can learn about children's initial introduction to place value. First, their understanding of numbers higher than 12 is representative of many children this age. They seem to grasp the meaning of 15 but do not connect the concept of the number 15 with the concept of place value. This exemplifies the cognitive processes of children's informal ideas of mathematics but a lack of understanding of the relationships between informal number concepts and formal, and potentially powerful, place value knowledge.

Next, teachers can be extremely helpful at this stage of mathematical development in making this connection. They could supply students with blocks or other similar objects to count. Students will need to learn that the 1 in the 15 is a symbolic representation of the number 10—hence 10 blocks. Similarly, the 5 in 15 is a symbolic representation of 5—hence 5 blocks. The key points here are: (1) manipulatives like small blocks, if used appropriately, can serve as tools in promoting mathematical understanding; and (2) using these manipulatives helps bridge the gap between children's informal and formal understanding.

Finally, the instruction of place value and number concepts to 100 merely through lecture or recitation often prevents children from learning and understanding more complex mathematics concepts. At best, teaching without emphasizing the connection between informal and formal concepts might produce students who can perform procedurally but do not understand the topic conceptually. At worst, it produces students who will be unable to succeed in more advanced mathematical topics.

OPERATIONAL USE OF PLACE VALUE KNOWLEDGE

Based on years of research in early formal mathematics, it is highly recommended that children obtain a strong conceptual base of addition and subtraction concepts before the introduction to formal symbols and procedures and well before they learn their number facts (Baroody 2003; Ginsburg 1989). When the connection between children's informal mathematical and formal mathematical structures in addition and subtraction mathematics curricula is articulated in the first grade, teachers set the stage for the addition and subtraction of two-digit numbers in the second grade.

A solid understanding and facility in addition and subtraction number combinations will foster a powerful means by which students develop knowledge of whole number computation. Effective teaching of two-digit addition and subtraction can complement the students' understanding of single-digit addition and subtraction that they learned prior to entering the second grade. For example, when teaching double-digit addition and subtraction, successful teachers often use problems that foster students' awareness and recognition of patterns as a way of emphasizing the properties of whole number in terms of addition and subtraction (e.g., $14 + 17 = 31$; $17 + 14 = 31$; $31 - 14 = 17$; $31 - 17 = 14$). Furthermore, when combined with what they learn formally in earlier grades, children still invent strategies based on what they know informally, whether they are learning concepts from Kindergarten or more advanced concepts in the second grade or later.

In addition to its potentially powerful characteristics, the concepts of two-digit addition and two-digit subtraction are rich in terms of their historical background. Recipes called algorithms in mathematics for "+" and "−" were introduced in Europe by Arab scholars after Hindu-Arabic numerals replaced Roman numerals; before that most calculation was done using some form of an abacus. The Romans used grooves cut in wood or stone instead of wires and pebbles instead of beads. In fact, the word "calculation" (and even the word "calculus") comes from the Latin "calculi" which means "small stones."

Modern abacuses with separate wires for units, tens, hundreds, and so on strung with bead counters are used by teachers in China, Korea, Japan, Russia, and also in the United States to teach place value and regrouping. For first and second graders, a modern teaching abacus may have more wires and beads than needed at those levels, and can cause confusion. Still, the place value, addition, subtraction and regrouping concepts are important enough to warrant the use of a classroom-made abacus with provisions for only units and tens or only units, tens, and hundreds. For this purpose the medieval English and German wooden abacus, with painted columns instead of grooves and wires and flat button-like counters, can easily be made by children using wooden shingles marked with a felt pen. Of course, paper can be used instead of a wooden shingle, but a wooden slab such as a shingle is more authentic historically.

In medieval England the wooden abacus was called a "counter," which we inherited as the location in a store where computation is done. In Germany, the wooden counter was called a "slab" or "bank"—another word still used to indicate a place of calculation. In medieval Germany, when a business failed, members of the same guild or union would seize the businessman's counter or "bank" and break it. The old German word for "break" was "rupt"—so the failed merchant was "bankrupt." If students make shingle abacuses, they can be used in calculating contests like spelling bees. In one sense, it is really more enjoyable to lose these contests than to win, since the losers get to break their shingles—they are "bankrupt"!

There are a variety of configurations for modern abacuses. In both Chinese and Japanese designs, beads are moved to the center bar to record numbers. In the Russian and American style, beads are moved from right to left—the wires or rods strung with beads indicate units, tens, hundreds, and so on, from top to bottom. Regrouping in either addition or subtraction is obvious if each column is restricted to no more than 9 beads. A button in the tens column is equivalent to ten buttons in the units column.

Like the learning of early counting and addition concepts, the concept of addition with two-digit numbers can be fostered through the proper use of manipulatives other than the abacus, namely, the base-10 blocks. Through the use of base-10 blocks and also while engaging in the activity "Race for a Flat," students will be able to build their understanding and knowledge of place value and addition concepts by linking their everyday knowledge of numbers with written formal arithmetic. Students will need: (1) a tub of base-ten blocks (units, longs, and flats); (2) a pair of game dice; and (3) a place-value mat for each student. Students should engage in Race for the Flat in pairs. Give each group two dice, each pair of students within the group a supply of base-ten blocks, and each individual a place mat, which serves as an organizer for the materials. The three columns on the place mats indicate where to put each kind of block. Explain to the students that the units are placed in the unit column at the right, and that once they have 10 units, they will exchange them for one long, which they will then put in the middle column, or longs column. Ask them what they think they will do when they get ten longs. Students take turns rolling the dice. The sum of the dice tells how many units to take from the group's base-ten supply. Students take the units they need, put them in the correct place on the place value mat, make any exchanges possible, and pass the dice to the next player. The first player to get a flat wins.

The students must make all exchanges before passing the dice and all of the other players need to watch to be sure they agree with what is being done. You may want to model a game first, perhaps you against the class. Before students begin to play, ask for questions. Sometimes students will ask what to do if they roll a ten or more. For example: "If I roll a 12, do I have to take 12 units, or can I take 1 long and 2 units?" Answer that taking a combination is fine as long as they can explain their choice to the other players. Another question might be: "Do you need to have exactly one flat, or can you go over?" For this game, allow students to go over, so that a winner must have at least one flat.

Students who are at the appropriate developmental level should try to connect the regrouping process to an algorithmic procedure for addition. After each roll, have players keep a written record of the additions and regroupings. If students apply a "traditional" algorithmic approach, then recordings may indicate regrouping with a "carry." (See Figure 25.8)

Figure 25.8 **Example of a "Race for a Flat" Player's Use of Addition and Place Value After each Role of a Die**

Round 1:	4		**Round 2:**	4
				+ 5
				9
Round 3:	9		**Round 4:**	11
	+ 2			+ 5
	11			16
	1			
Round 5:	16		**Round 6:**	22
	+ 6			+ 3
	22			25

The point to be made is that grouping can help us count and add numbers and, perhaps most important, grouping through Race for the Flat builds the concept of place value—namely, grouping by 10s. After this point, teachers should strive to have their students connect this informal procedure of base ten with formal, written arithmetic.

Assess what students know by walking around the classroom and listening to them as they play. Observe who is using shortcuts and who is counting out the units one at a time. Identify who is doing mental computation. Notice the language they use. For example, if a student has seven units and rolls a six, then how does the student handle the regrouping of ones to tens? Does the student place six units on the board and then make a group of ten units to trade for a long? Or does the student automatically reach for a long and take four units off the board? You might hear the following statements: "If Cathy rolls a six, she can get another long." "You only need 12 more to win." "I need four more longs to win and you only need three." "You have more than I do. You have 64 and I only have 48." "You have 14 more than I do." The point to be made is that grouping can help us count and add numbers.

RESEARCH AND EFFECTIVE PRACTICE

One way to foster students' solid understanding of subtraction with two-digit numbers and the concept of regrouping as it is related to place value is to conduct an activity called "Clear the Mat." Like Race for a Flat, the two-digit addition counterpart, Clear the Mat entails having students work in groups of two, and each student takes turns rolling a pair of dice. The idea is to develop and foster students' understanding of the place value concept and double-digit subtraction. Each pair of students will need: (1) a tub of base-ten blocks (units, longs, and flats); (2) a pair of game dice; and (3) two place-value mats. After students are comfortable playing Race for the Flat, introduce Clear the Mat. Ask students to place one flat, one long, and one unit on their place value mats. Then explain, "As in Race for the Flat, you will take turns rolling dice. But this time, the dice tell you how many units to remove. When you have done that, and your partner agrees you have made all possible exchanges, pass the dice to the next player. The first person to clear his or her mat wins." Explain further that they need to clear their mats with an exact roll of the dice. For example, if 7 units are left, a roll of 7 or less is good, but a roll of 8 or more is not. At any time, they may elect to roll just one die. Play at least one round with several students while the others watch, so that students can see that exchanges are necessary from the very first roll. Clear the Mat provides a good foundation for understanding the regrouping often required when doing subtraction. Students who are at the appropriate developmental level should try to connect the regrouping process to an algorithmic procedure for subtraction. After each roll, have players keep a written record of the subtractions and regroupings. If students apply a "traditional" algorithmic approach, then recordings may indicate regrouping with a "borrow." For example, see Figure 25.9.

The point to be made is that grouping can help us count and not only add, but subtract numbers, too. And perhaps most important, grouping through Clear the Mat builds the concept of place value—namely, grouping by 10s. Teachers should strive to have their students connect this informal procedure of base ten with formal, written arithmetic. As the teacher, you can identify strengths and weaknesses of various students by observing who is using shortcuts and who is counting out the units one at a time. Note who is doing mental computation, and also those students who tend to be more concrete—those who are counting by units. Notice the language they use. For example, if a student has 37 as three longs and seven units and rolls an "11," how, then, does the student handle the regrouping of tens to ones? The point to

Figure 25.9 **Subtraction through the Process of Borrowing**

Round 1:
$$\begin{array}{r} \overset{0}{11\!\!\!/1} \\ -\ \ 7 \\ \hline 104 \end{array}$$

Round 2:
$$\begin{array}{r} \overset{9}{10\!\!\!/4} \\ -\ \ 9 \\ \hline 95 \end{array}$$

be made is that grouping can help us count and subtract numbers as well as add them. So, as teachers, our observations are very important.

The success of Asian students in mastering computation skills is due in part to the extensive use of the abacus both in and out of school. This has a great deal to do with the ways in which computation is taught. In the American system, teachers often implement the "counting all" followed by the "counting on" strategies when teaching one and two-digit addition and subtraction. For example, when children solve $19 + 4$, they often count on from 19, the larger number. In the Asian method, students are asked to think: $19 + ? = 20$. So, $19 + 1 = 20$, and $4 = 1 + 3$; therefore, $19 + 4 = 23$.

As discussed above, the base-10 system has a rich history and serves as the base for most cultures throughout the world. In addition, children generally have difficulty learning place value in the early elementary grades, and often acquire knowledge of place value after 7 or 8 years of age, and even sometimes toward the end of the elementary school years. The concept of place value is central in the learning of more advanced mathematical skills in the later school years.

Chia-ling Lin

DEVELOPMENT OF SPATIAL AND GEOMETRIC CONCEPTS

The development of spatial and geometric concepts refers to an individual's earliest cognitive perceptions of space and shape, and the learned behavior and thinking processes that unfold from these perceptions. Some important terms must be addressed before discussion of spatial and geometric development. First, geometry is the study of space. Second, space, in the context of human development, refers to one's immediate, or local, environment and the objects within it. Spatial objects, whether real or imaginative, include points, lines, two- and three-dimensional shapes, grids, relationships between objects (e.g., congruent shapes and parallel lines), and transformations of figures. As infants, individuals perceive spatial phenomena initially. Only later do they develop ways to represent characteristics of space and geometry.

BACKGROUND AND PHILOSOPHICAL UNDERPINNINGS

Past discussion and research regarding the development of geometry and space concepts are rich in both content and context. Recorded history regarding this topic spans nearly 2,500 years to Greek (and Hellenic) times. One of the earliest discussions on the knowledge of spatial and geometric concepts can be found in one of Plato's dialogues entitled *Meno* (1937). In this dialogue, Socrates attempts to convince Meno that the young and uneducated servant nearby, through probing questions and gentle guidance by Socrates, possesses the knowledge that the area of a square is uniquely determined by the length of the diagonal drawn through it. In a sense, the boy knows the Pythagorean Theorem, though he never studied such subjects, nor did Socrates give him the answer. Socrates believed that the young boy "knew" these geometric relationships, not from experience or habituation, but solely based on universals.

Rene Descartes, the French rationalist philosopher of the early seventeenth century, argued that the concept of space is an ideal that is "given" innately to the child without prior experience (1994). George Berkeley, on the other hand (and to a great extent, the Scottish philosopher, Thomas Reid, several years later), took the empiricist stance, and argued that space is not an ideal, but a concept experienced in reality through sensation (1988). Unlike Descartes and Berkeley, Immanuel Kant, a German philosopher of the late eighteenth and early nineteenth century, felt that the concept of space is neither innate for the child, nor is it developed empirically through sensation. Instead, Kant believed that space is constructed by the child through experience and exposure to surrounding phenomena. For Kant, phenomena are based on experience; yet at the same time, he considered the form or origin of these phenomena as an *a priori* structure of sensory perceptions. Space is a self-evident truth, based on pure intuition, which forms the foundation of external intuitions. Principles of geometry are an example of external intuitions, according to Kant, which can only be derived from space (1902).

Ernst Cassirer, a dedicated follower of Kantian philosophy, identified three forms of spatial experiences: organic-active or sensorimotor space, perceptual space, and abstract-symbolic-contemplative space (1957). These forms of spatial experience are characteristic of both the animal and human kingdoms. Organic-active space is the form that ranks lowest in order. According to Cassirer, it is characteristic of the animal kingdom as well as human infants, and deals with space concretely, bereft of abstraction or differentiation. Perceptual space, the next spatial form in Cassirer's hierarchical classification, has to do with the ways in which the visual, auditory, tactile, vestibular, and kinesthetic senses are used as a means of interpreting or thinking about the spatial characteristics of objects. Abstract-symbolic-contemplative space, the third and highest form, was, according to Cassirer and the psychologist Heinz Werner who followed him, the level of spatial thought that differentiated humans from animals.

PIAGET AND THE THEORY OF TOPOLOGICAL PRIMACY

Perhaps the most extensive theoretical framework on the child's conception of space to date is that of the Swiss psychologist and epistemologist Jean Piaget. Piaget and his associate Bärbel Inhelder (1956) advanced a general theory of spatial and geometrical development—in particular, the theoretical underpinnings of the topological primacy thesis. Piaget's clinically and empirically based theory of the child's conception of space developed out of the tradition of the epistemological problems that philosophers like Descartes, Berkeley, Rousseau, Kant, and Cassirer faced when dealing with the fundamental concepts of space.

According to Piaget's theory, spatial thinking begins in infancy. From approximately the end of the first month of life, the infant begins to construct perceptual space, which refers to an individual's direct contact with an object or group of objects and their surroundings. Unlike older children and adults, infants are unable to conceive of objects as having a "life" of their own. Infants, then, are unable to consider objects beyond their immediate perception. Like representational space, which comes much later, perceptual space is not acquired passively; individuals develop perceptual space from experience and active engagement with objects or other individuals in their environment or immediate surroundings. These experiences, Piaget and Inhelder (1956) claim, begin with the infant's use of reflexes, and the subsequent development of primary circular reactions in the second stage of the sensorimotor period. The first and second stages in the sensorimotor period form the first of three periods in the development of perceptual space. It is in this first period that infants develop five elementary spatial relations: proximity, separation, order, enclosure, and continuity. In terms of the period of topological primacy (birth through age seven), Piaget designates the period from birth through two years and six months as Stage 0 because the young child overwhelmingly exhibits evidence of perceptual space in which objects, whose permanence is unstable, appear as fleeting, ephemeral images; there is little or no evidence of representational space in this earliest stage.

Continuing through the stages of spatial and geometric development, Piaget distinguishes between two substages of Stage I. Substage IA describes a child whose age is between two years six months and three years six months. Whereas children in Substage IA find it difficult to differentiate between different shapes, Substage IB children, ages three years six months to five years, are able to differentiate between shapes topologically, and not in Euclidean form. Like the previous stage, Stage II is divided into two substages. According to Piaget, although children between Substages IB and IIA demonstrate a crude recognition between rectilinear shapes (e.g., squares and rectangles) and curvilinear ones (e.g., circles and ellipses), they are unable to differentiate between the shapes themselves. This transitory period occurs between the ages of four years and four years six months. In the heart of Substage IIA—ages four years six months to five years—children seem able to differentiate between shape by angle and sometimes dimension. In Substage IIB, which usually commences at five years and ends at five years six months, children progress to the level of differentiating between similar shapes. Stage III, which begins at approxi-

mately six years six months of age, is the final stage in the "topological primacy" period. By stage III, children are able to synthesize and organize complex forms of shapes without hesitation. According to Piaget, Stage III of this period forms the beginning of the transition from topological thinking to projective thinking.

In short, although Piaget argued that "perceptual space" is constructed as early as infancy, it is only much later that children develop ideas regarding space as it relates to Euclidean geometry. This is what Piaget called "representational space." Further, Piaget argued that children's understanding about shapes does not come from passive learning. Instead, children develop knowledge of space and geometric concepts as a result of active engagement in different activities. Children do not learn about geometric shapes through recall or rote learning (Piaget and Inhelder 1956).

CURRENT PERSPECTIVES ON SPACE AND GEOMETRY IN THE FIELD OF PSYCHOLOGY

Many psychologists often refer to the term "space" as having two meanings: actual space, or space that can be "seen" in the sense of usable space; and abstract, mathematical space, or, the space created from an individual's mental constructs. Other psychologists have expanded on this definition. George Armitage Miller (1998) distinguishes between two types of space: perceptual space and conceptual space. Perceptual space deals with the mental schemas associated with an individual's senses—visual, auditory, olfactory, and tactile—and concerns our everyday manipulation of objects and all of our movements. In contrast, conceptual space deals with our understanding of the existence of spatial phenomena beyond our senses. The individual knows that on the other side of a wall there are familiar objects that cannot be seen or touched. Conceptual space is interpreted through particular representations, such as maps, pictures, or even ideas or mental constructions that may not necessarily be translated into symbolic form.

In his book *Perception*, Julian Hochberg (1964) demonstrates how perception, through visual stimuli, develops in terms of an individual's spatial and geometric cognitive level. For Hochberg, the perception of shape is more than merely observed shapes that an individual has experienced or learned. Instead, he argues that a shape is simply "the sum of the sensations of points of color and shade at a particular set of positions" (p. 58). This position seems to run counter to developmental theory, which suggests that the development of spatial perception and shape is based on recognition of shape due to prior experience. Hochberg also examined the meaning of two-dimensional pictures and their relationship to shape. His argument is as follows: The perception of objects that exist in the real world does not necessarily derive from one's perception of their three-dimensional form. At the same time, depth cues, which are pictorial pieces of information about depth, are not necessary for one's recognition of three-dimensional objects in two-dimensional pictures. The idea of depth cues, then, is not a critical factor when one perceives objects either as pictures or as real-world phenomena. As an example, a child does not need any pictorial training for recognizing any two-dimensional representation of an object or shape. Hochberg's position seems to support the notion that shape recognition or identification is not a learned phenomenon, but one merely related to sensation of points of color and shade as well as its positioning. Again, this view seems to counter the Piagetian topological primacy thesis, which maintains that humans, who construct perceptual space as early as infancy through direct contact with objects, develop meanings of shape and size through experience and learning.

Psychologists have also proposed the distinction between psychological space and physical space. They argue that for the psychologist and physiologist, psychological space is the subject of interest while, for the physicist, physical space is the subject of interest. Psychological space is defined as any space that is attributed to the mind and which would not exist if the mind did not exist. In contrast, physical space is any space attributed to the external world independent of the existence of minds. Other psychologists argue that the distinction between physical and psychological space should be made with caution: On the one hand, physical space is important for psychologists who believe that an individual's psychological space is learned directly from physical space; yet, at the same time, physical space cannot be learned or measured independent of one's mental construction of it.

Spatial and geometric development has played a crucial role in developmental psychology research.

One important research topic involves the role of searching for missing or hidden objects as it relates to early childhood spatial development. Theories of search, perhaps stemming from the Piagetian notion of object permanence and the six elementary spatial relations (mentioned above), involve a variety of aspects of space, such as location, shapes of objects, and direction. Research in this area also demonstrates that search is a universal characteristic among all people and all ages; all cultures possess and manipulate objects, and all individuals are faced with situations in which needed objects may not be in sight or are not readily available. Finally, psychologists whose works are devoted to this area believe that search, as it relates to spatial representation, sheds light upon other areas of cognition—namely, the development of memory, intuition and logic, and the role of planning.

Piaget's contributions to research concerning the child's conception of space, as well as those who have replicated his work, have had a far-reaching impact on current research in this area. However, this research does not examine the development of young children's conceptions of space and geometry in the everyday context. Recent studies in this have concluded that young children engage in proto-geometric activities—behaviors in which the investigator identifies the bridge between advanced spatial and fundamental Euclidean thinking—for nearly 33 percent of the time during free play (Ginsburg, Lin, Ness, Seo 2003; Ness 2001).

EFFECTIVE PRACTICE IN MATHEMATICS EDUCATION

It has become evident that researchers on spatial and geometric development have drawn a great deal from Piagetian theory. Pierre van Hiele (1986) and Pierre and Dina van Hiele (1953) proposed a hierarchy of five levels of spatial-geometric development in which each level is chronological (one does not skip levels) but not dependent on age (individuals who are several years apart in age may belong to the same level). The geometric knowledge of individuals classified under the first level (Level 0) is based on their perceptions of objects (e.g., a door is a rectangle because it looks like one). Second level (Level 1) individuals, however, can distinguish between what they see and their understanding that a rectangle can be classified as a four-sided figure. Third level (Level 2) individuals not only can classify rectangles as four-sided figures, but also understand that the properties inherent in a rectangle are different from those in a circle or a triangle. Fourth level (Level 3) individuals appreciate the relationships between properties of figures (i.e., Euclidean proof), while fifth level (Level 4) individuals study the relationships between various geometric systems (e.g., Euclidean versus Lobachevskyan geometric systems).

Douglas Clements and Michael Battista (1992) have researched extensively on the areas of space and geometry from a mathematics education perspective. Both Clements and Battista have examined the research in the development of spatial and geometric reasoning in the early years and students' understanding of the subject throughout elementary and secondary school. Further, much of their earlier work has examined computer software packages and programs like Logo™ and their benefits to children's geometric thinking skills. They have also proposed the concept of spatial structuring, which deals with the ways in which children manipulate mental schema as a means of solving problems in geometry.

Researchers of spatial-geometric cognition propose that successful understanding of concepts in Euclidean geometry is dependent on strong process skills, in particular, the ability to identify and justify relationships, and not simply memorize definitions. Educational goals with regard to the study of geometry for the early grades focus on analytical thinking skills which prepare students with the ability to compare and contrast geometric relationships and prove theorems that are related to these relationships.

Daniel Ness

DEVELOPMENT OF MAPPING CONCEPTS

Maps are graphic representations of space, shape, and location. Mapping concepts refer to an individual's level or ability to represent objects (material or abstract) of space in his or her environment. Some of these concepts include scale, perspective, direction, linking the written representation with its referent (for example, a roadmap of a town with the actual streets of that town), and the coordinate system.

The subjects of maps and mapping have gained a great deal of importance in education, especially within the last two decades, mainly for two reasons. First, we know much more now that mapping concepts are intrinsically linked to the development of children's thinking and cognitive structures. Second, since mapping concepts are developmental and are based on experience and learning, psychologists and educators believe that a strong content knowledge of mapping will help children learn concepts in geography—a subject only recently implemented in a number of state curricula (due to federal legislation published in *Goals 2000: Educate America Act*, Public Law 103–227). First and foremost, however, the routes of cognition regarding mapping concepts can be traced to early stages of mathematical development, particularly the origin and growth of spatial thinking.

MAPPING AND ITS ORIGINS IN DEVELOPMENTAL AND COGNITIVE RESEARCH

Like concepts of number, knowledge of maps stems from infancy and early childhood and emanates from an infant's or young child's experience with objects in space. James Blaut and David Stea's results indicate that children as young as three years of age are capable of producing maps when given miniature trees, houses, and cars (1974). It has been difficult, however, to identify the specific techniques and strategies young children use when demonstrating their abilities in mapping and navigation. Others have argued that although young children are capable of having some knowledge about maps, they will make mistakes if maps lack specific landmarks or cognitive indicators like the trees, houses, and cars mentioned in Blaut and Stea's example.

Research on spatial cognition also has addressed issues relating to young children's understanding of maps and their local environments as well. In agreement with Blaut and Stea, Liben and Downs (2001) have concluded that, for the most part, young preschool children have a minimal understanding of the general representational nature of maps and that a basic representational form of experience and knowledge is established by three years of age. Older preschool children are able to learn the relative distances between markers once they are familiarized with certain paths. Many older preschoolers may possess the ability to measure scaled routes as soon as they are familiar with them. Children between the ages of four and seven, like older children, adolescents, and adults, are able to learn from consulting maps. For example, children who consult maps in order to learn a route through a six-room house learn the route more quickly than those who use navigation (that is, searching by walking or traveling) alone. Younger children, on the other hand, have a great deal of difficulty extrapolating information from a map to determine where they need to go relative to their initial position.

A number of mathematics educators, like Douglas Clements (1999), argue that the ability of orienting one's self—that is, knowledge or understanding of mental or physical maps—is essential in improving spatial abilities and developing geometric concepts. However, children who process mathematical information visually or graphically do not necessarily perform better in geometric or geographic skills than those who process this information through verbal-logical means.

DIRECTION AND LOCATION

To date, we seem to know a good deal about children's acquisition of notions concerning direction or location. Children acquire knowledge of the front-back-side concept by age five; however, exactly how and when children acquire each of these concepts is not entirely conclusive. S. Kuczaj and M. Maratsos (1975) found that children seem to encounter the notions of "front" and "back" as opposites before they actually learn the meaning of each term. Children learn the meanings of these terms when they first apply each word to themselves before associating "front" and "back" to other objects. Further, they maintain that the notion of "side" appears last. Children's (and adults') notion of front is the most prominent side of almost all objects and living things. Certain characteristics of objects tend to represent notions of front: with moving objects, front is generally associated with the part of the object or being that is at the most forward point, such as the

head of a dog, or the headlights of a car; for stationary objects, front generally concerns the parts of the objects that are manipulated in some way, like the door of a refrigerator. Characteristics of "back" include the tails of animals, trunks of cars, and the like. The main point is that children generally do not learn the concepts of front and back in any particular order—they are learned simultaneously for the most part.

Despite what is known regarding children's understanding of "front" and "back," children's mastery of environmental directions, such as "above," "over," and "behind," navigational concepts, such as "left" and "right," or global directions, like "north," "east," "south," and "west" as well as scale and measurement have been shown to improve children's development of map reading.

One of the more advanced concepts related to mapping concerns the coordinate system. Students in the upper elementary grades have difficulty in mastering the coordinate systems because they lack experience working with two-dimensional systems. Students in the upper elementary and middle school levels might be able to strengthen these skills by familiarizing themselves with grid lines, points, and distance relationships between points.

MAPPING AND GEOGRAPHY EDUCATION

Since a rapidly growing body of studies supports the finding that cognition of maps and mappings occurs in the early preschool years, psychologists and educators have emphasized the importance of a strong geography education curriculum. Their eagerness to establish and promulgate a geography curriculum stems from a number of reports from the 1980s, offshoots of the infamous "A Nation At Risk" report of 1983, which allude to an unsatisfactory state of students' geographic knowledge. For example, one study reported that only 20 percent of U.S. students were able to locate the United States on a world map and even fewer knew how to identify the location of the U.S. capital (Liben and Downs 2001).

Nearly all researchers on mapping and geography will attest that geography is not merely a mundane set of facts and figures—that is, rote memorization of names of countries and their capitals, names of rivers, lakes, and other bodies of water, or identification of the highest peaks and the lowest points on earth. Rather, geography refers to the spatial characteristics of human existence that allow individuals to make important decisions about their environment with respect to maximizing efficiency for better living conditions (for example, ideal locations for the construction of schools, supermarkets, and the roads between them). Researchers have also noted that the unrelenting lack of geographic knowledge of most Americans has produced numerous social problems and imprudent decisions. Some of these problems include: the improper locations of waste sites without due consideration of environmental implications regarding the hazards associated with pollution; unnecessary urban sprawl, which may result in makeshift infrastructures of residential, commercial, and industrial structures; or making political decisions based on a poor understanding of a particular country's topographical environment and how the inhabitants use it.

Daniel Ness

PROCEDURAL KNOWLEDGE VERSUS CONCEPTUAL KNOWLEDGE

The question concerning the effectiveness of procedural knowledge over conceptual knowledge or vice versa in mathematical learning has been a main theme for debate among mathematics education and psychology researchers for several decades. The cognitive processes which determine one's method of solving problems and answering questions can be identified within the knowledge continuum, whereby procedural knowledge may account for one extreme, and conceptual knowledge may account for the other extreme in the continuum. By knowledge continuum, one refers to the way in which an individual goes about knowing anything. The important term here is "goes about," which can be interpreted as "how" one knows anything. In mathematical terms, we can add the sum of two sets using written symbolism in a highly efficient manner—that is, in a quick and accurate procedure. For example, without the use of a (non-human) calculator or computer, an individual

Figure 25.10   **Double and Single Digit Addition Problem Solved Procedurally**

$$\begin{array}{r} {}^{1} \\ 27 \\ +\ 5 \\ \hline 32 \end{array}$$

can calculate the above problem (Figure 25.10) procedurally rather quickly.

The idea behind solving the 27 + 5 problem in the above example is that we are unable to determine on face value whether the individual knows the meaning behind the "1" placed above the "2" of the 27, but we do know that the individual solved the problem correctly and efficiently, without demonstrating the conceptual underpinnings of the problem. The individual used the standard algorithm for addition with place value. A standard algorithm for any mathematical domain (a mathematical domain is defined here as any mathematical idea, for example, ideas of number, addition, subtraction, multiplication, division, the Pythagorean Theorem, statistical mean, integration, and so forth) is a method for solving a mathematical problem that has been commonly accepted in society for decades, centuries, or even longer (society is defined here as in the school, the university, the workplace, or at home).

When referring to the previous discussion, it was noted that the procedural method for solving 27 + 5 is not useful for determining one's knowledge of the concept behind addition with place value. We can identify an individual's knowledge of the concept of addition with place value, or any other mathematical domain, through a more conceptualized method of solving mathematical problems. Figure 25.11 illustrates the method of solving 27 + 5 through conceptual knowledge.

This method is conceptual because we can count all the members of each set; more specifically, all the diamonds of each set (27 in one set and 5 in the other) to arrive at the sum, namely, 32. This method summons the generalizable concept of addition—the combining of two (or more) sets to obtain a single sum. The early method of adding—counting all, which leads to counting on (and which can be interpreted as inefficient and time consuming, nevertheless accurate)—is demonstrated in solving a problem with a conceptualized approach.

Figure 25.11 **Double and Single Digit Addition Problem Solved Conceptually**

27+5=32

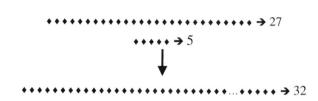

The topics of procedural knowledge and conceptual knowledge are discussed separately, and are followed by a discussion on how research in the area of procedural and conceptual knowledge affects practice.

PROCEDURAL KNOWLEDGE

One of the most recognized publications on the subject of procedural knowledge and conceptual knowledge is a landmark book, *Conceptual and Procedural Knowledge: The Case of Mathematics,* edited by James Hiebert (1986). In their introductory chapter, "Conceptual and Procedural Knowledge in Mathematics: An Introductory Analysis," Hiebert and Patricia Lefevre define the terms "procedural knowledge" and "conceptual knowledge" in quite broad terms. Hiebert and Lefevre argue that the definition of procedural knowledge consists of two parts. The first part deals with mathematical symbolism in terms of the ways in which we represent mathematical terms for the purpose of making sense for solving a problem. They contend that one part of the definition of procedural knowledge "is composed of the formal language, or symbol representation system, of mathematics. The other part consists of the algorithms, or rules, for completing mathematical tasks. . . . It includes a familiarity with the symbols used to represent mathematical ideas and an awareness of the syntactic rules for writing symbols in an acceptable form . . ." To illustrate the formal component of procedural knowledge, one can identify the syntactical accuracy of the multiplication problem: $17 \times 4 = 68$. In the same manner, one does not write "$17\boxed{4} \times = 68$" because it is syntactically incorrect.

The second part of the definition of procedural knowledge has to do with its algorithmic composi-

tion, that is, the set of rules or procedures used to solve various mathematical problems. For example, there is a very specific and systematic method in which to solve the problem $17 + 5 = \square$. We add the 7 and the 5 to yield a 12; but instead of writing the 12, we write "2." We then carry the "1," which stands for "10" and add it to the "1," which also stands for a "10," in the tens column, thereby yielding 20. The answer, 22, is the outcome of an algorithm—a structured and efficient method for solving a mathematical problem.

CONCEPTUAL KNOWLEDGE

Conceptual knowledge is much different from strict procedural knowledge in that it is not concerned with syntactical nomenclature, nor is it entirely concerned with algorithmic sequencing. In contrast, conceptual knowledge deals with the relationships between different elements of knowledge. (Although, one exception to this has to do with the relational element to the algorithmic part of procedural knowledge— namely, that x precedes $x + 1$.) This definition can clearly be traced to literature in cognitive psychology, which states that for one to understand a concept, one will first need to gain insight into factual knowledge. Only then will it be possible for one to make connections between factual content and create meaningful concepts. Conceptual knowledge, then, according to Hiebert and Lefevre, "is characterized most clearly as knowledge that is rich in relationships . . . and can be thought of as a connected web of knowledge, a network in which the linking relationships are as prominent as the discrete pieces of information." Conceptual knowledge can be attained, for example, when a child has memorized the standard algorithm for addition, and connected it with her knowledge of the numbers in the ones place, tens place, and so on. This connection, or network of individual concepts, is what makes conceptual knowledge a compelling form of cognitive development and growth.

RESEARCH AFFECTING PRACTICE

In the examples shown in Figure 25.12, we can identify the meaning of the process of multiplication by examining the problem: 23×4. The first example is strictly procedural, demonstrating the problem solved through the standard algorithm for multiplication.

Recall that a standard algorithm can be defined as "a commonly accepted procedure," and has been developed over a period of time—often several centuries or even millennia—and is generally the most efficient method of solving in a particular domain (the domain being multiplication in this case). The second example of the same problem is solved in a highly conceptualized form; clearly, the process of repeated addition—the conceptual definition of whole number multiplication (with the exception of 0 and 1)—is evident here. In the third example, we show the same problem being solved, yet in an entirely different manner from the previous two. In a sense, the third example can be interpreted as a combined form of procedural multiplication and conceptual multiplication. As seen in Figure 25.12, the third example exemplifies what Baroody (2003) would refer to as the investigative approach.

For several years, the gap between procedural knowledge and conceptual knowledge has remained wide. Only recently have researchers identified how a proper combination of both types of knowledge benefit genuine mathematical understanding. Baroody identified four approaches to mathematical instruction, which range in a continuum from entirely authoritarian to entirely democratic in teaching style. They are: (1) the skills approach; (2) the conceptual approach; (3) the investigative approach; and (4) the problem-solving approach.

The Skills Approach

The skills approach is a highly dualistic model—that is, doing mathematics is the production of either right or wrong answers; there is no gray, that is, no answer "in between." In addition, only one procedure will yield a correct answer. The teacher exerts absolute authority on the students and is the sole judge of correct and incorrect answers. The goal for instruction is for students to master basic skills in a more or less rote, mechanical manner through the use of mnemonic devices and other memorization strategies. The focus of the skills approach is to emphasize procedural knowledge. The general progression of the skills approach model is bottom-up—basic skills are mastered first, followed by more complex skills later. The general classroom environment is one in which the teacher directs all components of student learning. The lecture method is implemented on almost every occa-

Figure 25.12 **Double and Single Digit Multiplication Using: Example (1) the Standard Algorithm; Example (2) the Repeated Addition Concept; and Example (3) a Procedure Showing Partial Products**

Example 1

$$
\begin{array}{r}
{\scriptstyle 1} \\
23 \\
\times\,4 \\
\hline
92
\end{array}
$$

Example 2

$$
\begin{array}{r}
23 \\
23 \\
23 \\
+\,23 \\
\hline
92
\end{array}
$$

Example 3

$$
\begin{array}{r}
23 \\
\times\,4 \\
\hline
12 \\
+\,80 \\
\hline
92
\end{array}
\qquad
\begin{array}{l}
\\
\\
10 + 2 \\
80 + 0 \\
\hline
90 + 2
\end{array}
$$

sion and students generally work in isolation. Textbooks and worksheets are very common tools for teaching and learning, and manipulatives are almost never used. This approach was quite common throughout the history of formal schooling and even common to the present day. Its advocates were educational theorists and researchers who espoused behaviorist psychological research in educational practice.

The Conceptual Approach

The conceptual approach is a pluralistic model in that its proponents emphasize a continuum between right and wrong. There are usually several procedures to obtaining correct answers; however, there is usually one "best" procedure. Although the teacher has full authority over teaching and learning, there is an acceptance of diverse ways to solve basic and more complex problems. The teacher takes a somewhat authoritarian position; instruction is direct or semi-direct—that is, there is some imposition on the part of the teacher. The goal of the conceptual approach is to foster a meaningful environment for students as they learn facts, rules, and procedures. The focus of instruction under this approach emphasizes both procedural and conceptual content. Instruction is sequential and is based on the cognitive developmental level of students. Like the skills approach, the conceptual approach is didactic, however, not to such a great extreme. Textbooks are used, but teachers emphasize models for student learning as a means of explaining procedures and concepts. Oftentimes, manipulatives are used under this approach.

Investigative Approach

Baroody (2003) refers to the investigative approach as being instrumental in that it fosters an environment in which there are many procedures for obtaining correct answers or solutions. Teachers generally are open to a variety of viewpoints as long as they are effective. Incorrect responses often involve the teacher asking appropriate questions to tap into the student's understanding. This environment is democratic for the most part in that it is student centered. The goals of this approach are not only to provide meaning to skills and concepts, but also contribute to positive disposition (e.g., motivation and confidence), mathematical reasoning, and problem solving. The investigative approach differs from the previous two methods of instruction in that the teacher serves more as a guide. The teacher recognizes the students' informal knowledge and attempts to link students' inventive strategies with formal strategies. In addition, this approach is top-down in that the teacher poses a problem to promote student inquiry and investigation. Students have the opportunity to work in groups and on their own, and the use of manipulatives and technology plays an important role in learning.

Problem-Solving Approach

Baroody (2003) refers to the problem-solving approach as extreme relativism in that there is no right or wrong answer; rather all answers and solutions are equally valid because each student has his or her own viewpoint of what is true and logical. This approach differs greatly from the previous three instructional methods, especially the skills and conceptual approaches. The teacher and students evaluate their own answers and solutions based on their own belief systems. The teaching style is entirely democratic and student centered, and the main goal of the method is to promote mathematical inquiry. Thus, the focus of the problem-solving ap-

proach is to foster the processes of mathematical inquiry. Students are generally engaged independently in activities and the teacher generally participates as a monitor of activities and moderator of discussion. Activities are often open ended and the teacher makes little use of textbooks.

CHOOSING THE BEST APPROACH

With little research to support the "best" approach to teaching mathematics, Baroody (2003) espouses the investigative approach because it is the method that centers on conceptual knowledge, even more so than the conceptual approach. The investigative approach, more than the other three, promotes fluency of skills, conceptual understanding through appropriate probing methods, and even encourages a strong disposition toward mathematics.

Daniel Ness

PROCESS SKILLS ASSOCIATED WITH QUANTITATIVE AND SPATIAL THINKING

Although the National Council of Teachers of Mathematics (NCTM) lists only five process skills—problem solving, communicating mathematical ideas, reasoning and proof, connecting mathematical ideas, and representing mathematical ideas in a variety of ways—as standards (or what they categorize as "theme standards"), the number of processes associated with mathematical thinking abound. One can certainly add to this list of processes: estimating, conjecturing, analyzing, measuring—the list continues. Before the common process skills are discussed, however, it is necessary to gain insight into how and why these process skills are significant in the development of mathematical thinking.

PHILOSOPHICAL UNDERPINNINGS OF MATHEMATICAL PROCESS SKILLS

Mathematical process skills are crucial for cognitive development because they emanate from our senses. In the empirical tradition of how we come to know anything, if everything we know we can base on sensory perceptions, then any insight we gain with regard to mathematical thinking would be a product of the senses—our visual stimuli, for example, would allow us to proceed to solve mathematical problems, to reason or prove a theorem or to represent mathematical problems in several ways, while our auditory stimuli cause us to listen to others as they communicate their ideas or make mathematical conjectures. This is a perspective firmly rooted, as stated above, in the empiricist tradition, particularly in the works of Locke, and subsequently in the work of Hume.

PROBLEM SOLVING AND THE VARIETY OF MATHEMATICAL REPRESENTATIONS

Students' accuracy in solving mathematical problems in early and middle twentieth-century American education was not based on the identification of common or efficient problem-solving strategies. In fact, it was Edward L. Thorndike (1905), the Teachers College professor of psychology, who posited that transfer of mathematical ideas was negligible at best and nonexistent at worst, and that mathematical learning was an outcome of the association between external stimuli and an intended response. With this philosophical view, mathematical problem solving strategies basically took a back seat for several decades.

Problem-solving strategies and the promotion of estimation were proscribed by educators, whose emphases were rather on number fact and procedural memorization for the general school aged population. It was not until the 1980s when the standards movements in a number of academic fields were generally in place, and subsequently placed greater emphasis on a somewhat pseudo-constructivist framework for teaching subject matter knowledge. Prior to the 1980s, there was a sentiment among educational administrators and politicians that students were generally performing poorly, or underachieving, in the common branch subject areas. Much of this sentiment was a result of a number of factors, including one seemingly ignored by many educational scholars—increased access to education. Another critical factor had to do

with the role of teaching mathematics and science in the public schools.

From the late 1950s, after the Soviet Union's launching of Sputnik, to the end of the 1970s, American schooling adopted what is commonly referred to as the "new math." The new math curriculum, which included both the mathematics fields and the science-related fields (especially physics), included topics that tended to focus on students who were interested in higher-level mathematics and physics. Common mathematical topics in the elementary school included set theory, the study of number bases other than ten, and modular arithmetic. Instead of finding ways to promote the then established mathematics and science curricula, many conservative politicians within the Reagan administration condemned the new math curricula because, as they claimed, it was contributing to an increase in an underachieving student population. Critics have argued that these politicians were more interested, in a sense, in "dumbing down" the school-aged populace. As a possible repercussion to the somewhat fatalistic tone of the infamous right-wing publication, *A Nation at Risk,* in 1983, the education community decided to focus on key elements that promoted successful teaching and learning. One of these key elements had to do with the manner in which students solved mathematical problems. These elements were identified, and eventually led to the development of the standards movement, which exists in full form to the present day.

Despite the standards movements in recent days, research in problem-solving methods and strategies—known as heuristics—are far from novel enterprises. In fact, the topic of heuristics was burgeoning during the years of World War II, and was fully developed in George Pòlya's book entitled *How to Solve It* (1945). Shortly after Pòlya wrote his book, it was clear to most mathematicians that his heuristic methods were sound, and if followed correctly, would yield successful results when solving mathematical problems. However, Pòlya was not without his critics, especially in the 1960s and 1970s. Although Pòlya's methods were transparent to most mathematicians, a number of critics argued that research supporting his heuristic approach was lacking, and that there were hardly any data to support his problem-solving techniques, especially with regard to mathematics education. Pòlya's heuristic framework, however, had received a great deal of acceptance throughout the mathematics and education research community by the 1980s (incidentally, during the growth of the standards movement). By this time, researchers had collected several studies, including doctoral dissertations, on the topic of heuristical approaches in mathematics, and concluded that Pòlya's methods were successful in fostering achievement in mathematical problem solving.

Unfortunately, Pòlya's program for developing heuristical strategies was not entirely achieved in the contemporary classroom or in school curricula. Despite his popularity in this domain, Pòlya's problem-solving framework was oversimplified. First, the process of successful problem solving will involve individual students or small groups of students developing specific strategies based on the heuristics. Teachers generally follow what Burkhardt calls the "exposition, examples, exercises" mode, in which students are introduced to a new topic, work out examples with the teacher, and work on exercises at the end of the lesson or for homework. The content of each heuristic is taught—it is not presented for students' active engagement when working on problems.

Another dilemma produced by the way problem-solving strategies are carried out in the contemporary classroom has to do with the status of heuristic teaching in school. The heuristic is usually considered a separate activity, disconnected from so-called mainstream parts of mathematics textbooks. They are usually presented more as novelties, or "rewards and recreations" toward the end of each chapter. To follow Pòlya's program, teachers need to ensure that heuristic methods play a role in every aspect of mathematics learning.

COMMUNICATION THROUGH CONJECTURE AND REASONING AND PROOF

Like mathematical problem solving, the ability to communicate mathematical ideas was also generally proscribed in American schools in the early and middle parts of the twentieth century. Students were asked to memorize their number fact tables and operational procedures individually, oftentimes without the aid of an adult. Within the last decade, however, the role of communication in the mathematics classroom has become the *sine qua non* process-skill activity because it is believed to promote transfer of mathematical learning and both procedural and conceptual knowledge. Moreover, the increase in use of the Piagetian clinical method as being a successful means of tapping students' understanding of mathematical (and other) concepts, and the greater use of general psychoanalytical techniques as analogues to the classroom environment for promoting connections between one mode of thinking to other modes have greatly contributed to the role of communicating mathematical ideas in the classroom.

Another area in which mathematical communication has become a major element in mathematics learning is metacognition—the ability for an individual to interpret, and possibly analyze, her own thinking process. The identification of metacognitive ability can also be demonstrated through the Piagetian clinical method. Metacognition occurs in a social milieu—that is, a setting with more than one person—for if this were not the case, than it would be difficult to identify an individual who is engaged in metacognitive activity, and it would be futile to talk through one's thinking processes in an environment lacking other individuals. As Lester and his colleagues point out, metacognitive instruction is most efficient and valuable when it is practiced in a systematically controlled and structured situation under the direct guidance of the teacher.

THE INTERRELATIONSHIP OF MATHEMATICAL IDEAS

As stated above, with the psychological findings of Edward Thorndike, American educators at the turn of the twentieth century were not convinced that mathematical concepts involved transfer, and that one mathematical concept was distinct from any other mathematical concept. For example, it would be peculiar in the 1920s for a teacher to present a topic in Euclidean geometry by including material having to do with number operations and algebraic concepts. Teachers using current methods, however, inculcate these types of connections for the development of mathematical thinking; for example, it would be quite common nowadays to observe a lesson demonstrating the bisection of a rectangle to prove that two triangles are congruent (geometric thinking), and, at the same time, demonstrating congruence by presenting the equal proportions (arithmetic and algebraic thinking) of the corresponding legs of each triangle. Recent research studies have demonstrated otherwise—namely, that students' knowledge transfer involves a great many mathematical ideas.

ESTIMATING

NCTM did not include estimating as a process skill within their set of standards. This may very well have to do with the role of estimation in problem solving. This may have something to do with the fact that there was little, if any, research in mathematics education before 1980 on the topic of estimation in mathematical teaching and learning. During that time, and even today, teachers have downplayed the role of estimation. Perhaps this is due to the use of the term as a euphemism for "obtaining a close answer, but not the correct one." However, estimating is a powerful tool, which enables students to identify and appreciate mathematical patterns and relationships.

Estimation is powerful in a number of ways. First, it allows students to detect patterns and relationships with numbers. For example, if a student knows that $10 \times 6 = 60$, when she encounters the problem 102×59, the process of estimation will allow her to identify an answer that is quite close to the correct answer, namely, 6,000, without actually performing the problem on paper. Second, estimating abilities are helpful in tackling more complex forms of mathematics. And third, good estimation skills often lead to better performance in mathematical abilities; students who possess these skills use more strategies and appear to be more flexible in their thinking than other students.

It must be clarified, however, that estimation is not synonymous with the term "approximation." An individual might approximate a measurement or the answer to a problem without performing an estimation task. For example, an estimate of the number $\frac{5}{17}$ to the nearest thousandth might be 0.301 since $\frac{5}{17}$ is slightly less than $\frac{1}{3}$. But to approximate $\frac{5}{17}$ to the closest thousandth would require the use of pencil and paper or a calculator. In short, estimation is cognitively based while approximation is procedurally based (through the process of using algorithms). And finally, to estimate is not to guess. Estimating is not an arbi-

trary endeavor; when one estimates, he is not picking an answer arbitrarily out of a hat. Rather, there is a general organization to the thinking process with regard to the identification of patterns and relationships.

GRAPHING AND THE VARIETY OF MATHEMATICAL REPRESENTATIONS

NCTM includes "mathematical representations" as one of their so-called theme standards. There is a great deal of controversy with regard to the benefits (or the lack thereof) of one's use of a variety of representations of a mathematical idea or procedure for the purpose of gaining knowledge. On the one hand, educators espousing one constructivist perspective would argue that having more than one method to solve a problem, or the use of a number of mathematical representations for problem solving, allows for greater versatility in using mathematical symbols and ideas, and therefore builds knowledge and understanding. On the other hand, a number of educational researchers and psychologists have argued that children who use too many methods for solving a mathematical problem tend to use inefficient strategies and usually have slower processing speeds and limited long-term memory. These students are often diagnosed as mathematically disabled learners. Moreover, there is a rather high positive correlation between mathematically disabled individuals and overall learning disabled individuals. Despite this chasm, there is a general belief that any mathematical topic can be represented in more than a single way.

Chia-ling Lin

MATHEMATICAL ERROR ANALYSIS

Mathematical error analysis is one means by which teachers or psychologists can assess the developmental level of mathematical knowledge of a student. Rather than identifying the correct versus incorrect responses on most standardized criterion-referenced tests (e.g., Test of Early Mathematical Ability [TEMA], Test of Mathematical Ability [TOMA], Comprehensive Mathematics Abilities Test [CMAT]), mathematical error analysts identify the mistakes that occur—the common ones—among students. The intention of most error analysts is to demonstrate that a student's errors in computation are frequently consistent. Errors become predictable when they can be decoded to explain exactly why and under what circumstances an incorrect response was produced.

SOURCES OF ERRORS

There are three important factors to consider when encountering individuals who make consistent mathematical errors when attempting to solve problems. First, many students identify arithmetic and algebra merely as activities which are isolated from their everyday concerns. Thus, they think of these areas of study, and mathematics as a whole, as a topic with its own set of rules, completely unrelated to the general routine of their lives.

Second, errors that children make are more often than not based on organized strategies and rules. Many educational administrators and politicians base children's errors on a number of factors that have little if anything to do with the reasons behind those errors. In an earlier entry, a six-year-old child was asked to give the answer to $5 + 3$. Her response was "7," and she based her answer on a logical argument—if $7 - 3 = 5$, then $5 + 3 = 7$. In short, the child produced a sound, logical argument to an otherwise erroneous response. Unfortunately, many teachers, administrators, and politicians would think of these errors in terms of "low IQ" or the diagnosis of a learning disability.

And third, there may be very sensible origins to the faulty rules that underlie students' errors. Children do not produce consistent errors because they lack intelligence; rather, these errors are almost always the products of what children have been taught or what they have observed. This problem can certainly be compounded if a teacher is not entirely clear about how to teach certain mathematical topics. From an objective standpoint, the faulty rules children use may seem illogical; however, through analysis, it has been seen that most errors have sensible origins that make some sense to the child.

MATHEMATICAL BUGS

Given the sensible nature of most errors we can classify mathematical errors into two primary categories: Math-

Figure 25.13   **Mathematical Bug Produced When Ignoring Place Value with Double and Single Digit Subtraction**

ematical bugs and mathematical slips. The origin of the term "bug" goes back to the early days of computer programming, when computers filled the space of entire laboratories and programs were produced using punch cards. The term "bug" was applied to a faulty program, or a program that failed to produce output due to faulty logic or incorrect terminology.

The term "bug" was also appropriated for individuals who produced mathematical errors in a consistent manner. For example, consider the pattern of errors in the above three problems (Figure 25.13).

The analysis of this error pattern with respect to these three problems is clear: The individual's faulty rule clearly has sensible origins—namely, that when subtracting whole numbers, the smaller number is always subtracted from the larger number. In the first problem, the "1" is subtracted from the "4" to produce "3," and the "2" is either "brought down," or an assumed "0" in the tens place of the subtrahend (bottom number) is subtracted from the "2" in the minuend to yield "2," hence, the incorrect answer of 23. The second problem is produced in a similar manner, namely, $7 - 2 = 5$ and $1 - 0 = 1$. The third problem is quite similar with only one minor change: Although the larger number, "8" in the ones place, is in the subtrahend, the larger number in the tens place is in the minuend. Nevertheless, the same faulty rule is applied, thus producing the incorrect answer of 14. The student's answers to these three problems constitute what Brian Enright (1986) and other error analysts refer to as an error pattern, and which has been referred to as a mathematical "bug."

ERROR CLUSTERS AND PATTERNS

Researchers in mathematical error analysis measure mathematical errors in numerous ways. Based on his *Diagnostic Inventory of Basic Arithmetic Skills* (1986), Enright identified 233 error patterns in students' mathematical performance. Each of these patterns is grouped into seven error clusters. These clusters into which all of the error patterns appear fit into one of the following seven categories: regrouping, process substitution, omission, direction, placement, attention to sign, and guessing. Regrouping demonstrates a student's inability to solve an arithmetic problem due to a lack of place value knowledge. Process substitution is evident when a student changes the method of one or more of the computational steps when attempting to solve a problem. The student will create an entirely different algorithm that results in an incorrect answer. Next, an error cluster in which a student leaves out a step in an algorithm or leaves out part of an answer is called omission. An omission error differs from a process substitution error in that an incomplete algorithm is used, not a different one. The error cluster of direction is produced when the steps are performed in the wrong direction or order even if the computation is correct. Placement errors are often calculated accurately, but the answers are incorrect because the numbers are written in the wrong place. The attention to sign error cluster occurs when a student ignores the sign, and thus performs the incorrect operation. Guessing, the last error cluster in Enright's framework, is perhaps the only one of the seven that does not seem to be derived from faulty rules that have sensible origins. Guessing lacks logical coherence, and indicates a lack of knowledge of both content and process. Figure 25.14 shows examples of each error cluster.

This cluster method can be useful in at least two ways. First, the examiner can establish whether the student is making the same error in different skill assessments. This may suggest a basic weakness in a fundamental arithmetic process. For example, if on several skill tests a student demonstrates a number of error patterns that fall within a particular error cluster such as process substitution, the examiner can assume that the student needs remedial instruction in those areas.

Second, error analysis information for each skill test can be recorded, thereby providing data for setting individual instructional objectives and can be used during school conferences as a graphic record of the student's current performance in arithmetic. By reviewing the data sheet, the examiner can determine quickly and easily if there are students who can be grouped for instruction. The 233 error patterns in seven error clusters indicate that there are numerous ways to produce errors in mathematical computa-

tation. The error pattern given in Example 1 of Figure 25.14 involves regrouping because the individual failed to demonstrate knowledge of place value when subtracting. Therefore, proper instruction fixed upon an essential process that will be applied again and again can greatly reduce the repetition of student errors in computation.

ERROR ANALYSIS VERSUS CRITERION-REFERENCED TEST RESULTS

There are numerous differences between the identification of errors through mathematical error analysis and the results from criterion-referenced tests. First, as mentioned above, criterion-referenced tests are devised so that administrators can determine the developmental level of a student's mathematical knowledge based on the number of correct and incorrect responses. Mathematical error analysts, in contrast, are concerned primarily with the consistency of mathematical errors and, perhaps more important, the structure of these errors. Another important difference between the two has to do with the nature of the content that is being assessed. On the one hand, error analysts wish to understand how errors are produced from the standpoint of calculation and computation, and not from the standpoint of conceptual knowledge. On the other hand, researchers who use criterion-referenced tests use these tests because many questions identify whether a student recognizes the correct response to a question that is conceptually based.

MATHEMATICAL SLIPS

Mathematical bugs consist of only a single type of mathematical error. Another mathematical error type is referred to as a slip. It is often the case that individuals make errors due to sloppiness, carelessness, or a lack of attention to mathematical detail. These distinct behaviors are called slips. For example, a child may consistently obtain the correct answer to the problem $16 - 9 = \square$. However, on one particular occasion, the same child may erroneously conclude that $16 - 9 = 8$. Another individual might be quite adept in multicolumn multiplication, but for some reason, makes an error with the problem 16×21. Instead of obtaining 336 as an answer, the student overlooks the additional 10 that was carried over (from 2×6) to the tens column, thus obtaining the

Figure 25.14 Examples of Error Clusters in Mathematical Computation

1. Error Pattern from the "Regrouping" Cluster

```
    5   7
  + 1   5
    6  12
```

The student writes the entire sum of each column with no indication of regrouping.

2. Error Pattern from the "Process Substitution" Cluster

```
    3   4
  -     5
    8   9
```

The student adds the subtrahend to each digit of the minuend and also does not regroup with regard to place value.

3. Error Pattern from the "Omission" Cluster

```
       1  7
  0.4)6  8
```

The student ignores the decimal point in the divisor.

4. Error Pattern from the "Direction" Cluster

```
    2   3
  ×     2
    6   4
```

The student multiplies the tens place of the multiplicand before multiplying the ones place of the multiplicand.

5. Error Pattern from the "Placement" Cluster

```
    2   7
  - 1   5
    2   1
```

The student writes the digits of the difference in reverse.

6. Error Pattern from the "Attention to Sign" Cluster

```
        6
  -  ⊗  5
     1  1
```

The student adds the two numbers when multiplication should be utilized instead.

7. Error Pattern from the "Guessing" Cluster

$$\frac{4}{12} = 4$$

The student copies the numerator and designates it as the answer.

Source: Adapted from Brian E. Enright, *Tester Manual for Enright Diagnostic Inventory of Basic Arithmetic Skills* (with 10 books, student tests, and arithmetic record book). North Billerica, MA: Curriculum Associates, 1986.

incorrect answer of 236. Unlike bugs, slips are not systematic and are often associated with boredom, lack of effort, or attempting to process a calculation too quickly. Slips are much closer to randomness than are bugs. In terms of frequency, Kurt Van Lehn (1986) found that slips occur almost as frequently as systematic errors or bugs—that is, approximately 50 percent of all mathematical errors are slips. All remaining (approximately 50 percent) errors have systematic origins.

Daniel Ness

MATHEMATICAL THINKING AMONG OLDER CHILDREN AND ADOLESCENTS

The mathematical thinking strategies of older children and adolescents are founded and dependent on the mathematical development of infants, toddlers, and young children. From a Piagetian perspective, children commonly considered in the intermediate grade level (approximately seven to eleven years) can perform numerous mathematical tasks that would be otherwise untenable for the preschool aged child. Piaget referred to these children as concrete operational in that they were able to appreciate the relational nature of equivalence of two or more sets (conservation of number), classify shapes according to their properties, place straws of varying lengths in the proper order of size, and explain how they would solve a three-digit multiplication problem with a fairly clear description.

Children at the level of concrete operations are then able to demonstrate more organizational skills than children in previous levels. When comparing classroom investigations of early elementary school children, intermediate children, and adolescents, concrete students were asked to conduct an empirical activity where they were initially asked to predict what would happen if a tennis ball were to be dropped from the top of a meter stick. Some children concluded that they believed the tennis ball would reach one meter after the first bounce, while others believed the ball would reach half a meter after the first bounce. There were even a few other students who were unable to make predictions altogether.

They were then given meter sticks and tennis balls, and were asked to carry out their investigations. Their task at this point was to work in groups: One member of each group would hold the meter stick vertically, while another member would drop the tennis ball from a meter above the floor, while another student would measure the approximation of the distance between the tennis ball and the floor after the first bounce. Children at the preoperational level (kindergarten and first grade) generally had no idea how to proceed with the directions of the activity. The child in charge of the meter stick would typically hold it in a slight slant, the child dropping the tennis ball would add downward force to the ball (thereby adding an additional, and unnecessary, variable to the activity), while the child measuring the distance of the ball from the floor after the first bounce would not react quickly enough to approximate the measurement. Children at the concrete operations stage would be far more organized that the younger children. The child with the meter stick would hold it upright and perpendicular to the floor, the child dropping the ball would be careful in the way she dropped the ball, making certain that no extra force is applied and that it drops vertically (without a curve), while the third child takes rather accurate measurements. At this point, however, they did not know completely how to proceed. They did not know how to apply the approximated measure of the distance of the tennis ball to the floor after the initial bounce to any type of generalization with regard to patterns and relationships with measurement concepts. So, although their actions demonstrated careful and systematic treatment of the task at hand, their range of ability to generalize was limited.

Adolescents or young adults (approximately twelve years and older) are at the level of formal operations. Unlike the younger children, the adolescents were not only systematic and careful in their calculations, they also considered the general idea of the investigation in terms of all possibilities. After making several measurements of the first bounce after a tennis ball dropped from one meter, some students made similar kinds of predictions by dropping the ball at a new constant height. Others decided to drop the tennis ball at the same height, but now they wanted to drop the ball on a gymnasium mat to confirm their original hypotheses. In general, the older children and adolescents did not only hold the variables constant; they continued their investigations by changing some of the variables and then holding the new variables constant. That is, they tested their hypotheses by appreciating the relationships between variables and realizing that if any one variable is changed, the same conditions of the other variables must apply. In sum, formal operational individuals are able to generalize at a much higher level than preoperational or concrete operational individuals. These findings have significant implications for mathematics educators in terms of older children, adolescents, and adults and the processing and solving of mathematical problems.

PROBLEM SOLVING AMONG ADOLESCENTS AND ADULTS

Research examining mathematical acquisition and retrieval of basic number operations and more complex problems has demonstrated mixed results in terms of how adults process mathematical problems when compared to younger children. One classic study on adult mathematical thinking is that of M. Ashcraft and J. Battaglia (1978) who proposed that older children and adults retrieve answers to rather simple problems (e.g., $6 + 7$; 2×5) from memory, which then activate associative links between answers and binary (two numbers being acted upon through an operation) combinations.

Subsequent research in this area, then, has suggested that older adolescents and adults differ considerably on problem-solving techniques in that younger children employ a variety of techniques—both formal and informal—while the adult resorts solely to memory which then is transferred to a link between number combination and an answer. For example, the child of seven years will often solve the problems 23×4 using a number of procedures. Some of these procedures include: $23 + 23 + 23 + 23$ (repeated addition); $20 \times 4 + 3 \times 4$ (place value concept); the standard algorithm (see glossary); or simply counting all members of each set.

For the past two decades or so, research has suggested that the adult processes this problem in a different and singular manner, namely through memory: (1) the adult memorizes the answer to the number combination 23×4, or (2) performs the easier calculation through memory using the standard algorithm for multiplication. In short, the general development of arithmetic knowledge from childhood to adulthood went something like this: Young children use numerous strategies when solving mathematical problems. Over time, they learn more efficient methods and eventually dispense with the inefficient ones. They use flexible and adaptive methods acquired from a variety of procedures. Later, however, adults will use a single and "most efficient" method for solving various mathematical problems. In fact, most research on adult mathematical thinking up to the late 1990s has espoused this view.

CURRENT RESEARCH ON ADOLESCENT AND ADULT MATHEMATICAL THINKING

Research within the past five years presents a quite different picture with regard to adolescent and adult mathematical processing of procedures. Jo-Anne LeFevre and her colleagues (2003) provide evidence demonstrating that adults, like children, have multiple procedures from which to select when solving mathematical problems. In addition, it has been shown that adults do not solely rely on memory of combinations as has been put forth by earlier research. The following are some examples which illustrate similarity between children's and adults' cognitive processing when solving mathematical problems and carrying out less complex calculations.

First, adults' processing speed, like that of children's, is faster when working with ties—binary combinations in which the numbers being operated upon are the same (e.g., $5 + 5$, 7×7)—than when working with non-ties—binary combinations in which the numbers being operated upon are different (e.g., $2 + 9$, 6×3)—on both addition and multiplication combinations. Second, adults, like children, find it easier to solve problems with operands that involve the numbers 2 or 5 (e.g., 2×6, 2×7, 5×3, 5×4) than those that do not (e.g., 3×6, 4×7). One reason for this may have to do with the divisibility of 10; that is, our society, like most societies, works with base 10 in the everyday goings on of school, work, play, and so forth. Since the number 10 is divisible by 2 and 5, the faculties of the brain find it easier to work with these numbers than other numbers that do not divide the number 10 evenly—that is, into equal parts (e.g., 2 divides 10 into 5 equal parts; likewise, 5 divides 10 into 2 equal parts). In other words, the base 10 system can be parsed more easily with the numbers 2, 5, and of course 10, than other numbers.

In sum, adolescents' and adults' processing of arithmetic problems differs from children's processing perhaps only with regard to speed. With processing speed aside, however, there are few if any differences at all in terms of the use of single procedures or multiple procedures when comparing children's and adults' problem-solving methods. In fact, data suggest that adults use a greater variety of mathematical procedures than was originally posited by earlier researchers in the field of mathematical cognition and processing speed.

Chia-ling Lin

MATHEMATICALLY RELATED LEARNING DISORDERS

Difficulty with mathematics covers a wide range of conditions. These conditions, however, may have little to do with neurological deficit—that is, mathematically related learning disabilities due to physical deficiencies—and may have a great deal to do with affect (for example, problems with anxiety when encountering mathematical problems) or cognitive deficit (for example, difficulty with fact retrieval, conceptual insight, memory, and processing speed). Since learning problems related to affect are not characterized as disorders, discussion here focuses on neuropsychological deficits and cognitive deficits in mathematical thinking and problem solving.

NEUROPSYCHOLOGICAL DEFICIT

While cognitive deficit refers to procedural and fact-retrieval skills, conceptual knowledge, working memory, and processing speed, individuals experiencing neuropsychological deficit have suffered from either developmental or acquired physical conditions. Neuropsychological research has accounted for three types of conditions that affect arithmetic-related learning: (1) distinct fact retrieval; (2) procedural fact-retrieval; and (3) disruption of the ability to spatially represent numerical information. Despite some overlap with cognitive deficiencies, individuals who lack distinct fact retrieval are unable to produce solutions to factual arithmetic questions. For example, an individual who experiences deficiencies in distinct fact retrieval will be unable to identify the larger set when examining two sets—one with three dots and the other with seven dots. Individuals who lack procedural fact retrieval are unable to provide correct or accurate responses to relatively simple operations, for example, the sum of 5 and 3, or the difference between 9 and 8. Individuals who experience a disruption of the ability to spatially represent numerical information are unable to identify the meanings of mathematical symbols based on their spatial representation. For example, they will undoubtedly lack knowledge with regard to the convention of aligning decimals points when adding numerals containing decimal parts. Another example would be when individuals attempt to subtract one number from another with an arbitrary positioning of numerals. These three conditions are extremely common with individuals who possess a number of acquired or developmental neurological learning problems with regard to mathematics. Individuals who experience these and other related conditions may have the following neurological learning disorders in mathematics.

THE DYSCALCULIAS

The most common neurological condition related to mathematics learning is the disorder referred to as dyscalculia. This disorder is often diagnosed in two forms: acquired dyscalculia and developmental dyscalculia. Individuals with acquired dyscalculia experience problems associated with numbers, specifically arithmetic computation and calculation, that result from some form of brain injury, while individuals diagnosed with developmental dyscalculia experience problems in conceptual knowledge of number or arithmetic learning that are a result of a sequence of neurological events originating from early childhood. These individuals do not necessarily suffer from some form of overt brain injury, although evidence suggests that a neuropsychological deficit (e.g., lack of synaptic growth) underlies the mathematically related learning problems. According to a classic study of acquired forms of dyscalculia,

H. Hecaen and his colleagues (1961) classified acquired and developmental dyscalculia into three types: alexia and agraphia for numbers, spatial acalculia, and anarithmetia.

Alexia and Agraphia

Alexia (repetitive reversal of numeric symbols) and agraphia (the inability to read and write mathematical terms correctly) for numbers involve difficulties in the reading and writing of numbers, however, with adequate and intact skills in other areas of arithmetic. Alexia and agraphia for numbers are sometimes, but not always, associated with reading and writing in nonmathematical language-related disorders. Symptoms of alexia and agraphia often appear in young children—it is quite common to observe preschool-aged children who reverse numerals when writing them; however, reversal of numerals should not be an indicator of a neurological disorder in mathematics learning of an individual, especially during early childhood. Alexia and agraphia for numbers will be a problem, however, only if it persists well into the elementary school level (over seven or eight years of age). Lesions in the left hemisphere of the brain are the cause of alexia and agraphia of numbers.

Spatial Acalculia

Spatial acalculia refers to one's inability to reason mathematically as a result of arbitrary placement of mental or written mathematical symbols. Spatial acalculia is often caused by damage occurring in the posterior section of the right hemisphere of the brain. Examples of spatial acalculia are abundant: They include rotation of numerals, omission of numerals, the inability to construe the meaning and placement of operator symbols $(+, -, \times, \div)$, and deficient knowledge of place value as a result of numeral misalignment. In the latter instance, an individual will be unable to subtract $32 - 17$ because the "7" is either under the "3" or haphazardly placed below and to the right of the "2."

Anarithmetria

Anarithmetria, an acquired neurological deficit in mathematical thinking, does not involve problems in reading and writing of numbers or the spatial arrangement of numerals; rather, it involves an acute difficulty in retrieving basic number facts and arithmetic procedures. It is important to note, however, that individuals with anarithmetria usually understand arithmetic concepts, but arithmetic procedures are lacking, most often due to an inability to retrieve basic facts and procedures from memory. Two frequent problems associated with anarithmetria in young children are the confusion of operation signs and perhaps more frequently, the retrieval of arithmetic facts. Research in anarithmetria suggests that individuals who experience difficulty with arithmetic fact retrieval also experience procedural deficits in language. Damage to the posterior regions of the left hemisphere has been found to be the major cause of individuals who show signs of anarithmetria. N. Badian (1983) identified a fourth category, attentional-sequential dyscalculia, in which individuals make strings of careless errors when performing procedures and experience extreme difficulty when memorizing basic arithmetic number facts, particularly those involving multiplication.

COGNITIVE DEFICIT MODEL

Unlike neuropsychological deficit, individuals with cognitive deficit possess mathematical learning disabilities that are not a result of brain injury. Cognitive deficits in mathematical processing include the following: lack of counting knowledge; problems with working memory and memory development; developmental problems with regard to procedural and fact-retrieval knowledge, and the speed at which one processes information.

Counting Knowledge

Counting knowledge and counting skills provide the framework for early arithmetical development. It is therefore possible that mathematically disabled individuals' difficulties in basic arithmetic are related to a poor understanding of counting concepts. These difficulties may arise out of the inability for certain individuals to move beyond certain effective but inefficient counting strategies (counting all—counting all members of two or more sets to find a sum; or counting on—identifying the total number of one set and counting on from the other set to find a sum). Mathematically disabled individuals often use their fingers to count objects or numbers in their mind. However, it should be noted that finger counting is not an indication of mathematical disability. One's inability to procede beyond object counting will hinder that individual's success in formal arithmetic operations and more complex mathematical concepts in later years.

Working Memory and Memory Development

In general, mathematically disabled students who do not have any kind of neuropsychological disorder are usually poor with regard to memory and procedural and fact-retrieval skills. They often have difficulty in memorizing basic number facts, and often find it very difficult to memorize common conversions (e.g., $\frac{1}{2} = 0.5$) and important mathematical formulas ($a^2 + b^2 = c^2$, or even more basic than the Pythagorean Theorem, any number multiplied by 0 is equal to 0—the zero property). Similarly, their procedural skills are often fraught with errors. For example, they will be unable to calculate the sum or difference of two familiar fractions. Although research in the area of mathematical disability is consistent with regard to procedural knowledge, findings concerning conceptual knowledge among mathematically disabled individuals are mixed. In some cases, mathematically disabled individuals are unable to identify efficient strategies for solving problems; however, their conceptual knowledge may be clear. For example, nearly all mathematically disabled individuals will be unable to add 45 + 59. However, a large number of these individuals will tell you that the sum is around 100. So, the notion of number sense with regard to rounding is fairly strong.

Mental Addition Using Procedural and Fact-Retrieval Knowledge

In assessing students with learning disabilities, it is as important to identify strengths as it is to understand difficulties. Often, children with learning disabilities are surprisingly adept at informal mathematics. When asked to perform some simple mental addition problems, mathematically disabled individuals often have a great deal of difficulty. In one scenario, an interviewer asks a third grader to add 16 + 8 and 12 + 13. The child eventually reaches the correct answer. These children may seem as if they are thinking through each problem given to them; however, they do not seem to know the answers from memory.

Another child, a fourth-grader, is asked to add 14 + 15. He did several interesting things. First, he started with the larger number. In general, this is a good method and makes addition simpler. Although these numbers are so similar, it does not make a great deal of difference. Then, he broke the 14 into 6 + 6 + 2. Perhaps he invented this method himself; perhaps someone helped him develop it. In either event, the boy's procedure involves transforming the problem into more manageable chunks. This method of changing a difficult problem so it is easier and more manageable (a process known as "chunking") is common, and generally considered evidence of sound thinking. Again, this is a common characteristic of mathematically disabled children with regard to arithmetic operations. Further, this implies a great deal about assessment procedures.

Testing or assessment should go beyond evaluating whether or not a student has memorized facts and procedures. Assessment should provide some insight into a student's strategies, thinking ability, and potential for learning. Testing should also help us understand students' styles of learning, what they believe, and how they feel, because these factors too can have an important impact on learning.

Processing Speed

The general finding with regard to processing speed is that mathematically learning disabled children need more time to solve arithmetic problems than do their mainstream peers. A few reasons may account for this finding. First, one body of research suggests that mathematically disabled children are generally slower than mainstream peers with regard to the execution of all processes related to number and operation. Another finding is that since mathematically disabled individuals use different, and often inefficient, problem solving strategies, they will tend to spend a longer amount of time solving arithmetic related problems. Third, mathematically disabled individuals often rely more on less efficient counting strategies—for example, counting all when adding members of two or more sets—and do not frequently use faster fact retrieval strategies (Geary 1994).

Processing speed and working memory are interrelated, however. One particular area with regard to the interrelationship between processing speed and working memory in which researchers are interested is counting speed; the speed at which one counts might determine the speed and ease at which individuals can process basic arithmetic facts—a skill that is inextricably linked with long-term memory.

THE COGNITIVE-NEUROPSYCHOLOGICAL MODEL

Although the literature regarding mathematical disabilities developed into two distinctively different operational domains—namely, the neuropsychological model and the cognitive model—researchers within the last two decades have investigated the link between mathematical disability as a result of brain injury on the one hand, and cognitive deficit (not resulting from brain injury) on the other. This new domain is referred to as the cognitive-neuropsychological model. One of the primary concerns of researchers in this area is to show that a cognitive skill, for example, the concept of subtraction, can be organized into several processing components. Any form of brain damage that selectively disrupts any one of these components can be examined not only from a neurological perspective, but also from a cognitive-psychological perspective. One question that can be asked is: How might the roles of response time (i.e., processing speed) and working memory affect an individual's skill in solving a mathematical problem, when their mathematical knowledge base has been hampered or delayed as a result of brain injury?

A cognitive-neuropsychological framework can be useful for a few reasons. First, since the cognitive model may serve to help understand brain injured individuals' delayed performance in particular cognitive domains, the cognitive-neuropsychological model can be helpful in understanding the processing of information in individuals with a total lack of cognitive ability within a particular cognitive domain. In addition to illuminating our understanding of acquired disorders (e.g., acquired dyscalculia), a cognitive-neuropsychological model can be useful in terms of our understanding of developmental disorders as well (e.g., developmental dyscalculia).

DO GENETICS IMPACT MATHEMATICALLY DISABLED INDIVIDUALS?

To date, there is little, if any, evidence that suggests that mathematical disabilities are a result of heritability—that is, a genetic influence on mathematically disabled individuals. Research has substantiated, however, that approximately half of the variability in basic number and operations ability among young children is a result of a genetic influence. Nevertheless, the possibility that mathematical disability is associated with a genetic component is important to consider in that if most mathematically disabled children represent the left tail of the normal distribution curve with regard to arithmetic ability, then a lack of adequate performance in this area may have a great deal to do with a genetic influence, especially if these same children are reading disabled. Since there are common cognitive factors that influence both reading ability and arithmetic ability, more research is needed to verify a link among mathematical disability, reading disability, and other forms of learning disabilities.

Daniel Ness

Glossary

Associativity. An arithmetic and algebraic principle that verifies that an operation performed on two numbers (*a* and *b*), and the same operation performed on the outcome of *a* and *b* with another number c will yield the same total outcome as an operation performed on a with the outcome of the same operation performed on b and c. That is, *(a + b) + c = a + (b + c)*, or *(a × b) × c = a × (b × c)*. Associativity is applicable to the addition and multiplication operations only.

Abstraction principle. A rule which states that a counting procedure can be applied to individual objects or to whole groups of objects, and that counting objects of a different kind is applicable to the counting process.

Algorithm. A systematic method or procedure that is used to solve a quantitative mathematical problem that cannot otherwise be solved by number fact memorization alone. Standard algorithms are those that have been widely accepted by mathematicians and mathematics teachers.

Binary operation. A mathematical procedure involving two and only two variables or constants. For example, $3 × 4$ is a binary operation because the operation—multiplication—involves two constants (3 and 4); $q ♦ r$ is a binary operation because the operation involves two variables (*q* and *r*). The symbol "♦," however, must be defined.

Calculus. A means whereby one can obtain instantaneous velocity and whose fundamental ideas involve differentiation and integration.

Cardinality. The number that refers to the total number of objects in a set. For example, "five ducks" has a cardinality of five.

Cardinality principle. A rule that states that the last number word written or stated verbally refers to the number of objects in a set.

Cartesian coordinate system. A system of geometric representation based on two axes (*x* and *y*) and containing a finite number of units—a system developed by the seventeenth-century rationalist philosopher and mathematician René Descartes.

Commutativity. An arithmetic and algebraic principle that verifies that an operation performed on two numbers (*a* and *b*) will yield the same outcome if the operation were performed on the same numbers with b as the first number and *a* as the second. That is, a + b = b + a, or a × b = b × a. Commutativity is applicable to the addition and multiplication operations only.

Conceptual knowledge. Knowledge based on the recognition and identification of patterns and relationships. Conceptual knowledge is achieved by the construction of relationships between often factual pieces of information.

Conservation of number. The ability for an individual to distinguish between the cardinality of a set and the physical arrangement of the objects of that set.

Conservation of space. The ability for an individual to recognize the capacity of an uncountable object (e.g., water, clay, sand) as being the same regardless of the size of the container that is holding the object.

Counting all. Identifying the sum of the objects of two or more sets by counting each member of both sets. Compare with "counting on."

Counting on. The identification or recognition of a number of an initial set of an addition problem and the subsequent adding of each member of the second set to the initial set without the counting of the entire two sets. For example, a child is asked to add 14 + 5. The child replies: "fourteen . . . fifteen, sixteen, seventeen, eighteen, and nineteen" without counting the first fourteen numbers aloud. This procedure is more time efficient than counting all.

Declarative knowledge. See "conceptual knowledge."

Distribution. An arithmetic or algebraic principle that asserts that the sum of two products is equal to the product of two sums, or vice versa. That is, *ab + ac = a (b + c)*, and similarly, *a (b + c) = ab + ac.*

Enumeration. Knowledge of number concepts and operations on whole numbers.

Estimation. An answer to a mathematical problem based on an individual's reasonable approximation. For example, a second grade child might say the answer to $23 × 4$ is "about 100."

Euclidean geometry. A system of spatial representation dealing with axioms, postulates, and definitions, and whose initial proponents were Euclid and his collaborators. Common ideas regarding Euclidean geometry include the axiomatic constructions starting with a point (undefined), a line (two points determine a line), a plane (three points, two of which are not on the same line, determine a plane), and parallelism, or the parallel postulate (two lines [l and m] are parallel if the alternate interior angles created by a transversal [line n] are equal).

Everyday mathematics. Identification of an individual's mathematical thinking in out-of-school contexts (e.g., free play, work). Everyday mathematics can be spontaneous or gradual.

Function. An operation applied to a variable (or set of variables) that yields an entity known as the value for that particular variable. This is commonly exemplified by $y = f(x)$, where y is said to be a function of the variable x if for every x, there is one and only one value of y.

Grouping. The creation of two or more sets of objects for the purpose of combining all sets for determining the cardinality of the number of objects in all sets. A child separates a large set of 23 objects into four groups in order to determine the total number of objects in the set (informal addition): The first group contains 4 objects, the second group contains 6 objects, the third group contains 6 objects, and the fourth group contains 7 objects.

Iconic representation. A distinct mark not directly related to a particular object's appearance that is used to represent the object. For example, a child may draw eight Xs to represent eight checkers. Other forms of iconic representation include tally marks, dots (not circles or zeroes), checkmarks, or asterisks.

Invented strategy. A plan used to solve a mathematical problem that does not employ a standard algorithm. Invented strategies are not formal in that they are generally constructed on prior knowledge in the everyday environment.

Irrational number. a number that is not rational. Any number that *cannot* be expressed as a/b, where a is an integer and b is a nonzero integer. A nonrepeating decimal.

Logico-mathematical thinking. A term defined by Jean Piaget that refers to the processes undertaken by individuals who eventually reach a level of mathematical thinking associated with formal operations.

Manipulatives. Objects that are manufactured for the purpose of connecting an individual's informal knowledge of mathematics with formal or in-school mathematical knowledge. Examples abound and include Cuisenaire rods, Geoboards, and Base-10 Blocks.

Mapping. An individual's representation of objects (material or abstract) of space in his or her own environment. Some of these concepts include scale, perspective, direction, linking the written representation with its referent (for example, a roadmap of a town with the actual streets within that town), and the coordinate system.

Number. An abstract idea that can be used for representing cardinality when referring to a set of objects or for differentiating between two or more objects—or labeling (e.g., bus numbers, addresses, telephone numbers).

Number sense. One's knowledge of the number concept and the ability to use binary operations on those numbers. One's identification of patterns and relationships associated with different numbers.

Number facts. The answers to binary operations (based on the four primary operations of arithmetic—namely addition, subtraction, multiplication, and division) whose addends, minuends, subtrahends, factors, divisors (not always dividends), and quotients are not less than 0 and not greater than 12 (sometimes 10). A few examples include (see underlined) $5 + 2 = 7$; $9 - 4 = 5$; $3 \times 8 = 24$, and $30 \div 6 = 5$.

Numeracy. Computational fluency, or fluency in the identification or recognition of patterns and relationships among mathematical concepts.

Numeral. A symbol used to represent a number (e.g., "7" for seven objects).

Numerosity. A set of one or more objects that can lead to numerical reasoning for young children. Examples include three apples, two beach balls, one candle, five checkers, and the like.

One-to-one correspondence. The ability to recognize elements of a set such that each element corresponds to one and only one number.

One-to-one principle. A rule that states that only one number word can be associated with one and only one object when counting a set of objects.

Operation. A mathematical action that involves two or more variables or constants.

Order relevance principle. A rule that states that the assignment of a number to a particular object when counting is irrelevant.

Procedural knowledge. Knowledge consisting of (1) familiarity of mathematical symbols and syntax for writing those symbols, and (2) the rules, algorithms, or procedures used to solve mathematical tasks.

Protoquantitative knowledge. Young children's knowledge of numerical quantities in the form of amounts, but not in the form of numerosities.

Pushing aside. A memory-reduced technique that young children use to count that involves the exclusion of objects once they have been counted. For example, a child may push a penny aside, bend each finger, or collect objects while counting.

Quantitative knowledge. Young children's knowledge of numerical quantities with small numerosities.

Rational number. Any number that can be expressed as a/b, where a is an integer and b is a nonzero integer.

Seriation. The process of creating or ordering a sequence by a specific attribute such as length, weight, or time.

Spatial sense. One's knowledge of spatial relationships for interpreting both abstract and real-world geometric phenomena. One's identification of patterns and relationships associated with geometric figures.

Spontaneous mathematics. Mathematical cognition that emerges from activities during play. For example, two children building a structure with blocks demonstrate spontaneous mathematics in the following manner: Child 1 takes two long blocks and indicates that the blocks can be used to cover one side (or wall) of a four-sided structure. Child 2 says: "OK, we need 8 [blocks]." (See "everyday mathematics.")

Stable order principle. A rule that states that number words are written or verbally stated in a fixed sequence.

Standard algorithm. See "algorithm."

Subitizing. Instantaneous visual recognition of numerosities without the necessity of counting each member of individual sets or collections. Subitizing is not a primitive form of number development; young children subitize for the purpose of developing efficient mechanisms for solving arithmetic problems.

Symbolic representation. Numerals, regardless of system (e.g., hindu-arabic, Roman, Egyptian) used to represent a set of objects. For example, the child will write the number "5" to represent five teddy bears.

Tagging. The process of touching each object in a particular set (i.e., unit cubes, pennies, fingers) once and only once without movement of each object for the purpose of counting.

Topological primacy thesis. A theoretical model of Jean Piaget that argues that the earliest forms of spatial knowledge are plastic and dynamic in form and structure, not rigid in the sense of Euclidean geometry.

REFERENCES

Ashcraft, M.H., and J. Battaglia. (1978) Cognitive arithmetic: Evidence for retrieval and decision processes in mental addition. *Journal of Experimental Psychology: Learning, Memory, and Cognition* 4: 527–38.

Badian, N.A. (1983) "Dyscalculia and Nonverbal Disorders of Learning." In *Progress in Learning Disabilities*, vol. 5, ed. R. Myklebust, 235–264. New York: Grune & Stratton.

Baillargeon, Rene. (1995) "A Model of Physical Reasoning in Infancy." In *Advances in infancy research*, vol. 9, ed. C. Rovee-Collier and L. Lipsett, 305–371. Norwood, NJ: Ablex.

Balfanz, Robert. (1999) "Why Do We Teach Young Children So Little Mathematics? Some Historical Considerations." In *Mathematics in the Early Years*, ed. Juanita V. Copley, 3–10. Reston, VA: National Council of Teachers of Mathematics.

Baroody, Arthur. (1987) *Children's Mathematical Thinking: A Developmental Framework for Preschool, Primary, and Special Education Teachers.* New York: Teachers College Press.

———. (1998) *Fostering Children's Mathematical Power: An Investigative Approach to K–8 Mathematics Instruction.* Mahwah, NJ: Lawrence Erlbaum Associates.

———. (2003) "The Development of Adaptive Expertise and Flexibility: The Integration of Conceptual and Procedural Knowledge." In *The Development of Arithmetic Concepts and Skills: Constructing Adaptive Expertise*, ed. Arthur Baroody and Ann Dowker, 1–33. Mahwah, NJ: Lawrence Erlbaum Associates.

Baroody, Arthur. J., and Jesse L. Wilkins. (1999) "The Development of Informal Counting, Number, and Arithmetic Skills and Concepts." In *Mathematics in the Early Years*, ed. Juanita V. Copley, 48–65. Reston, VA: National Council of Teachers of Mathematics.

Berkeley, George. (1988) *Principles of Human Knowledge.* Originally published in 1710. New York: Penguin Books.

Blaut, James M., and David Stea. (1974) Mapping at the age of three. *The Journal of Geography* 73, no. 7: 5–9.

Bryant, Peter. (1995) Children and arithmetic. *Journal of Child Psychology and Psychiatry* 36: 3–32.

Cassirer, Ernst. (1957) *The Philosophy of Symbolic Forms.* Vol. 3, *The Phenomenology of Knowledge.* New Haven, CT: Yale University Press.

Clements, Douglas H. (1999) "Geometric and Spatial Thinking in Young Children." In *Mathematics in the Early Years*, ed. Juanita V. Copley, 66–79. Reston, VA: National Council of Teachers of Mathematics.

Clements, Douglas. H., and Michael T. Battista. (1992) "Geometry and Spatial Reasoning." In *Handbook of Research on Mathematics Teaching and Learning*, ed. Douglas Grouws, 420–464. New York: MacMillan.

Descartes, René. (1994). *A Discourse on Method, Meditations, and Principles.* Originally published in 1641. New York: Everyman's Library.

Enright, Brian E. (1986) *Tester Manual for Enright Diagnostic Inventory of Basic Arithmetic Skills* (with 10 books, student tests, and arithmetic record book). North Billerica, MA: Curriculum Associates.

Fowke, Edith. (1989) *One Elephant Balancing.* New York: Harcourt, Brace, Jovanovich.

Fuson, Karen C. (1988) *Children's Counting and Concepts of Number.* New York: Springer-Verlag.

Geary, David. (1994) *Children's Mathematical Development.* Washington, DC: American Psychological Association.

Ginsburg, Herbert P. (1989) *Children's Arithmetic: How They Learn It and How You Teach It.* Austin, TX: Pro-Ed.

———. (1997) *Entering the Child's Mind: The Clinical Interview in Psychological Research and Practice.* New York: Cambridge University Press.

Ginsburg, Herbert P., Chia-ling Lin, Daniel Ness, and Kyoung-Hye Seo. (2003) Young American and Chinese children's everyday mathematical activity. *Mathematical Thinking and Learning* 5, no. 4: 235–258.

Ginsburg, Herbert P., Sandra Pappas, and Kyoung-Hye Seo. (2001) "Everyday Mathematical Knowledge: Asking Young Children What Is Developmentally Appropriate." In *Psychological Perspectives on Early Childhood Education: Reframing Dilemmas in Research and Practice*, ed. Susan L. Golbeck, 181–219. Mahwah, NJ: Lawrence Erlbaum Associates.

Hecaen, H., R. Angelergues, and S. Houillier. (1961) Les varietes cliniques des acalculies au cours des lésions retrolandiques: Approche statistique du probleme. *Révue Neurologique* 105: 85–103.

Hiebert, James, and Patricia Lefevre. (1986) "Conceptual and Procedural Knowledge in Mathematics: An Introductory Analysis." In *Conceptual and Procedural Knowledge: The Case of Mathematics*, ed. James Hiebert. Hillsdale, NJ: Lawrence Erlbaum Associates.

Hochberg, J. (1964) *Perception.* Englewood Cliffs, NJ: Prentice-Hall.

Howard, Katherine. (1979) *I Can Count to 100 . . . Can You?* New York: Random House.

Hughes, Martin. (1986) *Children and Number: Difficulties in Learning Mathematics.* Oxford, England: Blackwell.

Huttenlocher, Jeanne, and Nora Newcombe. (1984) "The Child's Representation of Information about Location." In *The Origins of Cognitive Skills: The Eighteenth Annual Carnegie Symposium on Cognition*, ed. Catherine Sophian. Hillsdale, NJ: Lawrence Erlbaum Associates.

Jacobs, Allan D., and Leland B. Jacobs. (1971) *Arithmetic in Verse and Rhyme.* New York: Garrard.

Kamii, Constance. (1985) *Young Children Reinvent Arithmetic: Implications of Piaget's Theory.* New York: Teachers College Press.

Kant, Immanuel. (1902). *Critique of Pure Reason.* Originally published in 1781, trans. F.M. Müller. New York: Macmillan.

Kent, Jack. (1973) *Twelve Days of Christmas.* New York: Scholastic.

Kilpatrick, William H. (1951) *Philosophy of Education.* New York: Macmillan.

Kuczaj, S.A., II and M.P. Maratsos. (1975) On the acquisition of front, back and side. *Child Development* 46: 202–10.

LeFevre, Jo-Anne, Brenda L. Smith-Chant, Karen Hiscock, Karen E. Daley, and Jason Morris. (2003) "Young Adults' Strategic Choices in Simple Arithmetic: Implications for the Development of Mathematical Representations." *The Development of Arithmetic Concepts and Skills: Constructing Adaptive Expertise*, ed. Arthur Baroody and Ann Dowker. Mahwah, NJ: Lawrence Erlbaum Associates.

Lester, Frank, Joe Garofalo, and D. Kroll. (1989) The Role of Metacognition in Mathematical Problem Solving: A Study of

Two Grade Seven Classes. Final Report to the National Science Foundation of NSF Project MDR 85–50346.

Leutzinger, Larry P. (1999) Developing thinking strategies for addition facts. *Teaching Children Mathematics* 6, no. 1: 14–18.

Liben, Lynn S. (1981) "Spatial Representation and Behavior: Multiple Perspectives." In *Spatial Representation and Behavior across the Life Span: Theory and Application*, ed. Lynn S. Liben, A.H. Patterson, and Nora Newcombe. New York: Academic Press.

———. (1999) "Developing an Understanding of External Spatial Representations." In *Development of Mental Representation: Theories and Applications*, ed. Irving E. Sigel. Mahwah, NJ: Lawrence Erlbaum Associates.

———. (2001) "Children's Understanding of Spatial Representations of Place: Mapping the Methodological Landscape." In *A Handbook of Spatial Paradigms and Methodologies*, ed. N. Foreman and R. Gillett. Mahwah, NJ: Lawrence Erlbaum Associates.

Liben, Lynn S., and Roger M. Downs. (2001) "Geography for Young Children: Maps as Tools for Learning Environments." In *Psychological Perspectives on Early Childhood Education*, 220–252. Mahwah, NJ: Lawrence Erlbaum Associates.

Macaruso, Paul, and Scott M. Sokol. (1998) "Cognitive Neuropsychology and Developmental Dyscalculia." In *The Development of Mathematical Skills*, ed. Chris Donlan. East Sussex, UK: Psychology Press.

McCloskey, M., A. Caramazza, and A.G. Basili. (1985) Cognitive mechanisms in number processing and calculation: Evidence from dyscalculia. *Brain and Cognition* 4: 171–96.

McLeod, Douglas B. (1992) "Research on Affect in Mathematics Education: A Reconceptualization." In *Handbook of Research on Mathematics Teaching and Learning*, ed. D.A. Grouws. New York: Macmillan.

Miller, George Armitage. (1998) *Psychology: The Science of Mental Life*. New York: Addams Bannister Cox.

Miller, K.F., and D.R. Parades. (1996) "On the Shoulders of Giants: Cultural Tools and Mathematical Development." In *The Nature of Mathematical Thinking*, ed. R.J. Sternberg and T. Ben-Zeev. Mahwah, NJ: Lawrence Erlbaum Associates.

Miller, Kevin F., M. Perlmutter, and D. Keating. (1984) Cognitive arithmetic: Comparison of operations. *Journal of Experimental Psychology: Learning, Memory, and Cognition* 10: 46–60.

Mix, Kelly, Janellen Huttenlocher, and Susan Cohen Levine. (2002) *Quantitative Development in Infancy and Early Childhood*. New York: Oxford University Press.

National Council of Teachers of Mathematics. (2000) *Principles and Standards for School Mathematics*. Reston, VA: NCTM.

Ness, D. (2001) The Development of Emergent Spatial Thinking, Geometric Concepts and Architectural Principles in the Everyday Context. Ph.D. Dissertation. New York: Teachers College, Columbia University.

———. (2003) "Helping Teachers Recognize and Connect the Culturally Bound Nature of Young Children's Mathematical Intuitions to In-school Mathematics Concepts." In *Commitment to Excellence: Transforming Teaching and Teacher Education in Inner-City and Urban Settings*, ed. Linda A. Catelli and Ann Diver-Stamnes. Cresskill, NJ: Hampton Press.

Piaget, Jean. (1954) *The Construction of Reality in the Child*. New York: Basic Books.

Piaget, Jean, and Bärbel Inhelder. (1956) *The Child's Conception of Space*, trans. F.J. Langdon and J.L. Lunzer. London: Routledge and Kegan Paul.

Piaget, Jean, Bärbel Inhelder, and Anna Szeminska. (1960) *The Child's Conception of Geometry*. New York: Norton.

Plato. (1937). "Meno." *Dialogues of Plato*, ed. and trans. Benjamin Jowett. New York: Random House.

Polya, George. (1945) *How to Solve It*. Princeton, NJ: Princeton University Press.

Presson, Clifford C. (1982) The development of map-reading skills. *Child Development* 53: 196–99.

Reisman, Frances K. (1982) *A Guide to the Diagnostic Teaching of Arithmetic*. 3rd ed. Columbus, OH: Charles E. Merrill Publishing.

Reys, Robert, E., Nobuhiko Nohda, and Katsuhiko Shimizu. (1994) *Computational Alternatives for the Twenty-First Century: Cross-Cultural Perspectives from Japan and the United States*. Reston, VA: National Council of Teachers of Mathematics.

Schoenfeld, Alan. (1992) "Learning to Think Mathematically: Problem Solving, Metacognition, and Sense Making in Mathematics." In *Handbook of Research on Mathematics Teaching and Learning*, ed. Douglas Grouws. New York: MacMillan.

Seo, Kyoung-Hye, and Herbert P. Ginsburg. (2003) "'You've Got to Carefully Read the Math Sentence . . . ': Classroom Context and Children's Interpretations of the Equals Sign." In *The Development of Arithmetic Concepts and Skills*, ed. Arthur J. Baroody and Ann Dowker. Mahwah, NJ: Lawrence Erlbaum Associates.

Shaywitz, S.E., M.D. Escobar, B.A. Shaywitz, J.M. Fletcher, and R. Makuch. (1992) Evidence that dyslexia may represent the lower tail of a normal distribution of reading ability. *New England Journal of Medicine* 326: 145–50.

Simon, Tony J., Susan J. Hespos, and Philippe Rochat. (1995) Do infants understand simple arithmetic? A replication of Wynn (1992). *Cognitive Development* 10: 53–269.

Sinclair, H., and A. Sinclair. (1986) "Children's Mastery of Written Numerals and the Construction of Basic Number Concepts." In *Conceptual and Procedural Knowledge: The Case of Mathematics*, ed. James Hiebert. Hillsdale, NJ: Lawrence Erlbaum Associates.

Sisul, Jennifer S. (2002) Fostering flexibility with number in the primary grades. *Teaching Children Mathematics* 9, no. 4: 202–04.

Sophian, Catherine. (1984) "Developing Search Skills in Infancy and Early Childhood." In *Origins of Cognitive Skills: The Eighteenth Annual Carnegie Symposium on Cognition*, ed. Catherine Sophian. Hillsdale, NJ: Lawrence Erlbaum Associates.

Steffe, Leslie P., and Paul Cobb. (1988) *Construction of Arithmetical Meanings and Strategies*. New York: Springer-Verlag.

Sztajn, Paola. (2002) Celebrating 100 with number sense. *Teaching Children Mathematics* 9, no. 4: 212–17.

Thorndike, Edward L. (1905) *The Elements of Psychology*. New York: Seilor.

Van Hiele, Pierre. (1986) *Structure and Insight: A Theory of Mathematics Education*. Orlando: FL: Academic Press.

Van Hiele, Pierre and Dina Van Hiele-Geldof. (1953) *Werkboek der analytische meetkunde*. Purmerend, Netherlands: Muusses.

Van Lehn, Kurt. (1986) "Arithmetic Procedures Are Induced from Examples." In *Conceptual and Procedural Knowledge: The*

Case of Mathematics, ed. J. Hiebert. Hillsdale, NJ: Lawrence Erlbaum Associates.

Vandenberg, S.G. (1962) The hereditary abilities study: Hereditary components in a psychological test battery. *American Journal of Human Genetics* 14: 220–37.

Wei, Sun, and J.Y. Zhang. (2001) Teaching addition and subtraction facts: A Chinese perspective. *Teaching Children Mathematics* 8, no. 1: 28–31.

Wellman, Henry M. (1985) *Children's Searching: The Development of Search Skill and Spatial Representation.* Hillsdale, NJ: Lawrence Erlbaum Associates.

Whitenack, Joy W., Nancy Knipping, Jenine Loesing, Ok-Kyeong Kim, and Abby Beetsma. (2002) Starting off the school year with opportunities for all: Supporting first graders' development of number sense. *Teaching Children Mathematics* 9, no. 1: 26–31.

Willoughby, Stephen S. (2000) "Perspectives on Mathematics Education." In *Learning Mathematics for a New Century*, ed. M.J. Burke and Frances R. Curcio, 1–15. Reston, VA: National Council of Teachers of Mathematics.

Wittgenstein, Ludwig. (1967) *Remarks on the Foundations of Mathematics.* Cambridge, MA: MIT Press.

Wynn, Karen. (1992) Evidence against empiricist accounts of the origins of numerical knowledge. *Mind and Language* 7 (4): 315–32.

———. (1998) "Numerical Knowledge in Infants." In *The Development of Mathematical Skills*, ed. Chris Donlan. East Sussex, UK: Psychology Press.

Zvonkin, Alexander. (1991) Mathematics for the little ones. *Journal of Mathematical Behavior* 11, no. 2: 207–19.

V

EDUCATIONAL ISSUES CONCERNING DIVERSE POPULATIONS

26

Learner Differences

Individual differences among learners have been used to explain the ways in which students learn, to describe groups of students, and to provide guidance to educators in planning instruction for learners to maximize achievement outcomes. They have also been used to group students who fall at the extreme ends of the population distribution as gifted or in need of special education services. While there are obvious physical differences among children and adults (height, weight, manual dexterity, speed, agility, etc.), the focus on individual differences in the classroom is generally in the realm of cognitive differences and sometimes crosses over into behavioral domains that may impair the learning process. The cognitive differences that have been measured and used in decisionmaking in classrooms range from global concepts, such as general intellectual ability (IQ), to very specific differences in learning styles and interests.

Assessment of differences in human abilities and achievement is not a new phenomenon. The Chinese civil-service system established more than 4,000 years ago used a formal testing program to select candidates for government positions. Teachers in one-room schoolhouses in the United States clearly distinguished between the achievement levels of their students and assigned learning tasks accordingly. However, the history of the study of individual differences for the sake of understanding differences in learning, achievement, and ultimately the effects of educational intervention began with the work of psychologist Sir Francis Galton (1962).

Intelligence as a Dimension of Individual Differences

In the late nineteenth century Galton studied eminent men, their mental abilities and the hereditary and environmental influences on the development of "genius" (1962). His work influenced the work of the American psychologist J. M. Cattell who brought Galton's tests and research approaches to the United States, led the movement to include the study of individual differences in the science of psychology, and was instrumental in the spread of the testing movement in the United States (Anastasi 1988). At about the same time, Alfred Binet was charged by the French government to develop an assessment tool that would identify those children who were likely to have difficulty learning in school (Binet and Henri 1896). This led to development of the Binet-Simon Test of Intelligence that provided a measure of "mental age." The work of Simon and Binet was translated and adapted in the United States by Lewis Terman into an instrument known as the Stanford-Binet, and it was in this instrument that the intelligence quotient (IQ: the ratio between mental age and chronological age) was introduced. Terman used his instrument in the identification of gifted children whom he then studied for more than thirty-five years (1916).

The Stanford-Binet required individual administration by a trained examiner; hence, it was best suited to clinical use. The development of objective tests that could be administered to groups of individuals by the U.S. military became the model for most group intelligence tests that exist today and spurred a tremendous growth in intelligence-test development. Soon assessment programs were in place to measure the general intellectual ability of children and adults of all ages from preschool through graduate school. The widespread use of these tests was accompanied by parallel use of these tests in categorizing children, making selection decisions for admissions to schools, colleges, and universities, and for placement in special programs based on individual differences measured by these instruments.

While intelligence tests were shown to be a good

predictor of school achievement, they have been widely criticized for not measuring specific abilities that distinguish the performance or potential performance along other dimensions considered important for success in the various disciplines. Accordingly, other psychologists began work to develop tests of specific abilities. Early tests focusing on mechanical, clerical, musical, and artistic abilities were used primarily for vocational counseling and in the classification of personnel in industrial and military settings, but led quickly to the development of multiple aptitude batteries designed to yield information about individual differences on traits such as verbal comprehension, numerical aptitude, spatial visualization, arithmetic reasoning, and perceptual speed. The most extreme example of breaking down cognitive functioning into individual components that were then translated into instructional recommendations was the development of the Structure of Intellect Model by J. P. Guilford, which identified ninety different specific abilities (1967). The model was then used by Mary Meeker to create instructional materials to address each component of the model (Meeker and Meeker 1986).

Intelligence tests were widely used in schools to make decisions about student placements, to identify students who might be gifted or those who were categorized as mentally retarded. In some cases they were used to group students in classrooms, leading to a practice identified as tracking. Tracking occurred when students who were first grouped on some general aptitude measure were then identified as having a given level of potential and grouped accordingly in classrooms for instruction. These students then stayed in that group throughout their school careers with little or no opportunity for moving into another group. The result for many students was the loss of opportunity to take high-level high school courses that would lead to college or other opportunities following high school. Tracking was widely criticized in the 1960s as a means of restricting the opportunities of poor and minority students.

Widespread use of intelligence tests, especially in clinical diagnoses of children and the representation of mental ability as a single score, continues and the use of intelligence tests for grouping students continues to be criticized on many grounds. During the 1980s and 1990s the conception of intelligence was broadened through the work of two psychologists, Howard Gardner (1983) and Robert Sternberg (1985). Gardner

coined the term "multiple intelligences" for the dimensions of intelligence he identified as a result of his retrospective case analyses of gifted individuals, and he identified linguistic, logical/mathematical, spatial, musical, bodily/kinesthetic, interpersonal, and intrapersonal intelligences. He later added naturalistic intelligence and then, even later, posited existential intelligence. The first three initial intelligences (linguistic, logical/mathematical, and spatial) closely parallel domains sampled on conventional intelligence tests, and the first two, according to Gardner, are the domains emphasized in traditional assessment and instruction in schools. Linguistic intelligence taps the ability to use language to explain, to convince, to remember information coded as language, and to clarify meaning. To operate on relationships using abstract symbols and symbol systems and to evaluate ideas and quantities logically are considered to fall into the logical/mathematical domain. Spatial intelligence requires the skills of perceiving and transforming visual-spatial relationships.

Those who have profiles which are strongest in one or more of the remaining five intelligences are valued by most cultures, but are not traditionally measured by group intelligence tests or given equal emphasis in school. Those in whom musical intelligence is exceptional excel in sensitivity to musical nuance and are able to appreciate, produce, and combine pitch, tones, and rhythms. Skillful use of one's body to dance, mime, compete athletically, and so on, is considered bodily-kinesthetic intelligence, and exceptional understanding of and sensitivity to other people's motives, behaviors, and emotions characterizes interpersonal intelligence. Persons who excel notably in intrapersonal intelligence are those who reflect understanding of their own motives, emotions, strengths, and weaknesses. Finally, naturalistic intelligence requires understanding patterns found in the natural environment, and those who have gifts in existential intelligence are able to ask and reflect on important questions about life, death, and the ultimate realities.

Gardner's work was applied in the education literature to curricula and teaching guides that suggested that teachers should teach to develop the particular intelligence that dominated the child's profile. An industry developed around the production of materials that would teach the disciplines using strategies modeled on the descriptions of the individual intelligences. Gardner has debunked several myths that have arisen through schools' misapplication of the multiple intelligences (MI) theory, including the notion that there should be a separate intelligence test for each of the identified intelligences. Further, he did not support the development of activities to "teach" the intelligences or to treat them as discipline to be taught like science or social studies. Rather, he has suggested that the appropriate use of an understanding of individual differences in profiles is to capitalize on that knowledge by using the profiles to more effectively teach the disciplines. He suggests introducing topics in ways that most engage learners because of the connections they can make to the new ideas through examples drawn from the various intelligence domains, by drawing analogies using a model derived from areas where students may have stronger knowledge because of a more highly developed intelligence, and by providing multiple representations of the central or core ideas of a topic. He cautions, however, these uses of the intelligences must be congruent with high standards and true representations of the concepts and themes of the topic being taught (Gardner 1999).

Sternberg's conceptions of intelligence were triarchic in nature (1985). He identified three basic types of intelligence: analytic intelligence, synthetic intelligence, and practical intelligence. Those strong in analytic intelligence are those who would be identified by traditional assessments of intelligence and ability. They excel at analytic intelligence and are those who succeed in traditional school learning. They are able to identify a problem, define its nature, devise a successful solution, and monitor execution of the solution. Those who are strong in synthetic intelligence are those who are identified as creative—able to come up with unique ideas and unusual, but appropriate, solutions to problems. Finally, practical intelligence is characterized by the ability to solve the ill-defined problems that come up in everyday life and to implement solutions and make them work. Translating his conceptions of intelligence into assessment tools and curriculum, Sternberg has demonstrated that teaching using a curriculum that is structured to address the intelligence strength of a group of students results in greater learning. Those who excel in all three intelligence dimensions demonstrated the greatest success on tasks of all types.

Carolyn Callahan

LEARNER DIFFERENCES IN ACHIEVEMENT

Many other dimensions have been considered in the assessment of individual differences in students for the purpose of grouping students, developing tailored lessons, or motivating students. The most widely used are tests of achievement. Achievement is assessed informally daily in classrooms through observation and questioning of students, and on an intermittent basis by unit or end-of-year tests. The first standardized achievement tests were introduced in the United States in the 1920s, very soon after the introduction of intelligence tests. The use of standardized tests that measure very defined state goals through statewide competency testing or through standardized tests that attempt to compare students to carefully selected norm groups is usually conducted on a particular identified grade level in schools (every several years). The initial development of these tests was based on the notion that they would allow for comparisons of individual differences in learning using more objective measures than grades or individual teacher or local assessment. Parents, teachers, and administrators could compare an individual student to students across the nation. Expansion of the use of both nationally standardized and statewide assessments has led to their application to high-stakes decisions about student placements in special programs and for student advancement or graduation from high school.

Regardless of how achievement is assessed, learner differences in prior knowledge greatly affect the students' learning. Hence, attention to differences in three types of prior knowledge should guide instruction: declarative knowledge or knowledge that students can articulate about what they know; procedural knowledge or ability to act on what they can state; and conditional knowledge or the ability to use their declarative and procedural knowledge in new situations. Understanding learner differences in preexisting knowledge—both correct and incorrect knowledge—has been identified by the National Academy of Sciences as critical in planning effective learning experiences for children. Successful learning experiences are built on understanding a student's current knowledge, including incomplete understandings, false beliefs, and naïve conceptualizations of ideas, and then creating learning activities that will help students construct more mature understandings.

CREATIVITY

As a result of the presidential address to the American Psychological Association by J. P. Guilford in 1950, considerable attention was directed toward investigating individual differences in creativity. Debate surrounding assessment of individual differences in creativity focused on the multiple ways creativity was being defined and the modifiability of creativity through instruction. The literature variously defined creativity as part of the thinking process, as a personality variable, or as reflected by the ideas or creations of the individual. Accordingly, activity focusing on the measurement of differences among school-age children and adults resulted in the creation of measurement tools ranging from personality tests to evaluations of the processes and products of creative productivity. Self-report personality instruments assessing creativity included items intended to measure such factors believed to contribute to creativity as risk taking, tolerance for ambiguity, and perseverance—all personality characteristics that were found in creative producers. Other product-oriented instruments (e.g., the Torrance Tests of Creativity) focused on asking the students to complete such tasks as generating multiple alternative uses for common objects or modifying a toy to make it more fun to play with. The responses were scored on fluency (number of different responses), flexibility (number of different categories of responses), and originality (the statistical uniqueness of each response). Adult creativity assessments such as the Alpha Biographical Inventory matched attitudes, values, and behaviors of the examinee to a set of characteristics derived from the study of creatively productive persons. Research on creativity using the assessments based on products provides limited evidence that fluency, flexibility, and originality of responses (outcomes associated with the creative process) can be modified by instruction. Creativity is another dimension of learner differences that is sometimes central to definitions of gifted and talented students, and various assessments of creativity, including teacher ratings of creativity, creativity tests, and the creativity of student products as included in portfolios, are sometimes used in the identification of students as gifted and talented.

COGNITIVE STYLE/LEARNING STYLE

A decade after the focus on creativity, psychologists introduced the concept of cognitive style to the lexicon of cognitive differences. Messick (1993) provided a general definition of cognitive style as consistent individual differences in preferred ways of organizing and processing information and experience. The first introduction of cognitive style by Witkin (1977) was a study of the dimension of field independence and field dependence or the degree to which the immediate stimuli and conditions surrounding a problem influence the perceptions and strategies used to solve a problem. Since that time, more than fifty-four dimensions of learning style have been discussed including reflective/impulsive style and analytic/holistic styles, but some authors have claimed these all fall into a range of differences that can be categorized as spanning from analytic to intuitive. Analytic information processing is more compliant and adherent to rules, is structured in the decisionmaking process, and often follows step-by-step procedures for solving problems. Intuitive processing tends to be more nonconformist, uses more open-ended decisionmaking strategies, relies on more random methods of exploring potential solutions to problems, and uses a more holistic approach to problem solving.

Another view of learning style differences in students in classrooms, introduced by Rita and Kenneth Dunn (1978), incorporates many of the psychological dimensions of cognitive style, but goes beyond those dimensions to encompass the following domains: environment (light, sound, temperature, design), emotional (motivation, persistence, responsibility, need for structure or options), sociological (self, peer, team, adult, varied motivators), physical (time of day, need for mobility, etc.), and psychological (global/analytic, impulsive/reflective).

Joseph Renzulli and Linda Smith (1978) have also identified the degree to which students prefer one specific learning/teaching strategy to others as a learning style. While one might assume that children of certain ages, certain abilities, or from certain cultures might prefer to engage in learning in a particular way, the evidence suggests that in any group there is variability in the degree to which students prefer to listen to a lecture, participate in a discussion, be involved in a simulation activity, or engage in learning through other teaching strategies.

OTHER COGNITIVE LEARNER DIFFERENCES

Developmental differences in such areas as metacognition, the ability to monitor one's own learning and problem-solving strategies, may also affect learners' abilities to succeed in a given learning situation. While developmental theory provides guidance in the sequence of development and the approximate ages for attaining certain levels or stages of development, within any group of children there will be wide variation. For example, young children often fail to use effective strategies like rehearsal for remembering information because they believe that once they hear or read something they will remember it. As students mature they are likely to come to understand the importance of rehearsal, but not all children come to this realization and internalize it at the same age.

INTERESTS

Interests are grouped into the two categories of relatively stable interests and those that are generated in particular situations and may or may not last. The first type of interest, individual interests, are those that are associated with the predisposition to be attentive to and engaged in a topic. They have usually developed over time and are enduring and sustained. Situational interests are those stimulated by a set of environmental conditions that generate a more immediate short-term affective/emotional response in a particular context. Of course, situational interests may develop into individual interests. Students who are interested in particular topics either because of individual or situational interest pay closer attention, persist for longer periods of time, learn more and enjoy the learning process more than those who do not exhibit interest.

OTHER INDIVIDUAL DIFFERENCE VARIABLES

Researchers consider other noncognitive variables as important factors for school success. One of these is theory of mind—the ability of a person to predict and explain another person's behavior by considering the person's mental state and consequent response to that mental state. The development of this ability is considered important to the everyday social interactions of children and adults. The lack of appropriate social and communicative ability of individuals with autism is associated with very low levels of developed theory of mind. Further, higher levels of theory of mind are associated with more advanced cognitive functioning in such areas as executive functioning, creativity, and language.

Another individual difference that educators and psychologists have identified as an important element contributing to student success in the classroom is temperament. Rather than a characteristic that describes what a student does and how well the student does it, temperament describes how a student goes about learning and performing in the classroom. Differences in temperament are described on a continuum. On one end are the students who have a slow tempo, do things at an unhurried pace, and are slow to action. They are seen as students who have trouble finishing assignments, lag behind their peers, and are constantly being urged to "catch up." On the other end of the continuum are the highly active, impulsive, quick-to-respond children who are always starting an assignment before the directions are completed and rush to finish any task. Temperament is also described as difference in children who need changes in routine and those who find changes in routine upsetting, difference in those who persist at a task and those who give up easily, and those who are shy and those who join right in. While temperamental differences in individuals have always been noted, little attention has been given to the ways these differences have affected students' achievement, adjustment, and overall experience in school until recently. Recent research suggest that differences in students' temperaments affect the ways they approach learning tasks and interact with teachers' temperaments affecting their adjustment to the classroom, and the goodness of fit between the student and the school (Keough 2003). The research has led to suggestions for assessments for classrooms and for positive preventive strategies to help teachers avoid discipline, behavior, and learning problems in the classroom.

Carolyn Callahan

ABILITY GROUPING

The practice of ability grouping has been controversial for the last two decades. Part of the controversy stems from the confusion between the terms *ability grouping* and *tracking*. The term *ability grouping* refers to the practice of using test scores and/or other indicators of student ability and/or achievement to assign same-grade students to classes or instructional groups within a class or across classrooms. It may be used to group children into high, middle, and low classes or learning groups in elementary school or into varying levels of core classes at the middle school or high school level. It may be used by teachers to assign students to high, middle, or low reading or mathematics groups within the same classroom for instruction or it may be used to group students across several grade levels who are at the same level of achievement into groups for reading or mathematics instruction (cross-grade or cross-age grouping).

The term *tracking* was once restricted to the practice of recommending to students that they elect a course of high school studies leading to a particular vocational goal. The practice of tracking was considered to be a self-selection process left to the choice of students. However, the term has come to be applied to the practice of sorting students at an early age into high level, medium level, and low level classes, on the basis of measures of intelligence, where they remain through high school. As a rigid and immutable practice, tracking has received great criticism, which has been extended to the practice of ability grouping. The intention of ability grouping was not to create permanent configurations of students; however, when schools do not provide opportunity for students to gain the knowledge and skills necessary to move between groups or do not use frequent assessment to reassign students appropriately, tracking may result.

Clarification of terms used to discuss grouping is essential. Homogeneous grouping is the practice of using some pre-set criteria such as an aptitude test score, achievement test scores, or some other measure of academic ability or achievement to create instructional groups that contain only one level of student. Homogenous groups may be whole classes or they may be small groups within a class. Heterogeneous grouping arrangements result when students are systematically or randomly assigned to groups so that each group consists of students of a wide range of ability or achievement levels. Within-class grouping is the term often used to describe homogeneous small groups within a classroom. They are commonly used for mathematics and reading instruction in the elementary school. In Joplin and cross-grade grouping, a practice most common in reading instruction, students from heterogeneous classes at different grade levels, but at the same level of achievement or ability, are grouped for instruction. In whole-class ability grouping, students of like ability remain together for most of the instructional day. Accelerated classes of students (typically identified as gifted students) are provided a curriculum that allows them to advance through the traditional grade levels at a pace faster than their peers. Cooperative learning groups are usually small heterogeneous (although sometimes homogeneous) groups in which students are presented with specific instructional tasks to complete, and success of the group is as critical as individual success.

Ability grouping in most forms was widely practiced in the United States through at least the 1980s, and there is evidence that in some school districts tracking was also widely practiced. Accelerated classes are quite rare. There has been considerable attention to "de-tracking" students particularly at the elementary and middle school level, and the practice of heterogeneous classroom grouping at the elementary and middle school is now widely espoused by educators. However, there is evidence that grouping by subject area still is widespread at the high school level and at least in the discipline of mathematics in middle schools. The debate about the advantages and disadvantages of grouping is ongoing in the educational literature.

Arguments among educators supporting or not supporting grouping practices are based on whether or not they believe grouping improves achievement, whether or not grouping is inconsistent with the democratic ideal that all students should have equal opportunity to learn, whether the grouping practice promotes the notion that abilities are fixed, and whether or not ability grouping results in discrimination by race, ethnicity, or socioeconomic status.

The research on ability grouping is extensive, with the first studies as early as 1928. While hundreds of studies were conducted in subsequent years, researchers who tried to analyze the data across the accumulated evidence were unable to draw consistent conclusions. Some of the inconsistency in interpretation stems from the fact that many different types of grouping practices have been studied using many different measures of outcomes. Other reasons for the inconsistency may be related to the orientation of researchers who conduct the studies. A historical look at interpretations over the past seventy years provides some insight into this possibility. One group of researchers in the 1930s concluded, not surprisingly, that when students were grouped by intellectual ability and the ability groups worked with materials that matched their aptitude level, the instruction led to more positive school outcomes. When the same instructional and curriculum materials were used in all classes, there were no differences between students in homogeneous classes (ability grouping) and those in heterogeneous classes. Progressive educators who were followers of John Dewey in the later 1930s concluded from their reviews that grouping led to lower achievement and diminished self-concept and leadership. Reviews in the 1950s, when there was an emphasis on academic excellence, concluded that students with high aptitudes benefited from special accelerated and enriched classes with no detriment to social or emotional adjustment. Then, during the 1960s, coincidental with an emphasis on the issues of equity in schools, researchers concluded that no one benefits from ability grouping and that the achievement, academic motivation, and self-esteem of the lower and middle groups was adversely affected by grouping. The multiple interpretations of the research resulted in the application by educators of whichever findings suited an individual bias.

In the 1990s, using new methodologies, researchers did large-scale observational studies of tracking in junior and senior high schools, concluding that instruction was of higher quality in the higher-track classes. No quantitative data relative to student achievement was provided to support the observations in these studies and they have been criticized for attributing too much importance to very small differences and not separating the effects due to grouping and those due to student characteristics. A second approach used in recent studies is that of studying grouping by analyzing very large databases collected by the U.S. government. Researchers found that most high school seniors were in the track they wanted to be in; that the factor second in determining track placement (after personal preference) is academic ability; that social class does not appear to be important in determining curriculum except to the degree that social class influences test scores; and that race plays a small role in placement. In fact, when blacks and whites of equivalent aptitude and socioeconomic status are compared, blacks have a greater probability of being enrolled in the higher-track classes.

Other extensive analyses of all the grouping studies, using other strategies for analysis that had both experimental and control groups and which looked at grouping where the curriculum was adjusted and grouping where the curriculum was not adjusted by group, resulted in the following conclusions:

- When curriculum is not adjusted, lower and middle aptitude students learn about the same amount in grouped and mixed classrooms. Middle and lower classroom groups who earned about one year's worth of achievement in a mixed classroom would earn about one year's worth of achievement in grouped classrooms.
- In one analysis, when curriculum is not adjusted, grouping results in a slight positive effect on higher aptitude students. Students who would earn one year in mixed classes would earn 1.1 years in grouped classes. Another analysis failed to find an effect for any arrangement for any of the groups.
- When no adjustment was made for curriculum, self-esteem scores for the lower group went up slightly and the self-esteem scores for the higher group went down slightly.
- When curriculum is adjusted by accelerating the pace for high ability learners in grouped classes, the achievement of students in these classes exceeded that of students in the classes whose curriculum was not accelerated. When curriculum was adjusted by enrichment, children in these classes gained 1.4 to 1.5 years in achievement compared to 1.0 year for control groups.
- When cross-age grouping and within-classroom grouping using differential curriculum for the groups was compared to mixed group instruction, the average gain for the grouped students in one year was 1.2 to 1.3 years compared to 1.0 year for the control group.

James Kulik (1992) concludes in his review of all the analyses that have been done that if grouped classes where no curriculum differentiation occurs were eliminated, there would be a slight decrease in achievement for the brightest students and no discernable effect on other students. But, both higher and lower aptitude students would suffer academically if the grouped classes that have actually adjusted materials and methods to address the characteristics of the learner groups were to be eliminated.

Carolyn Callahan

EXCEPTIONALITIES AND SPECIAL EDUCATION

The concept of learner differences naturally leads to consideration of those who fall at the extremes of the population. Of particular note are the categories that have been established to incorporate those with exceptional cognitive abilities including the mentally retarded, those with learning disabilities, and the gifted. In addition, those who are physically impaired or exhibit behavior problems may be identified as exceptional students. Exceptional learners have been defined by Daniel Hallahan and James Kauffman (2003) as those who require special education and related services to realize their full potential.

The creation of programs of special education corresponded to the institution of compulsory schooling in the United States and the influx of immigrants to the United States. Compulsory education introduced large numbers of students who had never been part of the school system and were not able to succeed or conform to the demands of the classrooms. The influx of immigrants introduced a second new population of students who differed culturally, ethnically, and linguistically, and also had difficulty in succeeding in school. Lack of understanding of how to cope with these new students led administrators to create alternative means of educating them. Initially, students who exhibited severe intellectual deficiencies that were the consequence of biological/medical conditions that resulted in central nervous system damage and the lack of ability to function in

the school context were placed in isolated, ungraded classrooms. Over time, the concept of mental deficiency was broadened to include both those with severe retardation resulting from biological causes to milder cases of retardation associated with poverty. As indicated in the description of the early development of intelligence tests, the first directive given to Alfred Binet was to develop an assessment that would help identify those who would be likely to have difficulty learning. The use of the intelligence test became widespread in identification of the mentally retarded (and the gifted).

CATEGORIES OF STUDENTS SERVED IN SPECIAL EDUCATION PROGRAMS

The American Association on Mental Retardation (AAMR) defines the term mental retardation as "significantly subaverage intelligence functioning, existing concurrently with related limitations in two or more of the following adaptive skill areas: communication, self-care, home living, social skills, community use, self-direction, health and safety, functional academics, leisure, and work. Mental retardation manifests before age 18" (AAMR Ad Hoc Committee on Terminology and Classification 1992, 5). In the early twentieth century, the terms *moron, imbecile,* and *idiot* were used to identify subcategories of mental retardation based on IQ scores. These category labels were dropped because of their derogatory connotations and current classifications range from mild to profound retardation based on IQ scores. More recent definitions of mental retardation rely less on the concept of IQ and include deficiencies in adaptive behavior as part of the definition, particularly the individual's ability to communicate, to otherwise interact socially, and to engage in the basic activities of daily living. During the first half of the twentieth century there was a dramatic rise in the numbers and proportion of students identified as mentally retarded (MR). However, the incidence of mental retardation has declined steadily over the past twenty-five years to a prevalence of about 2.3 percent of the population nationally, but there is great variability among states in the rate of classifying students as MR. A disproportionate number of poor and minority students have historically been identified and placed in special classes for the mentally retarded. As of 1998, black children are more than twice as likely as their white counterparts to be identified as MR.

Learning disability was a term introduced by Samuel Kirk in 1962 to describe students who were not mentally retarded, but exhibited difficulty in achieving academically. The term has come to be an umbrella term that covers a broad range of learning problems that vary considerably from student to student. The term covers conditions that are highly variable in nature and degree, but generally indicates difficulty with information processing. Further, the term may be used to designate one deficiency in processing or it may indicate multiple processing difficulties. The following definition of learning disability was set forth in federal legislation in 1977 and reaffirmed in 1997 (Individuals with Disabilities Education Act Amendments of 1997, Sec. 602(26), p. 13):

(a) IN GENERAL: The term "specific learning disability" means a disorder in one or more of the basic psychological processes involved in understanding or using language, spoken or written, which disorder may manifest itself in imperfect ability to listen, think, speak, read, write, spell, or do mathematical calculations.

(b) DISORDERS INCLUDED: Such term includes such conditions as perceptual disabilities, brain injury, minimal brain dysfunction, dyslexia, and developmental aphasia.

(c) DISORDERS NOT INCLUDED: Such term does not include a learning problem that is primarily the result of visual, hearing, or motor disabilities, of mental retardation, of emotional disturbance, or of environmental, cultural, or economic disadvantage.

Federal regulations require that an IQ-achievement discrepancy be used to identify students with learning disabilities. Critics have called for revisions of the definition and identification process to eliminate the IQ-achievement discrepancy.

The rate at which students were identified as having a learning disability increased steadily from 1974 through 1994—nearly doubling between the beginning of the 1970s and the end of the 1990s. The rate of identification is now at about 6 percent of the population. Incidence of learning disabilities also varies greatly from state to state. In 1998 Rhode Island identified 9.75 percent of its students as having a learning disability, while Georgia identified only 3.10 percent.

Learning disabilities often occur in combination with other conditions, such as attention deficit hyperactivity disorder (ADHD). Children and adults with ADHD fall into one of three categories. One category is ADHD, Predominantly Inattentive Type. These students often fail to attend to detail or make careless mistakes, have difficulty sustaining attention, do not listen when spoken to directly, do not follow through on instructions, and fail to finish task and/or to organize tasks, avoid activities that require sustained mental effort, and are distracted and forgetful. Those who are categorized as ADHD, Predominantly Hyperactive-Impulsive Type, fidget, leave their seats in the classroom when expected to remain seated, often inappropriately run about or climb excessively, have difficulty playing or working quietly, talk excessively, blurt out answers, have difficulty waiting for their turn, and interrupt or intrude on others. Students who are Hyperactive-Impulsive do not qualify for special education services if there is no impairment in the learning process. Students may also be identified as ADHD, Combined Type, when they exhibit the characteristics of both the Inattentive and Hyperactive/Impulsive types.

The federal government has defined emotionally disturbed (ED) as a condition in which an individual exhibits one or more of the following characteristics over a long period of time and to a marked extent, and which adversely affects educational performance:

(1) an inability to learn that cannot be explained by intellectual, sensory, or health factors
(2) an inability to build or maintain satisfactory relationships with peers and teachers
(3) inappropriate types of behaviors or feelings under normal circumstances
(4) a general pervasive mood of unhappiness or depression
(5) a tendency to develop physical symptoms or fears associated with personal or school problems

In the federal definition, the child who is schizophrenic is included; children who are socially maladjusted are excluded unless they fit the other criteria above.

Fewer children are identified as ED than are identified as learning disabled or mentally retarded; however, black children are at a higher risk of being identified as ED (around 1.5 percent) than any other racial or ethnic group in the United States.

The other disability categories include speech and language impairments, hearing impairment, visual impairment, orthopedic impairment, other health impairments, deaf-blindness, autism, traumatic brain injury, and developmental delay (not all states use this category of disability). All of these categories have very low incidences with the exception of speech and language impairments. Annual reports of the numbers of students served under the federal law called the Individuals with Disabilities Act (IDEA) can be found at www.ideapractices.org on the Internet.

SERVING STUDENTS THROUGH SPECIAL EDUCATION PROGRAMS AND SERVICES

Through the 1970s teachers designated as special education teachers served most exceptional children in special, segregated, and self-contained classrooms. Public Law 94–142 was passed in 1977 and included provisions that individual learning needs should be specifically identified by careful and thorough assessment, that individual educational plans (IEPs) should be developed to guide the instruction and services provided to these students and that these students should receive instruction in the least restrictive environment. This led to the development of a variety of administrative plans for the education of exceptional learners ranging from a few special provisions made by the student's regular classroom teacher to full-time residential care in a special facility. Hallahan and Kauffman (2003) have identified levels of intervention from the most integrated to the most segregated. The most integrated is the regular classroom with instruction provided by the regular classroom teacher. At the next level, the regular classroom teacher may work with a special educator or other professional (e.g., school counselor) who consults with and/or provides the teacher with appropriate resources and demonstrates or gives guidance in the use of alternative instructional strategies, materials, or equipment. If further services are needed, students may receive direct services from the special educators who visit several schools and classrooms within those schools to instruct individuals or small groups within the classroom setting and continues to provide additional resources for the time when they cannot be there. At the next level, a resource teacher works with individuals or small groups in a special classroom for some designated part of the school day, but still serves as a consultant to the regular classroom teacher on resources and materials to use. More severely impaired students may require hospital or homebound instruction. This is most often required by students with severe physical disabilities or emotional or behavioral disorders, is usually for a short period of time, and regular contact continues between the regular classroom and the special educator to ensure smoother transitions back to the classroom. At the next levels of service, exceptional students are not served in the regular classroom. These arrangements include special self-contained classrooms where a child spends all day or nearly all day with other exceptional students, special day schools that are distinguished by special facilities, and residential schools. The range of arrangements is called a continuum of alternative placements. The concept of least restrictive environment is used to guide the decision as to which placement is most appropriate. Least restrictive environment implies that the student should be integrated with the nondisabled in the classroom, home, family, and community as much as is feasible; that the student's life should be as normal as possible, and the intervention should provide for meeting the student's educational needs with minimum interference with individual freedom.

A central feature of PL 94–142 and the Individuals with Disabilities Act (the replacement for PL 94–142 passed in 1990 and amended in 1997) was the requirement that every exceptional student in need of special education must have an individualized educational plan (IEP). This written plan must be approved by the student's parent or guardian and must include: (1) a description of the student's current level of functioning, (2) statements of annual goals, (3) short-term instructional objectives and benchmarks that indicate progress toward achieving those goals, (4) descriptions of the special services to be provided and indications of the degree to which a student will be part of the regular education program, (5) a clear statement of the plan for starting services and the duration of the services, and (6) a plan to evaluate the effectiveness of intervention. For older students, the IEP must include a description of how the student will make the transition from school to work or higher education.

In addition, the federal legislation regarding provision of services requires that all children with disabilities will in all cases be provided with a free, appropriate public education (FAPE) without cost to parents and at a level appropriate for the particular student. This requirement has had significant impact in not allowing schools to exclude or deny educational options to students with disabilities on the grounds that the school did not have services available.

The Individuals with Disabilities Act (IDEA) also states that students with disabilities should be removed from the general education classroom "only when the nature and severity of the disability is such that education in regular classes with the use of supplemental aids and services cannot be achieved satisfactorily." Passage of these acts led to great controversy surrounding the use of the special self-contained classroom and to widespread implementation of the practice of mainstreaming for those students with moderate or mild disabilities or handicapping conditions and led to the inclusion movement in special education.

GIFTED EDUCATION

Gifted was defined by Lewis Terman (1926) in the early studies of giftedness as those individuals with IQs greater than 135. Some authors further discriminated between moderately gifted students (IQs between 130 and 150) and profoundly gifted students (IQs greater than 150). While IQ scores and general intellectual ability continue to dominate definitions and assessment of giftedness in practice, the definitions of gifted in the literature have been expanded and modified in response to criticisms that traditional IQ tests fail to assess a broad array of human abilities or to predict exceptional performance in many of the areas valued by society, including creative performance. Many definitions of giftedness have reflected changes in conceptions of intelligence and the recognition of the limitations of a narrow conception of giftedness.

For example, the first federal definition of gifted (Marland 1972) included general intellectual ability as one area of giftedness, but expanded the definition to include specific academic aptitude, creative or productive thinking, leadership ability, visual and performing arts abilities, and psychomotor ability. Most states have adopted this definition or the later revisions. The most current definition of gifted and talented students reads: "The term 'gifted and talented students' means children and youth who give evidence of high performance capability in areas such as intellectual, creative, artistic, or leadership capacity, or in specific academic fields, and who require services not ordinarily provided by the school in order to fully develop such capabilities " (U.S. Department of Education 1993). The major difference between the earlier federal definitions and the current definition is the elimination of the category of psychomotor ability. Because of the evolution of the definition of giftedness from the IQ tests based on a normal distribution of scores, the incidence of giftedness is generally stated as between 3 and 5 percent of the population. Reliance on standardized assessments in the identification of gifted students has resulted in underrepresentation of minorities and children from lower socioeconomic groups in gifted programs. Accordingly, much attention has been directed recently at efforts to encourage talent development in the primary grades and the development and use of nontraditional assessments.

Joseph Renzulli (1978) criticized the federal definition for its artificial categories (asking how one can be creative outside of specific fields) and its failure to include all of the traits necessary to describe gifted behavior. Based on his analysis of the characteristics of creatively productive adults he offered a "three-ring definition" of giftedness. In his definition gifted and talented children possess above average ability, high levels of task commitment (bringing to bear a passion for productivity in a particular area), and high levels of creativity. When the individual has these three clusters interacting in the same performance domain, gifted behavior occurs. However, Renzulli recommends identifying students with above average ability and creativity in many general and specific areas and then providing learning activities in the areas of high interest for the child to bring out and nurture the task commitment as well as further the development of the abilities and creativity.

Renzulli (1977, Renzulli and Reis 1985) is also recognized for making one of the major contributions to curricular and programming recommendations for the gifted. Based on his model of giftedness, he developed a model that provided Type I activities as high-interest enrichment for students to use to explore areas of study outside the traditional curriculum and to invite those with task commitment to further study in that area, Type II activities which were oriented toward helping students develop the processing skills necessary to be creatively productive, and Type III activities in which students worked on real life problems to produce solutions that have real life audiences. The goal was to guide high-ability students to be producers of knowledge rather than consumers of knowledge. Identification in this model became known as a Revolving Door Model in which a fairly large "talent pool" (up to 20 percent) of high-ability students would participate in Type I and Type II activities and then "revolve" into the most intensive services when they are able to identify and commit to the completion of a Type III project. This model evolved into the Schoolwide Enrichment Model in which Type I and Type II activities are offered in every class in a school as a means to develop potential abilities and interests.

Renzulli (Renzulli and Smith 1978) was also noted for incorporating the instructional strategy of compacting into his model. Compacting is a process in which teachers pre-test high-achieving students prior to beginning a unit of instruction to determine which objectives the students have already mastered or identify areas in which quick mastery of new ideas is likely. The already mastered learning is eliminated from the instruction for these students and other objectives are addressed through accelerated instruction. The process of compacting "buys time" for student to engage in the enrichment activities offered. Research suggests that this process can be used to eliminate 40–50 percent of the content for high-achieving students with no loss in achievement gains (and some greater achievement in science) compared to a control group.

The issues of providing curriculum for gifted students have ranged from debate of the relative merits of acceleration or enrichment of curriculum to the appropriate emphasis on process dimensions versus product dimensions of curriculum. The acceleration of gifted students has taken on many forms. Students may be admitted to kindergarten early, may skip grades, may go to more advanced classes for instruction in a particular discipline (e.g., going from a first grade classroom to a third grade classroom for mathematics instruction, and/or entering college early). The arguments against acceleration have focused on the fears of social or emotional difficulties that may result from being removed from same-age peers. The research suggests that when acceleration is implemented with students whose needs clearly suggest that this modification in their school program is warranted, when careful monitoring and support are available, and when the practice is flexible, the students have been successful with no indication that social or emotional problems are an expected outcome.

Common administrative grouping arrangements for gifted students include self-contained classrooms (either within a school or as part of a special school), special instruction in resource rooms for some period of time each day or each week, and curriculum differentiation within the regular classroom setting. There are many arguments presented for and against each of these models. The arguments for self-contained classrooms include the importance of providing instruction at an appropriate level of challenge all day, the benefits for gifted students of being able to interact with intellectual peers, the need for specially trained teachers, and the need for specialized resources. At the high school level, the argument for specialized resources is particularly relevant in the creation of special schools of science, mathematics, and technology. Arguments against self-contained classrooms include the problems of elitism that may evolve among the students. The pull-out program advocates note that this arrangement allows for the gifted student to be both in the regular classroom with same-age peers and in the gifted resource room with specially trained teachers and intellectual peers with opportunities to engage in activities that the regular classroom teacher has neither the time nor the resources to create. The nonintegrated nature of the curriculum that has traditionally been offered, the disruption of classrooms, and the argument that gifted students need a challenging curriculum more than a few hours per week are offered as reasons that this alternative is not satisfactory. Differentiation in the regular classroom has become an increasingly popular model because of the opportunity for differentiated curriculum throughout the school day.

The lack of skill and will to differentiate curriculum for the gifted, combined with the many pressures of high-stakes testing and the inclusion of other children with exceptional needs in the general classroom, make implementation of this model difficult.

The curriculum to be offered to gifted students, regardless of setting, must be created by the teacher of the gifted student based on the beliefs of the school about the important goals for gifted programming. Many models of curriculum have been offered. Early models tended to emphasize the process-oriented curriculum that emerged from the study of creativity and intelligence by J. P. Guilford (1967) and the Taxonomy of Behavior Objectives developed by Benjamin Bloom and his colleagues (1956). For example, Mary Meeker (Meeker 1970; Meeker and Meeker 1985) developed instructional activities to match the dimensions of the Structure of Intellect Models with particular emphasis on the development of divergent thinking skills (generating many solutions to a given problem) with the goal of developing creativity. The Enrichment Triad Model and Schoolwide Enrichment Model offered by Renzulli (1977, 1985) moved the emphasis to more product-oriented curriculum with greater emphasis on the disciplines and productivity that emulated that of adult gifted productivity. More recently, the differentiated instruction model offered by Carol Tomlinson and the Parallel Curriculum Model developed by Tomlinson, Kaplan, Renzulli, Purcell, Lappien, and Burns (2002) both reflect a strong emphasis on curriculum designed to address high content and discipline standards and create challenges for gifted students by building on and extending the core curriculum. Learning activities and instructional units are developed by extending the intensity of challenge along a continuum leading toward expertise in learning and the disciplines.

Carolyn Callahan

INCLUSION

Few educational topics have generated the heated discussion that has surrounded the movement to include students with disabilities in general education classrooms. This movement originated in response to frustration over the ways in which educational services were being provided to special education students. The first attempts to serve students who were identified as needing special education services were largely structured to separate these students from the general population. Special education students were served in self-contained classrooms, often in separate buildings or sections of buildings. The alternate programming arrangement used to serve them was the resource room. Students would be assigned to a regular heterogeneous classroom and then leave the room for a designated part of the school day to meet with a specialist. The special education teacher would address the student's deficiencies in achievement through direct curricular modifications or would provide instruction in coping strategies that would assist in the learning process.

Both the special education self-contained and resource rooms were severely criticized educational options during the 1980s. They were criticized for the stigmatization that accompanied the assignment to the special class or the departure to attend a special class that was obviously for remediation. Advocates for these children also noted that instruction in special education segregated classes never afforded students the opportunity to interact with and learn the social skills of interacting with students without disabilities. The departure from the regular classroom also reduced the opportunity for the child with a disability to participate in the same learning opportunities available to other children. Most importantly, from the perspective of advocates of inclusion, special classes often failed to meet the high standards mandated by P.L. 94–142. The curriculum in the special classes and resource rooms was characterized as a set of disjointed activities that failed to coordinate with regular classroom goals or result in a cohesive curriculum. Advocates of inclusion also argued that the curriculum was mired in basic literacy and numeracy skills, lacked the richness of the general education curriculum, and failed to introduce or help students develop higher-level cognitive skills. A further contributing factor to negative perceptions of these administrative options was the fact that disproportionate numbers of students who were from racial/language minority groups or were from low-income families were identified for special education services, thus creating segregated instructional groupings. Hence, advocates called for greater integration of the special education student into the general education program.

Two parallel reform movements have been associated with the inclusion movement. First is the Regular Education Initiative which largely addressed the needs of students with mild disabilities such as learning disabilities and called for a merger of general education and special education to address the needs of these children and other children who were deemed at risk within the regular classroom with little or no segregation. However, there was a second movement aimed at changing the pattern of segregation and isolation of students with more severe disabilities. Advocates of these children focused on inclusion as the goal of special education and the full realization of the least restrictive environment mandate of PL 94-142. Inclusion refers to educating students with disabilities—regardless of severity—in general education classrooms for most or all of the school day. It is based on the tenet that students with disabilities have a right to participate fully in the general education classroom with peers of the same age. Advocates of these children were successful in incorporating language in the federal law which provides funding for special education students that called for these children to be provided educational interventions in "the least restrictive environment." From this provision stemmed the impetus to bring special services and the support for all special need children into the regular classroom.

Critics of the inclusive school movements acknowledge the criticisms offered of past special education practice, but they also claim that there are limits on how resourceful and responsive the general education teacher and classroom can be. They maintain that the full continuum of services model is better suited to meet the diverse needs of exceptional students. The debate has not been resolved despite studies of such variables as teacher attitudes and achievement outcomes. The only consistent finding of the research is the conclusion that students without disabilities seem to benefit academically from being in inclusive classrooms.

The debate around inclusion has also affected the services provided to gifted students. In early programming efforts, gifted students were often grouped in homogeneous classes or they were served through resource-room arrangements where they might be pulled together for some period of time each week (normally a very limited one to two hours per week). The gifted self-contained classrooms and resource rooms were criticized on other grounds. The self-contained classrooms were viewed as elitist and those opposing this grouping arrangement cited the literature that claimed that grouping resulted in detrimental achievement effects for low and middle groups. The resource room was criticized for offering enrichment options that were not rigorous and challenging and not a true extension in depth and complexity of the required curriculum. Second, many questioned the impact of the very limited time period. The result was a call from some educators to integrate the gifted into heterogeneous classrooms and to eliminate the enrichment class options. The advocates of these positions claimed that integration of the gifted into the heterogeneous classroom with differentiated services within that setting would provide for a more equitable class arrangement and, further, that gifted students could then benefit from provision of an appropriately differentiated curriculum for the majority of their school day rather than just several hours per day. The contrary argument is made that the regular classroom teacher has neither the skill and training nor the time to develop the curriculum appropriate for these high-end learners. These opponents to full inclusion of gifted students claim that the interpretation of least restrictive environment for gifted children should not parallel that used for children with disabilities. No research has demonstrated the advantage of inclusion over separate classes or resource rooms for gifted students or their classmates.

Carolyn Callahan

REFERENCES

Aiken, L.R. (1999) *Human Differences*. Mahwah, NJ: Erlbaum.

AAMR Ad Hoc Committee on Terminology and Classification. (1992) *Mental Retardation: Definition, Classification, and Systems of Support*. 9th ed. Washington, DC: American Association on Mental Retardation.

Anastasi, A. (1988) *Psychological Testing*. 6th ed. New York: Macmillan.

Binet, A., and V. Henri. (1896) La psycholgie individuelle [Individual psychology]. *L'Annee Psychologique* 2: 411–65.

Bloom, B.S. (1956) *Taxonomy of Educational Objectives, Handbook I: Cognitive Domain*. New York: McKay.

Callahan, C.M., S.L. Hunsaker, C.M. Adams, S.D. Moore, and L.C. Bland. (1995) Instruments used in the identification of gifted and talented students. Research monograph no. 95130. Storrs, CT: University of Connecticut, National Research Center on the Gifted and Talented.

Dunn, R., and K. Dunn. (1978) *Teaching Students through Their Individual Learning Styles*. Reston, VA: Reston Publishing.

Galton, F. (1962) *Hereditary Genius: An Inquiry into Its Laws and Consequences*. London: Collins. (Original work published 1869).

Gardner, H. (1983) *Frames of Mind: The Theory of Multiple Intelligences*. New York: Basic Books.

———. (1999) *The Disciplined Mind: What All Students Should Know and Understand*. New York: Simon & Schuster.

Guilford, J.P. (1967) *The Nature of Human Intelligence*. New York: McGraw-Hill.

Hallahan, D.P., and J. Kauffman. (2003) *Exceptional Learners: Introduction to Special Education*. 9th ed. Boston: Allyn and Bacon.

Keogh, B.K. (2003) *Temperament in the Classroom: Understanding Individual Differences*. Baltimore: Brookes.

Kirk, S. (1962) *Educating Exceptional Children*. Boston: Houghton Mifflin.

Kulik, J.A. (1992) *An Analysis of the Research on Ability Grouping: Historical and Contemporary Perspectives*. Storrs, CT: National Research Center on the Gifted and Talented, University of Connecticut.

Kulik, J.A., and C.C. Kulik. (1997) "Ability Grouping." In *Handbook of Gifted Education*, ed. N. Colangelo and G.A. Davis, 230–42. Needham Heights, MA: Allyn & Bacon.

Marland, S.P., Jr. (1972) *Education of the Gifted and Talented, Volume I. Report to the Congress of the United States by the Commissioner of Education*. Washington, DC: Government Printing Office.

Meeker, M. (1970) *Divergent Instruction: A Structure of Intellect Abilities Handbook*

Meeker, M., and R. Meeker. (1985) "The SOI System for Gifted Education." In *Systems and Models for Developing Programs for the Gifted and Talented*, ed. J.S. Renzulli, 194–215. Mansfield Center, CT: Creative Learning Press.

Messick, S. (1993) *The Matter of Style: Manifestations of Personality in Cognition, Learning, and Teaching*. Princeton: NJ: Educational Testing Service.

National Research Council. Committee on Minority Representation in Special Education. (2002) *Minority Students in Special and Gifted Education*. ed. M.S. Donovan and C. Cross, Division of Behavioral Social Sciences and Education. Washington, DC: National Academy Press.

Renzulli, J.S. (1977) *The Enrichment Triad Model: A Guide for Developing Defensible Programs for the Gifted and Talented*. Mansfield Center, CT: Creative Learning Press.

———. (1978) What makes giftedness? Reexamining a definition. *Phi Delta Kappan* 60: 180–84, 261.

Renzulli, J.S., and S.M. Reis. (1985) *The Schoolwide Enrichment Model: A Comprehensive Plan for Educational Excellence*. Mansfield Center, CT: Creative Learning Press.

Renzulli, J.S., and L.H. Smith. (1978) *The Compactor*. Mansfield Center, CT: Creative Learning Press.

Sternberg, R.J. (1985) *Beyond IQ: A Triarchic Theory of Human Intelligence*. New York: Cambridge University Press.

———. (1986) *Intelligence Applied: Understanding and Increasing Your Intellectual Skills*. San Diego: Harcourt Brace.

Terman, L.M. (1916) *The Measurement of Intelligence*. Boston: Houghton Mifflin.

———. (1926) *Genetic Studies of Genius*. Vol. I, *Mental and Physical Traits of a Thousand Gifted Children*. Stanford, CA: Stanford University Press.

Tomlinson, C.A. (2001) *How to Differentiate Instruction in Mixed-Ability Classrooms*. Alexandria, VA: Association for Supervision and Curriculum Development.

Tomlinson, C.A., S.N. Kaplan, J.S. Renzulli, J. Purcell, J. Leppien, and D. Burns. (2002) *The Parallel Curriculum: A Design to Develop High Potential and Challenge in High Ability Learners*. Thousand Oaks, CA: Corwin Press.

U.S. Department of Education. (1993) *National Excellence: A Case for Developing America's Talent*. Washington, DC: U.S. Government Printing Office.

Winner, E. (1997) Exceptionally high intelligence and schooling. *American Psychologist* 52: 1070–81.

Witkin, H. (1977) Role of the field-dependent and field-independent cognitive styles in academic evolution: A longitudinal study. *Journal of Educational Psychology* 69: 197–211.

27

Inclusion of Children and Youth with Severe Disabilities in School and Society

Persons with severe disabilities are those who need the most extensive instruction, adaptation, and assistance in order to perform and/or participate meaningfully and productively in everyday life activities of the home, community, and workplace. These individuals may experience one or more significant intellectual, physical, sensory or emotional disabilities. Under traditional classification systems severe disabilities usually refers to the presence of mental retardation, developmental disabilities, autism, pervasive developmental disorders, multiple disabilities, traumatic brain injury, or deaf-blindness. It is important to note that a diagnosis of any of the above does not necessarily mean that a person will be severely handicapped. Rather, individuals with severe disabilities constitute a subset of those diagnosed (the vast majority of individuals with mental retardation experience the need for only limited supports and are generally able to function independently in society's mainstream). It is estimated that persons with severe disabilities constitute approximately 1 percent of the general population.

The group of individuals generally regarded as having severe disabilities is very heterogeneous with a wide range of physical, behavioral, and learning characteristics. The concept of "severe disabilities" grew from the primary advocacy, professional, and research organization The Association for Persons with Severe Disabilities (TASH) during the mid-1970s. TASH developed in response to litigation and legislation establishing legal rights to education and other services for individuals with severe disabilities who traditionally had been excluded, segregated, and otherwise denied the right to access

education and to participate in mainstream American society.

During the Kennedy administration in the 1960s public awareness of individuals with mental retardation and other severe disabilities was heightened by the formation of the President's Committee on Mental Retardation, which provided an impetus for research, development, and training. At that time most families either had institutionalized their child with severe disabilities or kept the child at home because there were no educational or rehabilitation services available. As a result of the Kennedy administration and the growing national advocacy of organizations such as The Association for Retarded Citizens and United Cerebral Palsy, Congress began to authorize funds to support education and treatment programs.

Also at this time, a number of exposés in the national media cast light on the horrible conditions in large residential institutions where many children, youth, and adults lived. Burton Blatt and Fred Kaplan (1974) published "Christmas in Purgatory," a photographic documentary of life in institutions, and Geraldo Rivera captured the deplorable conditions at Willowbrook, a large institution in New York, on video tape and it was seen on national television. These exposés and others shocked the nation and rallied parents and advocates into political action.

During the same period, Wolf Wolfensberger (1972) and other writers from Scandinavia (which was far advanced in the humanistic treatment of persons with disabilities at that time) began to articulate the principle of "normalization" which affirmed the right of all persons to a dignified life. The normalization movement began as a foundation for attempts to improve the living conditions and quality of life in institutions and eventually evolved into the deinstitutionalization movement which saw thousands of persons with severe disabilities exit institutions to live in mostly smaller, more normal, familylike community residences. As the depopulation of institutions continued there was increased pressure on government to fully enfranchise these new community members who still were unable to access public education and had only meager "church-basement programs" sponsored by parents and advocacy organizations.

Everything changed in 1971 with the issuance of Judge Becker's ruling in the class-action case *The Pennsylvania Association for Retarded Children, PARC* vs. *Pennsylvania*, heard in federal court in Philadelphia. An excerpt of Judge Becker's decision is as follows:

It is the Commonwealth's obligation to place each mentally retarded child in a free, public program of education and training appropriate to the child's capacity, within the context of the general educational policy that, among the alternative programs of education and training required by statute to be available, placement in a regular public school is preferable to placement in a special public school class and placement in a public school class is preferable to placement in any other type of program of education and training.

Becker ruled in favor of the plaintiffs, who were parents of a class of children with mental retardation. Based upon the *Brown v. Board of Education* Topeka Kansas case in 1954, the PARC plaintiffs argued and won the right to education for their children. Known as "The Right to Education Case" PARC opened the door to a flood of litigations, state laws, and funding for programs for children and youth with mental retardation and other disabilities.

The next important chapter in the history of treatment and services for persons with severe disabilities was written by many of the same parent advocates from the PARC case. Together with politicians and educators, they took their case to the United States Congress where in 1977, after years of lobbying, the *Education for All Handicapped Children Act* (PL 94–142) was signed into law by President Nixon. Though

not a civil rights act, PL 94–142 made federal funding for special education contingent upon states' compliance with regulations set forth in the law. The law required: (1) a free appropriate public education, (2) an education provided in "the least restrictive environment," (3) an individualized education developed in an individualized education plan (IEP), (4) nondiscriminatory evaluation, (5) due process procedures to settle disputes between parents and the schools, and, importantly for children with severe disabilities, (6) a policy of zero rejection. The intent of the law was clear:

To the maximum extent appropriate, handicapped children, including children in public and private institutions or other care facilities, are educated with children who are not handicapped, and that special classes, separate schooling, or other removal of handicapped children from the regular educational environment occurs only when the nature or severity of the handicap is such that education in regular classes with the use of supplementary aids and services cannot be achieved satisfactorily.

During the ensuing decade, special education and rehabilitation programs flourished and proliferated across the nation, including public school and community services for children, youth, and adults with severe disabilities. However, even though the PARC case ruling and PL 94–142 provided mandates for the inclusion of children with severe disabilities, most were educated in separate schools or in separate classes in regular schools.

Another important law, passed in 1990, was the *Americans with Disabilities Act* (ADA), a civil rights law that prohibited discrimination against persons with disabilities in employment, public services, transportation, and telecommunications. This law affirmed the right of all Americans to access to many of the same aspects of life as those without disabilities. Perhaps the most important impact of the law was in employment, where hiring practices were required to provide opportunities to persons with disabilities who were otherwise qualified.

In 1997 the movement toward inclusion of children and youth with severe disabilities was given new life with the reauthorization of PL 94–142 into the *Individuals with Disabilities Education Act* (IDEA). IDEA contained new provisions requiring schools to address transition from school for adolescents and much stronger requirements for inclusion. The law also now required that students with disabilities have access to the general education curriculum and participate in district and statewide assessments. These provisions ensure new levels of accountability for a quality education for all students and strengthen the imperative to include students within general education classrooms and schools. Relatedly, the new "no child left behind" regulations require that school districts report levels of participation of students with disabilities in district and local assessments. Additionally, all students' scores are to be included in aggregate district and state assessment results. These provisions include assessment data from students with severe disabilities, many of who take an alternate form of the assessments. The importance of these provisions lies in the fact that the achievement of students with even the most severe disabilities is now part of the overall performance and accountability of a school and a school district, whereas in the past this has not been the case. As a result, schools and districts will need to be concerned about high expectations for achievement even for these students.

Over the past thirty years programs and services for children and youth with severe disabilities have changed dramatically. The field has gone from no services to segregated, limited services; to community-based services in separate schools and classes; to the present situation in which sweeping federal mandates not only provide strong support for access to and participation in general education classes and curricula, but also for access to most aspects of community life. These changes have been accomplished through many years of advocacy, litigation, and legislation and through various school-reform movements.

U.S. Department of Education statistics show that children and youth with severe disabilities increasingly are educated in regular schools and spend greater amounts of time in regular education classes being taught by general education teachers. All across the nation more and more students with severe disabilities are attending regular schools and classes where general education teachers are now required to participate in IEP meetings, adapt their curriculum and instruction, and manage a complex array of behavioral, medical, and other support needs of students with severe disabilities.

This chapter provides an overview of some of the most important areas relevant to the education of children and youth with severe disabilities. Ten areas of current best practices are discussed, each with an orientation toward providing a high-quality education utilizing inclusive practices. The first entry discusses the importance of parent and family involvement in the child's education. Parent involvement for these children is especially important given the impact of the child's disability on the family and the need to coordinate care and support practices between the home and school. Peer involvement and support is the subject of entry two, which provides a review of various approaches for organizing and supporting peers to participate and interact with children with severe disabilities. Research has shown that simply placing students with severe disabilities in physical proximity to nonhandicapped peers does not guarantee that interaction will occur. Communication and social interaction skills are also necessary for interaction to be fruitful for both students with severe disabilities and their nonhandicapped peers. Because students with severe disabilities usually do not acquire language in a typical fashion, alternative approaches known as augmented communication are necessary. Entry three addresses these issues. Entry four provides a description of methods and approaches for developing alternative ways these children can learn to communicate and interact with their peers.

Many times these students will exhibit social skills and behaviors that interfere with their learning and that of their peers. These challenging behaviors can be responded to through a process of positive behavioral support (PBS), which is delineated in entry five of this chapter. An alternative to more traditional behavior modification, PBS is used to develop a clearer understanding of the child's interaction with their environment, the reasons why the child engages in the behavior, and possible interventions and supports which will be used to alleviate the child's difficulties.

Entry six outlines the development and progression of approaches to assessment and curricula for students with severe disabilities and differences in content between the elementary and the secondary level. This entry also outlines how the *Individuals with Disabilities Education Act* and the *No Child Left*

Behind Act has affected assessment and curriculum development practices for teachers of students with severe disabilities.

For students with severe disabilities to receive a quality education using inclusive education it is also necessary that school and districtwide policies and practices be implemented. Entry seven discusses leadership, the development of a vision of inclusion, teamwork and collaboration, and district and school practices needed in order for inclusion to be effectively implemented.

The final three entries of the chapter deal with issues that confront these children and their families as they approach adulthood: developing choice and self-determination, the transition from school, and the adjustment to adult life in the community.

Steven R. Lyon, Becky A. Knickelbein,
and Paula J. Wolf

FAMILY INVOLVEMENT
AND SUPPORT

Parent and family involvement is critical to successful inclusion of children with severe disabilities. Families have much that is unique to contribute to the educational planning process. Parents know their child better than anyone and, therefore, are a valuable resource for helping others to learn about the child and his or her positive attributes, strengths, preferences, and needs. Parents and family members can provide a firsthand account of the child's developmental, communication, educational, behavioral, and medical treatment histories to help others to better know and understand the child's history and life experiences within the family, school, and community. Parents possess a wealth of information regarding what has and has not worked for their child and ways to successfully accommodate their child's learning and support needs. Only through input from and interaction with family members can educational personnel assure that instructional goals and methods are relevant for both child and family. It is parents and family members who can articulate a dream or vision of hope for their child that should guide the development of educational programs aimed at achieving those desired outcomes.

Often, it is the dreams and hopes that parents have for their child that influence their decisions to consider or seek inclusive educational opportunities. Many parents want their child to develop and maintain friendships and they believe that friendships are more likely to blossom in inclusive settings. Many parents express a desire for their child to be like other children, and they believe that specialized, self-contained settings emphasize their child's differences. Other parents want their child to develop to fullest potential. They believe that inclusive settings provide positive language and behavioral models as well as more frequent opportunities to practice and apply new skills. Parent (and family) involvement is a crucial component in the educational process, regardless of the preference for inclusive or other types of educational experiences for their child.

PARENTAL RIGHTS AND INVOLVEMENT

Parent involvement is one of the major provisions of Public Law 94–142. Subsequent amendments to the law extended services to infants, toddlers, and preschool children, and expanded and strengthened parents' roles in the educational planning process. The 1997 Amendments to IDEA provide for parent involvement via a number of protections and provisions. These include parental consent and due process. Schools are required to obtain parental consent before evaluating or reevaluating a child. Due process provides recourse for parents if they disagree with a school district about their child's eligibility, placement, program needs, or related services. The team process required by IDEA provides a mechanism for parental participation in eligibility determination, the development of the individualized education program (IEP), and transition planning. Additionally, IDEA requires that schools provide parents with regular reports of the child's progress in terms of performance on individual goals.

Under the current IDEA, parents of children of ages three to twenty-one are members of their child's school evaluation and planning teams. This means that parents take an active role as equal partners in the decisionmaking and IEP planning process. Rather than passively participating by providing consent to programs developed by professionals, or partially participating by providing information that professionals consider in the development of educational programs, parental involvement means that parents actively contribute to the planning process by collaborating with the other members of the team.

IDEA also provides for early intervention services for infants and toddlers from birth to three years and offers supports and services for their families as well. Unique to early intervention is the Individual Family Service Plan (IFSP), which details the early intervention services that will be provided. Unlike the IEP, which focuses primarily on the educational and related service needs of the eligible student, the IFSP details supports and services provided to the child and family. The IFSP is framed by the family members' concerns and priorities for the child and their conceptualization of his or her strengths and needs. Family resources and strengths are considered as well, and the services to be provided are based on family-identified outcomes and needs. Early intervention services are intended to enhance the capacity of the family to meet the needs of the child. Like the individual education planning process for school-age students with severe disabilities, the development of the IFSP is conducted in a partnership between family members and professionals.

The family's involvement in early intervention services may influence their interest in inclusive educational settings once their child reaches school age. The law requires delivery of early intervention services in naturalistic settings or environments. These include settings in the home as well as community settings such as parks, playgrounds, day care, and so on, and activities in which the family and child regularly participate. By providing early intervention services in this manner, families are supported in learning and applying needed interventions in everyday routines and activities, where they will be regularly used. Segregated classrooms may not be as appealing to parents following their child's earlier educational experiences in typical settings in the community.

MODELS OF FAMILY SUPPORT

The individual family supports provided by early intervention services constitute a family-oriented or family-centered approach. In earlier or more traditional service delivery systems, professionals focused on the child with a disability. Even when programs examined family interactions or included families

in the planning process, the focus of intervention remained exclusively on the child. In family-centered approaches, the child is considered within the context of the family, which means assessment, planning, and intervention address needs and preferences of the family. Rather than intervene directly with the child, family-centered services focus on providing supports that will increase or enhance the capacity of the family to better meet the child's needs.

The family-centered approach is based in part on family systems theory. In family systems theory, the family is viewed as a sum of its parts; the family comprises a whole unit, which consists of individual parts, that is, individual family members. Family membership is an interdependent phenomenon. All family members are in some way affected by what occurs to each individual member. That which affects one part of the whole affects all. Therefore, when one of the members of a family is a child with a severe disability, supports and services must consider and respond to the effects on each family member and the family system as a whole.

There are a number of practices that characterize family-centered approaches. First and foremost, family-centered approaches provide support to the entire family. These supports are based on and are respectful of family choice and preference. Second, family-centered systems are flexible. Flexibility is necessary in order to remain responsive to the individual family, as well as to a broader constituency. Family needs change over time, as do the roles and responsibilities of its individual members. Families differ significantly from one another, and family-centered approaches respect these differences, responding to the individual family's unique needs and culture. Finally, family-centered systems encourage the use of generic resources, that is, those supports and services that are utilized by the general population and not limited to a group with particular characteristics, such as disability-only services.

Rarely are school-based services family centered. For this reason, school districts can experience difficulty conceptualizing and supporting inclusion for children with severe disabilities. Though IDEA addresses children's transition from early intervention to preschool and from preschool to elementary school, these transitions are not intended to influence change in district practices, but rather to help the child adjust, and to ensure the availability of needed services. Once in school, the child will still receive the same kind of service, but how that service is delivered may differ significantly from how it had been provided under the family-centered system. For example, in a family-based system, physical therapy will be provided, for the most part, in the home, while in the educational system, the therapy would likely be provided at school.

FAMILY SUPPORT

Parents of children with severe disabilities may be at risk for personal and family difficulties, and siblings may experience difficulties as well. These difficulties can be associated with a number of factors, such as the increased responsibilities involved in the child's care, constraints on time or opportunity to focus on other family functions, strain on financial resources, lack of support, and so on. Children with severe disabilities often require extensive parental support on a day-to-day basis in order to meet basic needs and participate in the everyday activities of daily living. In addition, parents and families must attend to the child's medical, educational, and therapy needs, as well as interface regularly with case management and school personnel. The increased responsibilities can be isolating or exhausting for families.

Families also need support and a wide variety of family support services can be made available to them. Family support services are those formal and informal services and supports utilized by the family while the child with the disability lives in the family home. Formal services include case management, in- and out-of-home respite, parent training (i.e., for specific healthcare routines), parent support and advocacy groups, family and individual counseling, structural modifications to the home (e.g., construction of a ramp), and a variety of other services as well. Some services are provided directly to the child with the intent of easing the burden of care and allowing families to continue to participate in family routines and activities (e.g., overnight nursing care is provided so parents can sleep through the night; therapeutic support services are provided after school so parents can prepare the evening meal or assist siblings with schoolwork). Funding for formal services

is generally provided by the public sector or private medical insurance.

Families also receive assistance from informal supports, that is, a social network of unpaid supports that can be provided by extended family members, friends, neighbors, and volunteers. Informal supports are just as important if not more important than formal services. Informal supports may more readily match existing family routines and ways of doing things, especially when they are provided by others who experience a close relationship with family members. The family may view informal supports as less intrusive or impersonal than formal services. Informal supports may be just as elaborate and time-intensive as formal services, but for some families they may be preferable to those provided by agencies and service personnel.

Informal supports can be used to effectively supplement formal services and help the family preserve its way and quality of life. It is important for educational personnel to understand the importance of informal supports and be willing to include them in the child's educational program if the family so desires. This also means that those who informally support the family may also participate as members of the child's educational team if the family requests this.

Family support needs change with the passage of time. A range of services is available to meet changing needs of children with disabilities and their parents and families. Younger parents or parents of young and school-age children may need to utilize babysitting services that are provided by highly trained caretakers. Parents of older children may require information as their son or daughter experiences puberty. As life expectancies of individuals with severe disabilities continue to increase, support services may be required to meet the unique needs of aging parent caregivers. Such support may be intermittent—for example, estate planning or consultation and training regarding competency and guardianship. Parents who have supports available to them will be better able to participate in their child's inclusion planning.

Other supports available include advocacy and networking groups. These provide parents with assistance from parents of children with similar concerns or issues. Members of parent network groups may provide information or assistance in dealing with service agencies, IEP development, or the development of supports needed for inclusion.

SUPPORTING PARENT INVOLVEMENT

Because of the many demands on their time and attention, the parents and families of students with severe disabilities will often need support in order to participate consistently and meaningfully as a member of their child's educational team. Educational personnel must understand how the many constraints experienced by parents can pose significant barriers to parental participation, and they must be willing to adopt practices that support active parental involvement.

One means of supporting parent involvement is to provide information to parents about the array of options available to them and to their child. In response to the recognition of the need to support parental involvement, the revised IDEA of 1997 has provided for the creation of Parent Training Information Centers (PTIs) in each state. PTIs are part of a resource network whose purpose is to disseminate information and provide training on the IDEA to parents of infants, toddlers, and school-age children with disabilities. PTIs provide training to parents and teachers in order to help parents more effectively participate in shared educational and service planning; resolve problems between families and schools or other agencies; and facilitate in connecting children with disabilities to community resources that address their needs.

School districts can also support parental involvement by providing timely and well-organized information to parents. For example, providing parents with a school-year schedule or timeline of events related to special education is helpful to them in long-range planning. Parents of children with severe disabilities may need extended time to prepare information for IEP planning meetings or arrange for time off from work. Additionally, school districts can prepare fact sheets informing parents of the supports available to them from the school, community, and formal support system. School districts should be willing to disseminate information from other organizations and agencies that might provide assistance to parents as well.

Parents' participation in educational planning may

be compromised by easily overcome issues—such as the time or place meetings are held. When schools are willing to schedule meetings to accommodate parents' schedules and routines, parents may be able to more readily participate. Provision of childcare for siblings may also facilitate parent involvement as will arranging for transportation for parents who need it. School districts that are committed to ensuring active parent involvement in educational planning and decisionmaking will develop creative and effective ways of doing so.

Another way to support parental involvement in their child's educational team is to include them in teacher training and support efforts. Opportunities for parents and teachers to learn together can strengthen relationships and improve communication between them. Again, it is important to not only extend the invitation but to also provide supports needed so parents can participate. Finally, parents often express their frustration when professionals use technical language and jargon. Many parents report that they feel excluded when such terminology is used. School personnel must strive to use everyday language and avoid the use of acronyms, abbreviations, and buzzwords.

COMMUNICATING WITH PARENTS

It is generally accepted that successful inclusion of students with severe disabilities requires not just collaboration, but regular conferencing between the special and general educators and other members of the child's team. As members of the child's educational teams, as well as because they are the parents, it is imperative that schools engage in regular and effective communication with parents. The communication between school and parents may be initiated or coordinated by different members of the educational team, depending on the need or circumstances. For formal planning and educational decisionmaking, parents are contacted by whoever has been identified as responsible for coordination of the IEP process. This can be an administrator, such as a special education supervisor or director, a school psychologist or guidance counselor, or, as often is the case, the child's special education teacher. Communication that is intended to share day-to-day and routine information is generally initiated by the special education teacher. This includes notices of school activities, permission slips, and weekly schedules. Communication concerning the child can be initiated by either the teacher or parent, but most often is built in as a part of the child's educational program. The most common form of regular communication between teachers and parents of children with a severe disability is a daily communication log. A daily log provides a means for the teacher to provide regular feedback to a parent regarding the child's performance or behavior each day, to report a problem that may carry over to the home, to ask questions or to express general concern, to send a reminder, or to share an anecdote or story about something that occurred during the day. Parents can use them for the same purposes, and often will use daily logs to provide alerts regarding the child's health, behavior, or affective state on that particular day. Daily communication logs are commonplace and can be an important source of information as well as a highly efficient and effective means for parents and teachers to regularly communicate. Such daily logs can impede communication between parents and teachers when they focus exclusively on negative student behaviors; are used primarily to report problems; are too brief; are too lengthy, or require either the teacher or parent to spend excessive amounts of time responding to questions and concerns.

Steven R. Lyon, Becky A. Knickelbein, and Paula J. Wolf

PEER INVOLVEMENT AND SUPPORT

Examination of the critical involvement of peers in the successful inclusion of students with severe disabilities, and the supports required for inclusive education, is best understood from an educational and developmental level perspective. As the educational experiences of all students within general education settings change (i.e., from elementary to middle to secondary school), the expectations for peer involvement and the necessary supports must undergo change as well. As a result this topic is organized by educational levels and concludes with a summary of current best practice.

EARLY INTERVENTION AND PRESCHOOL PROGRAMS

The inclusion of students with severe disabilities had its beginning at the preschool level, and the research regarding socially inclusive programs at this level is more abundant and longitudinal. Initially many relationships at this age appear to be primarily based upon proximity and valued objects, suggesting opportunities for interaction could be easily accommodated by adapting the environment in a physical manner. The nature of social interactions among preschoolers allows adults to utilize simple interventions to assure the inclusion of all students. As a result associations between children with disabilities and classmates may occur in inclusive settings without formal interventions. Additionally, at the preschool level more emphasis is placed on pre-academic and play activities rather than on academics. Social play activities are more easily adapted and require less sophisticated cognition in order for the children with severe disabilities to participate. This may explain why teachers of younger students tend to be more optimistic when surveyed regarding positive outlooks for friendship development among students with and without disabilities.

Early emphasis was placed on simply teaching nonhandicapped students to prompt and reinforce the pro-social behaviors of their peers with disabilities. This reinforcement, however, did not result in increased interactions across settings. The approach is noteworthy because previous approaches with older students focused primarily upon the instruction of remedial social skills to the students with disabilities, not recognizing the social reciprocity in the students' natural environment.

In order to increase peer interactions, sociometric ratings have been used to identify several target behaviors for future curriculum consideration. The highly rated students of preschool age demonstrated a willingness to share materials, assist others with tasks, display affection, and respond to social initiations by peers in a positive fashion. Students with disabilities who were given lower sociometric ratings displayed many more negative interactions than their peers. Simple peer-mediated intervention that involved teaching students to suggest various play activities, offer to share desirable objects, and to provide assistance during play increased the positive social interactions among students with and without disabilities.

In summary, recognition of the interactive nature of the goal of social inclusion suggests the provision of reciprocal instruction to assure that the social initiations of students with disabilities be noticed and responded to appropriately. Questioning whether or not preschool children are able to interact in this fashion independently resulted in the initial attention on preschool students without disabilities. Types of interventions utilized at this age have been categorized based upon the source of the reinforcement maintaining the target behaviors. Peer or student-mediated interventions involve the use of skills specifically taught to students to increase social interactions. Adult-mediated interventions refer to the provisions of reinforcement by the adult in the setting in order to increase the interactions among students with and without disabilities.

The young child's dependence upon observable, concrete information indicates the need for providing direct information regarding students with disabilities, in order to explain observed traits that could set them apart. Ignored differences have the potential to separate some children from their peers. An open discussion regarding every child's strengths and needs may help students to realize how much they have in common.

While very young children may not naturally consider the viewpoints of others, certain experiences may accelerate their ability to put themselves in a classmate's shoes. Role playing, which children this age typically enjoy, could provide meaningful insight for children and carry over to their interactions with other children. Awareness of an individual student's particular personality style and careful planning of interactive opportunities may also be indicated to assure greater success.

Inclusive preschool program teachers should also consider the age-appropriate gender preferences of their students. During the preschool years companionship is sought regardless of gender suggesting that included students should be given the opportunity to interact with all of the students in the setting, regardless of gender. This comprehensive approach also recognizes the limited social skill level of all children at this age; however, friendship remains a reciprocal endeavor throughout life.

ELEMENTARY LEVEL PEER INVOLVEMENT AND SUPPORT PROGRAMS

As the inclusive philosophy has gained acceptance, several means of facilitation involving peers have become prominent at the elementary school level. These facilitation programs are encompassed by two general approaches, which may be described as those created specifically to bring students together and those which attempt to encourage relationships in a more natural way. Special programs are summarized below.

Circle of Friends

The Circle of Friends approach is a formalized peer support technique that involves several peers, rather than focusing on dyads. This approach has been most often utilized with younger children, but need not be limited to elementary settings. Nondisabled peers are asked if they would be willing to join or create a "circle," which meets regularly under the tutelage of a facilitator. The members of the circle are committed to caring about, and becoming involved in, the lives of their classmates with disabilities.

The Circle of Friends can also bring together family members, family friends, general and special educators, the student, and the student's friends to plan for full inclusion. This group meets several times, answering questions regarding the needs to be addressed by the individual education plan and friendship facilitation. The concept behind the Circle of Friends strategy has also been broadened to prepare individuals for full community inclusion.

Cooperative Learning

Cooperative Learning first gained prominence in school curricula to promote interactive learning among regular education students of varying ability levels. This method provides for small groups working together to accomplish shared goals in a cooperative structure, rather than the traditional competitive structure.

Each group member is given a very specific role to play and is held accountable. Whether the physical proximity and interaction that group work affords results in an increase in acceptance, or an increase in rejection of students with severe disabilities by their peers without disabilities, depends largely on how these situations are structured. Teachers can design these cooperative situations in order to achieve positive goals of interdependence, versus the negative outcomes that may result from competition in the classroom. Because the groups are heterogeneous and small, opportunity to interact is greatly increased. Positive interpersonal skill development is also a goal of this approach. Some cooperative learning models are very structured, specifically defining members' roles, and subsequent reinforcement; however, minimal accommodations may be sufficient to allow for the inclusion of students with severe disabilities. Structuring such cooperative activities in the classroom may be the most naturalistic technique to promote friendship among students with and without disabilities in inclusive classrooms.

Peer Tutoring Programs

Peer tutoring programs were originally utilized in both elementary and secondary schools in an effort to lower the pupil-teacher ratio among the regular education population; however, more recently they are being advocated as a means to promote interaction between students with and without disabilities in the inclusive setting. The peer tutor receives training in the provision of instruction to the student with a disability. The resultant role of the tutor closely parallels that of a teacher.

While such programs have reported universal acceptance among educators as a natural pathway to social relationships among students, others have questioned the use of peer tutoring to facilitate friendships, a purpose for which the program was not designed. Peer tutoring has been criticized for being overly formalized and for imposing new hierarchical roles on the peers involved.

Peer Buddies

Programs that organize peers to assist students with severe disabilities with less academically focused tasks than tutoring are typically referred to as *peer buddy programs*. Peer buddies accompany students with severe disabilities during activities such as lunch, assemblies, extracurricular activities, and so forth. The hierarchical relationship is less evident than the teacher-student relationship characteristic of peer tutoring. Peer buddies may help students learn appropriate ways to interact socially, and to participate in extracurricular activities.

Encouraging Relationships Naturally

One of the concerns with artificially designed programs, using volunteers to befriend students, is the fear that the relationships that result are unlikely to endure. This concern has led to the examination of more natural ways of relationship development among children with and without disabilities. Principles and practices need to be applied which develop accommodations, adaptations, and social support of students with severe disabilities enabling them to be a friend, even though they may never display some expected social behaviors, or communicate in the same way as their nondisabled peers.

As elementary students grow older and social interactions become more complex, the use of intervention packages is recommended. Intervention packages are comprised of sets of strategies designed individually for each student with disabilities. Information should be presented to classmates about communication systems, adaptive equipment, and educational activities of the student with disabilities within naturally occurring interactions. Various methods should be identified that can serve as a basis for social exchange. Ongoing facilitation by the education staff of social exchanges between students with disabilities and others is also recommended in a multiple strategies plan.

Relationships may also be encouraged by utilizing specialized curriculum designed to build a classroom community conducive to friendship development. Specific lessons may address topics such as belonging, keeping friends, including everyone, cooperating, and others. Observational data regarding interactions of students with and without disabilities in the regular classroom setting are also helpful in examining natural methods of friendship facilitation. Consistent encouragement provided by the teacher, the classroom climate, and the instructional practices comprise the multiple strategies approach to facilitating social inclusion in a natural setting. The increased reciprocity of friendships suggests the need to both educate the general education students regarding their expectations of students with severe disabilities, and to design specific programs for students with severe disabilities addressing interactive skills and necessary adaptations.

SECONDARY LEVEL INCLUSION APPROACHES

The social inclusion of students with severe disabilities in the secondary school setting is generally considered to be a more difficult process than that experienced during the preschool and elementary school years. Increased focus upon academic achievement and the preparation for postsecondary education as well as the departmentalized organization of most middle/junior and senior high schools may seriously complicate efforts to include students with severe disabilities at this level.

Peer Tutoring and Peer Buddy Programs

The peer tutoring and buddy programs described earlier are common strategies at the secondary level as well. Peer tutors provide instructional support, needed assistance, additional direct instruction, and training in communication. At this level many peer tutor programs are offered as graded elective courses for credit, and many secondary students are very comfortable in this role. Once again these interventions invite the criticism that such a hierarchical system reinforces status differences among students, and is not naturally interactive.

Group Formation

Strategies that allow students to interact as peers, without one student adopting a superior or helper role, requires a systemic paradigm shift. Friendship development is thought to be influenced by images of similarity, the opportunity to interact, and the ability to initiate and maintain social interactions.

To promote the recognition of similarities, the formation of groups around specific characteristics and interests provides students purposeful access to one another. The group's purpose and activities should be determined solely by the members in order to allow natural interactions. Students may participate in the design and implementation of social skills interventions to promote greater social inclusion of their classmates. This method places the students themselves in the role of expert regarding the

development of their existing friendships, and attempts to make use of this unique expertise. Friendships can be developed while social competence is systematically increased in natural contexts.

FACILITATION APPROACHES FOR ALL SCHOOL-AGE INDIVIDUALS

A peer support network for all school-age students may take the form of a welcoming committee, group leisure time, or school-sponsored clubs involving students with and without disabilities. Parental involvement and provision of support by staff or personnel are important components of any group approach. Facilitation of friendship development needs to be part of a broader values-based, system-wide undertaking. Too much control often results in formalizing relationships that are naturally informal. Small settings are favored over larger settings because they increase the involvement of all students. Interventions should strive to purposefully tap into the social skills of the students involved in order to promote favorable and natural outcomes. A systemic, multifaceted approach at all grade levels is clearly the most comprehensive means of addressing peer involvement and support of social inclusion in the true sense.

Perspectives of Nondisabled Peers

The goal of natural interaction among students requires serious recognition of the needs of both the student with disabilities and those without disabilities within the design of a successful support system. The critical role of the students without disabilities can no longer continue to be overlooked if the ultimate indicator of success involves their motivation to forge new relationships and friendships. Open recognition of the differences among all students is required to achieve inclusion beyond sharing the same physical space. In other words, approaching inclusion in the same fashion as other diversity issues such as multiculturalism, alienation, and underachievement is proposed.

In preschool, interaction may be temporarily encouraged by providing a student with severe disabilities an attractive and desirable toy; however, as the students grow older, the social supports provided should be continually checked against the age-appropriate expectations of their peers. Likewise, general education students need to be exposed to activities that promote their social development, and are congruent with their current social-cognitive abilities. It is not enough to expect students to interact in a desirable fashion because it is the right thing to do, or conversely to sell short the students' capability to understand the position of others.

Studies have provided insight into many issues related to peer involvement and support in inclusive education. For example, both the gender of the students without disabilities and the level of contact with students with severe disabilities are significantly related to later attitudes towards people with disabilities. Students who experienced the most contact with the students with disabilities in the past were more accepting of individuals with disabilities when interviewed later. Females were found to be more accepting of individuals with disabilities than males regardless of the level of contact they had experienced. Many elementary school relationships are not maintained throughout secondary school due to systemic issues that separate students who once spent most of their school day together. If nondisabled students are active participants in the design and implementation of interventions for specific situations, such as transition between classes and lunchtime, their investment in the success of these strategies may be increased. The novelty of inclusion has been observed to wear off as the school year progresses and the students with disabilities are likely to be treated more and more naturally by the nondisabled peers.

Current Implementation of Best Practices

Examination of several specific strategies results in the following suggestions for planning programs intended to promote peer interaction. Repeatedly, ability awareness has been cited as an early requirement for program planning. The means of providing awareness information should follow age appropriate practice. For example, young children can be easily introduced to awareness issues through the use of literature. Such knowledge is empowering to students and should be accompanied by active facilitation of social interactions and consistent encouragement from adults in the setting.

Building a sense of community in the environment and modeling acceptance are ongoing requirements for success. If incorporated as a comprehensive meth-

odology, the program becomes an integral part of a broader values-based, systemwide undertaking that will consistently strive to provide the most natural foundation for relationships to develop. In the past, the social-developmental needs of the students without disabilities had not routinely been considered in planning inclusive experiences. Because their critical role in successful program development cannot be overlooked, the needs and goals that motivate nonlabeled students to become active participants in these practices must be addressed.

While the point has been made that teaching social skills to students with disabilities is an inadequate approach used alone, it remains a vital part of the combination of strategies required to increase likely success. Functionally, social goals may be facilitated by organizing small groups to discuss similarities and differences among students and allowing students to make suggestions that could help their classmates with disabilities feel more a part of the school. The active assistance from adult facilitators requires educational and leisure time together within and outside of school, where behaviors can be both modeled and reinforced. Parental involvement and the provision of support for staff and personnel are important components of a comprehensive approach as well.

NATURAL SUPPORTS BEYOND SCHOOL

In order to plan for continuation of natural supports for social interaction beyond the school environment, the normative processes in place must be observed and setting-specific problem solving incorporated. Use of creative planning, which begins with the individual's ultimate goals and works backward, is suggested. This results-oriented method aligns well with IEP planning by beginning with long-range future goals and identifying the steps necessary to attain those goals, which would most certainly include the development of meaningful social relationships and friendships.

Searching for simple strategies to address such a complex process is certain to be unsuccessful and detrimental to real progress toward the goal of social inclusion and friendship development. Such efforts, however well intentioned, are making a false promise of friendship that can never be guaranteed or predicted. Addressing the social-cognitive needs of the individuals with and without disabilities may hold one key to developing the optimum breeding ground for the growth of genuine and lasting inclusion. Both the gender of the students without disabilities and the level of contact experiences during the school years have been shown to be significantly related to later attitudes towards people with disabilities. In other words, students who experience more contact with students with disabilities are more accepting of individuals later in life. This finding alone should motivate educators to promote the development of comprehensive inclusive cultures within their schools in order to positively impact greater acceptance in the community setting and society at large.

Steven R. Lyon, Becky A. Knickelbein, and Paula J. Wolf

INTERACTIONS AND FRIENDSHIP DEVELOPMENT

Traditional friendships are defined by several components that typically include enjoying one another's company; being of use to one another; and sharing common interests. Such relationships cannot be forced but may require intentional facilitation in inclusive settings in order to allow students to reach beyond barriers that have resulted from the social distance at which students with disabilities had been kept for many years. Inclusive practices allow students with and without disabilities to interact with one another. Parents of students with severe disabilities frequently report their desire for these interactions to develop further into friendships. *Belonging* is a term often used to describe the true membership of all students in the school environment that many believe is the ultimate goal of inclusive programming and a prerequisite for interactions becoming friendships.

Teaching social skills to students with disabilities, as a means of promoting the development of social interactions with nondisabled peers, has been a widely accepted practice. Such instruction is only one step in improving the social status of students with disabilities, however. Instruction of the child's nondisabled peers is also indicated, as noted earlier when discussing peer involvement and support. This process should be as unobtrusive as possible and ensure students are then given the opportunities to connect with peers. Friendship facilitation is a combination of many strategies that build a climate of concern for others and an interest in promoting the development of social relationships.

The reciprocal nature of social interactions that can result in the development of true friendship requires attention to not only the social skill levels of the student with severe disabilities, but also awareness of the typical students' cognitive-social development. This understanding is necessary in order to successfully facilitate the growth of friendships among students with and without disabilities within the context of realistic expectations. The needs and interest of students without disabilities involved in inclusive programs may influence the quality of interactions among students and their future participation. Examination of typical social development may provide valuable insights for planning successful facilitation through the years. An image of similarity is believed to affect the probability of developing friendships. Opportunities to interact and discover these similarities students have to each other increase the likelihood of making friends. The ability to make social discriminations and to initiate and maintain interactions are also helpful and perhaps necessary in developing relationships.

SOCIAL COGNITIVE DEVELOPMENT DURING THE PRESCHOOL YEARS

Very young children have difficulty distinguishing between their own values and those of others. Friends are merely others who happen to be present and willing to interact. Proximity appears to be the key to interaction, which focuses upon objects and space rather than feelings. Conclusions drawn by children at this age are thought to most often be based upon physical characteristics, due to the child's reliance upon concrete and observable information. Peers are viewed only in terms of the child's own needs.

Focusing on the issue of gender, unlike older children, preschool peer friendships appear to seek companionship regardless of gender. In other words, students show little or no gender preference in playmates. Specific experiences are believed to accelerate preschoolers' ability to put themselves in a classmate's shoes. Such experiences may be promoted by using role-play activities designed to provide meaningful insight for children.

Physical proximity and the use of valued objects are useful strategies in facilitating social interaction at the preschool level. In addition, positive behaviors should be modeled by the adults in the setting, and students displaying such behaviors on their own should be appropriately reinforced. When student social behavior is not positive, these occurrences should be treated as opportunities to teach more positive interactions. Information regarding differences among students should be explained, as students at this age depend heavily on observable traits.

SOCIAL COGNITIVE DEVELOPMENT DURING THE EARLY ELEMENTARY YEARS

As children reach primary school age they begin to realize that others may hold views different from their own. Even though young school-age children begin to differentiate their individual perspective from that of others, this differentiation is subjective and does not typically translate into cognitive understanding of the others' perspective. During the early elementary years, friends appear to be chosen who fulfill the student's expectation of providing one-way assistance, without reflection upon the friend's feelings or needs. Children are just beginning to distinguish between intentional and unintentional actions at this time. There is generally no realization or understanding that people, at times, hide their feelings. Children begin to learn to enter groups, control their aggression, and resolve minor conflicts as they grow socially. Early social development also requires the child to be able to recognize his or her own emotions, as well as others' feelings. The expression of emotion is also recognized as critical. Characteristics such as helping, sharing, and cooperation have been recognized as desirable at this age and throughout later development.

SOCIAL COGNITIVE DEVELOPMENT OF INTERMEDIATE ELEMENTARY SCHOOL AGE CHILDREN

Older elementary students can now reflect upon the thoughts and feelings of others, however, they do not hold their own perspective and that of another simultaneously, as is necessary to compare and contrast two viewpoints. During the middle elementary years, friendship is often based upon a shared interest and/or activity and the exchange of possessions. Demonstration of concrete supportive behaviors is also important to friendship at this time.

During the final elementary years, children tend to share in a more reciprocal fashion and to develop mutual trust. Children increasingly see themselves as others see them. Loyalty begins to receive greater emphasis within the relationship, which is now becoming a two-way entity. Children typically begin to prefer interacting with same-sex peers from approximately ages eight through twelve. They may in fact display some antagonism toward the opposite sex during this developmental stage.

The increased reciprocity of friendships suggests the need to both educate the general education student regarding their expectations of students with severe disabilities, and to design specific programs for students with severe disabilities addressing interactive skills and necessary adaptations. Opportunities should be provided that allow students of like gender to interact socially, as this is the preference of most children during these years. Students will continue to need assistance in seeing another's point of view from time to time, making role-play experiences helpful and successful means to increase social abilities. If facilitation approaches place students at this age into specifically defined roles, these roles are unlikely to change in the general education student's mind. In other words, peer tutors will most likely maintain their hierarchical roles throughout their interactions with students with severe disabilities. Students with severe disabilities may need to receive instruction regarding situation-specific supportive behaviors, in order to develop a reciprocal relationship that is satisfying to both students.

SOCIAL COGNITIVE DEVELOPMENT DURING THE SECONDARY SCHOOL YEARS

Beginning at approximately grade seven, the child's same-sex friends begin to share the critical support role previously filled by the student's parents. As supportive influences are changing, students begin to step outside of their own viewpoint, as well as their friends, and can now assume the perspective of a neutral third person. These new abilities parallel the individual's overall cognitive development, allowing students to support one another and share their problems.

Older secondary students display the potential for adultlike social understanding, which includes empathy. This concern also extends beyond personal relationships to include concerns for the environment, health issues, and conservation. Their social focus also moves to relationships of greater loyalty and intimacy with their peers. Increased independence is often reflected in the diminishing need for constant peer approval as adolescents grow. Friendships among adolescents are expected to offer understanding, reassurance, and emotional and social support in stressful situations.

Peer pressure constantly influences the secondary student's use of the social cognitive skills he or she has developed. The value given pro-social behavior by the peer group or school culture is critical to developing an atmosphere conducive to successful inclusion of students with severe disabilities. Students in this age group have far greater capabilities of perspective taking and empathy than they typically display. Interventions that purposefully tap into these skills should be very beneficial in achieving more favorable outcomes for social inclusion in secondary school.

Secondary school females are more often described as comfortable displaying caring behaviors. Because males place greater value upon independence, they may be less likely to display overprotective behaviors toward students with severe disabilities, and in fact provide included students greater opportunity for engagement in activities without assuming a predominately helping role in the relationship. The culture of the school environment obviously plays a critical role in influencing general education students' inhibitions regarding pro-social and accepting behaviors. Perhaps much of the pessimism surrounding social inclusion during adolescence is unwarranted and reinforced only by our inability to employ the appropriate multifaceted facilitation methods.

FROM INTERACTION TO FRIENDSHIP FACILITATION

Moving from short-term social interaction to long-term ongoing friendly relationships requires more

than choosing a best friend for a student, assigning a peer tutor, teaching social skills curriculum, establishing clubs or providing disability awareness. Facilitation is a combination of strategies that attempts to promote a climate of concern for all others in the environment. Most agree the role of facilitator should be shared by general and special educators, teaching assistants, classmates, family members, counselors, and community members. To become comfortable facilitating the development of friendships involves recognition of how often we help each other with all of our friendships every day.

Day-to-day facilitation may involve getting students together to allow them to get to know one another, encouraging budding friendships, modeling ways to include students with disabilities, and allowing them space to grow. Specific methodologies may involve special interventions or simply the encouragement of natural relationships between students. The research and proposed strategies suggest a general perception that facilitation of friendships between students with and without disabilities is less difficult in the preschool and elementary school setting than in the secondary environment. This may be due to the structure of the preschool and elementary school which allows the classroom teacher greater time with the students and autonomy to establish a consistent classroom climate. The highly competitive nature of high school is also identified as negatively affecting the likelihood of successful inclusion. Consideration of the changing stages of the social cognitive development of the general education student further complicates the process of facilitation. Peer tutoring and special friends programs have been criticized for their matchmaking qualities and oversimplification of what true friendship means. Singular strategies are unlikely to generate solutions for such complex undertakings, and many programs used to facilitate social relationships were not designed for that specific purpose.

Researchers have identified essential conditions to help students connect and increase the likelihood of building friendly relationships. These include the obvious prerequisites of full inclusion and the required communication supports. Use of creative problem solving and attention to age-appropriate activities are also necessary. *Inclusion* refers to a broad climate of acceptance and diversity that transcends any singular group.

UNIQUE DEMANDS ON FRIENDSHIPS AMONG STUDENTS WITH AND WITHOUT DISABILITIES

Communication difficulties are most often noted as one of the greatest hurdles to overcome in developing and maintaining friendships in the inclusive setting. Initial communication issues can often be addressed through adaptive technologies, and students often develop improved communicative interaction when afforded enough time together. These needs should be clearly addressed and progress monitored in the students' IEPs.

The hierarchical nature imposed upon student relationships in some settings can also result in unnatural consequences unique to such relationships. Even though friends are routinely accustomed to helping one another, should this helping relationship become one way only, the relationship is less likely to be described as a true friendship. The nature of these unique relationships may be better framed as reciprocal when the nondisabled students see their friendship as a social growth experience. Teachers have reported the observation of considerable growth in the social skills of nondisabled peers who actively interact and relate to students with disabilities. The advantages to nondisabled students that result from inclusive activities are being increasingly recognized by both the students themselves and the facilitators.

Steven R. Lyon, Becky A. Knickelbein, and Paula J. Wolf

DEVELOPING COMMUNICATION AND SOCIAL INTERACTION SKILLS

One of the most important reasons for inclusion of children and youth with severe disabilities in school, work, and community is to provide the opportunity for social benefits. These opportunities include belonging to a group and having membership, developing friendships, and acquiring a network of social support. In school, it is argued that for children with severe disabilities, the potential social benefits of inclusion are more important than the potential academic benefits.

However, early research on inclusion, particularly in early intervention programs, indicated that physical proximity of children with severe disabilities to normally developing peers did not ensure that the desired social interactions would occur or that friendships would develop. It has been noted that the reasons for this are due, in part, to lack of communication and social interactions skills of children with disabilities. As a result, much attention has been given, in research and in curriculum and program development, to the teaching of communication and social skills to children with severe disabilities. Although the benefits of inclusion for children with severe disabilities are not entirely dependent upon their ability to communicate and interact effectively (i.e., physical proximity alone may provide opportunities for normal peers to engage children with severe disabilities in various beneficial ways), the ability to communicate and interact socially, even at a rudimentary level, greatly enhances the potential social benefits of inclusion.

LANGUAGE, COMMUNICATION, AND SOCIAL SKILLS

Language, communication, and social skills are highly interrelated, mutually interdependent, and develop together. In normally developing children, language and communication development, as well as social development, occur in a generally predictable sequence, with generally predictable milestones at certain chronological ages (although there is some variability due to a variety of factors that may be internal or external to the child). Additionally, although there are a variety of theories (e.g., Skinner's behavioral, Chomsky's psycholinguistic, and Piaget's cognitive-developmental) about how and why language and social development occur, there is little disagreement over the actual path and chronological timeframe which is observed in most children.

Language is defined as a system of rules, structure, context, and vocabulary that combine together to form a coherent and universally understood system for communication. Normal development of language occurs in stages, progresses from simple to complex in structure, and progresses in vocabulary size and diversification as well as in semantic and contextual utilization. Understanding and utilization of a language requires the acquisition of knowledge about the various aspects of the rules which govern its use. For most, oral or spoken language is the vehicle used to communicate, and is the outer indication that inner language understanding exists.

Communication, on the other hand, is defined as the act of reciprocal interaction, involving intent on the part of the communicator, content to be communicated, and another individual to which the communication is directed. Communication may or may not involve the use or require the existence of language. As well, there are many forms of communication (e.g., spoken, manual signs, gestures, or other discrete behavioral acts). It is generally accepted that communication involves intent and serves a function for the person attempting to communicate. If the intent and/or the message is not perceived or correctly understood and function is not served then we have a failure to communicate. Unfortunately, it is often the case that children and youth with severe disabilities, who use gestures and discrete (and sometimes idiosyncratic) behavioral acts to attempt to communicate intent and to serve a function, the communication fails because others in the environment do not recognize the intent.

Social interaction can involve performing or participating in a variety of different behaviors, activities, or tasks, at different levels of complexity for a variety of different purposes. Developmental psychologists and educators have noted that in the norm social interaction skills and social development are aligned with cognitive and language development. Social development is also influenced greatly by experience, environmental context, and cultural mores.

Although language, communication, and social development are distinctly different phenomena, they overlap considerably and are highly interdependent. So much so that it can be said that all communication is social and all social interaction is communicative. Stated another way, this means that communication always is driven by a social context, and that social interaction always requires the use of some form of communication. The importance of the relationship is that, because of this, the teaching or promotion of communication and social skills must be contextually based in order to be effective.

COMMUNICATION AND SOCIAL SKILLS OF CHILDREN AND YOUTH WITH SEVERE DISABILITIES

Almost by definition, children and youth with severe disabilities are significantly deficient in communication and social skills in comparison to their normal peers. In a majority of cases this is due to the presence of significant cognitive or intellectual disabilities (formerly referred to as mental retardation). The presence of significant intellectual disabilities restricts one's ability to acquire, develop, diversify, and generalize all forms of knowledge and skills, including those involving communication and social interaction. Additionally, much of the conceptual development, representational logic, and higher-order thinking (which begins to evolve in most normal children from twelve to eighteen months of age) that is correlated with language and social development is either substantially delayed or does not develop. As a result, children and youth with severe disabilities are observed to have extremely limited cognitive and behavioral repertoires, which further hinders other learning. Language, communication, and social-skills development are critical learning outcomes but they are also important vehicles for other learning. Perhaps the best example of this is the fact that children with language disabilities also experience difficulty in learning to read due to the fact that reading is language based.

Several other factors are also often related to the lack of communication and social development in children and youth with severe disabilities. One such factor is the presence of sensory and/or physical disabilities and chronic health impairments. Being deaf or blind under many circumstances may affect one's learning how to communicate or interact with others. Several physical disabilities (e.g., cerebral palsy) may also make normal spoken language very difficult or impossible and may severely limit the effective use of other forms of communication such as sign language. Chronic health impairments may limit learning opportunities and reduce alertness or availability for learning. Another factor that may limit communication and social development is the presence of interfering behaviors. Although many types of interfering behaviors (e.g., self-stimulatory, self-destructive, disruptive, or aggressive) may serve some function for the individual (e.g., gaining attention or escaping from a situation), if the intent is not understood these behaviors may actually interfere with the development of constructive and more accepted forms of communication and social interaction. Research on the social inclusion of children with severe disabilities in school indicates that interfering behaviors are a significant obstacle to social interaction and friendship development with normal peers.

An additional reason why such a large proportion of children and youth with severe disabilities have very limited communication and social skills is because of lowered expectations and the associated social isolation that many of these children and youth experience. Despite multiple federal mandates in civil rights and education law requiring equal access and opportunity regardless of handicap, many children, youth, and adults with severe disabilities continue to be excluded from the mainstream and segregated into handicapped-only daycare centers, schools, recreation programs, residences, and work places. Unfortunately, these environments are impoverished with respect to the abundance of appropriate communication and social skills role models and opportunities to interact. As a result they do not foster communication and social development in ways that "normal" learning, living, and working environments do.

Although the limitations in communication and social skills in children and youth with severe disabilities are well documented, it is also the case that there is a wide range of skills within the population. Some individuals with severe disabilities have limited oral language and literacy; others do not speak but have an established repertoire of signs and gestures, while still others use electronic communication aids. Some children and youth with severe disabilities are instructed in (and use) "total communication" which may involve multiple input and output modalities (e.g., signing and speaking or gesturing and selecting a communication board icon). Given the importance of communication and social development, and the prevalence of substantial deficits and wide variation in communication and social skills in this population, it is critical that individualized assessment and intervention begin early and take pragmatic and contextually based approaches.

INDIVIDUALIZED ASSESSMENT OF COMMUNICATION AND SOCIAL SKILLS

Prior to the development of an intervention program to teach communication and social skills it is important to consider the child's personal-social context (i.e., home, family, community, school, work). Because communication and social development are so closely tied to these contexts, assessment should inform and help to align intervention with important factors in the child's life. For example, assessment of home and family characteristics and routines will allow for selection of communication methods and content that is relevant to and supported within the home and family.

There are a variety of other personal characteristics and circumstances that should be assessed initially. Chief among these is the child's cognitive, physical, and sensory status. The presence of significant cognitive, physical, and/or sensory disabilities will have implications for the approaches taken to teaching communication and social skills. Other factors which should be assessed include: the child's present communication and social interaction skills, the immediate communication needs, the contexts (environments) in which the child has opportunities for interaction, the child's interests and preferences, conceptual symbolic-representational understanding, available response modes, and possible initial communication content.

Assessments should be conducted in naturalistic settings, involve significant persons in the child's life, involve the use of multiple repeated measures, and be focused on relevant social contexts and activities. The child's parents, siblings, classmates, friends, and teachers should be involved; and assessment information should be collected through observations, interviews, and discussions. The primary goal of assessment is to gain a clear understanding of how the child communicates and interacts within important personal-social contexts so that an effective intervention program can be developed. The goal of intervention is to attempt to develop independent, interactive, and generalized communication and social skills usable within the environments and contexts where the child is expected to function. Given the developmental nature of communication and social skills, it is necessary that assessment be ongoing and frequent so that intervention goals and methods can be updated as the child learns skills and/or as the child's needs for communication and social skills change.

INTERVENTION STRATEGIES FOR TEACHING COMMUNICATION AND SOCIAL SKILLS

Historically, communication therapy and social skills instruction was carried out in situations and contexts different from where the child was expected to use the skills. For example, communication therapy was provided in therapy rooms and social skills were taught in simulated social skills training groups. The overwhelming preponderance of empirical evidence indicates that these strategies are not effective, due largely because of the failure of generalization or transfer of skills learned.

The widely accepted alternative is to situate or embed instruction into natural contexts, thereby eliminating the need for transfer. It has also been noted that naturalistic intervention embedded in familiar contexts provides greater support for the initial learning and maintenance of skills. Sometimes referred to as "milieu teaching," this approach places and distributes intervention and instruction within and across natural routines. Additionally, instruction involves teaching multistep or multicomponent and reciprocal patterns in which communication is intertwined with social interaction. Both expressive and receptive communication is promoted and vocabulary and structure is developed simultaneously. This approach to intervention is pragmatic, and draws upon a variety of specific techniques dictated by the particular needs of the child and the characteristics and demands of the context where the skills are to be learned and used.

Providing direct intervention to teach communication and social interaction skills is one of the most effective methods of improving the social opportunities for children and youth with severe disabilities in inclusive settings. However, in order to enhance the social outcomes of inclusion it may also be useful to focus the intervention on the environment rather than the child with the disability. The two most important methods for doing this are the use of instructional adaptations and peer-mediated interventions. Instructional adaptations involve changes in

any aspect of curriculum or instruction that enables a child to participate in an activity without possessing the requisite skills. Examples of adaptations include simplifying materials, giving more assistance, or lowering performance expectations. Adaptations may be used to compensate for physical, sensory, or cognitive disabilities on a permanent basis or they may be used until requisite skills are learned and then faded out and eliminated.

Peer-mediated interventions are also an effective means for promoting appropriate social participation and interaction in inclusive settings. Peer-mediated interventions are those that impact on outcomes for children with disabilities and that are delivered "through" peers (typically classmates or friends). Phillip Strain and his colleagues have demonstrated the effectiveness of peer-mediated interventions through a series of investigations aimed at developing social skills, play behaviors, and communicative interactions. Typically, the "normal" peer is taught roles or strategies used to interact with, instruct, or assist the peer with disabilities within a structured social play context. The peer with disabilities, in turn, has opportunities to participate and interact in activities and to learn important communication and social interaction skills.

AUGMENTIVE COMMUNICATION AND ASSISTIVE TECHNOLOGY

Additional effective methods of promoting communication and social interaction include the use of augmentive communication and assistive technologies. For many children and youth who are unable to acquire language or use speech, augmentive communication and assistive technology may be important alternatives. Augmentive alternative communication is "an integrated group of components, including the symbols, aids, strategies and techniques used by individuals to enhance communication" (American Speech-Language Hearing Association 1991). This could involve unaided augmentation (e.g., communication boards or booklets). User response modes could involve direct selection, scanning devices, or encoding. Symbol systems could involve the use of letters, words, pictures, symbols, or actual objects. Augmentive communication, which is sometimes referred to as "total communication," normally involves the use of multiple modalities for input, such as the use of speech and sign or pictures and sign. Similarly, output, or expression on the part of the user, may also involve multiple modalities. Augmentive or total communication is used to take advantage of redundancy and thereby increases the likelihood of comprehension for the listener.

Finally, assistive technology may provide a viable means of communication for children and youth who are unable to do so in traditional ways. Assistive technology is defined by the U.S. Department of Education as "any item, piece of equipment, or product system, whether acquired commercially off the shelf, modified, or customized, that is used to increase, maintain, or improve functional capabilities of individuals with disabilities." Although defined broadly here as useful for a variety of purposes (e.g., modality, environmental controls, etc.) assistive technology has been particularly important and effective for communication purposes. Assistive technology devices and systems may be high tech (i.e., electronic, computer-based) or low tech (i.e., mechanical, non-electric, or motorized). Since the passage of the Technology-Related Assistance for Individuals Act in 1978, and with the development of microcomputer technology, an entire industry has evolved with a whole range of systems that are available, including output, scanning, and selection devices. Interestingly, many of the same principles of assessment and intervention discussed earlier, such as the emphasis on individualized, pragmatic, and contextually based assessment and intervention, apply also to the assessment, development, and utilization of assistive technology for communication and social intervention. It is also often important, particularly for classroom peers, to demonstrate the use of these devices and systems in order to facilitate communication and social interaction with their peers with disabilities using the assistive technology.

Steven R. Lyon, Becky A. Knickelbein, and Paula J. Wolf

POSITIVE BEHAVIOR SUPPORTS

It is not unusual for students with severe disabilities to exhibit problem behavior. Problem behavior is gen-

erally defined as behavior that interferes with the health, safety, or functioning of the individual or others in his or her environment. Problem behavior jeopardizes the student's access to inclusive settings because it can disrupt school activities and interfere with the learning of other students in the classroom.

Positive Behavior Support (PBS) is an empirically validated approach for effectively influencing change in significant problem behavior that individuals with severe disabilities may experience in home, school, work, and community settings. Rooted in Applied Behavior Analysis, PBS originally emerged as an alternative to the use of aversive methods for reducing or eliminating undesirable behavior in individuals with severe disabilities. Sometimes referred to as functional behavior support, positive behavior supports are based on the premise that behavior occurs for a reason and discovery of that reason leads to the development of effective supports and interventions.

For example, behavior may be a form of communication—it may be the way the student indicates illness or displeasure. A student's behavior may effectively serve to initiate or terminate an activity or interaction. What parents or educational personnel regard as interfering behavior may help the student to acquire or avoid something, such as an object or attention. Behavior may be the student's only means of exerting control over an unstimulating or oppressive environment. What is viewed as behavior may actually be a symptom of a physical disorder. Fundamental to PBS is the assumption that most behavior serves some purpose or occurs for a reason. Exploration of those reasons is a major component of positive behavior support.

The aim of positive behavior support is to develop a thorough understanding of the person and the contextual variables that contribute to the behaviors in order to create positive, lasting change. Important information is gathered about the person and includes, but is not limited to, discovery of personal lifestyle preferences, an examination of factors that affect the student's quality of the life, and learning about the student's likes, dislikes, strengths, and skill needs. Rather than targeting behaviors to be reduced or eliminated, PBS interventions are based on changing environments and circumstances. Today, the primary aim of PBS is to bring about more inclusive and personally meaningful lifestyles for children, adolescents, and adults with severe disabilities. An underlying assumption of PBS is that behavior reduction is a by-product of intervention rather than its primary focus.

In the past, when an individual with severe disabilities exhibited challenging behavior, the accepted treatment protocol was based on topography and severity, that is, what the behavior consisted of, as well as the gravity of its effects. Intervention most often focused on decreasing or eliminating the behavior(s) of concern, using techniques that had been empirically validated for that particular topography. Behavioral interventions were grouped according to their level of intrusiveness; practitioners were to utilize a more restrictive procedure only when less restrictive ones proved to be ineffective. For individuals who exhibited high rates of extremely self-injurious, aggressive, or destructive behaviors, many practitioners began to rely heavily on punitive and aversive techniques, such as seclusion, visual masking, water or vinegar misting, mechanical restraint, and electric shock. Some practitioners and researchers began to question the humanity as well as the efficacy of such approaches.

The use of aversive procedures often inflicted physical and psychological pain or trauma. The application of aversive behavior-change methods most often prevented the individual's access to and participation in more stimulating opportunities, activities, and learning environments (in some cases, this can be said for less intrusive practices as well). Behavior-change interventions were often carried out in highly specialized environments, such as behavior-shaping units operated by institutions, clinics, or residential group-home providers. Individuals were not released until their behavioral problems diminished. Consequently, they were often forced to remain in environments that may have been contributing to their problem behavior. The quality of life for individuals with severe disabilities who also had significant behavioral issues was at one time extremely poor, compromised by their behaviors as well as the treatments intended to improve those behaviors.

Two frequently expressed criticisms of traditional behavior treatments were the lack of generalizability and durability of treatment effects. A growing body of research and meta-analysis of previously published studies supported these concerns. Results indicated that behavior change brought about by aversive approaches lacked durability over time and often did not generalize to other settings or social contexts.

FUNCTIONAL BEHAVIOR ASSESSMENT

Functional Behavior Assessment provides the foundation for the development of positive behavior interventions. There is a compelling body of research indicating that behavioral interventions that are based on functional assessment are significantly more effective than interventions that are not. Functional Behavior Assessment consists of information-gathering and team-based problem-solving activities which are conducted to (1) develop knowledge and an appreciation of the person, (2) develop an understanding of the contextual variables that influence the person's behavior, and (3) guide the development of effective behavior support interventions. Functional assessment is based on the premise that behavior occurs for a reason and discovery of that reason could lead to effective treatment approaches. Functional assessment helps to identify when, where, and under what conditions challenging behaviors are likely to occur and not occur, as well as identify those consequences that may be maintaining the behaviors. Functional assessment also considers lifestyle issues and other factors that may contribute to the behavior or jeopardize the individual's quality of life.

There are a number of models for functional behavior assessment reported in the literature. Each describes a multistep process that generally consists of the following activities: (1) describe the behavior of concern in clear, operational terms; (2) make decisions about the levels of behavior severity and which behaviors are priorities for intervention; (3) gather information; (4) develop a hypothesis as to possible functions of or reasons for the behavior; (5) design a positive support plan that addresses the hypothesized reason the behavior is occurring; (6) implement the plan; and (7) regularly monitor and evaluate the plan, and revise as needed.

Though it may appear to be, functional assessment is rarely a linear process. The information gathered during one step of the process may need to be revisited as new or additional information surfaces during another. For example, though the behavior support team may have clearly defined a particular behavior that they have targeted for assessment and intervention, subsequent observation (conducted during step three) may necessitate that they rewrite their definition (return to step one) or reverse their decision about treatment priorities (return to step two). The steps in the functional assessment process can be implemented separately or simultaneously, and usually they occur in a cyclical fashion.

GATHERING INFORMATION

Step three, the gathering of information, is the most important and time-consuming step in the functional assessment process. The kind, breadth, and depth of information to be gathered can vary considerably, depending on the student, the behavior, and the circumstances. Minimally, most researchers recommend the examination of specific contextual information (i.e., antecedents, setting events, and maintaining consequences) to help understand when, where, and under what conditions behavior is most likely to occur and not occur.

Antecedents are events that precede the occurrence of the target behavior(s). Antecedents, for example, can include a specific request, a termination of an activity, or removal of a preferred item. To illustrate, when told he must put away his Game Boy, Michael bites his hand. When the bell signals that recess is over, Jodi begins to scream.

Setting events are previous and current environmental issues and events that influence the occurrence of the target behavior. Setting events may be physiological (e.g., fatigue, hunger, pain, and physical discomfort); social (e.g., number of friendships or access to preferred or interesting persons); or physical (e.g., schedule changes, level of stimulation, access to preferred things or activities, daily routines). Some researchers also consider affective states to be a form of setting event. Setting events may be proximal, that is, present at the time the target behavior occurs (e.g., noise); they may be distal, that is, related to an event or condition that previously occurred or will occur at a different time (e.g., a previous fight with a significant other, or an upcoming hospitalization or holiday). For example, Mary is more likely to hit other students on days when she is not feeling well (proximal, physiological setting event). Joe is more likely to be verbally abusive in math class on those days that he rides the bus to school (distal, physical, or perhaps social setting event).

It is important to examine the relationship between setting events and antecedents. For example, on most days, Michael complies with the teacher's directive to put away the Game Boy. However, on days when it is extremely noisy in the classroom or when he is worried about the weather, Michael will usually bite his hand following the teacher's directive to put the Game Boy away. Often, a particular setting event or antecedent alone will not trigger the occurrence of a particular behavior; however, when a particular antecedent is paired in combination with a particular setting event, the target behavior is likely to occur.

A consequence is an event that occurs immediately following the occurrence of a behavior that serves to strengthen the behavior by making it more likely to re-occur. For example, when Sam throws his book on the floor during independent practice in math class, he is called to the teacher's desk for individual instruction and assistance. When Suzie forcefully spits out her food, the instructional aide stops feeding her.

It is extremely important to identify setting events and antecedents that trigger target behaviors and the consequences that maintain them. However, the behavioral difficulties of students with severe disabilities are generally more complex, and are often related to the interaction between their immediate environment and a number of other factors, such as the student's general skill levels, receptive and expressive communication, physical and psychological health, life experiences, quality of life, and so on. For students with severe disabilities, additional information is needed.

Functional Behavior Assessment should include an inventory of the student's functional skills and skill needs. In addition to knowing what the student can and cannot do, it is important to ensure that the student's current skill repertoire is well suited to the physical and social environments the student encounters at home, in school, and in the community.

Functional Behavior Assessment should also include assessment of the child's expressive and receptive language abilities. For students whose communication is limited, assessment should provide an inventory that indicates known ways in which the student produces certain messages (e.g., greetings, requests). Additionally, it should be determined whether adults and other students who share space or activities with the student understand and respond to these communication efforts.

Lifestyle issues should be considered as well during the functional assessment process. The depth and breadth of this information will vary across learners and their specific situations. It is important to know if and how the interfering behavior affects the student's physical and psychological well being, interactions with others (e.g., siblings, peers), and performance in school. It is important to examine how many and what kind of social relationships the student enjoys; how the student spends leisure time; and the kinds and frequency of activities in which the student participates (in the home, school, and community). The student's level of self-determination should also be assessed; this includes how much control the student is able to exert over the environment, and how such control is exerted.

In order to generate effective behavior interventions for students with severe disabilities, it may be important to develop an historical perspective so team members can better understand the student and his/her behavioral challenges in context, over time. The level of detail will vary, based on behavior, severity, and durability. Histories should summarize, from birth to present, significant life events, where and with whom the individual has lived, school and residential placements, medical issues, and the content and effectiveness of previous behavioral interventions. In cases of significantly challenging behavior, it is extremely important that the historical perspective include a review and analysis of each medical and psychiatric diagnosis, and the medications, treatments, and therapies prescribed for each.

TYPES OF FUNCTIONAL BEHAVIOR ASSESSMENT

There are three different types of functional behavior assessment used to collect information about the student and factors relating to the behavior(s) of concern: informant methods (also known as indirect methods), observation (also known as direct methods), and functional analysis (also known as clinical or analogue analysis).

Indirect methods are utilized to gather information that is provided by others who know or have contact with the student, using any of a variety of methods, such as review of records, discussions, person-centered planning activities, structured interviews, and the completion of checklists, rating scales, or surveys. Informant methods can yield a range of information that helps to develop an understanding of the person and the contexts surrounding the behavior.

Observational methods consist of any of a variety of techniques in which the person and behavior of concern are observed in settings in which the behavior does and does not occur, and the data is systematically recorded. Frequently used observational methods include A-B-C (antecedent-behavior-consequence), recording, and scatter plots.

Functional or analogue analysis is the intentional manipulation of one or more variables in a controlled setting to determine those variables that occasion and/or maintain a particular behavior or behavior set. While the literature indicates that analogue assessment is generally not used in applied settings, there is research that has demonstrated its effectiveness as a means of hypothesis testing (step four of Functional Behavior Assessment).

DEVELOPING AND IMPLEMENTING THE BEHAVIOR SUPPORT PLAN

Step four in the functional assessment process entails the formulation of a hypothesis about the purpose or function of the target behavior. If the information gathered and reviewed by the behavior team is comprehensive, it should not be difficult to generate reasonable hypotheses about why the behavior is occurring. At this stage, it is important to remember that one behavior may have multiple functions or that one function may be expressed by multiple behaviors. For example, Tia's team hypothesizes that her loud growls are communicative attempts to indicate illness, thirst, discomfort, or a wet diaper; to seek the attention of an adult or peer; and to initiate or terminate an interaction. Cole's team hypothesizes that his aggressiveness toward females in his age group is an expression of his interest in them: when Cole encounters a cute girl he wants to meet, he may slap her on the arm, spit at her, rush her, or grab something away from her and hit her with it.

In step five, the team develops a support plan, aimed to specifically address the hypothesized function of the behavior. At this point in the process, some researchers recommend that these hypotheses should first be tested by gathering data through direct observation of the student in the settings in which the behavior occurs, or by intentionally manipulating antecedents, setting events, and consequences. According to other researchers, if sufficient and accurate information has been collected and it appears to be corroborated by direct observations that were conducted during the gathering of information, there is no need to test the hypotheses.

Steps six and seven (implement the plan; and monitor, evaluate, and revise the plan) should occur simultaneously. Careful monitoring ensures that the plan is being implemented as written; ongoing evaluation determines if the plan is effective. If not, the behavior team must collect additional information, formulate new hypotheses, and develop an alternative plan.

MULTI-COMPONENT INTERVENTIONS

Positive behavior support plans should consist of multi-component interventions. As the name implies, multi-component interventions are behavior support plans that include a variety of elements. Multi-component interventions include but are not limited to: (1) antecedent and setting-event modifications, (2) teaching new skills, (3) consequence interventions, and (4) lifestyle enhancement. Some researchers recommend using only those that apply in each individual case while others caution that these four areas are interrelated, and therefore, must be considered and addressed simultaneously. For example, teaching new skills that replace or eliminate the need for an individual to use a particular behavior may be a logical component of a support plan. However, if appropriate use of the new skill does not produce the desired effect for the student (consequent interventions) or opportunities for the person to consistently use the skill are not provided (lifestyle enhancement), the positive behavior support plan may be ineffective over time because the student will most likely resort to the earlier, undesirable behavior.

Manipulation of antecedent and setting events (i.e., stimulus-based approaches) has recently been getting much attention in the literature. Several meta-analyses of behavioral-intervention studies have revealed that those that include manipulation of ecological and setting events and/or redesign of the environment were more successful that those that did not.

Interfering behaviors often result from skill deficiencies or failure to use a skill or skill set. The logical intervention in this case would be teaching a new skill to replace or compensate for the behavior of concern. Skill training can involve acquisition, fluency, and/or generalization of a new or alternate skill in a variety of areas, such as adaptive behavior, academics, communication, coping and tolerance, or others. Skill training may or may not be directly related to the target behavior.

Choice making is frequently recommended as an integral part of a multi-component intervention plan, though some consider choice to be a subset of skill development, lifestyle enhancement, or ecological manipulations. Choice-making interventions can take several forms: teaching students how to make choices, providing opportunities for choice making, and honoring choices that are made. Research supports the use of choice making as an effective intervention for individuals with severe disabilities.

Positive Behavior Supports for students with severe disabilities is a longitudinal endeavor. Because of the severity of their disabilities, they will require support over their lifetime, in a variety of areas and ways: gaining and maintaining reciprocal relationships, accessing and participating in preferred activities and events on a regular basis, and exerting choice and control over day-to-day and life decisions. This support is needed not just to maintain behavior change, but also to sustain a safe and personally meaningful lifestyle.

It has been predicted that the use of multi-component interventions will most likely increase, as will their scope and complexity. Parents of individuals with severe disabilities and challenging behavior have emphasized the need for multi-component support approaches that include additional elements. For example, parents have requested that interventions include the restructuring of home routines and strategies for reducing stress for themselves and other family members. For the child who is experiencing behavioral problems, parents believe interventions should also focus on enhancing communication, expanding relationships, and increasing choice making.

SYSTEMS-CHANGE ORIENTATION

More recently, PBS is being described as a systems-change approach, placing less emphasis on supporting the individual and more emphasis on building capacity to develop and sustain effective practices and supportive environments. This broadened application of PBS is attributed in part to provisions of the reauthorized Individuals with Disabilities Education Act (IDEA) of 1997, which recommends, without providing a clear definition and procedural guidelines, the use of positive behavioral interventions for interfering behavior.

Following the reauthorization of the IDEA, it has become more common for PBS to be characterized in the literature as a systems approach (i.e., one that emphasizes the development of environments that support positive behavior). There are, however, two distinctly different thrusts to the systems-orientation perspective on PBS. The first refers to collaborative and coordinated efforts to develop and sustain structures and environments that support positive behavior in the individual. The second refers to efforts to achieve and sustain pro-social student behaviors in the schoolwide community.

From the individual perspective, a systems approach focuses on changing problem contexts rather than problem behavior. It is meant to capitalize on and enhance the complex and interrelated relationships between all systems and stakeholders, including the person with challenging behavior. It includes activities such as establishing rapport with families, understanding how particular behavior is influenced by the environment, partnership and teamwork, and providing sufficient support for all involved. It also requires creation of a flexible system that includes interagency collaboration and a commitment to resource reallocation.

In the second approach, the entire school becomes the focus of intervention. PBS focuses on reorganizing and creating structures to nurture a supportive culture that values and applies effective practices for all students in the areas of instruction and discipline. This schoolwide system is based in a policy framework complete with procedures, protocols, and routines. It utilizes schoolwide teams, provides for ongoing staff and professional development, applies data-based decisionmaking practices, and uses research-validated practices.

Steven R. Lyon, Becky A. Knickelbein, and Paula J. Wolf

ASSESSMENT AND CURRICULA

Throughout the years the approaches to curriculum and assessment have evolved for all students. Regardless of the instructional level or content area of the curriculum, assessment and curricula are closely interrelated. In other words, assessment should drive instructional assessment practices, and both are dictated by carefully chosen learning outcomes.

EARLY CURRICULA

Most early curricular approaches for students with severe disabilities involved remedial approaches and essentially taught the same content (intended originally for students with mild disabilities) but in a simplified version. Based upon delayed developmental tasks presented later than typical, the expectations for students with severe disabilities were derived from this watered-down approach with little regard to meaningfulness, functionality, and transfer.

In the past it was also customary to approach organized school academic activities for students with severe disabilities as a building process from the bottom up. In other words, focus was placed upon discrete skills addressed in isolation with a goal to eventually chain these miniskills together into the more complex objective. As a result, an inordinate amount of time could often be expended on what were considered prerequisite skills, delaying student progress indefinitely. Such criticism, along with less than impressive results from these bottom-up methods, led to the progression of the opposite curricular approach.

TOP DOWN CURRICULA

Progressing from the ineffective adaptation of the developmental curriculum, taught in a piecemeal fashion, curriculum development for students with severe disabilities later moved into a stage of top down curricula. The top down approach to curriculum represents a movement toward functionality and the need to focus on preparing students for adult life and referencing curriculum to post-school and adult environments. This position was first presented by Lou Brown (Brown, Nietupski, and Hamre-Nietupski 1976) and his colleagues at the University of Wisconsin-Madison in a seminal paper titled "The Criterion of Ultimate Functioning." In a series of works that followed, this group delineated an approach to assessment and curriculum developed from analysis of current and future environments relevant to the student. With this approach, the content was typically divided between four comprehensive areas, which included skills related to: (1) domestic, (2) community, (3) vocational, and (4) recreational/leisure environments. These content areas address basic skills (i.e., those needed in the environment) and also included critical activities (i.e., activities unique yet critically important in one particular environment). The process of making curricular decisions typically involves the identifying of local environments of interest and need; conducting ecological inventories of those environments; performing a discrepancy analysis to identify the gap between needs and developed skills; and developing instructional plans as a result of these activities.

The focus upon the appropriate local environments is intended to satisfy the need to design a curriculum that directly meets the specific needs of the student in the familiar environments in which they must function. Ecological inventories provide the detail required to address specific skills necessary to effectively function within the student's specific environment. Discrepancy analysis describes the necessary initial assessment required to identify the difference between the students' strengths and needs regarding a specific skill inventory. The information gained through this specific skills assessment, which resembles a pre-test of sorts, is then the basis for the instructional plan designed to eliminate the gap between current functioning and the long-term goal.

The outcomes sought from the top down curricular approach are labeled *functional skills*. Functional skills are those skills which were accepted as important, useful, age-appropriate, socially valid, and enabling. These criteria are applied to all decisions regarding the student's individual educational goals.

THE IMPACT OF SCHOOL REFORM ON ASSESSMENT AND CURRICULA

The current school reform movement, which has focused upon specified standards and outcomes, has impacted the education of all students in America.

Heavy emphasis on testing and assessment and the accountability movement have resulted in new policies intended to measure student progress in a high-stakes environment. The reauthorization of the amendments to the *Individuals with Disabilities Education Act* (IDEA) of 1997 called for the inclusion of students with severe disabilities in general education and access to the general education curriculum for all students regardless of specific eligibility for special education services. The combination of the reform movement and the reauthorization of IDEA have had significant impact on the intended program planning for students with severe disabilities.

The changes in IDEA impacted the population of students with severe disabilities in several ways. The past and continued exclusion of this population within the educational setting was recognized as separate and unequal treatment. Additional changes were intended to address issues of belonging, valuing, friendship development, development of teacher expertise, and appropriate high expectations. While the promotion of such access and progress may be applauded, the specific needs of this population must be considered as all programs are revised and realigned to meet the requirements of the law. Recognition of the unique nature of students with severe disabilities accessing the general curriculum has led to experts calling for a multilevel model beginning with standards and moving through the IEP process, addressing instructional issues, and leading to appropriate individualized intervention.

Following closely behind the reauthorization of IDEA, the increased emphasis upon state and local assessment for accountability purposes has become widespread. In this context, educators of students with severe disabilities faced several problems. The standards address few areas for the population of students with severe disabilities, and the fact that full inclusion is not a reality for many students makes access to the general education curriculum more complicated. If students with severe disabilities are not included in the general education classroom then accessing the curriculum can, at best, be by proxy or through simulation. The options available in addressing access to the general education curriculum include modification or adaptation of the curriculum or development of a specially interpreted curriculum made up of functional skills and linked back to the same learning standards.

There are, however, other problems with general education curricula for students with severe disabilities. The general education curriculum is not functional or systematic for the population of students with severe disabilities; overall the level is too high and the pace of progression is unreasonable for them. Matching the general education curriculum and maintaining a level of functionality for this group of students is an exceptionally difficult challenge. In order to mesh the general education curriculum with the program planning for students with severe disabilities in a meaningful way, a curriculum inventory and a student inventory are required. The assessment component of a discrepancy analysis would then follow in order to address important learning goals in each student's Individual Education Plan (IEP).

INDIVIDUAL EDUCATION PLAN DEVELOPMENT

Efforts to incorporate the general education curriculum as required by IDEA 1997 and functional skills simultaneously into the IEP of each student with severe disabilities is a complex undertaking. Not every objective should be or can be addressed and learned at school. Some school experiences are not covered in the IEP specifically. Consequently, fewer, more comprehensive goals should be included in the IEP, remembering that as students grow older less of the general education curriculum is likely to be authentic and functional.

Each IEP objective and related criterion should be carefully chosen by the team. Task analysis of each discrete objective should then be matched to the appropriate teaching methods. The design of corresponding measurement and evaluation of the objective follows, as well as the outline of needed materials and the proposed schedule. The final step in IEP development for each objective would include a clear outline of the proposed fading, maintenance, and generalization methods planned. This complex process will require collaboration and consultation among all IEP team members in order to draw from the individual expertise of each.

Specific modifications to the general education curriculum employed by the IEP team may include adaptation of the amount of curriculum addressed, the length of time allotted to instruction, the amount of prompting and assistance provided to the student, modification of the difficulty level, materials provided, and the output required of the student at the conclusion of the instruction.

ADULT OUTCOMES

A balance is needed between each student's participation in the general education curriculum and teaching toward adult outcomes. Adult outcomes are those that will help the students ultimately function happily and productively in self-fulfilling and valued roles in adult society. These outcomes focus upon the basic skills essential to achieving the maximum amount of independence an individual can be realistically expected to achieve based on authentic assessment.

The detailed attention to the design of the IEP, one objective at a time for each student, will inevitably determine the level of participation for that student regarding their participation in the general education curriculum. Use of a matrix, coordinating each objective with the time proposed for instruction, should be incorporated into each IEP. Settings for instruction, including the regular classroom, special classes, the school setting, and the community, should also be identified. A well-designed IEP would also outline the instructional delivery plan, including direct instruction, incidental learning, indirect independent learning, and planned skill practice for maintenance and generalization.

IEP team members required in order to produce the highest-quality plan for each student should include the student, special educator, general educator, teaching assistants, related service personnel, parents, and fellow students. Any additional individuals potentially involved in the specific students' educational success should also be included.

ASSESSMENT OF FUNCTIONAL SKILLS

Despite the move toward access to the general education curriculum and the emphasis on academic content customarily associated with the general education of mildly handicapped populations, the progressive development of critical functional skills must continue to be authentically assessed. Classroom teachers are most often responsible for formative measurement of student progress within the functional curriculum. This is vital to achieving maximum independence and optimal participation levels. Frequent data collection has routinely allowed teachers to measure and visualize student progress, making necessary instructional alterations when substantial progress is not indicated. Measurement of the diminishing need for assistance, prompts and primary reinforcement for example, provides valuable information to parents as well.

GENERAL EDUCATION CLASSROOM ASSESSMENT

In order to juxtapose the child's IEP within the general education classroom environment and routines, it is necessary to conduct an analysis of the general education classroom and curriculum. Assessment of the classroom environment should include attention to the physical organization of the room, the use of appropriate grouping methods, the materials available and used, and the teaching methods employed. Physical organization refers to, in addition to the room layout, the classroom routines, climate, rules, and general use of time. Grouping choices may vary between whole-class, large- or small-group, and individual or one-to-one dyads. These organizational and instructional methods and choices should be analyzed to determine how they could align with the child's IEP.

STATE AND DISTRICT ASSESSMENTS LINKED TO ACCOUNTABILITY

The *No Child Left Behind Act* (NCLB) passed in 2002, like the reauthorization of IDEA mentioned earlier, requires the provision of alternate means of assessment for students who cannot participate in the state or district assessments as typically accommodated. As individual states design specific statewide assessments for general education students, the requirement for alternative assessment, affording the inclusion of all special needs populations in the accountability movement, are also being required. The inclusion of most students with disabilities in statewide assessments is now required. Students with mild disabilities may be provided some accommodations in administration of the general assessment, but are usually required to participate by completing the same assessment as their nondisabled peers.

The mandate requires states to develop meaningful alternate assessment tools for students with the most significant disabilities, as the statewide exams are impractical. The students' IEPs should address their participation in the alternative assessment. Such assessments are typically performance or portfolio based and derived from the applicable state standards.

Steven R. Lyon, Becky A. Knickelbein, and Paula J. Wolf

SCHOOL AND DISTRICTWIDE SUPPORT

In order for teachers to effectively include students with significant disabilities it is necessary that school building and school district-level organizational supports be developed and put in place. Michael Fullen a noted school reform authority, and many other authors, indicated that school reform efforts that are effective and sustainable are those that result in a change in the culture and organization of the school (Fullen, 2001). So it is with inclusion: teachers, principals, related services personnel, parents, and community people need to work together to change the organizational structures, management patterns, and social climate in order to achieve an environment where all children can receive an appropriate academic education and also be part of the social fabric of the school.

This change is necessary because traditionally, in most schools, the structure, pattern, and climate has not supported the inclusion of all students; quite the contrary, it was only as recent as the 1970s (corresponding to the enactment of the *Education of Handicapped Children Act*, PL 94–142) that students with severe disabilities were even permitted to access public education, much less receive their education in regular schools and regular classes. Although U.S. Department of Education (1996) data has shown a gradual and steady increase in the number of students and the percentage of time in general education classes, many students with severe disabilities still are educated full time in separate schools or separate classes within regular schools. Education that is separate is fundamentally different and when a school district or school building attempts, for the first time, to include a child with severe disabilities in the general classroom, different approaches are necessary. Often, changes in the organization, management, and climate of the school are necessary. Some of the more important elements of effective schooling that support inclusion are summarized below.

LEADERSHIP TO SUPPORT INCLUSION

A great deal has been written about the importance of leadership for effective organizations in general and for schools in particular. Traditional functions of leadership typically are described as including prioritization, goal setting, and planning; administering and managing operations; and supervision and evaluation of organizational and personal performance. Characteristics of effective leaders include important personal qualities such as organizational and interpersonal skills. Effective leaders also identify important themes, or a vision for the organization, that others can identify with and rally around. Good leaders are able to balance the responsibility for their own decisionmaking with the responsibility for developing organization-wide participation of others in decisionmaking at all levels in the organization.

More recent literature on school leadership emphasizes other functions, roles, and characteristics of effective leaders, many of which are the result of recent changes in the political and social contexts of education in our local communities and across the nation. Some of the more important changes in contexts which are impacting schools and school leaders are: the increased diversity in students and families; the globalization of the economy; the development of web-based and other digital technologies; the changes in structure and availability of funding; and the increased emphasis on accountability. Collectively, these factors have greatly increased the importance of student achievement outcomes and have, in turn, greatly increased the importance of school leaders being "instructional leaders." The role of the educational leader has changed significantly over the past decade. A contemporary and popular term for important and effective school leadership is "collaborative leadership," which is characterized by a more flexible, problem-solving style, built upon personal relationships and shared across the organization.

School leadership may come from a variety of individuals functioning in a variety of roles and situations throughout the school district. School leadership may be provided at the district level and may originate from a variety of positions and roles (e.g., superintendents, assistant superintendents, school board members, curriculum area directors, or supervisors). Leadership may also be situated at the building level (an increasing number of school districts vest leadership and decisionmaking authority at the building level), and often the building principal is called upon to assume many important leadership functions. Others at the building level, such as assistant principals, supervisors, school psychologists, social workers, counselors, other related services personnel, parents, or teachers may provide valuable leadership to the school.

The concept of "teacher leaders" is relatively recent and is based upon the notion that teachers, given support and the proper opportunities for professional development, may acquire a wide range of skills and areas of expertise to enable them to provide leadership. In this context, teachers of students with severe disabilities may provide training, consultation, and support to general education teachers in curriculum adaptation, instructional strategies, behavior support, progress monitoring, modification of grades, and many other areas. Experienced teachers may also provide important leadership in program development and changes in buildingwide policies and practices (e.g., development of a peer buddy program or infusion of ability awareness content into the curriculum).

A VISION OF INCLUSIVE EDUCATION

Because inclusion is so new to so many schools, it is often necessary for school districts to revisit their mission or vision. Most organizations in the public and private sectors have gone through a process of planning, leading to the development and adoption of a mission and vision statement. In strategic planning the mission and vision statements are intended to provide the basis for organizational goal setting and action planning. Strategic plans, ideally, become the engine of the organization that members can identify with and relate to their particular role. Some of the values fundamental to a vision of inclusive education are as follows:

Community

Central to the concept of inclusion is community or community building. This affirms that all students and staff within a school form a community whose members share the same environment and a certain set of experiences, values, and goals. Building a sense of community within a school reinforces collectivist values that transcend a focus on individual abilities.

Diversity

Although inclusion has developed primarily from the need to include those formerly excluded, inclusion has evolved more broadly to embrace all types of diversity among members of the school community. Inclusive schools welcome diversity in social, ethnic, and religious background as well as in cognitive, behavioral, and physical ability. Diversity in schools and in classroom groups provides a richer learning environment and enhanced learning opportunities for all.

Membership

In inclusive education, membership means that all students have a chance to belong and to be accepted as part of the community or group. With membership come the benefits of participation and the opportunity to make contributions and to be recognized and respected as a full member, regardless of one's capabilities.

Ownership

In the literature pertaining to inclusion, ownership refers to the degree to which general education teachers willingly accept responsibility for students who have been included in their classes. In order for inclusion to work effectively, general classroom teachers must assume responsibilities for teaching and supporting students with disabilities in ways similar to the ownership teachers feel for other students. Often, teachers need time, training, assistance, and ongoing support from other professionals in order to achieve ownership for a diverse range of students.

Acceptance

Similar to ownership and membership, acceptance on the part of teachers and students occurs when people come to understand each other. Understanding is accomplished most readily through sharing the same physical space, interacting and communicating with one another, sharing the same class projects and experiences, and developing relationships and friendships. It has been frequently noted, for example, that elementary students in particular will readily accept other children with visible physical, sensory, or cognitive disabilities once they learn about and can express similarities between themselves and those children.

Equity

Inclusion supports equity or equality of opportunity by allowing all students to participate and share in the same activities. Pull-out programs such as special education classes for students with mental retardation, remedial reading, gifted programs, or adapted physical education all represent educational opportunities that are conditional, based upon students' abilities or disabilities. Questions about the equity or fairness of these types of programs have arisen continually.

Support

Inclusive schools and classrooms are by their very nature supportive environments. Simply stated, support means giving someone something they need (e.g., assistance, help, consultation, etc.) in order to learn and to get along. Supports ranging in variety and intensity are developed and made available to all students based upon their needs. Additionally, teachers as well as students provide support to each other in inclusive schools.

Individualized Education

Special education services have always been defined as the development of individualized education. In designing an inclusive education program for a student with disabilities it is necessary to conduct an individualized assessment and develop individualized goals and objectives as a basis for providing an individualized sequence of learning activities based upon student needs and adapted from the regular curriculum. There is increasing interest, within the school reform literature, in developing more individualized assessment and instructional methods for all students. Margaret Wang developed the concept of adaptive instruction (Wang 1989) as an approach to providing an individualized education for all students.

Adaptation and Accommodation

Finally, inclusion means that although students will be educated in the regular class, not all students will be participating in the curriculum in the exact same ways, using the same materials, performing the same behaviors, or working toward the same goals, at least not all of the time. Adjustments in curricula and instructional practices (referred to here as adaptation and accommodation) are made, based upon individual student needs and abilities. In the inclusive school the regular classroom teacher works with the assistance and support of the special education support staff to identify, develop, and effectively use appropriate methods of adaptation and accommodation. Importantly, inclusive schools emphasize that since diversity in student abilities is accepted, differences in students needs will necessitate adaptation and accommodation, which is also accepted as a normal part of schooling (Lyon and Utley 1997).

TEAMWORK AND COLLABORATION

For inclusion to be successful the collective knowledge and skills of many different individuals is needed, and several different types of teamwork and collaboration are necessary. Collaboration in leadership has already been described as an important part of how the school district and school buildings should be run. Shared input and decisionmaking regarding the development and implementation of inclusive practices is particularly important: district policies affect schools, school practices affect classrooms, and classroom practices affect individual students. Therefore, it is important that participation and representation from all parts of the school district be secured so that the best interests of the students inform policies and practices.

Another important type of teamwork and collaboration is between special and general educators. The major focus of this is usually centered on rather specific instructional strategies, curriculum adaptations,

or other supports provided to students with disabilities in general education classes. Termed "collaborative teaming" this process includes a two-way dialogue in which the general educator shares knowledge and expertise about the general education classroom and curriculum; and the special educator shares knowledge and expertise about the adaptations and supports a child will need. In collaborative teaming the general and special educators (as well as other support staff) develop and negotiate an individualized plan for educating a child.

A third type of teamwork and collaboration is that which involves related services personnel. Related services personnel include physical, occupational, and speech-language and communication therapists, school psychologists, social workers, nurses, and others. Often, students with severe disabilities receive services from a variety of related services personnel due to the complexity of their educational, health care, and other needs. When children are included then related services personnel must collaborate with teachers so that needed services and supports may be provided within the regular education classroom. For many educators and related services personnel this requires a fundamental change from past practices in which therapies and other services were provided in isolated, separate settings. We now know that therapies and other support services provided within natural contexts and structured to support and not supplant the child's access to the curriculum is more effective. As a result, related services personnel and teachers need to share information (and sometimes skills) so that the needed services and supports may be fully integrated into the child's daily schedule.

Finally, collaboration with parents is an essential part of effective inclusion. Although home-school collaboration has long been viewed as an important role of special educators, the involvement of general educators with parents has traditionally been less intense. With the advent of students with significant cognitive, physical, sensory, and behavioral disabilities receiving their education within the regular class, the role of the general education teacher in collaboration with parents needs to be expanded. Often, parents have considerable knowledge and expertise about how to teach and care for their child and school personnel, including teachers, may benefit greatly from working closely with them.

DISTRICT AND SCHOOL PRACTICES

There are a number of districtwide and/or school building organizational practices which may impede or support the inclusion of students with severe disabilities. Among the most important are student placement, grouping, and staff assignment. Clustering student primary placements within particular schools or within particular classrooms usually makes effective inclusion extremely difficult. In a series of papers over the past decade Lou Brown and his colleagues (Brown, Long, Udvari-Solner, Schwartz, Vandeventer, Ahlgren, Johnson, Gruenwald and Jorgensen 1989) (formerly affiliated with the University of Wisconsin-Madison and the Madison Metropolitan School District) elaborated two important principles related to placement. The first is the concept of "natural proportions." Placement according to natural proportions dictates that in any given school or classroom there should be no more students with disabilities placed than what would normally occur. That is, students with severe disabilities constitute approximately 1 percent of the school population. Following the principle of natural proportions no school or classroom should have any more than 1 percent of these students. Congregate placements limit opportunities for students, complicate instruction and classroom management for teachers, and may reduce the quality of education students receive.

A second important principle related to student placement is the concept of the "home school." A home school is that school the child would attend if not disabled. In many communities home schools are located in neighborhoods where students live. Under this principle students with disabilities would follow the same attendance patterns and attend the same schools as their nonhandicapped brothers and sisters and neighborhood friends, rather than being bussed to separate special education centers or to other public schools where services are clustered into several self-contained classes. Following this principle requires staff, services, and supports to be dispersed throughout a school district. It also requires the development of a more widely dispersed array of expertise across a greater number of school buildings and classrooms. As indicated in the introduction to this chapter, beginning with the assumption that all students would receive their education in the regu-

lar class was really the underlying meaning behind the *Education for all Handicapped Children Act*.

Relatedly, the manner in which staff, including teachers and paraprofessionals, is assigned also has a great deal of impact upon efforts to develop inclusion. Under clustered or congregate arrangements teachers are given a class and paraprofessionals and, aside from a few limited opportunities (e.g., lunchroom, recess, gym class), students with severe disabilities spend most of their school day being taught in the self-contained class. An alternative arrangement is where, in elementary schools, support staff are assigned to a grade level and work closely with the students and teachers at that grade level. Middle school staffing patterns which are supportive of inclusion are sometimes organized by teams at grade level, including multiple-subject teachers (i.e., language arts, science, mathematics, social studies), special education teachers, and paraprofessionals. At the high school level teachers may be assigned to subject areas. These methods of organizing instructional resources and support lend themselves more readily to inclusion, primarily because support staff becomes more familiar with the curriculum and classrooms where they are supporting students.

There are a number of interrelated curriculum, instruction, and support practices that also impact on efforts to include students. Students should have access to participation in the regular curriculum and they should also participate in local district and state assessments (even though this is now a requirement of IDEA, many districts still struggle with implementation) for students with the most severe disabilities. In order for these students to participate meaningfully in class activities, projects, and other routines it will be necessary to make modifications. A variety of models and approaches to adaptation of curriculum and instruction have been developed and most proceed from the least intrusive or substantive to the more intrusive. The logic is, generally, that only those modifications are made that are necessary for a child's meaningful participation. Adaptations may be made to the goals and objectives, instructional materials, teaching methods and techniques, as well as the methods used to evaluate and grade student work. All of these types of adaptations are permissible under IDEA for students with IEPs. In this way efforts are made to provide the child as similar an education to that provided same-age nondisabled peers as possible. If a child needs more intrusive or substantial modifications to the curriculum or instruction in order to have her/his needs met and/or to participate meaningfully in the classroom, then those modifications are made. This approach makes it possible to provide access to the general curriculum, to allow for participation in ways that are meaningful to the child's needs, to involve the child in regular classroom activities and routines, and to receive the social benefits as well.

Steven R. Lyon, Becky A. Knickelbein, and Paula J. Wolf

DEVELOPING SELF-DETERMINATION AND CHOICE

When students without disabilities exit formal education, it is expected that they will begin to responsibly direct their own lives by making good decisions about personal goals and how to work toward attaining them. The assumption of personal responsibility for the direction and quality of one's life is referred to in the literature as *self-determination.* Self-determination consists of a number of skills and personal characteristics that develop over time as children, youth, and adults experience and reexperience day-to-day and major life events. It includes the development of skills in choice making, problem solving, decisionmaking, goal setting and attainment, self-regulation, and self-advocacy. Additionally, self-determination is influenced by individual levels of self-awareness, self-knowledge, and motivation. Though some researchers debate the likelihood that students with severe disabilities can become self-determining, most agree that educational programs for these students should focus on opportunities and experiences that promote the development of self-determined behaviors.

Students with severe disabilities can experience many immediate and long-term benefits when their individual programs incorporate instruction in the component skills of self-determination and provide opportunities for them to utilize those skills meaningfully for a variety of purposes, including their own educational planning. There is growing empirical evidence that indicates that increasing a student's level of self-determination can enhance student interest, motivation, and participation in the learning process; decrease interfering behavior; and positively influence post-school employment and adult living outcomes.

Inclusive environments can contribute significantly to the development of the self-determination of students with severe disabilities. First, in comparison to segregated educational classrooms and settings, inclusive environments provide a greater number and variety of experiences and opportunities that are reflective of certain quality-of-life indicators. These indicators include friendships and social relationships, membership and belonging, and citizenship. A priority adult outcome for students with severe disabilities is the realization and preservation of a satisfying and personally defined lifestyle. Exposure to the richness of activities provided in inclusive settings can serve to broaden students' experiences, increase their self-expectations, increase the expectations that others have of them, and ultimately expand the options available to them. Additionally, inclusive environments are far more complex than segregated ones, thus requiring students to utilize newly acquired self-determination skills, such as choice making or problem solving, on a frequent basis. These opportunities to contextually and regularly apply what is being learned will serve to strengthen the repertoire of skills needed to be self-determining.

DEFINITIONAL PERSPECTIVES ON SELF-DETERMINATION

Increasingly, reports in the current literature in severe disabilities emphasize the educational importance of self-determination. As more information emerges about self-determination, so do the number of ways to conceptualize what it is and how it pertains to children and youth with severe disabilities. Self-determination is a highly complex construct; researchers have yet to agree on how to define and classify it. Generally, there is consensus that self-determination is both an outcome and a means of outcome attainment. From there, points of view diverge and can be grouped into three broad categories: success, choice, and control. In other words, self-determination is either: (1) succeeding and experiencing personal success, (2) making and having choices, or (3) exerting and being in control. None of these perspectives, when viewed alone, presents a satisfactory picture of self-determination as it applies to students with severe disabilities. Rather, the integration of these three points of view provides a compelling rationale for parents and practitioners to support and facilitate self-determination. When considered together, these multiple perspectives can generate more positive expectations of children and youth with severe disabilities. Conversely, the adoption of only one point of view on self-determination could result in the creation of barriers that limit or prevent it.

The success point of view on self-determination emphasizes autonomy, self-awareness, self-regulation, and accomplishment. From this perspective, an individual cannot be considered to be self-determined (or exhibit self-determined behaviors) unless he or she:

1. is autonomous, that is, acts independently of others, free of unnecessary or excessive external influence;
2. is self-aware, that is, has developed considerable knowledge about his or her strengths and limitations and how his or her actions and inactions affect others;
3. can self-regulate, that is, possesses the ability to assess the demands of social and physical environments and choose responses appropriate to the setting or situation; and,
4. can accomplish goals, that is, successfully applies a variety of skills over time to achieve long-range outcomes that are personally defined.

Given that many individuals with severe disabilities require extensive and even pervasive support to function, one could interpret the success point of view to mean that there is little or no potential for such persons to become self-determined. Without the expectation that students can acquire the skills needed to develop and practice self-determination, it is unlikely that the experiences and opportunities needed to do so would be provided to them.

The primary element of the choice point of view on self-determination is choice. While it is certainly true that choice is a critical feature in educational programs that promote self-determination (choice will be discussed in more detail later in the entry),

many researchers caution that misinterpretations regarding choice can create significant barriers. First of all, the terms *choice* and *self-determination* are not synonymous. Simply providing opportunities for a student or adult to make choices does not mean that person is or will become self-determined. Secondly, choice (and self-determination for that matter) is often associated with the concept of personal rights and freedom. This is sometimes interpreted to mean that an individual has *carte blanche* to do or not do whatever he or she pleases, even when such action or inaction could have detrimental effects to health, safety, personal growth, or dignity. This is not self-determination; in fact, such practices are condemned in the literature as abusive, neglectful, and unethical. Finally, parents and educators who believe that individuals with severe disabilities are incapable of making good choices about their lives may reject self-determination when it is presented solely from the choice point of view. They may associate choice with risk for potential injury, victimization, or harm. This association can present a significant barrier to self-determination. Children, adolescents, and even adults with severe disabilities could experience restrictions imposed by caring but overly protective family members, teachers, and service providers who may intentionally limit the kind and number of choices an individual is permitted to make because of concerns for health, safety, and personal well being.

Finally, self-determination is often described from a control point of view, that is, the exertion of personal control over day-to-day and major life decisions and events. This perspective can evoke some of the same concerns as the success and choice points of view. If one interprets control to mean *total* control, it is relatively easy to dismiss self-determination as a viable outcome for individuals with severe disabilities. The word *control* has many negative connotations. One who associates control with manipulation, for example, may reject self-determination because of fears it will encourage or attempt to legitimize undesirable behavior.

As mentioned previously, some of the literature on self-determination presents an all-or-nothing perspective; that is, an individual cannot be said to be self-determined unless able to independently apply all of the various skill components of self-determination to produce personal outcomes that are both positive and socially acceptable. This view precludes the inclusion of many people with severe disabilities and most individuals with significant cognitive disabilities among the ranks of the self-determined. However, there is an ample body of empirical research that supports the ability of individuals with severe disabilities to influence control over their lives by communicating preferences, indicating choice, applying problem-solving approaches to influence decisionmaking, utilizing a variety of self-monitoring and self-management techniques, and setting and achieving goals.

Even so, some researchers, parents, and educational personnel continue to reject the notion of self-determination for students with severe disabilities simply because these students need some level of support to manage and participate in the myriad aspects of life. This need for support, however extensive, does not mean that individuals with severe disabilities, even those with significant cognitive disabilities, are incapable of participating in the management of their lives. Most people without disabilities, even though they are self-determined, need and accept some level of support in various aspects of life; they occasionally make mistakes or fail to learn from them; they sometimes make bad choices and decisions; and from time to time, they may flounder in the pursuit of an important personal goal. The skills and opportunities needed for self-determination are highly relevant and necessary in today's society. It is more likely that these important skills will be included and rigorously pursued as part of students' educational programs when parents and educators accept the notion that students with severe disabilities can become self-determined.

STRATEGIES FOR ASSESSING, TEACHING, AND SUPPORTING SELF-DETERMINATION

Individuals with severe disabilities can exercise self-determination. In order to do so, they need to have skills, opportunities, and appropriate support. Individual IEPs should include goals and objectives aimed at teaching skills needed for self-determination. Ample opportunities to use the skills needed for self-determination should be embedded in the curriculum and routines in the home and community.

Assessment Related to Self-Determination

Educational personnel must conduct assessments prior to the identification of educational goals relative to the development or improvement of self-determined skills and behaviors. The information that is needed is determined on an individual basis. Typically, assessment addresses abilities in communication and the expression of choice, the level of self-determination skills, and preferences.

Educators can use commercially produced or teacher-developed assessments to measure the various skills associated with self-determination. Though formal published assessments have primarily been designed for use with students with mild disabilities, they have been successfully adapted for use with students who have more significant disabilities. Many of these products are associated with curriculum packages in self-determination and preparation for transition; these can also be adapted.

Teacher-made assessment tools include checklists, questionnaires, and surveys that the teacher may use to organize observations regarding a student's current abilities or to obtain information directly from the student, family members, educational personnel, or others who know the student well.

One of the primary purposes of focusing on self-determination is to help the student attain a good quality of life that reflects personal lifestyle preferences regarding people, places, activities, and things, among others. Individual preference assessment is a valuable tool in promoting self-determination. For students with the most severe disabilities, it is crucial to also assess their ability to communicate their preferences and dislikes. Once preferences are known, parents and school personnel can provide regular access to them; likewise, they can help control the student's exposure to things not liked, thus increasing the student's personal pleasure and satisfaction.

Preference assessments are crucial in planning educational programs that promote self-determination. In order to be individually relevant, instructional goals and methods used for students with severe disabilities should reflect their preferences. Incorporating individual preferences into instruction in choice making, problem solving, and decisionmaking provides context for the student and has been shown to increase motivation. Teachers can arrange for more meaningful and frequent opportunities for students to generalize skills when they know with whom, where, when, and under what conditions students are more likely to engage in various activities.

Though there are formal assessments that inventory the known preferences of students with severe disabilities, these can be of limited use if the student has not had access or the opportunity to experience a wide array of activities, materials, settings, and experiences, or if the student lacks any skills that might have been needed in those experiences. Thus, assessment to identify preferences must also consider and document these factors. If it has been determined that a student has had limited exposure, or seems to have developed a very limited number of preferences, the student's individual educational program should include the systematic introduction and assessment of preferences for new opportunities across multiple conditions. It is also important to determine if a student's dislike or ambivalence is related to skill deficits. Teaching general skills is just as important as teaching those needed for self-determination.

Consideration of the student's mode of communication is important when planning to promote and support self-determination. For students who do not have access to or use an alternative or augmentative form of communication, educational personnel must be attuned to and learn how to interpret other communicative expressions. For example, one can learn to interpret nonverbal communication, such as vocalizations, gestures, facial expressions, body language, level of energy, visual regard, or behavior excesses or deficits as indicators of preference or dislike. For students whose impairments significantly impede discernable communication, educational personnel will need to spend significantly more time with the person to determine the subtle ways in which the individual may be expressing preferences.

Getting to know and developing a deeper understanding of the student as a person is an extremely valuable outcome that educational personnel should pursue. Person-centered planning provides one of the most powerful, enjoyable, and rewarding ways in which to accomplish this. Person-centered planning is a storied approach to understanding the student and articulating individual circumstances and personal perspective. Conducted in a gathering of people who know and care about the student, person-centered planning includes the student's family, friends, edu-

cational personnel, and any others who might contribute to the process.

Person-centered planning provides a powerful tool for helping to identify preferences. In addition to identifying known likes and dislikes regarding activities, tasks, materials, settings, and events, person-centered approaches attempt to identify preferences (and potential preferences) for people, daily routines, communication, and interaction. Because it relies on illustrative vignettes and graphics to share and record information, and avoids jargon and professional language, person-centered planning supports the active involvement of students with severe disabilities in educational decisionmaking and planning. Rather than emphasize skill deficits and instructional needs, person-centered planning approaches aid in the identification of experiences and contexts that will help enrich the student's life. Intended outcomes of person-centered planning include helping the student to (1) develop and deepen relationships, (2) increase meaningful community participation, (3) assume valued roles and responsibilities, (4) increase personal competence, and (5) expand choice and control.

Teaching and Supporting Choice Making

The term *choice* has many definitions and (as discussed earlier) connotations. Thus, one must apply multiple perspectives when considering the importance of choice for children and youth with severe disabilities.

Choice is the act of choosing. In order to choose, one must have both the ability and opportunity to do so. Learning how to make choices is important and will usually need to be taught to children with severe disabilities. Of equal importance is the assurance that once individuals are taught to make and express their choices, those choices will be honored (within reason). This also implies that students should be permitted to choose whether they want to participate in or terminate an activity, as is appropriate to the student's age group, the activity, and the circumstances.

A choice can also be described as an option, that is, the right or freedom to choose. Rather than having choices made for them, as is often the case, children and youth with severe disabilities should regularly make choices that are developmentally appropriate for their chronological age. Such experiences are crucial to the development of those self-determined behaviors needed for transition planning and adult life. Preschool-age children regularly make a variety of choices on a daily basis; however, their choice making is carefully monitored and controlled by adults. In later childhood, adult control gradually gives way to guidance and support. Once students reach elementary school, they begin to experience situations that involve some degree of problem solving in making their choices. By middle school, students are able to identify goals and develop action plans to achieve them. Once students reach adolescence, their choice-making skills have evolved to include the achievement of more complex, long-range goals and the ability to monitor, evaluate, and change plans as is needed.

Choice also refers to a sufficient variety or an array from which to choose. This suggests that children with severe disabilities should be regularly exposed to and experience a variety of activities and settings that are stimulating, interesting, and shared by others of the same chronological age who do not have disabilities. Specialized, segregated educational settings and classrooms often do not provide such opportunities.

A choice is also something that is chosen. Most often, those things chosen in inclusive settings will differ in kind and degree from those chosen in self-contained special education classrooms. Thus, access to inclusive settings will provide additional opportunities for students with severe disabilities to further develop abilities in choice making that are critical to self-determination.

Finally, choice refers to care in selecting. This means that students with severe disabilities will require instruction and a sufficient number and variety of experiences in order to learn to consider alternatives as well as any consequences of the choice and choices that are being made.

Instructional Considerations

It is imperative that educational programs for students with severe disabilities address self-determination. The specific skills needed for self-determination must be taught and opportunities to use them must be provided on a regular basis. Skills to be taught include choice making, decisionmaking, problem solving, goal setting, and self-management. Students should learn to use these skills to monitor and evaluate their circumstances and performance, and take appropriate action if necessary.

Students must also be provided with opportunities to exercise self-determination. This means that students should have direct input into what it is they will learn and how they will learn it. They should be actively involved in the development and coordination of their IEP goals and objectives. They should be supported in participating in and contributing to the IEP process.

Students with severe disabilities must experience frequent and sustained successes and learn to be less reliant on others. This means that instructional goals must be tailored to the specific needs, circumstances, interests, and desires of each individual student. Teachers must use empirically validated instructional methods that promote skill acquisition, fluency, and generalization. Because students' participation in inclusive settings is critical to the development of self-determining behaviors, special and general educators should collaborate to ensure that students have opportunities to learn and use self-determination and choice.

SELF-DETERMINATION AND SYSTEMS CHANGE

The term *self-determination* is also being used to describe systems change efforts to reform community-based supports and services for children and adults with severe disabilities. The current system is tied to eligibility, which is based on the kind and degree of disability. Such a focus has created a system that, for the most part, is not responsive to individual needs and preferences. This is because most services are congregate, that is, they consist of group living, work, and recreational arrangements. An eligible person may only access what is available; from that person's perspective, what is available may not be suitable. Because the current system funds programs and not individuals, the individual may be forced to make a take-it-or-leave-it decision. While this description presents a worst-case scenario, it is the prevailing reality for most people with severe disabilities in the United States.

Under a self-determination model of service delivery, individuals with disabilities (and their families) will be the primary decisionmakers in the management of their lives, the services and supports they need and want, and the public funds available to them. This will create more control and ultimately more choice for individuals with severe disabilities and their families, as they will be able to look beyond the existing service-provider system for support. In turn, service providers will become more flexible and responsive to consumer demands as they compete for consumer dollars.

Steven R. Lyon, Becky A. Knickelbein, and Paula J. Wolf

TRANSITION FROM SCHOOL

Transition is and should be the final chapter in a child's formal preparation for adult life; the final stage of preparation for community membership and the world of work. Unfortunately, however, transition is often one of the most difficult times in the life of a family with a child with severe disabilities. There are a number of reasons why this period is so often stressful for the family and for the child. First and foremost is the fact that completion of school means the end of the mandated public-school entitlement. With the early-intervention mandate, most children with severe disabilities have been eligible for educational services from the age of three years through the age of twenty-one in most states. Under federal legislation the right to a free appropriate public education is guaranteed and the rights of parents are protected by due process. Although most states do have adult services available to eligible youths who have left school, these programs are not mandated by law. As a result many families find that needed services are not available. Traditionally, adult services programs are often underfunded, resulting in wait lists.

Another challenge faced by families of youth with severe disabilities in transition is the difficulty they experience in learning and navigating the adult services system. After eighteen years of dealing with the public schools, with one set of rules, regulations, and nomenclature, parents are faced with having to learn how to access a variety of different agencies, each with their own eligibility, terminology, and services. Additionally, in many communities, adult services programs are administered by different individuals in different offices that have different geographic jurisdictions.

Even when families are able to figure out all of the complexities involved in identifying agencies, establishing eligibility, and deciding on the types of services and supports their child needs, they may find that the preferred services are not available. A major problem with the current adult services system is that in many states large proportions of local and state resources are used to continue supporting outdated segregated service models such as sheltered workshops, adult day programs, and segregated living arrangements. As a result, insufficient resources are available for more contemporary service models such as supported employment or independent living.

The difficulties that youth with severe disabilities and their families experience have been well documented (Lou Harris and Associates 1994) and consistently showed a rather bleak outlook for these youth as they approach adulthood:

1. Limited student/parent participation/leadership in transition planning;
2. Unclear/undeveloped visions for post-school adult community membership;
3. Lack of functional skills related to the demands of adult community life;
4. Insufficient social skills, relationships, and support networks;
5. Frequent physical and social isolation and segregation from mainstream community life;
6. Large-scale unemployment, underemployment, low-status employment, and job instability;
7. High rates of referral, placement, and long-term maintenance in workshops and developmental programs.

These outcomes indicated that even through a free appropriate education has been mandated since the mid-1970s, many students were not leaving school with the preparation necessary to become integrated into the community as adults.

FEDERAL LEADERSHIP AND THE TRANSITION MANDATE

In the face of these data things began to change under the Reagan administration with leadership from Madelyn Will, then assistant secretary of education and the parent of a child with mental retardation. Legislation was enacted by congress providing for research, model program development, and state-wide systems change related to public-school transition services. Several different groups of researchers under the leadership of Paul Wehman at Virginia Commonwealth University; Tom Belamy at the University of Oregon; and Frank Rusch at the University of Illinois were instrumental in conducting research on transition, developing and validating effective transition models and practices, and disseminating their findings to the public and to congress. The *Individuals With Disabilities Education Act* (1990) established "transition planning" as a mandated part of the IEP. Will defined transition as follows:

> Transition from school to working life is an outcome-oriented process encompassing a broad array of services that lead to employment. Transition is a period that includes high school, the point of graduation, additional post-secondary education or adult services, and initial years of employment. . . . The transition from school to work and adult life requires sound preparation in the secondary school, adequate support at the point of school leaving, and secure opportunities and services, if needed, in adult situations.

As can be seen from this definition, transition was conceptualized early on as a broad range of services and supports covering an extended period of time. Transition came to be understood as a process, beginning in the high school years and continuing past graduation thus providing a bridge to adulthood. Transition may be seen as consisting of three different periods: (1) the time leading up to transition (age fourteen to eighteen), (2) the time period during transition (age eighteen to twenty-one), and (3) the time period after transition from school (age twenty-one and over). During the time period leading to transition the focus of the child's program should be balanced between being included as a full member of middle and high school classrooms and school activities, and being provided whatever other instruction on functional life skills is determined to be needed that cannot be provided within certain academic classes. During the actual transition period, and depending upon the preferences of the child and parents, community involvement and exposure should be intensified. This could involve regular off-campus trips for various instructional or related purposes. Some school districts have even developed temporary living arrangements in the

community where students spend periods of time with school district personnel learning to live in and manage their own homes. After transition from school is also a period of adjustment for the students and family. This is a time when any needed long-term follow-up services (typically to support employment or community living) need to be fully secured and stabilized. One issue that arises for many families after their children begin employment is how to negotiate the social security system. Another major decision that many families face after their children leave school is whether they will remain living at home or consider moving into some type of independent/supported living arrangement. These and other types of post-school challenges mean that many youth with severe disabilities and their families will continue to need supports and services well beyond the school years.

TRANSITION PLANNING

When the *Individuals with Disabilities Education Act* was passed in 1990 new regulations were added that required transition planning for all eligible students beginning at the age of fourteen. The following definition is part of the law:

> The term "Transition Services" means a coordinated set of activities for a student, designed with an outcome-oriented process, which promote movement from school to post-secondary activities, including post-secondary education, vocational training, integrated employment (including supported employment), continuing and adult education, adult services, independent living or community participation. The coordinated set of activities shall be based upon the individual student's need, taking into account the student's preferences and interests, and includes instruction, related services, community experiences, the development of employment and other post-school adult living objectives, and, when appropriate, acquisition of daily living skills and functional vocation evaluation. (Sec. 602 [30])

Under these regulations school districts are required to include in the IEP, when the child is fourteen, a description of the type of curriculum the child will be studying for the remainder of high school. This has the effect of bringing together the family and school to begin a discussion about the child's future. Sometimes these discussions follow a particular personal planning model or format (such as Maps, Path, or Personal Futures Planning). At this stage, well before the child leaves school, it is important that the parents, child, and teachers begin to develop ideas about the child's future adult life and to plan for the educational activities that will prepare the child. For many families it takes a long time and many different experiences in order to arrive at a plan for transition to adulthood that is suitable, realistic, and attainable.

During the time the child is fourteen to eighteen years old, a major point of emphasis for transition planning is career development, also a long-term process. For students with severe disabilities career development is more challenging because students do not benefit from traditional career counseling provided to general education students (most students with severe disabilities do not read or write and are essentially unable to engage in discussions of abstract concepts).

Career development for students with severe disabilities should involve a series of more concrete and functional activities and experiences, organized and arranged to result in the child leaving school with a clear path toward employment. Parents should be closely involved with the program throughout the school years so that at the time of transition they will have developed positive and realistic expectations for their child's future. Along the way, efforts should be made by the school to provide various career awareness activities, for the student as well as the parents. It is also important that the child be included with and has opportunities for interaction with nondisabled peers.

This is vitally important since we know from a plethora of research on the employment of people with disabilities that their inability to maintain employment is most often the result of their inability to get along socially, rather than their inability to learn the work. Along with learning social skills, students' curricula should be grounded in important and functional skills, based upon real life expectations and taught in practical ways.

Part of the instruction transition-age students receive should be conducted off the school campus in actual community settings, referred to in the literature as community-based instruction (CBI). Teachers select sites based on the child's IEP goals; conduct a thorough analysis of those sites, including an inventory of activities and tasks performed there; bring the child to the site and perform an in-vivo assessment; develop an instructional plan based upon a discrepancy analysis (between the child's performance level and that expected in the norm); and subsequently do individual instruction with the child at the site until the targeted skills are learned or adapted. CBI could involve a number of skills domains including leisure/recreation, shopping, or vocational or job skills. Ideally, academic skills such as literacy and mathematics are integrated into the instructional routines and tasks to make them functional.

As the child approaches school exiting age, which is twenty-one in most states, extended training in a variety of work settings is conducted. Through a process of "rotational job sampling" students are exposed to a range of job types and work settings until a suitable potential career direction is identified. Under ideal circumstances the local vocational rehabilitation agency would be brought in to work with the child, family, and teacher while the child is still in school. Adult-agency personnel would assume responsibility for additional training and extended support in a paid job and the child would transition from school, be employed, and have the support of an adult service agency.

In addition to career development there are other important areas of transition planning, services, and support including continuing or adult education, community living, community leisure and recreation, and accessing other types of health or social services. The IEP team, with the assistance of relevant other outside agencies and with participation of the child and family, works to identify and secure the needed services and supports prior to the time the child exits school.

In order for the transition planning and services to be effective, parents and the student should be involved directly. Additionally, longitudinal efforts should be made to teach the child choice making, self-determination, and self-advocacy skills so that these skills may be used during transition and beyond, into adulthood.

Steven R. Lyon, Becky A. Knickelbein, and Paula J. Wolf

Beyond School—Community Living and Employment

Upon exiting secondary school, which generally occurs around the age of twenty-one, most young adults with severe disabilities will continue to require support and services throughout their lives. Supports may be necessary to assure health, safety, and well being, and to facilitate meaningful participation in adult life in the community. Supports can take many forms and may be available from a variety of sources.

Supports may be formal, provided systematically after careful planning, forethought, and training. They may be informal, that is, casual, spontaneous, or uncomplicated. Supports may be provided by service agencies and organizations, or by friends, family members, neighbors, co-workers, and acquaintances. Supports may require the use of specialized equipment, intervention programs, and expertise, or, they may require nothing more than the use of an ordinary, everyday object, spending a little extra time with someone, or the use of some common sense. Members of their families need support as well.

Regardless of the kind and degree of supports that are provided or who provides them, supports to adults with severe disabilities should help them assume adult roles and responsibilities and should promote their status (and the recognition of that status) as participating and contributing members of the community.

Adult Services

The formalized system of community-based supports for people with developmental and severe disabilities is referred to as adult services. These services are generally provided by public-sector, nonprofit, or for-profit agencies and organizations, and sometimes by individual entrepreneurs. Adult services include a variety of individual and group support or service models in housing, employment, transportation, personal assistance, leisure/recreation, and community participation.

Community-based adult services for individuals with severe disabilities began in the United States following the end of World War II, when the pre-dominant service model was institutional care. For the adults who remained in the community with their families, there were virtually no services available. The parents of these adult children formed advocacy organizations, such as The National Association for Retarded Children (now known as The Arc) and United Cerebral Palsy, which in turn developed sheltered workshops, day activity centers, and recreational programs.

In the 1970s, large numbers of institutionalized adults and children moved back to their communities of origin, in part because of growing concerns about the quality and appropriateness of institutional care. The small network of community-based vocational and day programs experienced tremendous growth as it accommodated individuals arriving from the institutions. Existing organizations expanded the scope of their programs to provide residential services; many new agencies were created for this purpose as well. As institutions continued to draw heavy criticism, attention began to focus on the benefits of community placements. Even though the results of comparison studies were inconclusive, the superiority of community-living arrangements over institutions became widely accepted.

As the adult system grew over the next twenty years, so did concerns about the services provided by it. Although community residential, vocational, and day services were generally considered to be preferable to institutional care, research conducted to measure consumer satisfaction consistently found that users of community-based services expressed dissatisfaction with their lives. Outcome and efficacy studies of group homes, workshops, and day treatment centers yielded some problematic results (Bellamy et al. 1986; Kishi et al. 1988). Though community-based services were seemingly free of the abuse, neglect, and poor living conditions that had been associated with some institutions, studies indicated that community programs were isolating and ineffective.

For example, consumers attending sheltered workshops and work activity centers rarely moved on to real employment. Neither did they experience improvement in job and work-related skills. Workshop participants were paid subminimum wages based on individual productivity; some earned less than one dollar per week. Many vocational and day-program service users had not chosen to attend these programs—their participation was mandatory as per local policy or state regulations. This scenario does not depict circumstances that are isolated to some provincial or economically depressed locale, but rather, illustrates the general state of affairs in vocational and day programming for individuals with severe disabilities across the nation at that time.

The majority of individuals attending vocational and day programs lived in group homes. Consequently, they lived with the same people with whom they worked, and they recreated with the same people with whom they lived and worked. They regularly shared many other life routines and events such as attending church services, celebrating holidays, shopping, and going out to eat with the same people with whom they lived, worked, and recreated, day in and day out. Again, these circumstances were not atypical.

The preceding descriptions led to some disturbing conclusions. Though many adults with severe disabilities were living in the community, they were not necessarily a part of the community. They were experiencing a group life, based on the perceived needs of a collective population (i.e., people living in the group home, adults with severe disabilities), instead of one in which they were able to exercise control over day-to-day and significant life events that were reflective of their own preferences and desires. The direction of their group lives appeared to be both influenced and limited by prevailing beliefs and expectations about people with severe disabilities and what they can accomplish.

CHANGING BELIEFS ABOUT DISABILITY

New ways of thinking about people with disabilities began to emerge that challenged the way adult services were conceptualized and provided. People with disabilities can be viewed from a person-centered perspective, that is, they are people first and it is important to get to know and understand each of them as individuals. The primary concern should not be on disability; this tends to connote that there is something wrong that needs to be fixed. Of primary interest should be discovering and appreciating the uniqueness of each person; this tends to draw attention to what people have in common with one another and what they can do. The focus on disability

separates and isolates people with disabilities; the focus on the person brings people together.

This does not mean that disability is unimportant or that it should be overlooked. Disability is secondary to the person; it does not define who she or he is as a human being. The person is not the problem. Instead, attitudes and misconceptions about disability (and people with disabilities) can create barriers to their acceptance and participation as members of the adult community. Low expectations can limit the opportunities that are afforded to them and prevent them from exercising control over their lives. Diminished opportunity and lack of control limit personal growth, which negatively affects competence and function. A vicious cycle ensues. If one believes that the negative effects of disability can be attributed to the interaction between the individual and the physical or social environment, it stands to reason that removal of those barriers can have a positive affect on the capacity of the individual.

These new ways of thinking drove two different kinds of change in the adult service system. Some people who shared this positive, capacity-focused view began to think about how changes to the organizational structures of adult service agencies could eliminate the separation and isolation of people with disabilities and contribute to more meaningful lives for them. From this emerged person-centered planning.

Others with this same perspective began to think about totally new kinds of services that could more fully support people with significant disabilities as competent, contributing members of the adult community. Soon new models and approaches began to appear, such as supported employment and supported living.

PERSON-CENTERED PLANNING

A central premise of person-centered planning is the expectation that change will occur, not to the individual, but in the systems and processes supporting the individual, so that meaningful lifestyle change occurs for the person. Person-centered processes seek to develop a shared understanding of the person, framed from a capacity perspective. This means that those who care about and provide services to the person strive to discover his/her strengths, abilities, gifts and talents, and those positive characteristics that draw others. Personal deficits and differences are not the focus of interest; intervention is not the intended outcome. Rather, person-centered approaches seek to develop an understanding and appreciation of the person; identify what may be missing in the person's life; and help the person identify how she/he might want to live, work, or may want out of life—then commit to action to help the person attain it in ways that are meaningful and satisfying to the person. Major outcomes of person-centered approaches are framed in terms of helping people to develop and expand reciprocal relationships and personal networks; have more opportunities to make choices and exercise control in their lives; assume valued roles in the family, workplace, school, and community; demonstrate competence; assume valued roles and responsibilities; increase community participation; and be recognized and respected. A change in any one of these areas can dramatically improve a person's life.

There are many different person-centered planning approaches available. They can be used for many different purposes, for example, to help a person make a change in his/her life; to help a person achieve a dream or an important goal; to explore why a person is experiencing behavioral difficulties; to help determine what kinds of supports a person might need, and so on.

OPTIONS FOR SUPPORT AND SERVICE DELIVERY

The emergence of two new models of service delivery, supported employment and supported living, are based in one simple idea: instead of placing people in specialized residential and vocational programs and facilities, provide them with supports and services that are relevant to their individual needs, so they can have real jobs and live in real homes (typical living and housing arrangements in the community). Take the service (or more appropriately, the support) to the person, rather than take the person to the service (or more accurately, the program). The following are very powerful but underutilized ways of promoting membership in the community.

Supported Living

Until recently, the alternatives available to adults with severe disabilities who wanted or needed to live in the community were very limited. Group home arrangements were and continue to be the prevailing residential option. They vary in size, accommodating two to fifteen persons. Group homes generally provide the advantage of twenty-four-hour supervision, and they are a moderately inexpensive form of housing. But as discussed earlier, group homes place limitations on one's choice, control, and privacy.

Supported living services provide a variety of supports to individuals living in the community. Supported living is not a residential or housing program; it provides personalized support needed by an individual in order to live in his/her own home or apartment. Funding for residential and supported living services is totally separate, thus allowing for a flexible array of housing and support options. Consumers can choose where and in what kind of home to live. If they prefer to live with others, it can be with people whom they have chosen to share their living quarters. Supported living services are designed on an individual basis. The kind of services and the number of hours of service provision vary for each individual. Some of the services available in supported living arrangements include attendant care, homemaker services, transportation, and assistance in connecting with the community.

People utilizing supported living services have more choice and control over their own lives than do those living in group homes. They can make and keep their own schedules, determine daily routines, and choose the kinds of activities in which they engage. They have control over who will live and work in their home. As their needs or preferences change over time, so can the type and intensity of the supports provided.

Supported Employment

Supported employment is competitive employment in an integrated employment setting for individuals with severe disabilities who, because of the severity of their disability, need some type of ongoing support and services to successfully perform and maintain their job. Supported employment reflects the assumption that skills are more readily acquired in the actual settings in which they are to be used. Therefore, supported employees are provided on-the-job training by fellow employees, or, as most often is the case, by professional job coaches.

There are four separate components of supported employment: individual assessment, job development, on-the-job training, and ongoing follow-up and support. The purpose of assessment is to ascertain the individual's strengths, abilities, aspirations, and preferences, and the conditions under which he or she is most successful. While traditional vocational assessment has not proven to be useful for people with severe disabilities, person-centered planning processes are an effective means of gathering and organizing the needed information. Since many individuals with severe disabilities have had limited exposure to the kinds of job and working conditions available, assessment may include on-the-job work exploration activities, during which the prospective employee can learn about the responsibilities and working conditions of various jobs, either by observing or trying them out in the workplace.

During the job-development phase, the information that has been gathered about individual interests and characteristics is carefully matched to the demands, conditions, and culture of a particular job. This may entail negotiating with employers to create or modify a position to match an individual's personal characteristics and situation, or simply helping the individual procure an existing job that matches the identified criteria.

Once a job has been procured, on-the-job training is provided and systematically faded as the worker learns to perform the job duties independently. Supported employees are paid the prevailing wage during their training. Once training has been completed, ongoing support is provided.

Natural Supports

To successfully perform their job duties and maintain their employment, individuals with severe disabilities will need support, either on an intermittent or regular basis. Rather than rely on intervention delivered by a job coach, it is recommended that supported employment personnel arrange for the development of natural supports. Natural supports are resources that naturally occur in the workplace (e.g., co-workers or some form of employer-provided training and assistance that is available to workers in that particular worksite or business). Natural supports also include the use of specially designed modifications or interventions that fit the physical and social context of the workplace. Additionally, natural supports can be applied to work-related activities and functions, such as getting to work, cashing one's paycheck, completing and updating employer-generated paperwork, and participating in social events associated with the workplace, among others.

Natural supports can be used successfully in any type of setting or situation when the need for ongoing support exists or is anticipated. Person-centered planning is an excellent tool for identifying current and future support needs and it facilitates the generation of creative and practical ways in which support can be provided.

Changes in the Lives of Adults with Severe Disabilities

Positive outcomes have been reported for people with severe disabilities who work and live in more typical settings and circumstances. There is ample research to indicate that people living in the community with supports can experience an improved quality of life across a number of areas, such as housing, economic status, and work. Families and consumers have both reported higher levels of satisfaction with services, and feel these approaches are beneficial because they increased family involvement and physical and psychological well being. Consumers have reported higher levels of lifestyle satisfaction and self-determination, as such arrangements provide many opportunities for decisionmaking and they are conducive to the exercise of personal choice.

Despite compelling evidence that quality of life is better for those in supported employment and typical community living-settings, the majority of people with severe disabilities continue to live and work in segregated settings.

Steven R. Lyon, Becky A. Knickelbein, and Paula J. Wolf

REFERENCES

American Speech-Language-Hearing Association. (1991) *Report: Augmentative and Alternative Communication.* ASHA, 33 (Supps.), 9.

Bambara, L., and T. Knoster. (1998) Designing positive behavior support plans. *Innovations* 13: 1–43. Monograph of the American Association on Mental Retardation.

Bartlett, L.D., G.R. Weisenstein, and S. Etscheidt. (2002) *Successful Inclusion from Educational Leaders.* Upper Saddle River, NJ: Merrill Prentice Hall.

Bellamy, G.T., L.E. Rhodes, P.E. Bourbeau, and D.M. Mank. (1986) Mental Retardation Services in Sheltered Workshops and Day Activity Programs: Consumer Benefits and Policy Alternatives. In *Competive employment issues and strategies,* ed. Frank Rusch, 257–271. Baltimore: P.H. Brookes.

Blatt, B., and F. Kaplan. (1974) *Christmas in Purgatory: A Photographic Essay on Mental Retardation.* Syracuse: Human Policy Press.

Brolin, D.E., and R.J. Loyd. (2004) *Career Development and Transition Services.* 4th ed. Upper Saddle River, NJ: Pearson Merrill Prentice Hall, 2004.

Brown, L., E. Long, A. Udvari-Solner, P. Schwartz, P. VanDeventer, C. Ahlgren, F. Johnson, L. Gruenewald, and J. Jorgensen. (1989) Should students with severe intellectual disabilities be based in regular or in special education classrooms in home schools? *The Journal of The Association for Persons with Severe Handicaps* 14, no. 1: 8–12.

Brown, L., J. Nietupski, and S. Hamre-Nietupski. (1976) Criterion of Ultimate Functioning and Public School Services for the Severely Handicapped Student. In *Hey, Don't Forget About Me: Education's Investment in the Severely, Profoundly, and Multiply Handicapped,* ed. M.A. Thomas, 2–15. Reston, VA: Council for Exceptional Children.

Carr, E.G., R.H. Horner, A.P. Turnbull, J.G. Marquis, D.M. McLaughlin, and M.L. McAtee. (1999) *Positive Behavior Support for People with Developmental Disabilities: A Research Synthesis.* Washington, DC: The American Association on Mental Retardation.

Cushing, L.S., and C.H. Kennedy. (1997) Academic effects of providing peer support in general education classrooms on students without disabilities. *Journal of Applied Behavior Analysis* 30: 139–152.

Donnellan, A.M., G.W. LaVigna, N. Negri-Shoultz, and Fassbender, L.L. (1988) *Progress without Punishment: Effective Approaches for Learners with Problem Behaviors.* New York: Teachers College.

Durand, V.M. (1990) *Severe Behavior Problems: A Functional Communication Training Approach.* New York: Guilford Press.

Evans, I.M., and L.H. Meyer. (1985) *An Educative Approach to Behavior Problems: A Practical Decision Model for Interventions with Severely Handicapped Learners.* Baltimore: Paul H. Brookes.

Flexer, R.W., T.J. Simmons, P. Luft, and R.M. Baer. (2001) *Transition Planning for Secondary Students with Disabilities.* Upper Saddle River, NJ: Merrill Prentice Hall.

Fullen, M. (2001) *Leading in a Culture of Change.* San Francisco: Josey-Bass.

Gaylord-Ross, R., ed. (1990) *Issues and Research in Special Education,* (Vol. 1). New York: Columbia University Teachers College Press.

Goetz, L., ed. (1998) Self-determination: Signaling a systems change? Special issue. *The Journal of the Association for Persons with Severe Handicaps* 23, no. 1.

Gray, D.B., L.A. Quatrand, and M.L. Lieberman. (1998) *Designing and Using Assistive Technology.* Baltimore: Paul H. Brookes.

Hughes, C., S.R. Copeland, C. Guth, L.L. Rung, L.B. Hwang, G. Kleeb, and M. Strong. (2001). General education students' perspectives on their involvement in a high-school peer buddy program. *Education and Training in Mental Retardation and Developmental Disabilities* 36: 343–356.

Individuals with Disabilities Education Act (IDEA). Public Law 105–17. C.F.R. 300 (1997).

Janney, R., and M.E. Snell. (2001) *Behavioral Support.* Baltimore: Paul H. Brookes.

Kerzner Lipsky, D., and A. Gartner. (1989) *Beyond Separate Education.* Baltimore: Paul H. Brookes.

———. (1997). *Inclusion and School Reform.* Baltimore: Paul H. Brookes.

Kishi, G., B. Teelucksingh, N. Zollers, S. Park-Lee, and L. Meyers, (1988) Daily decisionmaking in community residence: A social comparison of adults with and without mental retardation. *American Journal on Mental Retardation* 92: 430–435.

Koegel, L. K., R.L. Koegel, and Dunlap, eds. (1996) *Positive Behavior Support: Including People with Difficult Behavior in the Community.* Baltimore: Paul H. Brookes.

Kostelnik, M.J., ed. (1993) *Guiding Children's Social Development.* Albany, NY: Delmar.

Lou Harris and Associates. (1994) *National Organization on Disability: Harris Survey of Americans with Disability.* Washington, DC: National Organization on Disability.

Lyon, S.R., and B. L. Utley, (1997) "Issues and Strategies for Developing Inclusive Schools: Organizational Development, Curricular and Instructional Practices and Personnel Development." Proceedings of the Pittsburgh Symposium on the Renewal of Teacher Education in Boznia-Herzegovina. Pittsburgh, PA: International Institute for Studies, in Education, School of Education, University of Pittsburgh, 50.

Mastropieri, M.A., and T.E. Scruggs. (2004) *The Inclusive Classroom Strategies for Effective Instruction.* 2nd ed. Upper Saddle River, NJ: Pearson Merrill Prentice.

McDonnel, J., B. Wilcox, and M.L. Hardman. (1992) *Secondary Programs for Students with Developmental Disabilities.* Boston: Allyn and Bacon.

Meyer, L.H., H. Park, M. Grenot-Scheyer, I.S. Schwartz, and B. Haring, eds. (1998) *Making Friends.* Baltimore: Paul H. Brookes.

Mount, B. (1992) *Person-Centered Planning. Finding Directions for Change: A Sourcebook of Values, Ideals, and Methods Encouraging Person-Centered Development.* New York: Graphic Futures.

Mount, B., and K. Zwernik. (1988) *It's Never Too Early, It's Never Too Late: A Booklet about Personal Futures Planning.* St. Paul, MN: Metropolitan Council.

O'Neill, R.E., R.H. Horner, R.W. Albin, K. Storey, and J.R. Sprague. (1990) *Functional Assessment for Problem Behavior: A Practical Assessment Guide.* Sycamore, IL: Sycamore Publishing.

Pennsylvania Association for Retarded Children v. Commonwealth of Pennsylvania, 334 F. Supp. 1257 (E.D. PA. 1971).

Reichle, J., J. York, and J. Signfoos. (1991) *Implementing Augmentive and Alternative Communication.* Baltimore: Paul H. Brookes.

Ryndak, D. L., and S. Alper. (2003) *Curriculum and Instruction for Students with Significant Disabilities in Inclusive Settings.* Boston: Allyn and Bacon.

Ryndak, D.L., and D. Fisher, eds. (2003) *The Foundations of Inclusive Education.* 2nd ed. Baltimore: The Association for Persons with Severe Handicaps.

Sage, D.D., ed. (1997) *Inclusion in Secondary Schools.* Port Chester, NY: National Professional Resources.

Saleno, S.J. (2001) *Creating Inclusive Classrooms.* 4th ed. Upper Saddle River, NJ: Merrill Prentice Hall.

Schaffner, C.B., and B.E. Buswell. (1992) *Connecting Students: A Guide to Thoughtful Friendship Facilitation for Educators and Families.* Colorado Springs, CO: PEAK Parent Center, Inc.

Schalock, R. L., ed. (1990) *Quality of Life, Volume I: Application to Persons with Disabilities.* Washington, DC: American Association on Mental Retardation.

———. (1996) *Quality of Life, Volume II: Application to Persons with Disabilities.* Washington, DC: American Association on Mental Retardation.

Seligman, M. (2000) *Conducting Effective Conferences with Parents of Children with Disabilities: A Guide for Teachers.* New York: The Guildford Press.

Seligman, M., and R.B. Darling. (1997) *Ordinary Families, Special Children: A Systems Approach to Childhood Disability.*

2nd ed. New York: Guilford Press.

Selman, R. L. (1980) *Five Stages of Social Perspective-Taking: The Growth of Interpersonal Understanding, Development and Clinical Analysis.* New York: Academic Press.

Slavin, R.E. (1995). *Cooperative Learning: Theory, Research and Practice.* Boston: Allyn and Bacon.

Stainback, S., and W. Stainback. (1992) *Support Networks for Inclusive Schools.* Baltimore: Paul H. Brookes.

Technology-Related Assistance for Individuals with Disabilities Act of 1988, PL 100-407 (August 19, 1988). Title 29, U.S.C. 2201 et sey: U.S. Statutes At Large, 108,

U.S. Department of Education. (1996) *Eighteenth Annual Report to Congress on the Implementation of the Individuals with Disabilities Education Act.* Washington, DC: Publisher.

Wang, M.C. (1989) "Adaptive Instruction." In *Beyond Separate Education Quality Education for All,* 99–119. Baltimore: Paul H. Brookes.

Warren, S.F., and J. Reichle. (1992) *Causes and Effects in Communication and Language Intervention.* Baltimore: Paul H. Brookes.

Wehman, P. (1992) *Life Beyond the Classroom.* Baltimore: Paul H. Brookes.

Wehmeyer, M. L., M. Agran, and C. Hughes. (1998) *Teaching Self-Determination to Students with Disabilities: Basic Skills for Successful Transition.* Baltimore: Paul H. Brookes.

Will, M. (1984) *OSERS Program for the Transition of Youth with Disabilities: Bridges from School to Working Life.* Washington, DC: U.S. Department of Education, Office of Special Education and Rehabilitative Services.

Wolfensberger, W., ed. (1972) *The Principle of Normalization in Human Services.* Toronto: National Institute on Mental Retardation.

28

Mental Health and Education

Contemporary Western society has increasingly come to recognize that children and adolescents have psychological problems that can be treated through the methods of psychiatry and clinical psychology. As academic demands on children in schools grow, children with psychological difficulties have greater trouble in coping, and there is more pressure on parents to have their children assessed and treated by mental health professionals. Many people are ambivalent about this trend. On the one hand, we are glad to be able to identify problems and mental disorders and treat them appropriately in ways that help children perform better in their studies and avoid the dangers such as low self-esteem that come with most enduring psychological problems. Most obviously, if we have a way to help children who are suffering, we should use the advances of medical science to relieve that suffering. On the other hand, many are concerned that through labeling more children with mental disorders and putting them on medication or in some forms of therapy that have not been fully studied and proven safe and beneficial in the long term, we will be increasing levels of bureaucracy and surveillance of family life in an effort to ensure conformity to standards that are hard to measure and are of questionable value. The increasing rates of diagnosis of children and adolescents with mental disorders are sometimes interpreted as a symptom of our society's decreasing tolerance for individual difference and the normal difficulties associated with growing up.

THE RECOGNITION OF CHILDHOOD AND ADOLESCENT MENTAL DISORDERS

Parents and teachers faced with a child with emotional or behavioral problems are placed in a diffi-cult position because it is hard to know if and when to turn to the mental health profession. This difficulty is compounded by the huge variety of opinions and different and sometimes conflicting "facts" that are stated in different television programs, popular books, Internet websites, and even in literature provided by professional associations. (See the first entry for more detailed discussion of this issue.)

This introduction will spell out some of the issues relevant to negotiating the maze of information and ideas concerning child and adolescent mental disorders. The entries that follow present the most up-to-date information about current mental health practice and the data behind that practice. The entries are not exhaustive of all mental disorders and do not include all the relevant information concerning the disorders they do cover. They do cover most of the main mental disorders and they provide information that readers can use to follow up.

THE OBJECTIVITY OF DEFINING MENTAL DISORDERS

One of the central questions arising in child and adolescent psychiatry is the validity of the diagnostic categories. In short, the question is whether the criteria used by clinicians in assessing young people do in fact mark out real disorders. The fact that rates of diagnosis of many disorders have been increasing leads many to ask whether the numbers of people with those disorders are indeed increasing, or whether the increases are due to shifting definitions or interpretations of those definitions. If definitions are changing, we can ask whether those changes are scientifically and medically justified, or whether they are more related to changing social trends and values. As with many other medical disorders, most mental disorders are not diagnosed through laboratory tests but rather through signs and symptoms associated with the disorders. For mental disorders, the criteria used are mainly the behavior, emotions, and reported thoughts and feelings of the patient. While there is a good deal of agreement these days among clinicians about when a person qualifies for a diagnosis of a mental disorder, and modern diagnostic criteria must be proven to be reliable before they are adopted by professional organizations, the validity of the criteria as markings of a genuine disorder is a separate issue. Some have worried that the divisions of mental disorders into different groups such as mood disorders, anxiety disorders, schizophrenia, adjustment disorders, and personality disorders is at least rather arbitrary. When using criteria for children and adolescents, there is the added complication that they are developing both physically and psychologically. Actions, thoughts and feelings that might be symptomatic of a disorder at one age may not point to a disorder in a child at a different age. Furthermore, there is considerable variability among individuals in how they go through the development process, and this too can make it more difficult to spell out with objective criteria when to diagnose a mental disorder.

The American Psychiatric Association publishes *Diagnostic and Statistical Manual of Mental Disorders,* which is now in its fourth edition (DSM-IV-TR) (APA 2000). The DSM is the document generally referred to when justifying a diagnosis, and it is the document most often used by various health management organizations and health insurance companies. It has a chapter devoted to "Disorders Usually First Diagnosed in Infancy, Childhood, or Adolescence." The diagnostic criteria for most other disorders listed in this manual make little or no distinction between the appearance of the disorder in adults and young people. Each edition includes changes to some of the descriptions and criteria of disorders; sometimes, old diagnoses are dropped from the manual, and more often, new diagnoses are added. The process by which this decision is made includes both scientific research and consultation with clinicians and other professionals. Nevertheless, not all experts believe that the DSM provides the best categorization of child and adolescent mental disorders; suggested alternatives range from slight to radical revisionings of the nature of disorders in young people. Despite the disagreements among experts, the area of child and adolescent psychology and psy-

chiatry is relatively stable and indeed resembles much of adult psychology and psychiatry. Young people with individual psychological problems that significantly interfere with their family life, peer relations, and school functioning can generally receive a diagnosis of mental disorder from a health care professional, and treatments very often center around cognitive behavioral psychotherapy, medication, and family education. Occasionally, teachers play an important role in the diagnosis and treatment of mental health problems.

THE IDEOLOGY OF CONCEPTUALIZING MENTAL DISORDERS: BRAIN DISEASES, FAMILY PATHOLOGIES, AND SOCIAL PROBLEMS

In recent decades, there has been a growing tendency to describe serious mental disorders as brain diseases. This has been partially justified by growing scientific evidence of differences in brain structure and functioning between those with and without mental disorders. However, it is important to understand that this tendency has also been driven by a wish to move away from older models of childhood mental disorders, especially popular in the 1950s and 1960s, as fundamentally psychological problems caused by inappropriate parenting or dysfunctional family dynamics. Families often experienced great shame in having a child with a mental illness, and this shame was compounded when they were led to believe that they were the cause of the illness. Advocate groups for the mentally ill such as the National Alliance for the Mentally Ill (NAMI) have stressed that families should not be blamed for the mental disorders of their children, and they have embraced the understanding of mental disorders as brain diseases. This biological framework is thought to be less stigmatizing than psychological conceptualizations of problems.

Given the stigma and shame that still comes with psychological problems, clinicians, educators, and families need to be extremely sensitive to the language that is used to describe the people with those problems. Nevertheless, it is also important that choice of language does not distort the correct scientific understanding of mental disorders. It is helpful to keep in mind that psychologists and philosophers have not found any sharp distinction between the psychological and the biological, and that the causes of most mental disorders are still in fact not well understood. While some older theories such as Freudian psychoanalysis have declined in popularity due to lack of supporting scientific evidence, and there is strong evidence for a biological and especially a genetic component, scientific psychiatry is still far away from a complete well-confirmed account of the causes of mental disorders.

Furthermore, as educators well know, there is a strong link between the psychological and academic difficulties of students and the family and social conditions in which those students live. A young person's self-esteem, ability to focus, propensity to substance abuse, ability to relate to peers, and self-motivation are strongly influenced by family, peers, and life outside of school. Many social commentators have argued that problems that are generally identified as psychological or even mental disorders have their origin in the larger social environment. To speak of these as primarily social problems is to distort their nature. It may be appropriate to nevertheless treat the affected young people with the tools of psychology and psychiatry, but we should keep in mind the underlying social factors that caused or worsened them and form social and educational policies that aim to address those factors. (It can be helpful to remember that exactly the same is true of problems that are obviously medical, such as childhood obesity and type-II diabetes.)

THE GROWTH OF CHILDHOOD MENTAL DISORDER

Child and adolescent psychiatry only really started in the twentieth century and it only became professionalized after World War II. While cases of childhood mental illness were recorded in the eighteenth and nineteenth centuries, there was little general recognition of the problem and even less readiness to treat it. It was mostly seen as a private problem to be dealt with at home (Neve and Turner 2002). Since the 1940s, the rates of diagnosis of mental disorders in young people have increased and, correspondingly, so have the rates of psychological and psychiatric treatment for those problems. One study examined community treatment data from 1987 to 1996 and found that the use of psychiatric

medication in young people has increased by two to three times (Zito et al. 2003).

INFANTS AND VERY YOUNG CHILDREN

Currently, one of the main controversies in child psychiatry is in the diagnosis of babies, infants, and very young children with mental disorders. While the rates of diagnosis for this population are still low, there is some concern about the very possibility of making a reasonable diagnosis in the very young when they are pre-linguistic or have only very limited ability to report their feelings.

PROBLEMS IN GETTING CORRECT AND APPROPRIATE TREATMENT

Given the difficulties in establishing definitive diagnoses for mental disorders in young people, it is not surprising that in everyday practice, there is considerable variation in the diagnoses that individuals can receive from different physicians. In one survey of two hundred articles on severe childhood mental illness published between 1809 and 1982, a study of the case reports showed that about a half of the children who should have been diagnosed as manic had originally received another diagnosis (R. A. Weller et al. 1986; see also E. B. Weller et al. 1995). Much of the diagnosis of young people is done not by child and adolescent psychiatrists but by general practitioners and nonspecialist psychologists, and this compounds the problem of inaccurate diagnosis. If the diagnosis is inaccurate, then it is likely that treatment will also be inappropriate.

Even when there is no dispute about the diagnosis and appropriate treatment for children and adolescents with mental disorders, families often experience difficulty in getting appropriate treatment in the United States. According to one approximation, of the estimated 42–45 million Americans who are uninsured, about 17–18 million are children (Schreter 2004, 62). Many states provide care for children with mental illnesses when their parents cannot afford treatment, but this varies from state to state. Even for those who are covered by managed care or health insurance, mental health services may be inadequately provided. One authoritative commentator has recently expressed the problem as follows:

We are now in the age of managed care. Child and adolescent mental health and child, adolescent, and adult health care are being examined in terms of non-existent standards of cost-effectiveness. Poorly designed and conducted outcome studies are used to determine cost-effectiveness. It is clear that any concern for adequate health and mental health care for children, adolescents, and adults is being replaced by a primary concern for cost containment. (Berlin 2004, 9)

Thus there are powerful reasons to be troubled about the treatment that young people receive. It is often wise for parents and guardians to engage in self-education and to fight hard to ensure that their children receive the best possible treatment. At the same time, there are dangers in parents assuming that they know more than clinicians or acting on unreliable sources of information.

TOPICS NOT INCLUDED

The entries included in this chapter, in combination with the mental disorders discussed in other chapters of this encyclopedia, cover most of the main mental health problems of children, but it is not an exhaustive list. The selection is not meant to imply that other disorders are not as important.

There are also issues facing educators and third parties about when to make attempts to intervene in families to help children or adolescents with psychological problems. Of course, it is always possible to give advice or suggestions to parents and sometimes parents will follow through on them. One of the challenges facing educators is communicating with parents about their children's mental health problems in nonjudgmental ways. Sometimes such efforts are unsuccessful. Except when young people are in danger of abuse from family members, it can be very difficult to intervene in families. Parents generally have rights to determine their children's medical care unless there is risk of severe or permanent damage. Laws vary from state to state, however, and so full discussion of this issue would take up more space than available here.

Finally, one major concern, especially for children and adolescents who have prescriptions for medication or are seeing a therapist, is finding ways to ensure that they have a positive attitude towards the treatment and are willing to keep up with it. Again, this important issue is beyond the scope of this chapter.

Christian Perring

INFORMATION SOURCES ON CHILD AND ADOLESCENT MENTAL DISORDERS

Over and over again, parents of patients come to me, a child psychiatrist, with articles that they have read, or websites that they have found that have implications for their children, whom I am evaluating or treating for psychiatric disorders.

It is wonderful and speaks well for the future of the child when parents are interested enough to educate themselves in these matters. I must say, however: *caveat emptor!* A great deal of the advice available in print and on the Internet derives from misinformation. It is usually well intended, but it is often fallacious.

As an egregious and potentially lethal example, let me take the case of an "organic" agent currently marketed with some intensity on the Internet. The ads state that this medicine is wonderful for people with "ups and downs" or mood swings. The active ingredient in this agent is lithium. Lithium continues to be perhaps the best medicine available for the treatment of people with bipolar disorder. It is a very dangerous medicine and can cause thyroid and kidney problems. Sometimes it causes severe neurological problems. The good news is that, if lithium levels and thyroid and kidney status are monitored through blood tests, the adverse effects can be largely avoided and the medicine can work extremely well. Buying this medicine from the World Wide Web and using it without careful medical monitoring could cause disaster. Giving this medicine to a child who has mood swings (as most children do) could cause horrible problems.

SYNDROMES

As one examines the literature and the Internet sites, one realizes that the parents of young patients have access to a great deal of good and bad information about psychiatric disorders. A case in point is attention deficit disorder.

Attention Deficit Hyperactivity Disorder (ADHD)

Many books and websites point out, correctly, I believe, that this disorder is over-diagnosed. The diagnosis is made by teachers, friends of the family, parents, and physicians from almost all specialties. There are, in fact, rather rigid criteria for the diagnosis of attention deficit disorder as a clinical diagnosis. Parents who are completely convinced that their child has this disorder frequently go from physician to physician until they find one who agrees. Many parents of bright children who are doing well in school will also approach physicians, believing that better attention—even though baseline attention falls within the realm of normal—will help their child achieve better.

This may represent an initial surge of a push for "designer drugs" in the new century: a desire to have drugs to make normal people happier, smarter, and more fulfilled in many areas. Christian Perring (1997) has discussed this phenomenon. Perhaps this would be well and good—though serious philosophical and ethical arguments can be constructed against it—but the stimulants can have serious adverse effects, such as poor sleep, short stature, poor appetite, and eating patterns. They are not for the faint of heart or for normal children who do not need them.

Parents who have been informed by teachers that their child should be evaluated for this disorder often seek information in the printed and electronic literature. They may find excellent resources, or they may find polemical advice with distorted data. If one has a child with true attention deficit disorder, who could be seriously helped with medication, it is unfortunate to read that the medicines are "poisons," which is certainly not the case. If one has a bright child without attention deficit disorder who is not achieving quite as well as one would hope, it is unfortunate to read that the *only* cause of such a problem is attention deficit disorder and that the child should be placed on medicine immediately: there are certainly many causes of poor school achievement.

Eating Disorders

If parents have a child who has been losing a great deal of weight, with a restricting eating disorder such as anorexia nervosa, there is a baffling array of books and electronic media advice. Some of the books suggest that parents should "stand back" and not play any role in the child's eating. (It is immensely difficult for ordinary, good parents to watch a child starve!) Other books, with equally credentialed authors, urge that parents come forth and "take charge" of the child's eating. How are parents to know the best approach? If they go to the Internet, they may find one or more of a great many "pro-Ana" sites that promote anorexia nervosa as a healthy approach to life (even though it is in fact a deadly approach to life, with the highest mortality of any psychiatric disorder).

Childhood Bipolar Disorder

A young child may be ebullient at times and more negative at other times. This is completely normal developmentally, but parents who read a lot in an effort to learn about and help their children may think that the child has bipolar disorder. Bipolar disorder does occur in children. It is also, in fact, rare in children. I have very rarely seen a case of childhood bipolar disorder where a first degree relative (often several) does not have bipolar disorder. In a typical case of true bipolar disorder, a child is morose and depressed for at least several weeks at a time, and may make statements about wanting to be dead and may even make a suicide attempt such as impulsively running in front of a truck. These periods are interspersed with periods in which the child is truly "high," ebullient, perhaps grandiose and out of touch with reality as others see it. Children with this condition usually respond well to medical treatment.

On the other hand, all children and especially young children have alterations of mood. It is very sad that normal children with mood alterations are diagnosed by some as having bipolar disorder. The medicines used to treat this disorder are complex and have a great many adverse effects. This condition is grossly over diagnosed. Sometimes, very well-meaning parents read about bipolar disorder on the Internet or in magazines or books and go from doctor to doctor until they find one who is willing to treat the child for this rare disorder. This is very unfortunate.

I recently cared for a twelve-year-old girl who did, in my opinion, have bipolar disorder. Her parents were professionals and very highly achieving people. They cared immensely for this child. Her father had read almost everything there is to read about this disorder on the Internet, and would frequently tell the child, "I've been reading about this, and it's likely that the next thing that will happen is . . . ." Usually this terrible thing would indeed happen shortly after the verbal communication. The father seemed unable to understand the role of suggestion in the progression of his child's behavior and attributed all of it to the infallibility of his Internet resources.

SEPARATING TRUTH FROM FALLACY

Part of the problem we are facing is the reification of psychiatric syndromes. Clusters of behaviors do not necessarily imply a "disease," and many psychiatrists and psychologists would agree with me. Increasingly, from relatively ill-informed media presentations, parents are diagnosing a disease and are doctor-shopping until they find someone who will agree with them. I do not blame these parents: they have identified a problem with their child and are trying hard to get help, but the help may be worse than the initial condition.

I recently saw a little girl who was mildly retarded and quite hyperactive. Her well-educated single mother had briefed herself about possibilities on several websites, and had read many books. She had taken the child to many doctors. When I hospitalized this child, she was taking nine psychotropic medications each day—stimulants, mood-stabilizers, anti-anxiety agents, antidepressants, antipsychotics, and more. Ten days later, I dismissed her from the hospital taking a stimulant drug for attention deficit disorder, which she clearly had, and nothing else. Her mother marveled at how much better she was. Most of us would be "much better" if we were not on nine heavy-duty medicines with significant adverse effects!

Very caring parents of seriously afflicted children often develop websites about the child and/or the child's condition. I recently treated a young girl with severe autism. Her mother had put together one of the best websites on this disorder that I have seen. But for every excellent website, there is one with crackpot ideas about an approach to the disorder, and it is very hard for parents to discern which is which.

RESOURCES

Before going to websites, it is usually helpful for parents to go to a good, knowledgeable doctor, and educators are often in a position to recommend doctors who are expert at different sorts of behavioral problems.

The Web itself is useful for finding doctors. "Best Doctors in America" is helpful and lists physicians based on credentials and recommendations. In most states, the state Board of Medical Practice lists physicians who are in trouble for various complaints. Again, buyer beware.

There are some excellent books and websites about childhood psychiatric disorders. These are listed in the references section of this chapter, and I comment on some of them here.

Mina Dulcan and Claudia Lizarralde (2003) have written an excellent book about medicines for parents, children, and teachers, now in its second edition. Russell Barkley has written several excellent books about disruptive behavior disorders (see Barkley 1998, 2000), and Kathleen Nadeau (1997) has written an excellent book that complements some of Barkley's writing. David Mrazek (1993) has written a parents' guide to common behavioral problems in the first twelve years of life.

There are perhaps thousands of websites regarding childhood emotional disorder; several of them can be found in the references section of this chapter. Several of these provide general information. Except for the "Dr. Bob" site, which is a fine resource, all are sites maintained by impeccable professional societies and may be relied on. While the NAMI site takes a fairly strong position that psychiatric disorder in children is biological, it provides useful advocacy information and wonderful links to relevant and well-developed sites.

Some of the sites are important because they examine the interface between education and behavioral/emotional problems. Others are written and maintained for specific syndromes. Among the best of these are those for obsessive-compulsive disorders, attention deficit hyperactivity disorder, Tourette syndrome, and childhood bipolar disorder, among others. Of these, the attention deficit disorder site provides some information on so-called adult attention deficit disorder, which may be controversial—but the childhood part of this site is generally accurate. The childhood bipolar disorder site is wonderful, since it is quite interactive and also makes the repeated point that not all mood instability in children is bipolar disorder.

Sites of local academic medical centers can be especially helpful to parents and educators. Four of the best of these are included in the references section.

A warning: websites (and books) often can get out-of-date. Information about childhood psychiatric disorders is increasing very rapidly. Users should ascertain that the sources they are using are current.

I recently cared for a seventeen-year-old girl in the hospital. She weighed sixty-two pounds. She was very ill with Anorexia Nervosa. From misinformation gleaned from several websites her parents believed she had a severe gastrointestinal disorder, which had been ruled out at four medical centers. Because of misinformation on several websites, they removed her from our medical center, although I believe we could have treated her effectively. This also occurred at the other three medical centers, which could also have treated her effectively. This is a potentially tragic situation.

I hope that educators can help parents find useful information. I hope, too, that educators will not promulgate misinformation based on their favorite websites. They have an obligation to discern knowledge that has some research base. More importantly, I hope that they can discuss syndromes with parents so that the enormous potential harm of misinformation is not spread further.

Lloyd A. Wells

THE ROLE OF FAMILY AND COMMUNITY IN TREATMENT

For many years, psychiatry was different from other specialties in a major respect: it did not have accepted somatic methods of treatment. In the twentieth century, such methods of treatment as psychosurgery and electroconvulsive therapy were introduced, but these were applicable to few patients and "the talking cure" was the predominant approach to treatment for many decades. With the introduction of lithium and chlorpromazine and, later, the tricyclic antidepressants, pharmacological therapy became part of psychiatry's arsenal. With the later introduction of many medicines with relatively minor side effects, medical treatment of many common psychiatric illnesses became possible.

Ironically, as the rest of medicine moved away from a traditional medical model of illness and embraced the biopsychosocial model of George Engel (1980), many psychiatrists embraced the older medical model. This move was greatly enhanced and reinforced by "educational" efforts of pharmaceutical companies, who manufacture the medicines, and by the insistence of many managed care companies that only pharmacological approaches would be reimbursed.

CASES

Thus, we have an ironic situation, in my view, in which many psychiatrists only do "med management" or see "med checks." (Even the language is diminishing!) Yet patients come to us with enormously complicated situations, and this reductionistic approach simply doesn't work. The following are two cases.

Case One

A Cambodian boy, fourteen years old, was presented to our child and adolescent psychiatry unit after having been brought by the police to the Emergency Room. He had purchased a gun and was in the process of shooting himself when he was apprehended, after his friends had become concerned. When I first interviewed him he was extremely depressed and told me that he was having auditory hallucinations, which told him to kill himself. He also believed that he had been "a very bad little girl" in a past life, and that his current depression was a punishment for that.

His mother was dying of cancer and was unable to come to see him. He provided a great deal of the in-home care for his mother. His father had moved his wife, the patient's mother, to Minnesota to be near her own mother. He himself worked at a job in Illinois and had to drive several hundred miles twice each week to be at his job. He was absent, because of his work, for the first two days of the patient's hospitalization.

When I finally did get to talk to the father I

learned that all of the patient's family believed in reincarnation, though the idea of expiation in this life for sins of a past life were not a part of the family's belief system. The father also believed that mental illness was a condition caused by spirit possession. He absolutely refused to have his son treated with medicine, which the boy needed, and he refused any follow-up care for the boy after discharge.

The staff of the unit and I worked very hard with the father (and the boy). We explained our very different views of mental illness to him. Over a period of three days, he became quite interested in our beliefs and agreed to a trial of medicine for his son and to outpatient appointments for him. His county's social services were able to provide some in-home care for the boy's mother, which will be ongoing. Social Services also agreed to check on the boy regularly, at home and at school. Personnel at his school had been unaware that he was so troubled and offered to help substantively.

The patient himself improved and was no longer suicidal when he left the unit after five days. But his insurance company refused to pay for the last three days of this hospitalization because its protocol insisted that such a patient should have medicine initiated on day one, and "parent teaching" completed by day two. I thought it had been quite remarkable that we achieved as much as we did by day five, but the insurance company firmly disagreed and denied any payment after the first two days.

This case is illustrative of much that happens in inpatient child and adolescent psychiatry in the United States. Had we sent the boy home after two days, he would have been no better, and his family would have been no more understanding of his plight. There would have been no community support for him.

Case Two

A fifteen-year-old girl was admitted because of major depression, for which she fulfilled diagnostic criteria. There was a strong family history of major depression on both sides of her family, with a good response to antidepressant medicines.

In addition to the family history, however, the girl was living in horrific conditions. Her mother was very ambivalent toward her. Her mother's boyfriend, who lived with the patient and her mother, was a very violent man. When he became angry with the patient, which was frequently, he did such things as beat her about the head with a telephone. Indeed, he served time in prison for assaulting the girl, but was back in the home, hitting her again, at the time she was hospitalized.

THE BIOPSYCHOSOCIAL MODEL

The biopsychosocial model of illness, proposed by George Engel many years ago, fits very well with these two cases and should be an important part of formulation in child and adolescent psychiatry. Ironically, this approach has been widely adopted in medicine and is a cornerstone of the curriculum in most medical schools. Many child and adolescent psychiatrists, however, do not use it. It argues that all illnesses—in any specialty—have biological, psychological, and social roots and sequelae, and that one must consider biological, psychological, and social factors in order to effectively treat these syndromes. This model is easily applied to both of the cases I have just described.

In the first case, biologically, one can speculate that the boy was dealing with a neurologically mediated depression. Though the biological etiology of depression has not been entirely elucidated, we know that this type of depression runs in families and likely has some genetic basis. Indeed, the boy's father told us that he had had very similar symptoms as a young man. There is some evidence to suggest that this type of depression is caused by relative deficiencies and/or excesses of certain neural transmitters in parts of the brain, though much work remains to be done.

Psychologically, the boy was dealing with his perceived need not just to care for but somehow to save his desperately ill mother and to fill his father's role in the family during the father's absence at work in a different state, many hours away. He had a strong sense of himself as a weak person and an ineffective one.

Socially, the boy was dealing with a great many issues: a move away from his childhood home, efforts to start a new school with peers who knew nothing of his culture and were often highly prejudiced, his own poor cultural fit with his very traditional family—he was caught between two cultures and didn't think he fit well in either—as well as his mother's rapidly deteriorating health and his father's absence.

As for the second case, the girl had an incredible family history of depression on her mother's side, with a great many relatives who were or had been depressed and a grandfather, aunt, and uncle who had all killed themselves. The phenomena associated with her depression are those we believe to be related to biologically mediated depressions.

Psychologically, she dealt with many issues. She had very poor self-esteem and viewed herself as a worthless person—and this view of herself preceded her depression by many years. She had come to believe that she deserved the horrific abuse meted out by her mother's boyfriend.

Socially, she was on the fringe. The family had no money and was frequently evicted from low-rent apartments. Her peer group consisted of adolescents with similar backgrounds and dilemmas and was heavily involved, as was the patient, in alcohol and drug abuse and promiscuous sexual behaviors. There were no positive adults in this girl's life.

Once one begins to formulate a case using a biopsychosocial model, it is possible to develop a rational approach to treatment using the same model.

In the case of the boy, treatment with an antidepressant medicine was highly warranted, biologically. Psychologically, he will need psychotherapy, which addresses his sense of deracination and ineffectiveness. Socially, he will benefit a great deal from county-provided case management, which will help him get to his appointments. Social Services will also provide an in-home aid to help with his mother's illness, and it will help his father try to acquire a job closer to home.

The girl's case is similar, in many ways. She is taking an antidepressant medicine. Her drug and alcohol abuse interfere with the efficacy of the medicine and may well worsen the depression, and she is getting help with that problem as well. Psychologically, she will get—and badly needs—psychotherapy over a long period, as well as family therapy with her mother and younger sister. Socially, the mother's boyfriend violated his parole by again beating the patient with a telephone and he is back in jail. If the mother opts to have him return to her home after his term is finished, the girl will be placed with a relative or in foster care. County Social Services are also sending someone to the home twice each week to supervise its safety.

MORE SUBTLE SITUATIONS

Let me present a third case. The patient is a thirteen-year-old girl who presented with a fear of being in public, especially at school. This fear is longstanding but has been getting worse. She feels harassed by a few peers at school, and many others make fun of her for her shyness and avoidance, the abruptness of some of her mannerisms and comments, as well as her poor fit with the norms of early adolescent dress and style. She saw a psychiatrist who correctly diagnosed social anxiety disorder and placed her on a medicine that is usually helpful to people with social anxiety disorder.

Nothing changed very much, and four months later the girl made a serious suicide attempt and nearly died of an acetaminophen overdose.

In our hospital unit, she was socially awkward and very bright and creative. She found it hard to conceptualize a good future.

I spent a lot of time with her parents. Her mother, too, was a very anxious person, and a highly dependent one. Her father was passive and tried to be uninvolved, often pacing the hospital hallways during visiting hours, rather than spending them with his daughter. The mother projected many of her own issues onto this girl: "She's going to have a bad marriage"; "She's going to view herself as worthless and unloved," and so on. Both parents predicted that the girl would commit suicide before she was fifteen, with the father saying, "I've just accepted it—she won't live to grow up."

The first two cases presented here demonstrated overt social problems, but this situation is more subtle and in some ways more typical. The parents are well-intended people who care for their daughter. The initial psychiatrist who saw this patient, months before her suicide attempt, did a reasonable evaluation and correctly diagnosed social anxiety disorder, but other features of her syndrome were not clear to her. The choice of medicine was reasonable, but it was not enough.

Psychologically, this girl has a very heavy load to bear, with conscious and unconscious parental expectations that grow out of their own pathologies, caring as they are.

Socially, she is an outcast at school and truly hates it in spite of her high intelligence and achievement.

A reasonable approach to this patient is to treat

her with a powerful anxiolytic medicine but also to engage the parents in their own therapies (which they have agreed to do), as well as some family therapy to include the girl. I had two lengthy and useful discussions with the patient's middle school principal, who did a thorough investigation and determined that she is in fact being bullied and harassed. The principal promises to deal with these issues definitively. This will not make school a wonderful place for the girl, but it is a start. It is particularly important to speak with parents and school officials very directly and honestly in these situations.

FRAGMENTATION OF CARE

The mental health care of children has become fragmented in the managed-care era. Even when child and adolescent psychiatrists are able to evaluate a child comprehensively, the treatment is often broken up, with a psychiatrist managing the medicine, a psychologist or social worker—or, too often, someone without credentials—managing the therapy, and county workers managing the social aspects of the case. Too frequently, these different providers do not even talk with each other about the patient and her or his progress.

To approach a child or adolescent reductionistically, or to view his or her problems as entirely biological in nature, can be very harmful practices. Even when they are not harmful, the result is to see one small part of a child's dilemma and struggle, and this is surely not satisfying to professionals who care about children.

Educators are in a unique position to observe which practitioners take a comprehensive approach to patients and which do not. Their recommendations can be extremely helpful.

Lloyd A. Wells

EATING DISORDERS IN ADOLESCENTS

In the last thirty years, eating disorders have emerged as a considerable risk to the psychological and physical health of adolescents (Lewinsohn, Striegel-Moore,

and Seeley 2000). Social and public health costs of these disorders include adverse physical consequences (Pike and Striegel-Moore 1997), emotional disturbances such as depression and anxiety (Lewinsohn et al. 2000; Rowe, Pickles, Simonoff, Bulik, and Silberg 2002), social isolation (Striegel-Moore, Seeley, and Lewinsohn 2002), relationship and family problems (Humphrey 1986; Strober, and Humphrey 1987), and difficulties in social and emotional development (Fisher et al. 1995; Striegel-Moore et al. 2003). Frequently, eating disorders develop into chronic illnesses with many patients undergoing multiple hospitalizations and long-term treatment (Kreipe and Uphoff 1992; Steiner and Lock 1998). In light of these serious consequences, it is important for educators to be able to identify students at risk for eating disorders and guide these students and their families towards appropriate treatments.

To assist teachers in this process, this entry will focus on the identification and treatment of eating disorders. After describing the signs and symptoms of eating disorders, it will address gender, developmental, and family influences that place girls at risk for an eating disorder. Moreover, the standard of care for the treatment and prevention of these disorders will be described. Specifically, this entry will explain how teachers can support their students who present with these difficulties and how they can best address these issues in prevention efforts with their students.

EATING DISORDERS: SIGNS AND SYMPTOMS

Eating disorders encompass a wide range of clinical phenomena that are classified in the American Psychiatric Association's (1994) Diagnostic and Statistical Manual–Fourth Edition (DSM-IV) into two discrete disorders, Anorexia Nervosa (AN) and Bulimia Nervosa (BN). Anorexia Nervosa is derived from *anorexia*, the Greek term for loss of appetite. However, this term is somewhat of a misnomer given that individuals with anorexia do not lack a desire to eat, but rather harbor a fear of weight gain. Nevertheless, this term does seem to be descriptive of the intense weight restriction efforts of these patients, which lead them to lose weight far beyond what is acceptable. As such, one of the chief diagnostic criteria of this disorder is the refusal to maintain weight at a minimally acceptable level or, for younger children, a failure to achieve expected weight gain. Moreover, a second criterion involves an intense fear of becoming fat. Individuals with this disorder are so preoccupied with losing weight that they often fail to see that they have gone far beyond the culturally accepted standard of thinness toward a serious state of semi-starvation. In fact, disturbance in the way in which one's body weight is perceived or the inability to perceive the seriousness of one's low body weight represents a third criterion of the disorder. Clearly, the physiological consequences of starvation can be serious and involve the disruption of puberty or regression toward a prepubertal state. This is reflected in the fourth diagnostic criterion, amenorrhea, or the loss of one's menstrual cycle. Although approximately 0.5 percent of women and girls meet the diagnostic criteria for AN, the rate may be higher for adolescent girls (Striegel-Moore and Marcus 1995). Unfortunately, given that few individuals with anorexia recognize the seriousness of their low body weight, treatment efforts with these patients tend to be exceedingly difficult.

Bulimia Nervosa is derived from the Greek term for *ox hunger* to describe the frequent episodes of binge eating in which these individuals engage. In spite of this description of overeating, the diagnostic criteria for BN shares many features with AN. In particular, similar to patients with AN, diagnostic criteria for BN involve placing an undue emphasis on weight and shape in one's self-evaluation. Individuals with BN also resemble those with anorexia in their fear of gaining weight, the level of dissatisfaction they experience with their bodies, and attempts at restrictive eating. However, for individuals with BN, periods of fasting are frequently punctuated by episodes of binge eating. According to the DSM-IV, binge eating is an episode in which a person eats more food than others would consume under similar circumstances. Individuals with Bulimia Nervosa can often consume thousands of calories in one sitting (Rosen, Leitenburg, Fisher, and Khazam 1986). However, what distinguishes a binge episode from other periods of large food consumption—such as the social eating common to high school and college students—is the feeling of a loss of control over eating. Given the value that these individuals place on thinness, to compensate for binge eating they often resort to extreme and inappropriate weight loss

measures. These compensatory behaviors represent another diagnostic criteria of the disorder and range from vomiting and abusing laxatives to intense fasting and excessive exercise. BN is more common than AN, afflicting about 1 percent of girls and women (APA 1994), and almost certainly more adolescents (Striegel-Moore and Marcus 1995).

Subthreshold eating disorders fall into the category of *eating disorder not otherwise specified* (EDNOS). Individuals with EDNOS are missing one or more of the diagnostic criteria for an eating disorder. For example, an adolescent presenting with all of the features of bulimia, yet who binge eats infrequently, would fall into this category. Another example of a patient who would fall in this category is a girl who engages in intense weight restriction to avoid gaining weight, has lost her menstrual cycle, yet does not fall below 85 percent of her expected body weight. Clearly, EDNOS includes a diverse group of patients who, because of less stringent diagnostic criteria, represent the majority of patients presenting to clinical settings (Shisslak, Crago, and Estes 1995).

GENDER, CULTURE, AND DIETING

Although the causes of eating disorders are unknown, most researchers suggest that the development of eating disorders involves a complex interplay of developmental, biological, social, and psychological factors. One of the most striking features of eating disorders is that they occur almost exclusively in girls and young women, with males representing less that 10 percent of the patients presenting in clinical settings (APA 1994). Given the disproportionate prevalence of these disorders among girls and young women, researchers have looked to gender specific influences in the development of these disorders. In particular, girls and women in Western culture are exposed to messages from peers, family, and the media about the slender ideal body and experience a great deal of pressure to conform to the culturally prescribed thin ideal (Striegel-Moore et al. 1986). Consequently, sociocultural factors have received considerable attention in the study of both body dissatisfaction and eating disorders.

As a result of these pressures to be thin, body dissatisfaction and dieting are extremely pervasive among adolescent girls. To explain the widespread nature of this problem, some theorists have referred to body dissatisfaction among adolescent girls as a "normative discontent" (Striegel-Moore et al. 1986). In fact, nearly 25 percent of nine- to fourteen-year-old girls think they are overweight, with nearly as many on a diet at any one time (Field et al. 1999). Moreover, research suggests that many adolescent girls engage in extreme and unhealthy dieting behaviors (Killen et al. 1996). In addition to dieting, 13 percent of girls engage in purging behavior to control their weight (Killen et al. 1996).

Despite the fact that preoccupation with weight and dieting are pervasive among adolescent girls, they are not a benign rite of passage. Research suggests that dieting is strongly linked to the development of both anorexia and bulimia nervosa. Although the precise relationship between dieting and the onset of eating disorders remains to be determined, dieting can have a variety of physical, cognitive, and emotional consequences that serve to perpetuate restriction and, in many cases, trigger binge eating (for a review see Heatherton and Polivy 1992; Polivy and Herman 1993).

DEVELOPMENT

Although eating disorders occur in adulthood and in rare cases childhood, they most commonly begin during adolescence (APA 1994). In fact, eating disorders most often have their onset at two points in adolescent development—early and late—periods that represent unique developmental junctures in the lives of adolescent girls (Smolak and Levine 1996). Given that eating disorders are tied more than any other psychological disorder to specific developmental periods, researchers have looked to adolescence to understand the unique factors that contribute to the development of these disorders (Smolak and Striegel-Moore 1996).

Developmental research has established that adolescence seems to be a time when girls are particularly vulnerable (Halmi, Casper, Eckert, Goldberg, and Davis 1979). During the transition to adolescence, girls experience an increased risk for depression (Nolen-Hoeksema 1994), decreased self-esteem (Byrne 2000), and increased body dissatisfaction (Thompson, Heinberg, Altabe, and Tantleff-Dunn 1999). Several theorists have suggested that adolescence includes age-specific demands that present unique challenges for girls (Hsu 1990; Smolak and

Levine 1996; Smolak and Striegel-Moore 1996). In early adolescence, girls are accommodating pubertal changes, as well as the transition to junior high school, often simultaneously. In late adolescence, girls are preparing to go to college or leave home. These challenges require girls to develop autonomy from parents and increasingly get their emotional and social needs met from peers. Most girls navigate these challenges successfully. However, some girls are unprepared to meet these challenges, placing them at risk for eating disorders.

FAMILY FACTORS

Several researchers have examined family functioning to understand the development of eating disorders. A number of studies have found that girls and women with eating disorders, compared to those in control groups, perceive less family cohesion, including less emotional support, empathy, and understanding (Calam, Waller, Slade, and Newton 1990). In addition, compared to women in control groups, those with BN perceive higher levels of conflict and hostility (Humphrey 1986; Johnson and Flach 1985). Parents of women with eating disorders also report more family conflict than parents of those without an eating disorder (Stern et al. 1989). This has been supported by observational studies of women with BN and their families (Humphrey 1989). In addition, several theorists have suggested families of patients with AN display less tolerance and support for autonomy (Bruch 1973; Minuchin, Rosman, and Baker 1978). Observational research finds support for this suggestion, finding parents of girls with AN, tending to ignore their daughter's self-expression (Humphrey 1989). Despite these findings, it is unclear whether such disruptions in family communication and support were present prior to the development of the disorder or reflect difficulties coping with a child who has a serious chronic illness.

In addition to family communication patterns and support, evidence suggests that girls and women who have a relative with anorexia nervosa are more likely to develop an eating disorder, compared to females without a relative with an eating disorder (Strober, Lampert, Morrell, Burroughs, and Jacobs 1990). In addition, maternal attitudes about weight have been found to be associated with disordered eating in adolescent girls (Pike and Rodin 1991). These findings not only suggest a biological predisposition, but also the influence of being raised in an environment that stresses the value of being thin and one that provides modeling for dieting behaviors.

TREATMENT

Few controlled treatment studies of children and adolescents with eating disorders have been conducted. For the treatment of AN, the research literature is relatively modest, offering few clear treatment directions. Nevertheless, practice guidelines for the treatment of AN generally recommend a multidisciplinary approach (American Psychiatric Association 2000b). This recommendation is due to the multifaceted origins of anorexia, as well as the very serious consequences of this disorder. Within this context, patients are typically treated by a number of professionals (e.g., individual therapist, group therapist, family therapist, psychiatrist, dietitian), who function more or less independently, and who direct their interventions toward the individual patient. For the treatment of BN, research with adults generally recommends cognitive behavior therapy (CBT) (for a review see Fairburn, Agras, and Wilson 1992). The goal of CBT is to decrease the patient's reliance on restrictive eating patterns and modify the extreme personal value they attach to an idealized body shape (Fairburn, Marcus, and Wilson 1993).

Despite the standard of care for adults with anorexia and bulimia, it is unclear whether these models can be successfully applied to the treatment of adolescents. Because few adolescent patients present for treatment on their own accord and many harbor denial about the seriousness of the problem, it is unclear whether working with the adolescent directly is beneficial. In addition, many adolescents do not have the cognitive and abstract thinking skills necessary to participate actively in therapy and to take perspective on their own thinking. Furthermore, there is little research on whether seeing a number of professionals simultaneously is necessary or even effective.

It is possible that the direct involvement of several practitioners may impede the recovery of these girls (Sim, Sadowski, Whiteside, and Wells 2004). First, the attendance of these girls at several appointments per week may interfere with normal adolescent development, reducing the time or availability to develop age-appropriate social relationships. In

addition, the involvement of several practitioners may decentralize therapeutic guidance, which can have the unintended consequence of the patient receiving contradictory advice. Disparate advice is not only frustrating to the patient and her parents, but can also be problematic when working with patients who may seize upon these inconsistencies to continue restricting eating and weight loss. Lastly, the focus of these treatments tends to be on the individual patient and treatment effectiveness is founded on the patient's motivation for change. Unfortunately, focusing on personal commitment of the patient as a requisite for success can suggest that the patient is then responsible for treatment failure. Besides being inconsistent with the widely accepted disease model of the disorder, such a presumption can have the untoward effect of influencing care providers and families to effectively give up on these patients.

As an alternative to the multidisciplinary method for the treatment of anorexia nervosa, a family-based approach has gained currency in recent years (Dare, Eisler, Russell, and Szmukler 1990; Eisler, Dare, Hodges, Russell, Dodge, and le Grange 2000; Eisler, Dare, Russell, Szmukler, le Grange, and Dodge 1997; Robin et al. 1999). This alternative approach entails a specific form of family therapy in which the family is enlisted as a resource in the treatment of the patient, and is described in a recently published treatment manual (Lock, le Grange, Agras, and Dare 2001). In this therapy, the adolescent with AN is viewed as no longer capable of making sound choices regarding her health, and thus requires help from parents to overcome the illness. Therapy involves: (1) mobilizing the family in the re-feeding of the adolescent, (2) negotiating a new pattern of family relationships, and (3) helping the family to support and nurture their daughter's adolescent development, particularly regarding autonomy. In general, this treatment has demonstrated good outcomes for adolescents with anorexia nervosa (Dare et al. 1990; Eisler et al. 2000; Eisler et al. 1997).

As many of the treatment components of this intervention seem to be relevant for adolescents with bulimia, Lock (2002) has suggested that the family can play an important role in CBT. In particular, the parents can alter the environment in the service of behavioral change. In addition, families can support and assist their child who may not have the cognitive abilities, motivation, or emotion management skills to participate actively in treatment (Lock 2002). In preliminary research, this treatment has shown promising results comparable to those expected for CBT with adults (Lock 2002).

In addition to identifying students who present with these disorders, educators can guide families to approaches that involve the family in treatment. In addition, educators can assist students by providing support and acceptance, helping them to feel comfortable in seeking help and sharing their feelings. Moreover, they can keep parents apprised of their daughter's eating behavior. To keep adolescents in school during their treatment, teachers can assist parents with meal monitoring. For example, to prevent girls in treatment from restricting in school, some families have asked a guidance counselor, school nurse, or teacher to supervise their daughter during lunchtime. This typically involves the parents sending an approved lunch to school with a list of the contents enclosed in the lunch bag. The lunch supervisor can assist the family by unpacking the student's lunch, verifying the items enclosed, and monitoring the adolescent's meal in a room free from receptacles or places where food can be hidden. Other ways that school personnel can be helpful is in staying apprised of programming limitations for girls with eating disorders such as any restrictions they may have in physical education or team sports participation.

Prevention of eating disorders in the classroom can be challenging as research has shown that prevention education programs that focus on the signs and symptoms of eating disorders can have the unintended effect of drawing ones attention to them, providing "how to" information for losing weight, and potentially glamorizing eating disorders (Mann et al. 1997). As such, educators should refrain from providing education that focuses specifically on eating disorders education. Instead, they can strive to create an environment where all students are treated equally, regardless of size, and teach respect for a diversity of body sizes and shapes. In addition, teachers should educate children about the ineffectiveness of dieting, as well as teach them to be critical consumers of media so that they can resist harmful messages. This prevention education can and should be delivered to all age groups and modified for the developmental level of the classroom.

Leslie A. Sim

MOOD DISORDERS

The American Psychiatric Association's *Diagnostic and Statistical Manual* (DSM-IV-TR) (APA 2000) splits mood disorders into different groups: Depressive Disorders, Bipolar Disorders, and then mood disorders due to general medical condition or as the effect of substance use. The depressive disorders are further divided into major depressive disorders (sometimes referred to as "clinical depression"); dysthymic disorder, which is essentially a chronically depressed mood that lasts for at least two years; and then those disorders that are "Not Otherwise Specified." Bipolar disorders are better known as forms of manic depression, and some clinicians still prefer that older label. These are divided into Bipolar I, Bipolar II, Cyclothymic Disorder, and again, those that are "Not Otherwise Specified." Bipolar I is essentially characterized by the occurrence of one or more manic episodes or what are known as "mixed episodes," a combination of both a manic episode and a major depressive episode. Bipolar II, by contrast, only requires a major depressive episode accompanied by a "hypomanic episode." A hypomanic episode is defined as "a distinct period during which there is an abnormally and persistently elevated, expansive, or irritable mood that lasts at least 4 days" (APA 2000, 365). During this period, the individual will show a number of other symptoms such as inflated self-esteem, grandiosity, decreased need for sleep, pressure of speech, flight of ideas, distractibility, or risky but pleasurable activities. Cyclothymia is characterized by "chronic, fluctuating mood disturbance involving numerous periods of hypomanic symptoms . . . and numerous periods of depressive symptoms" (APA 2000, 398). The DSM is the best source for the precise listings of the diagnostic criteria for these different disorders (APA 2000).

The DSM does not, broadly speaking, specify different sets of symptoms for children, adolescents, and adults in diagnosing mood disorders, although many clinicians have argued that these illnesses do present rather differently depending on a sufferer's age. What is clear is that mood disorders are a serious problem among children and adolescents and that they are being increasingly recognized and treated. In the United States, there is evidence that there is still significant underdiagnosis of depression. Among those whose problem has been identified, a significant proportion lack full health insurance or their managed care policies provide only minimal mental health coverage, which means that the problem is often not properly addressed. Some observers have expressed concern about the increasing use of antidepressant medication in young people—because of lack of evidence that antidepressants are an effective treatment in children, worry about the drugs' possible short- and long-term side effects, or because of a belief that using pills leaves the underlying psychological or social causes of the mood disorder unaddressed.

CRITERIA

While modern psychiatry has not achieved consensus about the causes of mental illness, it has achieved wide agreement about how to classify the major mental disorders using associated signs and symptoms. The lists of indicators provided in the DSM (APA 2000) provide the most authoritative ways of deciding whether someone has a mental disorder.

Major Depression

The essential features of major depression are similar at all ages, but there are nevertheless important variations. Clinicians generally distinguish between preadolescent or child depression on the one hand, and adolescent depression on the other.

The main criteria for a major depressive episode in children and adolescents are:

- depressed or irritable mood for most of the day, nearly every day
- markedly diminished interest in pleasure in all, or almost all, activities most of the day, nearly every day
- weight gain or significant weight loss or failure to make expected weight gain when not dieting
- insomnia or hypersomnia nearly every day
- fatigue or loss of energy nearly every day
- feelings of worthlessness or excessive or inappropriate guilt nearly every day
- diminished ability to think or concentrate, or indecisiveness, nearly every day
- recurrent thoughts of death or suicide (Adapted from APA 2000)

Preadolescent Children Diagnosing mood disorders in preadolescent children is a challenge for a number of reasons. Since young children often find it difficult to explain their emotions, mood disorders can be expressed as bodily symptoms or vague complaints about feeling unwell. There have been reports of depression in infants and preschool children, primarily characterized by a depressed look, crying, slow reactions and movements, and sleep and appetite disturbances. However, such diagnoses are somewhat controversial.

Adolescents Unsurprisingly, the symptom profile of depression in adolescents is closer to that in adults. Adolescent depression tends to be characterized by more irritable mood than depressed mood compared to adult depression.

Mania

The following are the main criteria for a manic episode for any individual, child, or adult, as given in the American Psychiatric Association's Diagnostic Manual:

1. A distinct period of abnormally and persistently elevated, expansive, or irritable mood, lasting at least 1 week (or any duration if hospitalization is necessary).
2. During the period of mood disturbance, three (or more) of the following symptoms have persisted (four if the mood is only irritable):

- inflated self-esteem or grandiosity
- decreased need for sleep
- more talkative than usual or pressure to keep talking
- flight of ideas or subjective experience that thoughts are racing or distractibility
- increase in goal-directed activity or psychomotor agitation
- excessive involvement in pleasurable activities that have a high potential for painful consequences

3. The mood disturbance is severe enough to cause marked impairment in occupational functioning or in usual social activities or relationships with others, or to necessitate hospitalization to prevent harm to self or oth-

ers, or there are psychotic features. (Adapted from APA, 2000, p. 362).

However, there can be great difficulty in assessing what counts as mania in children. Behavior that would be symptomatic of mania in adults may be within the normal range for young children, and it can be challenging to distinguish mania from other mental disorders. Children also tend to have a different symptom profile from adults; they tend to experience irritability rather than euphoria, with what are evocatively called "affective storms" and prolonged and aggressive temper outbursts, worsening of disruptive behavior, moodiness, difficulty sleeping at night, impulsivity, hyperactivity, inability to concentrate, explosive anger followed by guilt, depression, and poor school performance (E. B. Weller et al. 2004a, 415). Some preschool-age children have been diagnosed with mania when displaying explosive and unmanageable temper tantrums, sexual joking, and nightmares with violent imagery, but again, diagnosis at such a young age is controversial.

PROGNOSES

The wide agreement on the classification of mental disorders has helped researchers to collect information about the typical courses of those disorders. It is now possible to assess the likelihood of different outcomes once someone has received a particular diagnosis.

Pre-Pubertal Depression

The prospects for recovery from first-episode depression are good, but the younger a child is at the age of onset, the more serious the problem and the longer the depressive episode. Factors such as gender and class seem to make little difference to recovery. One study found that the average time for recovery in children aged eight to fourteen with major depressive disorder was within one year for 74 percent, but 33 percent had a recurrence within two years, and 72 percent had a recurrence within five years. (E. B. Weller et al. 2004a, 414).

Adolescent Depression

Adolescents with major depression have a much higher risk (two to four times) of going on to de-

velop depression when they become young adults. Adolescent depression occurs more often in individuals who also have conduct, anxiety, and substance abuse disorders.

Bipolar Disorder

The prognosis for children with bipolar disorder is somewhat bleak. The condition tends to be chronic and continuous, often characterized by rapid cycling with mixed manic states. Children with this condition tend to have fewer episodes of remission than adults (E. B. Weller et al. 2004a, 416). As they grow into adults, they are likely to experience further mood disorders.

PREVALENCE

Until the 1970s, it was thought that children and adolescents were not prone to disorders of mood (Harrington 2002, 463). It is still thought that childhood mood disorders are underdiagnosed (E. B. Weller et al. 2004a, 411). No large studies have been performed to discover the prevalence of depressive disorders in pre-pubertal children, although some have estimated that 0.3 percent of preschoolers and 1–2 percent of elementary school-age children are affected.

The rates of major depression in adolescents are higher, and are estimated to be between 2 percent and 5 percent at any particular time. One estimate is that each year, 1.3 percent of young people between fifteen and nineteen suffer from depression each year, and the lifetime prevalence rate of major depressive disorder ranges from 15 percent to 20 percent. Many surveys show that adolescent females experience depression considerably more often than males (E. B. Weller et al. 2004b, 448). Furthermore, a large proportion of adolescents suffer from "subclinical depression," in which they exhibit several symptoms of depression, but not enough to qualify for a diagnosis. Those individuals are at high risk for developing major depression (E. B. Weller et al. 2004b, 439). There is some indication that the prevalence of depressive disorders is increasing among adolescents with each passing decade, although there is debate as to how rapid the increase is (Harrington 2002, 466).

There is less information available on the prevalence

of bipolar disorder in adolescents, but it is far less common than major depression. One estimate suggests that the lifetime prevalence for high school students is about 1 percent (E. B. Weller et al. 2004b, 449).

TREATMENTS

There has been an astonishing increase in the use of antidepressant medication with children in recent years. For example, in the United States from 1996 to 1997 the number of children age five and younger taking selective serotonin reuptake inhibitor (SSRI) medications, such as Prozac, went from 8,000 to 40,000. In that time period, children from six to eighteen years old received 792,000 prescriptions for such medications (E. B. Weller et al. 2004a, 411). Despite this, there has been relatively little study of the effectiveness of psychiatric medications in treating mood disorders in children and adolescents. As Elizabeth Weller et al. (2004, 425) comment, "It should be remembered that fewer than 300 children and adolescents have been studied in well-designed double-blind, placebo controlled studies of antidepressants, whereas thousands of adults have been treated in such controlled studies." Nevertheless, there is some evidence that antidepressants can be helpful in treating depression in young people. On the other hand, there is also serious concern that some of these medications may increase the likelihood of self-destructive behavior and suicide and, in 2003, the British government withdrew authorization for most such medications for children and adolescents. In the UK, in 2003, the Government's Medicines and Healthcare Products Regulatory Agency advised, concerning most of the new antidepressants, that "the balance of risks and benefits for the treatment of major depressive disorder in under-18s is judged to be unfavourable." (Medicines and Healthcare Products Regulatory Agency 2003). In March 2004, the FDA recommended the strengthening of the warnings section with regard to antidepressant medications used for both adults and young patients (U.S. FDA 2004).

There has been more study of the efficacy of lithium carbonate, a mood stabilizer, in adolescents then in pre-pubertal children, but it has nevertheless been used in the treatment of children of all ages. A few studies have noted that it can cause cognitive impairment in some children. For those who do take lithium, studies have suggested that long-term maintenance on the medication is more effective than short-term use. (E. B. Weller 2004a, 425) There have been some studies of anticonvulsant drugs (carbamazepine, valproate) used as mood stabilizers for children and adolescents with bipolar disorder, with some indications of success, but none of them was a controlled study and so they are of limited scientific value. These medications can have significant side effects.

Some forms of psychotherapy have been found effective by clinicians for treating children and adolescents. Firm scientific evidence for its efficacy is difficult to find, partly because it is hard to provide a good control group, but there have been studies showing that children who received psychotherapy fared better than those who did not. It is important to be clear that it is possible for psychotherapy to also have negative effects, and clinicians tend to recommend forms of therapy in which the therapist is passive and waits for the child to express thoughts and feelings. There still needs to be more research on what kinds of psychotherapy are most effective for particular problems in particular populations. For mood disorders, experts recommend psycho-education, school intervention, and family treatment (E. B. Weller et al. 1995).

Christian Perring

SCHIZOPHRENIA AND THOUGHT DISORDERS

While schizophrenia is often understood among the general public to be one of the most serious mental illnesses, with symptoms thought to be allied to the popular images of "madness," there are many popular misconceptions about the nature of the disease. It should not be confused with what is often known as "multiple personality disorder" or other disorders of dissociation. As with most other mental disorders, it can be difficult to provide definitive diagnoses, and schizophrenia can be confused with bipolar disorder or pervasive developmental disorders. Furthermore, while schizophrenia is certainly a very serious and often chronically disabling disease, it is a mistake to assume that any young person diagnosed with the condition will be incapable of having a rewarding life.

For a considerable part of the twentieth century, it was often assumed that schizophrenia was related to the behavior of the affected individual's family, and parents felt a great deal of guilt and shame as a result of this. Modern psychiatry has changed considerably since then, and schizophrenia is mostly described as a disease of the brain. There have been many studies showing that genetic factors make individuals predisposed to developing the disorder, but while there has been considerable speculation and study as to why one person will develop the condition while another will not, no simple causes have so far been identified. Considering the wide variation of symptoms displayed by people with different types of schizophrenia, some theorists have argued that the condition will ultimately come to be seen as a cluster of different but related disorders.

From the 1930s up until the early 1970s, the general concept of "childhood schizophrenia" was a broad one, including not only what we now call schizophrenia and allied disorders, but also autism and other developmental disorders. It was only in the 1970s that schizophrenia in childhood was conceptualized in its current form, as continuous with the adult illness. The Diagnostic Manual DSM-IV-TR (APA 2000) draws no distinction between childhood, adolescent, and adult expressions of the illness. Nevertheless, there are some differences between the characteristic forms of the disorder depending on age.

CRITERIA

There is a great deal of variation in symptoms among those diagnosed with schizophrenia. Characteristics such as hallucinations, delusions, thought disorder, and disorganized behavior are known as the "positive symptoms," while lack of emotion, lack of communication, and lack of action are called the "negative symptoms." The positive symptoms tend to predominate during the most acute phases of the illness, while negative symptoms tend to appear at other points. It is not unusual for people with schizophrenia to have been diagnosed with other serious mental disorders such as bipolar disorder or personality disorder, either because their symptoms did not cleanly fit with one mental illness or because they had more than one disorder concurrently. The essential DSM-IV-TR criteria for schizophrenia are:

1. Characteristic symptoms include two or more of the following, each present for a significant portion of time during a one-month period (or less if successfully treated):

   - delusions
   - hallucinations
   - disorganized speech
   - grossly disorganized or catatonic behavior
   - negative symptoms, i.e., emotional flatness, lack of speech or lack of action

Note: only one of these symptoms is required if delusions are bizarre or hallucinations consist of a voice keeping up a running commentary on the person's behavior or thoughts, or two or more voices talking with each other.

2. For a significant portion of the time since the onset of the disturbance, one or more major areas of functioning such as work, relationships with others, or self-care are significantly below the level prior to the onset (or when the onset is in childhood or adolescence, failure to achieve expected levels of interpersonal, academic, or occupational achievement).
3. The signs of the disturbance are exhibited continuously for at least 6 months.
4. Some other psychotic disturbances have been ruled out as diagnoses. (Adapted from APA 2000, 312.)

Determining what counts as a symptom is not always a simple matter. As with other mental disorders, behavior and mental phenomena that might be symptomatic in adults can be normal in children. Standards for what counts as a delusion will be different in an adult and a preadolescent child, and similarly, standards of disorganization of speech and behavior will also depend on age. Furthermore, hallucinations are not necessarily symptoms of schizophrenia, but can instead be associated with sleep disturbances or even normal parts of childhood development such as imaginary friends. Sometimes unusual beliefs may have a cultural basis, resulting from a family's religion, and this should not be mistaken for schizophrenia.

Child and adolescent onset cases of schizophrenia are less often characterized by paranoia than in adults, but more often exhibit the negative symptoms, disorganized behavior and hallucinations (Hollis 2002, 616). Large proportions of children and adolescents with schizophrenia experience visual or auditory hallucinations. Studies suggest that children with schizophrenia do show more illogical thinking and loose associations than psychiatrically healthy children, but that there is no significant difference in the richness of the content of speech. The IQs of children with a diagnosis of schizophrenia tend to be lower than the mean (Tsai and Champine 2004, 387).

PROGNOSES

There is some debate over the long-term prognosis for those with schizophrenia. It has been characterized by some as a chronic disease from which only a minority of patients recover. One study of children with schizophrenia documented that a quarter of the subjects recovered completely, and about one half recovered to some degree (Tsai and Champine 2004, 338). On the other hand, other studies have pointed to evidence that more than half of those who suffer from the disease can recover completely (see Whitaker 2002, and also Warner 2003). Without settling this debate, it is very clear that schizophrenia is an extremely serious condition, with a high rate of morbidity. One survey showed that those with child and adolescent onset schizophrenia have a twelve-fold increase in risk of death compared with the general population of children of similar age and sex, and this is higher than for adult schizophrenia (Hollis 2002, 618).

PREVALENCE

There have been no well-confirmed studies of the rates of incidence of childhood and adolescent schizophrenia and related disorders, but the rates are lower than in adults. Among adults, the prevalence is about 1 percent of the population. The illness seems very rare among preadolescent children, although estimates vary. Some studies suggest that schizophrenia is more common among children from families of lower socioeconomic status (Tsai and Champine 2004, 381).

TREATMENTS

Very often, the main treatments for schizophrenia and psychotic disorders are medications. As with many other psychiatric medications, the "antipsychotics" used for schizophrenia have received little testing specifically on children and adolescents. However, they have been tested on adults and it is generally assumed that the effects of the medications are similar in adults and young people, although there are some significant differences.

Antipsychotic medication is broadly divided into two groups, the typicals and the atypicals. Some of the main typicals are haloperidol, chlorpromazine, and trifluoperazine, better known under their brand names Haldol, Thorazine, and Stelazine. These have been available for several decades now, and their effects are familiar. Some of the main newer atypical medications, which became widely used in the 1990s, include clozapine, risperidone, and olanzapine, better known under their brand names Clozaril, Risperdal, and Zyprexa. There is less research on these newer medications, but they have a reputation for causing fewer unpleasant side effects and for being more effective. Psychiatric opinion has not reached uniform agreement concerning which medications are most effective in a young population, and so there is considerable variation among clinicians. One estimate suggests that about 70 percent of patients benefit from antipsychotic medication, although it can take between six and eight weeks until the benefit is noticeable (Hollis 2002, 628). While most psychiatrists believe that medication is an essential form of treatment for schizophrenia and psychotic disorders, it should never be forgotten that all these medications, both old and new, have powerful side effects that are sometimes long-lasting, and even when they are helpful, it can take a good deal of trial and error until the right combination of medications is found for any patients, including children and adolescents.

Nonbiological treatments are also used, including cognitive-behavioral therapy and psycho educational interventions for patients and their families. There has been little study of the effectiveness of psychotherapy for young people with psychotic disorders, although some forms have been shown to be helpful in adult populations. While family interventions by highly trained professionals may well be helpful, one authority cautions that it may be unproductive and expensive to use them as a routine form of treatment (Hollis 2002, 629).

Christian Perring

CONDUCT, OPPOSITIONAL DEFIANT, AND ANTISOCIAL DISORDERS

While educators often do not encounter students with major depressive disorder or schizophrenia because children with those illnesses tend to be rather reclusive and may stop attending school altogether, they are more likely to be confronted by students with conduct disorders of various forms. These disorders are essentially defined by the disruptive behavior of children and adolescents. Often they are grouped with attention deficit hyperactivity disorder (ADHD) and both involve problems with self-control. There is considerable overlap in the symptoms of the ADHD, conduct disorder (CD), and oppositional defiant disorder (ODD). However, CD and ODD are essentially characterized by patterns of behavior that are willfully antisocial. This makes the category of CD and ODD somewhat controversial, since some are inclined to count such problems as intrinsically moral rather than medical or psychiatric. Nevertheless, the psychiatric approach has become firmly entrenched in both educational settings and society in general.

CRITERIA

Conduct Disorder is essentially characterized by a persistent pattern of behavior that violates the basic rights of others or major age-appropriate societal norms for a year or more. These forms of behavior are placed in four groups: aggression to people and animals, destruction of property, deceitfulness or theft, and the serious violation of rules (APA 2000, 98–99). Oppositional Defiant Disorder, generally considered a less severe condition, is essentially characterized by a pattern of negative, hostile, and defiant behavior lasting at least six months, where the symptoms do not meet the criteria for CD. Those diagnosed with

ODD must frequently exhibit at least four of the following: losing temper, arguing with adults, actively defying adult requests or rules, deliberately annoying people, blaming others for his or her mistakes or bad behavior, touchy or easily annoyed, angry and resentful, and spiteful or vindictive (APA 2000, 102). One should note that since irritability is a central symptom of depressive disorders, which can lead to hostile interactions with adults and peers, it can be hard to distinguish ODD from major depressive disorder in children and adolescents. Indeed, it is possible for individuals to be diagnosed with both conditions. There is a similar overlap between ODD and psychotic disorders, and also between ODD and bipolar disorder (Hendren and Mullen 2004, 512).

Experts agree that when making diagnoses of these disorders, it is important to seek reports from both teachers and parents. Studies have found that children and parents largely agree when the children are displaying the symptoms of CD, but agree less on attention deficit, lack of impulse control, and opposition. School records may provide clinicians with useful information in assessing a child's level of performance, both academically and socially (Earls and Mezzacappa 2002, 427).

PREVALENCE

In one study, the prevalence among ten- to eleven-year-olds of conduct disorder was 6.2 percent in boys and 1.6 percent in girls (Earls and Mezzacappa 2002, 421–22). Some studies have found considerable variations depending on socioeconomic class and geographical location. Different estimates range from less than 1 percent to more than 10 percent of children, and CD is one of the most common disorders diagnosed in children (APA 2000, 97). Estimates of rates of ODD vary from 2 percent to 16 percent of children.

TREATMENTS

Multimodal treatments are generally recommended for children and adolescents diagnosed with CD and ODD. These can involve working with the family, improving the social skills of the child or adolescent, medication, cognitive-behavioral treatment, and addressing the related medical and psychological problems, especially substance abuse. The family, educators, and other community resources may all be brought in to help with treatment. The legal system will also sometimes be involved. The problem of conduct disorder is often chronic, and so treatment is likely to be lengthy. Nevertheless, treatment is also able to lead to long-term improvement, especially if parents are actively involved. For preadolescent children, it is helpful to train the family and educators on how to mold the child's environment so as to reduce and prevent problematic forms of behavior, on how to respond to such behavior when it occurs, and how to teach the child the skills that will enable him or her to become more self-controlled. When it comes to adolescents, there are additional considerations, especially in regards to the peer groups of the young person. It can be difficult to force a youth to associate with different people, and thus it is more effective to instill a desire to associate with different friends who will not lead him or her into trouble. It can also be helpful to help the youth to develop skills to interact with peer groups more functionally.

Various forms of family therapy have been shown to be effective. Parental management training (PMT) has gained credibility in recent years. PMT to help parents manage their children's behavior has been shown to be successful in reducing the conduct disorders of young people (Earls and Mezzacappa 2002, 429). However, it may not be helpful in all cases, and can possibly lead to further parent-child conflict (Altepeter and Korger 1999, 131). There are other family system interventions that might be productive in cases where PMT is inappropriate.

Individual cognitive-behavioral treatment for conduct disorder will focus on problems such as impoverished communication and problem-solving skills, lack of impulse control, and anger and aggression. The focus on skills leads to an enhancement of self-control, and this in turn enables the young person to reduce his or her impulsive and disruptive behavior.

There is a lack of strong evidence that psychotropic medication is helpful in the specific treatment of conduct disorder (Hendren and Mullen 2004, 519). Nevertheless, it is not unusual for medication to be used when treating individuals with the disorder and this is partly justified because individuals with conduct disorders very often have other psychological problems such as ADHD or mood disorders that do demonstrably benefit from medication. Stimulants such as Ritalin have been found to reduce opposi-

tional behavior, impulsivity, and aggressive behavior in young people who have both ADHD and ODD/CD. Powerful antipsychotic medications such as Haldol have been used to reduce aggressive behavior, but they generally have severe and sometimes long-lasting side effects. One study has suggested that a newer atypical antipsychotic drug with fewer side effects is effective in reducing aggressive behavior. There is little indication that antidepressants are helpful as a treatment for conduct disorder. Mood stabilizers and anticonvulsants (such as lithium or halperidol) have been shown to reduce aggressive behavior in some populations of young people. Furthermore, there is some evidence the antianxiety drug Buspar may help with the aggressive symptoms of ODD and CD.

PREVENTION AND PROGNOSES

Children who later develop symptoms of CD and ODD often display warning signs even in preschool and early elementary school, and it can be very helpful to catch the problems early. Multimodal treatment of such psychological problems is generally essential. Furthermore, long-term follow-up is also of great benefit. The outcome for children is improved when the mental disorders of parents are addressed.

One Canadian experiment examined the benefits of a community-based preventative program. Aimed at boys between ages five and fifteen, it offered a program of non-academic skills development. It led to a reduction in vandalism and police and fire calls in the local area, and the reduction in expenses of local government agencies was far greater than the cost of the program (Earls and Mezzacappa 2002, 431).

One form of prevention that has been popular is school-based intervention. One program combined the training programs of teachers and parents in developing social skills development in children between the years of six and eight. It was effective for white children, but not for African Americans. Other programs have also had mixed results with different populations, and show the counteracting effects of problematic policy decisions in schools, such as clustering aggressive children in the same classroom. Nevertheless, there is clear evidence that prevention programs can have powerful effects in reducing aggressive behavior in young people (Earls and Mezzacappa 2002, 431).

For those children who do develop conduct disorder, the long-term outcome tends to depend on the initial severity of the condition and the age of onset. Those with mild forms generally recover, but those with more severe forms have more difficulty overcoming the problems. The more aggressive forms of the disorder have a worse prognosis. According to one study, between 23 percent and 41 percent of highly antisocial children grew up to engage in antisocial behavior as adults, while between 17 percent and 28 percent did not become antisocial, and the rest did not fall into either category (Hendren and Mullen 2004, 521).

Christian Perring

ANXIETY DISORDERS

There are a variety of ways of conceiving of the scope of anxiety disorders. In its chapter on Anxiety Disorders, the American Psychiatric Association's diagnostic manual DSM-IV-TR (APA 2000a) includes panic attacks, various phobias, obsessive-compulsive disorders (OCD), posttraumatic stress disorder (PTSD), and stress disorders. Other approaches treat OCD and PTSD separately. It is somewhat arbitrary how to group these different conditions. Here, DSM-IT-IV will be followed and OCD and PTSD will be included. Furthermore, there is considerable overlap between mood disorders and anxiety disorders, especially in young people for whom irritability tends to be a marker of depression. Even for adults, the common condition often known as neurotic depression combines anxiety and unhappiness. So there is no sharp and obvious distinction between pure anxiety disorders and other related conditions. Nevertheless, the concept of anxiety is relatively easy for most people to understand, and thus the notion of an anxiety disorder has an intuitive straightforwardness that makes it a useful category.

One of the best-known phenomena concerning anxiety is a panic attack. Note that a panic attack is not itself a disorder, although it may be a symptom of a disorder. A panic attack is characterized by a person having at least four of the following symptoms that develop abruptly and reach a peak within 10 minutes: palpitations, pounding heart, or faster heart rate; sweating; trembling or shaking; feelings of shortness of breath or smothering; sensations of choking; chest pain or discomfort; nausea or abdominal discomfort; feeling dizzy, unsteady, lightheaded or faint; feelings of unreality, of detachment from self; fear of losing control or going crazy; fear of dying; numbness or tingling sensations, or chills or hot flushes (APA 2000, 432). Panic attacks may occur as a result of stress or a particular event, or they can occur spontaneously. Panic disorder is essentially the condition of recurrent, unexpected panic attacks followed by at least a month of persistent concern about having another one, worry about the possible implications of the attacks, or significant change in behavior related to them. The condition can occur at any age, and often occurs in conjunction with separation anxiety disorder.

Another central condition related to anxiety is that of Specific Phobia. This is characterized by a marked and persistent excessive or unreasonable fear triggered by the presence or anticipation of a particular object or context. Exposure to the phobic stimulus nearly always triggers an immediate anxiety response. In children, the anxiety may be expressed by crying, tantrums, freezing, or clinging. While it is necessary in adults that the person recognizes the fear is excessive or unreasonable, this is not a requirement for children. For all sufferers, the phobic object or context is avoided or endured with intense anxiety or distress. These symptoms must significantly interfere with the rest of the person's life. For those under eighteen years, the symptoms must last at least six months (APA 2000, 449). For children, phobias are very often directed at animals and natural occurrences such as storms. Note that not all irrational fears count as phobias, especially for younger children. Furthermore, avoiding contexts such as school may not necessarily be a result of a phobia, but could be a symptom of a different kind of problem such as another anxiety disorder, depression, conduct disorder, substance abuse, or even family psychopathology (Black et al. 2004, 593).

A related disorder is Social Phobia, also known as Social Anxiety Disorder. There has been increasing public awareness of this disorder, partly due to advertising campaigns for medication used to treat the condition, and recent studies have revealed the incidence of the disorder in children and adolescents (Kashdan and Herbert 2001). The diagnostic criteria for the disorder are parallel to those for specific phobia, and are essentially characterized by a "marked and persistent fear of one or more social or performance situations in which the person is exposed to unfamiliar people or possible scrutiny by others." The person fears humiliation or embarrassment. In children, the criteria include the requirement that the child have "the capacity for age-appropriate social relationships with familiar people and the anxiety must occur in peer settings, not just in interactions with adults" (APA 2000, 456). Adolescents with this phobia may have great difficulty with dating, and may drop out of school. The condition has a greater risk of associated alcohol abuse and other mental health problems.

Separation Anxiety Disorder is a condition of the young and tends to occur soon before adolescence. It is essentially characterized by excessive anxiety concerning separation from the home or primary caregivers, and involves persistent and excessive worry about losing or possible harm occurring to caregivers (APA 2000, 125). It may be harder to identify the disorder in younger children since they have more difficulty in expressing their fears, and even older children may hide them. It is estimated that about 4 percent of young people experience this disorder, with equal proportions of males and females.

Generalized Anxiety Disorder, as its name suggests, is characterized by excessive and uncontrollable worry not focused on just a few objects or situations, which lasts for more than six months. For diagnosis in children, this must be associated with just one of the following: restlessness or feeling on edge; being easily tired; difficulty concentrating or mind going blank; irritability; muscle tension; and sleep disturbance (APA 2000, 476). About 9 percent of girls and 4 percent of boys experience this problem (Bernstein and Layne 2004, 560).

There has been greater awareness of Obsessive-Compulsive Disorder (OCD) on the part of the general public in recent years, partly spurred by the 1989 bestseller *The Boy Who Couldn't Stop Washing* by psychiatric researcher Judith Rapoport. When psychiatry was dominated by psychoanalytic theory and behaviorism, OCD was thought to be a result of poor parenting, and especially perfectionistic demands. However, this belief has now changed, and the disorder has come to be seen more as a biological illness. Although those with the disorder still fear the judgment of others, the new understanding has diminished the shame associated with the condition. The distinc-

tion between compulsions and obsessions is not strict, but compulsions are more associated with behavior while obsessions are more associated with thoughts. Often, compulsive behavior aims at preventing some imagined event or outcome over which the subject obsesses, including contamination, danger to self or others, lack of symmetry or moral wrongs. The most common behavior symptomatic of OCD is compulsive hand washing and other self-cleaning activities. Children with OCD often display repeating rituals such as repeating phrases, preoccupations with entrances to rooms, sitting behavior, and checking behavior. Counting, ordering, arranging, and hoarding are also common symptoms. The disorder normally creates distress in the sufferer, especially when he or she is unable to complete the symptomatic rituals or actions, or the actions come to significantly interfere with the rest of the person's life. Furthermore, in OCD the compulsions and obsessions are themselves typically ego-dystonic, meaning that the person does not see them as justified or reasonable, despite feeling that they need to be performed and experiencing great anxiety if they are not performed. (Note that this is one way to distinguish OCD from Obsessive-Compulsive Personality Disorder, in which the symptomatic obsessions and compulsions are more integrated in the sufferer's personality, which means that they are then ego-syntonic.) Patterns of symptoms generally change over time, generally starting with just a single obsession or compulsion, and then becoming more diverse. Young people with OCD are more likely to also suffer from ADHD and behavioral tic disorders (Freeman et al. 2004, 577). When young people with OCD are prevented from carrying out their rituals, they may react with powerful emotions, including anger. Due to the secrecy with which they perform their compulsions and rituals, it is likely that the disorder is only discovered once it has become quite serious and disabling.

The category of posttraumatic stress disorder (PTSD) has undergone a number of name and conceptual changes; it has also been known as battle fatigue, shell shock, and even nervous breakdown. The term PTSD was first explicitly termed to describe the condition of some soldiers who had served in the Vietnam War, and it is used to characterize the disorder that occurs as a reaction to extreme stress and trauma. It remains somewhat controversial as a diagnosis of adults, and its application to young people is even more contested and unproven. Nevertheless, this is an area of psychiatric and psychological research, and there is a growing consensus that PTSD can be validly diagnosed in children and adolescents. The characteristic symptoms are intrusive thoughts concerning the original traumatic event, emotional numbness, and a tendency to avoid reminders of the original event, and physiological hyperarousal. There has been debate whether PTSD is best characterized as an anxiety disorder or is better understood as a form of dissociation (Yule 2002, 520). Furthermore, although the official psychiatric criteria of the DSM make very little distinction between adults and the young, there is debate whether the criteria are equally relevant when applied to young people. For example, it may be hard to be clear about what counts as "emotional numbing" in children, and young people may exhibit this in different ways from adults. Some accounts suggest that young children will engage in repetitive drawing and play around themes based on the traumatic event. Children and adolescents are likely to display separation difficulties with caregivers after a very frightening experience. They may well experience repetitive and intrusive thoughts about the event, flashbacks, sleep disturbances, fears of the dark, nightmares, irritability, pressure to talk, difficulties in concentration, and memory problems. They are especially aware of possible dangers. Many experience survivor guilt and feel a need to protect their families from their unhappiness and external dangers. Diagnostically, the fear of children may be expressed through disorganized or agitated behavior. If the symptoms last for less than four weeks but longer than two days, then a diagnosis of acute stress disorder is given instead of PTSD. PTSD has high rates of both false negative and false positive diagnosis due to the complexity of the possible symptoms and the number of associated mental disorders such as depression (Donnelly et al. 2004, 616).

PREVALENCE

It is estimated that about 2 to 3 percent of young people experience OCD at some point in their development. Fifty percent of those who experienced the disorder as adults first developed symptoms as children or adolescents (Rapoport and Swedo 2002, 571). Males tend to have earlier onset of first symptoms than females. It is likely that children are often secretive about their symptoms and this can lead to underestimates of prevalence.

Estimates of the prevalence of PTSD vary widely, depending on a great variety of factors. Some estimate that a large proportion of young people who experience a traumatic event will go on to develop a related disorder, while other studies offer far lower estimates for the development of PTSD. Overall, somewhere between 10 percent and 40 percent of children and adolescents in violence-ridden neighborhoods experience PTSD (Donnelly et al. 2004, 616). One study of Chicago middle and high school students showed remarkably high levels of exposure to violence, with 35 percent of students having witnessed a stabbing, 39 percent having witnessed a shooting, and 25 percent having witnessed a murder. Forty-six percent had been a victim of a highly violent crime (Donnelly et al. 2004, 617). Furthermore, news media makes people far more aware of violence going on both in local neighborhoods, nationally, and internationally. Not all children who experience violence will develop PTSD, and the risk factors are not well understood, but it does seem that a large proportion of children exposed to violence are at significant risk for the trauma and stress.

TREATMENTS

In many cases, when treating anxiety disorders, it is helpful for clinicians to seek information about a young person's behavior from a variety of sources, including the young person him or herself, the family, the school, and other therapists who are familiar with the young person. The main treatment options are medication and cognitive-behavioral therapy. Since the advent of the new generation of antidepressants such as Prozac, Zoloft, and Paxil, they have been the preferred drugs used to treat anxiety disorders. Studies have shown that these are generally efficacious and safe, at least in the short term (Bernstein and Layne 2004, 564). The popularity of this approach is especially tied to the fact that these medications tend to have fewer side effects that are better tolerated than those associated with older drugs, although it is important to note that the side effects were still not negligible. For example, stomachaches, headaches, and abdominal pain were all reported in one study of Prozac (p. 565).

Obsessive-Compulsive Disorder is addressed through a number of treatments. Cognitive-behavioral treatment (CBT) is often used, with much confidence, even though its efficacy has not been strictly proven in children and adolescents. Indeed, it is often the treatment of choice, and is thought by some to have longer lasting effects than medication. This treatment includes exposure and response prevention, cognitive therapy, and relaxation training. There is growing interest in the use of interactive computer programs for self-assessment and self-help, largely because this presents a relatively inexpensive option (Rapoport and Swedo 2002, 582). Nevertheless, drugs, especially the newer medications such as Prozac, Zoloft, and Paxil, are increasingly popular as a treatment and there have been studies pointing to their efficacy in reducing symptoms. Psychiatrists recommend initially using a medication for twelve weeks to assess whether or not it is effective (Bernstein and Layne 2004, 582). Once a patient has found a medication that is helpful, long-term use of the medication is often maintained. Sometimes medication is combined with the use of CBT. Other forms of psychotherapy and family therapy are also used to help patients deal with problems such as family arguments and lowered self-esteem caused by their mental disorder. Family education indeed can be an essential element in a treatment program. Teachers are occasionally included when the young person's disorder is significantly interfering with schoolwork.

As with many other mental disorders, there has been little specific research into the most effective treatment for PTSD in children and adolescents. Approaches that have been successfully used with adults have been adapted to use with young people. It is important to clarify the aims of treatment; it is unlikely that it will be possible to eradicate the experience of involvement in a traumatic event, so the ultimate goal is probably best seen as the return of the individual to healthy functioning with appropriate feelings about the event. The main mode of treatment is cognitive-behavioral therapy for which there is some evidence of efficacy. Other forms of psychotherapy, family-supportive work, and medication are also used. Families and, indeed, teachers may need help in facing the child's distress and in dealing with reminders of the traumatic experience. Many experts agree that the period immediately following the experience of trauma is crucial for the prevention or

reduction of PTSD. Debriefing and psychological first aid are commonly used both in crisis centers and schools. Yet there has been concern that the use of "grief counselors" and other such clinical interventions after major events of trauma are ineffective or could even worsen the psychological reaction to the event. Thus, it is clear that such interventions need to be done carefully and with follow-up to make sure that they have been as helpful as possible.

Medication is often used for those with PTSD as a way to enable the effectiveness of psychological treatment, although there has been little study of the scientific validity of this approach. Medication can decrease intrusive thoughts, avoidant behavior, sleeplessness, and the hypervigilance associated with PTSD and stress disorders. The most frequently used medications are the selective serotonin reuptake inhibitors such as Prozac, Paxil, and Zoloft. Many other medications are also used.

PROGNOSES

There has been little study of the long-term prognosis for young people with OCD, but what evidence there is suggests that while for some the problem clears up and treatment is helpful, for a large proportion of those afflicted it can remain a long-term trouble.

For young people diagnosed with PTSD, their troubles can be chronic and debilitating, and there is a great deal of individual variation in how they cope. The outcome partly relates to their previous mental health before the traumatic event, and the seriousness and number of traumas experienced.

Christian Perring

ATTENTION DEFICIT HYPERACTIVITY DISORDER

Attention Deficit Hyperactivity Disorder (ADHD) is the most common referral of children to mental health practitioners in the United States. It is a behavioral disorder that is manifested by inattention, hyperactivity, and impulsivity. It is the most common disruptive behavioral disorder of childhood and is recognized as a devastating contributor to academic underachievement and social rejection. The prevalence of students diagnosed with ADHD in the school-age population is estimated at 3–5 percent (American Psychiatric Association 1994).

The primary symptoms of inattention, hyperactivity, and impulsivity are exhibited at developmentally inappropriate levels and over a consistent period of time, at least six months. All children will generally show evidence of these types of behavior at some time in their development, however, the child with ADHD presents these continuously and most likely the symptoms were present early, usually before seven years of age.

With respect to inattention, a child with ADHD shows significant deficits in sustained attention and effort. The child is unable to remain on task, has difficulty paying attention or following directions, can be easily distracted, is forgetful and often loses things. Even playful activities can be short lived because of the attention factor, which can have implications for poor social interactions. Schoolwork can suffer because of lack of attention to detail or the inability to complete a task. Organization of work and personal care can become a very real problem.

Hyperactivity associated with ADHD is characterized by excessive motor activity and an inability to regulate this activity level. It is very difficult for the child with ADHD to sit still. The tendency is to be on the go and moving constantly.

Impulsivity in a child with ADHD emerges as difficulty inhibiting behavior, whether it is in school, at home, or in any environment. Children with ADHD tend to be high risk takers but are unable to delay gratification. It is difficult for them to wait their turn or to share with others. This behavior is often perceived as antagonistic or at least selfish. However, with ADHD it is believed this behavior is the result of a neurological deficit that interferes with the normal ability to inhibit impulses. This lack of inhibition often appears as a lack of patience and frustration while working on a project or playing games.

All of these symptoms change with development. Younger children are more apt to show hyperactivity whereas attention span in early childhood is limited for most children. A hyperactive youngster may appear to outgrow the hyperactivity but it may, in turn, manifest itself in puberty and/or adolescence as impulsivity.

The effects of these symptoms can be devastating when left unchecked. Children with ADHD are at risk for peer rejection because they are in other children's faces constantly. By nature of their inability to inhibit actions they do not acquire social skills as easily or as naturally as other children do. They also are at risk for and can present co-morbid symptoms of conduct disorder. When children are not helped to deal with the inattention, impulsivity, and hyperactivity, they stand out in a group, or in a classroom. Constant negative attention not only labels them but often times causes them to use disruptive behavior to gain needed attention.

Children with ADHD tend to be very creative. Learning with a multisensory approach works well for all children but especially for the child with ADHD. Participation in the arts and physical education activities both in school and out allows for expression of special talents and gives outlets for expenditure of excessive energy.

Low-esteem can be another by-product of ADHD. Constant negative attention can lead to depression and a bruised self-concept.

It is believed that the core problem present in ADHD is a deficit in inhibiting behavior (Barkley 1998). There is a control mechanism in the brain, so to speak, that allows most children to control behaviors, to one degree or another. Children with ADHD do not have that control. The understanding of this factor is key in working with the child with ADHD. It is essential to give children with ADHD strategies to learn how to control various behaviors, a control that will not come automatically to this child as it would to another child without the deficit.

Recognition of the lack of this inhibitor gives the proper perspective to the child's sometimes uncontrollable and exasperating behavior. Most often, children with ADHD are accused of "bad" behavior when in fact the behavior is often not intentional or at least not controllable and usually not directed at anyone.

What causes ADHD? Research is unveiling more evidence of a strong biological factor that is closely associated with and perhaps causal of ADHD. Neurological studies show less activity in the frontal lobe regions of the brain, which involve behavioral inhibition, persistence of responding, resistance to distractions, and control of one's activity level. These are all factors involved in ADHD.

What does not cause ADHD? Research indicates that although poor parenting can exacerbate ADHD, it does not cause the disorder. There are strong support systems for parents with children who have ADHD. Children and Adults with Attention-Deficit/Hyperactivity Disorder (CHADD) is one such organization. Their website is www.chadd.org/index.cfm. Diet and allergies have been thought to affect ADHD. There is no conclusive evidence to date that the cause of ADHD can be attributed to either allergies or diet. Again, there is the possibility that they can exacerbate ADHD.

The assessment and diagnosis of ADHD involves a focus on the child in his or her developmental and environmental context. Because often times there is a hereditary component of ADHD, a history of the child, including family history, is essential. A medical history and evaluation are needed to rule out a physical disorder that could be a source of problem behaviors. An emotional, social, and family evaluation is necessary to rule out depression and behavior resulting from poor childrearing practices. Parent and teacher rating scales are used to assess the child's behaviors in environmental settings. Learning disabilities are common among children with ADHD. Therefore, an assessment for academic achievement and a screening of general intelligence is protocol.

The medical history and evaluation component of the multidisciplinary diagnostic process is critical. A family history scans the possibility of hereditary link to ADHD in a child. The physician's role is to search for any remediable medical causes of ADHD. Medical diagnostic testing ranges from blood analysis to MRI scans in order to exclude any medical illness disguising ADHD. Appropriate physical and neurological examinations are protocol. When medication is indicated, the physician is critical in supervising the medication interventions program.

Detecting ADHD early is important. There is no treatment that has proven to be a cure for ADHD. Some treatments provide symptomatic relief. However, no treatment has produced any enduring effects once the treatment is withdrawn. The rationale for the early identification of ADHD is the prescription of early interventions to limit the severity of the behaviors of ADHD. A multimodal treatment plan combines medication, behavior management strategies, effective instruction, and counseling for the child and the family. The goal of intervention is to create a better fit between the child with ADHD and the demands made by the social environment at home and at school. Medication, when appropriate, is recommended as only one part of a broader treatment plan. Rarely is it enough to treat ADHD alone. Other interventions are needed to assist children with ADHD who have behavioral, social, and learning difficulties.

The most widely used medications to treat the symptoms of ADHD are stimulant drugs, among which are methylphenidate (Ritalin), dextroamphetamine (Dexedrine), and pemoline (Cylert). These drugs have helped many children with reducing hyperactivity and improving attention, as well as with inhibiting impulsivity. If these drugs are not helpful to the child with ADHD sometimes antidepressants or antihistamines are tried. In any case, a physician works closely with patient and family to find appropriate treatment.

In cases where medication is prescribed, when improvement is noted due to the use of medication, the drug is usually applauded for causing the change. But there is an alternate view: "These changes are actually the child's own strengths and natural abilities coming out from behind a cloud. Giving credit to the medication can make the child feel incompetent. The medication only makes these changes possible. The child must supply the effort and ability. To help children feel good about themselves, parents and teachers need to praise the child, not the drug (National Institute of Mental Health 1996, 14).

Parent training and behavioral management programs are a means for parents to become effective advocates and role models for their children. Research indicates that nonsocial behaviors such as aggression, impulsivity, and noncompliance decrease through parent training (Barkley 1998).

Because teachers play a critical role in the successful school experience of the child with ADHD and with the almost certain knowledge that every teacher will someday find a child with ADHD in his or her classroom, there is a tremendous need for teacher understanding, knowledge, and training in the management of the disorder. Proper placement and management in the classroom can aid the child with ADHD in having a positive and successful school experience.

There are several publications, organizations, and support groups that help individuals, teachers, and parents to understand and live with ADHD. For a list of these resources consult The National Institute of Mental Health (NIMH) at www.nimh.nih.gov.

Sandra Buck Loughran

ASPERGER'S SYNDROME

Asperger's syndrome is a neurological disorder named after an Austrian physician who described a number of children who were his patients during the 1940s. Subsequent research supported his findings and the disorder was added to the *International Classification of Diseases and Related Health Problems* (World Health Organization 1992) and *Diagnostic and Statistical Manual of Mental Disorders–Fourth Edition* (American Psychiatric Association 1994). The disorder is sometimes considered a form of high-functioning autism.

The underlying deficit in Asperger's Syndrome (AS) is the inability to sustain social interaction. Children with AS lack social skills and a basic understanding of how social relationships work. They often miss body language cues, do not make eye contact, and lack a certain affect in expression and reaction. AS causes a significant impairment in social situations, work settings, and other important areas of functioning.

A common characteristic of children with AS is a preoccupation with certain patterns of behavior, an obsessive interest in certain objects, and repetitive actions, for example, hand or finger tapping and twisting. Routines can become inflexible. Change becomes very stressful for children with AS.

Interestingly, early development of language takes a normal progression, making it difficult to detect the underlying symptoms at an early age. Although armed with sufficient verbal ability to speak at home or in public, children with AS in preschool and elementary school will often be the observer, not readily engaging in conversation with peers and/or adults. They have trouble reading social situations and body language. They can often appear to be the odd person out and are subjected to teasing and bullying.

Although intellectually competent, these children have a neurological difference that makes their way of seeing and reacting to the world different. It can be difficult for a child with AS to show empathy or understand what another child may be feeling, as well as difficult to give outward evidence of his or her own feelings.

Although the behavior of a child with AS can be unusual, it is a result of a neurological uniqueness, not "bad" behavior or behavior resulting from poor parenting. Children with AS tend to respond to stress more with emotions than with logic, causing the child to blurt out inappropriate words and exhibit a lack of self-control.

Because a child with AS has difficulty with change, sameness in routines becomes a needed element in their daily schedule. A child with AS can become compulsive about routines and schedules.

With age, children become aware of their differences and may develop a sense of isolation. Depression can also accompany these feelings. They become aware that they have difficulties making friends but still experience the normal desire to have friendships.

The cause or causes of AS are still being researched. Evidence strongly suggests that the disorder may be caused by physical factors involved in brain development. Childrearing or emotional factors are not the cause. There is the possibility of a hereditary factor. Histories of family members with similar symptoms are common.

There is no specific treatment or medication for AS. Depending on the severity of symptoms, medication can be prescribed to offset specific symptoms. What is most important for the child with AS at all stages of development is social-skills training. Children need to learn how to make eye contact, how to converse with peers, and how to judge and respect the space needed to relate with peers and others in their environment. It is recommended that these skills be learned in small groups with children with similar problems.

The child with AS presents different cognitive abilities so that school programs should be individualized. Teachers and parents need to understand the difficulties involved, such as difficulties with eye contact, the need for consistent routines, and difficulties with change. Karen Williams (1995) offers an excellent treatise on guidelines for teachers working with Asperger's Syndrome. Parents and teachers can keep current with support groups and information through Online Asperger Syndrome Information and Support (O.A.S.I.S.) at www.udel.edu/bkirby/asperger.

As with remedies in any disorder, the therapy needs to be tailored to the individual child. A child with AS prospers with less intense emotional demands and proceeds better with concrete, step-by-step behavioral techniques. AS is a lifelong disorder, however, with early intervention, individuals with AS are capable of living full lives with self-sufficiency and with gainful employment.

Sandra Buck Loughran

REFERENCES

Altepeter, Thomas, and John N. Korger. (1999) "Disruptive Behavior: Oppositional Defiant Disorder and Conduct Disorder." In *Child and Adolescent Psychological Disorders: A Comprehensive Textbook*, ed. Sandra D. Netherton, Deborah Holmes, and C. Eugene Walker, 118–38. New York: Oxford University Press.

American Psychiatric Association. (1994) *Diagnostic and Statistical Manual of Mental Disorders–Fourth Edition.* Washington DC: APA.

———. (2000a) *Diagnostic and Statistical Manual of Mental Disorders–Fourth Edition, Text Revision.* Washington DC: APA

———. (2000b) Practice guideline for the treatment of eating disorders. *American Journal of Psychiatry* 157: 1–39.

Barkley, R.A. (1998) *Attention-Deficit Hyperactivity Disorder: A Handbook for Diagnosis and Treatment.* 2nd ed. New York: Guilford Press.

Barkley, R.A. (2000) *Taking Charge of ADHD, Revised Edition: The Complete, Authoritative Guide for Parents.* New York: Guilford Press.

Berlin, Irving N. (2004) "Development of the Subspecialty of Child and Adolescent Psychiatry in the United States." In *The American Psychiatric Publishing Textbook of Child and Adolescent Psychiatry*, 3rd ed., ed. Jerry M. Wiener and Mina K. Dulcan, 3–12. Washington, DC: American Psychiatric Publishing.

Bernstein, Gail A., and Ann E. Layne. (2004) "Separation Anxiety Disorder and Generalized Anxiety Disorder." In *The American Psychiatric Publishing Textbook of Child and Adolescent Psychiatry*, 3rd ed., ed. Jerry M. Wiener and Mina K. Dulcan, 557–73. Washington, DC: American Psychiatric Publishing.

Black, Bruce, et al. (2004) "Specific Phobia, Panic Disorder, Social Phobia, and Selective Mutism." In *The American Psychiatric Publishing Textbook of Child and Adolescent Psychiatry*, 3rd ed., ed. Jerry M. Wiener and Mina K. Dulcan, 589–607. Washington, DC: American Psychiatric Publishing.

Bruch, H. (1973) *Eating Disorders: Obesity, Anorexia, and the Person Within.* New York: Basic Books.

Byrne, B. (2000) Relationships between anxiety, fear, self-esteem, and coping strategies in adolescence. *Adolescence* 35: 201–15.

Calam, R., G. Waller, P. Slade, and T. Newton. (1990) Eating disorders and perceived relationships with parents. *International Journal of Eating Disorders* 9: 479–85.

Dare, C., I. Eisler, G.F.M. Russell, and G. Szmukler. (1990) Family therapy for anorexia nervosa: Implications from the results of a controlled trial of family and individual therapy. *Journal of Marital and Family Therapy* 16: 39–57.

Donnelly, Craig L., John S. March, and Lisa Amaya-Jackson. (2004) "Pediatric Posttraumatic Stress Disorder." In *The American Psychiatric Publishing Textbook of Child and Adolescent Psychiatry*, 3rd. ed., ed. Jerry M. Wiener and Mina K. Dulcan, 609–36. Washington, DC: American Psychiatric Publishing.

Dulcan, M., and C. Lizarralde. (2003) *Helping Parents, Youth and Teachers Understand Medications for Behavioral and Emotional Problems*, 2nd ed. Washington, DC: American Psychiatric Press.

Earls, Felton, and Enrico Mezzacappa. (2002) "Conduct and Oppositional Disorders." In *Child and Adolescent Psychiatry*, 4th ed., ed. Michael Rutter and Eric Taylor, 419–36. Oxford, UK: Blackwell Publishing.

Eisler, I., C. Dare, M. Hodges, G. Russell, E. Dodge, and D. le Grange. (2000) Family therapy for adolescent anorexia nervosa: The results of controlled comparison of two family interventions. *Journal of Child Psychology and Psychiatry* 41: 727–36.

Eisler, I., C. Dare, G. Russell, G. Szmukler, D. le Grange, and E. Dodge. (1997) A five-year follow-up of a controlled trial of family therapy in severe eating disorders. *Archives of General Psychiatry* 54: 1025–30.

Engel, G.L. (1980) The clinical application of the biopsychosocial model. *American Journal of Psychiatry* 137: 535–44.

Fairburn, C.G., W.S. Agras, and G.T. Wilson. (1992) "The Research on the Treatment of Bulimia Nervosa: Practical and Theoretical Implications." In *The Biology of Feast and Famine: Relevance to Eating Disorders*, ed. G.H. Anderson and S.H. Kennedy, 317–14. San Diego: Academic Press.

Fairburn, C.G., M.D. Marcus, and G.T. Wilson. (1993) "Cognitive-Behavioral Therapy for Binge Eating and Bulimia Nervosa: A Comprehensive Treatment Manual." In *Binge Eating: Nature, Assessment, and Treatment*, ed. C.G. Fairburn and G.T. Wilson, 361–404. New York: Guilford Press.

Field, A.E., C.A. Camargo, C.B. Taylor, C.S. Berkey, A.L. Frazier, M.W. Gillman, and G.A. Colditz. (1999) Overweight, weight concerns, and bulimic behaviors among girls and boys. *Journal of the American Academy of Child and Adolescent Psychiatry* 38: 754–60.

Fisher, M., N.H. Golden, D.K. Katzman, R.E. Kreipe, J. Rees, J. Schebendach, G. Sigman, S. Ammerman, H.M. Huberman. (1995) Eating disorders in adolescents: A background paper. *Journal of Adolescent Health* 16: 420–37.

Freeman, Jennifer B., et al. (2004) "Obsessive-Compulsive Disorder." In *The American Psychiatric Publishing Textbook of Child and Adolescent Psychiatry*, 3rd ed., ed. Jerry M. Wiener and Mina K. Dulcan, 575–88. Washington, DC: American Psychiatric Publishing.

Halmi, K., R. Casper, E. Eckert, S. Goldberg, J. Davis. (1979) Unique features associated with age of onset of anorexia nervosa. *Psychiatry Research* 1: 209–15.

Harrington, Richard. (2002) "Affective Disorders." In *Child and Adolescent Psychiatry*, 4th ed., ed. Michael Rutter and Eric Taylor, 463–85. Oxford, UK: Blackwell Publishing.

Heatherton, T.F., and J. Polivy. (1992) "Chronic Dieting and Eating Disorders: A Spiral Model." In *The Etiology of Bulimia Nervosa*, ed. H. Crowther, D.L. Tennenbaum, S.E. Hobvfoll, and M.A.P. Stephens, 133–55. Washington, DC: Hemisphere.

Hendren, Robert L., and David J. Mullen. (2004) "Conduct Disorder and Oppositional Defiant Disorder." In *The American Psychiatric Publishing Textbook of Child and Adolescent Psychiatry*, 3rd ed., ed. Jerry M. Wiener and Mina K. Dulcan, 509–27. Washington, DC: American Psychiatric Publishing.

Hollis, Chris. (2002) "Schizophrenia and Allied Disorders." In *Child and Adolescent Psychiatry*, 4th ed., ed. Michael Rutter and Eric Taylor, 612–35. Oxford, UK: Blackwell Publishing.

Hsu, G. (1990) *Eating Disorders.* New York: Guilford Press.

Humphrey, L.L. (1986) Family relations in bulimic-anorexic and nondistressed families. *International Journal of Eating Disorders* 5: 223–32.

Humphrey, L.L. (1989) Observed family interactions among subtypes of eating disorders using structural analysis of social behavior. *Journal of Consulting and Clinical Psychology* 57: 206–14.

Johnson, C., and A. Flach. (1985) Family characteristics of 105 patients with bulimia. *American Journal of Psychiatry* 142: 1321–24.

Kashdan, T.B., and J.D. Herbert. (2001) Social anxiety disorder in childhood and adolescence: current status and future directions. *Clinical Child Family Psychology Review* 4: 37–61.

Killen et al. (1996) Weight concerns influence the development of eating disorders: A four-year prospective study. *Journal of Consulting and Clinical Psychology*, 64: 936–940.

Kreipe, R.E., and M. Uphoff. (1992) Treatment and outcome of adolescents with anorexia nervosa. *Adolescent Medicine* 3: 519–40.

Lewinsohn, P.M, R.H. Striegel-Moore, and J.H. Seeley. (2000) Epidemiology and natural course of eating disorders in young women from adolescence to young adulthood. *Journal of the American Academy of Child and Adolescent Psychiatry* 39: 1284–92.

Lock, J. (2002) Treating adolescents with eating disorders in the family context: Empirical and theoretical considerations. *Child and Adolescent Psychiatric Clinics of North America* 11: 331–42.

Lock, J. D. le Grange, W.S. Agras, and C. Dare. (2001) *Treatment Manual for Anorexia Nervosa: A Family-Based Approach.* New York: Guilford Press.

Mann, T., S. Nolen-Hoeksema, K. Huang, D. Burgard, A. Wright, and K. Hanson. (1997) Are two interventions worse than none? Joint primary and secondary prevention of eating disorders in college females. *Health Psychology* 16: 215–25.

Medicines and Healthcare Products Regulatory Agency (MHRA). (2003) MHRA News in 2003 (December). Available at: www.mhra.gov.uk/news/2003.htm#ssri.

Minunchin, S., B. Rosman, and L. Baker. (1978) *Psychosomatic Families: Anorexia Nervosa in Context.* Cambridge, MA: Harvard University Press.

Mrazek, David. (1993) *A to Z Guide to Your Child's Behavior: A Parent's Easy and Authoritative Reference to Hundreds of Everyday Problems and Concerns from Birth to Twelve Years.* New York: Perigee Books.

Nadeau, Kathleen G. (1997) *Learning to Slow Down and Pay Attention.* Washington, DC: Magination Press.

National Institute of Mental Health. (1996) Publication No. 96–3572. Originally printed 1994, 14.

Neve, Michael, and Trevor Turner. (2002) "History of Child and Adolescent Psychiatry." In *Child and Adolescent Psychiatry*, 4th ed., ed. Michael Rutter and Eric Taylor, 382–95. Oxford, UK: Blackwell Publishing.

Nolen-Hoeksema, S. (1994) An interactive model for the emergence of gender differences in depression in adolescence. *Journal of Research on Adolescence* 4: 519–34.

Perring, C. (1997) Medicating children: The case of Ritalin. *Bioethics* 11: 228–40.

Pike, K.M., and J. Rodin. (1991) Mothers, daughters, and disordered eating. *Journal of Abnormal Psychology* 100: 198–204.

Pike, K.M., and R. Striegel-Moore. (1997) "Disordered Eating and Eating Disorders." In *Women's Health Book*, ed. S.J. Gallant, G.P. Keita, and R. Royak-Schaler, 445–87. Washington DC: American Psychological Association.

Polivy, J., and C.P. Herman. (1993) "Etiology of Binge Eating: Psychological Mechanisms." In *Binge Eating: Nature, Assess-ment, and Treatment*, ed. C.G. Fairburn and G.T. Wilson, 173–205. New York: Guilford Press.

Rapoport, Judith. (1989) *The Boy Who Couldn't Stop Washing: The Experience and Treatment of Obsessive-Compulsive Disorder.* New York: E.P. Dutton.

Rapoport, Judith L., and Susan Swedo. (2002) "Obsessive-Compulsive Disorder." In *Child and Adolescent Psychiatry*, 4th ed., ed. Michael Rutter and Eric Taylor, 571–92. Oxford, UK: Blackwell Publishing.

Robin, A.L., P.T. Siegel, A.W. Moye, M. Gilroy, A.B. Dennis, and A. Sikand. (1999) A controlled comparison of family versus individual therapy for adolescents with anorexia nervosa. *Journal of the American Academy of Child and Adolescent Psychiatry* 38: 1428–89.

Rosen, J.C., H. Leitenberg, D. Fisher, and C. Khazam. (1986) Binge-eating episodes in bulimia nervosa: The amount and type of food consumed. *International Journal of Eating Disorders*, 5: 255–67.

Rosen, J.C., N.T. Silberg, and J. Gross. (1988) Eating attitudes test and eating disorders inventory: Norms for adolescent girls and boys. *Journal of Consulting and Clinical Psychology* 56: 305–08.

Rowe, R., A. Pickles, E. Simonoff, C.M. Bulik, and J.L. Silberg. (2002) Bulimic symptoms in the Virginia twin study of adolescent behavioral development: Correlates, comorbidity, and genetics. *Biological Psychiatry* 51: 172–82.

Schreter, Robert K. (2004) "Economic Issues in Child and Adolescent Psychiatry." In *The American Psychiatric Publishing Textbook of Child and Adolescent* Psychiatry, 3rd ed., ed. Jerry M. Wiener and Mina K. Dulcan, 57–67. Washington, DC: American Psychiatric Publishing.

Shisslak, C., M. Crago, and L. Estes. (1995) The spectrum of eating disturbances. *International Journal of Eating Disorders* 18: 209–19.

Sim, L., C. Sadowski, S. Whiteside, and L. Wells. (under review). Comparison of conventional care to a family based approach for the treatment of anorexia nervosa in adolescents. *Mayo Clinic Proceedings.*

———. (2004). Family based therapy for adolescents with anorexia nervosa. *Mayo Clinic Proceedings*, 79: 1305–1308.

Smolak, L., and M.P. Levine. (1996) "Adolescent Transitions and the Development of Eating Problems." In *The Developmental Psychopathology of Eating Disorders: Implications for Research, Prevention, and Treatment*, ed. L. Smolak, M.P. Levine, and R. Striegel-Moore, 207–34. New Jersey: Lawrence Erlbaum Associates.

Smolak, L., and R. Striegel-Moore. (1996) "The Implications of Developmental Research for Eating Disorders." In *The Developmental Psychopathology of Eating Disorders: Implications for Research, Prevention, and Treatment*, ed. L. Smolak, M.P. Levine, and R. Striegel-Moore, 183–204. New Jersey: Lawrence Erlbaum Associates.

Steiner, H., and J. Lock. (1998) Eating disorders in children and adolescents: A review of the last 10 years. *Journal of the American Academy of Child and Adolescent Psychiatry* 37: 352–59.

Stern, S., K. Dixon, D. Jones, M. Lake, E. Nemzer, and R. Sansone. (1989) Family environment in anorexia nervosa and bulimia. *International Journal of Eating Disorders* 8: 25–31.

Striegel-Moore, R., and M. Marcus. (1995) "Eating Disorders in Women: Current Issues and Debates." In *Women's Health*, ed.

A. Stanton and S. Gallant, 445–90. Washington, DC: American Psychological Association.

Striegel-Moore, R., J. Seeley, and P.M. Lewinsohn. (2002) Psychosocial adjustment in young adulthood of women who experienced an eating disorder during adolescence. *Journal of the American Academy of Child and Adolescent Psychiatry* 4: 587–93.

Striegel-Moore, R., L.R. Silberstein, and J. Rodin. (1986) Toward an understanding of risk factors for bulimia. *American Psychologist* 41: 146–63.

Strober, M., C. Lampert, W. Morrell, J. Burroughs, and C. Jacobs. (1990) A controlled family study of anorexia nervosa: Evidence of familial aggregation and lack of shared transmission with affective disorders. *International Journal of Eating Disorders* 9: 239–53.

Strober, M., & Humphrey, L. L. (1987). Familial contribultions to the etiology and course of anorexia nervosa and bulimia. *Journal of Consulting and Clinical Psychology* 55: 654–59.

Thompson, J.K., L.J. Heinberg, M. Altabe, and S. Tantleff-Dunn. (1999) *Exacting Beauty: Theory, Assessment, and Treatment of Body Image Disturbance.* Washington, DC: American Psychological Association.

Tsai, Luke Y., and Donna J. Champine. (2004) "Schizophrenia and Other Psychotic Disorders." In *The American Psychiatric Publishing Textbook of Child and Adolescent Psychiatry*, 3rd ed., ed. Jerry M. Wiener and Mina K. Dulcan, 379–409. Washington, DC: American Psychiatric Publishing.

U.S. Food and Drug Administration. (2004) Questions and Answers on Antidepressant Use in Children, Adolescents, and Adults (March). Available at www.fda.gov/cder/drug/antidepressants/Q&A_antidepressants.htm.

Warner, Richard. (2003) *Recovery from Schizophrenia Psychiatry and Political Economy.* New York: Brunner-Routledge.

Weller, Elizabeth B., Ronald A. Weller, and Arman K. Danielyan. (2004a) "Mood Disorders in Prepubertal Children." In *The American Psychiatric Publishing Textbook of Child and Adolescent Psychiatry*, 3rd ed., ed. Jerry M. Wiener and Mina K. Dulcan, 411–35. Washington, DC: American Psychiatric Publishing.

———. (2004b) "Mood Disorders in Adolescents." In *The American Psychiatric Publishing Textbook of Child and Adolescent Psychiatry*, 3rd ed., ed. Jerry M. Wiener and Mina K. Dulcan, 437–81. Washington, DC: American Psychiatric Publishing.

Weller, Elizabeth B., Ronald A. Weller, and M.A. Fristad. (1995) Bipolar disorder in children: Misdiagnosis, underdiagnosis, and future directions. *Journal of the American Academy of Child and Adolescent Psychiatry* 34: 709–14.

Weller, Ronald A., Elizabeth B. Weller, and S.G. Tucker, et al. (1986) Mania in prepubertal children: Has it been underdiagnosed? *Journal of Affective Disorders* 11: 151–154.

Wells, L. A. (1998) Psychiatry, managed care, and crooked thinking. *Mayo Clinic Proceedings* 73: 483–87.

Whitaker, Robert. (2002) *Mad in America: Bad Science, Bad Medicine, and the Enduring Mistreatment of the Mentally Ill.* New York: Perseus Publishing.

Williams, K. (1995) Understanding the student with Asperger Syndrome: Guidelines for teachers. *Focus on Autistic Behavior* 10, no. 2: 9–16.

World Health Organization. (1992) *International Statistical Classification of Diseases and Related Health Problems.* 10th ed. Geneva, Switzerland: WHO.

Yule, William. (2002) "Post-Traumatic Stress Disorder." In *Child and Adolescent Psychiatry*, 4th ed., ed. Michael Rutter and Eric Taylor, 520–28. Oxford, UK: Blackwell Publishing.

Zito, Julie Magno, Daniel J. Safer, Susan dosReis, James F. Gardner, Laurence Magder, Karen Soeken, Myde Boles, Frances Lynch, and Mark A. Riddle. (2003) Psychotropic practice patterns for youth: A 10–year perspective. *Archives of Pediatric and Adolescent Medicine* 157: 17–25.

WEBSITE RESOURCES

General

www.bestdoctors.com/en/default.htm
www.healthfinder.gov
www.dr-bob.org
http://psychcentral.com
www.mentalhealth.org
www.mayoclinic.com
www.nami.org

Education

www.schoolcounselor.org
www.ashaweb.org
www.ideapractices.org
http://psychcentral.com
www.mentalhealth.org
www.ed.gov/offices/OSERS/index.html
www.ffcmh.org
www.nichcy.org

Societies

www.aacap.org
www.psych.org
www.apa.org

Syndromes

www.tourettesyndromesupport.com
www.autism-society.org
www.cabf.org
www.chadd.org
www.ocdresource.com
www.udel.edu/bkirby/asperger/

Medical Centers

http://childpsych.columbia.edu/Centers/centers
http://rtckids.fmhi.usf.edu/
www.georgetown.edu/research/gucdc/cassp.html
www.aboutourkids.org/index.html

29

HEALTH AND PARENTING ISSUES IN CHILDHOOD AND ADOLESCENCE

For centuries, philosophers, psychologists and educators have debated the nature-nurture controversy. At the heart of the controversy lie questions about how much of the child's development is predetermined by genetic and organismic traits of the individual, and how much is malleable and shaped by the environment in which the individual lives. In relatively recent history psychologists, including Uri Bronfenbrenner (1979, 2000), Ronald Seifer and Arnold Sameroff (1987) have reframed this debate to focus on the interplay between organic and environmental influences in determining developmental outcomes. Their work has spawned a growing body of research that highlights the dynamic and ongoing nature of the interaction between characteristics of the individual and the environment. In some instances, the influence of particular characteristics varies with their timing, as illustrated in the case of maternal substance abuse during pregnancy. The effects are most deleterious to the child's development during the first trimester, and this initial early exposure may have a direct and specific impact on development. Its significance in the life of an individual, however, is realized through the response of the environment over time to the endowments, capacities, and inclinations of the particular child, as well as through the influence of the child's changing needs and behavior on the environment.

The classic work of Albert Thomas and Stella Chess demonstrated that it is not the particular characteristics of the child that determine developmental outcome, so much as the *goodness of fit* between the child's endowments and the environment. A child who is highly persistent, for example, may have difficulty in an environment that is very fluid and changes quickly. However, in an environment that provides opportunities for the child to extend an activity over time and follow tasks through to completion, cognitive development may be enhanced by the child's persistence.

This chapter explores two key aspects of the broader nature-nurture framework: children's health and parenting. Examining these in tandem acknowledges the critical links between them in the lives of children. The child's health is a fundamental aspect of nature; it constitutes a significant part of what the individual child brings to the process of development, and defines the readiness of the organism for growth and learning. In the most basic sense, the child's health sets limits on growth and development, and defines the resources and supports that the child seeks from the environment. At the same time, the child's health has a significant influence on the expectations and care that children receive. For example, children's chronic illnesses are associated with caregiver behavior that is restrictive and anxious, in other words, overprotective. Parenting is a central component of nurture; it represents one of the primary environmental contexts in which development unfolds. Parental behavior has a direct impact on the child, and also mediates the child's access and exposure to other environmental domains. Children's access to healthcare, for example, is in many ways dependent on parental behavior.

CHILD HEALTH

Currently there is a stark contrast between the health issues confronting children in industrialized versus developing countries. Children in developing countries continue to struggle with health problems that have been largely eradicated in the industrialized world. In 2002, the Child Health Research Project of the United States Agency for International Development reported that in developing countries, 2 million children under the age of five die each year from pneumonia; another 2.2 million from diarrheal disease; and 5 million newborns from infections. This means that 9.2 million children in developing countries are dying annually from causes that are preventable, and readily treated in industrialized countries (Children's Health Research Group 2002a). Moreover, while HIV/AIDS constitutes a serious health concern for all nations, the severity of its impact on children in the developing world profoundly exceeds circumstances in industrialized countries. In an overview of policy issues related to HIV/AIDS, Jennifer Kates and colleagues (2002) noted that by 2010, more than forty million children in the developing world will have lost one or both parents to AIDS. These children also are themselves at heightened risk for AIDS.

This chapter focuses on health and parenting issues facing children in the industrialized world. During the twentieth century, the United States and other industrialized countries made dramatic strides in provisions for the basic health needs of children. There were significant overall decreases in the rates of infant mortality and increases in the availability of preventive vaccines for serious childhood illnesses including measles, mumps, rubella, chicken pox, pneumonia, and meningitis. The potential of these advances in medical knowledge to enhance survival rates and health has increased concern with ensuring all children have access to adequate healthcare.

Access to healthcare is closely linked to child poverty and also to racial and cultural barriers. In 2003, the United States Health Resources and Services Administration reported that 64 percent of children in the United States were white, non-Hispanic; 16 percent were Hispanic; 15 percent were black, non-Hispanic; 4 percent were Asian/Pacific Islander; and 1 percent were Native American/Alaska Native. The racial and ethnic disparities in child healthcare and health outcomes, some of which will be described later in this chapter, reflect continuing problems in ensuring equal access and utilization of health services by all groups. Even when healthcare is available, gaps in understanding across cultures and languages interfere with the delivery of optimal care. Anne Fadiman provided a case study of what she described as the "collision of two cultures" in the life of a Hmong girl, Lia, born with severe epilepsy

(1997). The inability of family members and medical care providers to effectively communicate about symptoms and treatment protocols seriously undermined the care that Lia received. Fadiman emphasizes the need for "cultural brokers" who can place linguistic translations within the broader contexts of cultural traditions and practices to facilitate communication and thereby ensure better access to healthcare for diverse populations.

PARENTING

Early development is characterized by dramatic changes in social, emotional, and cognitive functioning that occur within the context of the child's caregiving environment. Parental behavior plays a key role in shaping this environment and providing the experiences through which the child constructs a sense of self and expectations about the world. Parenting does not have a simple, unequivocal influence on child outcomes; parenting provides a context for development, but does not determine it. Anne Okongwu documented the ways in which constraints on available resources lead families to focus their energy on basic survival issues, such as procurement of food and shelter, and to neglect other needs including emotional availability for parenting and monitoring of children's health status and needs. Moreover, Victor Bernstein and Sydney Hans demonstrated that disturbances in emotional availability compromise development across multiple domains, interfering with the child's achievement of regular milestones in language and cognitive development (1994). At the same time as parenting is a significant contributor to the environmental context for the child's development, there is also increasing recognition of the impact that the child has on parenting behavior. This is illustrated in the work of psychologists Gerald Patterson, Tom Dishion, and Lawrence Bank (1984) who found that coercive parental behavior emerged in response to children's chronic aggression and noncompliance.

Changing patterns of family constellations have made untangling the influence of parenting on development more complex. The stay-at-home mother who provides nurturance and supervision is an increasing rarity. In 2002, the Children's Defense Fund reported that 79 percent of mothers with school-age children were working. In 1999, 71.5 percent of single mothers were working. Overall, by 2001, 13 million preschoolers, 60 percent of all young children in the United States, were in childcare (Children's Defense Fund 2001b).

SCHOOLS AND PREVENTION

Changing structures of family and childcare have resulted in expanded roles and responsibilities for schools in the lives of children as well as their families. Parents rely increasingly on schools as caregivers for their children. In April 2001, the Children's Defense Fund found that 65 percent of mothers in the labor force had children under age six, and 78 percent had children between the ages of six and thirteen. Nearly seven million school-age children stay home alone unsupervised after school, in the afternoon hours, when incidents of juvenile crime occur most frequently. Access to after-school activities, which varies significantly by income, is an important predictor of children's involvement in smoking, early sexual activity, and other high-risk behaviors (Children's Defense Fund 2001b).

In the second half of the twentieth century, as schools assumed more responsibility for caregiving, their role in relation to children's health issues also changed significantly. For children growing up in the 1950s, health education consisted of little more than a few class lessons in the early grades about the food pyramid, and in the upper grades about human sexual maturation and reproduction. By the 1990s, the health-related topics in school curricula had grown to include strategies for handling stress and peer pressure, alcohol and substance abuse, sexual practices, contraception, pregnancy, AIDS, and violence. This expansion reflects growing awareness of the links between how children are feeling and their ability to learn. It also reflects the changing role of the school in children's lives.

Schools have assumed responsibility for education that in previous generations was provided within family contexts. This shift has occurred partly in response to an explosion of knowledge about health-related issues, and concomitant concern about disseminating that knowledge as broadly and consistently as possible. The growing racial and ethnic diversity of America's children has heightened the importance of schools as a source of universal access to information about health resources and practices.

Schools have assumed an increasingly prominent role in educating children and families about health issues. Although there is not always a clear consensus about how much information should be provided about sensitive issues such as sexual behavior, AIDS prevention, and substance abuse, recent research indicates that the majority of American parents would prefer that schools address these issues with their children. Many of the more effective and comprehensive prevention programs currently in use, and reviewed at the end of this chapter, include work with parents to improve their communication with their children around these sensitive topics. Schools also have become enforcers of health strategies, through such policies as requiring immunizations for entry, or psychotropic medications for continued enrollment.

The present chapter examines a series of issues related to children's health and parenting. The first three entries address basic health concerns for children. While the emphasis in these entries is on the "nature" domain, the contribution of environmental factors to the emergence as well as the alleviation of childhood health problems is also considered. "Perinatal Health Issues" presents an overview of infant mortality and neonatal risk factors. It also reviews maternal behaviors during pregnancy that increase the risk of complications and developmental problems for the child. "Health Issues in Childhood and Adolescence" provides a profile of the changing health issues for American children. Despite the elimination of many of the common diseases of childhood through vaccines, other chronic conditions, including asthma and obesity, pose increasing health problems for children. Aside from health problems that are primarily physical in nature, many childhood disorders are defined in terms of disruption of the child's emotional and cognitive functioning. "Mental Health Disorders in Childhood and Adolescence" reviews these disorders, highlighting their links to physical symptoms and treatment, as well as to environmental influences.

The next four entries deal with a continuum of nurture issues. "Parenting Behavior" examines changing family constellations and childcare patterns. Key dimensions of parenting style and discipline techniques are highlighted. In "Family Stress and Coping," the impact of stress on the individual as well as on family functioning is considered. The importance of stress to the development of effective coping strategies is highlighted. Strategies for helping children develop more effective coping skills are presented. Extreme cases of ineffective coping are explored in "Child Maltreatment," which examines the antecedents and consequences of child abuse. The impact of child maltreatment on emotional regulation, peer relationships, and school achievement is considered. "Families of Children with Special Needs" explores the issues and stresses confronted by families with children who have particular physical and/or developmental needs. The family's role in ensuring appropriate care and services for the affected child, and the impact of the child's special needs on family functioning, are considered.

The final two entries of this chapter address issues that reflect the intimate connections between children and adolescents' health, behavior, and education. For the child, adolescence marks an increasing engagement in peer relationships and susceptibility to peer influences. At the same time, there is experimentation with behaviors, such as smoking, drinking, and early sexual activity, that pose health risks. In fact, these behaviors pose threats to the individual's physical and emotional well being, as well as to educational and occupational success. Changing family constellations and diminishing parental supervision, combined with parental uncertainty about how to handle these sensitive topics, have resulted in a growing reliance on schools to handle these issues. "Risky Behaviors in Adolescence" reviews current findings on adolescent involvement in smoking, drinking, substance abuse, and early sexual activity. "Adolescent Health Education and Prevention" provides an overview of research on effective strategies for preventing adolescent initiation of risky behavior.

Helen L. Johnson and Micheline Malow-Iroff

PERINATAL HEALTH ISSUES

The living conditions and medical care for mothers and children vary dramatically between industrialized and developing countries. The impact of these differences is highly apparent in the health issues and risks surrounding pregnancy and newborn outcomes. In 2002, the Child Health Research Project of the United States Agency for International Development reported that approximately five million infants under the age of one month die annually, the majority of these within the first week of life. Of these deaths, 98 percent occur in developing countries. It is difficult to obtain precise information about the cause of death in many of these cases, because most of the births occur at home without medical personnel or assistance. One known cause of these early deaths is infection, which accounts for almost 40 percent of the cases (Children's Health Research Group 2002b).

These findings contrast starkly to perinatal health issues and outcomes in the United States and other industrialized nations. Over the past several decades, general attitudes have moved from viewing pregnancy as an illness to be treated to viewing it as a medical condition that requires monitoring and support. The move away from a disease model of pregnancy has been associated with assigning a more active and less medicated role for the mother, and much more involvement of other family members in prenatal care and the processes of labor and delivery. There have also been major advances in medical procedures and technology to support the survival of infants who would not have survived in previous generations or under the conditions still prevalent in developing countries, because they were born very early, very small, and/or with serious impairments. One result of these advances, however, has been an increase in the number of newborns and infants who face difficulties that threaten both their immediate well being and their long-term chances for healthy development and learning. This entry will examine some of the key issues surrounding the health of American mothers and newborns during the time right around birth, commonly referred to as the perinatal period.

INFANT MORTALITY

Infant mortality refers to the rate of deaths among babies less than one year of age. In the United States, the Office of Minority Health of the Centers for Disease Control and Prevention (CDC 2004) reported that the infant mortality rate declined steadily from 26.0 deaths per 1,000 in 1960 to 6.9 deaths per 1,000 in 2000. The most frequently cited causes of infant death were preterm/low birth weight, Sudden Infant Death Syndrome (SIDS), complications of pregnancy, respiratory distress syndrome, and congenital abnormalities (CDC 2004).

The CDC reported that in 1998, the United States ranked twenty-eighth in the world in infant mortality (CDC 2004). This low ranking is due primarily to racial disparities in infant mortality. Specifically, the infant mortality rate among African Americans (14.1 deaths per 1,000 live births) was slightly more than double the national average (6.9 deaths per 1,000 live births). SIDS deaths were 2.3 times more frequent among Native American and Alaska Native infants than among non-Hispanic white infants.

PRETERM AND LOW BIRTHWEIGHT INFANTS

Babies born within two weeks of their due date (forty weeks from the mother's last menstrual cycle) are considered full term. Babies are considered "preterm" if they are born before the thirty-seventh week. The March of Dimes reported that the rate of preterm births in the United States increased more than 10 percent from 1991 to 2001. In 2001, 11.9 percent of live births in the United States were preterm. This means that in an average week, 9,159 babies were born preterm; 1,493 were born very preterm, at thirty-two weeks gestational age or younger. Recent medical advances have extended the point of viability down to twenty-three weeks, and improved the survival rates for infants born very preterm. However, in 2003 the March of Dimes reported that prematurity/low birthweight remains the leading cause of death in the first month of life. Moreover, although advances in medical treatment have reduced the mortality rates among preterm infants, these infants still face many other difficulties, including developmental delays, chronic respiratory problems, and impairments of vision and hearing.

As with infant mortality, there are significant racial and ethnic disparities in the rate of preterm births, as indicated in Table 29.1.

These racial disparities are even more striking with regard to extremely low birthweight infants (ELBW). ELBW is defined as birthweight less than 1,000 grams (2 lbs., 3 oz.), and generally involves infants born very preterm, at twenty-seven weeks or less. In 2002, Drs. Siva Subramanian, Helen Yoon, and Juan Toral reported that while African Ameri-

Table 29.1

Rates of Preterm Birth

Group	Percent
African American	17.6
Native American	12.8
Hispanic	11.4
Non-Hispanic White	10.6
Asian	10.2

Source: March of Dimes (2003).

cans accounted for 15.5 percent of live births in the United States, they accounted for 36.8 percent of the ELBW births. Although overall survival rates have improved, the proportion of ELBW infants who suffer severe impairments, including mental retardation, cerebral palsy, and deafness, has not changed. Subramanian, Yoon, and Toral reported that major impairments occur in as many as 48 percent of ELBW infants.

MATERNAL HEALTH DURING PREGNANCY

Maternal health and medical history are important predictors of the course of pregnancy and the likelihood of preterm delivery. There are a number of factors that increase the risk for preterm and low birthweight births, including the mother's history of prior preterm delivery, overall health status, and nutrition. Maternal age also is a factor, with increased risk for preterm and low birthweight births among women younger than twenty or older than thirty-five. Preterm and low birthweight births occur more frequently in multiple births. In 2003, the National Center for Infants, Toddlers and Families reported that the rate of triplet and higher order multiple births has increased 400 percent over the past twenty years. Maternal smoking, infections, and unplanned pregnancy also increase the risk of preterm/low birthweight births. The impact of these factors is heightened by the large number of women of childbearing age who are uninsured, do not obtain regular medical care, and have low incomes.

For many of the factors that jeopardize prenatal development, exposure during the first trimester of pregnancy has particularly negative effects. Women who do not realize that they are pregnant may engage in behaviors that compromise the development of their unborn child. Many women, especially those living in poverty and not receiving regular medical care, do not become aware that they are pregnant until the second or third trimester. In 2001, the Children's Defense Fund reported that one in six infants is born to a mother who did not receive prenatal care during the first three months of pregnancy; and one in twenty-six is born to a mother who received late or no prenatal care (Children's Defense Fund 2001a).

Prenatal care is particularly important for identifying maternal medical conditions that may pose a threat to the infant. This need is most urgent for mothers with HIV/AIDS (Acquired Immune Deficiency Syndrome). In 2001, AIDS was the sixth leading cause of death among one- to four-year-olds in the United States (Santrock 2004). Of the infants born to women infected with AIDS, between 15 and 30 percent become infected with the virus. With proper medical treatment and supervision, the rate of transmission can be reduced to 10 percent. Transmission of the virus from the mother to her baby can occur in one of three ways: (1) During pregnancy, the virus can cross the placenta; (2) During delivery, the virus can be transmitted through contact with the mother's blood or fluids; and (3) Postpartum, the virus can be transmitted through breastfeeding.

In addition to these concerns about maternal physical health, there are particular maternal behaviors that increase the likelihood of preterm/low birthweight births, as well as of complications during the newborn period and neurological and learning disorders in later development. Most notable among these behaviors are smoking, drinking, and substance abuse. The negative consequences of maternal smoking during pregnancy have been extensively documented (Burguet et al. 2004). Smoking is associated with higher rates of preterm delivery, infant mortality, and lower birthweights. Soren Ventegod and Joav Merrick recently noted the growing evidence that links exposure to tobacco to developmental delays and early behavioral problems in school (2003).

There has also been extensive documentation of the negative impact of maternal alcohol consumption during pregnancy. In 2002, the CDC published a report that described prenatal exposure to alcohol as "one of the leading preventable causes of birth defects, mental retardation, and neurodevelopmental disorders in the United States." Examining trends from 1991 to 1999, the CDC found that while overall, the rate of drinking during pregnancy had declined, the rates of binge drinking (five or more drinks on one occasion) and frequent drinking (seven or more drinks weekly) had not changed. This means that although fewer women now drink during pregnancy, those who do drink have continued previous patterns of heavy drinking. The data also indicated that women who drank at all during pregnancy, in comparison to those who did not, were more likely to be older than thirty, employed, and unmarried. Moreover, whereas women under age thirty tended to reduce their drinking upon learning that they were pregnant, women over age thirty did not. The CDC interprets this as indicating that the older women had greater alcohol dependency, and consequently were unable to reduce their consumption during pregnancy.

Maternal alcohol consumption during pregnancy has shown a range of negative effects on the infant and developing child. Fetal alcohol syndrome (FAS) is reported in approximately three in 10,000 births. The American Academy of Pediatrics (2000) describes the symptoms of FAS as including: small body size, low birthweight, slow development without catch-up, skeletal malformations, facial abnormalities, organ defects, and irregularities of the central nervous system, such as small brain, mental retardation, and poor coordination. In some children, FAS appears as a full-blown syndrome; in others, only a few symptoms are present (fetal alcohol effects, or FAE). While the early research documenting FAS was conducted with infants born to heavy drinkers, more recent evidence has suggested that prenatal exposure to even small amounts of alcohol can have negative effects.

Research on maternal substance abuse during pregnancy has sought to identify a syndrome of effects comparable to those associated with alcohol. Thus far, it has not been possible to identify a consistent pattern of symptoms that constitute a prenatal substance abuse syndrome. However, there is substantial evidence linking maternal substance abuse during pregnancy with negative consequences including preterm and low birthweight births; complications of labor and delivery; higher incidence of SIDS and neurological abnormalities; impaired emotional regulation; as well as delays in language and representational play. Marilyn Lewis and colleagues recently reported a dose-related effect of prenatal cocaine exposure on toddlers' mental and psychomotor development, indicating that more severe effects were associated with higher levels of maternal cocaine use (2004).

PREVENTION AND INTERVENTION

Although there have been major improvements in infant mortality rates, serious threats to maternal and infant health remain. Strikingly, many of these threats are behavioral rather than organic, which makes them natural targets for prevention and education efforts. The Special Supplemental Nutrition Program for Women, Infants, and Children addresses the nutritional needs of women, infants and children determined to be low income and nutritionally at risk. In fiscal year 2000, the WIC program served over seven million women and children (March of Dimes 2003). Maternal smoking, drinking, and substance abuse pose different problems for prevention and intervention. Over the past several decades, there have been nationwide efforts to heighten public awareness of the special risks associated with these behaviors during pregnancy. While the overall numbers of women who smoke and drink during pregnancy have declined, it appears that the behaviors continue among those women with greater dependence on these substances, making more negative effects likely. While monitoring the smoking and drinking habits of women during pregnancy can be incorporated into regular prenatal care, the abuse of illicit substances poses special challenges. Pregnant women frequently fear that disclosing their use of illicit substances will result in losing custody of their children. The move in some states to prosecute pregnant women who are using cocaine or heroin has heightened this concern and made it more difficult for doctors to get accurate prenatal information. Fear of prosecution also has exacerbated the tendency of substance abusing women to access prenatal care erratically, or not at all.

The challenge for prevention efforts is to provide information in ways that are accessible and believable to those most at risk. Since a large number of women do not learn that they are pregnant until after the first trimester, all women ages fifteen through forty-four must be included in the target population for information about perinatal health. The broad cultural, socioeconomic, educational, age, and occupational diversity of this population requires that prevention and education efforts be implemented in multiple settings (schools, community health centers, media) and from multiple perspectives.

Micheline Malow-Iroff and Helen L. Johnson

HEALTH ISSUES IN CHILDHOOD AND ADOLESCENCE

Children's health has both direct and indirect consequences for children's development and learning. A child who is hungry is likely to be less attentive in class; a child with chronic ear infections is more likely to show delays in speech and language. While advances in pharmacology have yielded a new generation of antibiotics, vaccines, and other drugs for preventing and treating many childhood illnesses, serious problems remain. A growing number of American children are dealing with health issues, including asthma, poor nutrition, obesity, and AIDS, that interfere with their school attendance and participation, and place special demands on their families and teachers. After a brief overview of current trends in immunizations, which have led to a significant shift in the profile of childhood illnesses, this entry will examine two areas in which the challenges to child health are increasing most rapidly across all income and racial/ethnic groups: asthma and nutrition.

CHILDHOOD IMMUNIZATIONS

In the twentieth century, vaccine-preventable illnesses were a major cause of infant mortality. In the United States, medical and public health agencies have made significant efforts to increase access and utilization of childhood immunizations. Through the Vaccines for Children Program, which was implemented in 1994, the government purchases vaccines at a discount, and distributes them to states so that they can be allocated to physicians and health clinics that serve children who are uninsured or enrolled in Medicaid. The program's success was apparent in the Children's Defense Fund report (2001c) that by 1999, 80 percent of two-year-olds were fully immunized against diphtheria, tetanus, pertussis, measles, mumps, rubella, and polio. In 2003, the Centers for Disease Control and Prevention indicated that the number of American children receiving immunizations remained at an all-time high (Medical Letter on the CDC and FDA August 2003). Moreover, the CDC reported significant increases in the number of children receiving the immunizations for chicken pox and pneumonia, which have become available more recently.

Despite the overall success of immunization programs, however, racial, ethnic, and regional disparities in immunization rates remain. Concern about possible side effects leads some parents to decide against immunizations for their children. Most recently, there has been public concern over possible links between childhood immunizations and autism. Although no clear evidence supporting this link has been presented to date, the concern has generated some public support for parental choice about immunizations. Psychologists Abigail Wroe, Nikki Turner, and Paul Salkovskis (2004) examined parental decisions about immunizations. They found that parents who decided against immunization were concerned about possible side effects, believed that the body's natural immune system should not be disrupted, and were more likely to distrust information about immunizations offered by the government and healthcare professionals. Elaine Larson (2003) recently emphasized the need for practitioners to employ culturally competent education and outreach approaches to improve access and utilization of immunization programs by underserved populations.

Immunization requirements for school entry have been implemented in all fifty states, resulting in vaccination rates of 95 percent for children entering school. Children exempted from vaccinations for religious or medical reasons are thirty-five times more likely to contract measles than those who have been vaccinated. These unvaccinated children pose a health risk to others in their communities who may be particularly vulnerable to these contagious but preventable diseases.

ASTHMA

Ironically, at the same time as the incidence of many contagious diseases has been reduced dramatically through childhood immunizations, the rate of asthma has nearly doubled in the United States over the past ten years. Citing data from the CDC, the Children's Defense Fund reports that asthma has become one of the most common chronic health problems of childhood (Children's Defense Fund 2001d). Their data indicate that 4.4 million children are currently affected by asthma.

There is increasing awareness across the health professions that many illnesses have roots in both biological and psychosocial factors. Researchers Mary Klinnert, Marcella Price, Andrew Liu and JoAnn Robinson (2002) examine childhood asthma from this perspective, suggesting that asthma is the result of genetic susceptibility combined with environmental exposures. It is the environmental exposures that appear to account for the prevalent patterns of childhood asthma in the United States. This suggests prevention and intervention could have a significant impact on childhood asthma rates.

There are significant racial and economic disparities in both the rates of asthma and the consequences associated with it. Prevalence and morbidity of asthma are greatest among African American children living in low-income households in large urban communities. The Children's Defense Fund (2001d) reports that recent increases in asthma rates have been highest among children of color living in low-income communities. Among non-Hispanic children ages five to fourteen, African American children are five times more likely than white children to die from asthma. Other factors associated with higher prevalence of childhood asthma include young maternal age, single parenthood, poor prenatal care, and low birthweight in infants. Klinnert and colleagues note that all of these factors occur more frequently in low-income families, and are characteristics associated with increased family stress (Klinnert et al. 2002). Similarly, problems with parental functioning, stress, and mental health, all associated with asthma prevalence and morbidity, are also more frequent in low-income families.

There have been mixed findings regarding the risk and protective factors for childhood asthma. Recently, Jouni Jaakkola and Mika Gissler (2004) sought to clarify the relationship that has been reported between maternal smoking during pregnancy and childhood asthma. Specifically, they examined the relation between the incidence of asthma at age seven and three perinatal variables, all of which have well-documented associations with maternal smoking during pregnancy: birthweight and small for gestational age (both measures of fetal growth), and preterm delivery. The findings of their large-scale study of Finnish children indicated that both birthweight and preterm delivery increased the risk of childhood asthma, although being small for gestational age did not. Overall, Jaakkola and Gissler conclude that fetal growth mediates only a small portion of the association between maternal smoking and childhood asthma. These findings again highlight the importance of environmental factors in predicting childhood asthma.

Klinnert and colleagues sought to identify racial/ethnic differences in the "patterns of covariation of family history, environmental allergens, and psychosocial stressors" associated with childhood asthma (Klinnert et al. 2002). They concluded that it was difficult to clearly delineate the effects of individual variables because the variables tend to occur in clusters. Specifically, the groups with the highest levels of exposure to maternal smoking and environmental allergens also had the greatest proportion of young single mothers and the highest incidence of stressful life experiences. Klinnert and colleagues suggest that intervention strategies must acknowledge the clustering of these variables in the lives of children and their families. This means that in addition to addressing biological vulnerabilities and exposures, intervention efforts must ameliorate the psychosocial factors that contribute to these biological conditions and exposures.

Interestingly, recent studies have suggested a "hygiene hypothesis" to explain the origins of childhood asthma. According to this approach, children's vulnerability to asthma may result from their lack of early exposure to infections. This early exposure triggers the child's development of immunities to common infections; without the exposure, the child is more susceptible to later respiratory difficulties, and more likely to develop asthma (Lima et al. 2003). Rosangela Lima, Cesar Victora, Ana Menezes, and Fernando Barros (2003) recently corroborated this relationship in a large-scale study of Brazilian adolescents. In their findings, being of high socioeconomic status, living in an uncrowded household, and being breastfed for nine months or longer were all related to higher

risk for asthma. Lima and colleagues conclude that many of the health practices that serve to reduce the spread of serious illnesses in developing countries may inadvertently place the child at higher risk for asthma. The implications of this paradoxical finding for intervention strategies are currently being explored. At the same time, some promising school-based interventions for helping children regulate their asthma are emerging, and will be discussed in the entry on intervention at the end of this chapter.

NUTRITION, OBESITY, AND EATING DISORDERS

Nutrition

The United States is lauded as the land of plenty. Yet in 2003, the Children's Defense Fund projected that in 2004, one out of six American households with children will have trouble "putting food on the table." Researchers Cheryl Wehler, Linda Weinreb, Nicholas Huntington, Richard Scott, David Hosmer, Kenneth Fletcher, Robert Goldberg and Craig Gundersen (2004) cite government findings that 10.1 percent of all American household are food insecure, which means that they did not have enough money or other resources to obtain sufficient food to enable all family members to have active, healthy lives. Of these 31 million food-insecure Americans, 3 million households experience hunger.

Recent data from the third National Health and Nutrition Examination Survey illustrate the links between children's nutrition and health. In an analysis of the data on young children, food insufficiency was defined as a family member's report that the family sometimes or often did not have enough to eat. Not surprisingly, poor-fair health status and iron deficiency were both more prevalent among low-versus high-income children. Even after the effects of confounding variables including poverty were controlled, food insufficiency increased the likelihood that children would have poorer health status and more frequent headaches and stomachaches. In preschool children, food insufficiency also was associated with more frequent colds.

Wehler and colleagues (2004) examined socioeconomic and psychosocial factors that contribute to food insufficiency. Their findings indicate that while lack of economic resources contributes significantly to hunger, these effects are exacerbated by maternal physical and mental health. Mothers with fewer health problems and better emotional functioning were more able to protect their children from hunger, despite constrained resources.

Obesity

At the same time as procuring sufficient food is difficult for many American children and their families, excessive food consumption has resulted in a growing problem of childhood obesity and associated health risks. Researchers Jennifer Nelson, Mary Ann Chiasson and Viola Ford (2004) found that from 1974 to 2000, the prevalence of overweight children increased from 4 percent of the population to 15 percent for children ages six through eleven, and from 5 percent to 10 percent in two- to five-year-olds. In 2003, noting that the number of obese children had doubled over the past two decades, the American Academy of Pediatrics reported that "the prevalence of childhood overweight and obesity is increasing at an alarming rate in the United States as well as in other developed and developing countries." The pediatric evaluation of overweight and obesity status is based on body mass index (BMI), a ratio of body weight to height. Children with BMIs between the eighty-fifth and ninety-fifth percentile for their age and gender are considered at risk for overweight; those with BMIs over the ninety-fifth percentile are considered obese.

Childhood obesity is associated with serious health problems, both in childhood and adulthood. In children, these problems include increased risk of cardiovascular problems such as hypertension, endocrine problems such as type 2 diabetes and menstrual irregularities, and mental health problems such as depression and low self-esteem. Childhood obesity, as well as the symptoms associated with it, is likely to persist in adulthood. Because of the intractability of adult obesity, the American Academy of Pediatrics recommends increasing efforts to prevent childhood obesity as the best strategy for alleviating this major American health risk (AAP 2003). Studies of children's eating and exercise patterns suggest that childhood obesity results from a combination of both. The diets of American children generally do not meet the recommended requirements for fruits, vegetables,

and calcium, and reflect excessive consumption of highly processed, salted, and sweetened foods. Working mothers increasingly rely on fast-food meals, which are particularly laden with more caloric than nutritional value. Moreover, children's engagement in physical activity has diminished as recreational time has focused more on computers and television.

The depression and low self-esteem associated with childhood obesity have particularly deleterious effects in adolescence. Concerns about self-image and social status may lead obese adolescents to impose extreme limits on their caloric intake, which create additional health problems. There is increasing evidence of links between adolescent dieting and the initiation of health-compromising behaviors, including smoking, drinking, substance abuse, and unprotected sex.

Eating Disorders

Over the past twenty years, there has been a significant increase in cases of eating disorders. These disorders are defined in terms of: (1) maladaptive attempts to control body weight, (2) serious disruptions in eating behavior, and (3) abnormal attitudes about body shape and weight, and may occur in people who are overweight, normal weight, or underweight. Eating disorders may include binge eating, in which the individual consumes an unusually large amount of food in a limited time period, and feels a lack of control about the eating. Individuals with eating disorders seek to control their weight through either restricting intake or purging.

The two main categories of eating disorders are anorexia nervosa and bulimia nervosa. Individuals with anorexia nervosa have an intense fear of gaining weight, have bodyweights less than 85 percent of expected weight, and have distorted body images that lack recognition of the low bodyweight. Anorexics experience disruption of the menstrual cycle, and can place themselves at risk of death from the extreme restrictions on caloric intake that they impose. Anorexics do not perceive their low bodyweight as posing a health risk. In Hilda Bruch's classic work on anorexia, some patients perceived their refusal to eat as an indicator of personal control and autonomy (1979). Whereas anorexics restrict their intake, bulimics engage in binge eating and then purging. Eating disorders generally begin in adolescence, and occur most frequently in white females from middle- to upper-income households.

In the twentieth century, the profile of health issues facing American children changed significantly. The broad availability of immunizations and antibiotics has drastically reduced, and in some cases eliminated, contagious diseases that once posed serious threats to children's survival. At the present time, the most pervasive and rapidly growing challenges to children's health have strong environmental components that interact with genetic predispositions and vulnerabilities. The complexity of these disorders will require more comprehensive approaches to prevention and intervention.

Micheline Malow-Iroff and Helen L. Johnson

MENTAL HEALTH DISORDERS IN CHILDHOOD AND ADOLESCENCE

The number of children diagnosed with mental health disorders is soaring. Public debate frequently rages over the trend to diagnose and treat children and adolescents who may deviate from behavioral expectations. But are children truly over-diagnosed and medicated so that parents and teachers can manage them better? Or, are parents and clinicians more aware of normal development and behavior, enabling them to identify early symptoms of problems? The answer to these questions can only be answered on a case-by-case basis. However, all medical professionals utilize the criteria of symptoms and exclusions listed in the Diagnostic and Statistical Manual–IV (DSM-IV) to diagnose children and adolescents with a mental health disorder (American Psychiatric Association 1994). As the DSM-IV is a medical system of classification, most educators and parents are not familiar with the behaviors, symptoms, and exclusions listed as indicators of the various disorders. Moreover, adults who are well informed as to the distinction between typical behaviors and exceptional behaviors in children are in a better position to know when to seek professional help and how to participate actively in the diagnostic process.

Recent estimates indicate that 3–4 million Ameri-can children under the age of eighteen are prescribed and take psychiatric drugs. This number has doubled since a decade ago, partially due to the fact that children at increasingly younger ages are being prescribed psychiatric drugs (Zito 2000). The problem with this trend is that most of the psychiatric drugs prescribed to children have not been tested in these young patients. Concerns about method of action, side effects, and long-term consequences of using these substances abound, yet the medications are being prescribed at ever-increasing rates. How is this possible? Drug companies tend to pursue the simplest route to market for their medications and this generally means obtaining approval by the Food and Drug Administration (FDA) for the adult use of medications. Back in 1970 the FDA declared that the medications doctors prescribed for children must be tested in children. However the FDA's limited power and influence is unable to monitor prescription practices and the organization estimates that between 70 percent and 80 percent of all drugs prescribed to children have not been approved for use by children (Brown 2003). Although the use of what is called "off-label" treatments is common medical practice, the FDA and the U.S. Department of Health and Human Services continue to push for studies on pediatric patients. Slowly, things are changing. Organizations such as the National Institute of Mental Health are leading the way by funding investigations into basic drug biology and clinical trials that look into how these drugs affect children's brains.

The etiology of mental health disorders is unclear. Experts agree that they develop out of a complex set of risk factors that include genetic predisposition, brain chemistry, personality and temperament, parent and family interactions, as well as life experiences. What is clear is that the early diagnosis and treatment of mental health problems in children is a trend that is around to stay. Professionals concur that the earlier a condition is recognized, the sooner an appropriate course of treatment can begin and the better the long-term prognosis. Treatment options include parent training, family and individual psychotherapy, behavioral therapy, and medications. Once diagnosis occurs, families and educators can utilize treatment options to begin to counter the negative effects of having a child with a mental health disorder such as family stress, lowered self-esteem, learning difficulties, and socialization issues. Therefore, we as educated participants in society need to be armed with an awareness of the early indications of a variety of mental health disorders that are present in childhood and adolescence. Three of the most common mental health disorders will be briefly reviewed: attention deficit hyperactivity disorder, mood disorders, and anxiety disorders.

ATTENTION DEFICIT HYPERACTIVITY DISORDER

Attention deficit hyperactivity disorder (ADHD) is one contributor to the current increase in the diagnosis of mental health disorders. ADHD has become the most common neuropsychiatric syndrome diagnosed in children. ADHD is reported to affect between 3 percent and 5 percent of school-age children (American Psychiatric Association 1994), a figure that represents approximately 2 million children nationwide. Despite the growing numbers of children who are diagnosed with this disorder, ADHD continues to evade efforts to pinpoint a universally accepted definition. The DSM-IV states that the atypical behavior observed in the individual must be present for at least six months, that the child must display six or more symptoms from the inattention (Attention Deficit Disorder) or the hyperactivity/impulsivity (Attention Deficit Hyperactivity Disorder) categories prior to the age of seven, and that the behavior must be present in at least two settings (e.g., home and school). Complicating these guidelines is the fact that ADHD is a multifaceted disorder, encompassing a variety of behavioral symptoms that manifest differently in individual children. Children with ADHD include those with symptoms of difficulty sustaining attention, distractibility, lack of task persistence, and disorganization. However, it can also include children with excessive motor activity and impulsive responding behavior. Russell Barkley, one of the primary and leading researchers in the area, provided one of the most helpful definitions of ADHD in 1990 indicating that it is a "developmental disorder characterized by inappropriate degrees of inattention, over-activity, and impulsivity. These often arise in early childhood; are relatively chronic in nature; and are not readily accounted for on the basis of gross neurological,

sensory, language, motor impairment, mental retardation, or severe emotional disturbance" (p. 47). Despite the rise in research investigating this disorder over the last two decades, ADHD still remains a challenge to diagnose as there are frequently coexistent conditions complicating the diagnosis. These conditions include anxiety disorders, mood disorders, learning disorders, conduct disorder, and oppositional defiant disorder.

EDUCATION AND TREATMENT FOR ADHD

Without early intervention and treatment, ADHD-type behaviors interfere with developmentally appropriate socialization, learning, and parent-child interaction. However, parental concerns about the rising rate of stimulant prescription, potential side-effects of long-term medication, and the growing use of psychostimulant medication in preschool children make professional consultation for ADHD difficulties an option of last resort. Prior to seeking professional help, parents usually try a variety of home-cure approaches that might include behavior modification techniques, dietary restrictions (e.g., limiting sugar or preservatives), corporal punishment, activity scheduling, and religious interventions. Some home-cure techniques may be consistent with evidence-based behavioral principles; however other strategies may add undue stress to the parent-child relationship. Thus, the home-cure strategies implemented by the parents should be discussed and assessed as to their efficacy with medical professionals when it is determined that professional help is needed. Medical professionals spend a limited amount of time interacting and observing the children they are charged with serving, therefore the judgments and observations of parents and teachers become crucial in the diagnostic process. Once identified as ADHD, interventions and treatments for this disorder include the highly researched and reviewed psychosocial therapies and psychostimulant medication. These two well-researched treatments will be discussed briefly.

Psychosocial therapies include the development of behavioral strategies to help families and educators work with the child's present level of functioning. The goal is to make the necessary accommodations within the child's environment in order to maximize the child's performance. One model of psychosocial therapy that has proven effective is parent training. In a recent investigation, which utilized a community sample, parent training was found to increase the mothers' sense of well being and improved clinical symptoms in 53 percent of the children whose parents received it (Edmund et al. 2001). Another common behavioral intervention is the development of a plan that all adults involved with the child agree to implement in various settings. This may include changes to the environmental arrangements at home or in the classroom, it may provide suggestions for the parents and teachers in their interactions with the child, and it may provide for the administration of consequences for inappropriate behavior. Environmental arrangements should be individualized as much as possible to allow for a structure and routine that permits the child to engage in developmental experiences that provide the adults with numerous opportunities for positive interaction. Techniques to facilitate the acquisition of appropriate behavior include the application of behavior management principles. These principles include clear and consistent expectations with an abundance of opportunities to provide positive reinforcement and feedback in order to increase desirable behaviors. While at the same time, these principals provide for the ability to reflect and gain composure through time-outs, and other procedures with the goal of decreasing undesirable behaviors.

Although many parents of children with ADHD do not support the use of psychostimulant intervention, research has proven that it is more effective in reducing children's ADHD symptoms than psychosocial therapies alone (Bussing and Gary 2001). Between 70 percent and 90 percent of children prescribed medication for ADHD will have a positive response to the medications. The most commonly administered medications are stimulants that include Ritalin and Dexedrine. Although administering stimulants to a child who already may exhibit excessive motor activity is counterintuitive, research is providing insights into their mechanism of action. Stimulant medications are thought to alter the chemical functioning in the frontal lobe region of the brain, increasing the child's ability to attend to and focus on a task. Ritalin specifically works by increasing the extracellular dopamine levels, which in turn activates the motivation and drive of the individual.

The Multimodal Treatment Study of Children with Attention-Deficit/Hyperactivity Disorder (the MTA study) is a cooperative treatment study performed by six independent research teams (MTA Cooperative Group) in collaboration with the Division of Services and Intervention Research, National Institute of Mental Health, and the Office of Special Education Programs, U.S. Department of Education. The MTA Cooperative Group conducted an investigation of treatment practices used in children diagnosed with ADHD over fourteen months, at six different sites in the United States, and utilized children from 7 to 9.9 years of age (MTA Cooperative Group 1999). Each child was randomly assigned to one of four treatment groups: medication, intensive behavioral treatment, combined medication and behavioral treatment, and standard care offered by providers in the community. Results indicated that there was a reduction in symptoms in all groups but that the medication and the combined medication/behavioral therapy groups showed significantly greater improvement. The combined group did not differ significantly from the medication group on ADHD symptoms, but behavioral therapy did help to reduce other coexisting symptoms that included oppositional/aggressive behavior and internalizing behavior. Given that research has found medication to be one of the most effective treatments, it stands to reason that the trend to prescribe stimulants for ADHD will continue.

MOOD DISORDERS: DEPRESSION AND BIPOLAR DISORDER

Mood disorders have been called the "common cold" of psychiatric illnesses. While everyone experiences shifts in moods from time to time, most of us do not understand the depths of depression or the highs and lows of bipolar disorder. It is estimated that more than 20 million Americans will suffer a mood disorder episode during their lifetime, however only one in three people who experience this debilitating disorder will seek treatment. Although it was once commonly thought that children did not experience mood disorders, clinical opinion has turned and it is now known that individuals throughout the lifespan can and do experience the helplessness that accompanies them. As with all psychiatric disorders, mood disorders are diagnosed with the use of the DSM-IV, which divides them into depressive disorders and bipolar disorders.

Depression is a mood disorder that is characterized by changes in emotion, motivation, physical well being, and thoughts. The emotional state of individuals experiencing depression can be characterized as overwhelming feelings of sadness or worthlessness. Changes in motivational states are recognized as a change in an individual's behavior. These behavioral changes may include changes in friendships or stopping associations with friends altogether, changes in recreational activities or stopping the participation in these activities, and changes in school work, most often resulting in a decline in grades. The changes in physical well-being are often observed through a behavioral change in the individual that is different from their normal pattern of behavior. These can include alterations such as eating and sleeping too much or too little, disregarding personal hygiene and appearance, and having vague physical complaints such as aches and pains that have no origin. Changes in thought and cognition also occur which help to sustain the disorder in the individual as they believe that they are worthless, ugly, unable to do anything right, and that life is hopeless for them.

Research has found that symptoms of depression manifest differently in children, adolescents, and adults, fueling the debate over whether children actually experience depression. In children, depression is mixed with a larger array of behavioral characteristics that are often misunderstood leading to the difficulty in diagnosis. Depressed children often display aggression, irritability, undifferentiated anxiety, antisocial behavior, and school failure. In addition, depression often occurs in conjunction with other disorders such as conduct disorder, substance abuse, eating disorders, and anxiety disorders. According to the American Academy of Child and Adolescent Psychiatry, approximately 5 percent of children and adolescents experience depression (American Academy of Child and Adolescent Psychiatry 2004b).

Bipolar disorder, known throughout most of the twentieth century as manic-depressive illness, is experiencing rising rates of diagnosis in children and adolescents. Just as it was thought that children did not experience depression, it was also believed that bipolar illness did not occur in individuals until late adolescence or early adulthood. Although it is estimated that between 1–2 percent of adults worldwide are affected by bipolar disorder, due to co-morbid conditions, estimates of children afflicted

with the disorder are presumed to be inaccurate. Current diagnosis of bipolar disorder indicates that approximately 1 million children and adolescents in the United States are affected. However, according to the American Academy of Child and Adolescent Psychiatry, up to one-third of the children and adolescents currently diagnosed with depression may actually be experiencing early-onset bipolar disorder. In addition, it is suspected that many of the children currently diagnosed with ADHD may also have early-onset bipolar disorder (Papolos and Papolos 1999).

While depression is characterized by mood states that are low, individuals who suffer from bipolar disorder experience exaggerated mood states. An individual with bipolar disorder is depressed at times and then swings to the other end of the mood spectrum and has heightened levels of activity, ideas, and energy known as mania. Bipolar disorder presents itself differently in adults and children, which initially led to the belief that children and adolescents did not experience it. The DSM-IV criteria for the classification of bipolar disorder requires that the manic and depressive episodes that the individual experiences last for a prescribed number of days or weeks. However, this is not the pattern that is generally demonstrated by children. Children with bipolar disorder experience a chronic and erratic course with many shifts in mood throughout a day. Thus, many children and adolescents do not meet the diagnostic criteria specified in the DSM-IV. Additionally, as there is a great deal of overlap in the demonstration of symptoms in children and adolescents, frequently these individuals are diagnosed with other psychiatric labels such as ADHD, depression, oppositional defiant disorder, obsessive-compulsive disorder, or separation anxiety disorder.

EDUCATION AND TREATMENT FOR MOOD DISORDERS

For diagnosis and treatment of mood disorders, the involvement of parents, teachers, and other important adults in a child's life cannot be overstated. As with many psychiatric disorders, there is no conclusive medical test for these disorders. The observation, recording, and accurate reporting of behaviors to medical professionals are necessary in order to receive an accurate diagnosis and the proper treatment. This is especially important with mood spectrum disorders as the treatment for depression can facilitate the onset of mania in an incorrectly diagnosed individual. For this reason, it is essential to incorporate an educational component into any diagnosis and treatment of mood disorders; both the individual with the disorder and his or her family need to be educated about the course, symptoms, patterns, treatment options, and side effects of medications. As with many of the psychiatric disorders, both psychological interventions and medical treatments have proven effective in the treatment of mood disorders. In addition, new research indicates that interactions within the family setting may be indicative of poorer social functioning in depressed adolescents. A high level of expressed emotion by one or both of the parents is associated with the presence of more depressive symptoms in the adolescent. Expressed emotion is assessed on an individual basis, utilizing a standardized tool. A family with high expressed emotion as an interactional style would display excessive criticism, hostility, or emotional over involvement. In these circumstances, a familywide intervention would be appropriate to assist the depressed individual in their recovery.

Two of the individual psychological interventions that have proven effective in treating depressed individuals are cognitive therapy and interpersonal psychotherapy. Both interventions are structured and time-limited in their approaches, geared toward developing the increasing competence of the individual. Dr. Aaron Beck detailed his view of depressive symptomatology in 1973 when he described individuals as having acquired cognitive schemas that are characterized by self-devaluation and lack of confidence about the future. The habitual negative thoughts magnify and expand depressed individuals' negative experiences as they begin to attend to only the negative cues in the environment. Cognitive therapy teaches the depressed individual to challenge the persistent negative thoughts. Drs. Gerald Klerman and Myrna Weissman developed interpersonal psychotherapy (Klerman and Weissman 1986). Interpersonal psychotherapy differs from cognitive therapy in that it works to improve an individual's self-concept, communication skills, and social relationships.

Individual and family therapies are an important part of treatment for bipolar disorder as well. Individuals who are bipolar need lifestyle management strategies. Keeping schedules are extremely impor-

tant as fluctuating schedules can destabilize circadian rhythms. Time zone changes and sleep deprivation can cause many difficulties so that regular bedtimes and wakeup times are necessary to keep children stable. Diet management can also be important as caffeine, alcohol, and recreational drug use can trigger a manic episode. In addition, families need to learn how to reduce environmental stress that may trigger episodes. A stable, steady home that avoids too much negatively expressed emotion is essential and therapists can teach parents and children how to minimize discord within the family.

Antidepressants are the medical treatment for depression. There are numerous antidepressants on the market and current research has brought more effective treatments with fewer side effects. Medications such as Prozac, Zoloft, Paxil, and Elavil have been used to reduce the symptoms of depression in both children and adolescents with successful results. However, as with all medications there are side effects that may occur within individuals and need to be monitored. These side effects can include insomnia, agitation, nausea, dizziness, and headache.

The use of antidepressants for individuals experiencing a mood disorder is very risky. This is a major concern due to the frequency with which bipolar illness is misdiagnosed as depression. For individuals with bipolar disorder, antidepressants may trigger bouts of mania, increased irritability, and aggression. Thus, the possibility of bipolar disorder must be ruled out before antidepressants are prescribed. For bipolar disorder, mood stabilizers are the main medical treatment. The mood stabilizer with the most history of use is lithium carbonate, however many new mood stabilizers have become available. One of the most important new drugs to be made available in the treatment of bipolar disorder is the anticonvulsant Lamictal. The FDA approved this medication in 2003 for long-term treatments. In addition to these medications, there are many antipsychotic drugs that have been used to treat psychotic symptoms, anxiety states, and to break up rapid mood-cycling swings.

One last important point to be made about individuals experiencing mood disorders is the connection with suicide. According to the American Academy of Pediatrics, suicidal adolescents often display depressive symptoms (2001). In 2000, the National Center for Health Statistics indicated that suicide was the third leading cause of death in adolescents between the ages of thirteen and nineteen. Additionally, although suicide is rare, 1,921 individuals between the ages of ten and nineteen committed suicide in the United States in the year 2000. However, far more than that number either contemplated suicide or attempted it unsuccessfully. Although females have higher rates of depressed moods and are more likely to attempt suicide than males, males are more likely to be successful in their attempts. Depressed adolescents are particularly at risk for suicidal behavior and it is crucial for them to be seen immediately by a physician who has expertise in this area. Pediatricians, general practitioners, and psychiatrists are the first line of treatment for depressed and suicidal children. Frequently these children are prescribed antidepressants to combat their illness. Controversy over the efficacy of this practice has been widely discussed in recent news reports. Ultimately, the FDA will determine whether the newest class of antidepressants, selective serotonin reuptake inhibitors (SSRIs), will be approved for prescription to children. Concerns over the practice specifically relate to increased risk of suicidal behavior in children and adolescents. With research and investigations ongoing, the American Academy of Child and Adolescent Psychiatry has advocated for enhanced warnings on SSRI medications. Additionally, this organization emphasizes the need for close monitoring of children and adolescents being treated with these substances (2004a).

ANXIETY DISORDERS

All individuals experience anxiety to some degree. Low levels of anxiety can help a person to remain alert in situations that require focus and can also improve performance. In fact, anxiety is considered normal at specific points in development. One example of this is the anxieties that infants exhibit starting at about eight months of age upon separation from individuals to whom they are attached. However, high levels of anxiety can be debilitating and cause interference with the daily activities of life such as separating from parents, going to school or work, and making friends. Attacks of anxiety can arise suddenly and last for a few seconds, or they can develop gradually, over a period of days and last for years. Anxiety that lasts for a longer period of time and interferes with daily functioning is known as an anxiety disorder. Anxiety dis-

orders are among the most common childhood and adult mental health disorders. The understanding of anxiety in childhood and adolescence has increased within the past decade due in part to the development of new assessment measures that differentiate among types of chronic anxiety. Approximately 12–20 percent of children and adolescents are afflicted with this disorder (Costello and Angold 1995). Anxiety disorders are characterized by excessive amounts of fear, worry, and uneasiness, and cause significant impairment in academic, social, and familial functioning. The anxiety that is experienced by some individuals is so distressing that depression can occur, or anxiety and depression can coexist, or depression can come first and trigger an anxiety disorder.

There are many types of anxiety disorders. Table 29.2 presents a brief description of each subtype. Children and adolescents can develop any of these subtypes; however some of the subtypes are more common in childhood than others. Younger children tend to have separation anxiety disorder, specific phobias, and early symptoms of obsessive-compulsive disorder, while generalized anxiety disorder and social anxiety disorder are more common to middle childhood and adolescence, and panic disorder usually occurs in adolescence. Another subtype of anxiety disorder, post-traumatic stress disorder, can occur at any point that a trauma is experienced. The DSM-IV is used to diagnose anxiety disorders based on the clinical judgment of presenting symptoms, while utilizing specific diagnostic criteria to determine the subtype of the anxiety disorder and to rule out other coexisting disorders. In addition, new measures used to diagnose anxiety in children include diagnostic interviews based on DSM-IV symptomology.

EDUCATION AND TREATMENT OF ANXIETY DISORDERS

Much like other mental health disorders, anxiety disorders are caused by a combination of biological, familial, and environmental factors. Thus, education and treatment follows a similar course. The individuals and their families learn about the specific anxiety disorder, how it manifests in the individual, early signs and symptoms, and ways to control or handle the anxiety. Treatments can follow one of the many psychosocial therapies available for anxiety disorders, medical intervention can involve using a variety of

Table 29.2

Anxiety Disorder Subtypes with Brief Descriptions

Separation Anxiety Disorder	Persistent thoughts and fears about safety for self and parents, school refusal, physical complaints, extreme worry over sleeping away from home, trouble sleeping, and nightmares.
Specific Phobia	Irrational fear reaction to a specific object or situation such as spiders or heights. Can lead to the avoidance of everyday situations.
Generalized Anxiety Disorder	Characterized by excessive, chronic, and unrealistic worry that lasts six months or more. Symptoms may include trembling, physical complaints, insomnia, and irritability.
Social Anxiety Disorder	Extreme anxiety at the thought of being judged by others. Irrational fear of behaving in a way that will cause embarrassment. Physical symptoms may include heart palpitations, faintness, trembling, and profuse sweating.
Panic Disorder	Severe attacks of panic that can occur in a variety of situations and results in physical symptoms such as heart palpitations, chest pain, sweating, fear of dying, fear of losing control, and fear of unreality.
Obsessive-Compulsive Disorder	Persistent recurring thoughts (obsessions) that reflect fears or anxiety. Obsessions lead the individual to perform a routine behavior (compulsions). Examples of compulsions include washing hands, repeating phrases, and turning lights on and off a certain number of times.
Post-Traumatic Stress Disorder	Follows exposure to a traumatic event such as assaults, death, and natural or man-made disasters. Symptoms include reliving the event through flashbacks or nightmares, avoidance behaviors and emotional numbing, and physiological arousal such as irritability and poor concentration.

Source: Anxiety Disorders Association of America (2004).

medications specifically oriented toward the individual's manifestation of the disorder, or treatment can involve a combination of approaches. As with all mental health disorders, involvement of the family is necessary to enhance treatment outcomes. Poor treatment outcomes in children have been associated with high rates of psychopathology in the family. Some investigations have proposed that poor treatment response is linked to parent-child relational factors and specifically that children of depressed mothers are at high risk for poor outcomes. Thus, investigation of family psychopathology and interactional patterns should be a part of a comprehensive evaluation for a child with anxiety disorder.

Psychosocial treatments for anxiety disorder have shown positive results, contributing to the development of a variety of therapy modalities, which include behavior therapy, relaxation techniques, cognitive therapy, and cognitive-behavior therapy. The goal of these treatments is to help the individual modify and gain control over unwanted behavior and/or to change harmful thought patterns. Within behavioral therapies, a very useful procedure has been to provide individuals with support and guidance during controlled exposure to the anxiety-provoking situation. The exposure, or systematic desensitization, to the anxiety-producing situation can be pre-sented either as mental images or in real life, depending on the degree of anxiety and the individual's willingness to be exposed to the various situations. Frequently, this exposure will be paired with relaxation techniques that will allow the individual to develop the ability to cope with the stress of anxiety while controlling the physical symptoms. Relaxation techniques may involve breathing retraining, biofeedback, and exercise. Cognitive therapy used in anxiety disorders has the same goal as the cognitive therapy utilized for people diagnosed with depression. The individual examines his/her own feelings and learns to separate realistic from unrealistic thoughts. Combining behavioral therapy and cognitive therapy results in what is known as cognitive-behavioral therapy and provides the individual with a way to target not only their behavioral patterns but also their thought patterns.

Medication therapy for anxiety disorders includes the full range of antidepressants available, as well as anxiolytics (antianxiety medications), anticonvulsant medications, antipsychotic medications, and beta blockers. The most widely used class of drugs for the treatment of anxiety disorders, both in children and in adults, are selective serotonin reuptake inhibitors (SSRIs). This class of drug affects the concentration of the neurotransmitter serotonin in the brain. Commonly used SSRIs include Prozac, Zoloft, Paxil, and Luvox. The FDA has given approval to use the SSRIs Prozac, Zoloft, and Luvox in pediatric obsessive-compulsive disorder; however, it is frequently used off-label in the treatment of other anxiety disorders, with or without coexisting depressive symptoms. Although improvement in symptom severity can occur after one week of SSRI treatment, treatment trials are generally given for four to six weeks to assess the clinical response. Although SSRIs generally have minimal side effects, the typical side effects that do occur are similar to the physical symptoms experienced as a result of the anxiety disorder. These can include headache, nausea, sleep changes, jitteriness, and agitation. Therefore, careful monitoring of physical complaints while undergoing SSRI treatment is essential (Anxiety Disorders Association of America 2004).

Although both psychosocial and medication treatment regimens have been proven effective for anxiety disorders, often it is medical practice to utilize a combination of both. As medication therapy generally produces a quick reduction in symptoms, it is often the first line of defense against the anxiety disorder. However, whether medication intervention is a short-term or long-term treatment option, medication therapy should be paired with both family and individual psychosocial therapy in order to teach the skills that will be useful in the management of their specific anxiety disorder.

Micheline Malow-Iroff and Helen Johnson

PARENTING BEHAVIOR

The configuration of the American family has changed drastically over the last several decades due to the proliferation and acceptance in society of what constitutes family. Several widespread practices have propelled changing conceptions of family such as the increased incidences of divorce rates, single-parent families, mothers working outside of the home, blended families, extended families, and culturally and racially diverse families. As a result, the typical American family is a conglomerate of attitudes and behaviors that are as diverse as the cultures that make up the people in those families.

Divorce is a social problem that is estimated to af-fect 40 percent of children born to married parents in the United States. Research indicates that approximately 25 percent of the children of divorce will show evidence of more adjustment difficulties than their counterparts from nondivorced families (Hetherington and Jodl 1994). These adjustment difficulties include academic problems, externalizing behaviors, internalizing behaviors, substance abuse problems, and social problems. As more divorces occur, so do more remarriages and the rate of remarriage has steadily grown producing a variety of blended families. As in divorced families, children in stepfamilies experience a higher level of adjustment problems than their counterparts in nondivorced families. Again, not all children will experience these difficulties. In fact the majority will not, with only 25 percent of the children in blended families experiencing adjustment difficulties like those associated with divorce (Heatherington and Stanley-Hagan 2002). Another result of the increased divorce rate is the rise in single-parent families. Mothers with custody of their children experience the most difficult transition during a divorce as they lose more income than a custodial father, resulting in a significant change in lifestyle for both the mother and her children. In addition, custodial mothers typically experience increased workloads, high rates of job instability, and residential moves to less desirable neighborhoods. Researchers emphasize the need for the continuation of a positive relationship between the divorced spouses in order to help children adjust during this stressful situation.

Maternal employment is also part of modern life in the United States. Women may choose to work outside of the home, in addition to their roles as mothers, for a variety of reasons. For some women, it may be a necessity of life in order to provide for their families. This may be due to the employment instability of their spouse, divorce, single-parent responsibilities, or the desire for increased income for their families. However, for an increasing majority of women, working outside of the home is a choice that they make in order to fulfill their own personal needs and career goals. Overall, research has found that maternal employment does not impact negatively on child development. However, in specific circumstances research has detected effects that relate to maternal employment. Jeanne Brooks-Gunn and colleagues (2002) reported detrimental cognitive effects for three-year-old children whose mothers went back to work full time prior to the infant turning nine months old, as compared to mothers who stayed at home during the first nine months. These effects were less pronounced when the mothers worked less than thirty hours a week, were sensitive in their caregiving and had high-quality childcare outside of the home.

Another area of concern due to the rise in mothers working outside the home is "latchkey children." *Latchkey children* is the term for the population of children who are home alone after school or when school is not in session. Latchkey children may be at risk for more difficulties due to the lack of adult supervision and guidance that they experience. Children left alone can engage in unsupervised peer contact, delinquency, and other externalizing behaviors. However, just as the experience of children who have working mothers varies, the experience of latchkey children varies. Working mothers need to find ways to effectively monitor their children's behavior. Parental monitoring can help children cope more effectively with their latchkey experience. In addition to parental monitoring, successful latchkey experiences often include community after-school programs. After-school programs with warm supportive staff, flexible schedules, multiple activities, and opportunities for positive interaction have been associated with better academic achievement and social adjustment for latchkey children.

Parenting practices are a mix of behaviors that are acquired in interaction with the environment, culture, and individual. This view represents the ecological systems perspective as proposed by Uri Bronfenbrenner (1979). The ecological-systems perspective views parents and their practices as part of a broader system which takes into account the reciprocal, bi-directional influences of individual, family, school, workplace, and community practices, as well as state and national policies and legislation. A leading expert on parenting, Diana Baumrind, formulated a classification of parenting styles that has been widely used and validated in research on parenting (1971). The classification system posits that there are four main styles of parenting—authoritarian, authoritative, neglectful, and indulgent (Baumrind 1971). Each style is described as follows:

- An authoritarian parent is strict and punitive; placing firm limits and controls on the child while allowing for little verbal exchange. Authoritarian parents may use physical punishment and coercion techniques with their children, often relying on negative interactions. Research has found that children of authoritarian parents frequently engage in more aggressive interactions.
- The authoritative parent encourages the mature, independent, and age-appropriate behavior of the child while maintaining rules but allowing for verbal exchange. Baumrind asserts that an authoritative parenting style is the best as it encourages parents to behave in a supportive, affectionate manner with their children while developing rules that govern their functioning.
- A neglectful parent is very uninvolved in the child's life, not knowing where the child is or what he/she is doing. Children of neglectful parents tend to be socially incompetent and display low self-esteem.
- The indulgent parent is very involved in the child's life, but places very few demands or restrictions on the child. These children may have difficulty regulating their behavior, displaying traits of egocentrism and noncompliance while maintaining difficulties in peer relations.

Authoritative parenting has been shown to be the most effective parenting style for several reasons. First, it allows for the parent to adopt a balance between autonomy and control. Children are given opportunities to develop independence within a framework of standards, limits, and guidance. Also, authoritative parenting allows children to engage in verbal interaction with parents. Within this type of atmosphere, children learn to express their views, knowing that their opinions are welcome and heard. Finally, the parental involvement that is characteristic of this style of parenting renders the child more receptive to parental influence. The links between child competence and authoritative parenting have been found across ethnic groups, social strata, and family structure.

DISCIPLINE

While parental demands and controls have been indicated as part of the most effective parenting style, it is also important to consider the methods parents use to enforce those limits. This is often termed parental discipline. Martin Hoffman, an early researcher into parental discipline, identified three types of discipline styles (1970). These discipline styles include love withdrawal, power assertion, and induction. Love withdrawal and power assertion are the two discipline styles associated with poor child outcomes. Love withdrawal is a discipline technique in which the parents either refuse to interact with the child or verbally states their dislike for the child. It often incorporates an emphasis on losing a parent's love. Hoffman contends that this style of discipline fosters considerable anxiety in the child. The discipline style of power assertion is an attempt to gain control over the child. It is frequently associated with corporal (physical) punishment such as spanking. Due to the negative child outcomes associated with both of these discipline styles, researchers sometimes combine them into a spectrum of behaviors known as overreactive discipline. Overreactive discipline includes yelling, physical aggression, name-calling, criticism, threats, and unreasonable expectations. This form of discipline results in aggressive acting-out and antisocial behaviors that can lead to school difficulties, delinquency, substance abuse, and adult antisocial behavior.

The use of corporal punishment by parents is legal in every state in the United States; however, many other countries throughout the world have passed laws forbidding parents to physically punish their children. Sweden was the first country to pass this law in 1979, but has since been joined by Finland, Denmark, Norway, Austria, Cyprus, Latvia, Croatia, Germany, and Israel. Since the enactment of the antispanking law in Sweden, rates of juvenile delinquency, alcohol abuse, rape, and suicide have declined, although these trends may also be representative of changing social attitudes throughout Sweden. The message that this sends to the United States and like-minded countries is that corporal punishment may not be necessary to improve the well being of children. Corporal punishment has been associated with higher rates of immediate compliance in children, but is also associated with higher levels of aggression and problem behavior, and lower levels of behavioral control, concern for the welfare of others, and conformity to social rules. Despite research that indicates the contrary, parents from the Caribbean, the United States, Canada, and many other parts of the world continue to engage in corporal punishment as a means to discipline and control their chil-

dren. Physical punishment does not teach appropriate behavior, however it does provide a model of an out-of-control, aggressive, and potentially abusive parent. Thus, educating parents in culturally sensitive ways to alternative methods of discipline is good not only for the well being of the child, but also for the well being of society.

The last discipline technique—induction—is the one endorsed by psychologists, other mental-health professionals, and informed individuals around the world. Induction promotes the use of reason and explanation when disciplining children. It utilizes the warm, supportive relationship that exists between a child and an adult, incorporating time for interaction and reflection. The idea is to explain to the child the effect his or her action had on others. Induction does not focus the attention on the child's shortcomings and misbehavior, but instead teaches appropriate behavior, thought processes, and emotions. This allows the child to develop a sense of empathy for other people.

Inductive techniques are what parenting education programs focus on. These programs involve teaching parents more adaptive ways of interacting with children at various developmental stages in order to promote healthy functioning in children. Although parenting programs vary in their specific details, they generally provide parents with the opportunity to learn parental monitoring skills, how to engage in age-appropriate interactions with their children, and techniques for providing positive feedback to promote desirable behavior. Additionally, these programs teach parents how to give clear, reasonable instructions to their children and provide a variety of techniques for brief, nonphysical discipline. Changing parental discipline styles has been effective in mediating behavioral problems in children. Parental education is the key to informing parents about discipline style and what works and what does not work to facilitate healthy growth and development in children at every age.

Micheline Malow-Iroff and Helen Johnson

FAMILY STRESS AND COPING

Learning how to handle the circumstances and events of life is an ongoing process that all people share. As children, our emotional abilities develop in response to our biological temperament, interaction with others, and the environmental conditions in which we have been placed. Stress is the individual's response to these life events and the events themselves are the stressors. Life events can be good or bad, challenging or easy; however, our interpretation of them and our ability to deal with these events vary. Not all stress impacts negatively on children and families. Low levels of stress can add excitement and challenge to life, prodding us to move ahead in school or work and to engage in new activities. Life events, and the stress they place on the individual, are not a problem until the individual finds he or she can no longer handle the situation competently and engages in poor coping skills. Symptoms of stress can include irritability, fear, depression, aggression, and substance use. Thus stress reactions occur on an individual level and are determined by a combination of cognitive and situational influences.

The interpretation of life events as stressful is what researcher Richard Lazarus (1996) has termed *cognitive appraisal*. A cognitive appraisal occurs when an individual interprets an event as harmful, threatening or challenging, and determines whether he/she possesses the resources necessary to cope with the event. According to Lazarus, appraisals of life events occur in a two-step process. First the individual engages in a primary appraisal to determine whether the event involves harm that has already occurred, is a threat that involves future danger, or is a challenge to be overcome. In the next step, the secondary appraisal, the individual evaluates his/her resources and determines how to cope with an event. Coping involves the strategies, skills, and abilities that the individual possesses to handle the stress. Thus for Lazarus, an individual's experience of stress is the balance between the primary and secondary appraisals; if a threat is perceived as high and the secondary appraisal determines that the challenge and resources are low, then the stress experienced by that individual is likely to be high.

Martin Seligman is another researcher who investigates how cognitive factors impact on coping with stress. Seligman classifies individuals into two categories, optimistic or pessimistic. Optimists tend to classify bad experiences as a temporary setback and realize that their behavior and the outcomes of a situation are changeable. However, pessimists generally relate bad experiences to flaws within themselves. These individuals are more likely to feel hopeless and depressed, and have a tendency toward poor health and underachievement at school or work (Seligman 1995).

The spectrum of situational stresses experienced by any individual can range from ordinary to extreme. Ordinary stressful experiences for children include taking exams at school, arguing with friends, and feeling jealous over another's success. When these events occur, a parent, trusted teacher, or competent friend can provide the guidance and skills necessary to help the child past these normal events. However, when stress is severe, the coping skills for this event may not be clear and the significant adults in a child's life may not have the ability to foster or implement effective strategies to handle these situations. Experiences of extreme stress can occur after one traumatic event such as the death of a loved one, an experience of victimization, or the divorce of a child's parents. It can also be present in children who live for years in abusive or neglectful families, in children who experience foster care placement, and in homes where there are individuals who have special physical, academic, or emotional needs. Additionally, researchers are documenting the detrimental effects of stress in children who live with the chronic conditions of poverty, family tension, and prejudice (Duncan and Brooks-Gunn 1997). Although these chronic conditions do not register as major life events in children's development, the accumulation of stress over time in these situations can lead to psychological disorders, physical illnesses, and destroyed lives in the same manner that stress experienced due to traumatic life events can lead to similar impaired health and functioning.

EDUCATION AND INTERVENTIONS FOR STRESS

Everyone experiences stressful events; however, how each person handles that stressful experience will vary from individual to individual. Parents and teachers can help children to cope effectively with stressful events in a number of ways. One way is to recognize that the significant adults in a child's life serve as models of behavior for how children will cope. Lev Vygotsky, a preeminent educational psychology theorist, proposed that all mental functions have an external or social origin (1962). Young children acquire meaning and understanding of events through the communication and behavior of those around them. Thus, if a child's parents react to the daily stress at work by coming home, getting drunk, and/or yelling at their family members, the message communicated to the child will be to find ways to avoid or escape stressful situations. However, if the parent communicates to the child in a calm way the strong emotions and frustration they feel, their children will learn to express their feelings in increasingly normal and healthy ways. Learning that everyone has strong emotions at times and modeling appropriate methods of coping with those feelings will allow children to begin to express their own feelings.

Many researchers believe that children who approach stressful events with a problem-solving approach, rather than an avoidance strategy, will cope better with the event (Bridges 2003; Lazarus 1996; Seligman 1995). Additionally, children who have learned a number of coping strategies to handle life's ups and downs are placed in the most optimal situation for handling stressful events. As children age, they begin to see more alternatives for coping and tend to use more cognitive coping strategies. Research has found that by ten years of age, most children are able to use cognitive strategies such as shifting thoughts to a less stressful event and reframing situations so that every event is not personally directed. The adults in the child's life often model these techniques, so the child has learned in context what to do when things go awry. Additionally, as it is natural for children to tend to use these skills only in the stressful situations that they have learned to apply them toward, the adults can help them to generalize the use of these skills in other situations by adapting a problem-solving approach.

Difficulty occurs when children have not learned effective coping skills through experience or interaction in their environment. When families are overwhelmed by the stress, turmoil, and trauma present in their own lives, they do not engage in healthy coping strategies or resort to effective problem solving. Children in these families are trapped by the circumstance of their experience. In these cases, other, more competent adults and peers can step in to provide support and teach more effective prob-

lem-solving skills to the individual. One way to help children in these situations is to remove as many barriers to effective functioning as possible. This can lighten the child's load, enabling him/her to feel stronger and more successful in other situations. Gregg Duncan and Jeanne Brooks-Gunn (1997) have illustrated the need for this type of approach in their research on the pervasive negative developmental effects associated with children growing up in extreme poverty. Children who grow up in poverty are more likely to be born at a low birth weight, have higher infant mortality rates, experience learning disabilities, and drop out of high school, among other disturbing correlations. The physical and cognitive implications of residing and developing in this chronically stressful environment indicate a need for reform to educate and support children and families in this high-risk situation. Obviously, all stressful life events cannot be remediated by outside influences; however, teachers and other adults involved with children have the opportunity to interact in ways that can remove extra stressors whenever possible, and teach coping and problem-solving skills.

Some events that occur in life are beyond the control of the individual. When this happens repeatedly, children may take on a "learned helplessness" approach to situations. Learned helplessness is a theory proposed by Martin Seligman in 1975 to account for the depression that resulted from an individual's exposure to prolonged stress, negative experiences, or pain. Reformulations of the learned helplessness theory have propelled work on the impact of cognitive attributions on stress. Lazarus' ideas on cognitive appraisal and Seligman's work with optimistic and pessimistic children have expanded the understanding of why some individuals give up in situations where they feel they have no control (Lazarus 1996; Seligman 1995). It is important to note that Seligman believes that children's pessimistic attributions can be modified by adults who model effective coping skills, provide explanations that encourage further effort, and teach realistic ways of handling disappointing life experiences.

Recent events in the United States and around the world have left many children and adults feeling particularly vulnerable to stress. Traumatic events such as the Oklahoma City bombing and the terrorist attacks on the World Trade Center in New

York City and the Pentagon leave all individuals feeling defenseless. Exposure to traumatic experiences, whether a single event or chronic exposure to environmental stressors, have both short- and long-term consequences in children's lives, and the symptoms of post-traumatic stress disorder can contribute to physical, emotional, and educational impairments. Indicators of post-traumatic stress disorder include fears, repetitive nightmares, thought reenactment, and thought suppression. Often the numbing effect of the stress, combined with fear and depression, make it hard for teachers or other adults to identify a child in crisis, because they too have experienced the debilitating effects of stress. As the adults in the child's life become more irritable and less responsive or tolerant of others, this is when professionals are needed to step in. When an individual can no longer utilize normal coping and problem-solving approaches to handle the stress and negative emotional states in their lives, they need to seek the help of a psychologist, psychiatrist, or a professional therapist. The recognition of individual differences in the response to stress or trauma is especially important as variations in feelings and functioning are dependent on many factors including developmental level and access to support systems. After the Oklahoma City bombing in 1995, professionals made recommendations to teachers and other caring adults for dealing with individuals who are experiencing high levels of stress. A summary of these recommendations made by R. Gurwitch and colleagues (2001) is included below:

- Reinforce the safety and security of the child.
- Allow children to retell events in their own way.
- Encourage children to talk about their feelings and worries. Young children may not have words to express their feelings; help them to develop their expressive language skills through hands-on activities.
- Help children to develop a realistic understanding of what happened by providing age-appropriate information.
- Provide reassurance to children and help them to develop skills to handle stressful feelings over time.
- Protect children from reexposure to frightening or traumatic situations.

Micheline Malow-Iroff and Helen Johnson

CHILD MALTREATMENT

Although it is difficult to imagine, many children each year are killed or injured by their parents, caregivers, or other adults with whom they come in contact. Child abuse is the product of a disturbed environment. Personality characteristics of the adults present in the home interact with environmental stress and the characteristics of the child to produce harmful negative developmental effects. Each year in the United States, child welfare agencies receive more than three million allegations of abuse. Laws in many states in the United States make "mandated reporters" of teachers, doctors, law enforcement officials and mental health professionals, to name just a few of the professionals required to report the suspicion of any form of abuse directed toward a child. The mandated reporter is not required to have proof of the alleged abuse or neglect; the law requires only that there is "reasonable cause to suspect" that a child has been maltreated. Many school systems set their own policies for reporting concerns of child maltreatment. These policies support the state guidelines and provide teachers with a system of reporting through the school. Due to the procedural guidelines that now govern the reporting of maltreatment, cases of maltreatment can be identified and the children helped. The 2002 statistics from the National Clearinghouse on Child Abuse and Neglect reported that 879,000 children were identified as victims of abuse and neglect in 2000.

The conditions suffered by maltreated children are varied. Abuse can be everything from sporadic physical abuse to long-term, severe neglect. Among the types of maltreatment are physical and sexual abuse; the fostering of delinquency; lack of supervision; medical, nutritional and educational neglect; and drug or alcohol abuse. The National Clearinghouse on Child Abuse and Neglect estimates that caregivers kill two thousand children every year. However, the most common abuser is not an uncontrolled physical abuser who ends up killing his/her child. Most physical abuse is mild to moderate in severity and represents approximately 23 percent of the maltreatment cases reported. Sexual, emotional, and other forms of abuse represent another 23 percent of reported maltreatment. The most common abuser is an impoverished single mother who, due to her social circumstance and poor coping skills, neglects her child or children. Issues of neglect involve approximately 54 percent of the maltreatment cases nationwide.

Maltreatment is also thought to be a process of intergenerational transmission. Parents who use physical punishment to control their children often were physically punished themselves as children. Approximately one-third of parents who abuse their children were victims of abuse themselves. Parents who respond using overreactive disciplinary measures may not have sufficient resources or the necessary support from others to see them through difficult periods. Breaking the intergenerational cycle is difficult, but possible if there are models of loving, caring parenting in the adult's background as well as adequate social and emotional support in their present relationships.

Martin Teicher, an associate professor of psychiatry at Harvard Medical School and a leading researcher into the field of neurobiological effects of maltreatment, is a proponent of the view that early exposure to various forms of maltreatment alters the development of the limbic systems in these patients (2000). The limbic system is a neural center that is integral in the regulation of emotion and memory. Two of the important structural components within the limbic system are the amygdala and the hippocampus, both of which are in the temporal lobe of the brain. The amygdala functions to create the emotional content of memories and is responsible for the conditioning of fear and aggression. The hippocampus is important in the creation and retrieval of both emotional and verbal memories. Dr. Teicher proposes that both structures could be damaged through heightened electrical activity or the excessive exposure to stress hormones that victims of maltreatment experience.

Maltreated children are at high risk for displaying many medical problems and psychological disorders. The developmental consequences of child maltreatment include poor emotional regulation, attachment difficulties, problems in peer relationships, difficulty in school, anxiety disorders, depression, conduct disorder, aggression, substance use and delinquency. Two specific medical conditions observed in maltreated children are "failure to thrive" and "psychosocial dwarfism." Up to 5 percent of children admitted to pediatric hospitals suffer from failure to thrive syndrome. Infants afflicted with this condition are generally of low weight, small size, and poor physical development. The condition is diagnosed as feeding disorders of infancy and early childhood due to the limited nourishment that the child has received in infancy. However, the condition is complicated by psychosocial factors of poverty, lack of education, neglect, and sometimes abuse. If medical and social-service interventions are obtained in a timely fashion, the infant with failure to thrive can recover, although if not treated the child can be left with lifelong disabilities or die.

While failure to thrive is a condition of infancy and early childhood, psychosocial dwarfism is the result of severe and prolonged stress due to physical and psychological abuse. In this condition, also known as Kasper-Hauser syndrome, the child's physical, cognitive, and social development is impaired due to the effects of prolonged stress on endocrine function. The abuse depresses the endocrine function, which in turn slows the child's physical and mental growth. A child with psychosocial dwarfism often appears to be many years younger than his/her actual chronological age.

Reliable data on the proportion of children that survive abuse and become developmentally disabled due to the maltreatment is not available. One estimate indicates that child maltreatment may be responsible for 15 percent of new cases of developmental disabilities each year. Children with disabilities are a vulnerable population due to reporting difficulties, language barriers, and the isolation that they and their families often experience. A related issue is the maltreatment of children who are already disabled. The increased stress placed on a family when there is a child with developmental disabilities cannot be underestimated. This is an area of great concern suggesting that child maltreatment contributes to developmental disabilities and that children with disabilities are at high risk for child maltreatment.

PREVENTION AND INTERVENTION

Early researchers took a psychological perspective when trying to understand the consequences of maltreatment. It was thought that the emotional and social difficulties perpetuated by adults who had suffered child maltreatment could be remediated via therapy. Indeed, individuals who successfully break out of the pattern of abuse have received therapy and do have positive models and a support system to draw upon. Thus, the importance of receiving professional help in these circumstances cannot be overstated. However, new insights into childhood maltreatment, such as those asserted by Dr. Teicher, indicate that the brain is physically altered by the horrific experience of maltreatment. The permanent alteration of the brain, through molecular and neurobiological effects that alter the neural developmental pathways, suggests a grim prognosis for those exposed to maltreatment. Thus, the effort to educate and prevent maltreatment before it begins may be the best way to alleviate this harmful state.

As indicated above, the best way to eradicate and treat victims of abuse is to prevent it before it occurs. In order to do this, programs must be put into place that provide support and assistance to the most vulnerable part of our population. As the most common area of maltreatment is the neglect of children within single-mother households, this is a population of individuals that need to be targeted for intensive support. The 2000 U.S. Bureau of the Census report indicates that single-mother families with children under the age of eighteen signify the largest segment of the population living in poverty, representing 26.5 percent (Clark et al. 2003). Expressed in 1999 dollars, the poverty threshold for families with children under the age of eighteen was $13,410. Thus, individuals living in families with total cash income below this level were counted as poor. This represents 12.4 percent of the U.S. population, approximately 34 million people. Furthermore, the Current Population Survey indicates that 44.2 percent of children under the age of fifteen, related and unrelated to the families they live with, exist in poverty (Clark et al. 2003). The consequence of these high rates of poverty on children and families is catastrophic and avoiding the persistent poverty that plagues many families is key to facilitating healthy outcomes. Greg Duncan and Jeanne Brooks-Gunn (2004), two researchers in the field of adverse outcomes on children due to poverty, recommend that families with young children be exempted from the time limits, sanctions, and categorical restrictions that are currently part of welfare re-

form. Additionally, they suggest that well-designed parenting programs can help to alleviate problems. Reducing stress, providing support, teaching problem-solving strategies, and offering assistance through publicly funded programs for families and children will go a long way toward preventing the maltreatment of children.

Micheline Malow-Iroff and Helen Johnson

FAMILIES OF CHILDREN WITH SPECIAL NEEDS

Increasing attention has been given to the role of the family when working with children with special needs. This shift in focus represents an increased attention paid to the ecological perspective of development. The child's disabilities are not seen in isolation, but the development of the child is seen within the context of the family and the community. The reaction to having a child with special needs will vary across families. Families of children with special needs were once thought to progress through a grieving process, much like a person does at the loss of a loved one. Often the response to the birth or diagnosis of a child with special needs will be one of shock, denial, sadness, anxiety, or anger. However, research does not support the idea that families progress through these emotions in a specific order before they move on to an acceptance phase. In truth, a family's response to learning that their child has special needs will be as varied as the personalities of the individuals within that family and will also be impacted by the developmental status of the child, the support available at home and in the community, the attitudes of the culture, and the family's economic resources.

EDUCATIONAL SERVICES FOR CHILDREN WITH SPECIAL NEEDS AND THEIR FAMILIES

Families of children with special needs are mobilized into action to provide for their child in different ways. The identification of a disability can come from a pediatrician, a teacher, the parents, other caring friends, or members of the child's family. After the recognition that a disability is present, state and local agencies provide for medical and developmental evaluations to determine the need for intervention services. Once a family has acknowledged that they are living with a child who has special needs, a new world of service delivery and intervention practices opens up to them. Families must embrace the role of their child's advocate, as the only way for their child with special needs to receive services is through the federal- and state-funded agencies. Family involvement in the process to obtain special services for children with special needs began in 1974 when congress passed the *Family Education Rights and Privacy Act* (FERPA), also known as the Buckley Amendment. In addition to the rights of knowledge, the ability to challenge decisions, and the guarantees of privacy within the administration of educational services, this amendment legally empowered parents to take an active role in the determination and provision of a child's educational services. Subsequent legislation over the last thirty years has reauthorized the family's, the student's, and the school's rights and obligations to provide services to children with special needs.

With the passage of the *Education for All Handicapped Children Act of 1975* (Public Law 94–142), Congress asserted that the national interest was served when the federal government supported programs for children with special needs. This law provided for a free and appropriate public education (FAPE) for all children aged five through twenty-one. In addition, the law required a comprehensive, nondiscriminatory evaluation to identify the child's needs, a written individualized education plan (IEP), and stated that the child's educational services be provided in the least restrictive environment (LRE). Passage of each new law has reauthorized and extended these basic rights. In 1990, the *Individuals with Disabilities Education Act* (IDEA), also known as Public Law 101–476, passed in Congress. This law updated terminology to reflect the ideology that the disability does not define the person, but that they are individuals with disabilities that need to be served. IDEA was amended in 1997 with the passage of Public Law 105–17, also known as IDEA 97. IDEA 97 provided an expanded role for parents in the decisionmaking process, including parents on the team that makes educational placement decisions. Additionally, schools were required to create and bear the cost of a system of mediation to resolve conflicts between schools and families. Although

IDEA 97 is up for reauthorization, it is uncertain when this will occur. Figure 29.1 details the important components mandated by IDEA 97.

The implementation of federal laws involves agencies at the federal, state, and local levels. Each state must present a plan to the U.S. Office of Special Education Programs to ensure compliance with federal regulations in order to receive federal funding. Although the state laws must comply with the federal laws, the implementation, description, and criteria for classifying children with special needs is slightly different from state to state. At the local level, departments of education and early-intervention agencies are responsible for the delivery of special education services. As a result of the many layers of governmental involvement for the implementation of special education services, the laws related to special education are complex. For many families this complexity proves to be a barrier to the services that each child is entitled to by law. These barriers become even greater when the family is from another culture and/or for whom English is not their primary language. Efforts are being continually made to reach out and expand the opportunities of families in the education of their children. The latest version of the *Elementary and Secondary Education Act of 1965* is an example of this. The *Elementary and Secondary Education Act of 2001*, also known as the *No Child Left Behind Act of 2001* (Public Law 107–110), redefined the federal role in education from kindergarten through grade twelve. It provides for stronger accountability of academic results, more flexibility on how local school districts can allocate their federal funding, gives more options to parents from disadvantaged backgrounds on how and where their children will be educated, emphasizes the use of proven teaching methods and curricula, dictates the need for highly qualified teachers in every classroom, and focuses on enabling limited English proficient students in the acquisition of English. *No Child Left Behind 2001* has several implications for students with special needs. First it dictates that children with disabilities will participate in the same curriculum content as general education students. In addition, it states that all children must show adequate yearly progress. This means that each child must show a year's worth of progress in a year's time. Frequently adequate yearly progress will be measured with standardized state assessments. Individuals with disabilities have four options in regard to state assessments: 1) they can take

Figure 29.1   **Major Provisions of IDEA 97**

Purpose:
To assure a free and appropriate public education to all children with provisions for special education to meet individual needs.

Type of Programs:
An individualized family special education plan (IFSP) for children birth–2.
An individualized education plan (IEP) for children 3–5 and 5–21.

Parent Participation:
Parents participate in all aspects of process, from identification to eligibility and modifications. Due process procedures must be followed.

Evaluations:
Nondiscriminatory with students tested in native language.

Ages served: Birth–21
Downward Extensions:
    Part B—Special Education Preschool: 3–5 years old.
    Part C—Early Intervention: birth–2 years for children and their families.

Definition of Disability: 13 Federal Categories
Autism
Deaf-Blind
Emotional Disturbance
Hearing Impairment
Specific Learning Disabilities
Mental Retardation
Multiple Disabilities
Orthopedic Impairment
Other Health Impairments
Speech or Language Impairment
Traumatic Brain Injury
Visual Impairment
Developmental Delay (3–9 years of age only)

Placement:
Least Restrictive Environment: Attempts to educate child with their special education services in the general education setting must be demonstrated before a more restrictive placement can be made.

Source: Individuals with Disabilities Education Act Amendments of 1997.

the regular assessment with everyone else, 2) they can take the regular assessment with modifications, 3) they can take an alternative assessment that is aligned to their grade level standard, or 4) they can take an alternative assessment aligned to alternate achievement standards as set forth in their individualized education plan.

The most important component to successful family involvement in the provision of services to children with special needs is information. If the family is kept informed and the lines of communication are open between the home and the school then there are greater opportunities for successful collaboration between the various individuals working with the child. All too often, barriers to family participation in schools get in the way of active family involvement. These barriers include logistical concerns such as transportation or time of meetings, communication problems such as language differences or professional jargon, and lack of understanding about schools and their complex set of rules. It is essential for teachers and service providers to overcome these barriers in order to work with both the children who have special needs and the families that love them.

Micheline Malow-Iroff and Helen Johnson

RISKY BEHAVIOR IN ADOLESCENTS

In adolescence, significant changes in the developmental status and tasks of the individual propel the individual toward behaviors, including initiation of drinking, drug abuse, and early sexual intercourse, that entail significant health risks. Indeed, one of the striking aspects of these behaviors is that they pose threats to both the individual's physical and emotional well being, as well as to educational and occupational success. The classic work of psychologists John Donovan and Richard Jessor (1985) on problem-behavior theory demonstrated that these behaviors tend to occur in clusters within individuals, which means that adolescents are likely to be engaged in more than one type of risky behavior, if they are engaged in any. The initiation and maintenance of problem behaviors in early adolescence is a significant predictor of the educational and occupational trajectories of individuals. Psychologists John Schulenberg and Jennifer Maggs (2002) have documented the importance of early involvement in problem behaviors to these diverging life paths.

The rapid pace of physical and cognitive changes during early adolescence influences all aspects of life, and places children at heightened risk for the development of maladaptive coping strategies that include drinking, substance abuse, and the early initiation of sexual behavior. Dramatic shifts in the organization of families and the workplace have increased risk factors to children in all social groups and income levels. Children and young adolescents spend more hours of unsupervised activity than at any time in

Table 29.3

Monitoring the Future Survey 2002/2003 Data: Marijuana/Hashish

	8th grade	10th grade	12th grade
Lifetime	19.2/17.5	30.3/28.2	36.2/34.9
Past year	14.6/12.8	30.3/28.2	36.2/21.2
Past month	8.3/7.5	17.8/17.0	21.5/21.2

Source: National Institute on Drug Abuse, Monitoring the Future Survey (2003).

Table 29.4

Monitoring the Future Survey 2002/2003 Data: Cigarettes and Smokeless Tobacco

	8th grade	10th grade	12th grade
Ever used	31.4/28.4	47.7/43.0	57.2/53.7
Past month	10.7/10.2	17.7/16.7	26.7/24.4
Daily use	5.1/	10.1/	16.9/
(past month)	4.5	8.9	15.8

Source: National Institute on Drug Abuse, Monitoring the Future Survey (2003).

Table 29.5

Monitoring the Future Survey 2002/2003 Data: Alcohol

	8th grade	10th grade	12th grade
Lifetime	47.0/45.6	66.9/66.0	78.4/76.6
Last year	38.7/37.2	60.0/59.3	71.5/70.1
Last month	19.6/19.7	35.4/35.4	48.6/47.5

Source: National Institute on Drug Abuse, Monitoring the Future Survey (2003).

recent decades. Early onset of substance and alcohol abuse, and involvement in sexual behavior, is associated with problems that continue to be more severe and prolonged in adulthood.

ALCOHOL AND SUBSTANCE ABUSE

During early adolescence, the majority of students have their first encounter with substance use in social settings. Although in many American communities some experimentation with substance use is "normative" for adolescents, there is strong evidence of links between early onset of substance and alcohol abuse and involvement in violence. There is also strong evidence that this early-onset population is particularly vulnerable to extended involvement in problem behavior.

In the United States, drug abuse trends among students in eighth, tenth, and twelfth grades are studied annually through the Monitoring the Future Survey (MTF) (Johnston et al. 2004). MTF collects data from students on past-month, past-year, and lifetime drug-abuse experiences. The 2003 responses indicate an overall decline in the use of illicit drugs among eighth and tenth graders. This is exemplified by the data on marijuana/hashish use in Table 29.3.

It is worth noting that despite the overall declines in use of marijuana, almost 50 percent of twelfth graders had experimented with it.

While lifetime smoking rates declined among students in all three grades (see Table 29.4), the rates of smoking within the past month did not decline among eighth and tenth graders. This suggests that the decline in smoking that has been observed over the past few years is dissipating.

Furthermore, the MTF 2003 data with regard to

alcohol and prescription painkillers revealed no improvement. Alcohol use remained stable, with no significant changes in any grades on any measure (see Table 29.5).

Use of OxyContin and Vicodin also remained stable at rates that are of concern. In fact, among twelfth graders, Vicodin was the second most frequently used drug after marijuana.

It is apparent from these data that drinking and drug abuse pose persistent health challenges for American adolescents. Although many of these negative health consequences do not appear until adulthood, there is growing evidence that substance use can compromise adolescent health as well. For example, Patrick Johnson and Linda Richter's recent analyses of the National Household Survey on Drug Abuse data found that adolescents who used alcohol reported lower self-perceived health than adolescents who abstained (2002). Johnson and Richter also found that overnight hospitalizations occurred more frequently among adolescents who consumed alcohol than among those who abstain.

Use of alcohol and painkillers has proven particularly impervious to prevention and intervention efforts. The fact that these substances are available legally to individuals based on age and medical criteria heightens the difficulty of controlling access. Aside from direct health dangers that these substances pose, there is also extensive evidence that adolescents involved with drinking and drugs are more likely to become involved in risky sexual behavior as well as violence.

SEXUAL BEHAVIOR AND SEXUALLY TRANSMITTED DISEASES

Over the last few decades, there has been increasing concern about adolescent sexual behavior, pregnancy, and parenthood in the United States. Despite declines in the adolescent birth rates in the United States since World War II, the rates remain two to ten times higher than in other industrialized nations. There has also been a progressive increase in adolescent childbearing outside of marriage. A recent report from the Department of Health and Human Services (DHHS) indicated that between 1986 and 2000, the birth rate among adolescents increased by nearly 25 percent (Moore et al. 2002). This is of particular concern because the overwhelming majority of adolescents do not wish to become parents. According to recent DHHS data, 84 percent of adolescent pregnancies are unintended. In addition to the risks of pregnancy and unintended parenthood, sexually active adolescents are at very high risk for sexually transmitted infections (STIs) and exposure to human immunodeficiency virus (HIV). Dr. David Schonfeld (2000) reported that each year, approximately one of every four sexually active adolescents contracts an STI. Because the majority of sexual encounters before age fifteen are coercive, they are associated with poor protection from pregnancy and transmission of STIs. Alcohol and substance abuse also increase the likelihood of engaging in unprotected sexual behavior, which in turn increases the risk of transmission of STIs.

Adolescents and young adults are now a major risk group for the incidence of sexually transmitted diseases (STIs). Of the 18.9 million new cases of STIs occurring in 2000, 9.1 million (48 percent) were among those aged fifteen to twenty-four. Sixty percent of the 359,000 new reported gonorrhea cases in 2000 were among those aged fifteen to twenty-four. Because half of new infections are typically undiagnosed or unreported, this would mean that in 2000,

the estimated number of new gonorrhea cases among fifteen- to twenty-four year olds was actually 431,000.

Chlamydia is the most common STI among adolescents. In 2000, approximately 1.5 million of the 2.8 million new chlamydial infections were among fifteen- to twenty-four-year olds. The majority of individuals with this STI are unaware of their infection. Without screening to identify these infections, many remain unnoticed and untreated. Researcher Steven Belenko (2004) noted recently that in addition to heightened risk for HIV, untreated STIs place the individual at risk for other negative long-term health consequences. Up to 40 percent of women with untreated chlamydial infections experience pelvic inflammatory disease. Untreated STIs also are a risk factor for transmission of HIV; individuals with STIs are three to five times more likely to contract HIV. At the same time as biological factors make individuals with STIs more likely to contract HIV after exposure, HIV-infected individuals with STIs are more likely to transmit HIV to their sexual partners.

The incidence of adolescent HIV infection has been increasing. HIV destroys the body's immune system, and causes acquired immune deficiency syndrome (AIDS). There is an average of five to seven years between becoming infected with the virus and showing signs of illness. Consequently, most infected adolescents will not become ill until they are adults, and adolescent AIDS cases result from exposure earlier in childhood.

It is estimated that 850,000 to 950,000 Americans are HIV-infected, and that 25 percent are unaware of their infection. There are significant racial and ethnic disparities in HIV/AIDS cases in the United States. Approximately 78 percent of HIV-infected women are minorities. According to the U.S. Office of Minority Health, in 2000 HIV infection was the fifth leading cause of death for people between the ages of twenty-five and forty-four (2002). Many of these individuals became infected during adolescence. The Centers for Disease Control and Prevention (CDC) recently reported that approximately half of the new HIV infections were among fifteen- to twenty-four-year-olds, and the majority of these cases were infected through sexual contact (CDC 2002). According to the CDC, in 2000, young people accounted for a much greater proportion of HIV cases (13 percent) than AIDS cases (3 percent). In adolescents between ages thirteen and nineteen, a greater proportion of HIV cases occurred among females (61 percent) than males (39 percent). African Americans have been disproportionately affected by HIV, accounting for 56 percent of all cases ever reported among thirteen- to twenty-four-year-olds. One very problematic issue is that most infected youth are not aware that they have HIV. Belenko cites a recent survey of seven cities in which only 18 percent of infected adolescents knew they had the virus.

The choices that adolescents make about risky behaviors have serious consequences for both their immediate and long-term health. Education, prevention, and intervention efforts to address these critical issues will be considered in the next entry.

Micheline Malow-Iroff and Helen L. Johnson

ADOLESCENT HEALTH EDUCATION AND PREVENTION

The fundamental connection between education and prevention was highlighted in the 1989 report of the Carnegie Task Force on Education of Young Adolescents entitled *Turning Points: Preparing American Youth for the 21st Century.* This influential document emphasized the integral connection between health and education. The report indicted schools for failing to address adolescents' developmental, emotional, and cognitive needs, stating:

> Caught in a vortex of changing demands, the engagement of many youth in learning diminishes, and their rates of alienation, substance abuse, absenteeism, and dropping out of school begin to rise. (Carnegie Task Force on Education of Young Adolescents 1989, 8–9)

Peer group affiliation and academic performance during early adolescence are powerful predictors of school completion and college attendance, as well as of involvement in risky behaviors. Children who experience academic difficulties, feel alienated from school, and/or engage in minor acts of delinquency during early adolescence are prone to become involved in more problematic behav-

ior, including substance abuse and risky sexual activity, in later adolescence. Consequently, prevention efforts have focused increasing attention on early adolescents, between the ages of ten and fourteen years.

ALCOHOL AND SUBSTANCE ABUSE PREVENTION

At the same time as school experiences may contribute to the initiation of problem behaviors, schools also play a central role in prevention efforts. School-based programs have the greatest potential to deliver cost-efficient, broad-based prevention to students from diverse socioeconomic and ethnic backgrounds. Findings from the Institute of Medicine (2002) indicate that school-based prevention programs are especially important in helping minority youth who are at risk for major negative health consequences associated with substance use later in life. This is because many minority youth avoid tobacco, alcohol, and other substances not because they understand their dangers, but because they fear the negative parental sanctions that will ensue should they be caught. When these youths become independent and the threat of parental sanctions is removed, they are at greater risk for experimenting with these substances to counteract their negative mental health states, and less likely to possess alternative coping strategies.

In the 1990s, the implementation of school-based alcohol and substance abuse prevention programs increased significantly. The Centers for Disease Control and Prevention (CDC) School Health Policies and Programs Study reported that in 2000, 93 percent of all schools cover the long-term health consequences of alcohol use and addiction, and 89 percent cover the long-term consequences of illegal drug use (National Center for Chronic Disease Prevention and Health Promotion 2002). Short-term health consequences of alcohol use were covered by almost 93 percent of schools, and those of illegal drug use by almost 89 percent of schools. The impact of these programs has been limited. Rates of initiation of alcohol and substance abuse behaviors and incidence of related problems have remained fairly constant, while age of first involvement extended downward for most substances, to include children in upper elementary and middle school. The National Institute on Alcohol Abuse and Alcoholism (NIAAA) recently concluded that the small effects associated with school-based programs demonstrate the need for more comprehensive prevention efforts (NIAAA 2000).

In its guidelines for prevention, the National Institute on Drug Abuse (NIDA) emphasizes that the primary targets in effective prevention programs are the risk and protective factors that exist in the child's family, school, and community. Prevention programs are defined in terms of their audience:

1. *Universal* programs are designed for the general population; for example, all the students in a school.
2. *Selective* programs focus on subgroups that are considered to be at risk; for example, children with academic problems, or children with substance-abusing parents.
3. *Indicated* programs address individuals who are already engaging in substance abuse. (NIDA 2003)

Universal programs emphasize strengthening protective factors. Current research-based programs accomplish this through various routes, including:

1. *The Caring School Community Program*—reinforcement of children's sense of the school community.
2. *Classroom-Centered and Family-School Partnership Intervention*—improvement of communication patterns.
3. *Guiding Good Choices*—improvement of parents' communication and disciplinary skills.
4. *Life Skills Training*, *Project Alert*—teaching middle school students social and resistance skills. (NIDA 2003)

Echoing the NIAAA recommendations, NIDA reports that multicomponent programs that occur in more than one setting, for example home as well as school, are generally more effective than programs in single settings. A few research-based comprehensive programs that incorporate children, parents, and teachers have been implemented, most notably: Project STAR and SOAR (Skills, Opportunity, and Recognition).

EDUCATION AND PREVENTION FOR SEXUAL BEHAVIOR, STIs, AND AIDS

The prevention issues and principles outlined by NIDA are also applicable to education about sexual behavior, STIs, and AIDS. To date, the evidence is mixed on the long-term impacts of AIDS and STI prevention efforts. It is clear, however, that more comprehensive and interactive rather than didactic approaches increase the impact of prevention programs.

Public controversy about appropriate sexual information for children of different ages, and misconceptions about HIV/AIDS, complicate education and prevention efforts. The CDC identifies comprehensive health education as an essential aspect of successful HIV/AIDS prevention. According to health educators Susan Telljohann, Cynthia Symons, and Beth Pateman (2004), misconceptions and stereotypes about HIV/AIDS have generated a misguided complacency among some groups regarding the need for universal HIV/AIDS education. Complacency among "low risk" groups, combined with the sense of invulnerability that is characteristic of adolescence, contribute to risky behavior. Telljohann, Symons, and Pateman emphasize the importance for children and adolescents of integrating information about transmission of STIs and HIV/AIDS into more broad-based considerations of sexual behavior. This point is underscored by the increasing percentage of cases of HIV transmission that occur through heterosexual contact.

Drs. Darby McElderry and Hatim Omar (2003) note that the federal government currently favors abstinence-only sex education programs. McElderry and Omar cite evidence that although such programs result in immediate reductions in sexual activity, these reductions are transitory, lasting for only a few months. Research indicates that comprehensive sex education programs that include information about contraception and STIs, as well as abstinence, result in better outcomes. While specific results vary between studies, comprehensive programs are associated with delay of intercourse, increased contraceptive use, and decreased sexual risk-taking behavior.

McElderry and Omar's findings also highlight the importance of the individual presenting the sex education program. Adolescents reported that the sex education instructor often was someone with whom they did not feel comfortable discussing sexual issues. Although learning of factual material about AIDS was not affected by the rapport between students and teacher, discussion of sexual behavior was.

IMPROVING THE EFFECTIVENESS OF HEALTH EDUCATION AND PREVENTION

Dr. David Schonfeld (2000) notes that many teachers and principals are reluctant to discuss risky behaviors, especially sexual activity, with students. Their reluctance stems in part from concern about parental reactions, as well as from their own feelings about these issues. Most teachers receive very little, if any, preparation for addressing these sensitive issues in their classrooms. This is unfortunate since the majority of school districts rely on classroom teachers to implement prevention programs. The lack of teacher preparation for this task is particularly significant because teacher attitudes toward adoption and implementation of these programs have been shown to impact their effectiveness. Phyliss Levinson-Gingiss and Rita Hamilton (1989) found that teachers who perceive limited responsibility for student outcomes in prevention, and are not comfortable using interactive teaching techniques or teaching the content of the prevention curriculum, are less likely to implement the program thoughtfully, if at all.

Beyond strengthening the commitment of teachers to delivering the message, though, it is important to ensure that the message itself addresses the concerns and life circumstances of the target audience and offers them constructive strategies for handling high-risk situations. M. Newcomb and P. Bentler (1989) report that telling children and adolescents that a behavior such as smoking, drinking, or sex will be acceptable when they are older suggests that these behaviors are indicators of maturity. In this way, the behaviors become more attractive. In addition, the Office of Substance Abuse Prevention found that while messages about the negative effects of high-risk behaviors varied, according to the individual's level of sensation seeking most children and adolescents chose to avoid behavior that was linked to negative consequences. However, the response of those who were high in sensation seeking was that "Anything that sounds really bad must be good" (OSAP 1991, 65).

At the beginning of the twenty-first century, America's children face serious challenges to their health and well being. For the most part, these challenges are preventable. The findings reported here indicate that simply providing information is not an effective deterrent of risky behavior. Young adolescents do not usually pause to deliberately weigh the pros and cons before deciding to drink beer, smoke marijuana, or engage in sexual activity. These decisions are made in social contexts in which the negative social consequences of saying no may be at least as salient as the potential health hazards of saying yes. Prevention researchers and educators have the opportunity to use what has been learned about children's understanding of health issues and risky behavior, and about how children learn, to improve the quality of outcomes for all children.

Micheline Malow-Iroff and Helen L. Johnson

REFERENCES

Alaimo, K., C.M. Olson, E.A. Frongillo, and R.R. Briefel. (2001) Food insufficiency, family income, and health in U.S. preschool and school-aged children. *American Journal of Public Health* 91: 781–86.

American Academy of Child and Adolescent Psychiatry. (2004a) "AACAP Supports Stronger Warnings Not Black Box For Antidepressants." Available at www.aacap.org/press_releases/2004/0928.htm.

———. "Facts for Families – Depression." (2004b) Available at www.aacap.org/publications/factsfam/depression.htm.

———. "Facts for Families – The Anxious Child." (2004c) Available at www.aacap.org/publications/factsfam/anxious.htm.

American Academy of Pediatrics (AAP). (2000) Policy statement: Fetal alcohol syndrome and alcohol-related neurodevelopmental disorders. *Pediatrics* 106: 358–61.

———. (2001) Suicide and suicide attempts in adolescence. *Pediatrics* 105: 871–74.

———. (2003) Prevention of pediatric overweight and obesity. *Pediatrics* 112: 424–30.

———. (2004) "Fetal Alcohol Syndrome Fact Sheet." Available at www.aap.org.

American College of Preventive Medicine issues immunization statement. (2003) *Health and Medicine Week* 585 (September 15).

American Psychiatric Association. (1994) *Diagnostic and Statistical Manual of Mental Disorders.* 4th ed. Washington, DC: APA.

Anxiety Disorders Association of America. (2004) "Anxiety Disorders in Children and Adolescents." Available at www.adaa.org/AnxietyDisorderInfor/ChildrenAdo.cfm.

Austin, S.B., and S.L. Gortmaker. (2001) Dieting and smoking initiation in early adolescent girls and boys: A prospective study. *American Journal of Public Health* 91: 446–50.

Azar, S.T. (2002) "Parenting and Child Maltreatment." In *Handbook of Parenting,* ed. M.H. Bornstein. 2nd ed., volume 4. Mahwah, NJ: Erlbaum.

Baledarian, N.J. (1991) *Abuse Causes Disabilities. Disability and the Family.* Culver City, CA: Spectrum Institute.

Barkley, R.A. (1990) *Attention-Deficit/Hyperactivity Disorder: A Handbook for Diagnosis and Treatment.* New York: Guilford.

Barlow, D.H., and V.M. Durand. (1995) *Abnormal Psychology: An Integrative Approach.* Boston: Brooks/Cole.

Baumrind, D. (1971) Current patterns of parental authority. *Developmental Psychology Monographs* 4 (1, Part 2).

Baumrind, D., R.E. Larzelere, and P.A. Cowan. (2002) Ordinary physical punishment: Is it harmful? Comment on E.T. Gershoff. *Psychological Bulletin* 128: 590–95.

Beck, A. (1973) *The Diagnosis and Management of Depression.* Philadelphia: University of Pennsylvania Press.

———. (1993) Cognitive therapy: Past, present and future. *Journal of Consulting and Clinical Psychology* 61: 194–98.

Beers, M., and R. Berkow, eds. (2005) *The Merck Manual of Diagnosis and Therapy.* 17th ed. Available at www.merck.com/mrkshared/mmanual/home.jsp.

Belenko, S. (2004) "Sexually Transmitted Infections In Incarcerated Adolescents." Technical report, Treatment Research Institute, University of Pennsylvania.

Belle, D. (1999) *The After School Lives of Children.* Mahwah, NJ: Erlbaum.

Bernstein, V.J., and S.L. Hans. (1994) Predicting the developmental outcome of two-year-old children born exposed to methadone: The impact of social-environmental risk factors. *Journal of Clinical Child Psychiatry* 23: 349–59.

Berson, I., and M. Berson. (2001) The trauma of terrorism: Helping children cope. *Social Education* (October): 341–43.

Bissada, A., and J. Briere. (2001) "Child Abuse: Physical and Sexual." In *Encyclopedia of Women and Gender,* ed. J. Worell. San Diego: Academic Press.

Borowsky, I., M. Ireland, and M. Resnick. (2001) Adolescent suicide attempts: Risks and protectors. *Pediatrics* 107: 485–93.

Bridges, L. (2003) "Coping as an Element of Developmental Well-Being." In *Well-Being,* ed. M.H. Bornstein, L. Davidson, C.L.M. Keyes, and K.A. Moore. Mahwah, NJ: Erlbaum.

Bronfenbrenner, U. (1979) *The Ecology of Human Development: Experiments by Nature and Design.* Cambridge, MA: Harvard University Press.

———. (2000) "Ecological theory." In *Encyclopedia of Psychology,* ed. A. Kazdin. Washington, DC and New York: American Psychological Association and Oxford University Press.

Brooks-Gunn, J., W.J. Han, and J. Waldfogel. (2002) Maternal employment and child cognitive outcomes in the first three years of life: The NICHD study of early child care. *Child Development* 73: 1052–72.

Brown, K. (2003) The medication merry-go-round. *Science* (March 14): 1646–49.

Bruch, H. (1979) *The Golden Cage: The Enigma of Anorexia Nervosa.* New York: Vintage.

Burguet, A., M. Kaminski, L. Abraham-Lerat, G.C. Schaal, J. Fresson, H. Grandjean, P. Truffert, L. Marpeau, M. Voyer, J-C. Roze, A. Treisser, B. Larroque, and the EPIPAGE Study Group. (2004) The complex relationship between smoking in pregnancy and very preterm delivery. *BJOG: An International Journal of Obstetrics & Gynaecology* 111: 258.

Bussing, R., and F.A. Gary. (2001) Practice guidelines and parental ADHD treatment evaluations: Friends of foes? *Harvard Review of Psychiatry* 9: 223–33.

Carnegie Task Force on Education of Young Adolescents. (1989) *Turning Points: Preparing American Youth for the 21st Century.* Washington, DC: Carnegie Council on Adolescent Development.

Centers for Disease Control and Prevention, National Center for HIV, STD and TB Prevention. (2002) Young people at risk: HIV/AIDS among America's youth.

Centers for Disease Control and Prevention, Office of Minority Health. (2002) Eliminate disparities in HIV and AIDS.

———. (2004) Fact Sheet: Racial Ethnic Health Disparities.

Centers for Disease Control and Prevention. (2002) Alcohol use among women of childbearing age—United States, 1991–1999. *The Journal of the American Medical Association* 287 (April): 2069–71.

Children's Defense Fund. (2001a) "25 Key Facts about American Children." In *The State of America's Children Yearbook 2001* Washington, DC: Children's Defense Fund. Available at www.childrensdefense.org.

———. (2001b) "Child Care and Early Education." In *The State of America's Children Yearbook 2001.* Washington, DC: Children's Defense Fund. Available at www.childrensdefense.org.

———. (2001c) "Child Health: Immunizations." Children's Defense Fund. Available at www.childrensdefense.org.

———. (2001d) "Child Health: Asthma." Children's Defense Fund. Available at www.childrensdefense.org.

———. (2002) "Facts on Youths, Violence, and Crime." Fact Sheet. Washington, DC: Children's Defense Fund. Available at www.childrensdefense.org.

———. (2003) "2002 Facts on Child Poverty in America." Children's Defense Fund. Available at www.childrens defense.org.

Children's Health Research Group. (2002a) Avoiding child deaths: A call to action. *Synopsis* 6. United States Agency for International Development (USAID).

———. (2002b) Major causes of death in young infants. *Synopsis* 6: United States Agency for International Development.

Cicchetti, D., and S.L. Toth. (1998) "Perspectives on Research (USAID) and Practice in Developmental Psychology." In *Handbook of Child Psychology,* vol. 4, ed. W. Damon. New York: Wiley.

Clark, S.L., J. Iceland, T. Palumbo, K. Posey, and M. Weismantle. (2003) *Comparing Employment, Income And Poverty: Census 2000 and the Current Population Survey.* Housing and Household Economic Statistics Division Report (September). Washington, DC: U.S. Census Bureau.

Compas, B.E., J.K. Connor-Smith, H. Saltzman, A.H. Thomsen, and M.E. Wadsworth. (2001) Coping with stress during childhood and adolescence: Problems, progress and potential in theory and research. *Psychological Bulletin* 127: 87–127.

Costello, E., and A. Angold (1995) "Epidemiology." In *Anxiety Disorders in Children and Adolescents,* ed. J.S. March. New York: Guilford.

Curran, K. J. DuCette, J. Eisenstein, and I.A. Hyman. (2001) "Statistical Analysis of the Cross-Cultural Data: The Third Year." Paper presented at the meeting of the American Psychological Association, San Francisco (August).

De Haan, L., and R. Trageton. (2001) Relationships between substance use information and use prevalence and attitudes. *Adolescent and Family Health* 2: 55–62.

Donovan, J.E., and R. Jessor. (1985) Structure of problem behavior in adolescence and young adulthood. *Journal of Consulting and Clinical Psychology* 53: 890–904.

Duncan, G., and J. Brooks-Gunn, eds. (1997) *Consequences of Growing Up Poor.* New York: Russell Sage Foundation.

———. (2004) "Family Poverty, Welfare Reform, and Child Development." In *Annual Editions. Child Growth and Development 04/05,* ed. E. Nunn and C. Boyatzis. Guilford, CT: McGraw-Hill/Dushkin.

Durrant, J.E. (2000) Trends in youth crime and well-being since the abolition of corporal punishment in Sweden. *Youth and Society* 31: 437–55.

Edmund J., D. Daley, M. Thompson, C. Laver-Bradbury, and A. Weeks. (2001) Parent-based therapies for preschool attention-deficit disorder: A randomized, controlled trial with a community sample. *Journal of the American Academy of Child and Adolescent Psychiatry* 40: 402–08.

Egeland, B., D. Jacobvitz, and L.A. Sroufe. (1988) Breaking the cycle of abuse. *New Directions for Child Development* 11: 77–92.

Fadiman, A. (1997) *The Spirit Catches You and You Fall Down.* New York: Farrar, Straus and Giroux.

Field, T. (2000) "Child Abuse." In *Encyclopedia of Psychology,* ed. A. Kazdin. Washington, DC and New York: American Psychological Association and Oxford University Press.

Gallagher, P.A., J. Fialka, C. Rhodes, and C. Arceneaux, (2002) Working with families: Rethinking denial. *Young Exceptional Children* 5: 11–17.

Gershoff, E.T. (2002) Corporal punishment by parents and associated child behaviors and experiences: A meta-analysis and theoretical review. *Psychological Bulletin* 128: 539–79.

Golden, M.H., M.P. Samuels, and D.P. Southall. (2003) How to distinguish between neglect and deprivational abuse. *Archives of Diseases in Childhood* 88: 105–07.

Goldman L., M. Genel, R. Bezman, P. Slanetz. (1998) Diagnosis and treatment of attention-deficit/hyperactivity disorder in children and adolescents. *JAMA* 279: 1100–07.

Gurwitch, R., J. Silovsky, S. Schultz, M. Kees, and S. Burlingame. (2001) *Reactions and Guidelines for Children Following Trauma/Disaster.* Norman, OK: Department of Pediatrics, University of Oklahoma Health Sciences Center.

Hallfors, D., and R.A. Van Dorn. (2002) Strengthening the role of two key institutions in the prevention of adolescent substance abuse. *Journal Adolescent Health* 30: 17–28.

Hart, D., D. Burock, B. London, and R. Atkins. (2003) "Prosocial Development, Antisocial Development and Moral Development." In *An Introduction to Developmental Psychology,* ed. A.M. Slater and G. Bremner. Malden, MA: Blackwell.

Heatherington, E.M. and K.M. Jodl. (1994) " Stepfamilies as Settings for Child Development." In *Stepfamilies: Who Benefits? Who Does Not?,* ed. A. Booth and J. Dunn. Hillsdale, NJ: Erlbaum.

Heatherington, E.M., and M. Stanley-Hagan. (2002) "Parenting in Divorced and Remarried Families." In *Handbook of Parenting,* 2nd ed., vol. 3, ed. M.H. Bornstein. Mahwah, NJ: Erlbaum.

Hoffman, L.W., and L.M. Youngblade. (1999) *Mothers at Work: Effects on Children's Well-Being.* New York: Cambridge.

Hoffman, M.L. (1970) "Moral Development." In *Manual of Child Psychology,* ed., P.H. Mussen, New York: Wiley.

———. (1988) "Moral Development." In *Developmental Psychology: An Advanced Textbook,* 2nd ed. M.H. Bornstein and E. Lamb. ed. Hillsdale, NJ: Erlbaum.

Individuals with Disabilities Education Act Amendments of 1997, P.L. 105–17, 105th Congress, 1st Session. Available at www.ed.gov/policy/gen/guid/fpco/pdf/ferparegs.pdf.

Institute of Medicine (2002) *Unequal treatment: Confronting Racial and Ethnic Disparities in Health Care.* Washington, DC: National Academy Press.

Jaakkola, Jouni, and Mika Gissler. (2004) Maternal smoking in pregnancy, fetal development, and childhood asthma. *American Journal of Public Health* 94: 136–40.

Johnson, P.B., and L. Richter. (2002) The relationship between smoking, drinking, and adolescents' self-perceived health and frequency of hospitalization: Analyses from the 1997 National Household Survey of Drug Abuse. *Journal of Adolescent Health* 30: 175–83.

Johnston, L.D, P.M. O'Malley, J.G. Bachman, and J.E. Schulenberg. (2004) *Monitoring the Future National Results on Adolescent Drug Use: Overview of Key Findings, 2003.* (NIH Publication No. 04-5506). Bethesda, MD: National Institute on Drug Abuse.

Juvenile Bipolar Research Foundation. "About Juvenile-Onset Bipolar Disorder." Available at www.bpchildresearch.org/juv_bipolar/index.html.

Kates, J., R. Sorian, J.S. Crowley, and T.A. Summers. (2002) Critical policy challenges in the third decade of the HIV/AIDS epidemic. *American Journal of Public Health* 92: 1060–63.

Klerman, G. and M. Weissman. (1986) "The Interpersonal Approach to Understanding Depression." In *Contemporary Directions in Psychopathology,* ed., T. Millon, New York: Guilford.

Klinnert, M.D., M.R. Price, A.H. Liu, and J.L. Robinson. (2002) Unraveling the ecology of risks for early childhood asthma among ethnically diverse families in the Southwest. *American Journal of Public Health* 92: 792–98.

Langley, A., L. Bergman, and J. Piacentini. (2002) Assessment of childhood anxiety. *International Review of Psychiatry* 14: 102–13.

Larson, E. (2003) Racial and ethnic disparities in immunizations: Recommendations for clinicians. *Family Medicine* 35: 655–60.

Lazarus, R.S. (1996) *Psychological Stress and the Coping Process.* New York: McGraw-Hill.

Levinson-Gingiss, P.L., and R. Hamilton. (1989) Determinants of teachers' plans to continue teaching a sexuality education course. *Family and Community Health* 12: 40–53.

Lewis, M.W., S. Misra, H.L. Johnson, and T.S. Rosen. (2004) Neurological and developmental outcomes of prenatally cocaine-exposed offspring from 12 to 36 months. *American Journal of Alcohol and Drug Issues* 30: 299-320.

Lima, R.C., C.G. Victora, A.M. Memezes, and F.C. Barros. (2003) Do risk factors for childhood infections and malnutrition protect against asthma? *American Journal of Public Health* 93: 1858–64.

March of Dimes. (2003) "Peristats: An Interactive Perinatal Data Resource. Available at www.marchofdimes.com/peristats/.

McCleary, L., and M. Sanford. (2002) Parental expressed emotion in depressed adolescents: Prediction of clinical course and relationship to comorbid disorders and social functioning. *Journal of Child Psychology and Psychiatry* 43: 587–95.

McElderry, D.H., and H.O. Omar. (2003) Sex education in the schools: What role does it play? *International Journal of Adolescent Medical Health* 1: 3–9.

McLoyd, V.C., and J. Smith. (2002) Physical discipline and behavior problems in African American, European American, and Hispanic children: Emotional support as a moderator. *Journal of Marriage and Family* 64: 40–53.

Moore, K.A., B.C. Miller, B.W. Sugland, D.R. Morrison, D.A. Glei, and C. Blumenthal. (2002) Adolescent sexual behavior, pregnancy and parenthood. U.S. Department of Health and Human Services.

More U.S. children are getting their shots. (2003) *Medical Letter on the CDC and FDA* 12 (August 24).

MTA Cooperative Group. (1999) A 14-month randomized clinical trial of treatment strategies for attention-deficit/hyperactivity disorder. *Arch Gen Psychiatry* 56: 1073–86.

National Clearinghouse on Child Abuse and Neglect. (2002) *National Child Abuse and Neglect Data System Summary of Key Findings from Calendar Year 2000.* Washington DC: The Administration for Children and Families.

National Center for Chronic Disease Prevention and Health Promotion. (2002) Alcohol and other drug use prevention. Centers for Disease Control and Prevention.

National Center for Health Statistics. (2000) CDC Office of Minority Health (www.cdc.gov).

———. (2002) "National Vital Statistics Report: Death Statistics." Bethesda, Maryland: National Center for Health Statistics.

National Center for Infants, Toddlers and Families. (2003) "First-Ever Data Book on Babies and Toddlers." (November) Available at www.zerotothree.org.

National Institute on Alcohol Abuse and Alcoholism. (2000) Highlights from the Tenth Special Report to Congress. *Alcohol Research and Alcohol Health* 24.

———. (2001) Prevention of alcohol-related problems among adolescents. RFA: AA-01–001. Alexandria, VA: National Institutes of Health.

———. (2003) Preventing drug abuse among children and adolescents. Bethesda, MD: National Institute on Drug Abuse.

National Institute on Drug Abuse. (2004) "High School and Youth Trends." *NIDA Infofacts.* Revised June. Available at www.drugabuse.gov/Infofax/HSYouthtrends.html.

National Institutes of Health. (1998) Diagnosis and treatment of attention deficit hyperactivity disorder. *Consensus Development Conference Statement* 16, no. 2: 1–37.

Nelson, J.A., M.A. Chiasson, and V. Ford. (2004) Childhood overweight in a New York City WIC population. *American Journal of Public Health* 94: 458–62.

Neumark-Sztainer, D., M. Story, L.B. Dixon, and D.M. Murray. (1998) Adolescents engaging in unhealthy weight control behaviors: Are they at risk for other health-compromising behaviors? *American Journal of Public Health* 88: 952–55.

Neumark-Sztainer, D., M. Story, P.J. Hanna, MStat, and J. Croll. (2002) Overweight status and eating patterns among adolescent: Where do youths stand in comparison with the *Healthy People 2010* objectives? *American Journal of Public Health* 92: 844–51.

Newcomb, M.B., and P.M. Bentler. (1989) Substance use and abuse among children and teenagers. *American Psychologist* 44: 242–48.

Nolen-Hoeksema, S. (2004) *Abnormal Psychology.* 3rd ed. New York: McGraw-Hill.

Office for Substance Abuse Prevention (OSAP). (1991) A key to prevention: What kids think other kids are doing. *Prevention Pipeline* 4: 65.

O'Leary, S.G., A.M. Smith Slep, and M.J. Reid. (1999) A longitudinal study of mothers' overreactive discipline and toddlers' externalizing behavior. *Journal of Abnormal Child Psychology* 27: 331–41.

Okongwu, F.A. (1995) Looking up from the bottom to the ceiling of the basement floor: Female single-parent families. *Urban Anthropology* 24: 313-363.

Papalos, D., and J. Papalos. (1997) *Overcoming Depression.* 3rd ed. New York: Harper Collins.

———. (1999) *The Bipolar Child.* New York: Broadway Books.

Patterson, G.R., T.D. Dishion, and L. Bank. (1984) Family interaction: A process model of deviancy training. *Aggressive Behavior* 10: 253–67.

Pelham, W.E., H.R. Aronoff, M.A. Midlam, et al. (1999) A comparison of Ritalin and Adderall: Efficacy and time-course in children with attention-deficit hyperactivity disorder. *Pediatrics* 103: 1–14.

Perhats, C., K. Oh, S.R. Levy, B.R. Flayand, and S. McFall. (1996) Role differences in gatekeeper perceptions of school-based drug and sexuality education programs: A cross-sectional survey. *Health Education Research* 11: 11–27.

Pettit, G.S., J.E. Bates, K.A. Dodge, and D.W. Meece. (1999) The impact of after-school peer contact on early adolescent externalizing problems is moderated by parental monitoring, perceived neighborhood safety, and prior adjustment. *Child Development* 70: 768–78.

Pillow, D.R., A.J. Zautra, and I. Sandler. (1996) Major life events and minor stressors: Identifying mediational links in the stress process. *Journal of Personality and Social Psychology* 70: 381–94.

Pugach, M.C., and L.J. Johnson. (2002) *Collaborative Practitioners; Collaborative Schools.* 2nd ed. Denver, CO: Love.

Saarni, C. (1999) *The Development of Emotional Competence.* New York: Guilford Press.

Saavedra, L., and W. Silverman. (2002) Classification of anxiety disorders in children: What a difference two decades make. *International Review of Psychiatry* 14: 87–101.

Santrock, J.W. (2004) *Child Development.* Boston: McGraw-Hill.

Schonfeld, D.J. (2000) Teaching young children about HIV and AIDS. *Child and Adolescent Psychiatric Clinics of North America* 9: 375–87.

Schulenberg, J., and J. Maggs. (2002) A developmental perspective on alcohol use and heavy drinking during adolescence and the transition to young adulthood. Washington, DC: Task Force of the National Advisory Council on Alcohol Abuse and Alcoholism.

Seifer, R., and A.J. Sameroff. (1987) "Multiple Determinants of Risk and Invulnerability." In *The Invulnerable Child,* ed. E.J. Anthony and B.J. Cohler, 51–69. New York: Guilford.

Seligman, M. (1975) *Learned Helplessness.* San Francisco: Freeman.

———. (1995) *The Optimistic Child.* Boston: Houghton Mifflin.

Smith, D.E., and G. Mosby. (2003) Jamaican child-rearing practices: The role of corporal punishment. *Adolescence* 38: 369–81.

Southam-Gerow, M.A., P.C. Kendall, and V.R. Weersing. (2001) Examining outcome variability: Correlates of treatment response in a child and adolescent anxiety clinic. *Journal of Clinical Child Psychology* 30: 422–36.

Steinberg, L., and J.S. Silk. (2002) "Parenting Adolescents." In *Handbook of Parenting,* ed. M. Bornstein. 2nd ed., vol. 1. Mahwah, NJ: Erlbaum.

Steinberg, L., N.S. Mounts, S.D. Lamborn, and S. Dornbusch. (1990) "Interdependence in the Family: Autonomy, Conflict, and Harmony." In *At the Threshold: The Developing Adolescent,* ed. S. Feldman and G. Eliot. Cambridge, MA: Harvard University Press.

Subramanian, Siva K.N., and Helen Yoon. (2002) "Extremely low birthweight infants." Emedicine. Available at www.eMedicine.com.

Teicher, M. (2000) Wounds that time won't heal: The neurobiology of child abuse. *Cerebrum* 2, no. 4 (fall): 50–67.

Telljohann, S.K., C.W. Symons, and B. Pateman. (2004) *Health Education: Elementary and Middle School Applications.* Boston: McGraw-Hill.

Thomas, A., and S. Chess. (1979) *Temperament and Development.* New York: Brunner/Mazel.

Thomas, S.B., and C.A. Denzinger. (1993) *Special Education Law: Case Summaries and Federal Regulations.* Topeka, KS: National Organization on Legal Problems in Education.

Turnbull, A.P., and H.R. Turnbull III. (2001) *Families Professionals, and Exceptionality.* 4th ed. Columbus, OH: Merrill.

U.S. Department of Health and Human Services, Center for Mental Health Services. (1999) *Mental Health: A Report of the Surgeon General.* Rockville, MD: National Institute of Mental Health.

U.S. Office for Substance Abuse Prevention. (1991) A key to prevention: What kids think other kids are doing. *Prevention Pipeline* 4, no. 3: 65.

Federal Interagency Forum on Child and Family Statistics (FIFCFS). (2003) *America's Children: Key National Indicators of Well-Being, 2003.* 7th Report to the Nation. Washington, DC: FIFCFS. Available at www.childstats.gov.

Ventegod, Soren, and Joav Merrick. (2003) Long-term effects of maternal smoking on quality of life. *The Scientific World Journal* 3: 714–20.

Vygotsky, L.S. (1962). *Thought and Language.* Cambridge, MA: MIT Press.

Wehler, C., L. Weinreb, N. Huntington, R. Scott, D. Hosmer, K. Fletcher, R. Goldberg, and C. Gundersen. (2004) Risk and protective factors for adult and child hunger among low-income housed and homeless female-headed families. *American Journal of Public Health* 94: 109–15.

Wicks-Nelson, R., and A.C. Israel. (2000) *Behavior Disorders of Childhood.* Upper Saddle River, NJ: Prentice Hall.

Wilson, C.M., L.C. Wilson, and C.A. Fox. (2002) Structural and personal contexts of discipline orientations of Guyanese parents: Theoretic and empirical considerations. *Journal of Comparative Family Studies* 1–13.

Wroe, A.L., M. Turner, P.M. Salkovskis. (2004) "Understanding and predicting parental decisions about early childhood immunizations." *Health Psychology* 23: 0278–6133.

Zito, J. (2000) Trends in the prescribing of psychotropic medications to preschoolers. *JAMA* 283: 1025–60.

VI

PEOPLE

30

PEOPLE

In this section, we present a thorough examination of twenty-five eminent figures in education and human development. The assignment of selecting the "most eminent" individuals who impacted the fields of education and human development was by no means an easy task. Indeed, there is no magic formula or quantitative methodology that will determine who is "most eminent"; and this rule of thumb holds for the meaning of "eminence" in any field or discipline, not merely in education and human development. As the editors, we are fully aware that the list of eminent individuals in the field of education goes well beyond twenty-five. In fact, our original list surpassed the "one hundred" mark. However, with length and time limitations in mind, we needed to make some important decisions with regard to the individuals we were to include. Moreover, we had no intention to make mere mention of a hundred or more individuals of, say, 100 or so words each; that would do more of a disservice to each of the individuals than not including some of them at all. Rather, we wanted to include full-length entries (of approximately 1,000 words or more), in which each individual's life and work are examined in detail. At the same time, we are delighted to have identified several hundred renowned individuals—not included in this section—to be discussed in nearly all of the twenty-nine chapters in Part I of this encyclopedia.

So, how did we determine "eminent" individuals in education? To begin with, we asked a number of our colleagues to identify who they think to be the five "most eminent" individuals in education. Next, we determined how many times a particular figure was mentioned by each of our colleagues. It became evident that some figures focused their attention to educational practice, other figures were devoted to developing theoretical frameworks, and a third group of a more radi-

cal nature were interested in transforming dominant bureaucratic, and often times racist and sexist educational systems. Clearly, names like Paulo Freire, Maria Montessori, Jean Piaget, Jean-Jacques Rousseau, and Lev Vygotsky were mentioned most frequently.

Despite their eminence, the educational thinkers discussed in this section demonstrated, for the most part, both strengths and weaknesses in their output. Although we highlight all their contributions to education and human development, we also draw clear attention to the flaws in each thinker's philosophical, theoretical, or practitioner-based framework. For example, despite limited primary sources, we have some knowledge of Aristotle's views on education; he strongly believed that the pursuit of education is a sine qua non activity in order for one to achieve the good life—that is, to flourish and engage in skills that strengthen the mind, body, and soul. At the same time, Aristotle did not believe that girls and women should receive formal education (Everson 1996). As another example, for decades, William Kilpatrick's work on the Project Method served as a foundational model in schools. However, critics of Kilpatrick's method argued that he overwhelmingly emphasized trait and character at the expense of cognitive development and general content knowledge (Beyer 1997).

It is evident from the biographies that being human renders a variety of attributes such as intellect, creativity, perseverance, and charisma—some or all of which can be identified in the twenty-five selected individuals. The transformation of a field of study and the creation of a revolution in thought and practice are never easy. History often demonstrates that one's influence may not be recognized until posterity. We have identified four generalizations that support this notion. First, there must be a societal readiness for change as a means of acceptance of one's work or ideas. Second, there needs to be some type of mass distribution of an individual's work. The work must not only be translated into a variety of languages, but must be adapted to a common vernacular for the general public. Third, there needs to be some recognition of the work and general debate of its premises. Finally, good theories and practices are formative in nature and evolve under a variety of conditions. We believe that the twenty-five people who were selected for this section have transformed thought and practice in their related interests in the fields of education and human development.

Stephen J. Farenga and Daniel Ness

REFERENCES

Beyer, Landon E. (1997) William Heard Kilpatrick. *Prospects: The Quarterly Review of Comparative Education*, (Paris, UNESCO: International Bureau of Education), vol. XXVII, no. 3, p. 470-485.

Everson, Stephen. (1996) *Aristotle: The Politics and The Constitution of Athens*. New York: Cambridge University Press.

PETER ABELARD

Peter Abelard (1079–1142) is perhaps the best known educator in the medieval era that embraced scholasticism as a method of teaching. Scholastic educators applied classic philosophical approaches—including Platonism, Aristotelianism, Skepticism, Epicureanism, and Stoicism—to theology that were to eventually become the method of discourse in the earliest universities. The contributions of Abelard are important for several reasons. To begin with, he was not only a teacher, but also one of the first teachers to train individuals in the teaching profession. Second, he introduced the teaching methods associated with scholastic education. Third, his evidently stimulating and poignant delivery and style as a teacher is said to have been incomparable to his contemporaries. He drew throngs of students wherever he taught (Copleston 1962). Fourth, Abelard's achievements are contrasted with his difficulties in pedagogical practice. Moreover, these difficulties nearly one thousand years ago are similar to the problems that remain to the present day. And fifth, Abelard identified

cognitive development as a higher level of thinking to basic fact and concept mastery.

HISTORICAL BACKGROUND

Abelard was born in 1079 in the community of Le Pallet, France, not far from Nantes. At about the turn of the century (1100) he traveled to Paris, where he studied under the tutelage of William of Champeaux at the school of Notre Dame. Perhaps William's most outspoken critic, Abelard criticized his master's realist philosophy. Abelard eventually became a master at the school of Notre Dame and, in 1112, he taught at the school of Mont-Ste-Geneviève, not far from Paris. Abelard's fame as a dialectician attracted great numbers of students to Paris. Unlike several well-known educational thinkers before and after him, Abelard lived during his fame. Abelard's recognition, however, did not come until he was thirty-seven years of age in 1116. However, his fame was soon cut short.

After his romance with Heloise, with whom he bore a son, his relationship with a number of his colleagues became bitter, to the point that his reputation was diminished. Believing that Abelard would leave her and her son, Heloise's uncle sent a band of men after him. Abelard then sought refuge as a monk at Saint-Denis, where he remained until 1120. Finding that the monks at Saint-Denis would not accept him, Abelard created a hermitage near Troyes. In Troyes, Abelard built the monastery, the so-called Paraclete, where students would stay to study with him. Abelard gave the Paraclete to Heloise when he became abbot of Saint-Gildas-en-Rhuys, Brittany. Once again, in 1140, Abelard was condemned by the Council of Sens for allegedly having a negative influence on youth. He subsequently retired to Cluny. When he died in 1149, he was buried at the Paraclete. Later his body, along with Heloise (who died in 1164), was transported to Père-Lachaise in Paris. The events in Abelard's life are well documented, partly due to the fact that he himself wrote an autobiography, *Historia Calamitatum* (1974). Abelard was perhaps most important as a teacher. Some of his most celebrated pupils include John of Salisbury and Arnold of Brescia. In addition to his treatises on philosophy and education, Abelard also was an established poet. Although a prolific poet, only Latin hymns have survived.

Controversy between Religion and Philosophical Inquiry and Learning

As a result of a revival of the works of Aristotle, Abelard espoused a Aristotelian dialectic approach. This approach considered the overarching idea that the methods of logic are universal and are perhaps the *sine qua non* element for nonsectarian philosophical inquiry and human thought. Abelard, however, was one of the first individuals that believed Aristotelian dialectic could be applied to the universals of faith. This view was in radical opposition to the mystical views of St. Bernard, the ultra realist views of William of Champeaux, and the universalistic views of Roscelin. Abelard, however, attempted to ground universals as entities existing only in the abstract, yet with a basis in particulars. He referred to this as moderate realism. Although he was unsuccessful in reconciling the philosophy of Aristotle and methods of logic with faith, Abelard's ideas influenced a number of philosophers after him, particularly St. Thomas Aquinas approximately a century later.

Perhaps Abelard's most influential work was *Sic et Non* (Yea and Nay), in which he devised 158 questions about the Trinity, the idea of redemption, and the sacraments. In his introduction to *Sic et Non*, Abelard set a method of resolving the apparent contradictions between the church and the academy, thereby making the work significant for the development of the scholastic method. One important contribution to philosophy and education that Abelard presents is his method, which was employed in the teachings and treatises of a number of his predecessors, including Alexander of Hales and St. Thomas Aquinas. With the 158 questions, Abelard placed a column on one side that indicated an affirmative answer to a question and a column on the other side of each question that indicated a negative answer. In general, Abelard wished to place before the student the reasons for and against the principle that truth is to be attained only by a dialectical discussion of apparently contradictory arguments and authorities. In the problem concerning universals, a topic that occupied a large number of dialecticians in those days, Abelard reproached what he referred to as crude nominalism of Roscelin on the one hand, and the flagrant realism of his former mentor William of Champeaux on the other. It is not entirely clear, however, what Abelard's position really was with any accuracy. However, from the statements of his pupil, John of Salisbury, it is clear that Abelard's doctrine, while expressed in terms of a modified Nominalism, was very similar to the moderate Realism that began to be official in the schools about half a century after Abelard's death. This work formed the basis for the widely read *Sentences* of Peter Lombard, who may have been Abelard's pupil.

Abelard's genius was his ability to combine Platonic forms or essences with Aristotelian logic and with cognitive inquiry (Nominalism). To be sure, he posited that universals presuppose actual things (in the Platonic realm) and they are in such things as their discernible likenesses (as Aristotelians would maintain). He also argued that universals exist even after the objects they represent are no longer in sight or are no longer existing. This is evidenced, according to Abelard, in the cognitive domain—in other words, the learner becomes acquainted with something by name or in an abstract way. The cognitive argument—that the learner knows through thinking—is an essential component to the learning process.

Later Influence

Disgrace and humiliation aside, Abelard still managed to attract a multitude of students, many of whom became prominent figures. Before his death in 1142, Abelard attracted students from all areas of Europe. Hastings Rashdall (1936) states that twenty of Abelard's pupils became cardinals and fifty became bishops. Abelard's contributions to education influence contemporary practices in a number of ways. First, although he attempted to reconcile the distinction between human thought and inquiry (i.e., philosophy) and Christian faith, he insisted that in order to prevent dogmatic practices from prevailing in dispute and debate, it is necessary to development human knowledge through the methods of logic. Abelard's support for his ideas was the philosophical works of Aristotle. Next, he is one of the first individuals whose professional responsibilities dealt with the art and science of pedagogy. Abelard not only was deeply familiar with teaching style, but also was a teacher who motivated his students to a great extent.

Stephen J. Farenga and Daniel Ness

REFERENCES

Abelard, Peter. (1978) *Sic et Non.* Rev. Ed. Chicago: University of Chicago Press.

———. (1998) *The Letters of Abelard and Heloise,* trans. Betty Radice. New York: Penguin.

———. (2002) *Historia calamitatum,* trans. and ed. Dag Nikolaus Hasse. New York: Walter de Gruyter.

Copleston, F.J. (1962) *A History of Philosophy.* New York: Doubleday.

Rashdall, Hastings. (1936) *The Universities of Europe in the Middle Ages.* 3 vols. Ed. M. Powicke and A.B. Emden. Oxford, UK: Oxford University Press.

MARY AINSWORTH

Mary Ainsworth (1913–1999) is commonly referred to as one of the pioneers in the theory of attachment. Prior to Ainsworth, theorists such as John Bowlby and James Robertson contributed a great deal to our understanding of attachment as it pertained to institutional separation (e.g., separation from parents of a child who might be hospitalized). However, Ainsworth is perhaps one of the first researchers to investigate the effects of different forms of childrearing on attachment behaviors. Her primary interest was to examine infants' behavior when present with their mothers—a secure base for them from about eight months—and when left with a stranger for a few minutes. Her subjects include parent-child relations in different parts of the world and from a variety of social settings.

BACKGROUND

Ainsworth was born in Glendale, Ohio. At the age of twenty-six, she received her Ph.D. from the University of Toronto. Ainsworth served in the Canadian Army during World War II, and rose to the level of major. Prior to 1950, Ainsworth worked primarily alone. In 1950, however, she and John Bowlby exchanged ideas and influences on each other's theory. Throughout the remainder of her life, Ainsworth repeatedly reconnected with Bowlby to further develop theoretical ideas and share data. After World War II, Ainsworth traveled to Uganda with her husband, where she conducted numerous studies on mother-child interactions. There she discovered different patterns of attachment, which contributed to her general theory on the subject.

In 1956, Ainsworth went to Johns Hopkins University where she had conducted an intensive investigation of mothers and children in Baltimore County, Maryland. She found that the parent-child classifications that were evident among Ugandans applied to American mothers and children as well. In 1976, Ainsworth became a faculty member of the University of Virginia, and eventually retired there. Her later research investigated attachment beyond infancy and into adulthood.

ATTACHMENT THEORY

Ainsworth's key ideas were born during her time at the University of Toronto under the guidance of William Blatz, who developed a theory of the role of security in humans. Ainsworth developed her idea of a secure base in infant attachments on Blatz's framework. She argued that having a strong attachment provided the child not with a dependent and helpless relationship to the parent, but a sense of security as a base. From this secure base, the child could then explore, take risks, and in fact, behave more independently rather than being dependent and helpless. This view is compatible with Erikson's view of autonomy as an outcome of a foundation of trust. Ainsworth argued that one could never be too securely attached because attachment continues to be adaptive throughout one's life, while dependence is not.

As a means of assessing the type of attachment that had formed between a parent and a child, Ainsworth developed a technique she coined the "strange situation task." This task consists of a series of events for the infant and parent, usually the mother. The infant is first placed in a room with the mother alone. In one phase, the mother leaves the infant alone. In another phase, the mother returns. In another, a stranger enters. In another, the mother and stranger are both present with the infant. The task presents several chances to observe the infant's reactions to separation from the mother, to a stranger, and to reunions with the mother. Certain patterns of distress shown by infants on separation from their mothers and on encountering strangers were observed. Most important, certain patterns of reactions of the infant to reunion with the mother were also observed.

Based on extensive research, Ainsworth classified the patterns found during the strange situation task into three main types of infant attachment: Type A—insecure-avoidant attachment; Type B—secure attachment; and Type C—anxious-ambivalent (insecure-ambivalent) attachment or resistant attachment. In the Type A pattern (Insecure-avoidant attachment), the infant seems to ignore the mother, to show minimal distress when she leaves, and avoid her upon reunion. The infant seems to be detached from the mother. In the Type B pattern (secure attachment), the infant shows distress when the mother leaves and seeks her proximity, affection, and contact when she returns. The infant shares feelings easily and is easily comforted by the mother. Most children show this type. In Type C, the anxious-ambivalent attachment (also referred to as insecure-ambivalent, or resistant attachment), the infant seems to be ambivalent and inconsistent in his or her distress and reunion responses. Upon reunion with the mother, the infant often moves toward the mother, then away from her; the infant sometimes acts as if he or she is attempting to punish the mother.

Based on the results of the strange situation task, Ainsworth, among other researchers, concluded that its classifications predict children's future patterns of attachment. Children who possess secure types of attachments generally form close bonds with peers in the early childhood years. Those who demonstrate insecure types of attachment are more likely to have problems in preschool or elementary school related to poor behavior. Those who possess avoidant forms of attachment will more than likely exhibit various types of mood disorders and possibly depression. According to Ainsworth, attachment is evident at some point during infancy, and that behavior problems arise as a result of insecure attachments with the mother. Insecure attachments are likely the result of inconsistent or mixed-signal interactions between the parent and the child.

Ainsworth's groundbreaking work had a great deal of influence on subsequent researchers. For example, research emanating from Ainsworth's theory includes results that show how infants whose mothers do not respond in any way to their children (stone faced mothers) attempt to avoid their mothers. Other subsequent research includes the attachments of pre-term infants. Infants who are pre-term are generally at greater risk in developing secure attachments with their parents. Signs of insecure attachments, especially with insecure infants and young children, include delays in demonstration of release mechanisms, such as smiling, laughing, or making eye contact. In addition, their responses are generally less stable and predictable than young children with secure attachments. Another factor that may contribute to insecure attachments has to do with pre-term infants who are hospitalized for long periods. In this case, the parents may be separated from the child for significant amounts of time. Thus, pre-term children can form insecure attachments, and parents may have a more difficult time forming secure attachments.

AINSWORTH'S CONTRIBUTIONS TO EDUCATION AND HUMAN DEVELOPMENT

Ainsworth's contributions to psychology have influenced education and human development in that her theoretical positions have led individuals to be able to predict future behavior of children. One case in point is day care. One argument can be made in favor of day care in that it provides a supportive environment for young children from low-income households. A similar line of argument can be made in support of mothers who wish to pursue their careers. However, Ainsworth would most likely question this position by arguing that very young children who are placed in day-care facilities run the risk of losing secure attachments with their parents (or parent—usually the mother). Current research seems to indicate that the extent to which the bond between young child and mother deteriorates is not significant. Only about 7 percent of the young children who are raised in day care run the risk of insecure attachment. Related studies have indicated that there is no negative effect at all when the caregivers are of high quality. But this poses a problem for low-income households, where affordable and high-quality day care is difficult to find.

Like most theorists, Ainsworth too has had her share of critics. Jerome Kagan, for example, has argued that Ainsworth ignores possible innate characteristics of the child that might make her avoidant of her mother. More recent studies, which seem to argue in favor of both Ainsworth's position and those of her critics, indicate that children's emotional development is influenced in part by the parents and also possibly some innate characteristic of the child.

Stephen J. Farenga and Daniel Ness

REFERENCES

Ainsworth, Mary D. (1978) *Patterns of Attachment: A Psychological Study of the Strange Situation.* Mahwah, NJ: Lawrence Erlbaum Associates.

———. (1979) Infant-mother attachment. *American Psychologist* 34, no. 10: 932–37.

Bretherton, Inge. (1992) The origins of attachment theory: John Bowlby and Mary Ainsworth. *Developmental Psychology* 28, no. 5: 759–75.

Crain, William, C. (1999) *Theories of Human Development: Concepts and Applications.* 4th ed. Englewood Cliffs, NJ: Prentice Hall.

ALCUIN

Alcuin (c.735–c.800) was an eminent medieval educator. He was born about 735 in northeastern England near York. He played a singular role in the Carolingian revival of learning on the European continent after nearly four centuries of disorder in the educational systems. Alcuin's influence as a teacher and stimulant to the intellectual life of his times was especially great because of his talents. It was also great due to his life as a teacher in many lands, for example, at Tours and at Aachen in Gaul. Alcuin held the office of Scholasticus in the Cathedral school at York when he was invited by Charles I, king of the Franks—henceforth, Charlemagne—in 782 to assume charge of the palace school at Aachen.

ALCUIN'S LIFE AND CONTRIBUTIONS TO EDUCATION

The decline of church and state had been pervasive in Gaul. Despite differences in ethnicities, customs, institutions, and language, all its inhabitants under Charles's rule professed common goals, and the Church, then, would serve as the common institution for instructing the populace. Since the beginning of his reign, Charlemagne had wanted to raise the educational level of his subjects and the overall improvement and progress of intellectual life throughout the land (Duckett 1951). With the exception of the clergy and the monasteries, there were no institutions that could promote Charlemagne's plan. The first task, then, was to reform church discipline and to improve the educational preparation of the clergy. These tasks were assigned to Alcuin.

The main purpose of the palace school of the Frankish kings prior to the time of Charlemagne was to train court attendants in proper manners, but the boundless energy and intellectual curiosity of Charlemagne, coupled with his sense of mission in spreading religion and knowledge throughout his kingdom, changed all that (Sharpes 2001). During Charlemagne's reign, few priests knew Latin and even fewer knew Greek; this, according to Charlemagne, put the role of the Church in danger. Nonetheless, Charlemagne was devoted to the value of education, not merely for the upper classes, but for the masses as well. He searched throughout Europe for a Latin and Greek speaking scholar. In 782, Charlemagne found Alcuin, and brought the teacher from York to educate himself, his family, and court, and through the clergy, the entirety of his kingdom to ensure that the threat of pagan gods might be banished.

Alcuin and his fellow teachers were asked to teach a diverse crowd of students at the palace school. At times, all members of the immediate royal family were present, together with other family members (uncles, aunts, cousins, and so forth). It was difficult to distinguish the court life from the school operation because the personnel of court and school were nearly identical. The physical maturity and social status of most of the students, together with the heterogeneous nature of the classes, was undoubtedly responsible for the rather relaxed atmosphere that prevailed in the classroom. Nevertheless, Alcuin viewed each member with great affection and served as counselor and confidante.

ALCUIN'S PEDAGOGICAL STYLE

Alcuin used clever teaching devices as a means of creating a conducive learning environment at the palace school. In a document entitled *Problems for Sharpening the Wits of Youth*, credited to Alcuin, fifty-three puzzles are provided with methods of calculation for each. The following is one of Alcuin's puzzles:

A ladder has 100 steps. On the first sits one bird, on the second two birds, on the third three, and so on up to the one hundredth step. How many birds are there in all?

Legend has it that as a boy, the mathematical genius Carl Friedrich Gauss was asked to find the sum of the sequence 1, 2, 3, ... 98, 99, 100 as a penalty for a misdeed. The tutor was astonished when the boy answered so quickly. Alcuin, over one thousand years earlier, used a similar method where he considered all the pairs of numbers between 1 and 100 that added to 100 (1+99, 2+98, 3+97, ... 48+52, and 49+51). Since there are 49 such pairs, one simply can multiply 49 by 100 and add the leftover numbers that were not included in the pairs—namely 50 and 100—resulting in a total of 5050.

Alcuin was particularly talented as a teacher in that (given his prowess in instructing relatively well-prepared boys in the strict atmosphere of the school at York) he was able to make numerous adjustments in order to teach the mature and influential but largely boorish court members. Alcuin is sometimes referred to as one of the first teachers of adult literacy or adult education. Numerous palace students, realizing their roles in the economic and social life of the country were already firmly established, had neither desire nor opportunity to become scholars, but were satisfied to acquire the most elementary attribute of culture at the time—proficiency in Latin.

Based on his writings in education, Alcuin did not develop novel ideas; instead he compiled a great deal of compendia for the purpose and use of exercise and drill. His most significant contribution, however, was as a pedagogue. In surviving letters, Alcuin is described in terms of affection and grateful admiration (Allott 1988). Alcuin's great challenge as a teacher was to educate a large number of individuals in a most diverse setting. He was asked to teach elementary knowledge to adult students who lacked formal educational experience. Alcuin's experiences during the Carolingian period still rings true today; the American educational system, as well as those of other countries, clearly include huge populations that are deprived from an economic standpoint.

One of Alcuin's shortcomings was that, in his teachings, he did not employ instructional methods and the arts of rhetoric that were so much a part of the Greek and Roman periods more than seven to eleven centuries earlier. Perhaps the zeitgeist of the Carolingian period and the early medieval era in general was partially to account for this. However, Alcuin's goals in bringing learning to the Franks and his technique of complementing drill and practice with riddles and other challenges to the students' creativity should not be overlooked. While the students may have recognized the elementary character of much of what they did, Alcuin gave them a sense of intellect by encouraging them to compose poetry, answer riddles, and solve puzzles.

Stephen J. Farenga and Daniel Ness

REFERENCES

Allott, Stephen. (1988) *Alcuin of York: The Life and Letters of the Saxon Scholar.* New York: Hyperion Books.

Duckett, Eleanor S. (1951) *Alcuin, Friend of Charlemagne.* New York: Macmillan.

Sharpes, Donald K. (2001) *Advanced Educational Foundation for Teachers: The History, Philosophy, and Culture of Schooling.* New York: Garland Publishing.

ARISTOTLE

Aristotle (384–322 B.C.E.), a student in Plato's Academy, is considered by many philosophers to be one of the greatest thinkers in the field of philosophy. One primary reason for this has to do with his rich corpus of contributions to the development of numerous fields in the scientific, artistic, literary, and ethical realms. In addition to these contributions, Aristotle's prolific output covered the three major domains of philosophical inquiry: the problem of knowledge (what it means to know anything); the problem of conduct (what it means to be virtuous); and the problem of governance (what it means to lead and be led). Philosophers also seem to concur that Aristotle's work serves as the bedrock of modern social and physical science disciplines (e.g., psychology, political science, biology, and physics). He also emphasized the importance of education through the questioning of the meaning of knowledge. Although Aristotle's work impacted a wide range of subject areas, only about 20 percent of his written work has survived. Moreover, a good part of the extant writings of Aristotle is in the form of lectures and note-taking material. Jonathan Barnes's edition (1982) of Aristotle's complete works is an excellent compendium of what is known to exist in written form.

HISTORICAL BACKGROUND

Aristotle was born in Stagyra, a Greek colony and seaport on the coast of Thrace, in the area known as Macedon. The son of Nichomachus, the court physician to the Macedonian royal family, Aristotle was initially trained in medicine; however, in his mid-teen years, Aristotle left Stagyra for Athens, and entered Plato's Academy at the age of 17. Aristotle left the academy shortly after Plato's death in 347 B.C.E., and went to Assos and Lesbos. It was in these regions that Aristotle collected a great deal of data in the areas of physical and life sciences. Shortly thereafter, in 342 B.C.E., he was invited to the court of Philip of Macedon, where he tutored Alexander the Great. In 335 B.C.E., Aristotle returned to Athens, where he founded the Lyceum, an institution that admitted students who wished to pursue study in a newly founded discipline in the arts or sciences. The institution's mission was that of a university—research was pursued as an extension of higher education. Courses for enrolled students were usually held in the morning. In the afternoons and evenings, the Lyceum served the general public as an open university.

Upon a sequence of Macedonian victories led by Alexander, Macedonian-born Athenian civilians, like Aristotle, fell into disrepute with the Athenian military. Realizing the destiny of Socrates nearly eighty years earlier, Aristotle fled Athens for the island of Euboea in 323 B.C.E. to avoid a possible trial and perhaps a death sentence. In Euboea, Aristotle retired in the town of Chalcis where he lived in the house that had once belonged to his mother and was still retained by the family. He died there in the following year, most likely from a stomach ailment at the age of sixty-two.

ARISTOTLE ON EDUCATION

Unlike Plato's dialogues, which alluded to knowledge through education and learning, Aristotle's work on the subject of education is fragmented. The majority of Aristotle's output comes to us in the form of treatises. These treatises consist of both notes from his lectures and notes from his observations in the field. After the fall of the Roman Empire toward the end of the sixth century, there seems to have been a lack of interest in Aristotle's work along with the work of other classical Greek thinkers. It was not until the end of the ninth century that Muslim thinkers revived interest in Aristotelian philosophy.

Although only fragments of his work *On Education* exist, we have some understanding of his ideas on education from surviving works. In essence, Aristotle believed that education was the crucial key to becoming a flourishing individual. The following are elements of his thought that continue to play an important part in his philosophical agenda on education.

First, his work is a testament to the belief that our thinking and practice as educators must be infused with a clear philosophy of life. There has to be a deep concern for the ethical and political. For Aristotle, the best life is lived by one who flourishes in his or her endeavors. Accordingly, one must be conscientious with regard to what is good in terms of both intellect and virtue, not merely what is correct. The second element has to do with a broad curriculum. Aristotle underscored the necessity of an extensive program of study. Rhetoric, mathematics, physical development, musicianship, and the sciences (among other subjects) were equally important in strengthening the body as well as the mind. Next, education for Aristotle meant that the individual should be engaged in both contemplative (psyche) and practical wisdom (phronesis). Clearly an individual is capable of thinking methodically and with wisdom. However, practical wisdom is achieved when the individual is actively engaged in a particular activity. As Aristotle argues, "Anything that we have to learn to do we learn by the actual doing of it. . . . We become just by doing just acts, temperate by doing temperate ones, brave by doing brave ones" (Aristotle 1972, Book II, 91).

Unlike Plato's dialogues, Aristotle's work does not elaborate in great detail on issues in education. The most pervasive discussion on the subject is in his treatise entitled *The Politics*, particularly in Books 7 and 8 (1981). Of the little that remains of Aristotle's corpus, we know that his explicit remarks on the goals and objectives of education convey education as a practical—not theoretical—endeavor because it is a means by which individuals can pursue a good and happy life—the ends. Education is also a skill in that the process of teaching and learning is something that people not only pursue, but also engage in the act of making. People engage in labor and use their skills and crafts in order to "make" something happen.

ARISTOTLE ON PEDAGOGY AND LEARNING

Aristotle's ethical treatises are based on the concepts of happiness, the mean, leisure, and wisdom. These concepts are also encountered in his discussions on education. For Aristotle, all forms of education should focus on the mean. The last of the eight books of *The Politics* ends with a discussion of these concepts. Aristotle says, "Clearly, then, there are three standards to which musical education should conform. They are the mean, the possible, and the proper." The concept of the mean does not only apply to the ends of education; it is also an instrumental component, a pedagogical imperative. Although Aristotle makes reference to music, his point is this: Education should be based on good sense; that is, extremes are to be avoided. Music education should be based less on technical ability and more on listening. Physical education should not be based on producing top athletes; rather, it should be based on engaging the individual in physical training for the purpose of improving health and well being and even the soul.

With regard to pedagogy and learning, Aristotle also made reference to two harmonizing, and corresponding, educational categories: education as a form of habit and education as a form of reason. Aristotle argues that education through habit does not mean that someone is engaged in mindless repetition of a distinct task or group of tasks. Rather, habit involves what we refer to today as "active learning." In order to produce a consistent behavior, assuming that this behavior is virtuous—for the good of all humanity—we must engage in habit;

that is, we learn how to do something before we are able to do it. And, in order to learn how to do something, we create a good habit through repetition and practice. So a person becomes a flutist by playing the flute, an architect by creating and designing models of structures, and so forth. So, education in the form of habit is founded for the most part on experience.

In contrast, yet at the same time complementary to habit, education as a form of reason deals with universal principles. For Aristotle, this form of education is the primary basis for all knowledge. It is based on universals. That is, while learning through habit employs the role of experience in learning, it focuses primarily on specificities and particulars. For example, one may be adept in speaking and writing in a particular language. But can this individual identify and appreciate the general principles, rules, and concepts, of the grammar that accounts for the systematic structures of numerous languages? Without education for reason, engaging in scientific inquiry would be futile because hypothesis testing and experimentation must be conducted systematically and be based on evidence for support. In short, the purpose of educating for reason is to search for an understanding of the causes of things, not merely the disposition. Aristotle then distinguishes between two methods of educating for reason: learning by induction (epagoge) and learning through demonstration. Epagoge is a manner in which the individual initially learns from experience and then moves toward knowledge and the abstract; the individual identifies how several things in a particular category behave and subsequently generalizes about all things in the same category. Learning through demonstration, however, differs from epagoge because it involves universal principles and generalities for the purpose of instruction.

Stephen J. Farenga and Daniel Ness

REFERENCES

Aristotle. (1976) *The Nicomachean Ethics*. London: Penguin.
———. (1981) *The Politics: A Treatise on Government*. London: Penguin.
Barnes, J. (1982) *Aristotle*. Oxford, UK: Oxford University Press.
Jaeger, W.W. (1948) *Aristotle*. Oxford, UK: Oxford University Press.

BENJAMIN BLOOM

Benjamin Bloom (1913–1999) was an eminent American educational theorist, perhaps best known for his development of frequently cited taxonomy of learning objectives. Bloom's contributions to education influenced numerous present-day cognitive researchers and educational practitioners. His research in improving education was based on the following issues: (1) the influence of innate ability on human cognitive traits like intelligence and determination and the extent to which these traits can be influenced by experience; (2) the types of educational objectives that can be employed in the classroom setting; (3) the possibility of obtaining similar cognitive results in a full classroom of students as one would in one-on-one tutoring; and (4) the ways in which certain individuals reach the highest levels of achievement in their fields.

HISTORICAL BACKGROUND

Born in Lansford, Pennsylvania, in 1913, Bloom was the son of Russian immigrants who made their living as picture framers. Bloom was an excellent student in his formative years, and graduated as valedictorian of his high school class. He then went on to receive his baccalaureate and master's degrees from Pennsylvania State University, where he completed both degrees in four years. After college, Bloom was hired as a researcher by the Pennsylvania State Relief Organization. After a few years, he worked for the American Youth Commission (AYC). It was at AYC where he met his future mentor, Ralph Tyler, who was a professor of curriculum studies at the University of Chicago. Through Tyler's recommendations, Bloom entered the doctoral program at the University of Chicago, and completed a Ph.D. in Education in 1942. During his graduate study in Chicago, Bloom worked for the Board of Examinations, and remained with the organization until 1959. It was at the Board, which was initially under Tyler's supervision, that Bloom organized a conference around the topic of identifying levels of learning outcomes frequently encountered by teachers and examiners. In 1948, Bloom invited college and university personnel throughout the country for this conference. As a result, Bloom spent the next eight years on his well-known *Taxonomy of Educational Objectives* (1956).

Bloom's contributions to education during his time with the Board of Examinations were mainly publications on testing, measurement, and assessment. In 1959, however, Bloom spent approximately two years at the Center for Advanced Study in Behavioral Sciences at Stanford University where he completed his study on the effects of the environment on human cognition and published a book entitled *Stability and Change in Human Characteristics* (1964). In 1960, he returned to the University of Chicago and remained there for the majority of his career. At Chicago, he moved through the ranks from Instructor in 1944 to Charles H. Swift Distinguished Service Professor in 1970. In the 1960s, Bloom's work was referenced frequently in Lyndon B. Johnson's administration as a means of support for a number of educational programs. One in particular was the Head Start program for preschool children. A large part of his research and publications during the late 1960s and 1970s had to do with the extent to which students can master subject matter knowledge. His later works consisted mostly of works having to do with creativity and the means by which certain individuals—like well-known musicians, artists, mathematicians, and the like—have attained their achievement and success. Bloom died in 1999.

COGNITIVE TAXONOMY

The *Taxonomy of Educational Objectives* (Bloom and Krathwohl 1956) served as a springboard for Bloom's career as a preeminent leader in the field of curriculum and assessment in education. This work has been referenced in nearly every study having to do with student learning and assessment and is a staple in most curriculum, instruction, and assessment courses in schools of education for the past fifty years.

As Eisner (2000) points out, Bloom's taxonomy is not simply a classification of cognitive levels. Nor is it a system of categorizing stages of development, for it is not stage dependent like Jean Piaget's theory of intellectual development. Rather, Bloom wanted to demonstrate that reaching any subsequent level is dependent on one's ability to master the preceding levels. Evaluation—the highest level in the taxonomy—means that

Table 30.1   **Benjamin Bloom's Cognitive Taxonomy of Educational Objectives**

Higher-Order Objectives			
Level	**Structure of Content**	**Process Skills**	**Example**
Evaluation	Judgment, Appraisal	Judging, Assessing	An individual weighs the evidence supporting two separate arguments to determine the strengths and weaknesses of each.
Synthesis	Composition, Creation	Developing, Creating	An individual composes music for piano and string orchestra.
Analysis	Examination, Investigation	Comparing, Contrasting	An individual dissects two different organisms to compare the respiratory system of each.

Lower-Order Objectives			
Level	**Structure of Content**	**Process Skills**	**Example**
Application	Emulation, Simulation	Modeling, Simulating	An individual demonstrates the transition of a solid into a gas by using dry ice (CO_2).
Comprehension	Description, Explanation	Defining, Explaining	An individual explains the commutative principle for addition and multiplication of integers.
Knowledge	Facts, Labels, Indicators	Labeling, Identifying	An individual identifies the parts of speech for each word of a sentence.

Source: Stephen Farenga and Daniel Ness. Adapted from Benjamin Bloom and D. Krathwohl, *Taxonomy of Educational Objectives: Handbook I, The Cognitive Domain.* New York: David McKay and Company, 1956.

an individual is able to judge and make prudent decisions on selecting appropriate ideas or systems of knowledge within a particular subject area. For one to be able to reach the level of evaluation, that individual must be able to create or synthesize disparate concepts, facts, ideas, or symbol systems. Moreover, in order to reach the level of synthesis, one must be able to analyze— that is, compare and contrast—the parts of a given whole concept or idea. Next, in order to reach analysis, one must be able to apply a given concept to a particular context or situation. And in order to reach the application level, one must be able to understand the ideas behind a given concept. Finally, at the bare minimum, one must have the ability to name or identify various pieces of information. Table 30.1 identifies the six levels of Bloom's taxonomy, along with each of their meanings and an example of an individual reaching a particular cognitive level.

STUDENT SUCCESS AND LEARNING FOR MASTERY

Bloom's work during his hiatus at Stanford University proved to be significant, and his book *Stability and Change in Human Characteristics* (1964) turned out to be another landmark publication. In this book, Bloom argues that at around the second grade one can predict what a student's cognitive and academic level will be once that individual reaches adolescence. Further, his reliability index turned out to be quite precise (namely, 0.8, or 80 percent accuracy). In general, Bloom concluded that cognitive achievement as a result of one's physical environment diminishes over time. Nevertheless, he did not consider genetic determinism to be the cause of this stability in an individual's academic performance. Rather, he strongly embraced the idea that through effective teaching and curriculum development, cognitive levels can actually increase. At the same time, Bloom did not believe that the rate in which one completes a cognitive task has any value with regard to achievement. Instead, educational institutions must pay more attention to specific benchmarks in student learning.

In his well-known coauthored book, *Developing Talent in Young People* (Bloom and Sosniak 1985), Bloom demonstrated that although the influence of physical environment may decrease over time, it is a major factor in student achievement and high-achieving adults. More than likely, individuals who have become well-known writers, artists, mathematicians, athletes, and the like did not begin their careers as child prodigies. Nevertheless, the attention that these individuals have received in their formative years, according to Bloom, will have played an important part in their success as adults. High achievement, then, is the result of learning through both environmental factors like parental attention and individual effort, and not simply genetics alone.

Bloom also researched the extent to which whole-class instruction would have the potential to match the benefits of one-on-one instruction. In his article "The 2 Sigma Problem: The Search for Methods of Group Instruction as Effective as One-to-One Tutoring" (1984), Bloom investigated this question and arrives at the following conclusions. First, students who receive one-on-one tutoring score well above other students (namely, two standard deviations, hence the name "2 sigma problem") who receive solely the typical whole-class instruction. In addition, it is not impossible to simulate an environment in which whole-class instruction can provide similar benefits to personalized tutoring.

ADDITIONAL CONTRIBUTIONS TO EDUCATION

Bloom's career spanned more than five decades. During that time, he was a prolific author; he authored books with several currently distinguished figures in education including George Madaus and Lauren Sosniak. He also served as an educational adviser to numerous educational organizations and national educational systems worldwide. He served as president of the American Educational Research Association (AERA) from 1965 to 1967 and was chairperson of a number of committees at the College Entrance Examination Board (College Board). Despite Bloom's influence on the improvement of student learning throughout the world, he was quite skeptical and circumspect with regard to the issue of international comparisons and the issue of standardized testing in general (Eisner 2000). For Bloom, studies on international comparisons of student learning must be dealt with carefully because often times the researchers oversimplify the comparison by comparing test scores in only particular subject areas. Bloom also argued that standardized testing did not serve the student appropriately. He believed that the educator's role was to focus on the attainment of particular objectives and goals rather than a preoccupation with a student's speed in completing an examination.

Stephen J. Farenga and Daniel Ness

REFERENCES

Bloom, Benjamin. (1964) *Stability and Change in Human Characteristics.* New York: Wiley.
———. (1984) The 2 sigma problem: The search for methods of group instruction as effective as one-to-one tutoring. *Educational Researcher* 16, no. 6: 4–16.
Bloom, Benjamin, and D. Krathwohl. (1956) *Taxonomy of Educational Objectives: Handbook I, The Cognitive Domain.* New York: David McKay and Company.
Bloom, Benjamin, and Lauren A. Sosniak. (1985) *Developing Talent in Young People.* New York: Ballantine Books.

Eisner, Elliot W. (2000) Benjamin Bloom. *Prospects: The Quarterly Review of Comparative Education* 30, no. 3: 1–7. Paris: UNESCO, International Bureau of Education.

NOAM CHOMSKY

Noam Chomsky (1928–) is perhaps best known for his work in two areas: The first is his groundbreaking work in the field of psycholinguistics, and the second is his preeminence as one of the most critical political and social analysts of our time. Although Chomsky's work has not directly focused on educational issues per se, through his research and writings he contributed immensely to what we know about the emergence of language in children and how this affects education as a field and an institution.

BACKGROUND

Chomsky's innovations in the field of linguistics changed our view of how language develops in humans. Born in 1928, Chomsky's first acquaintance with linguistics was through his father, who was a highly respected Hebrew scholar. Chomsky spent his college and graduate school years at the University of Pennsylvania where he studied with the well-known linguist Zellig Harris. He completed his B.A. and Ph.D. degrees there, but found it difficult to obtain positions in most universities because his new theory, which combined linguistics with mathematics, was seen as uncharted territory in most traditional linguistics departments. One of his only offers came from the Massachusetts Institute of Technology (MIT). He took the post in 1955 and remains there to this day.

LINGUISTIC ANALYSIS AND UNIVERSAL GRAMMAR

In 1957, Chomsky completed his book entitled *Syntactic Structures*. It is in this book that we are initially acquainted with his view on the innateness of grammatical structure. In his theory of universal grammar, Chomsky argues that one's acquisition of a language—particularly in association with the grammar of that language—is innate. It is not something that develops, unfolds, or is reconstructed (as the developmentalists would have it), nor is it something that emerges through repetitive behavior (as the behaviorists would have it).

Before Chomsky's theory became known to the intellectual community, most theorists, researchers, and educators believed in the so-called storage bin theory. According to this theory, children begin to develop grammatical rules through imitation of adults. Through imitation, they acquire strings of sentences that they can store in their minds. And when they need to use a particular sentence, they summon the sentence from memory, and use it.

Chomsky shows through his theoretical work that this storage bin model of grammatical development is flawed. If it were true, according to Chomsky, humans would have very limited language abilities; they would simply summon sentences from memory, and at the same time, would have great difficulty in communicating to others who use structures that are novel. This is because the perpetual retrieval of previously stored sentence structures would not allow us to understand sentences that we have never heard before. When we write stories, novels, essays, or even research articles, we don't resort to a set number of grammatical structures; instead, although we often use the same words over and over, we create new sentences (hence, new ideas) each time. For Chomsky, we have internal rules that guide us to have the ability to do this.

According to Chomsky, it is difficult to explain the development of grammar through inputs from the external environment because the child's linguistic achievements over short periods of time are too great. How is it possible to explain the fact that children, on the whole, are acquainted with only a limited body of grammatical structure but are able to master somewhat complex grammatical structures beyond that of what they experience? Chomsky's conclusion is that there is a genetic blueprint that enables humans to employ more complex forms of grammar at early ages than the forms that they are used to hearing. This is what Chomsky refers to as the "innateness hypothesis." In 1986, Chomsky proposed his most novel position on language acquisition. He proposed that children acquire language innately through the guidance of universal grammar (UG). At some point, the child will automatically recognize the form that the language spoken (almost always the so-called native language) will take.

Chomsky was a strong opponent of learning theory and the Skinnerian approach to the development of language. In no way, according to Chomsky, does language emerge from excessive baby babble, until the point when a word is uttered and "reinforced." There is no way that one can verify that a stumbled-upon word is reinforced in the first place.

Although Chomsky's theoretical work had a great deal in common with the work of Piaget, the former happened to be one of the latter's most famous critics. Both Piaget and Chomsky, for example, do not believe, as the Lockeans and subsequently the behaviorists would have it, that children develop passively through external environmental agents. Rather, humans develop physically and cognitively through active and spontaneous engagement with the external environment. Chomsky's concern with Piaget's theory of intellectual development, however, stems from the latter's position that cognitive development has almost everything to do with the child's own active constructions of previously learned ideas as a means of making sense of the world. In contrast, Chomsky argues that language is wired, for the most part, in the genes of the human child. Based on a genetic plan, the child then will create grammatical structures automatically.

CHOMSKY'S POLITICAL AND SOCIAL VIEWS AND THEIR IMPACT ON EDUCATION

Chomsky made a clear mark in the field of education with his contribution to the origins of language acquisition. But Chomsky's contributions to education go well beyond the subject of linguistics and the emergence of grammar. Chomsky is perhaps one of the most outspoken social critics of our time. His position on the current (and past and future) education system serves primarily as an example of the greater problems of society as a whole. Similar to Paulo Freire or Ivan Illich's view of the educational system, for Chomsky, the idea of "school" as an institution for educating youth is a fallacy. Instead, schooling only serves to suppress knowledge as a free-thinking enterprise. Teachers are trained—not educated—to impose knowledge onto students. The system belittles the field of education to the point where teachers are identified not in terms of their academic skill and knowledge in various content areas, but in terms of their level of obedience to the system. They are trained not to challenge the system. Terms like "diversity," "for all," and "constructing knowledge" are only used as catch phrases but are not practiced within the context of the classroom. Most teachers possess a cookie cutter mentality that only serves as a vehicle for strengthening system doctrine.

Chomsky views education as an institution whose constituents—high-level administrators and policymakers—are members of the status quo. "Leaders" in the field of education is a misnomer. For Chomsky, they do not lead at all. If anything, they serve as followers of the establishment. In the book entitled *Chomsky on Miseducation* (2004), he states, "If you're following the party line you don't have to document anything; you can say anything you feel like. . . . That's one of the privileges you get for obedience. On the other hand, if you're critical of received opinion, you have to document every phrase" (p. 173). This statement can be applied to any institution in our society, not just education. In reference to education, however, this statement is clear: If you follow the strictures of the educational system, you need not document anything; if you follow the official policy, you are free to say anything you wish, so long as what you say is not critical of the educational establishment.

Another problem with the educational establishment, according to Chomsky, is that institutions of education fail to recognize or outright ignore the genuine ills of educational achievement. Rather than focusing on the negative influences of the home environment, such as poverty, poor health care, unsanitary conditions, and poor nutrition, education officials and policymakers place most, if not all, of their emphasis on agents of accountability—i.e., teachers, low-level administrators (e.g., principals, district leaders), budgetary issues (e.g., low school or district funding), or contextual issues (e.g., class size), which have been shown to have virtually no impact on student achievement.

CHOMSKY'S INFLUENCE ON EDUCATORS

Although Chomsky's work with children is relatively limited, his theory of universal grammar (UG) has far-reaching implications for the classroom. First, and perhaps contrary to popular opinion, Chomsky believes that young children should not be corrected when they produce incorrect grammatical structures (e.g., "Jill runned to the store"). For Chomsky, whatever the child lacks with regard to linguistic capabilities does not remotely compare with what the child masters in terms of the complex grammatical system in any language. Accordingly, Chomsky believes that, given the innate wiring of language with a genetic blueprint, children are capable of learning language on their own. They will triumph over the trivial limitations and idiosyncrasies of a language. In addition, by five or six years of age, we have gathered, through Chomsky's theory, that children grasp parts of speech whether or not the teacher includes the subject in the curriculum. So, although tree diagramming was favored before Chomsky's theory was recognized, it is seen by many educational researchers and practitioners as a futile endeavor in the classroom.

As one of the key intellectual thinkers of our time, Chomsky raises important questions concerning the institution of education and how it affects society. First, why does it seem as if schooling is meant as a vehicle for promoting knowledge and free thinking when in fact, as Chomsky would posit, it does precisely the contrary? And second, why do institutions of education seem to be predisposed to holding teachers or low-level administrators accountable for the low achievement of students, when in fact it has been shown that the pervasiveness of problems like poverty and lack of healthcare are the sole factors of students' poor academic performance? These questions have not been addressed by local, state, or federal officials. Time will tell whether Chomsky's ideas, both in the psycholinguistic and sociopolitical realms, will be taken more seriously.

Stephen J. Farenga and Daniel Ness

References

Chomsky, Noam. (1957) *Syntactic Structures*. The Hague, Netherlands: Mouton.

———. (2004) *Chomsky on Miseducation*, ed. Donald Macedo. Lapham, MD: Rowman and Littlefield.

Crain, William, C. (1999) *Theories of Human Development: Concepts and Applications*. 4th ed. Englewood Cliffs, NJ: Prentice Hall.

Comenius

Comenius (1592–1670) was a preeminent theologian of the seventeenth century who was the first to develop a science of education and use this framework as a general philosophy to be attributed to all socioeconomic levels (Piaget 1957). The life and works of Comenius are remarkable reflections of an individual whose life seemed to have been rife with paradoxes. First, theologians of the late Renaissance were not generally associated with scientific development and innovation. Second, and parallel to the first seemingly conflicting characteristic, theologians during Comenius's time had a rather difficult time reconciling religious doctrine and the problem of knowledge in philosophical terms. And third, as a philosopher, Comenius's ideas seemed to have run counter to most Western philosophers of his time, whose philosophical ideas seemed disassociated with the majority of the population (Spinka 1943). As an educator, Comenius hoped to bring education to the masses rather than keeping it a privilege for the elite classes.

Historical Background

Comenius (Johann Amos Komensky) was born in 1592 in Nivnitz, a city in Moravia (Czech Republic). He was the third child and only son of a miller who belonged to a Hussite sect and was a member of the Moravian Brethren, a religious group. Orphaned at the age of twelve, his guardians misappropriated his savings, thereby leaving the young Comenius destitute. Nevertheless, he did receive a strong education with the usual Latin elementary school preparation. He received his higher education at the University of Herborn in Nassau, where he prepared for the ministry. It was at Herborn where Comenius met John Henry Alsted, a Calvinist theologian, who supposedly influenced him greatly. Shortly thereafter, in 1613, Comenius entered the University of Heidelberg, where he studied astronomy, especially focusing on the works of Copernicus. This experience may have contributed to his interest in reconciling religious doctrine with philosophy and science.

In 1616, Comenius was ordained and subsequently returned to Nivnitz where he became chief bishop of the Moravian Brethren. During his time in Moravia, he became a very prolific writer and well-known teacher. As a result of the Thirty Years' War, Comenius was exiled from his native Moravia, and served as a schoolmaster in Hungary, Poland, Prussia, and Sweden. By 1642, his fame as a well-known educationist of his day almost led to the creation of a university in England based on his ideas. He was even asked to serve as president of the then young Harvard University. Comenius spent his final years in Amsterdam, revising and editing his earlier writings, and urging peace and political reform throughout the European continent.

KNOWLEDGE THROUGH LANGUAGE AND THE ORDER OF NATURE

Comenius earned his fame through a series of textbooks used to teach Latin. These textbooks differed from other textbooks of his day in that they included some of the new sciences. These works also reflected the emphasis on observation with regard to science. With language aside, observation, according to Comenius, was the foundation of all knowledge and inquiry, even with regard to scientific discovery.

One of his well-known publications, *Orbis Sensualium Pictus* (1970), discusses the earth, the sky, fire, various animal species, eclipses, geometry, and numerous other categories. The students of Comenius would learn Latin through the study of various subject areas (like the ones mentioned) as well as the natural environment. What made this work outstanding is the use of pictures to represent the actual phenomena. With 150 illustrated chapters, Comenius designed the work as a means of teaching Latin with the aid of short mnemonic sentences that a child would understand. The pictures were to serve as surrogates for the direct perception or observation of the phenomena themselves. Comenius did not simply write his texts to demonstrate collections of informational items. Rather, his pictures would serve as central themes whereby vocabulary and language would be learned. *Orbis Sensualium Pictus* was initially published as a German-Latin text in 1658 in Nuremburg. Many medievalists, philosophers, and scholars of education consider this work to be the first picture book for children. In sum, the work brought numerous subjects from all over the world into the home as a means for children to learn language through thematic essays.

THE GREAT DIDACTIC

Comenius began his most famous work, *The Great Didactic* (1896), in 1627 and completed it approximately five years later in 1632. However, it took nearly eighteen years for this grand work to be printed in its original Czech. A few years later, Comenius added several new chapters to the work, when it was finally translated into Latin. The work as a whole, *Opera Didactica Omnia* was published in Amsterdam in 1657. Unfortunately, Comenius did not achieve fame from this work, and it was not a work appreciated during his lifetime.

The Great Didactic (1896) served as the theoretical foundation of Comenius's educational program. In this work, Comenius devised a system in which he proposed universal education that was based on principles, and what he referred to as natural development. Because of *The Great Didactic*, many present day educational theorists refer to Comenius as the forerunner of educational thinkers who embraced a democratic view of the common school and provided insight into a universal educational process that would not be appreciated until several generations later. In this work, Comenius demonstrates his psychological insight into the development of thinking and learning by emphasizing the importance of a pupil's prior preparation to acquiring knowledge, the necessity of considering one's age when presenting particular concepts, and the teaching of the same subjects in different ways, depending on the learning style of the individual. This argument clearly anticipates the stage theories of the twentieth-century developmental psychologists such as Heinz Werner and Jean Piaget.

Through *The Great Didactic* (1896), we also find Comenius to be one of the first thinkers to examine everyday, spontaneous knowledge and how it benefits learning. Comenius identifies three rules, which serve as the foundation of learning:

1. Class instruction should be curtailed as much as possible, namely to four hours, and the same length of time should be devoted to private study.
2. Pupils should memorize as little as possible, that is, only the most important things; the remainder should be devoted to general meaning (i.e., conceptual understanding).

3. Curriculum should be arranged in order to suit the capacity of the pupil; the curriculum should increase naturally with study and age. (1896, p. 289)

To be sure, Comenius emphasizes the understanding of what is to be learned—the concepts—rather than the mere memorization of facts like verbal patterns or number computations. Today, the rules stated above are discussed and utilized often in schools of education and possibly in laboratory schools, where students of education and researchers of education can identify optimal learning experiences for pupils. However, it is unfortunate that they are rarely, if at all, used in general practice—that is, in most public and private schools.

CONTRIBUTIONS TO EDUCATION

The general impact of Comenius's works on education starkly differs today from that during his lifetime. In his own day, his contemporaries found him distinctive in writing Latin textbooks that included pedagogical technique in the teaching and learning of the academic subject areas. However, in posterity, Comenius left his mark as a forerunner of developmental and cognitive psychology. He emphasized the importance of what we refer to today as "developmentally appropriate practice," which refers to the pedagogical procedure of identifying what a student can learn at a particular age level and basing that knowledge on what the individual has already learned. Comenius also was committed to developing a philosophical program whose mission would be to make education less a privilege for the few and more a universal entitlement. However, despite his supposed influence on contemporary educational practice, his ideas are still unfamiliar to most educational researchers and practitioners. There are few biographies of Comenius in the English language. In addition, educators and developmentalists often attribute the idea of prior knowledge as a necessary component for developmental learning practice to Jean-Jacques Rousseau, who was born forty-two years after Comenius died. Rousseau's credit may have something to do with the intentions of the French philosophers to expand the role of philosophy and education to include not merely the elite classes,

but the general public as well. Nevertheless, the works of Comenius that remain have served as a foundational corpus in education circles for the past three hundred years.

Stephen J. Farenga and Daniel Ness

REFERENCES

Comenius, Johann Amos. (1657) "Didactica Magna" (The Great Didactic). In *Opera Didactica Omnia*. Amsterdam: D. Laurentii de Geer.

———. (1896) *The Great Didactic*. Originally published in 1657. London: Adam and Charles Black Publishers.

———. (1970) *Orbis Sensualium Pictus*. London: Scolar Press.

Piaget, Jean. (1957) "The Significance of John Amos Comenius at the Present Time." In *Selections*, Introduction. Paris: United Nations Educational, Scientific, and Cultural Organization (UNESCO).

Spinka, M. (1943) *John Amos Comenius: That Incomparable Moravian*. Chicago: University of Chicago Press.

CONFUCIUS

Confucius (551–479 B.C.E.) is universally acclaimed as one of China's—and, along with Socrates, Plato, and Aristotle, some believe the world's—most influential philosophical and educational figures of all time. Sinologists, students of Eastern philosophy, and modern scholars in general contributed to a revival of Confucius's ideas because his influences and contributions to life and more specifically to teaching and pedagogy seem to have impacted cultures and societies throughout history, even to the present time. Moreover, many believe that his contributions to philosophy and education cross cultural and societal boundaries. His overall influence is recognized in China as well as in the Western philosophical traditions.

HISTORICAL BACKGROUND

Confucius was born in 551 B.C.E. in Lu (which in modern times would be Qufu in the province of Shandong). His family name was Qui and given name was Zhongni. Due to political instability, his family, mostly aristocrats, left the region of Song for Lu in pursuit of safety. His father, originally a government official in Song, died when Confucius was a child. After his father's death, Confucius, his mother, and siblings lived in poverty for a number of years. As a young adult, Confucius worked mostly as a manual laborer, often in substandard conditions. These positions were typically related to livestock and agriculture. Nevertheless, Confucius pursued a governmental career, and slowly rose through the ranks. By the age of forty, Confucius had become the prefect and head of public works of the city of Zhongdu, and subsequently the minister of defense and law for Lu, his home principality. There, he began to develop his political and ethical philosophy, which attracted a somewhat large group of followers. He and his students subsequently traveled to many parts of China, attempting to attract more adherents. However, with little or no success, Confucius returned to the principality of Lu, and spent his remaining years as a writer and teacher.

CONTRIBUTIONS TO EDUCATION

Prior to Confucius, education was a privilege and reserved almost exclusively for the upper classes. Before his time, the purpose of education in the Zhou dynasty was to prepare individuals for careers in government. This formal education would take place within government housing and would be carried out by the officials themselves. To do this, individuals would complete civil and military training through the so-called six arts (Yang 1993). These included archery, calligraphy (writing), chariot driving, mathematics, music, and formal rites.

What made Confucius a significant force in education, let alone in Eastern philosophical tradition, was his role as a dominant leader in the shift in education as a privilege for the primarily aristocratic class to one that would eventually benefit all people. Confucius lived in a turbulent time, one in which he witnessed society moving from slave ownership to a feudal system. With the upper class monopolizing education, Confucius was considered the first individual to garner a large group of students both rich and poor. He began to take students in his thirties, well before he became Prefect of Zhongdu, and had a total of more than three thousand during his lifetime. In addition, seventy-two of his students completed the six arts.

Confucius believed that all individuals, regardless of social class, were entitled to an education. This belief had implications for both political and cultural reform. His work resulted in an acceleration of general education practices in China at the time.

Confucius was one of the first individuals to call into question the differences in human behavior and characteristics. He argued that humans are generally the same, and it is only the culture in which they live that molds a behavior and psychological disposition (with regard to ethics and intellect) different from others.

Confucius maintained that the two primary goals of any formalized system of education are moral and ethical instruction, and content or knowledge-based instruction. In addition, moral instruction would take precedence over instruction that imparted knowledge. This is because, Confucius argued, in order to build any form of stable government, the individuals in leadership roles must hold virtue as their primary objective in governing the lands (Ames 1999).

Despite his perseverance in emphasizing morality as the primary goal of education, Confucius was also resolute with regard to the importance of the growth of the intellect. In order to promote a feudal system as a replacement for oligarchic rule, Confucius believed that content knowledge was an essential part of developing a new form of society—one founded on the principle that all individuals can succeed in their goals and aspirations with a strong educational foundation. On these grounds, Confucius developed six manuals that were to serve as the foundation for learning and pedagogy. They are the Book of Odes, the Book of History, the Book of Rites, the Book of Music, the Book of Changes, and the Spring and Autumn Annals. Although these books deal primarily with leading a virtuous life, a large part of their content has to do with intellectually based subject areas that include economics, history, musicianship, philosophy, and political study. Since these books are believed to be the first set of works in Chinese history to cover a wide range of subject areas, they are often referred to as the Chinese classical canon, or "jing."

CONFUCIAN PRINCIPLES, PEDAGOGICAL MODELS, AND EDUCATIONAL ENDS

What we find in present-day formal schooling, in many ways, are essentially staples of the pedagogical principles developed by Confucius. These principles follow a somewhat pragmatic style with regard to educational outcomes. First, Confucius believed that students varied in aptitude and ability with regard to subject matter, and to some extent conduct and ethical habit. Accordingly, he believed that all students, despite his urge for universal education, did not necessarily learn the same way, and therefore required different methods and approaches. Each student needed an education that matched the respective aptitude. Second, students required inspiration as a means for guidance. Today, teachers often use the term "motivation." Third, Confucius anticipated Hegelian dialectic nearly 2,400 years later with his determination to combine theory with practice. For Confucius, applied study was necessary in practice, but could not be affective without abstract contemplation. Fourth, he espoused independent and free thinking and did not believe that the teacher's role was to subordinate the students. The habit of independent thinking encouraged self-analysis and introspection. Additional principles have to do with developing virtue as a student. These include respect for students of different ages, accepting criticism, the ability to set examples for less experienced students, and the realization and correction of mistakes (Yang 1993).

There is little doubt that Confucius was a profound teacher and bestower of knowledge. Confucius argued that a teacher must be fully engaged and committed to the practice of teaching. This prerequisite alone encapsulated the virtuous teacher. Moreover, he believed that the best teachers had a broad scope of subject area knowledge, and intimately cared for each student. It was the teacher's responsibility to know the student's disposition and psychological and intellectual idiosyncrasies in order to help that individual succeed in society.

In addition to pedagogical concerns, Confucius maintained that one of the most important ends of an education is to reach prosperity. In fact, in his writings, he would often state that reaching prosperity is more important than the formal education because the latter is only a means to an end. For Confucius, a healthy state is one in which its inhabitants live prosperous lives. And this can only happen if the educational system is strong and reaches the entire population.

CONFUCIUS TODAY

Although research on his output is relatively scant, Confucius's contributions to education are momentous. His ideas have been universalized and the utterance of his name is often associated with virtue and prudence. Moreover, his contributions span numerous fields of inquiry, which include intellect and how we think (psychology), how to conduct ourselves (philosophy), learning from events (history), mathematics, music, and a host of other areas as well. The ideas of Confucius became widely known throughout the East well before they reached Western nations. During the Qin and Han Dynasties, more than 2,000 years ago, his work reached the Korean peninsula and Japan. It was not until the middle to late 1500s that his ideas reached the West. When they did, numerous individuals realized the potential influence of the Confucian philosophical and educational perspective. In fact, many Western thinkers were associated with Confucius. For example, the great poet and playwright Johann Wolfgang van Goethe is sometimes referred to as the "Confucius of Weimar" (Yang 1993).

It is somewhat remarkable that Socrates, the eminent Greek philosopher, would be born approximately ten years after the death of Confucius. What makes this remarkable is twofold. For one, the approximate 500–year period between 700 B.C.E. and 200 B.C.E. seems to have marked an epoch that gave rise to some of the most productive thinkers of world history. And second, both Confucius and Socrates, although using different approaches, emphasized the necessarily important role of virtue and conduct in human life. Moreover, similar to the Western philosophical tradition in education, particularly outlined in the work of Aristotle, we see in Confucius, who of course preceded Socrates and subsequent thinkers, a determination to promulgate both morality and content knowledge as the two primary goals of education. However, Confucius, unlike the classical Greek thinkers during and after his lifetime, believed that a formal education was obtainable by anyone who pursued it, not just members of the upper classes.

Daniel Ness and Stephen J. Farenga

REFERENCES

Ames, Roger T. (1999) *The Analects of Confucius: A Philosophical Translation.* New York: Ballantine Books.

Shen, Jian-ping. (2002) "Confucius." In *Fifty Major Thinkers on*

Education: From Confucius to Dewey, ed. Joy Palmer. pp. 1–4. New York: Routledge.

Yang, Huan-yin. (1993) Confucius (K'ung tzu). *Prospects* 23, no. 1–2: 211–19. Paris: UNESCO, International Bureau of Education.

JOHN DEWEY

The philosopher and educator John Dewey has been acclaimed as one of the most influential American personalities in the realms of philosophy and education. Perhaps one of the most discussed and cited thinkers in the field of education, Dewey had established himself as a philosopher at the university at a time in history (the late nineteenth century) when the field of philosophy had just begun as a professional discipline. For the most part, Dewey's philosophy follows a pragmatic approach in which a social ideal is where each individual finds his or her own maximal potential through development. He was both an innovator and an iconoclast who sounded the clarion call for change. His contributions toward this goal are outstanding; and his impact on philosophy and education is enduring.

BIOGRAPHICAL BACKGROUND

John Dewey, the third child of Archibald Dewey and Lucina Rich, was born in Burlington, Vermont, on October 20, 1859. Dewey's father was a practical man and a successful shopkeeper who was respected in the community. His mother was an intense, independent, and religious woman with a spirit of social consciousness. His father's sense of the pragmatic and his mother's love of higher education and social consciousness were absorbed by young John and would later be reflected in his writings and his life.

Dewey attended public school in Burlington and graduated in 1874. After receiving his BA from the University of Vermont, he taught high school for three years. He entered Johns Hopkins University for advanced study in philosophy and received his PhD in 1884. There, he studied with leading philosophers of the late nineteenth century—Charles Peirce, George Sylvester Morris, and G. Stanley Hall.

Dewey's long and influential career in the field of education began at the University of Michigan. Except for a year at the University of Minnesota, he taught there from 1884–1894. During his tenure at the University of Michigan, he became interested in educational philosophy and psychology. In 1894 Dewey moved to Chicago and served as the chairman of the combined departments of Psychology, Philosophy, and Pedagogy at the University of Chicago. It was at the University of Chicago where Dewey and Alice Chipman Dewey (his wife) directed a laboratory school consisting of kindergarten children. A good deal of his empirical research emanated from that experience. In 1904, Dewey left the University of Chicago for Columbia University in New York and taught there until his retirement in 1931. A number of Dewey's most influential writings were published during his time at Columbia University. However, Dewey did not stop working upon retirement; to the contrary, he published a number of seminal works during the last twenty years of his life. Dewey also traveled around the world, gave lectures, acted as a consultant, and studied educational systems in Mexico, Turkey, the Soviet Union, Japan, and China. He died in 1952. With nearly 750 publications—forty books and over seven hundred articles—to his name, Dewey remains one of the most prolific writers in the fields of philosophy and education.

PHILOSOPHICAL IDEAS

Dewey's initial contribution to philosophy was Hegel's idealism, at a time when Hegel's work was disparaged by empirical philosophers and physical scientists. Philosophy, according to Dewey, is an intellectual attempt to work out the conditions in which human beings can attain their highest fulfillment. This fulfillment is not attained in isolation but in mutuality and interaction with the environment.

Dewey observed that the traditional world concept was very static, dualistic, hierarchical, and idealistic. He saw the world not in isolation, but in connectedness; not in duality, but in dialectics; not static, but in progress. He, therefore, eventually abandoned his earlier philosophy of Hegelian idealism and subscribed to "instrumentalism." Instrumentalism is founded on experimental methodology and it uses reason as an instrument to solve human problems. He emphasized the importance of the experiential and the practical. Truth, in this context, is that which works in one's experience. In this, he was greatly influenced by Charles Darwin and William James. Some critics labeled his philosophy as pragmatism but he favored the term instrumentalism or "experimentalism."

For Dewey, the scientific method or scientific inquiry is not to be owned by any particular discipline, say, in biology, physics, or any other branch of science. Rather, scientific thinking is to be used in any field of inquiry—it is a tool used for thinking, argumentation, deliberation, and arriving at conclusions. This, of course, poses a somewhat contradictory position to the Hegelian outlook. Nevertheless, Dewey argued that the field of philosophy needed to meld the two diametrically opposed strands of thought.

Human beings, according to Dewey, are organically interrelated to nature and the society they live in. He did not view the individual and society in opposition, but as complementary to each other. The individual was a "social individual" and society was an organic union of individuals. Democracy was the best way of overcoming the individual and the social dichotomy; it gave the best opportunity to maximize the optimal growth of the individual and society. Democracy, observed Dewey, should not be taken in its narrow sense as a form of government. For Dewey, democracy was a way of life. In *Democracy and Education*, Dewey (1966) stated: "A democracy is more than a form of government; it is primarily a mode of associated living, of conjoint communicated experience" (p. 87). It touches every aspect of human life: family, community, industry, school, and government.

EDUCATIONAL VISION AND PRACTICE

Dewey observed that there was an intimate relationship between philosophy and education. Education, according to him, was a laboratory in which philosophical ideas were tested and verified. When Dewey moved to Chicago he established a laboratory school. He was dissatisfied with the traditional schools. They were failing to adapt to the changing times and the demands of a democratic society. The new developments in child psychology and sociology prompted him to apply the findings to his school, which he headed until 1904.

Education, for Dewey, was growth. It is a continual renewal and re-adaptation to the environment. Central to Dewey's philosophy of education and pedagogy was his unique concept of experience. Education was reconstruction of experience. He applied the theory of organism and the environment in child's education. A child has instincts, impulses, and needs. This produces conflicts. It demands initiative, inventiveness, adaptation, and active participation. In education, therefore, a child is not a passive recipient of knowledge, but actively involved in the learning process.

School, for Dewey, was a form of community living and a reflection of the democratic society. In the traditional school, the teacher was an authoritarian figure. The teacher knew everything and the student was an empty pail to be filled. Dewey challenged this concept. According to him, a teacher was a guide who facilitated the learning process. He held the view that the method of teaching should be based on child psychology. A child's natural instincts and needs should be taken into consideration in teaching and learning. He emphasized the importance of experiential and experimental methods. Dewey (1966) observed, "An ounce of experience is better than a ton of theory" (p. 144). Occupational methods such as gardening, cooking, sewing, and carpentry were some of the examples he used in his school.

Dewey viewed curriculum as life itself. He did not subscribe to a concept of curriculum that was separate from real life. The curriculum in his laboratory school revolved around the child. The child's experience was the starting point from which learning experiences continually expanded in ever-growing circles.

Dewey did not approve of vocational education in its narrow sense, that is, training of an individual for industrial occupation. He approved of it in the broader sense of students having occupational experience as a slice of life. The division of curriculum into liberal education and vocational education, according to him, was "a plan of social predestination totally foreign to the spirit of democracy" (Dewey 1962b, 227).

RELEVANCE OF DEWEY'S IDEAS TODAY

Dewey's educational vision challenged and impacted the theory and practice of education, more specifically, in the United States. His emphasis on abandoning the traditional ways of teaching and learning and incorporating the latest findings in psychology and sociology paved the way for modern education. One of his great contributions to education was his focus on the centrality of experience in educational theory and practice. He insisted on having student-centered and experience-oriented education. The "progressive movement" seized upon this opportunity and some took liberty to go to the other extreme where learning became catering to the children's whims. In his book *Experience and Education*, however, Dewey (1963) explained his position on this issue and stressed the importance of organized subject matter and discipline in the classroom. He, in fact, disassociated himself from any particular "ism."

Dewey's war on dualism and unrelenting insistence on integrating experience and reasoning, child and curriculum, school and society, and the individual and society had far reaching impact on education. Emphasizing the mutuality and dependence of the individual and society, Dewey (1897) remarked: "Society is a society of individuals and the individual is always a social individual. He has no existence by himself. He lives in, for and by the society, just as society has no existence excepting in and through the individuals who constitute it" (p. 55). In an atmosphere of rugged individualism and ruthless business culture, Dewey's concept of the maximum individuality within maximum community is very important today.

In this post–9/11 world of religious intolerance, ethnic violence, and social discrimination, Dewey's vision of democratic education is very relevant. Respect for multiculturalism and individual difference, cultivating spontaneity and creativity, and nurturing of diversity and individuality are derived from the same democratic ideal. Thus, another great contribution of Dewey to educational philosophy and practice is his democratic vision and its every day application to life. His seminal thought on experience and education, the social individual, and the democratic ideal have impacted American education and education around the world. Dewey, therefore, is considered one of the great philosopher-educators of the modern world.

Francis A. Samuel

REFERENCES

Dewey, J. (1897) "Ethical Principles Underlying Education." *The Third Yearbook of the National Herbert Society.* Chicago: National Herbert Society.

———. (1956a) *The Child and the Curriculum.* Chicago: The University of Chicago Press.

———. (1956b) *The School and Society.* Chicago: The University of Chicago Press.

———. (1957) *Reconstruction in Philosophy.* Boston: Beacon Press.

———. (1958) *Experience and Nature.* New York: Dover Publications.

———. (1962a) *Individualism Old and New.* New York: Capricorn Books.

———. (1962b) *Schools of Tomorrow.* New York: E.P. Dutton.

———. (1963) *Experience and Education.* New York: Collier Books.

———. (1966) *Democracy and Education.* New York: Macmillan.

———. (1980) *Art as Experience.* New York: G.P. Putnam's Sons.

Dykhuizen, G. (1973) *The Life and Mind of John Dewey.* Carbondale: Southern Illinois University Press.

Hook, S. (1971) *John Dewey: An Intellectual Portrait.* West Point: Greenwood Press.

Rockefeller, S.C. (1991) *John Dewey: Religious Faith and Democratic Humanism.* New York: Columbia University.

Roth, R.J. (1962) *John Dewey and Self-Realization.* Englewood Cliffs, NJ: Prentice-Hall.

PAULO FREIRE

Paulo Freire (1923–1997) is regarded by contemporary educationists, social critics, and sociologists as one of the most influential thinkers in the field of education during the second half of the twentieth century. Since the 1950s, few individuals have made such sweeping impact throughout the world on the promotion of literacy, mathematics, communication skills for purposes of liberation, critical pedagogy, and education in general as Paulo Freire. As a social and political activist, Freire became known for his creation and development of literacy programs that promoted an anti-capitalist, anti-imperialist stance on behalf of oppressed peoples throughout the world. His seminal work *Pedagogy of the Oppressed* (1970) was one of the first publications in which the role of the dominant educational system of schooling and administration is challenged.

HISTORICAL BACKGROUND

Paulo Freire was born on September 19, 1921, in Recife, which is the capital of Pernambuco, one of Brazil's northeastern provinces. Born into a middle-class family, his father was a military officer. Both his parents were educated through the Catholic Church, and decided to educate their children in the same way. Freire reflected upon his childhood and viewed his father as someone who would always listen to what any member of the family had to say. This habit seemed to have influenced Freire a great deal and served as a foundation for his strong interest in communication skills.

As a result of the world economic crisis in 1928, the Freire family moved to the neighboring city of Jaboatão, a less-expensive area to live in and to educate children. After high school, Freire had an initial interest in law; however, financial difficulties forced him to work and provide for his immediate family. Nevertheless, he eventually earned his law degree and became employed, initially teaching Portuguese in secondary school from 1944 to 1945. Freire also served as a lawyer for the trade unions in Recife, where he organized union members and lectured on topics relating to the rights and entitlements of workers. His success as a trade union lawyer eventually helped him succeed to the post of director for the Department of Education and Culture for the Serviço Social da Indústria (Social Service for Industry [SESI]). Unlike other directors at SESI, Freire attempted to identify the needs of children and older students by involving parents of all socioeconomic levels and having them participate in discussions about educational and social issues that concerned society in general. Freire was no conformist. Despite his general success at SESI he eventually resigned from his post after much criticism with regard to his democratic, egalitarian form of administration.

In the early 1960s, Freire became a professor of literacy at the University of Recife. During the country's national literacy campaign, Freire worked with the peasants of the northeastern part of Brazil to help foster and promote their ability to communicate effectively. From this work, he developed a theory of literacy that identifies the use of literacy and communication as the primary conduit for critical thinking and dialogical discussion with the em-

powered class. When Brazil fell under military rule in 1964, government officials were wary of Freire's critical theoretical perspective and his desire to promote and teach critical techniques and practices to the peasants and other oppressed peoples for the purpose of liberation. As a result Freire was jailed for seventy-five days, and subsequently sent into exile. Freire left Brazil for La Paz, Bolivia, where the Bolivian government sought his services and made him an educational consultant. But, only twenty days after his arrival, the Bolivian government fell under a coup d'état. Chile was the second country to take Freire. He sought refuge in Santiago, Chile, and remained there for almost five years. In Santiago, Freire was given a professorship at the Catholic University and also worked on special assignment at the Santiago regional office of UNESCO. It was here that Freire wrote his well-known book *Pedagogy of the Oppressed* in 1970. Freire also lived in Mexico, the United States, Switzerland, and the islands of São Tomé and Principe. In the United States, Freire served an appointment at the Harvard University Center for Studies in Development and Social Change from 1969 to 1970. He subsequently served as a consultant to the Office of Education of the World Council of Churches in Geneva, Switzerland. While in Geneva, Freire served as consultant for a number of national educational systems including Guinea-Bissau, Angola, and Mozambique (Gerhardt 1993).

Freire finally returned to Brazil in 1980, where he served as a professor at the Pontificia Universidade Catolica de São Paulo and the Universidade de Campinas also in São Paulo. After 1980, Freire also provided consultancies in literacy education for numerous educational institutions throughout the world, including Fiji, Australia, and Italy (Gerhardt 1993). Further, in his later years, he worked with various oppressed cultural groups, fostering literacy programs on their behalf. He also served as honorary president for the International Council for Adult Education from 1985 to his death in 1997.

BANKING VERSUS PROBLEM POSING: THE PEDAGOGY OF THE OPPRESSED

Freire identified numerous problems with institutions of education in preparing students of differing socioeconomic levels. One of the most glaring incongruities of education was the manner in which content knowledge was provided for students. Using Freire's own terminology, teachers attempt to deposit bits of knowledge into students' minds. The students are presumed to have absolute ignorance on the topics discussed. The role of the teacher is to bestow what is considered to be knowledge, and the role of the students is to be passive listeners. Freire refers to this traditional form of educational practice as banking.

In contrast to the banking practice, Freire refers to the problem-posing method. Through this method, the teacher does not exert dominance or authority over students. Rather, they serve as collaborators in the search for knowledge. The banking model assumes that all students, regardless of socioeconomic status and level of oppression, must be guided by so-called self-evident universal truths that are inherent in nature. Unlike this model, problem posing assumes that different groups of students, regardless of age, have different sets of circumstances, and therefore different sets of goals. And for this, the education for a particular group or culture must address the problems that afflict these individuals, and the purpose of this education is to enhance their lives and well being. The necessary key component for promoting and fostering problem posing is dialogue through the process of argumentation, whereby the teacher and student dyad is a dual learning relationship, not one in which the teacher imposes knowledge on the students.

Freire is clear when he discusses the importance of dialogue in the process of communication and liberation. As he argues in *Pedagogy of the Oppressed* (1970):

If people, as historical beings necessarily engaged with other people in a movement of inquiry, did not control that movement, it would be (and is) a violation of their humanity. Any situation in which some individuals prevent others from engaging in the process of inquiry is one of violence. The means used are not important; to alienate human beings from their own decision-making is to change them into objects. (1970, p. 66)

This excerpt also expresses Freire's devotion to the formation of a nonoppressive program in education. This program would engage, rather than prevent, individuals of all backgrounds in the process of inquiry and investigation. It would also include all forms of education for all purposes—for example, general education for youth, education for liberation from oppression and poverty, and general adult education.

PRAXIS AND PEDAGOGY

The term "pedagogy" in the general sense refers to a method of teaching. This term is often used colloquially to describe a teacher's method of delivering instruction to students. The Webster's New Universal Unabridged Dictionary (1983) defines "pedagogy" as "the profession or function of a teacher" and "the art or science of teaching; especially, instruction in teaching methods" (p. 1320). In a more organizational sense, teachers and even faculty of schools of education use the term in a structured manner to refer to various teaching styles. Examples include teacher-centered pedagogy, student-centered pedagogy, or any of their derivative forms. In general, pedagogy used in this manner places the students as objects of manipulation, who are controlled by the strictures of larger entities—a municipality, a state, or a national government. That is, pedagogy is implemented in order to maintain national status quo—as objects, students must conform to the guidelines of society. Freire, in contrast, did not use the term pedagogy in this way. For Freire, pedagogy means to free oneself from the oppression of the dominant society, no matter how minimal or severe that oppression may be. Pedagogy, according to Freire, is a political tool used to acculturate students and to prevent a one-sided, culturally dominant perspective on any given learning situation.

Like the term pedagogy, the term "praxis," too, has been used by educators in a very loose manner. Unlike pedagogy, however, the general meaning of praxis is not necessarily diametrically opposed in meaning to Freire's own interpretation of the word. In a general sense, praxis refers to the act of using theoretical models in practice. Webster's Dictionary defines the term more broadly as "practice . . . distinguished from theory" (1983, 1414). But again, this definition is not quite what Freire had in mind. Praxis, for Freire, is similar to the manner in which the term would be defined in philosophical terms—namely, engaging in something with well-informed actions. That is, in order to act upon something, one must be knowledgeable and, at the same time, moral in the manner in which the action takes place. In light of the Freirean view, phronesis, which in Greek refers to practical knowledge of any given situation, presupposes one's engagement in praxis. That is, to engage in praxis, one must have the appropriate knowledge and moral disposition before acting upon something (McLaren 1998).

The ideas of praxis and pedagogy complement each other in that both serve as prerequisites for problem posing. In the banking model, neither praxis nor pedagogy, from Freire's perspective, are implemented; clearly, if pedagogy is a tool for liberation, then its use would not accommodate the banking model. Similarly, if one engages in praxis, then it is assumed that the individual is informed and knowledgeable not solely from an intellectual standpoint, but from a social and practical perspective that has a great deal to do with the problems and situations of the students.

SUMMARY OF CONTRIBUTIONS TO EDUCATION

Freire was undoubtedly a key figure in the field of education in the latter half of the twentieth century. His ideas are still strong with progressive educators to the present day, and serve as a springboard for efforts in the liberation of oppressed peoples throughout the world. Despite his place in the field of education and his numerous contributions to literacy and the use of education as a tool for promoting critical consciousness and liberation, Freire has been criticized by educators and social theorists from the feminist perspective. First, Freire's writings, especially from his work in the early years to the 1970s, seem to have either ignored women's rights or have subordinated women's issues. However, since that time, his books and articles have gone through a number of revisions; Freire himself admitted that this was a problematic issue in his earlier writings (Freire 1996).

Stephen J. Farenga and Daniel Ness

REFERENCES

Freire, Paulo. (1970) *Pedagogy of the Oppressed*. New York: Herder and Herder.
———. (1996) *Letters to Cristina: Reflections on My Life and Work*. New York: Routledge.
Gerhardt, Heinz-Peter. (1993) Paulo Freire. *Prospects: The Quarterly Review of Comparative Education* 23, no. 3/4: 439–58. Paris: UNESCO, International Bureau of Education.
McKechnie, Jean L. (1983) *The Webster's New Universal Unabridged Dictionary*. 2nd ed. New York: Simon and Schuster.
McLaren, Peter. (1998) *Life in Schools: An Introduction to Critical Pedagogy in the Foundations of Education*. 3rd ed. New York: Longman.

FRIEDRICH WILHELM FROEBEL

Friedrich Wilhelm August Froebel (1782–1852), an eminent German philosopher and educator, is widely known as the inventor of kindergarten. In addition to his numerous contributions to early childhood development and learning, Froebel, among others of his day, influenced the direction of education as both a professional and academic field in Europe and eventually in the United States and Canada. Froebel was the author of numerous publications. Perhaps the most noteworthy with regard to his educational mission is his work *On the Education of Man*, first published in 1826, in which he outlines and defines pedagogical principles (Froebel 1911).

HISTORICAL BACKGROUND

Born on April 21, 1782, at Oberweissbach in the Thuringian principality of Schwarzburg-Rudolstadt, Froebel was the sixth child of a local pastor. It is somewhat poignant to consider that Froebel, commonly considered the inventor of kindergarten, documents his own early childhood experiences as dark and melancholic. As Wichard Lange (1862) chronicled in his biography, Froebel speaks of the "awful dawn of [his] early life." His mother died from complications of his birth when he was six months old. Moreover, nearly three years later, Froebel's new stepmother took little interest in the young boy. In fact, Froebel indicated his feelings of neglect when referring to both his father and stepmother. Life seemed to have changed for the better when, in 1793, Froebel moved in with his maternal uncle at Stadt-Ilm. There, he attended a local elementary school for nearly three years. His father, who still believed his son lacked the ability to attend college, insisted that he consider a vocational career. So, for approximately two years, from 1798 to 1799, Froebel trained as a forester and surveyor. However,

Froebel was more interested in an academic career. He thus enrolled at the University of Jena, where he studied natural sciences.

It is after this point that Froebel's interests in education and philosophy began to emerge. In addition to his contributions to pedagogy, Froebel was a lifelong learner. After his brief encounter with architectural study in Frankfurt in 1805, which incidentally had a profound influence on his later work with early childhood development, Froebel was hired as a teacher at the Frankfurt Model School. In preparation, Anton Grüner, the school's headmaster, sent Froebel for a brief period to study with the well-known educational thinker of the time Johann Pestalozzi at Yverdon. With a strong interest in the Pestalozzian notion of an "object lesson," which allowed teachers to instruct students through direct observation of various objects, Froebel returned to Yverdon in 1808 to study with Pestalozzi for two more years. Having a deep interest in the structure of language and wishing to apply linguistic theory to his pedagogical principles, Froebel pursued study at the University of Göttingen from 1810 to 1812. In addition to language, he was also devoted to the study of earth science and its various subdisciplines, and pursued this course from 1812 to 1816 at the University of Berlin.

Froebel's career as an educator flourished after 1817, after which point he established a number of schools and institutes of learning. During this time, he initially established schools in Germany and later in Switzerland, where he lived from 1831 to 1836. In 1837, at the age of 56, Froebel returned to Germany where he established the child's garden, henceforth kindergarten, which was devoted to early childhood development. With a mixture of Rousseauan, Hegelian, and Pestalozzian influence, kindergarten was seen as an initial educational experience for children that merged both informal (learning in one's everyday context) and formal (learning in an educational institution) environments. With the profound influence of nature and the ideas of Pestalozzi, Froebel believed that young children need a conducive environment in order to fully develop in both cognitive and social domains. His creation of more than twenty objects for learning, known as Gifts, propelled his early childhood program and gained the interest of educators throughout Germany. Although kindergartens blossomed throughout the German regions, they seemed to have waned for a while, especially in Prussia. Froebel's free-thinking pedagogy was criticized by the more dogmatic and doctrinaire Prussian government. They eventually banned kindergarten altogether. Nevertheless, after Froebel's death in 1852, kindergartens sprouted up throughout the region, and eventually throughout Europe and the North American continent.

THE IMPORTANCE OF OPPOSITES AND UNITY IN EDUCATIONAL PROCESSES

For Froebel, the role of opposition was very important in the development of all things. The principle of opposites means that one looks for causes of behavior not in what resembles this behavior, but rather in what is radically different from it, a procedure that anticipates psychoanalytic theory, which is to appear almost one century later. As Froebel clearly states, "In good education, then, in genuine instruction, in true training, necessity should call forth freedom; law, self-determination; external compulsion, inner freedom; external hate, inner love" (1911, 13–14).

THE KINDERGARTEN AND THE GIFTS: FROEBELIAN INFLUENCE ON BLOCK PLAY

Froebel believed that in order to maximize cognitive and social development, an environment must be created in which young children can learn through free-thinking activities. Perhaps the most important aspect of Froebel's connection with young children's early formal educational experiences in general, and their involvement in mathematical activity in particular, is his invention of more than twenty Gifts. These gifts consisted of both two- and three-dimensional objects created specifically for the purpose of allowing young children to explore and develop their minds through both mental and physical manipulation of objects. Froebel's gifts included the following objects:

1. Six soft spherical objects of different colors
2. A sphere, cube, and cylinder all made of wood
3. A large cube made up of eight smaller cubes
4. A large cube made up of eight oblong blocks (rectangular prisms)

5. A large cube made up of three sections: 21 smaller cubes, 6 cubes that were half the size of the 21 cubes, and 12 cubes that were half the size of the 6 cubes
6. A large cube comprised of 18 oblong blocks
7. Rectangular and triangular tablets used for the purpose of arranging different geometric figures
8. Sticks for the purpose of outlining geometric figures
9. Rings comprised of wire, both whole and half pieces, for the purpose of outlining figures
10. Arts and crafts materials for the purpose of braiding, drawing, embroidering, modeling, perforating, and weaving objects or cutting and folding paper

With the profound influence of Froebel's gifts, blocks have become one of the most popular of toys and play materials for children in both Europe and the United States (Provenzo and Brett 1983). For example, in the late nineteenth century, influenced by Froebel's Gifts, the Crandall family had become one of the most successful manufacturers of children's blocks, and was credited for the creation and development of the interlocking block. Friedrich Richter, another Froebelian, developed the Anker-Steinbaukasten, or anchor block (made of highly compressed sand), which had become quite popular in the United States in the late nineteenth century after its success in Germany and the rest of Europe. The importance of the Richter blocks, which were founded on the principles of Froebel's Gifts and Occupations, lay in their construction, which is said to have fostered young children's intellectual development and flexibility in geometric thinking (Brosterman 1997). Richter's article "Stereometry Made Easy" (stereometry refers to the measurement of solid geometric figures) allowed children to explore with solid geometric blocks and also extend the notion of shape identification to the actual measurement of solid bodies (see Brosterman, 1997).

Froebel was perhaps one of the first individuals to connect young children's cognitive skills with their use of hands-on block materials—the Gifts or Occupations. After Froebel, one of the most noted individuals who encouraged the inclusion of blocks (particularly unit blocks) in the educational curriculum was Caroline Pratt.

Pratt made unit blocks the centerpiece of her educational curriculum and agenda (1948).

FROEBELIAN INFLUENCE

Froebel's contributions are evident in most school settings today, and, unlike other educational theorists, his ideas were put into practice in the years following his death. Balfanz (1999), for example, discusses how Friedrich Froebel's Gifts, both two- and three -dimensional materials that were designed and intended to promote young children's understanding of geometric concepts, influenced numerous individuals in different mathematically related fields. In addition, his ideas seem to have impacted the lives and careers of well-known architects and designers. In architecture, as shown in Brosterman (1997), Frank Lloyd Wright expressed his indebtedness to Froebel's ideas and techniques on numerous occasions. In one of his autobiographies, Wright recalled working with Froebel's Gifts to create geometric designs and models of buildings, which he further contended had a profound impact on his career. Wright was not the only architect who explicitly recognized Froebel's influence on later thinking. The Swiss architect Le Corbusier (whose birth name was Charles-Édouard Jeanneret) also acknowledged the importance of Froebelian Gifts as an important catalyst for his later endeavors in architecture. Le Corbusier, whose kindergarten experience included a great deal of Froebelian influence, designed buildings that explicitly demonstrated Froebel's creative approach to the learning of geometry.

Stephen J. Farenga and Daniel Ness

REFERENCES

Balfanz, Robert. (1999) "Why Do We Teach Young Children So Little Mathematics? Some Historical Considerations." In *Mathematics in the Early Years,* ed. by Juanita V. Copley pp. 3–10. Reston, VA: National Council of Teachers of Mathematics.

Brosterman, Norman. (1997) *Inventing Kindergarten.* New York: Harry N. Abrams.

Froebel, Friedrich. (1911) On *The Education of Man,* trans. W.N. Hailmann. International Education Series. Vol. 5. New York: Appleton.

Lange, W. (1862) *Friedrich Fröbels gesammelte pädagogische Schriften. Erste Abteilung: Friedrich Fröbel in seiner Erziehung als Mensch und Pädagoge. Bd. 1: Aus Fröbels Leben und erstem Streben. Autobiographie und kleinere Schriften* [Friedrich Froebel's collected educational writings. First part: Friedrich Froebel's education as a human being and teacher. Vol. 1: On Froebel's life and early endeavors. Autobiography and short texts]. Berlin: Enslin.

Pratt, Caroline. (1948) *I Learn from Children: An Adventure in Progressive Education.* New York: Simon and Schuster.

Provenzo, Eugene F. Jr., and Arlene Brett. (1983) *The Complete Block Book.* Syracuse, NY: Syracuse University Press.

JOHANN FRIEDRICH HERBART

Johann Friedrich Herbart (1776–1841) was a German philosopher who made significant strides in the emergent fields of education and psychology. Herbart emphasized a full examination of the psychological processes of learning as a means of devising educational programs based on student aptitude, ability, and interest. By asserting that a science of education was possible, Herbart furthered the idea that education should be a subject for university study. His perspective of education was one whose most important goal was to develop individuals' inner freedom and moral character. He is often considered the first individual to organize the field of pedagogy into a full-scale discipline of study. Herbart's interest in pedagogical methodology was not incidental; pedagogy was of primary (not secondary) interest to him. He was a prolific writer in the field of professional education and established an experimental school in which he tested his theories. Herbart then connected his theoretical approaches to education with his work in metaphysics, ethics, and psychology.

BACKGROUND

Herbart was born on May 4, 1776, in the north German town of Oldenberg. While attending the University of Jena between the years 1794 and 1797, Herbart's mentor was Johann Gottlieb Fichte, the philosopher from whom Herbart would eventually distance himself as he developed his own practical philosophy. Herbart rejected the idealistic philosophy of Fichte and Georg Wilhelm Friedrich Hegel on grounds that he believed it failed to explain a form of knowing founded on experience. Despite his departure of thought from Fichte, Herbart would still be true to his mentor's style. Herbart's career began in 1797 after his university studies at Jena, when he accepted the position as a private tutor in Bern, Switzerland. He left Bern in 1800 to become an independent scholar and tutor. Two years later, Herbart accepted a position as professor of philosophy and pedagogics (a term to refer to a scientific study of education and teaching) at the University of Göttingen, and was to remain there for seven years. As a university professor, his name had become synonymous with his methodological approaches in education and philosophy. He attracted masses of students at the University of Königsberg, where he served as the chair in philosophy, a position vacated by Immanuel Kant in 1809. Herbart served as university professor at Königsberg until 1833, at which time he returned to Göttingen. He remained at Göttingen for the rest of his life.

THE HERBARTIAN APPROACH TO PSYCHOLOGY

According to Herbart, the most essential sphere of psychological activity is that of cognition. All other psychological spheres, for example that of emotion or will, are subordinate to cognitive behavior. This Herbartian position thrusts the field of education into motion because it presupposes knowledge as the fundamental core of learning. He believed that human experience emanates from what he referred to as presentations (Vorstellungen). Presentations arise from the use of the senses and the realms of pain and pleasure. Moreover, Herbart categorized the presentations. Those that derive from the idea or object that caused the presentation, through acts of comparison, abstraction, or generalization, develop into concepts. Herbart's view parallels that of Rousseau in that he believes that children develop presentations from experience. As Herbart states, "Capacity for culture then, depends not on a relation between several primordially distinct capacities of the soul, but on a relationship amongst each other of presentations already acquired, and again between them and the physical organization. In both respects the pupil will need careful observation" (Herbart 1898, 114).

Experience and reflection are central to Herbart's philosophy of education, and serve as starting points for his idea of educational teaching. Like his predecessors, Herbart recognized the distinction between education and teaching. He argued that education has to do with the shaping and even the modification of one's character with the aim of improving the individual and, therefore, improving society. Teaching, however, deals with the realities of presenting knowledge, imparting skills, and demonstrating relationships. The instructor's ability to teach was the central activity of education. Unlike his predecessors, however, although he recognized the distinction between education and teaching, Herbart made the effort to link the two ideas. Through these efforts, he concluded that teaching played a subordinate role to education. For Herbart, the external influences (more or less punitive measures) did little to advance the student's moral and intellectual character. Instead, appropriate teaching, which emphasized cognitive development, was the most effective means of fostering student success in the field of education.

HERBART'S TEACHING METHOD

Herbart's teaching methodology is based on five chronological steps: preparation, presentation, association, systematization, and application. Each of the five steps is discussed in detail below. However, given their somewhat reciprocal relationship, association and systematization are discussed together.

Preparation

Preparation is the first step in Herbart's method of teaching. For Herbart, preparation was a quintessential attribute of teaching because it allowed for two important components—a motivational component and a cognitive component. Motivational devices were both intrinsic and extrinsic. Intrinsic motivational devices involve the instructor's ability to tap into her students' interests, ambitions, and pursuits. Extrinsic motivational devices have to do with the teacher's use of punitive measures for keeping students' attention on track with the topic under investigation. In addition to motivational devices, Herbart argues, cognitive devices are also employed under preparation. This involves what the student has learned leading up to the present topic. It can be recollection of ideas that are similar to the one being discussed, or it may have to do with causal relationships to the topic at hand. The teacher's task is to turn old lessons that might

seem nebulous or out of balance with the new material into useable material so that students have the opportunity to establish connections between what they have learned and what is being taught.

Presentation

The second step in Herbart's method of teaching is presentation. The main objective of presentation has to do with a clear awareness of what is to be learned as an object or unit of instruction. Examples of a single object or idea would be a story, experiment, poem, or an algebraic principle. Rousseau's influence on Herbart can be seen here because presentation involves the apperception—the process of fully understanding something based on knowledge of prior experience—of the object in question. Herbart did not relegate presentation solely to sense perception; all objects of presentation would be advanced through verbalization.

Within the component of presentation, Herbart discussed the symbiotic relationship between experience or concentration (Vertiefung) and reflection (Besinnung). He referred to these two additional areas as "mental respiration"; the student would learn new material of a topic as if it were an element having its own quality. The student would then think of the new element with respect to what he has learned from prior experience, thus allowing reflective practice.

Association and Systematization

The third and fourth steps in Herbart's method of teaching are association and systematization. These steps are intended to foster the student's conceptual ability by comparing and contrasting between instances of a phenomenon under study. While association deals with the analysis of instances of a phenomenon, systematization, on the other hand, has to do with the grouping of information and principles so as to organize parts and structures into a unified whole (e.g., parts of the body, the generalization of past tense formation). It may seem as if association and systematization are reciprocally related in that, with association, one deals with the analysis of an object while with systematization there is a grouping together of component parts to make a whole. In short, association and systematization involve the analysis and synthesis of new experiences. Although

Herbart parted with Hegelian philosophy, he seems to have incorporated it here, as the interaction between association and systematization heralds Hegel's dialectic of thesis and antithesis. Through the interrelated nature of association and systematization, the theoretical position anticipates future educationists like Friederich Froebel in the nineteenth century and Benjamin Bloom in the twentieth century.

Application

The fifth and final step in Herbart's method of teaching is application. In this phase, students are given projects (teachers often refer to projects as tasks, worksheets, or exercises) in which they are tested so that teachers can identify strengths and weaknesses of current and previous knowledge. To possess strengths, according to Herbart, students must possess cognizance with regard to new material, establish connections between new material and prior knowledge, and have the ability to summon what has been learned for future learning. Students may be asked to identify a set of concepts, or they may be asked to provide a generalization of the content learned.

HERBARTIANISM AND EDUCATION

In many ways, Herbart's worldview with regard to education and pedagogy established the framework for several countries' educational systems and served as a starting point for future educationists' theories and philosophies. Although his work seems to be quite familiar in schools of education and psychology, his development of a pedagogical science did not appear to influence educators in his own day. A number of years after his death, however, there have been numerous revivals of his method of pedagogics. An educational movement known as Herbartianism followed as numerous societies and centers focusing on his work were established in both European and American cities.

The underlying structure of lesson planning seems to have had its precursor in Herbart's pedagogical framework. We see this in various steps of his teaching method. For example, he discusses motivational and cognitive components in the preparation step. Today, we would see these ideas in the beginning of any "procedures" section of a lesson plan. Sections titled "Focus and Review" or "Anticipatory Set" are almost always used as a means to motivate students on the one hand, and identify their prior knowledge on the other. Herbart's philosophy on education and pedagogy, however, was not intended to promote teachers' dependence on models at the expense of avoiding knowledge of the content. On the contrary, teachers are to be proficient and skilled in their fields of interest and should not use models of teaching as surrogates for general knowledge.

Stephen J. Farenga and Daniel Ness

REFERENCES

Blass, Josef Leonhard. (1972) *Paedagogische Theoriebildung bei Johann Friedrich Herbart* (Johann Friedrich Herbart's Theory of Pedagogy). Meisenheim am Glan: A. Hain.

Herbart, Johann Friedrich. (1898) *Letters and Lectures on Education,* trans. H. M. Felkin and Emmie Felkin. Syracuse, NY: Bardeen Publishers.

Hilgenheger, Norbert. (1993) Johann Friedrich Herbart (1776–1841). *Prospects: The Quarterly Review of Comparative Education* 23, no. 3/4: 649–64. Paris: UNESCO, International Bureau of Education.

JOHN CALDWELL HOLT

John Caldwell Holt (1923–1985), a well-known educator and critic of compulsory schooling, was best known as an outspoken opponent of public or private educational institutions and mass education in general. Holt was an unequivocal advocate of home schooling, and left an estimable legacy to his followers and to education in general. He believed that children who were provided with a rich and stimulating learning environment would learn what they are ready to learn only when they are ready to learn it. This philosophical approach to educative practices may seem obvious to many people. However, in his day it was considered radical or progressive thinking. Today it is referred to as "unschooling" and "child-led learning" (not to be confused with child-centered learning, which is a pedagogical practice embraced in many school settings).

HISTORICAL BACKGROUND

Holt was born on April 14, 1923, in New York City to fairly affluent parents. The family moved to Boston when Holt was very young; his parents sent him to private schools in the United States and in Europe. Holt attended Yale University where he majored in industrial engineering. He subsequently lost interest in the engineering route. As an adult, Holt would never reveal the names of the schools he had attended because it was his strong conviction that the institution of school, both public or private, does not prepare students with what they need to know, both socially and intellectually. After serving on a submarine base in the Pacific Ocean during World War II, Holt moved to New York where he worked for the American Movement for World Government and subsequently with the United World Federalists, an organization whose mission was to prevent the proliferation of nuclear weapons in countries worldwide. After spending almost two years in Europe, Holt returned to the United States in 1953 and settled for a brief time with his sister in Taos, New Mexico. It was in the United States that his career as an educator seems to have blossomed. Although Holt was eager to become a teacher, he knew at this point that he had little knowledge of pedagogical technique. He soon became a teacher of the Colorado Rocky Mountain School, where he admittedly conformed to the systemic practices of schooling (i.e., following the strictures of a bureaucratic culture of schooling).

Holt spent the next decade in Massachusetts from 1957 to 1967 teaching at both elementary and secondary school levels. During this time, Holt became convinced that compulsory schooling was the problem and not the solution to children's development and learning. He served on the faculties of the University of California at Berkeley and at Harvard University, and wrote numerous books on the subject of alternative ways to educate children. He spent his remaining years thinking about how children can maximize learning potential through teaching and learning settings that were alternatives to compulsory schooling. Holt died on September 14, 1985, at the age of 62. A number of his books and articles, uncompleted at the time of his death, were later finished by close colleagues and students.

THE PROGRESSIVE EDUCATOR

Holt is not simply known as a critic of public schooling practices; his agenda, which was much broader in scope, included private schooling and parochial schooling practices as well. In fact, he was incredulous, let alone troubled, over the manner in which the culture of schooling undermined children's social, physical, and intellectual development. Holt was a teacher in private schools between the end of the post–World War II period and the time he wrote his first book. His first book, *How Children Fail* (1964), is a sharp critique of the educational system of schooling in the United States and even abroad. In short, Holt was disturbed by the way that public and private schools conform to institutionally mandated doctrinaire practices that have little or nothing to do with young children's proclivities, curiosities, and motivations to learning. Moreover, he was unnerved by teachers who, based on what they wanted to hear, praised students' performances at the expense of questioning and critical examination in a subject. Both *How Children Fail* and his subsequent book *How Children Learn* (1967), which denounces large class size, are classics among the many diatribes critiquing educational schooling practices during the 1960s and 1970s. At present, they have sold over 1.5 million copies and serve as required reading in many introductory education courses. In the late 1960s, Holt's ideas became widespread among critical educators. With the aim of reaching a wider audience, Holt founded Holt Associates, Incorporated, in 1969, and subsequently became its first president.

THE ALTERNATIVE-SCHOOLING MOVEMENT

During the 1970s, Holt realized that the schooling system in its present state could not be reformed. Holt's dissatisfaction with the dicta of his contemporaries (who included Jonathan Kozol, Herbert Kohl, and Ivan Illich)—a group with which Holt's name was commonly associated—became so pervasive that he disassociated himself from any type of schooling that was configured to accommodate mass numbers of students. Of course, this was the case with nearly the entire national school system. By the early 1970s, Holt arrived at the conclusion that education involving learning for the sake of learning, teaching and learning by transforming the mind, and the facilitation of creative thinkers could never be accomplished in the typical school setting.

Although Holt's position on education and

schooling was similar to that of his former colleagues, he identified key characteristics as to how his ideas differed from other thinkers of education. For example, in 1976, Holt published his book *Instead of Education* in which he argued that an individual or group's will to change the educational system is futile. Rather, the aim of change agents should be "unschooling," that is, educating in the home, where bureaucratic agendas play little if any role in the education of youth. Holt distinguished himself from Illich, who coined the term "deschooling" in his book *Deschooling Society* written in 1971 (Illich, however, did not support the home schooling movement).

SUMMARY OF CONTRIBUTIONS TO EDUCATION

Holt is remembered as perhaps the sharpest critic of compulsory education. Indeed, there were numerous educators who have vehemently opposed typical schooling practices whose constituents embrace conformity and compliance. However, these individuals, like Paulo Freire and Ivan Illich, were well known as a result of their contributions to the empowerment of underrepresented populations. In strengthening his position on the role of education in society, Holt was, on the one hand, revolutionary in the liberal sense in defining the importance and necessity of children's inquisitiveness and facilitation of childhood creativity in the school setting. On the other hand, Holt was dismayed with the positions of a number of critics in the so-called progressive camp—a philosophical school to which he once belonged. He was bitterly dissatisfied with mass education, whether in a public or private setting. For Holt, the expressions "the teacher as facilitator" or "the child's construction of knowledge" merely became catchphrases in the progressive movement in mass education. Gradually, the use of these terms became associated more with the political agendas of educational administrators and far less with the education of children and adolescents.

Holt's beliefs about schooling and education are not without critical examination. First, his belief, developed clearly in his book *How Children Learn* (1967), that small class size maximizes learning potential, is not supported by evidence. Although students may be learning in a teacher-centered environment, a number of school settings in the United States, Europe, and particularly in East Asian countries produce high-achieving results in many subject areas.

Stephen J. Farenga and Daniel Ness

REFERENCES

Holt, John C. (1964) *How Children Fail.* New York : Pitman.
———. (1967) *How Children Learn.* New York: Dell.
———. (1976) *Instead of Education: Ways to Help People Do Things Better.* New York: Dell.
———. (1990) *Learning All the Time.* Reading, MA: Addison-Wesley.
Illich, Ivan. (1971). *Deschooling Society.* New York: Harper and Row.

IVAN ILLICH

Ivan Illich (1926–2002) is perhaps one of the most overlooked progressive scholars in the field of education. As a theorist, he became well known for his sharp critiques of modern schooling and institutions of education in general. Although Illich's entire corpus of contributions did not emphasize educational issues per se, his well-known book *Deschooling Society* (1971a), as well as a number of subsequent works, greatly influenced the progressive education movement throughout the world. Along with Paulo Freire, Ivan Illich stands as one of the most progressive reformers of world education.

HISTORICAL BACKGROUND

Born in Vienna in 1926, Ivan Illich was one of three sons of Peter Illich, a prosperous civil engineer. Due to his somewhat well-to-do upbringing, Ivan and his two younger brothers received a good education and were able to travel throughout the European continent. In 1936, Illich attended the Piaristengymnasium, but was forced to leave in 1941 because the Nazis claimed that his mother was of Jewish ancestry, despite the fact that his parents were Roman Catholic (Smith and Smith 1994). After completing his pre-college studies in Florence, Illich went on to study histology, the anatomical study of animal and plant tissues, and crystallography at the University of Florence. However, entering the priesthood was more interesting to him than the biological sciences. As a result, he entered the theology and philosophy program at the Gregorian University in Rome in 1943. Illich graduated from the Gregorian University in 1946 and, five years later, in 1951, he decided to pursue a doctorate at the University of Salzburg, where he wrote a dissertation having to do with the history of knowledge. It was through his pursuit of a Ph.D., in studying the institutionalization of the church since medieval times, that Illich became interested in the underlying problems with modern institutions—a topic which would resonate in his critiques on formal education nearly twenty years later. Upon receiving his Ph.D., Illich moved to Washington Heights in New York City, where he served as a priest. As a priest of mostly Puerto Rican immigrants, Illich became fluent in Spanish, and began to speak strongly on behalf of the rights of Puerto Ricans by challenging the dominant culture (Smith and Smith 1994).

Illich left New York to become vice rector of the Catholic University in Ponce, Puerto Rico. However, by 1960, he was asked to leave his post because he opposed the bishop of Ponce's mandate that forbade Catholics in the diocese to vote for Luis Muñoz Marín, a governor who supported positions that were contradictory to the Catholic Church. Illich returned to New York and founded the Center for Intercultural Formation at Fordham University. The center was created to prepare American missionaries to work in Latin American countries.

During this time, Illich was vehemently opposed to Pope John XXIII's call for the modernization of the Latin American church in 1960. Instead, Illich urged missionaries to learn Spanish and to recognize that their own experiences are limited, especially when they are visiting peoples of cultures other than their own. Although the center was founded in New York, Illich insisted that it be based in Latin America. Illich and some of his associates renamed it The Centre for Intercultural Documentation (CIDOC). Given its mission to question past practices, especially if these practices led to bureaucratization, some elements of the Catholic hierarchy criticized the center and its challenge of authority. The Vatican eventually ordered Illich to dismantle CIDOC. Illich's strong views on the liberation of the church and democracy as well as his critique of the bureaucratization of the

church, and eventually with schooling, led him to leave the priesthood in 1969. The period between 1969 and 1980 were formative years for Illich with regard to his most significant contributions to education. Perhaps his most famous work, *Deschooling Society* (1971a) took a critical look at the institution of schools. During this same period, he wrote *Energy and Equity* (1974), a critique on energy consumption, and *Medical Nemesis* (1976), which investigated the institutionalization of medical treatment. Illich's interests shifted somewhat after this period from the institutionalization of schooling to a rigorous examination of the problems of institutionalization as a societal concern. For example, *Tools for Conviviality* (1973b) calls for a reorganization of societal structures and institutions in general.

By the 1990s, Illich eventually spent part of his time in three countries: Mexico, the United States, and Germany. He was a visiting professor of philosophy and science, technology, and society at Pennsylvania State University and taught philosophy at the University of Bremen. At the same time, he collaborated with numerous individuals who wished to work with him on projects that dealt with education as an egalitarian endeavor. Ivan Illich died in 2002.

DESCHOOLING SOCIETY

The precursor to *Deschooling Society* (1971a) was a short article originally published by CIDOC in 1968, and subsequently included in the book *Celebration for Awareness* (1971b), entitled "School: The Sacred Cow." In this article, Illich contends that the purpose of public schooling is not to educate students, but to limit their cognitive and social abilities so that they maintain the status quo. He was strongly opposed to the centralization of public schooling, the internal bureaucratic leadership, and the gross inequities that public schooling imposes on students. Another work that led to *Deschooling Society* was a book entitled *Who Does the School Serve in Latin America* (1973a). Originally written in Spanish, this book elaborated on the topic presented in his 1968 article.

Deschooling Society (1971a) is a remarkable polemic that investigates and challenges the assumptions of mandatory, state-run schooling procedures. A number of arguments are presented in this book. Illich's main argument with educational practice is that the individual's right to learn is greatly limited by obligatory schooling. For Illich, schooling is dehumanizing and does not serve as an appropriate model for universal education because the systemization of schooling fails to recognize and appreciate the values of nondominant cultures.

Many students, especially those who are poor, intuitively know what the schools do for them. [The system] school[s] [the students] to confuse process and substance. Once these become blurred, a new logic is assumed: the more treatment there is, the better are the results; or, escalation leads to success. The pupil is thereby 'schooled' to confuse teaching with learning, grade advancement with education, a diploma with competence, and fluency with the ability to say something new (p. 1).

As an alternative, Illich believed, first, that different, unconventional institutions needed to be formed. Second, the schooling system's reliance on accountability as a measure of student progress is futile. Illich strongly criticized the schooling system for attempting to modify individual elements—teachers, administrators, teacher education institutions—as a means of attracting the public's attention. The success of a student's education does not depend on a single change of a teacher's disposition, a change in administration, or more educational materials. In sum, bureaucracies of any kind (e.g., schooling, welfare, transportation, health) only serve to preserve the status quo—protecting administrative positions—and to subjugate the people who they are serving by having them believe that they are being assisted. Third, new formal educational institutions would provide enough resources for students to access any information they wanted. Fourth, these institutions would also provide the students with the opportunity to study with experts in a particular field of interest. And finally, these institutions would also serve as a venue for students to present their own ideas through the process of dialogue and argumentation.

In promulgating the vision of an alternative institution of education, Illich identified three methods by which it could promote an alternative learning process. He refers to these methods as "learning webs." These learning webs include the following:

1. Reference services to educational objects, which facilitate access to things or processes used for formal learning (e.g., libraries, museums, theaters, factories, farms, etc.).
2. Skill exchanges, which permit persons to list their skills, the conditions under which they are willing to serve as a model for others who want to learn these skills.
3. Peer matching, a communications network which permits persons to describe the learning activity in which they wish to engage.
4. A directory giving the addresses and self-descriptions of professionals, paraprofessionals and freelancers, along with conditions of access to their services. (1971, pp. 50–51).

ILLICH'S IMPACT ON CURRENT EDUCATIONAL SYSTEMS

Although Illich's contributions may not necessarily seem to influence the systemic concerns of schooling, there are a number of ways in which his ideas have contributed to the learning process. First, through his ideas regarding learning webs and with the advent of the Internet age, individuals who wish to broaden their knowledge in particular areas of inquiry can do so through virtual learning. In particular, one of the main purposes of virtual chat rooms and blogs is to present a topic to other parties, some of whom would be experts in the field of inquiry in question, who would then possibly be able to critique or expound on the writer's ideas. In addition, through the Internet, experts can be identified in different parts of the world. With regard to Illich's call for "skill exchanges, peer matching, reference services to educators at large, and reference services to educational objectives" (1971a, pp. 50–51), various chat rooms and Internet sites offer peer to peer, novice to expert, and expert to expert interactions. Second, current research on school achievement and poverty (Epstein and Sanders 2000; Johnson, Johnson, Farenga, and Ness 2005) appears to support Illich's view that "nowhere else should it be so evident that poverty—once it has become modernized—has become resistant to treatment with dollars alone and requires an institutional revolution" (1971a, 4). Finally, Illich's critique of the bureaucratization of society highlights the self-promoting function of welfare related institutions. Illich broadly claims that the result of such policies establishes "a professional, political, and financial monopoly over the social imagination, setting standards of what is valuable and what is feasible" (1971a, 4).

Stephen J. Farenga and Daniel Ness

REFERENCES

Epstein, Joyce L., and Mavis G. Sanders. (2000) "Connecting Home, School, and Community: New Directions for Social Research." In *Handbook of the Sociology of Education*, ed. Maureen T. Hallinan, 285–306. New York: Kluwer.

Illich, Ivan. (1971a) *Deschooling Society*. New York: Harper & Row.

———. (1971b) "School the Sacred Cow." In *Celebration of Awareness*. New York: Doubleday.

———. (1973) *En América Latina, para qué sirve la escuela?* [Who does the school serve in Latin America?]. Buenos Aires, Argentina: Ediciones Búsqueda.

———. (1973) *Tools for Conviviality*. New York: Harper and Row.

———. (1974) *Energy and Equity*. New York: Marion Boyars Publishers.

———. (1976) *Medical Nemesis: The Expropriation of Health*. New York: Pantheon.

Smith, L. Glenn, and Joan K. Smith. (1994) *Lives in Education: A Narrative of People and Ideas*. New York: St. Martin's Press.

Johnson, Dale D., Bonnie Johnson, Stephen J. Farenga, and Daniel Ness. (2005) *Trivializing Teacher Education: The Accreditation Squeeze*. Lanham, MD: Rowman and Littlefield.

ISOCRATES

Isocrates (436–338 B.C.E.), a contemporary of Plato, was a philosopher of the Sophist tradition in that, like nearly all other Sophists, Isocrates received payment for his services as an instructor and bestower of knowledge. His major accomplishment and educational contribution was to combine two distinct lines of activity with regard to education: (1) the study of rhetoric, and (2) encyclopedic knowledge. The study of rhetoric was an important and practical part of the male Athenian educational tradition in that it served as the means to a successful career as a politician on the one hand and, in a more practical sense, it shaped the student's ability to speak and persuade the public in an effective manner. An encyclopedic knowledge, the Sophists believed, was one of the answers to an ever-changing and more complex society, a way of providing the citizen with a broader educational base.

EDUCATION AS A SOURCE OF EMPOWERMENT

The later Sophists, like Isocrates, lived during a period of political and social crises that marked the decline of Athens as a political power shortly after the Peloponnesian War. As a result of the Spartan victory over Athens, Isocrates viewed instruction in rhetoric as the primary vehicle for reforming the state, educating politicians to undertake the challenges of the post-Peloponnesian era of Athens. To achieve a successful form of instruction for rhetoric, Isocrates, like other Sophists, attempted to combine ethics with the practicalities of political and social action. Isocrates believed he had accomplished this through pan-Hellenism—the unification of all of the Greek states—for which he was able to provide both an ethical and a practical justification.

ISOCRATES'S APPROACH TO INSTRUCTION

To date, no detailed account of Isocrates' instructional procedures has been found. However, historians and educators have identified a number of his methodological programs through his literary works. In fact, at the present time, the literary works of Isocrates are the earliest known evidence of instructional method through imitation. In *Against the Sophists* (1959), Isocrates argues that the teacher must combine the art of instruction with setting an example for students. For Isocrates, students learn not only through imitative techniques, but also by identifying patterns through the teacher's didactive methods. This is perhaps the first instance in which we see an expert—the teacher—and a novice—the student—in a setting where the teacher is the master and bestower of all knowledge and the student must follow the teacher's instruction in a rigid manner.

The words of Isocrates, then, can be seen as a precedent to one of the major themes of educational practice in the nineteenth and twentieth centuries—namely, that the teacher possesses full authority over students, who learn content in a more or less passive manner. In his literary work *Antidosis* (1929), Isocrates makes a number of points, comparing the education of the mind to that of the body, which implicitly suggests his method of student instruction. Since repetitive techniques strengthen the body in preparation for athletic contests, Isocrates argues that physical trainers must instruct their students through repetition of proper technique. Along similar lines, teachers of philosophy—that is, of the mind—must impart knowledge to their students through discourse. The teacher takes what he has taught his students in their initial lessons and prepares exercises that the student will learn and practice through habit and repetition. Unlike Plato, who viewed many forms of knowledge as universal truths, Isocrates saw knowledge as a collection of empirical instances in which one can identify truth through the number of times that something occurs. For Plato, knowledge was viewed as certainty, while for Isocrates, knowledge was viewed as probability.

Isocrates' method of instruction can be divided into three parts. The first was instruction in something he referred to as "ideas," or the thought elements, the styles or manners of presentation, the general principles or theories behind composition or speech. The second part of the method was the presentation and analysis of models or exemplary speeches. The third part wove the learning products of the first two phases together to form a speech appropriate to the requirements of a given situation or subject.

Stephen J. Farenga and Daniel Ness

REFERENCES

Isocrates. (1929) *Antidosis,* trans. G. Norlin. London: Loeb Classical Library. Original work from 354 B.C.E.

———. (1959). *Against the Sophists (Contro i sofisti),* ed. Sergio Cecchi. Milan, Italy: Società editrice Dante Alighieri. Original work from 390 B.C.E.

Poulakos, Takis. (1997), *Speaking for the Polis: Isocrates' Rhetorical Education.* Columbia: University of South Carolina Press.

WILLIAM KILPATRICK

William H. Kilpatrick (1871–1965) was a prominent educational thinker in the early and middle twentieth century who was responsible for introducing the activity curriculum and problem-solving style of teaching into the American school system. He became known in the field of education as the primary architect of the project method; however, it is often overlooked that Kilpatrick was one of the principal activists during the turn of the century in that his program contributed to the shift from a foundation in creationism to one of evolution. Kilpatrick's method of teaching has a good deal of its origins in the philosophy of John Dewey, who, in his book *How We Think* (1933), argued that the processes of thinking and that of learning are inseparable. Anecdotal evidence suggests that Kilpatrick was an outstanding teacher and had a profound influence on the very people who were to help both the moral and intellectual capacities of youth—the teachers in the classroom (Tenenbaum 1951). One of Kilpatrick's most influential publications was an article written in 1918 called "The Project Method." In this article, Kilpatrick proposes that schools should set subject matter aside (e.g., mathematics, the sciences, history, geography, language) and focus their attention on students' character and personality traits.

HISTORICAL BACKGROUND

Born in White Plains, Georgia, in 1871, Kilpatrick was the first child of the Reverend Dr. James Hines Kilpatrick and his second wife, Edna Perin Heard. Kilpatrick was greatly influenced by the stern character of his father and the more gregarious, yet balanced disposition of his mother. He gained a strong educational background at an early age. In 1888, Kilpatrick enrolled in Mercer University in Macon, Georgia, his father's alma mater. Although not overly expressive as a child, Kilpatrick had become increasingly innovative in his formative years. Charles Darwin's On *The Origin of Species* (1859) had a profound influence on the young Kilpatrick. Eventually, he rejected the religious orthodoxy that had once played a significant role in his childhood. Kilpatrick's time pursuing graduate study at Johns Hopkins University only intensified his rejection of religious dogma. Kilpatrick was also influenced by Francis Parker, an educator and philosopher who was well versed in the philosophical works of Johann Pestalozzi, Johann Herbart, and Friedrich Froebel (Beyer 1997).

Kilpatrick returned to Macon as a mathematics professor at Mercer University in 1897. Kilpatrick's prominence at Mercer University, a religiously oriented institution, made a number of Mercer administrators feel uneasy because of his religious skepticism. In 1898, he met John Dewey at a summer institute at the University of Chicago, where he enrolled in a course with the well-known philosopher, a course that was described by Kilpatrick as "disappointing." In Macon, Kilpatrick served as vice president of Mercer University from 1897 to 1899 and served as an interim president in 1904. Antagonistic sentiment forced Kilpatrick, an outspoken challenger of religious dogma, to resign from Mercer University in 1906 (Beyer 1997).

Both concurrent with and subsequent to his time at Mercer University, Kilpatrick worked as a teacher and served as a principal at a public school in Blakely, Georgia. With an interest in formal pedagogical theory and practice, Kilpatrick audited two courses with two professors, Percival R. Cole and Edward L. Thorndike, both from Teachers College, Columbia University. Kilpatrick subsequently moved to New York to study and eventually become a professor at Teachers College, an institution that had a profound impact on his work and served in sharp contrast to the more parochial atmosphere of the locale of his former academic appointment. Kilpatrick had become dissatisfied with the nature of subject matter knowledge instruction—so much so, that he shifted from a concern with what was to be taught to how learning takes place. His interests, then, centered on form rather than content. Kilpatrick was not so much interested in the emphasis on what was to be taught, but how learning was to take place. His earlier disappointment with Dewey changed in New York. There, Kilpatrick became an advocate of Dewey's work, and expanded on Dewey's notion of the activity curriculum (Beyer 1997). At Teachers College, Kilpatrick developed his education curriculum, and became what Kliebard (1986) argues as the "most popular professor in Teachers College history" (p. 159).

Kilpatrick retired from Teachers College in 1938. However, his recognition as a profound educator and theorist only heightened. He was one of the founders of Bennington College in Vermont and served as president of the New York Urban League from 1941 to 1951. Kilpatrick died on February 13, 1965. Yet his legacy as an educator lives on to this very day.

THE PROJECT METHOD

In order to fully grasp Kilpatrick's Project Method, it is necessary to understand what it proposes. First and foremost, the Project Method diminishes the level of importance that schools attribute to subject matter knowledge, namely the emphasis on content related to mathematics, history, the sciences, language, geography, the social sciences, and so forth. Instead, the Project Method proposes that school outcomes should focus on both character and personality traits. In his book, *Philosophy of Education* (1951), Kilpatrick states:

> The aim and process of teaching as now best conceived differ significantly from what formerly prevailed—and, as we have seen, still largely prevail in high school and college. In the older outlook the almost exclusive teaching emphasis was, and is, on imparting knowledge. In the newer outlook the emphasis is on helping to develop desirable, inclusive character and personality, with especial regard to the dynamic quality of such a character. Does the person being taught grow as a total personality? Does he grow, as a result of the teaching, more sensitive to possibilities inherent in life around him so as to seize upon these fruitfully? Does he grow more disposed to take hold effectively to bring things to pass? Does he meanwhile become practically better informed and wiser about such matters as he works with? Does he become more creative in his approach? Does he grow in the tendency to consider thoughtfully what he does? Has he adequate knowledge from present and past with which so to consider? (p. 300)

This passage clearly illustrates what Kilpatrick believed to be the appropriate order of priorities of education. It is also noticeable that character and disposition is discussed first and knowledge of content is discussed last. For Kilpatrick, knowledge is the means to reach good character—the ends.

In addition to the hierarchical nature of the components of learning, Kilpatrick believed in the notion of wholeheartedness. That is, the student is completely involved in what she is doing. The complete, or wholehearted act is the fundamental unit of living a worthy life. This outlook is analogous to the overarching Socratic maxim that an examined life is one worth living. The curriculum that Kilpatrick devised became a series of tasks that benefited students. The following are the types of projects associated with Kilpatrick's method:

1. Where the purpose is to embody some idea in external form, for example, to present a play or build a boat;

2. Where the purpose is to enjoy some aesthetic experience, for example, listening to a story or a symphony;

3. Where the purpose is to straighten out some intellectual difficulty, that is, to solve a problem;

4. Where the purpose is to obtain some item or degree of skill or knowledge (Kilpatrick 1918, 333–34).

Accordingly, Kilpatrick's philosophical perspective on education seemed to be in sharp contrast to the educational thinkers of the tradition of Jean-Jacques Rousseau. In fact, Kilpatrick, along with his mentor Edward L. Thorndike, was a rather harsh critic of the work of Maria Montessori, whose educational program focused on the intellectual development of the young child, oftentimes at the expense of social development.

In terms of teaching method and style, Kilpatrick was mostly interested in "wholeheartedness." This increasingly became his *sine qua non* for teaching practice. That is, the teacher's role was to focus attention not on what the student learns, but how the student is involved in the learning process. His goal for teachers was to identify the appropriate character and disposition of students for the maximization of learning.

SUMMARY OF CONTRIBUTIONS TO EDUCATION

Kilpatrick's general educational program has been a staple of the schooling and educative process in the United States and abroad for several decades. To be sure, for the most part, content knowledge has not been the priority for schooling in the early years. Rather, personality and character traits take precedence over content knowledge with younger students. Content becomes increasingly significant during the elementary school years, and later in the middle and high school years. Kilpatrick found the learning of content to be futile for young children if they do not have the wherewithal to know how to live a worthy life. At the same time, critics, many of whom are cognitive scientists and developmental psychologists, have argued in favor of content knowledge to a certain extent. Tapping a child's knowledge of a subject can provide very telling evidence of the processes of intellectual development.

Stephen J. Farenga and Daniel Ness

REFERENCES

Beyer, Landon E. (1997) William Heard Kilpatrick. *Prospects: The Quarterly Review of Comparative Education* 27, no. 3: 470–85. Paris: UNESCO, International Bureau of Education.

Darwin, Charles. (1859) *On the Origin of the Species by Means of Natural Selection, or: The Preservation of Favoured Races in the Struggle for Life.* London: John Murray.

Dewey, John. (1933) *How We Think.* Boston: Heath.

Kilpatrick, William H. (1918) The project method. *Teachers College Record* 18: 319–35.

———. (1951) *Philosophy of Education.* New York: Macmillan.

Kliebard, Herbert M. (1986). *The Struggle for an American Curriculum 1893–1958.* New York: Routledge.

Tenenbaum, S. (1951) *William Heard Kilpatrick: Trail Blazer in Education.* New York: Harper.

JOHN LOCKE

John Locke (1632–1714), an important English philosopher who developed strongly founded and well-substantiated arguments in support of the empiricist tradition, was a physician and academic by profession. Locke was clearly influenced by the so-called renaissance of science and inquiry. Locke was a contemporary of the renowned physical scientist and mathematician, Sir Isaac Newton, and was highly influenced not only by Newtonian mechanics, but by the novel approaches of English academics and philosophers of the time—most importantly, Sir Francis Bacon (1561–1626). Bacon in particular was outspoken about the need for change in the perspective and outlook of the methodological approaches to the sciences, which were, for the most part, ignored or censured centuries earlier. Locke's philosophical program included the methods of experimentation put forth by Newton and certainly Francis Bacon before him.

LOCKE'S NEWTONIAN VIEW OF LEARNING

In parallel with Newton, who devised cogent methodologies (most importantly, experimentation) for finding evidence in physical scientific phenomena, Locke applied a number of these very methods to the psychological sciences, which, in turn, had vast implications for the development of human learning. Locke devised a program in which an experimenter would be able to determine an individual's knowledge of reality through sense perception. A wooden table, for example, possesses characteristics that, through the senses, can be construed as real phenomena (a point that is challenged by subsequent philosophers who have espoused the rationalist tradition)—such as hardness. Moreover, data can be collected to indicate the verity of hardness as applied to wooden tables. These data are derived from a sample of individuals who are tested to determine characteristics of an object (such as hardness) through their sense of touch. In short, Locke's program emulates the Newtonian model in that it is applied to psychological rather than physical phenomena.

In 1690, Locke completed and published his well-known work, *An Essay Concerning Human Understanding,* soon to be followed by another important work, namely, *Some Thoughts Concerning Education,* written and published in 1693. In these works, Locke challenged the view that humans enter the world with many predetermined ideas and skills. Employing his empiricist position to philosophical problems and to the development of human thinking, Locke believed that humans are born as "blank slates," a term Aristotle had coined, and which Locke expounded upon in *Some Thoughts Concerning Education* nearly two thousand years later. In Locke's view, individuals have the potential to develop any ability or personality trait depending on how they are influenced by the world. Locke, then, believed that children are born neutral and society, or some other external force, molds them. That is, young humans are blank tablets on which society and the local environment write. This, in turn, is the mechanism (to use a term associated with the work of Isaac Newton) for human development and learning.

EMPIRICISM AND THE REDUCTIONIST APPROACH

Although not the first to hold this view, Locke's position became known as the empiricist approach because its application to child development suggests that all human knowledge and understanding is based on sense perception. This model can be associated with characteristics that are believed to describe human nature. Through this position, humans are seen as passive and reactionary entities that are intrinsically at rest until they react to external stimuli. That

is, some external element must have the authority to "make humans think." In the Lockean worldview, the environment in which one lives is the primary element that fosters an individual's learning—the environment is the nurturing device for development. Moreover, Locke believed that humans acquire a copy of reality when they set out to gain knowledge; that is, humans internalize facts and concepts that are brought to them from the outside world and react to these ideas in various ways.

Locke's view on learning and knowledge has been viewed by many subsequent philosophers and psychologists as reductionist in that it implies that humans are seen as wholes that can be divided into individual components, much in the same way that a computer or washing machine can be reduced to individual parts. To use a metaphor, Locke believed that it is possible to understand human nature by "breaking" humans into component parts. By repairing the parts, we then can repair the person. In sum, the main question in Locke's program is: How can we manipulate the environment in order to alter human development and learning? Locke's position, however, differs from the nativist (or materialist) position in that the Lockean worldview is based on sense perception and not the notion of innateness or that humans are prewired at birth.

LOCKEAN CONTRIBUTIONS TO PSYCHOLOGY AND EDUCATION

Locke's arguments have been vehemently criticized by a number of subsequent philosophers, such as Jean-Jacques Rousseau (who was born approximately two years prior to Locke's death) and Immanuel Kant who, during the late eighteenth century, argued against Locke's *tabula rasa* view of the young child's knowledge. On the other hand, numerous philosophers and psychologists even to this present day have espoused Locke's philosophical position on education—particularly the ways in which humans form knowledge bases. To be sure, Locke's associationist model has been emulated by many philosophers and researchers and can be identified as a model for the behaviorist (and pre-behaviorist) research of Edward L. Thorndike and, subsequently, B. F. Skinner. While Locke and other philosophers viewed associationism as the connection between two or more things possibly having a causal relationship, the nineteenth- and twentieth-century associationists viewed associationism as the connection between the external environment and one's actions—a highly experimental approach to the discipline of psychology. This approach has had a tremendous influence on the various subfields of education. For example, through positive or negative reinforcements, the teacher can have great impact on each student's subsequent behavior within the learning experience.

Stephen J. Farenga and Daniel Ness

REFERENCES

Crain, William C. (1999) *Theories of Human Development: Concepts and Applications.* 4th ed. Englewood Cliffs, NJ: Prentice Hall.

Locke, John. (1690/1994). *An Essay Concerning Human Understanding.* New York: Prometheus Books.

———. (1693/1999). *Some Thoughts Concerning Education.* Oxford, UK: Oxford University Press.

Miller, George. (1998) *Psychology: The Science of Mental Life.* New York: Adams, Bannister, and Cox.

MARIA MONTESSORI

Maria Montessori (1870–1952), often considered one of the greatest thinkers in education, was one of the few developmental theorists who were actually involved in the teaching of children. Her contributions to both the theoretical and pragmatic approaches to education make her one of the most preeminent educationists in modern times. In addition to her writings, she developed numerous types of objects or manipulatives for the purposes of learning and instruction. Montessori's following grew considerably during her lifetime and continues to grow even to the present day with thousands of schools throughout the world that follow more or less her methods of instruction. Her own theoretical positions aside, Montessori was a profound lecturer on the pedagogical implications of the work of the philosopher Jean Jacques Rousseau and, later, of Jean Piaget. Beyond her contributions to education, Maria Montessori will be known for generations to come as the first female physician of Italy.

HISTORICAL BACKGROUND

Born near Ancona, a province in Italy, in 1870, Montessori came from a rather affluent household. Her father was a successful civil servant who, like most men at that time, had a quite traditional perspective with regard to the role of women. In contrast, her mother was quite supportive of her daughter, and asked her to pursue her interests. Montessori followed her mother's advice, and became well known for her accomplishments as the first female physician in Italy.

Montessori's initial interest in education stemmed from her expert knowledge of the human body and its different systems. From this breadth of knowledge, she had become particularly interested in working with mentally retarded children. As a specialist in pediatrics and psychiatry, Montessori was appointed director of a school for mentally retarded children in 1901, where she installed a program to teach them to care for themselves and their environment. Montessori was influenced a great deal by the physicians Jean Itard (1802) and Edouard Seguin (1895), whose work convinced her to develop a scientific approach to education, based primarily on observation and experimentation. By 1903, a number of her students were able to pass the standard tests given by the public schools. She felt that given the right environmental conditions, children with mental disabilities could be taught and possibly lead healthy and productive lives. Montessori's interest in Seguin stemmed from his finding that mentally retarded children generally learn best when stimulated through the senses. Through Itard and Seguin, Montessori embraced Rousseau's philosophical perspective on human learning—that is, humans are born good, and environmental and societal conditions will affect the development of young children.

Shortly after her initial experiences as a director of a school, Montessori began coordinating a series of day care centers for children of working class households in the poor districts of Rome. Montessori concluded that young children between the ages of two and five were fascinated by the cognitive devices (i.e., manipulatives) she had developed. They were also involved in the learning of practical living skills. The older children would eventually help the teacher with the younger students—this general practice is an important feature in the modern Montessori classroom. By age four, most of her students were reading, writing, and performing four-digit mathematics calculations. From these observations,

Table 30.2 **Montessori's Sensitive Periods with Relation to Age**

Age Interval (in years)	Sensitive Periods					
	Order	Detail	Hand Use	Walking	Early Language	Conventional Language
0-1	✓				✓	
1-2	✓	✓	✓	✓	✓	
2-3	✓		✓		✓	
3-4			✓			✓
4-5			✓			✓
5-6						✓

Source: Adapted from Crain (1992).

Montessori concluded that children were equally happy to engage in both learning and play.

Montessori's method waxed in popularity in Europe at the turn of the century, and by 1912, had become a success in the United States. By the beginning of the 1920s, Montessori's pedagogical method fell into disrepute, particularly with the critiques of several educational psychologists like William Kilpatrick (1914) and Edward L. Thorndike (1932), both from Teachers College, Columbia University. While interest in educational theories in associationist psychology rose in popularity, the acceptance of the Montessori method, despite its earlier successes, had begun to wane. Kilpatrick wrote a critique of Montessori's methods, describing them as insensitive to the social needs and development of the child. Moreover, he believed that her materials lacked a sense of differentiation and did not allow for creative expression on the part of the child. Thorndike, too, was a leading critic of the Montessori method, and any other method or theoretical position emphasizing intellectual development at the expense of social development and personal hygiene in the early years. Nevertheless, despite overwhelming criticism, Montessori's method was not without merit in terms of the way her program and materials helped shape young children's thinking and competencies. Although Montessori's contributions were seen as too radical and idealistic, a revival of her program took place in the 1960s and became increasingly accepted ever since.

THEORY OF DEVELOPMENT: SENSITIVE PERIODS

Unfortunately, the popular press has underscored Montessori's contributions to educational practice while disregarding for the most part her contributions to theory and research. Nevertheless, since the 1960s, her theoretical position has been aptly studied and examined. Possibly due to her commitment to the Rousseauan tradition, a large part of Montessori's theoretical position anticipates several theories of intellectual development—for example, the contributions of Heinz Werner, Jean Piaget, and even those of Noam Chomsky. In line with Chomsky's universal grammar (1957), Montessori believed that human intellectual or cognitive development is to some extent genetically programmed. So, although young children learn by actively engaging with their environment, general cognitive tendencies are seen to be predetermined by nature. With regard to the work of Werner and Piaget, Montessori emphasized the growth of humans within particular stages of development.

The concept of sensitive periods of development plays an essential role in Montessori's writings. According to Montessori, sensitive periods of development are genetically determined, and occur during critical times during early childhood when children are engaged in painstaking efforts to master certain tasks. These periods include predisposition to order, detail, hand use, walking, and language. Although Montessori clearly distinguishes between different sensitive periods, her identification of age ranges for each period is hazy. A somewhat general correlation of age and sensitive period appears in Table 30.2 and is discussed in the following subsections.

Order

The sensitive period for order occurs rather early in the child's life, as soon as he demonstrates bodily movement. This period, which usually lasts until the end of the second year, is defined by the young child's insistence on the placement of various objects. To the young child, this placement is a form of order, which does not serve the same purpose as the meaning of order for adults. For example, the young child might cry when an object is placed in a location where it may typically not belong.

Detail

The sensitive period of detail occurs usually from twelve months to twenty-four months (two years) of age, and signals the point when a young child focuses on minute details of a particular situation or object. For example, an adult may place a large toy in a playroom. When the adult expects the child to play with the toy, the child's attention may instead be diverted to focus on a small piece of lint on the floor that may be situated near the toy. Adults find this behavior puzzling. This is yet another example that demonstrates Montessori's Rousseauan position that young children are not simply miniature adults, but instead think and behave in entirely different ways from that of the adult.

Hand Use

The sensitive period for the use of hands commences after the beginning of the first year and ends by age five, longer than any of the other sensitive periods. Shortly after twelve months, the young child increasingly makes use of the hands. The child grabs objects, puts smaller objects into larger ones, creates piles of objects, engages with things that open and close, and explores different objects through the tactile sense. From about three to five years of age, the child's touch becomes more sophisticated and he is able to manipulate new objects that at one time were difficult to handle.

Walking

Within the second year of life, the young child engages in her first walking experience. This period is perhaps the most visible to an adult because it begins with the child having a helpless appearance to one who is an independent active being. Given a much greater increase in mobility, the initial experience in walking allows the child to experience the world at a much higher level than ever before. Here again, Montessori clearly emphasizes the Rousseauan philosophical perspective on human development. This can be identified through her differentiation between the child's reason for walking and that of the adult. The adult walks for the main purpose of moving from one destination to another. In contrast, the child engages in the task of walking for its own sake. Families with young children who live in two-story homes may often encounter a child continually walking up and down a staircase. For Montessori, this indicates the child's interest in perfecting the skill of walking, and not walking for some other purpose.

Early and Conventional Language

The fifth sensitive period has to do with the development of early language. Adults often underestimate the complexities involved in learning language and how quickly the young child masters it. The child must learn not only the vocabulary of the language but the grammar that sets the vocabulary in a more effective framework for communicating with others. Due to its elusive nature, researchers and educators have had a difficult time understanding the role that language plays in children's intellectual development. This problem is very similar to our current challenges in understanding brain behavior. Nevertheless, children master vocabulary and grammar with little if any difficulty. Montessori also posited that children of households where more than one language is spoken master each language.

Adults who appreciate the challenges that children must encounter in order to learn find it perplexing to learn that grammar comes quite easily for young children. While the adult must pay great attention to rules and syntax when learning a new language, the young child does none of this—learning almost unconsciously. Here is where Montessori's writings seem to anticipate the work of Chomsky. She argues that young children have a built-in mechanism that allows them to absorb language without memorizing terms, learning syntax, or anything an adult is required to do to acquire a new language.

Montessori was clear about the importance of cognitive development within the first three years of life. From birth to the age of 2 ½ or 3 years of age, the child is equipped with what she needs in order to absorb the language or languages spoken in her environment. Montessori goes on to say that adults find it quite difficult to imagine what the child is experiencing at this point. After the three-year mark, this aptitude tapers off, and the child will no longer have this innate ability. Montessori believes this innate, maturational ability occurs for all children, regardless of environmental conditions. In addition, the progression of learning a language is consistent—the child begins with babble, continues to learn single words (vocabulary), moves on to strings of two words, three words, and eventually whole sentences.

Montessori also posited that each level of language learning is not gradual. Instead, the young child learns a language in spurts; that is, for a long period, the child may not be demonstrating any progress until a certain moment where he begins to say several new words, strings of words, or semi-complete syntactically accurate sentences. Although the sensitive period for language lasts for approximately six years, Montessori identifies a transition between two language periods. In Table 31.2, the sensitive period for language is divided into "early language" and "conventional language," where early language, discussed above, occurs from birth to about three years and conventional language occurs from three years to approximately six years of age. In contrast to early language, in the conventional language period the child is completely conscious when learning new vocabulary or grammatical structures.

MONTESSORI'S CONTRIBUTIONS TO SCHOOLING

In the Montessori tradition, since a large number of children do not enter school until 2 ½ to 3 years of age, parents and caretakers are essentially the first educators. Montessori believed that in order to help young children's cognitive structures, parents need a positive attitude. This is not done by ignoring children's interests or by directing the learning process. Instead, parents need to provide opportunities and environments for children that are conducive to learning and which will allow adults the occasion to observe children's everyday, spontaneous interests, inclinations, and motivations. Now that 2 ½ years have passed, the child may be ready for the Montessori school.

The representative Montessori school generally enrolls children between the ages of 2 ½ to 6 years of age, when most of the sensitive periods are still maturing and developing. In addition, Montessori did not mind mixing children of different ages because they tend to interact in ways that foster cognitive and social development. Within the Montessori school, a number of factors are found that are starkly different from the typical early childhood (grades K through 2) setting in the elementary school.

The first factor has to do with the child's independence. In general, elementary school children have little if any independence—they are told where to sit, when to ask questions, and when to leave their seats. With regard to content, children are often involved in drill and practice, instructed and told what to read or to say, and even engaged in recitation. In contrast, the Montessori school emphasizes the child's independence. Montessori argued that in order to stimulate vitality during the sensitive periods, the school must have the appropriate materials so children will engage in activities (often times without the assistance of an adult). In order to determine which materials were most suitable for the classroom, Montessori observed children in their everyday setting within the school. The materials which seemed to engage children the longest and which demonstrated children in total concentration were those that were used within the classroom. Based on one of her initial observational findings of children's concentrative efforts, Montessori developed cylindrical blocks ranging in size that fit into their respective holes in a large wooden block. Montessori implemented building blocks in her program as a means of developing geometric thinking and reasoning in the early years. Unlike earlier educators, Montessori instilled an element of free choice in her method of facilitating young children's learning. Through her method, children developed ideas of various geometric figures (e.g., circles, rectangles, triangles, ellipses, trapezoids, rhombuses, hexagons, and so forth) through exploratory activity. This is not to say, however, that her exercises and activities for children were deprived of structure; in fact, the Montessori method contains nearly 400 pages of sequenced lessons that are to be balanced with the child's free choice activities. She found numerous children engaged in the process of finding the appropriate holes for each of the different sizes of cylinders. Montessori observed that after several repetitions of a particular activity, the child would develop a sense of satisfaction and pleasure when accurately solving a problem using any of the materials. This was the point that Montessori referred to as *normalization*.

Montessori also emphasized children's rights to select the materials with which they wish to engage. For Montessori, this meant that the child would have a more productive time reaching the point of normalization. Most very young children will engage in activities in which attention to order or detail is evident, whereas children between ages 2 and 4 will most likely be engaged in activities which are associated with drawing (hand use) or writing and reading (hand use and language). Given the emphasis on children's independence, concentrative efforts, and free choice, reward and punishment is unnecessary in the Montessori school. Montessori felt that in the general elementary school, children become submissive to the adult, almost to the point that they will say and do anything for approval from the teacher. This process, then, limits children's ability to think independently. Instead, the Montessorians refrain from telling children what to do through reward and punishment, and instead provide them with the environment in which they are able to select their own materials and work independently or in collaboration with others.

It is frequently the case that young children wish to tie their own shoes or button their own clothes appropriately as a means of seeking greater independence from the adult. In anticipating young children's motor skill development, Montessori devised several subskills that prepared young children for some of the major tasks they would choose. In helping them build their dexterity for such fine motor tasks as tying shoelaces, Montessori prepared young children with subskills that included the proper holding of a crayon or pencil for the purpose of writing or drawing and even the washing and cleaning of fruit and vegetables.

In addition to issues of independence, free choice, concentration, rewards and punitive measures, and motor skill development, the Montessori school also includes childhood preparation in the areas of reading, writing, and (as seen above) arithmetic and geometric thinking. Montessori believed that the most favorable time to introduce these subjects is no later than 4 or 4 ½ years of age because it is at this time when the sensitive period for language is at its peak. Once the peak has passed, say, by ages 6 or 7, it will

be more difficult, according to Montessori, for the child to develop skills in these areas.

In her writings, Montessori also discussed the issues of moral misconduct, fantasy, creativity, and nature as educational devices. Moral misconduct, as Montessori asserted, results when the child's engagement in work or play is unfulfilled. Unlike the traditional classroom scenario where the teacher gains complete external control of behavior, the Montessori teacher emphasizes internal control by the child. The teacher instead engages in student observation to identify materials and activities that suit individual students. In addition, students learn respect for neighbors as opposed to merely being told to stop a bad behavior.

Montessori often emphasized that adults must learn to follow children's natural inclinations. She went on to say that one of these natural inclinations is fantasy. Montessori argued that children at first believe in the content of stories because they are unable to distinguish between a fantasy and reality. However, she believed that fantastic events and storytelling eventually leads the child to the ability to discriminate between the two. Further, children's involvement in creative tasks like painting and drawing alludes to some form of reality in the child's life, and is therefore a necessary component of the Montessori curriculum. Nature, too, plays an important part of the Montessori curriculum. For Montessori, the outdoors stimulates the young child perhaps more than any other environment. The young child has a much stronger predilection toward things in the natural environment than the adult does, and will often exhibit greater attention and patience when engaged in naturalistic activities outdoors than in a number of indoor activities, most of which are unnatural and contrived.

Montessori's contributions in education do not merely span the early childhood years (birth through five or six years of age), that is, the full durations of each of the sensitive periods. Montessori also wrote extensively on children in the elementary years (approximately six to twelve years of age), and to some extent, the adolescent period. Her primary goal with elementary school age students was the development of intellectual capacities as well as the child's outlook on the external environment. Montessori urged teachers in these age levels to emphasize student questioning and research for finding answers. She developed a curriculum called the "cosmic plan" which consisted of stories on important subjects for growth, such as the origin of life, why (and how) plants and animals grow, how buildings are constructed, and so on. Montessori believed that as children grow and become young adults, their involvement in responsible tasks, such as balancing household budgets, working on the farm, or working in a maintenance position will prepare them adequately for the real world.

MONTESSORI'S INFLUENCE IN TODAY'S SCHOOLS

Montessori has influenced schools of the late twentieth and now the twenty-first century, even in the non-Montessori elementary school. As stated above, the Montessori method has seen a number of revivals, particularly in the United States during the 1960s and 1970s. Educators in the United Kingdom and Australia have also seen the effectiveness of the Montessori school. Presently Montessori schools can be found in numerous countries throughout the world, mostly in many East Asian countries (e.g., Taiwan and Japan). The late twentieth-century revivals were most likely in response to the need for alternatives to the typical nursery or elementary school systems, which limited student autonomy and did not seem to serve critical points within early childhood. It was also during these decades when Piagetian theory became prominent in the United States. And, as indicated above, Montessori's theoretical framework seems to have anticipated the work of Piaget and other developmentalists in early childhood.

Nevertheless, Montessori also had her share of critics. Her approach was seen as radical by a number of behaviorist theorists and advocates who put social development well before cognitive or intellectual development. Thus, Montessori's critics seemed to have greatly influenced the educational panorama for the first several decades of the twentieth century, and although her methods are quite popular today, the educational system in the United States and in most other countries favor teacher-centered classrooms, whereby students are directed and instructed and have virtually no free choice at all. Regardless of her shortcomings, Montessori was one of the first

theorists and practitioners to put the philosophical perspective of Rousseau into practice. In addition, unlike the famous theorists who succeeded her, Montessori was perhaps the first to recognize the spontaneous capabilities of young children and appreciate the relationship between these capabilities and intellectual development in general.

Stephen J. Farenga and Daniel Ness

REFERENCES

Balfanz, Robert. (1999) "Why Do We Teach Young Children So Little Mathematics?: Some Historical Considerations." In *Mathematics in the Early Years*, ed. Juanita V. Copley. Reston VA: National Council of Teachers of Mathematics.

Chomsky, Noam. (1957) *Syntactic Structures*. The Hague: Mouton.

Crain, William. (1992) *Theories of Development: Concepts and Applications*. Upper Saddle River, NJ: Prentice Hall.

Itard, Jean. (1802) *An Historical Account of the Discovery and Education of a Savage Man : or, the First Developments, Physical and Moral, of the Young Savage Caught in the Woods Near Aveyron in the Year 1798*. London: R. Phillips.

Kilpatrick, William, H. (1914) *The Montessori System Examined*. Boston: Houghton Mifflin.

Kramer, Rita. (1988) *Maria Montessori*. Boston: Addison-Wesley.

Montessori, Maria. (1949/1967) *The Absorbent Mind,* trans. C. A. Claremont. New York: Holt, Rinehart, and Winston.

Seguin, Edouard. (1895) *Rapport et Mémoires sur l'Éducation des Enfants Normaux et Anormaux*, Préface par Bourneville. Paris: Alcan.

Thorndike, Edward L. (1932) *The Fundamentals of Learning*. New York: Teachers College Press.

JOHANN HEINRICH PESTALOZZI

Johann Heinrich Pestalozzi (1746–1827) is one of the most widely renowned educational thinkers of the late eighteenth and early nineteenth centuries. His influence is noticed in the works of later educational theorists and practitioners including Friedrich Froebel, Johann Herbart, and William Kilpatrick, as well as present day educational researchers. Although Pestalozzi is referred to frequently in educational circles, his ideas in general are obscure, partly because his writing style is somewhat complex. Nevertheless, if it were not for Pestalozzi, numerous common practices in education today would seem more like novelties than norms. For example, Pestalozzi was one of the primary architects of whole class instruction (in contrast to tutorship—the common pedagogical setting of his time). He is also recognized for promulgating the use of slates and pencils. In addition, Pestalozzi is credited for the well-known "object lesson," which today is often construed as a lesson in which students, through the use of objects, learn from modeling, and subsequently emulate or replicate a given cognitive task. In general, Pestalozzi can be credited for a number of educational practices that have been inculcated into an educational system still in place today in almost every post-industrial nation.

HISTORICAL BACKGROUND

Pestalozzi was born in Zurich, Switzerland, in 1746 to a middle-class family. His mother was Susanna Hotz Pestalozzi and his father, Johann Baptiste Pestalozzi, was a physician. Pestalozzi seems to have been influenced to some extent by his grandfather, Andreas Pestalozzi, a Protestant minister in the rural village of Hongg, who embarked on an undertaking to improve conditions for Swiss peasants.

Pestalozzi apparently led a somewhat unstable childhood in the sense that he was overprotected by his parents, particularly his mother (DeGuimps 1895). Nevertheless, as a resident of Zurich, Pestalozzi was influenced by a number of movements in the mid-eighteenth century. For example, through the Collegium Carolinum in Zurich, he was introduced to the work of Johann Breitinger, a scholar of classics, and Johann Bodmer, an expert in Swiss history. Pestalozzi was brought up in a pre-industrial world that had witnessed the malevolent effects of early industry on farmers and skilled craftspeople. As DeGuimps (1895) noted, Pestalozzi, along with other youth of his day, boycotted the burgeoning industrial movement by sleeping on bare ground and eating nothing but bread and vegetables in contempt of the materialistic agenda of early industrialists.

Pestalozzi, like other young and educated individuals of his day, studied for the ministry, but failed to complete his theological studies. Instead, he decided to turn to farming as a means of sustenance and happiness and, in 1769, Pestalozzi married and settled on a farm at Neuhoff near Zurich. As an agriculturalist, Pestalozzi gained his initial experience in educational practice. At Neuhoff, he employed young individuals who had mostly been orphaned or born into peasant families. In challenging the nascent industrial movement, Pestalozzi established a self-supporting agricultural and handicraft school on the Neuhoff farm in 1774. It was at this time, between 1774 and 1779, that Pestalozzi developed the idea of simultaneous instruction, in which he taught the farm hands reading, writing, and arithmetic, sometimes nearly fifty students at a time. By 1780, however, his business as an agriculturalist failed due to lack of funding. As a result, he turned to writing. He published his first book, *Leonard and Gertrude*, in 1781 (published in English in 1801), in which he outlines his ideas about pedagogy, and concluded that his role in life was to be an educationist. He was highly influenced during this time by the well-known philosopher Johann Gottlieb Fichte, who was interested in establishing a regeneration of the German state through a proper education (DeGuimps 1895).

Although his efforts at Neuhoff failed, Pestalozzi pursued teaching again in the city of Stanz, where he established a school for homeless children in 1798. This venture, like the one at Neuhoff, did not prove successful, but his major opportunity came in Burgdorf, from 1800 to 1804, when he developed a philosophical and methodological approach to pedagogical technique. He then opened his Institute at Yverdon in 1805. By this time, Pestalozzi had reached the peak of his career, attracting numerous individuals throughout Europe as students of his institute, one of them being Friedrich Froebel. Pestalozzi died in 1827.

NATURE AND THE LINK BETWEEN CONCRETE AND ABSTRACT

Pestalozzi identified human nature with the natural world. That is, he believed people behaved according to unalterable laws, almost in a similar tone to Sir Isaac Newton who had identified physical laws nearly a century earlier. However, unlike physical laws, the unalterable laws of humans have to do with the course of cognitive development. For Pestalozzi, *Anschauung*, or intuition, underlies all elements of cognitive process from the early stage of sense perception to the later stage of full cognitive awareness of a concept. In sum, the entire intellectual process starts with an obscure and possibly confused experience to a clear and definite cognition.

Pestalozzi believed that form, number, and language are the three elementary conduits for instruction. This is because the entire sum of the properties of any object was comprised of its appearance (form), its quantitative characteristic (measurement or number), and the elementary grammatical and syntactical structures involved in discourse (language). For example, any object considered must have a spatial orientation of some kind. The question is: Can the object be represented in simpler terms, namely, by breaking it down to simpler forms, like a rectangle or a line? Further, we can discern the specific object from other objects through the process of measurement. This is how the element of number is involved. For Pestalozzi, form and number are symbiotically related. That is, what we see (form) can be quantifiable through measurement (number); likewise, the reverse is also true—if we can measure something, then we can conclude that it has spatial characteristics and therefore can be seen. Next comes language, how we learn it and how we use it to discuss objects or to communicate. Pestalozzi used phonemes and syllables as units of language. He expounded on these units and developed elaborate systems of instruction that led to the child's learning of combinations of speech sounds and syllables, to words and phrases, and then to complete sentences.

THE OBJECT LESSON

In understanding Pestalozzi's philosophical program for education, it is not very difficult to identify the influence of both John Locke and Jean-Jacques Rousseau, individuals with two opposing philosophical views. For Locke, the foundation of what we as humans know has to originate with the senses. In seeming agreement with the Lockean perspective, Pestalozzi argued: "When I now look back and ask myself, what have I specially done for the very being of education? I find I have fixed the highest, supreme principle of instruction in the recognition of sense impression as the absolute foundation of all knowledge" (1894, 200). Yet, at the same time, Pestalozzi was greatly influenced by the work of Rousseau. According to Soëtard (1981), Rousseau's well-known treatise on education, *Emile*, was Pestalozzi's bedtime book for most of his life. Despite his steadfast belief that sensory perception is the underpinning of knowledge, Pestalozzi also believed strongly in liberating childhood. By this, he meant that children think in ways much different from how adults view the world, and he insisted on the Rousseauan belief that children are not merely miniature adults.

For Pestalozzi, then, the results of instruction were to be a clear and wholesome account of what was true, moral, and practical from an intellectual perspective. That is, the key to efficient learning had to do with a set of images or sensorimotor patterns of affect that could possibly stimulate the learner's interest and thought processes. Pestalozzi concluded that the teacher should be concerned with helping the student acquire a model, which would guide the process of trial responses. So, the concrete, spontaneous, and familiar objects of experience are what the student needs to develop and nurture his or her intuitions.

With a real, concrete object, Pestalozzi insisted that the object lesson be used to transform the student's thinking from sensory perception to one of abstraction and formal definitions of concepts with regard to the object being studied. The objects, then, were not the primary focus in the educational process; rather, the method of presentation was central and was to encourage the student's formation of concepts. The lesson would end with the formulation of a rule, a definition, or precept of a larger concept or idea. Pestalozzi's influence in this regard was far reaching in Europe and in the United States after his death. Individuals like Warren Colburn in mathematics and Lowell Mason in music based teaching techniques of their respective disciplines on Pestalozzi's object lesson.

PESTALOZZI'S LEGACY AS AN EDUCATIONIST

Pestalozzi and Comenius, a famous educationist a century earlier, had one most important thing in common: Both individuals' contributions to education were appreciated in posterity. Although both were well known during their own lifetimes, their contributions were seen more for their means rather than ends. Comenius was known in his day for his Latin picture books, yet his contributions to education that would come to seem far more important were his attempts at making education a universal enterprise. Pestalozzi, too, was known as an educator during his lifetime as an instructor and tutor of children of the middle and upper classes. But his contributions to education as a universal enterprise were recognized only posthumously. These contributions included a philosophical program for instruction and assessment as well as a keen interest in educating underprivileged children.

Pestalozzi may also be seen as the father of the manipulative—that is, the hands-on object, which serves to connect informal, everyday, or spontaneous ideas with formal concepts and definitions. His influence in this regard is clearly discernable in later educational thinkers, from Friedrich Froebel in the early nineteenth century to Maria Montessori in the early twentieth century, to scholars of education in the present day whose research demonstrates an important positive link between the use of manipulatives and genuine learning.

Stephen J. Farenga and Daniel Ness

REFERENCES

DeGuimps, R. (1895) *Pestalozzi: His Life and Work,* trans. James Russell. New York: Appleton.

Pestalozzi, Johann Heinrich. (1801) *Lienhard und Gertrud.* [Leonard and Gertrude]. Philadelphia, PA: Joseph Groff.

———. (1894) *How Gertrude Teachers Her Children.* Originally published in 1801, trans. L.E. Holland and F.C. Turner. Syracuse, NY: Bardeen Publishers.

Soëtard, Michel. (1981) *Pestalozzi ou la naissance de l'éducateur.* Berne: P. Lang.

JEAN PIAGET

Jean Piaget (1896–1980) was a Swiss psychologist and genetic epistemologist whose contributions to research and practice are far reaching in nearly all educational domains. Piaget was born in 1896 in Neuchâtel, Switzerland, and died in that city in 1980. As a child, Piaget had a keen interest in biology, particularly Darwin's theory of evolution. In particular, Piaget was interested in how various species change through adaptation to varied environmental conditions. Piaget was a precocious child. At ten years old, he published his first scientific article on his observations of an albino sparrow.

During adolescence, Piaget was particularly influenced by one of his uncles, a philosopher. It was through his uncle that Piaget was acquainted with the field of epistemology, the study of knowledge and how we know what we know. Piaget's primary philosophical influences were the works of Jean-Jacques Rousseau, Immanuel Kant, and Henri Bergson. Piaget attempted to reconcile the ideas of these thinkers with the Darwinian theory of evolution. After several years, Piaget invented a novel field known as genetic epistemology, namely, the origins of knowledge, particularly the origins of knowledge from the earliest periods of human life. Piaget's experiences in the biological sciences led him to believe that the nonempirical approach in philosophy (e.g., in the realm of Hegel and other Romantic philosophers) was unsuitable for determining the origins of knowledge. Instead, he proposed to combine philosophy with the empirical, scientific approach.

In 1917, at the age of twenty-one, Piaget completed his Ph.D. thesis (on the developmental changes of mollusks in Lake Lucerne) at the University of Neuchâtel. He subsequently worked in Paris for a few years on the development of intelligence tests (which were originally created by Alfred Binet). Although the purpose of the research was to develop norms and scoring for the test questions—determining the number of correct responses—Piaget was more interested in the errors children made and how their errors seemed to fit specific patterns at different ages. This led to his discovery that children's thinking was not at the adult level, but was nevertheless organized and had a form of logic of its own.

In 1921, Piaget became the director of the Jean-Jacques Rousseau Institute at the University of Geneva, where he remained for the rest of his life. The Institute was aptly named; Piaget was one of the first writers after Rousseau himself who followed Rousseau's philosophy on child development to such a great extent. Piaget followed Rousseau's belief that children who were allowed to follow their own course of development achieved optimal abilities as opposed to others who were not. Piaget, then, was an organismic thinker; he looked at the human as an organism acting on the world, and not simply a passive entity. He thought of the organism functioning as a structured whole entity, in which the whole is greater than the sum of its parts.

Piaget believed that children went through a sequence of reorganizations of their mental structures. This sequence of reorganizations, or systems of processing information, were distinctive from one another and led Piaget to think of development in terms of stages. Piaget had become one of the most sensitive observers of children's behavior. He kept highly detailed accounts of systematic observations of his own three children over a period of several years. As a result, he discovered important features of infant and child development that other thinkers spanning centuries had overlooked.

Piaget rejected the basic behaviorist traditions of thinking, which were put forth primarily by American psychologists (for example, E. L. Thorndike and B. F. Skinner). Instead, he believed that children should develop at their own rates and learn things for themselves, whereas the behaviorists, who rejected age or stage differences, believed that it is possible to hasten development and make it more efficient with the appropriate conditioning techniques. Piaget's answer to the possibility of speeding development is the following: Anything you tell children (what most teachers do) will prevent them from the process of discovery on their own terms. If a child developed more slowly, thinking things through, that child would develop more adaptive, scientific, and logical abilities.

SCHEMES

Piaget's theory of intellectual development is founded on a basic developmental process that he posited was at work throughout the life cycle. Piaget called the basic unit of knowledge a scheme (the scheme in Piagetian terms is called schema [singular] and schemata [plural]. The terms "scheme" [singular] and "schemes" [plural] will be used here). A scheme is a pattern of behavior in which we know something or gain knowledge of something. It is the most basic structure in Piaget's developmental theory and is composed of our frame of reference. According to Piaget, it is impossible to know anything without a frame of reference or structure that serves as a means of processing incoming information. He therefore posits that, as humans, we are equipped with some basic schemes that are the foundations of future knowledge. We are born with three schemes that are forms of reflexive actions when encountering the world for the first time: looking, grasping, and sucking. The infant uses these schemes in an automatic and reflexive manner. These basic schemes, however, are modified over time and develop and expand into newer and more complex schemes.

ASSIMILATION AND ACCOMMODATION

The development of schemes throughout the lifespan unfolds through two key processes: assimilation and accommodation. Since we only know what we can process through prior knowledge (basic structure of constructivist philosophy), we apply our current schemes to a new piece of information from the environment and incorporate that new piece of information into our existing scheme. This is the process of assimilation, that is, the new piece of information is being assimilated into the preexisting knowledge base. Take the sucking scheme as an example. A baby has the reflex of sucking, and therefore sucks anything that is placed in her mouth. She may recognize a nipple (an old object) by sucking it. If she then places her finger in her mouth, she will apply the sucking scheme to the finger (a new object). An older individual may have developed a scheme for a dog— a four legged creature, usually with a long tail, that you find on a leash or running in a park. So, if the child sees a collie, he may apply the dog scheme and refer to the collie as a dog.

However, we are constantly in the process of modifying our schemes because no two situations or entities are the same. So, we must adjust the way we look at something, the way we move our lips or hold something when encountering a different object (e.g., sucking a nipple compared to sucking a finger). Although assimilation allows us to generalize and apply our knowledge to many different conditions, it distorts reality and does not adapt to it because assimilative processes defy restructuring and modification of schemes. At this point, the process of accommodation is necessary and serves as a complementary process to assimilation.

Accommodation is the process of reorganizing or modifying our current schemes to be able to handle new incoming information or changes with regard to an object or idea. In this respect, we adjust to reality instead of distorting it. It allows us to alter existing schemes so that they can be applied to more varied situations. Accommodation is not completely the process of modification of existing schemes; it can also involve the creation of new schemes as well. For example, the infant who sucks his finger may encounter a rubber duck. Since the sucking reflex will not yield the results for which the infant is search-

Table 30.3 **The Four Stages in Piaget's Theory of Intellectual Development**

Stage	Characteristics	Age Range
Sensorimotor	Schemas—which emerge from the innate processes of sucking, grasping, and looking—are associated with the development of motor skills. Learning initially takes place locally and through bodily functions, and subsequently becomes externalized.	Birth through 24 months (2 years)
Preoperational	As the child matures, learning takes place externally (i.e., learning is not primarily based on bodily functions, or interest in an activity through happenstance). The child is unable to succeed in tasks involving conservation and seriation.	2 years through 7 years
Concrete Operational	The child has the ability to succeed in tasks involving conservation, seriation, and some aspects of order relationships involving logic. The child, however, is unable to make abstractions about concrete situations. For example, the child might be able to determine the next number in a sequence, but might not be able to generalize about the sequence as a whole. More specifically, in the sequence 2, 4, 8, 16..., a concrete operational child might know that the fifth number is 32, but will more than likely not know that the general rule has to do with the power of 2.	7 years through 12 years
Formal Operations	The individual can think abstractly. The individual is able to make generalizations when given specific tasks. For example, when given that A is older than B, C is younger than A, and C is older than B, the individual will be able to generalize that B < C < A.	12 years to adulthood

Source: Stephen J. Farenga and Daniel Ness. Adapted from (1) Piaget, Jean (1926). *The Child's Conception of the World*, trans. J. Tomlinson and A. Tomlinson. Savage, MD: Littlefield, Addams; (2) Inhelder, Bärbel, and Jean Piaget (1964). *The Early Growth of Logic in the Child*. New York: Harper and Row.

ing, he may decide to bite the rubber duck instead. This is evidence of an entirely new scheme. Likewise, the older child who refers to a cat as a "dog" because "it has four legs and a long tail" will be told by an adult that the animal does not belong in the "dog" family and is therefore labeled "cat." The child at this point must reorganize his knowledge of animals in such a way that he differentiates between dogs and cats. Assimilation also allows us to generalize between different phenomena and to develop a sense of classification.

Piaget's complementary processes of assimilation and accommodation refer to the system of equilibration. For Piaget, as living organisms, we desire equilibrium. As a result, we are always motivated to assimilate and accommodate objects and ideas in our environment. Doing so leads to the state of equilibrium. When we are unable to assimilate or accommodate new objects or ideas to a full extent, we are instead in a state of disequilibrium.

THE STAGES OF DEVELOPMENT

As stated above, Piaget outlined four primary stages of intellectual development: the sensorimotor stage; the preoperational stage; the concrete operational stage; and the formal operational stage. One stage is intrinsically different from another due to the differences in cognitive levels within particular age groups (see Table 30.3).

Sensorimotor Period

The sensorimotor stage occurs from birth to twenty-four months (two years of age). The basic theme here is that the cognitive abilities of children in the sensorimotor stage are confined to tasks and skills associated with bodily reflexes within the first four months of life to the discovery of external objects in the next eight months and finally to the development of language abilities in the second twelve-month period. Again, all knowledge learned during this period is generated from the three innate schemes given at birth—looking, grasping, and sucking. The end of the sensorimotor period serves as the transition to the next period of development in which the infant is able to use mental symbols and words to refer to absent objects. Piaget refers to the origin and continued use of mental and written symbols as the semiotic function.

Preoperational Period

Children begin to use symbols when they use one object or action to represent or supplement an absent one—the sixth stage of sensorimotor development. Initially, the child uses nonlinguistic symbols, or natural language, prior to the learning of an artificial language (e.g., Arabic, English, Japanese). To illustrate natural language, a child might pretend that a piece of cloth is a pillow and go to sleep on the cloth. Perhaps more basic than this, a very young child will cry if she scrapes her knee while attempting to learn how to walk; the adult, on the other hand, will use artificial language to indicate pain from scraping a knee or elbow ("Ouch, that hurts! I'll need to put a bandage on that.").

A major source of symbols is language (artificial language), which develops rapidly during the early preoperational years (two to four years). Language vastly widens the child's horizons. Through language, the child can relive the past, anticipate the future, and communicate events to others. But precisely because the young child's mind is so rapidly expanding, it initially lacks the properties of a coherent logic. This is apparent in the young child's use of words. He or she does not use words to stand for true classes of objects, but merely as preconcepts. For example, Jane, a three-year-old, has two brothers—Ron and Mike. She says, "My daddy has lots of Rons and lots of Mikes and lots of Janes." She does not yet possess the concept of a general class—children—within which those with the names Ron, Mike, or Jane comprise only a small subset. Because children lack general classes, their reasoning is frequently transductive, shifting from the particular to the particular: "I haven't had my nap yet so it isn't afternoon."

Another characteristic of a preoperational child is his inability to conserve. Take the conservation of continuous quantities (liquids) as an example. A child is shown two glasses, A1 and A2, which are filled to the same height. The child is asked if the two glasses contain the same amount of liquid, and the child almost always agrees that they do. Next the experimenter (or the child) pours the liquid from A2 to the glass P, which is lower and wider. The child is asked if the amount of liquid is still the same. At the preoperational level, the responses fall into two substages:

Substage I: The children clearly fail to conserve—that is, they fail to realize that the quantity is the same, e.g., "A1 has more because it is taller. . . ."

Substage II: The child takes steps toward conservation but does not achieve it. A boy might at one moment say that A1 has more because it is taller, then change his mind and say that P has more because it is wider, and then become confused. The child is showing "intuitive regulations"—beginning to consider two perceptual dimensions, but cannot reason the two dimensions simultaneously.

In another example of conservation, a child is unable to conserve number (better known as conservation of equivalence relations) if she is unable to distinguish between the number of objects present and the spatial arrangement of those objects: "I have four checkers and you have five checkers, but I have more because they're spread out . . . " A related number conservation task involves the use of a select number of small toy dolls and the same number of toy hats to go with each doll. If each hat is placed next to each doll, the preoperational child will undoubtedly agree that there are a same number of dolls and hats. However, if one group, say the hats, are spread apart, while the dolls are close

Figure 30.1   **Piaget's Conservation of Equivalent Relations Problem (Also Known As Conservation of Number)**

The typical preoperational individual will say that for every person there is one hat.

The typical preoperational individual will say that there are more hats than there are people.

Source: Stephen Farenga and Daniel Ness. Adapted from Jean Piaget's Task for the Conservation of Number. See Jean Piaget and A. Szeminska, *The Child's Concept of Number,* trans. Caleb Gattegno and F. M. Hodgeson. New York: Norton, 1941.

together, the typical preoperational child will say that there are more hats than dolls (See Figure 30.1). Other conservation experiments include conservation of substance, weight, volume, and length. Conservation of substance involves the use of clay or play dough. Two balls of clay are approximately the same size. One of the two balls of clay is rolled into a longer, thinner shape—like a hot dog. Preoperational children believe that the two objects have different amounts of clay. Seriation is another Piagetian task that allows a researcher to classify children into particular stages. Seriation involves placing objects of different lengths in order of size. Young children center on one aspect of the relationship of length. Concrete operational children are able to decenter, that is, they are able to take in two or more components of an idea or concept simultaneously (see Figure 30.2).

Concrete Operational Period

One can define children in the concrete-operational stage through comparison with children in the ear-

lier preoperational level. Concrete operational children generally can solve conservation tasks, seriation tasks, and are able to generalize to a greater extent than younger children. That is, their language capabilities generally increase and, they are therefore able to base their observations on real-life phenomena or concepts. They are able to deal with more than one component of a particular task simultaneously. Preconcepts generally disappear, and transductive thinking becomes more inductive in nature.

Formal Operations

At the level of concrete operations, children's actions showed more organization. In one experiment, children were given four flasks containing colorless liquids labeled 1, 2, 3, and 4. They also were given a small container of a colorless liquid, labeled C. Their task was to mix these liquids to make the color yellow. At the level of preoperational intelligence, children typically were messy and disorganized. They poured the liquids in and out of the

Figure 30.2   **Unsuccessful Attempt (a) and Successful Attempt (b) in the Seriation Task**

(a) Centration—The child's attention is limited to individual characteristics of a given

phenomenon at a time.

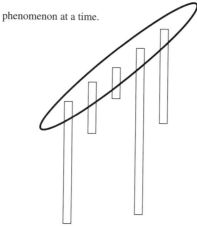

(b) Decentration—The child's attention broadens and includes most characteristics of a

given phenomenon or task.

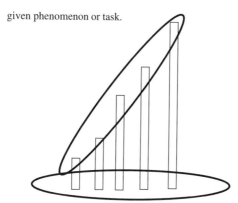

Source: Stephen Farenga and Daniel Ness. Adapted from Jean Piaget, *The Origins of Intelligence in Children*. New York: International Universities Press, 1936.

bottles haphazardly. At concrete operations, children's actions demonstrated more organization—a typical strategy was to pour C into each flask. However, they would then decide to discontinue the activity. When questioned, these children usually said that there wasn't anything more they could do. Thus, their actions revealed some organization, as we could have expected from their systematic behavior on conservation tasks. But they entertained only a limited range of possibilities.

At the level of formal operations, however, the adolescents worked systematically in terms of all possibilities when attempting to find the liquids that will make yellow. Some started out by trying various combinations and then realized that they had better make sure that they would include all possible combinations, so they wrote them down before acting further. Formal operational individuals are able to generalize at a much higher level in that they seek patterns without having to observe the results. For example, in another task, a sequence of ten squares going from left to right will have the following colors—green, blue, red, green, blue, red, and so on. Formal operational individuals are able to determine the color of the thirtieth red square, the forty-first green square, the nth blue square, and so forth, by identifying patterns and writing them down.

PIAGET'S METHODS OF INQUIRY

Piaget utilized two prominent forms of data collection for the development of his research program: systematic observation and the clinical interview. Despite his vast body of literature, Piaget discusses the methods of systematic observation and the clinical interview only briefly in the introductory chapter of his book entitled *The Child's Conception of the World* (1960).

Systematic Observation

For Piaget, the method of observation was perhaps the only way to tap into the development of organisms that do not possess any form of language capacity (i.e., speaking, reading, or writing). Infants, of course, would be categorized in this manner. Piaget's well-known observations (what he referred to as "pure observation") were with his own three children (Lucienne, Jacqueline, and Laurent). Piaget kept painstakingly extensive records on each one of his children as infants and young children—a process which took the course of several years. It was during this period (1930s) that Piaget developed a thorough progression of the cognitive development of infants. At this time, he discovered the six substages of the sensorimotor period of intellectual development.

Clinical Interview

Piaget used the clinical interview for a number of purposes. Perhaps the most important purpose of conducting the clinical interview was to identify specific characteristics of the primary stages of intellectual development, particularly the last three (preoperational, concrete operational, and formal operational). Piaget investigated several intellectual domains as a means of identifying these characteristics, for example, mathematical thinking, scientific thinking, language development, and moral development. Whether for purposes of exploration or supporting hypotheses for the establishment of a theory, Piaget structured the clinical interview in a very clear and concise manner. Piaget was an expert interviewer. His strategies as an interviewer entailed a number of elements. First, he would structure the interview without telling the child the answer to a particular problem. Doing so would indeed defeat the purpose of conducting the interview because, as stated above, according to Piaget, telling or teaching impedes learning and discovery. Likewise, Piaget would not provide hints or leading questions, for this, too, would prevent the researcher from tapping a child's knowledge of a particular domain. Second, Piaget would provide an organized structure, or protocol, for the interview. Doing so avoids digression from the main topic of discussion. In addition, Piaget used counter suggestion as a means of identifying a child's genuine understanding of a subject or an idea. Counter suggestion is used by an interviewer when a child produces a correct response to a problem, but may not verify the response in any way. For example, in the problem 25 + 16, the child might point to the 5 and 6 as the ones column and the 2 and 1 as the tens column. The interviewer will subsequently ask the child if the 5 and 6 is the tens column and the 2 and 1 is the ones column as a form of counter suggestion—the incorrect response. The child's subsequent response will then determine whether she has genuine knowledge of the ones label and the tens label.

Present-day researchers in developmental psychology and education make use of the clinical interview in several ways. The first way is to validate an accepted theory. For example, a researcher can perform an interview on a four-year-old child to determine the validity that children less than seven years of age lack the ability to conserve number or mass. A second reason for conducting a clinical interview is to support one's hypothesis concerning an individual's cognitive level or ability. Conducting several clinical interviews of this kind may lead to the establishment of a theoretical framework. For example, a researcher might establish the hypothesis that adults without formal schooling do not surpass the informal deductive stage of geometric thinking (level 3 in Dina and Pierre Van Hiele's theory of geometric development, which states that in the third level of geometric development, individuals are capable of identifying and comparing geometric figures based on their properties—e.g., rectangles have four right angles and opposite sides which are parallel (see Woodward and Hamel 1994). To test the researcher's hypothesis, several clinical interviews can be conducted on adults in, say, two or more age groups.

PIAGET AND EDUCATION

Piaget's theoretical framework has had a tremendous impact on educational programs throughout the world. First, many past and present scholars and practitioners consider him the pioneer of constructivism. Although Rousseau is credited with an alternative view of Locke's blank tablet view of humans at early stages of development, Piaget was perhaps the first (Heinz Werner is one possible exception) to support the organismic perspective with empirical data. The organismic perspective led to the view that children are not born as blank slates; rather, their experiences with the environment foster their cognitive development. The constructivist approach altered American education from a primarily behaviorist model prior to the 1970s to a more developmental approach in recent decades.

Stephen J. Farenga and Daniel Ness

REFERENCES

Ginsburg, H.P., and S. Opper. (1989) *Piaget's Theory of Intellectual Development.* Englewood Cliffs, NJ: Prentice Hall.

Phillips, J.L. (1981) *Piaget's Theory: A Primer.* San Francisco: Freeman Publishers.

Piaget, Jean. (1960). *The Child's Conception of the World.* New York: Routledge Kegan and Paul.

Piaget, Jean, and Barbel Inhelder. (2000) *The Psychology of the Child,* trans. Helen Weaver. New York: Basic Books.

Woodward, Ernest, and Thomas Hamel. (1994) *Visualized Geometry: A Van Hiele Level Approach.* Portland, ME: J. Weston Walsh.

PLATO

Plato (427–347 B.C.E.) was a preeminent Greek philosopher who had great influence on the conception of the observable world and its imperfections in comparison to the unobservable and unchanging forms. Born in Athens and raised in a wealthy aristocratic family, Plato pursued a strong interest in entering a career as a politician or statesman. As an adolescent, Plato served under the tutelage of his teacher and mentor Socrates. His decision to enter the field of politics was cut short at the age of twenty-eight in 399 B.C.E., when he found out that Socrates was sentenced to death for a number of allegations, including the suspected corrupting of youth. Plato was greatly influenced by his travels to Italy and Sicily, where he became acquainted with mathematics and its connections with philosophical inquiry. He was particularly intrigued with the camaraderie of Pythagoras and his associates and their development of a deductive approach to mathematical thinking and its application to philosophy. Upon his return from Sicily in 387 B.C.E. Plato founded the Academy, perhaps the most renowned school of philosophical thought. It was at the Academy that Plato worked with his most famous student, Aristotle, who entered the Academy at the age of seventeen.

A "FIRST" PHILOSOPHY OF EDUCATION

Bertrand Russell's famous remark was that the entire corpus of post-Platonic philosophical discussion is only a footnote to the dialogues of Plato. When we consider the philosophy of education, however, Russell's maxim still holds—namely, that the entire corpus of writings in the philosophy of education is but a footnote to the work of Plato, in particular, the dialogue entitled "Meno." In "Meno," (translated by Jowett in the 1937 edition of Plato's *Dialogues*) Plato's view on educative processes is clearly demonstrated. In this dialogue, Socrates interrogates his acquaintance Meno on a servant boy's knowledge of the relationship between the sides of a square and a diagonal that bisects it. In Pythagorean terms, the square of the length of the diagonal—also the hypotenuse of each of the two congruent triangles formed—is equal to the squares of the sum of two sides of the square. This knowledge, Socrates points out, is a self-evident truth that even the servant boy can deduce by himself. Philosophers and historians cannot agree on whether Plato's dialogue "Meno" is historically accurate. The main point here, however, is that Plato's position on the origin of knowledge is demonstrated through discourse between either a real Socrates or a fictional one.

In addition to knowledge, in the dialogue "Meno," Plato also asks whether virtue is teachable. For Plato, the pursuit of knowledge, which is founded on self-evident truths, assumes the paradox that we always knew what we learn—that is, our knowledge of something we learn is not based on what we see, hear, or touch. Rather, it is based on recollection and making connections between what we already know and what the problem is at hand. Meno, then, serves as the foundational text to the ongoing debate between the rationalist, empiricist, and material schools of thought in the philosophical enterprise. It is evident, then, that Plato believed that the role of education should presuppose one's pursuit of justice. The individual and the state are both responsible for maintaining and preserving a strong educational system because without one, the state runs the risk of corrupting society through immorality, thus affecting both personal conduct and the governance of the land.

Plato also believed that one can achieve a high level of intellect and a strong moral base through mathematics. He asks how it is possible to teach the youth to apprehend the most general and absolute norms and, at the same time, employ them for the purposes of self-examination in developing both knowledge and conduct. In preadolescence, Plato emphasized the importance of virtue. For Plato, the development of habit was the only way to lead a virtuous life. The health of soul and body, according to Plato, was to be conditioned through music and literature and by diet and exercise. However, he stipulated that certain forms of art and literature lead to the corruption of society. Upon adolescence, the educated person would then enter a second form of education—one that consisted of arithmetic, geometry, music, and astronomy, all to be studied from their theoretical perspectives rather than in their practical applications to industry or to the military.

Plato defends this form of curriculum in "Republic" (See Jowett's translation, 1937) because, through abstraction, the educated person can seek the truth through unchanging forms. Aside from his conviction that reality is mathematical in nature since it could be measured, he was fascinated by the notion that mathematics was a system of concepts predisposed to precise definition and rigorous development. Plato was interested in the ease with which mathematics could transform the concrete attributes of objects (i.e., size, shape, color, thickness) into abstract immutable ideas, free of material existence. For Plato, mathematics was seen as the penultimate rank with regard to knowledge: through mathematics, one can draw necessary conclusions within the rules and limitations of the idea discussed. From a theoretical perspective, music and astronomy, too, exhibited mathematical structures and thus qualify as educating in abstraction. The highest level of knowledge, according to Plato, was dialectic, for it is in this domain that deductive relations characteristic of mathematics were discovered to obtain reality itself.

PLATO'S VIEW OF INSTRUCTION

Plato was a contemporary of Isocrates (436–338 B.C.E.), the well-known Sophist philosopher. Unlike Plato, Isocrates was remunerated for his services as a teacher and as an instructor and advisor to well-to-do Athenian youth whose parents (mostly fathers) encouraged their sons to become public servants and statesmen. One of the key issues of disagreement between Plato's philosophy and that of Isocrates had to do with how humans come to know things. For Plato, knowledge has to do with self-evident truths that are based almost entirely on certainty. Isocrates, on the other hand, purported to the beliefs of the other Sophists in that he posited that what humans come to know has little to do with absolute outcomes, and instead are much more probabilistic in nature. Plato also distinguished himself from the Sophist tradition by dichotomizing knowledge with opinion. It was not the separation of these ideas that contrasted Plato from Sophistic thinkers like Isocrates; rather, it was Plato's definitions of these terms that set him apart from the Sophists. Knowledge, Plato says, is based on certainty and eternal principles while opinion lacks reliability and validity and merely serves ephemeral ends. The Sophists would probably not disagree with Plato with regard to the meaning of opinion. In contrast, they defined knowledge to be far from certain and probabilistic—that is, one cannot apply absolute terminology (e.g., all, none, never, always) to situations or events (Barrow 1976).

Plato also made strong use of the cave metaphor in the allegory of the cave from the dialogue "Republic." Scholars seem to concur that the Socrates in "Republic" may not be historically accurate (Blankenship 1996). A number of classical Greek scholars refer often to this Socrates, usually discussed in the middle and late dialogues, as "Plato's Socrates." Nevertheless, Socrates presented the hypothetical scenario of prisoners who have been chained and are unable to move; they can only "see" the shadows that have been cast by artificial light, and interpret the shadows as real entities. For Plato, the initial goal of education was to avoid the artificiality of shadows, and instead approach the actual representations of objects and ideas. Although objects were considered unreliable due to their ephemeral and empirical (that is, sense driven) qualities, ideas and what we understand and know are not. Concepts of things do not have any physical qualities. Thus, in order to transcend the senses as they are related to objects and one's sensual experiences with them, the individual must make use of abstract thinking. This form of thinking, most effective through the postulates and axioms associated wit mathematical logic, allows one to identify the universal nature of an object or concept.

We know of the so-called Socratic Method not through Socrates, who incidentally wrote nothing, but through Plato. Plato argued that in order for one to search the truth, an appropriate method of questioning must be devised and employed. The pursuit of knowledge is not achieved solely through directives, or the dicta of so-called authoritative figures like the Sophists. Rather, learning takes place through discourse and the ability to engage in self-examination.

PLATO AND EDUCATION TODAY

Without question, Plato's views with regard to metaphysical characteristics of animate and inanimate beings are staples of Western culture and in many respects serve as one of the bedrocks of the modern education system. However, Plato's ideas, not unlike any of the other educational thinkers discussed, have been critiqued throughout history. First, unlike a number of philosophers before and after him (the Chinese thinker Confucius included), Plato did not believe that all people were capable of leading prosperous, introspective lives and possibly filling leadership positions. Instead, Plato reserved the leadership role, and thus formalized education, to the elite class, which he believed was both ethically and intellectually capable of rule and leadership. The majority of the citizens were to obey and follow the set of laws put forth by the ruling class. Consequently, Plato's ideas have often been considered authoritarian in nature. For example, urging the cultivation of morals in society, Plato believed that most infants should be removed from the guardianship of their biological parents and instead be raised by the state, which would then provide youth with a proper education whose curriculum would consist of both in-

tellectual subjects—mathematics, literature, music, natural studies (i.e., the sciences)—and physical and athletic training. This so-called proper education would cultivate knowledge (intellectual ability), conduct (ethics and morality), and preparation for leadership (governance). He argues in favor of censorship of any form of art that disparages good behavior and fosters unethical conduct. Only an elite class of philosopher-kings possesses the ability to preside over a state or nation. In addition, although Plato believed that women were capable of leadership positions, his writings seem to be biased toward male rule of the state.

With the criticisms aside, Plato's contributions to the field of education cannot be overestimated. His exhortation for the emphasis of both intellectual and moral education is often seen as self-evident by most leaders of education and educational administrators today (Dominic 1995). Plato's beliefs influenced a number of twentieth-century thinkers, like Edward L. Thorndike and William Kilpatrick, who helped shape the course of conventional educational practices, and at the same time, impacted the thinking of contemporary constructivists, like Jean Piaget and Jerome Bruner, who have advocated the importance of self-reflection and the two-way discourse between student and teacher as a means of searching for the truth.

Daniel Ness and Stephen J. Farenga

REFERENCES

Barrow, Robin. (1976) *Plato and Education.* London: Routledge and Kegan Paul.
Blankenship, J. David. (1996) Education and the arts in Plato's Republic. *Journal of Education* 178: 67–98.
Plato. (1937) *The Dialogues of Plato,* 2 vols, trans. Benjamin Jowett. New York: Random House.
Scott, Dominic. (1995) *Recollection and Experience: Plato's Theory of Learning and Its Successors.* New York: Cambridge University Press.

JEAN-JACQUES ROUSSEAU

Jean-Jacques Rousseau (1712–1778) was perhaps one of the most influential philosophers of the eighteenth century whose work on human nature and child development carved a niche for future educators of the so-called constructivist tradition. Educational researchers and philosophers of education have generally pitted Rousseau's view of human development in diametric opposition to that of his English predecessor, John Locke (1632–1714).

For Locke, in terms of coming to know the world, the infant or young child is viewed as *tabula rasa*— a blank slate. That is, the young human being must be "turned on" (analogous to a machine) by an adult so that he or she will be able to learn about the world. The child, then, becomes neutral as he or she is "sculpted" by society. In stark contrast to Locke's worldview of human development, Rousseau saw children as being born good, but society will have an effect on keeping them good or corrupting them.

ROUSSEAUNIAN VIEW OF CHILD DEVELOPMENT

Rousseau published his world famous novel, *Emile*, in 1762, in which he established his premise that the natural state of humans at birth is good. For Rousseau, infants have an innate capacity that will serve as a means to help them develop into good and valuable adults. What we find in *Emile* is an entirely diametric view of child development compared to what we find in the work of Locke. Rousseau argues that society as a whole and its agents—parents, educators, and clergy—corrupt the young child and serve as the vehicles that exacerbate the problems of youth. Rousseau, then, concludes that the best way to raise children into valuable and virtuous adults is for parents and other adult figures to clear the path for the young child and remove society's obstacles so that each child can develop at his or her own rate. Children do not need the ills and evils of society thrust upon them as they develop into adults.

Moreover, unlike earlier mechanistic, materialist views of child development, Rousseau did not view young children as miniature adults. Nor did he view young children as blank slates, whose minds are seen as empty cells until the adult imposes or thrusts ideas upon them. Rather, the infant is viewed, in Rousseaunian terms, as a perfect organism that adapts to each stage in life in a positive manner. This view clearly serves as a foundational position for future stage theorists—like Heinz Werner and Jean Piaget—

who became towering figures in the fields of epistemology, cognitive, and intellectual development.

ROUSSEAU'S ORGANISMIC WORLDVIEW

Rousseau presented a second philosophical position known as the organismic worldview. In this view, humans are seen as organisms in a holistic sense. The organismic worldview can be described by several characteristics. First, unlike the mechanistic, Lockean worldview, the organismic worldview identifies humans as inherently active agents in the world. The basic structure of their nature is one of change, not stability or inactivity. Second, humans are viewed as self-motivating agents in the world. They need not be turned on or provoked by external influences. In the Rousseaunian worldview, then, nature—the internal, biological influences of the human—is the key function of human behavior. Third, in order to know something that is new, we do so by reconstructing what we already know. Humans create reality rather than absorbing copies of it. So, as the Lockeans would view human knowledge as the absorption of information, the Rousseanians would view knowledge as reconstruction and creation.

A fourth characteristic of Rousseau's organismic approach has to do with viewing humans in a holistic manner. That is, human behavior should be understood as an entire system or as a structural whole rather than using an atomistic or corpuscular theory whereby human behavior is studied in terms of its component parts. The whole, then, is not equal to the sum of its parts. Rather, it is greater than the sum of its parts. And finally, generalizations and universals are seen as having greater importance than individual differences. Accordingly, the organismic worldview focuses on what is typical of human development, not on environmental interventions that serve as obstacles to developmental processes.

IMPLICATIONS OF THE ROUSSEAUNIAN WORLDVIEW

Without question, Rousseau's philosophical approach to human development served as a springboard for later philosophers (e.g., Henri Bergson and John Dewey), developmental theorists and epistemologists (e.g., Heinz Werner and Jean Piaget), and educators (e.g., Johann Friedrich Herbart, Friederich Froebel, Maria Montessori). His ideas were also foundational for theories related to human development in terms of stages or periods.

Although Rousseau's worldview served as the groundwork for future theorists, it was by no means the first philosophical approach that embraced an active, organismic model as the primary representation of human behavior. Even in the fourth century B.C.E., Plato's metaphysical identified human behavior in this light. One primary example can be found in his dialogue entitled *Meno,* in which we find Socrates questioning Meno about the young servant boy's knowledge of the length of a diagonal bisecting line of a square and its relationship to one of the sides. The boy knew the answer to this relationship (i.e., the Pythagorean Theorem) not because he was told or taught it, but because he constructed this understanding through the self-evident, inherent structure of the relationship. Other later pre-Rousseaunian philosophical discussions that embraced humans as active agents in the world included those by other so-called rationalist thinkers like René Descartes and Benedict Spinoza.

Stephen J. Farenga and Daniel Ness

REFERENCES

Crain, William C. (1999) *Theories of Human Development: Concepts and Applications.* 4th ed. Englewood Cliffs, NJ: Prentice Hall.
Goldhaber, Dale E. (2000) *Theories of Human Development: Integrative Perspectives.* Mountain View, CA: Mayfield Publishers.
Plato. (1937). "Meno." In *Dialogues of Plato,* ed. and trans. Benjamin Jowett. New York: Random House.

SOCRATES

Socrates (469–399 B.C.E.) was a preeminent Greek philosopher, whose well-known saying was that an examined life is one worth living. Although classical Greek scholars are fairly clear as to how Socrates lived his life and the contributions he made, there is little, if any, evidence that he wrote anything at all. This point in and of itself is remarkable, given that society generally associates intellectual contributions with written output. Socrates, teacher of Plato and often informally referred to as the greatest of all teachers, is a clear example of a teacher whose educational goal or end was that of searching for a virtuous life, and not of immediate success as a politician or acquiring immediate skills for a temporary purpose. Without question, this very theme of Socrates' agenda distinguished him from his counterpart philosophers of the time, such as Protagoras, Isocrates, Thrasymachus, and other members of the Sophist tradition. In contrast to Socrates, however, the Sophists were paid for their services as teachers, and were highly regarded as the best teachers for careers in the most esteemed occupations at the time—law, politics, and even art and music. Socrates became known for the pursuit of teaching virtue because the very subject was so elusive in terms of observable evidence (Broudy 1963). Nevertheless, Socrates often questioned Sophist philosophers about whether they taught virtue. Although the Sophists claimed that they did, Socrates demonstrated that they could not even define virtue let alone teach it. At best, Socrates argued, the Sophists taught a set of skills that could only be applied to ephemeral success.

Socrates is often referred to as a gadfly; part of what contributed to Socrates' eventual trial and subsequent execution had to do with his approach to finding the truth. Through his general delivery and questioning methods, he angered numerous individuals and embarrassed them, many of whom were Sophist philosophers. Socrates was sent to trial in 399 B.C.E. Classical scholars have indicated that he was permitted to select his punishment: (1) he could be banished from Athens, or (2) he could select execution by drinking poison hemlock. Socrates chose the latter more out of necessity and principle than of will.

EXHORTATION AND THE SOCRATIC METHOD

The problem with identifying Socrates' life work has a great deal to do with the reliability and consistency of primary resources. We know of Socrates' life contributions from two primary sources: (1) Plato, perhaps his most famous student, and (2) the written records of his neighbor Xenophon. His role in education emanates from his approach to argument and rhetoric. Researchers of classical Greek thought, and society seemed to agree, that the early extant dialogues of Plato are perhaps the most reliable, in part because some were written during the period when Plato was a pupil of Socrates. Regardless of the time in which a particular dialogue was written, Plato demonstrates Socrates in highest form with his interlocutors and even with his pupils. For example, while walking to the home of Callias to hear the well-known rhetorician and sophist Protagoras speak, Socrates interrogates his pupil Hippocrates:

But are you aware of the danger which you are incurring? If you were going to commit your body to some one, who might do good or harm to it, would you not carefully consider and ask the opinion of your friends and kindred, and deliberate many days as to whether you should give him the care of your body? But when the soul is in question, which you hold to be of far more value than the body, and upon the good or evil of which depends the wellbeing of your all—about this you never consulted either with your father or with your brother or with any of us who are your companions. But no sooner does this foreigner appear, than you instantly commit your soul to his keeping. (Plato 1953, 137–38)

As this passage indicates, Socrates, through the use of exhortation, seems to have put Hippocrates into a state of anxiety by questioning his pupil's state of mind by insisting to follow the words of Protagoras. Socrates uses exhortation effectively as a means of illuminating reality and bringing out the truth during conversation and debate. Oftentimes, this resulted in jolting or even unnerving his interlocutor or pupil to the point where the listener feels uneasy and fails to support his argument. This notion of "illumination" can be seen in *Republic* of Plato, specifically in the famous allegory of the cave (see Jowett's translation of "Republic," 1937). The chained prisoners—who reflect the general public—must overcome their passions and desires in order to be unchained. After bondage, the prisoners will leave the dark cave and be jolted by the light outside. This action may contribute to a radical change in one's mindset and perspective on life. Based on this format of argumentation, Socrates was thus seen as a provoker and a gadfly, especially to those individuals, like the Sophists, who felt satisfied with their skills and knowledge.

Socrates is often seen not only as a philosopher and teacher but also as perhaps the first psychoanalyst. He would often begin conversation with an interlocutor, who would view the initial question as something too obvious for continued discussion. Nevertheless, Socrates would demonstrate that the subject of discussion—oftentimes about virtue, courage, or justice—was actually not so obvious after all. The opponent of Socrates would unveil his ignorance, even to the point of eliciting embarrassment and anger. When the anger was directed at oneself, Socrates would employ positive discussion as a form of dialectical self-examination and reflection. As seen from this scenario, the teacher is not merely a stimulus or an individual who merely provides a ripe environment for growth and development; rather the teacher is a leader who guides the student. The student must follow the teacher because the teacher's life is dedicated to scholarship and learning.

SOCRATES AND THE ROLE OF TEACHING AND LEARNING

An accurate way to identify the educational method of Socrates (and subsequently Plato) as it differs from those of other thinkers is to compare and contrast his teaching doctrine with those of his contemporaries—namely, the Sophists themselves. Due to their systematic documentation of rhetorical form, the Sophists viewed the act and practice of teaching as a systematized, mechanized operation that fostered imitation. That is, a teacher becomes a teacher through a great deal of imitation. For the Sophists, then, the practice of teaching was algorithmic; you follow specific steps in all teaching situations, and a certain set of steps was associated with specific skills to be learned.

Not so for Socrates and his followers. For them, the role of the teacher was far from mechanistic. The product of any lesson for any subject was not merely a correct or incorrect response or answer. Rather, the interaction between teacher and pupil was one in which intellectual development was paired with dispositional consciousness. For example, in addition to strong content knowledge, to become an architect, one must have good judgment when embarking on a project. So, for Socrates, the role of education was to seek the truth in any subject one wishes to study. Education does not consist of a set of steps to follow, for this does not yield perfection in a particular discipline.

Daniel Ness and Stephen J. Farenga

REFERENCES

Broudy, Harry S. (1963) Socrates and the teaching machine. *Phi Delta Kappan* 44: 243–47.
Plato. (1937) *The Dialogues of Plato.* 2 vols. Trans. Benjamin Jowett. New York: Random House.
———. (1953) "Protagoras." In *The Dialogues of Plato,* 4th ed., trans. Benjamin Jowett. Oxford: Oxford University Press.

BURRHUS FREDRICK SKINNER

Perhaps the most recognized behaviorist in the history of the psychological learning theory movement was Burrhus Fredrick Skinner (1905–1990). Skinner spent most of his time at Harvard University with a short hiatus in the 1940s at the University of Minnesota and another at the University of Indiana. The behaviorism of John B. Watson, one of Skinner's predecessors, succeeded chiefly at the level of polemic; a behavioral science could not be developed using no more than classical (Pavlovian) conditioning techniques. As discussed below, Skinner went far beyond classical conditioning techniques to support behaviorism and, in fact, influenced the field of education for several decades during the twentieth century.

EARLY YEARS AND INTERESTS

Burrhus Frederick (henceforth, B. F.) Skinner was born in 1905 in the small town of Susquehanna, Pennsylvania. Skinner was fascinated with building and construction as a child. He also developed an intimate liking for literature and composition. As a graduate of English literature from Hamilton College in New York, Skinner tried to earn a living as a writer. His other deep interest was psychology and eventually he decided to enter that field. He was considerably influenced by the work of Ernst Mach, one of the great physicists of the second half of the nineteenth century. When planes fly faster than the speed of sound, they fly in terms of Mach numbers. In addition to physics, Mach wrote influentially in the philosophy of science. It was Mach's conviction that philosophy and metaphysics should be removed from science. Science was concerned with the ob-

servable world and with a systematic treatment of what is observed. When addressing the definition of scientific law, Mach argues that a scientific law is solely a systematic description of experience. For Mach, the grounding of science is at the level of observation and experience. This strongly influenced not only B. F. Skinner but also an entire generation of scientists in the twentieth century.

Skinner was committed to a descriptive science of behavior; that is, a non-theoretical science of behavior, something akin more to engineering than to a form of theoretical physics. He was interested in how to build behavior into a system and how to predict and control that behavior. The first development of Skinner's thought to reach the public was a book written in 1938 entitled the *Behavior of Organisms.* It became a classic for generations of behaviorists, who would refer to it as the B of O. The book served as an argument for what the subject matter of psychology should be, a statement of what constitutes reliable data in the field of psychology, and perhaps most important, something of a declaration of independence in the discipline.

A scientific psychology based on observable behavior does not have to tie itself to physiology or chemistry or any other subject. It can prosecute its own agenda with its own tools at hand. This was a clarion call for any number of psychologists at the time. Psychology even before Wilhelm Wundt (discussed below) was always seeking scientific status and always seeking to define itself in ways that would allow one to distinguish between it and medicine, physiology, ethology, and so forth.

PSYCHOLOGY'S BREAK FROM PHYSIOLOGY

Skinner questioned the historic dependence between psychology and physiology. Wilhelm Wundt, often considered the first experimental psychologist, used physiology to influence his psychological method. Throughout the nineteenth century, the scientists we would identify as influential in the history of psychology were tying psychological processes with brain processes as they do today. A developed and scientific psychology would be a functional neuroanatomy, determining how different events in different places in the brain give rise to thoughts, dreams, associations, learning, memory, and the like.

When Skinner questions the nature of the relationship between a scientific psychology and physiology, he answers "none." It is nothing with which a psychologist needs to be concerned. The facts of behavior will survive any theoretical construction we impose on them. For Skinner, from the perspective of a behavioral scientist who has studied the conditions that established behavior (i.e., conditions in the environment), if you opened the zipper of the animal and looked inside and found nothing all, you would still have the facts of behavior. You would still know the relationship between events in the environment, and systematic alterations in the behavior of organisms—nothing is added to the information by finding out that there are nerves, blood vessels, and the like; nothing would detract from these findings if their were nothing inside at all.

Skinner argues that scientific behaviorism can be developed without waiting for the physiologists to solve their problems. One does not have to wait to know everything about the brain in order to figure out what it is that determines the course of behavior. A purely descriptive science of behavior has to be a science that is extremely lean in its terminology; it cannot make use of theory terms as if they had some actual ontological standing. Problems of definition have to be solved for this discipline to develop. Mentalistic, or unquantifiable, terms (or those terms that are associated with idiosyncratic sensations) must be avoided. These terms presuppose an independent private mental life that only the introspective mental individual has access to, and you only find out because the individual tells you (e.g., "I'm hungry!" or "I understand . . .").

To shun these terms, one adopts operational definitions: you define your chief terms by reference to the actual operations or methods you would use to realize or produce whatever it is to which that term is referring. Take the motivational term "hunger." In casual discourse, the way you explain why someone is going to the counter and ordering something and eating it is "they must be hungry." When one says, "they must be hungry," there is a reference to some internal state, something that only they can know about for certain; it is quite private. You cannot see hunger or anything about it. The term hunger, then, becomes some a type of mentalistic term.

Suppose you want to study the relationship between behaviors of consumption like eating or drinking. The question, then, is whether it is possible to observe hunger. This is not possible. Instead, one is going to study hunger in relation to some other observable element—namely, time. By hunger, Skinner refers to the number of hours of food deprivation. The interesting thing about defining hunger that way is from laboratory to laboratory, country to country, year to year, hours of food deprivation is hours of food deprivation, no matter where you are. One does not have to ask whether the organisms are equally hungry. To determine whether they were equally anything, it would be necessary to look for equality in their behavior. Again, it is all external—not internal. The determinants of behavior are found outside the organism, not inside the organism. Behavior is a response to events in the environment. What an organism has to do is to survive in a real, physical world; it does this by behaving in response to the challenges presented by that world. Operational definitions are helpful in that they allow you to establish comparable laboratory procedures from one laboratory to another, and they also allow you to understand the meaning of terms as different investigators use them.

LEARNING THEORY

Learning theory follows the philosophical tradition of John Locke, which claims that behavior is formed by the external environment. Ivan Pavlov is credited to have identified the basic tenets of learning theory. Pavlov's work served as a springboard for future theorists like Edward L. Thorndike, John B. Watson, and Skinner, soon after. In 1938, when *Behavior of Organisms* was published, the world was not ready for Skinner's behaviorism and theory of learning, possibly as a result of its association with genetic psychology. By 1945, no one was interested in genetic psychology, that is, predetermined types. It was not until the 1950s that interest picked up. Keller and Schoenfeld (1950) decided that the way to put behaviorism and learning theory on the map was to arrange an entire psychology curriculum around principles of behavior. By the middle and late 1950s, Skinner became a nationally and internationally recognized figure in the field of psychology.

Early Influences

To identify what is involved in Skinner's behaviorism, we first look at studies from the end of the nineteenth century by Edward L. Thorndike (1898), the well-known professor of educational psychology from Teachers College, Columbia University, who studied the behavior of cats inside cages with little loops hanging down. If the cat puts a paw through the loop and pulls on it, the cage opens up and the cat can get a piece of food. Thorndike published the first animal learning curves. He plots the amount of time it takes the cat to get out of the cage as a function of the number of trials (*Animal Intelligence* 1898).

Skinner identified some problems with Thorndike's approach, however. First, Thorndike used mentalistic language: The behavior that gives rise to a satisfying state of affairs tends to be repeated; the behavior that gives rise to an unpleasant or painful state of affairs tends never to be repeated. He refers to this as a law that covers all behavior—law of effect. Skinner says that Thorndike had the right idea in that he was looking at the right kind of behavior. He was looking at the kind of behavior an animal uses to get through the world and to secure what is necessary for survival. That is what psychology should be studying. Not the Pavlovian kind—not with a dog locked in a cage, powdered food in the mouth, and saliva measured. What does this represent? This has nothing to do with the Darwinian context in which creatures have to adapt themselves to the demand characteristics of the situation. In that latter realm, the behavior that counts is musculoskeletal behavior—the moving, the grasping, and the running (Bjork 1997). Another problem, according to Skinner, is Thorndike's laboratory setup. Thorndike picked the wrong form of species (cat) and the wrong type of environment. Skinner believed that in order to precisely measure animal behavior, it is necessary to identify a laboratory animal that does not need a large space to move around. A cat, for example, often runs too fast for an experimenter to measure behavior. Moreover, a smaller space is more conducive for measuring behavior since the experimenter does not have to spend time moving from one location to another (Bjork 1997).

The Skinner Box and Fixed Ratio Schedule

Skinner developed a box, commonly referred to as a Skinner Box, that allowed for the limitation of behavior. He would put an animal (most often a rat) in

this relatively confining enclosure. He wanted to limit responses to those that were readily measurable and quantifiable. The following scenario illustrates Skinner's method of observing behavior based on stimulus response.

A lever is sticking out of the box—and the rat is in the box. You only find this animal in psychology laboratories. The rat has been deprived of food in the box. The rat sniffs around the inner sides of the box, tries to get out of the box—the lever is sticking out. The animal might lean on it for balance or sit on it. And the microswitch is closed. A little food magazine tray is turned and a pellet of food drops down into a food well just underneath the lever. The animal then goes to the food well, lifts up the pellet, and eats it. One notices that there is a little less time sniffing around the top corners of the cage, and more time spent around the lever. Within an hour, the animal will be pressing the bar, in fact leaning back and pressing continuously. (Crain 1999)

This is the result of what Skinner calls "continuous reinforcement" (Crain, 1999). This is where every bar pressed results in a reinforcement. An operational definition of reinforcement is the following: A stimulus is a reinforcer when it alters the probability of the behavior that produces it. Any stimulus that significantly increases the likelihood of the behavior that brings it about is a positive reinforcer. And any stimulus that significantly decreases the likelihood of the behavior that brings it about is a negative reinforcer. In short, it is the animal's behavior that defines the reinforcer, not the psychologist trying to get into the mind of animals (as a psychoanalyst would).

When Skinner was in Minnesota and using pigeons in his experiments, he developed a method of delivering a reinforcer per peck and every other peck—and you can rearrange the food portions for every three pecks. This is an example of partial reinforcement. Not every response is reinforced but every fraction of responses. These are referred to as schedules of reinforcement. For FR3—fixed ratio three—you get a reinforcer for every three responses (or pecks). You could have an FR20, FR50, and so forth. Skinner was able to show that you can increase response rates to very high levels.

Variable Ratio Schedule

The most remarkable of the schedules of reinforcement is the variable ratio schedule. The animal starts out on continuous reinforcement. Every response receives a pellet. You now build in a fixed ratio schedule with a low FR value and then you start to stretch out the FR requirements, to an extent where one now moves to a low variable ratio schedule. What that means is this: If one moves to a VR2, over a long run of numerous trials, every second response (e.g., a pigeon's peck, a rat touching a lever) will receive a reinforcer, a food pellet. But one never knows from trial to trial which response will receive one. This is determined randomly.

The experimenter can then change from VR2 to VR5, or any other variable ratio. Virtually for the rest of the animal's life, you can disconnect the feeder, put the animal in a test chamber, and it will press the bar ad infinitum. Skinner refers to this as gambling behavior. Variable Ratio Reinforcement is the sort of schedule that will maintain stable rates of behavior indefinitely. To use introspective, mentalistic language: How does someone at a slot machine know when to stop pulling the lever—the answer is "never" because it may pay off next time, next time, next time. Nothing in the acquisition of the behavior provides a cue as to what condition must be satisfied for a reinforcer to be delivered. For example, if you take fixed ratio reinforcement you know that for every three pecks of a pigeon, a reinforcer is delivered. Now, if the feeder is disconnected and the pigeon pecks three more times and nothing happened, then the pigeon will eventually stop pecking. But suppose this behavior has been reshaped by variable ratio reinforcement. It is then difficult to determine what the contingency is that must be met in order for a reward to be given. This is one of the most powerful displays that behaviorist psychology was able to produce: the ability to maintain behavior over long stretches of time in an animal that is virtually untiring in responding even if a reinforcer has not been delivered in days, weeks, and even months. This is a powerful illustration of how events in the environment can impose extraordinary reliability on the behavior of organisms.

AVOIDANCE CONDITIONING

An animal is put in a box that has an electrified floor; a light comes on, and ten seconds after the light goes off, the floor is electrified. There is a little barrier that the animal can jump over and thereby escape from the shock. After one or two of these trials, the animal is put in the box, the light is turned on, and he jumps over the barrier. When put back into the box at a later time, he jumps over the barrier, and jumps over the barrier continually—whether the floor is electrified or not. Perhaps there were only one or two punishing stimuli.

The rat stands on the floor, the light comes on, and 15 milliamps come through the paws, and he is half a foot off the ground. The next time the light comes on, the rat is not sensing whether the shock is going to come this time. Instead, he runs. And he keeps running. This is again a powerful illustration of how an event in the environment can get a controlling hold on behavior indefinitely. There are parents who cannot determine why an offspring stops a particular behavior. One scenario might include the following dialogue: "Is there any physical abuse in this family?" The parents say, "No." Do you use corporal punishment? The parents say, "No." Did you ever hit your child? The parents say, "Well, only once." This is the classical example of avoidance conditioning. One does not have to do it more than once in order for the organism to behave in such a way as to avoid that environment.

SKINNER'S INFLUENCE ON LEARNING WITH REGARD TO THE FIELD OF EDUCATION

According to Skinner, there are three variables that influence the process of learning. First, there must be a situation in order for a behavior to occur. Next, a behavior must take place. The third variable is the consequence of the behavior. If, in a particular situation, a person exhibits a distinct behavior or response from a class of responses known as an operant, and if this individual is reinforced by this response, then it is likely, according to Skinner, that learning will occur.

In one of his well-known books on human behavior, *The Technology of Teaching* (1968), Skinner concludes that within the first four years of schooling, a young child will need in the area of 25,000 reinforcements in order to succeed as a student; however, children receive only about 3,000 to 4,000 such reinforcements. In this important book on teaching and learning, Skinner builds the theme around learning as a science and teaching as an art. He provides an overview as to why teachers fail and why students often lack motivation. At the same time, he provides insight into how his theoretical approaches can be applicable to the classroom environment.

Skinner's research on learning and how teaching affects learning suggests many reasons why students finish grade levels without necessarily learning concepts in a variety of subject areas. First, many students attempt to learn subject matter as a means of escaping punishment or negative consequences (e.g., parental disappointment, peer comparisons, teacher discontent). This aversion, according to Skinner, impedes improvement of skills. Second, teachers often fail to use positive reinforcements to the fullest extent in their classrooms. One reason for this might have to do with the fact that teachers often have very large numbers of students. Second, teachers might provide positive reinforcements several minutes after a student's response. According to Skinner, a short time lapse between a student's positive response and the teacher's positive reinforcement will adversely affect the student's behavior. And third, as mentioned above, the frequency of reinforcement might be deficient.

SKINNER'S HISTORIC INFLUENCE

Indeed, Skinner's influence in the fields of psychology and education is remarkable. As a behaviorist and experimental psychologist, he perfected and even superseded, from a scientific standpoint, his predecessors—such as Thorndike, Watson, and Pavlov—with regard to theoretical approaches of behaviorism. This is not to say, however, that Skinner's work was not scrutinized by his contemporaries. To be sure, Skinner was not a developmentalist by any means. Nowhere in his work does he refer to "stages of development" or "intellectual or cognitive levels." Developmental psychologists in particular often criticized his work on grounds that he based all learning not on growth or periods of development, but on microcosmic changes—stimuli and responses—that alter behavior, and that this position fails to consider human actions that take place over a significant amount of time.

Stephen J. Farenga and Daniel Ness

REFERENCES

Bjork, Daniel W. (1997) *B.F. Skinner: A Life.* Washington, DC: American Psychological Association.

Crain, William C. (1999) *Theories of Human Development: Concepts and Applications.* 4th ed. Englewood Cliffs, NJ: Prentice Hall.

Keller, Fred S., and William N. Schoenfeld. (1950) *Principles of Psychology: Systematic Text of the Science of Behavior.* New York: Appleton-Century-Crofts.

Milhollan, Frank, and William E. Forisha. (1972) *From Skinner to Rogers: Contrasting Approaches to Education.* Lincoln, NE: Professional Educators Publications.

Skinner, Burrhus F. (1938/1966) *Behavior of Organisms.* New York: Appleton-Century-Crofts.

———. (1968) *The Technology of Teaching.* Englewood Cliffs, NJ: Prentice-Hall.

Thorndike, Edward L. (1898) *Animal Intelligence: An Experimental Study of the Associative Processes in Animals.* New York: Trustees of Columbia University.

LEV VYGOTSKY

Lev Semyonovich Vygotsky (1896–1934) was a Russian lawyer, art historian, and philosopher-turned-psychologist whose influence on cognition and education has gained a great deal of momentum in American psychological and educational circles during the last two decades. Although he appeared as precocious and prolific as another well-known contemporary—Jean Piaget—Vygotsky succumbed to tuberculosis at the early age of thirty-seven, leaving behind a vast theoretical body of literature that would be revived by American psychologists nearly thirty years after his death.

HISTORY

Vygotsky was born near Gomel, a city near Minsk in 1896. Born into a middle-class Jewish household, Vygotsky was acquainted early with the works of numerous philosophers. The ideas of the so-called rationalist philosophers, particularly the ideas of Rene Descartes and Benedict Spinoza, fascinated him. Vygotsky's precocity was evidenced by his fluency in at least eight languages other than Russian, and his ability to memorize almost all of the plays of Shakespeare. In the early part of the twentieth century, nearly all the colleges and universities in Russia invoked a quota system that limited the number of Jewish students enrolling in higher education institutions. Fortunately, Vygotsky won a lottery to attend Moscow University, where he graduated in 1917.

With the belief that the Bolshevik Revolution would end Jewish discrimination in Russia, Vygotsky became strongly influenced by the works of Georg Hegel and Karl Marx. These philosophies strongly emphasized the importance of society and the value of labor in increasing the potential of human ability. Vygotsky believed that the Marxist perspective, in which technology and tools (defined as any object or idea that allows a human being to act on something) transform society and help humans to evolve socially, could be the foundation for a new theory of human development that would account for human functioning in a more constructive manner.

One aspect of the Marxist perspective on human development that Vygotsky espoused was a dialectic view of change. In dialectic reasoning, one begins with a thesis—the argument. An antithesis is presented to challenge the thesis, and by the combination of thesis and antithesis, a person constructs a synthesis, a new level of argument or understanding. This combination has already been seen in complementary and often conflicting processes found in other theories—namely, Erikson's notion of perpetual interplay between seeking connectedness and independence, and Piaget's balancing processes of assimilation and accommodation. For Vygotsky, however, this dialectic was between the individual and the nonindividual, that is, the individual versus others. In synthesis, they combined to move development to higher levels of thinking and functioning. These principles became the foundation of Vygotsky's cognitive theory known as cognitive mediation.

By the early part of the 1920s, Vygotsky settled on psychology as his primary field of inquiry. His initial publication was on the psychology of art. Incidentally, his Ph.D. dissertation was on the subject of the psychology of art. His other interests in human development were on the early stages of language, intelligence testing, and principles of education. One of Vygotsky's major contributions during his lifetime, however, was his work on "defectology"—the study of severe physical disorders that affect learning and intellectual abilities. Vygotsky's interest in intelligence testing was along paths similar to those of Binet, namely, to identify levels of intelligence for the purpose of maximizing the cognitive potentials of individuals, regardless of level of performance.

In his final years and for over two decades after his death, Vygotsky's work was banned from nearly all Russian libraries and universities. Despite his overall Marxist perspective on human development, the Bolshevik Soviet government purged his work on the grounds that Vygotsky's writings supported the bourgeois class. The censorship of Vygotsky's work, particularly the writings during his last ten years, was the reason why most of his writings were unpublished during his lifetime. Most of what we have today comes from posthumously published works that were kept by his closest students and his family. The first work by Vygotsky, in fact, to appear in the United States, was the publication *Language and Thought* in 1963. With the collapse of the Soviet Union, there has been an increased interchange between American and Russian scholars that has provided even more details of and insight into Vygotsky's thinking.

It is important to note, however, that Vygotsky's realization of his ultimate fate (given his more than a decade long illness) led him to write at a feverish pace. His data collection was meager. His writing, therefore, was highly theoretical. And instead of spending his time collecting data, his agenda was primarily to find appropriate methods for supporting his theoretical framework. So, unlike Piaget, who spent very little time developing a method of inquiry (namely, the clinical interview and systematic observation), Vygotsky's agenda was broader in that it looked beyond the individual's cognitive abilities and instead was focused on society's influence on the cognitive levels of human beings. For this, then, Vygotsky's search for method was of primary importance.

COGNITIVE MEDIATION THEORY

Vygotsky's general theoretical framework is referred to as cognitive mediation theory. Vygotsky believed that we share our lower mental functions with animals. We differ greatly, however, from animals in that we possess mental, psychological tools to enable us to think. It is important to consider Marx's influence here, in that Vygotsky believed that tools are the mediators of progress. According to Vygotsky, we acquire tools from our culture and the prior learning of our species. In comparison with learning theory, external stimuli elicit responses from individuals; however, when we acquire a psychological tool, like language, the tool itself mediates between the external stimuli and the subsequent responses. Our psychological tools help us compare, classify, and even plan events; that is, psychological tools create intentionality. Therefore, we learn not to respond directly to external stimuli as do nonhuman animals.

Culture is passed on to us through society, which is passed on to us through the adults in our society. What we identify in our culture is what we incorporate into our cognitive structures, which thereby determines the psychological tools we use (e.g., if we are born and raised in an English-speaking country we will develop knowledge of speaking, reading, and writing English as a means to various ends).

What are psychological tools, where in culture do they come from, and why are they so important for the development of what Vygotsky refers to as higher cognitive processes? First, psychological tools are symbols. Next, the symbol systems used by other developmental theorists, like Piaget, are Vygotsky's primary tools for cognitive development: language, play, art, writing, mathematics, and so forth. These symbol systems differ from Piaget's use of them in at least two ways: (1) they are derived from society—the people around us—not necessarily from within ourselves, and (2) these symbol systems are not merely the means by which we think, rather they can completely reorganize the manner in which we think.

For Vygotsky, language is the primary psychological tool. Vygotsky outlined the process by which children internalize language as a personal tool. At first, adults in our culture provide the child with a particular language and set of symbols. As the child masters the use of language, she begins to use language both to communicate with others and as a form of egocentric speech—talking to oneself, usually out loud. As time progresses, the child is able to eliminate the overt nature of speech and internalize egocentric speech. Vygotsky referred to this internalization as inner speech. The child is still talking to herself but only mentally. We find adults doing this as well. In time, the inner speech becomes the mediating tool for the child's thinking. She begins to use automatic and truncated speech to think and plan. Although language is the primary tool, other symbolic tools become internalized as well, like mathematical thinking or visual thinking.

The following are two examples of inner speech used by a child and by an adult. In the first example, a father tells his preschool aged daughter that mail is delivered every morning at around ten o'clock. During afternoon playtime, the young girl is playing "house" by herself and repeats, "Mommy and Daddy, it's time to get the mail! It just turned ten [o'clock]!" The adults heard this and realized that the girl was repeating what her father had told her about the timing of mail delivery. In a second example, an adult is learning a new recipe. He says to himself: "If I remember correctly, I add two teaspoons of butter to the mix before I add the sautéed vegetables . . . "So, whether a child or an adult, we use these symbolic devices which are derived from inner speech to guide our thinking, planning, and actions.

Curriculum experts and educational psychologists have promoted Vygotsky's view that society, through the aid of adults, helps children regulate their actions at first until they have internalized the mediating devices. Only then will they be able to regulate the devices themselves without adult guidance or intervention. This process of internalization of egocentric speech does not carry the connotations of conditioning or behavior modification as effective processes. Vygotsky outright rejects the stimulus-response framework of learning theory because the behaviorist model is reactive and focuses solely on external properties. Instead, to understand the essence of someone's behavior, overt response is not important. You must focus on an underlying process and particularly on the genetic or initial history of the process.

Like Piaget, Vygotsky examined the process and the history of the organism. Any psychological process is one going through changes right before one's eyes.

SPONTANEOUS VERSUS CONVENTIONALLY SYSTEMATIC CONCEPTS

Vygotsky makes the distinction between spontaneous, or everyday, concepts on the one hand and scientific, conceptually systematic concepts on the other. Spontaneous concepts are concepts that children develop within their everyday environment. These concepts are like little reflections, strong in what concerns the situational, empirical (what the child sees with her own eyes), and the practical. In contrast, scientific concepts, also generally identified as conventionally systematic concepts, refer to a hierarchical system of interrelated ideas. Scientific concepts are highly organized and systematic. School instruction, for example, makes a child self-conscious of particular concepts.

Rudiments of systematization enter the child's mind through scientific concepts. Vygotsky argued that instruction in scientific concepts is very helpful because it provides children with broader frameworks in which to place their spontaneous concepts. For example, a seven-year-old boy might have developed the spontaneous concept of grandmother, but his concept is primarily based on his image of his own grandmother. If we ask him to define the term, he might reply, "She always makes cake for me." Formal instruction, in which the teacher diagrams family trees (including concepts such as grandparents, parents, and children) can give the child a broader framework in which to place his spontaneous concept and help him understand what a grandmother really is (Vygotsky 1978).

Vygotsky, then, believed that spontaneous concepts moved in an upward manner while scientific concepts had a downward movement. In Vygotsky's own words: "The upward everyday [spontaneous] concept clears a way for a scientific [conventionally systematic] concept and its downward development. Scientific concepts provide structures in turn for everyday concepts by making them conscious and deliberate."

THE ZONE OF PROXIMAL DEVELOPMENT

One of the most significant contributions of Vygotsky's theory of cognitive mediation has been the concept of the zone of proximal development. According to Vygotsky, the zone that covers an individual's current developmental level stretches from the level at which the child has already completely mastered lower level skills and knowledge to the level at the upper limit of the individual's capacity, where the child can use a skill or know something only in the best of circumstances. The lower level of the zone is defined by Vygotsky as the actual level of development. Everything below this level has already been mastered—prior knowledge. Everything above this level is as yet unachievable by the person and beyond his or her limits (the future). Everything between these two levels is in the zone and is potentially achievable by the person (the present). This area is called the zone of proximal development because this range covers the problems, challenges, and tasks that are proximal, or next to, the person's last fully developed level of abilities.

Vygotsky proposed a zone rather than a distinct point in the course of an individual's cognitive development because whether a person can perform a task or successfully solve a problem depends on many environmental factors—for example, whether a problem is written clearly, whether a problem has a simple solution or a complicated one, whether there is another person serving as a facilitator, or whether aids, cues, or hints are provided.

Stephen J. Farenga and Daniel Ness

REFERENCES

Kozulin, Alex. (2001) *Psychological Tools: A Sociocultural Approach to Education.* Cambridge, MA: Harvard University Press.

Tudge, Jonathan. (1992) "Vygotsky, the Zone of Proximal Development, and Peer Collaboration: Implications for Classroom Practice." In *Vygotsky and Education: Instructional Implications and Applications of Sociohistorical Psychology*, ed. Luis Moll pp. 155–172. New York: Cambridge University Press.

Vygotsky, Lev. (1963). *Language and Thought.* Cambridge, MA: MIT Press.

———. (1978) *Mind in Society: The Development of Higher Psychological Processes.* Cambridge, MA: Harvard University Press.

VII

ORGANIZATIONS

31

ORGANIZATIONS

The tenth amendment to the United States Constitution reserves the right of education to the states. This has produced fifty decentralized state agencies and other governmental regulatory bodies in territories that develop educational requirements. Over time, there has been an increase in organizations that are interested in education at the local, state, and national levels. At the national level, Public Law 96–88 established the federal Department of Education. The stated purpose of the Department of Education Organization Act–Title I: General Provisions is:

(1) to strengthen the Federal commitment to ensuring access to equal educational opportunity for every individual; (2) to support more effectively States, localities and public and private institutions in carrying out their responsibilities for education; (3) to promote improvements in the quality and usefulness of education through federally supported research, evaluation, and the sharing of information; (4) to improve the management and efficiency of Federal education activities; (5) to increase the accountability of Federal education programs to the President, the Congress, and the public; (6) to encourage the involvement of the public, parents, and students in Federal education programs; [and] (7) to improve the coordination of Federal education programs. (Public Law 96–88, 1979)

Since the establishment of the U.S. Department of Education, constant reform initiatives have been established to formalize and centralize the field of education. Direct federal intervention in the field of education can be observed since *A Nation At Risk* (1983). From that point forward each successive administration had their own brand of reform. At present, the No Child Left Behind Act has had far reaching impact on students, teachers, administra-

tors, parents, and educational-related agencies. Many of the agencies and organizations that comprise this chapter are the conduits that develop, conduct, and promote the educational initiatives of the U.S. Department of Education. Much of the incentive to comply with the department's mandates comes through grants and other monies.

The National Educational Association (NEA) is the largest group concerned broadly with the education of teachers and their practices in the United States. The NEA has far-reaching influence in the field of education. This is demonstrated by its investment in other organizations such as the National Board of Professional Teaching Practices (NBPTP) and the National Council for the Accreditation of Teacher Education (NCATE). The NEA has provided financial or advisory board support to these organizations. Parallel to the NEA would be the American Federation of Teachers. The American Federation of Teachers is firmly grounded with its roots in organized labor and remains active in promoting educational reform. Other associations that are also broadly concerned with the education of teachers would include the American Association of Colleges for Teacher Educators (AACTE) and the Association of Teacher Educators (ATE). Other teacher organizations such as the National Science Teachers Association (NSTA), the National Council of the Social Studies (NCSS), the National Council of Teachers of English (NCTE), and the National Council of Teachers of Mathematics (NCTM), are involved with a variety of subject matter in grades Pre-K through college. A third group of organizations is affiliated with national certification and accreditation of educational programs and schools. These would include the National Council for the Accreditation of Teacher Education (NCATE), Teacher Education Accreditation Council (TEAC), and the National Board for Professional Teaching Standards (NBPTS).

These associations collectively exercise a large degree of control over the field of education. This occurs through the development of curriculum, instruction, licensing, assessment or accreditation. Above all, in this chapter, we discuss the role of educational organizations and associations that affect the development of teachers and students.

Stephen J. Farenga and Daniel Ness

REFERENCES

National Commission on Excellence in Education. (1983) *A Nation at Risk: The Imperative for Educational Reform.* Washington, DC: United States Government Printing Office.

Public Law 96–88. (October 17, 1979) "Bill Summary and Status for the 96th Congress." Available at http://thomas.loc.gov/cgi-bin/bdquery/z?d096:SN00210:@@@D|TOM:/bss/d096query.html.

SUBJECT MATTER ORGANIZATIONS

Subject matter-based teacher organizations include associations that foster and promote teacher and student support and enrichment in a distinct subject area. This entry includes seven organizations. They are the American Council on the Teaching of Foreign Languages (ACTFL), the International Reading Association (IRA), the International Society for Technology in Education (ISTE), National Council for the Social Studies (NCSS), National Council of Teachers of English (NCTE), National Council of Teachers of Mathematics (NCTM), and the National Science Teachers Association (NSTA). As indicated in the profiles below, these organizations vary in size, educational missions, contributions to the field, and financial status.

AMERICAN COUNCIL ON THE TEACHING OF FOREIGN LANGUAGES

The American Council on the Teaching of Foreign Languages (ACTFL) was established in 1967. It is a nonprofit professional organization with approximately 8,000 members. ACTFL's vision statement asserts that: "All Americans should be proficient in at least one language and culture in addition to English. For this

reason, foreign language education must be part of the core curriculum and be treated as central to the education of all children. To realize the vision, foreign language educators must strive for unity of purpose and they must take steps to realize fully the potential of professional status." ACTFL publishes the journal *Foreign Language Annals* as well as a national newsletter.

CONTRIBUTIONS TO EDUCATION

ACTFL contributes to the field of education by disseminating information on the requirements for effective learning of a foreign language. The organization publishes *Foreign Language Annals* four times per year. The journal focuses on the advancement of foreign language teaching and learning, and serves the professionals in the field, including classroom instructors, researchers, and administrators who are involved both directly and indirectly in the teaching of foreign languages at all levels of instruction. The organization holds an annual conference around a specific theme such as "Celebrating our International Spirit." There are five broad areas that address issues in the learning and understanding of foreign language. These are communication, culture, connection, comparisons, and communities. The Standards for Foreign Language Learning address the performances expected of students for each standard, and are elaborated upon below (ACTFL 2005).

STANDARDS FOR FOREIGN LANGUAGE LEARNING

1. Communication

   • Students engage in conversations, provide and obtain information, express feelings and emotions, and exchange opinions.

   • Students understand and interpret written and spoken language on a variety of topics.

   • Students present information, concepts, and ideas to an audience of listeners or readers on a variety of topics.

2. Culture

   • Students demonstrate an understanding of the relationship between the practices and perspectives of the culture studied.

- Students demonstrate an understanding of the relationship between the products and perspectives of the culture studied.

3. Connection

- Students reinforce and further their knowledge of other disciplines through the foreign language.
- Students acquire information and recognize the distinctive viewpoints that are only available through the foreign language and its cultures.

4. Comparisons

- Students demonstrate understanding of the nature of language through comparisons of the language studied and their own.
- Students demonstrate understanding of the concept of culture through comparisons of the cultures studied and their own.

5. Communities

- Students use the language both within and beyond the school setting.
- Students show evidence of becoming lifelong learners by using the language for personal enjoyment and enrichment.

FINANCIAL INFORMATION

The most recent information filed by ACTFL indicates that the organization has over $600 thousand in assets, $2 million in expenses, $700 thousand in liabilities, and over $2 million in revenue for the 2001 calendar year (IRS 2002). The actual amounts for assets, expenses, liabilities, and revenue are shown in Figure 31.1. In general, revenues are derived from direct public support through membership dues and assessments, program service revenue including government fees and contracts, interest on savings and securities, and rental income.

ACTFL receives a large part of its revenue from membership dues. Individual membership dues are $65 annually. Institutional membership dues are $100 annually. Additional information can be obtained online at www.actfl.org or at the following address:

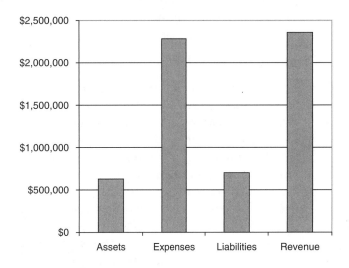

Figure 31.1   Financial Information for the American Council on the Teaching of Foreign Languages, Fiscal Year Ending 2002

Assets (holdings): $629,833
Expenses (amount paid): $2,284,386
Liabilities (amount owed): $701,530
Revenue (income): $2,356,960

Source: IRS (2002).

ACTFL, 70 South Washington Street, Ste. 210, Alexandria, VA 22314.

INTERNATIONAL READING ASSOCIATION

The International Reading Association (IRA) was established in 1956. It is a nonprofit international organization conducting its business in English, French, and Spanish. The organization has approximately 90,000 members. Members of the IRA include teachers, reading specialists, psychologists, supervisors, librarians, parents, and administrators. It is the goal of IRA to promote literacy worldwide. The organization publishes five hard-copy journals (*The Reading Teacher, Journal of Adolescent and Adult Literacy, Reading Research Quarterly, Thinking Classroom/ Peremena,* and *Lectura y Vida*) and one online journal (*Reading Online*). The numerous publications disseminate information relating to research on literacy development in early childhood, childhood, adolescence, and adulthood. The IRA is active in teacher education and professional development in both national and international venues.

CONTRIBUTIONS TO EDUCATION

IRA contributes to the field of education by disseminating information on teaching, learning, and assessment related to literacy. The organization's journals are designed to make the teaching of language accessible to professionals and parents in a variety of related fields. The IRA journals target specific age ranges (e.g., *Reading Teacher*, early childhood to age twelve), and integrate issues related to theory and practice in the teaching of reading. They have research-based suggestions that address issues and concerns related to instruction, curriculum, and assessment. The organization holds an annual conference, a one-day research conference, a world congress held biennially, and national and international meetings. IRA's standards have served as a model for numerous state and local agencies. These standards are used to guide the development of curricula, assessment, and instruction from preschool through college level literacy. There are five standards that address the professional development of individuals involved in literacy education. Each standard addresses what each professional needs to know and do in order to be effective in promoting literacy. The Standards for Reading Professionals are as follows (IRA 2004):

STANDARDS FOR READING PROFESSIONALS

1. Foundational Knowledge

   • Demonstrate knowledge of psychological, sociological, and linguistic foundations of reading and writing processes and instruction.
   • Demonstrate knowledge of reading research and histories of reading.
   • Demonstrate knowledge of language development and reading acquisition and the variations related to cultural and linguistic diversity.
   • Demonstrate knowledge of the major components of reading (phonemic awareness, word identification and phonics, vocabulary and background knowledge, fluency, compre-

hension strategies, and motivation) and how they are integrated in fluent reading.

2. Instructional Strategies and Curriculum Materials

   • Use instructional grouping options (individual, small group, whole class, and computer-based) as appropriate for accomplishing given purposes.
   • Use a wide range of instructional practices, approaches, and methods, including technology-based practices, for learners at different stages of development and from differing cultural and linguistic backgrounds.
   • Use a wide range of curriculum materials in effective reading instruction for learners at different stages of reading and writing development and from different cultural and linguistic backgrounds.

3. Assessment, Diagnosis, and Evaluation

   • Use a wide range of assessment tools and practices that range from individual and group standardized tests to individual and group informal classroom assessment strategies, including technology-based assessment tools.
   • Place students along a developmental continuum and identify students' proficiencies and difficulties.
   • Use assessment information to plan, evaluate, and revise effective instruction that meets the needs of all students, including those at different developmental stages and those from differing cultural and linguistic backgrounds.
   • Effectively communicate results of assessments to specific individuals (students, parents, caregivers, colleagues, administrators, policymakers, policy officials, community, etc.).

4. Creating a Literate Environment

   • Use students' interests, reading abilities, and backgrounds as foundations for the reading and writing program.
   • Use a large supply of books, technology-based information, and non-print materials representing multiple levels, broad interests, and cultural and linguistic backgrounds.

- Model reading and writing enthusiastically as valued lifelong activities.
- Motivate learners to be lifelong readers.

5. Professional Development

- Display positive dispositions related to reading and the teaching of reading.
- Continue to pursue the development of professional knowledge and dispositions.
- Work with colleagues to observe, evaluate, and provide feedback on each other's practice.
- Participate in, initiate, implement, and evaluate professional development programs.

FINANCIAL INFORMATION

The most recent information filed by IRA indicates that the organization has over $28 million in assets, $15 million in expenses, nearly $5 million in liabilities, and over $15 million in revenue for the 2002 calendar year (IRS 2003). The actual amounts for assets, expenses, liabilities, and revenue are shown in Figure 31.2. In general, revenues are derived from direct public support through membership dues and assessments, program service revenue including government fees and contracts, interest on savings and securities, and rental income. IRA receives a large part of its revenue from membership dues. Individual membership dues are $61 annually, and student membership is $37 annually. Dues increase $25 for each journal subscription. Additional information can be obtained online at www.reading.org or at the following address: IRA, 800 Barksdale Road, Newark, DE 19714.

INTERNATIONAL SOCIETY FOR TECHNOLOGY IN EDUCATION

The International Society for Technology in Education (ISTE) was established in 1979 by the merger of the International Association for Computing in Education and the International Council for Computers in Education. It is a nonprofit professional organization with approximately 10,000 members. ISTE's mission is to "Provid[e] leadership and service to improve teaching

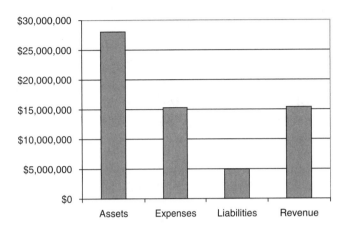

Figure 31.2 **Financial Information for the International Reading Association, Fiscal Year Ending 2003**

Assets (holdings): $28,050,372
Expenses (amount paid): $15,290,533
Liabilities (amount owed): $4,964,656
Revenue (income): $15,390,658

Source: IRS (2003).

and learning by advancing the effective use of technology in education." ISTE publishes three quarterly refereed journals dedicated to technology and education (*Learning and Leading with Technology, Journal of Computing in Teacher Education, Journal of Research on Technology and Education*).

CONTRIBUTIONS TO EDUCATION

ISTE has made an extensive investment in the development of standards in technology. The organization has developed standards for students, teachers, and administrators. The student standards are divided into three performance categories that introduce, reinforce, and are to be mastered by students. The standards for teachers are designed to meet the needs of the initial teacher who is beginning a professional career. The standards address the application of technology in educational settings. The goal of the teacher education standards in technology is to develop basic concepts, knowledge, skills, and dispositions. The educational technology standards and performance indicators for administrators deal with broad issues that affect the integration of technology at a systems level. The technology standards for administrators cover concepts such as leadership and vision, learning and teaching, productivity and professional practice, assessment and evaluation, support, management, operations, and social, legal, and ethical issues. The eighteen ISTE standards, six in each area mentioned above, are as follows:

TECHNOLOGY FOUNDATION STANDARDS FOR ALL STUDENTS

1. Basic Operations and Concepts

   - Students demonstrate a sound understanding of the nature and operation of technology systems.
   - Students are proficient in the use of technology.

2. Social, Ethical, and Human Issues

   - Students understand the ethical, cultural, and societal issues related to technology.
   - Students practice responsible use of technology systems, information, and software.
   - Students develop positive attitudes toward technology uses that support lifelong learning, collaboration, personal pursuits, and productivity.

3. Technology Productivity Tools

   - Students use technology tools to enhance learning, increase productivity, and promote creativity.
   - Students use productivity tools to collaborate in constructing technology-enhanced models, prepare publications, and produce other creative works.

4. Technology Communications Tools

   - Students use telecommunications to collaborate, publish, and interact with peers, experts, and other audiences.
   - Students use a variety of media and formats to communicate information and ideas effectively to multiple audiences.

5. Technology Research Tools

   - Students use technology to locate, evaluate, and collect information from a variety of sources.

   - Students use technology tools to process data and report results.
   - Students evaluate and select new information resources and technological innovations based on the appropriateness for specific tasks.

6. Technology Problem-Solving and Decision-making Tools

   - Students use technology resources for solving problems and making informed decisions.
   - Students employ technology in the development of strategies for solving problems in the real world.

EDUCATIONAL TECHNOLOGY STANDARDS AND PERFORMANCE INDICATORS FOR ALL TEACHERS

1. Technology Operations and Concepts. Teachers demonstrate a sound understanding of technology operations and concepts. Teachers:

   - Demonstrate introductory knowledge, skills, and understanding of concepts related to technology (as described in the ISTE National Education Technology Standards for Students).
   - Demonstrate continual growth in technology knowledge and skills to stay abreast of current and emerging technologies.

2. Planning and Designing Learning Environments and Experiences. Teachers plan and design effective learning environments and experiences supported by technology. Teachers:

   - Design developmentally appropriate learning opportunities that apply technology-enhanced instructional strategies to support the diverse needs of learners.
   - Apply current research on teaching and learning with technology when planning learning environments and experiences.
   - Identify and locate technology resources and evaluate them for accuracy and suitability.
   - Plan for the management of technology resources within the context of learning activities.
   - Plan strategies to manage student learning in a technology-enhanced environment.

3. Teaching, Learning, and the Curriculum. Teachers implement curriculum plans that include methods and strategies for applying technology to maximize student learning. Teachers:

- Facilitate technology-enhanced experiences that address content standards and student technology standards.
- Use technology to support learner-centered strategies that address the diverse needs of students.
- Apply technology to develop students' higher order skills and creativity.
- Manage students' learning activities in a technology-enhanced environment.

4. Assessment and Evaluation. Teachers apply technology to facilitate a variety of effective assessment and evaluation strategies. Teachers:

- Apply technology in assessing student learning of subject matter using a variety of assessment techniques.
- Use technology resources to collect and analyze data, interpret results, and communicate findings to improve instructional practice and maximize student learning.
- Apply multiple methods of evaluation to determine students' appropriate use of technology resources for learning, communication, and productivity.

5. Productivity and Professional Practice. Teachers use technology to enhance their productivity and professional practice. Teachers:

- Use technology resources to engage in ongoing professional development and lifelong learning.
- Continually evaluate and reflect on professional practice to make informed decisions regarding the use of technology in support of student learning.
- Apply technology to increase productivity.
- Use technology to communicate and collaborate with peers, parents, and the larger community in order to nurture student learning.

6. Social, Ethical, Legal, and Human Practices. Teachers understand the social, ethical, legal, and human issues surrounding the use of technology in PK–12 schools and apply those principles in practice. Teachers:

- Model and teach legal and ethical practices related to technology use.
- Apply technology resources to enable and empower learners with diverse backgrounds, characteristics, and abilities.
- Identify and use technology resources that affirm diversity.
- Promote safe and healthy use of technology resources.
- Facilitate equitable access to technology resources for all students.

EDUCATIONAL TECHNOLOGY STANDARDS AND PERFORMANCE INDICATORS FOR ADMINISTRATORS

1. Leadership and Vision. Educational leaders inspire a shared vision for comprehensive integration of technology and foster an environment and culture conducive to the realization of that vision. Educational leaders:

- Facilitate the shared development by all stakeholders of a vision for technology use and widely communicate that vision.
- Maintain an inclusive and cohesive process to develop, implement, and monitor a dynamic, long-range, and systemic technology plan to achieve the vision.
- Foster and nurture a culture of responsible risk taking and advocate policies promoting continuous innovation with technology.
- Use data in making leadership decisions.
- Advocate for research-based effective practices in use of technology.
- Advocate on the state and national levels for policies, programs, and funding opportunities that support implementation of the district technology plan.

2. Learning and Teaching. Educational leaders ensure that curricular design, instructional strategies, and learning environments integrate appropriate technologies to maximize learning and teaching. Educational leaders:

- Identify, use, evaluate, and promote appropriate technologies to enhance and support instruction and standards-based curriculum leading to high levels of student achievement.
- Facilitate and support collaborative technology-enriched learning environments conducive to innovation for improved learning.
- Provide for learner-centered environments that use technology to meet the individual and diverse needs of learners.
- Facilitate the use of technologies to support and enhance instructional methods that develop higher-level thinking, decisionmaking, and problem-solving skills.
- Provide for and ensure that faculty and staff take advantage of quality professional learning opportunities for improved learning and teaching with technology.

3. Productivity and Professional Practice. Educational leaders apply technology to enhance their professional practice and to increase their own productivity and that of others. Educational leaders:

- Model the routine, intentional, and effective use of technology.
- Employ technology for communication and collaboration among colleagues, staff, parents, students, and the larger community.
- Create and participate in learning communities that stimulate, nurture, and support faculty and staff in using technology for improved productivity.
- Engage in sustained, job-related professional learning using technology resources.
- Maintain awareness of emerging technologies and their potential uses in education.
- Use technology to advance organizational improvement.

4. Support, Management, and Operation. Educational leaders ensure the integration of technology to support productive systems for learning and administration. Educational leaders:

- Develop, implement, and monitor policies and guidelines to ensure compatibility of technologies.
- Implement and use integrated technology-based management and operations systems.

- Allocate financial and human resources to ensure complete and sustained implementation of the technology plan.
- Integrate strategic plans, technology plans, and other improvement plans and policies to align efforts and leverage resources.
- Implement procedures to drive continuous improvement of technology systems and to support technology replacement cycles.

5. Assessment and Evaluation. Educational leaders use technology to plan and implement comprehensive systems of effective assessment and evaluation. Educational leaders:

- Use multiple methods to assess and evaluate appropriate uses of technology resources for learning, communication, and productivity.
- Use technology to collect and analyze data, interpret results, and communicate findings to improve instructional practice and student learning.
- Assess staff knowledge, skills, and performance in using technology and use results to facilitate quality professional development and to inform personnel decisions.
- Use technology to assess, evaluate, and manage administrative and operational systems.

6. Social, Legal, and Ethical Issues. Educational leaders understand the social, legal, and ethical issues related to technology and model responsible decisionmaking related to these issues. Educational leaders:

- Ensure equity of access to technology resources that enable and empower all learners and educators.
- Identify, communicate, model, and enforce social, legal, and ethical practices to promote responsible use of technology.
- Promote and enforce privacy, security, and online safety related to the use of technology.
- Promote and enforce environmentally safe and healthy practices in the use of technology.
- Participate in the development of policies that clearly enforce copyright law and assign ownership of intellectual property developed with district resources.

Figure 31.3 **Financial Information for the International Society for Technology in Education, Fiscal Year Ending 2003**

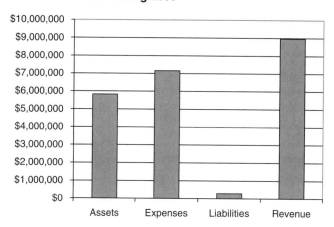

Assets (holdings): $5,828,417
Expenses (amount paid): $7,155,411
Liabilities (amount owed): $296,224
Revenue (income): $8,973,862

Source: IRS (2003).

FINANCIAL INFORMATION

The most recent information filed by ISTE indicates that the Organization has over $5.8 million in assets, $7 million in expenses, nearly $300 thousand in liabilities, and $9 million in revenue for the 2002 calendar year (IRS 2003). The actual amounts for assets, expenses, liabilities, and revenue are shown in Figure 31.3. In general, revenues are derived from direct public support through membership dues and assessments, program service revenue including government fees and contracts, interest on savings and securities, and rental income.

ISTE receives a large part of its revenue from membership dues as well as both private and government grants. Individual membership dues are $58 annually. Additional information can be obtained online at www.iste.org or at the following address: ISTE, 480 Chamelton Street, Eugene, OR 97401.

NATIONAL COUNCIL FOR THE SOCIAL STUDIES

The National Council for the Social Studies (NCSS) was established in 1921. It is a nonprofit profes-

sional organization with approximately 25,000 members. NCSS's mission is to examine the problems inherent in the teaching of social studies at the elementary and secondary levels, and in programs of initial and professional teacher education. NCSS publishes a monthly refereed journal, entitled *Social Education*, dedicated to the issues and interests in teaching the social studies, and two quarterly journals entitled *Social Studies and the Young Learner* and *Theory and Research in Social Education*. They also publish yearbooks, bulletins, curriculum series, and a variety of pamphlets on issues dealing with matters of pedagogy.

CONTRIBUTIONS TO EDUCATION

NCSS contributes to the field of education by sponsoring public discussions, articles, reports, surveys, and research related to the teaching of social studies. The organization's journals deal with aspects of social studies education, such as curriculum, content, pedagogy, and the review of materials that can be used in the teaching of social studies. The organization has a large interest group that includes many individuals from the social sciences such as civics, economics, political science, psychology, sociology, anthropology, history, geography, and law. NCSS holds an annual conference around a specific theme such as "Democracy and Diversity: Social Studies in Action." NCSS published *Expectations of Excellence: Curriculum Standards for Social Studies* (1994). The publication presents ten thematic standards for achieving excellence in social studies, and explains the purpose, organization, and the application of the standards. The standards deal with issues related to culture, geography, change, environments, individuals, institutions, governance, consumerism, technology, and civics. The ten standards are:

NCSS Standards

1. Culture. Social studies programs should include experiences that provide for the study of culture and cultural diversity.
2. Time, Continuity, and Change. Social studies programs should include experiences that provide for the study of the ways human beings view themselves in and over time.
3. People, Places, and Environments. Social stud-

ies programs should include experiences that provide for the study of people, places, and environments.

4. Individual Development and Identity. Social studies programs should include experiences that provide for the study of individual development and identity.

5. Individuals, Groups, and Institutions. Social studies programs should include experiences that provide for the study of interactions among individuals, groups, and institutions.

6. Power, Authority, and Governance. Social studies programs should include experiences that provide for the study of how people create and change structures of power, authority, and governance.

7. Production, Distribution, and Consumption. Social studies programs should include experiences that provide for the study of how people organize for the production, distribution, and consumption of goods and services.

8. Science, Technology, and Society. Social studies programs should include experiences that provide for the study of relationships among science, technology, and society.

9. Global Connections. Social studies programs should include experiences that provide for the study of global connections and interdependence.

10. Civic Ideals and Practices. Social studies programs should include experiences that provide for the study of the ideals, principles, and practices of citizenship in a democratic republic.

FINANCIAL INFORMATION

The most recent information filed by NCSS indicates that the organization has over $1 million in assets, $3 million in expenses, $1 million in liabilities, and $3 million in revenue for the 2002 calendar year (IRS 2003). The actual amounts for assets, expenses, liabilities, and revenue are shown in figure 31.4. In general, revenues are derived from direct public support through membership dues and assessments, program service revenue including government fees and contracts, interest on savings and securities, and rental income.

NCSS receives a large part of its revenue from membership dues as well as private and governmental grants. Individual comprehensive membership dues are $70

Figure 31.4 Financial Information for the National Council for the Social Studies, Fiscal Year Ending 2003

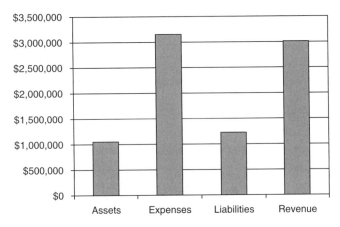

Assets (holdings): $1,052,795
Expenses (amount paid): $3,152,388
Liabilities (amount owed): $1,228,406
Revenue (income): $3,010,175

Source: IRS (2003).

annually. Annual dues for retirees and students are $29. Institutional membership dues are $87 annually. Additional information can be obtained online at www.ncss.org or at the following address: NCSS, 8555 16th Street, Ste. 500, Silver Spring, MD, 20910.

NATIONAL COUNCIL OF TEACHERS OF ENGLISH

The National Council of Teachers of English (NCTE) was established in 1911. It is a nonprofit professional organization with over 60,000 members. The organization is devoted to improvement, instruction, and learning of English and the language arts. NCTE's mission is the following: "The Council promotes the development of literacy, the use of language to construct personal and public worlds and to achieve full participation in society, through the learning and teaching of English and the related arts and sciences of language." NCTE publishes a variety of journals and periodicals that discuss issues related to teaching English and language arts. NCSS publishes refereed journals entitled *English Journal, Language Arts, College English, College*

Composition and Communication, English Education, Voices in the Middle, English Leadership Quarterly, Talking Points, Classroom Notes Plus, Research in the Teaching of English, School Talk, and *Teaching English in the Two-Year College*. Each publication is dedicated to the issues and interests in teaching English and language arts from preschool through college and initial to professional programs in teacher education.

CONTRIBUTIONS TO EDUCATION

NCTE contributes to the field of education by disseminating information on the teaching, learning, and assessment of English and language arts. The organization's twelve journals are designed to make the teaching of English and the language arts accessible to all professionals interested in the development and promotion of literacy. Each journal targets a specific grade band (e.g., *Language Arts*, preschool through grade 8) and focuses on novel ideas that address issues and concerns in the teaching of English and related areas. The organization holds an annual conference around a specific theme such as "Significance." NCTE's national standards are used to guide the development of curricula, assessment, and instruction from preschool through college level English. It should be noted that the NCTE standards are not strict prescriptions for instruction and learning. Rather, they were designed to allow for the expression of creativity and experimentation, which is considered essential to teaching and learning. In total, there are twelve NCTE standards:

NCTE STANDARDS

1. Students read a wide range of print and non-print texts to build an understanding of texts, of themselves, and of the cultures of the United States and the world; to acquire new information; to respond to the needs and demands of society and the workplace; and for personal fulfillment. Among these texts are fiction and nonfiction, classic and contemporary works.

2. Students read a wide range of literature from many periods in many genres to build an understanding of the many dimensions (e.g., philosophical, ethical, aesthetic) of human experience.

3. Students apply a wide range of strategies to comprehend, interpret, evaluate, and appreciate texts. They draw on their prior experience, their interactions with other readers and writers, their knowledge of word meaning and of other texts, their word identification strategies, and their understanding of textual features (e.g., sound-letter correspondence, sentence structure, context, graphics).

4. Students adjust their use of spoken, written, and visual language (e.g., conventions, style, vocabulary) to communicate effectively with a variety of audiences and for different purposes.

5. Students employ a wide range of strategies as they write and use different writing process elements appropriately to communicate with different audiences for a variety of purposes.

6. Students apply knowledge of language structure, language conventions (e.g., spelling and punctuation), media techniques, figurative language, and genre to create, critique, and discuss print and non-print texts.

7. Students conduct research on issues and interests by generating ideas and questions, and by posing problems. They gather, evaluate, and synthesize data from a variety of sources (e.g., print and non-print texts, artifacts, people) to communicate their discoveries in ways that suit their purpose and audience.

8. Students use a variety of technological and information resources (e.g., libraries, databases, computer networks, video) to gather and synthesize information and to create and communicate knowledge.

9. Students develop an understanding of and respect for diversity in language use, patterns, and dialects across cultures, ethnic groups, geographic regions, and social roles.

10. Students whose first language is not English make use of their first language to develop competency in the English language arts and to develop understanding of content across the curriculum.

11. Students participate as knowledgeable, reflective, creative, and critical members of a variety of literacy communities.

12. Students use spoken, written, and visual language to accomplish their own purposes (e.g., for learning, enjoyment, persuasion, and the exchange of information).

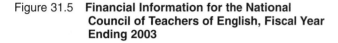

Figure 31.5 **Financial Information for the National Council of Teachers of English, Fiscal Year Ending 2003**

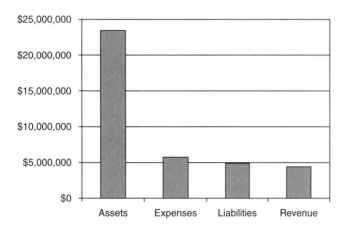

Assets (holdings): $23,451,970
Expenses (amount paid): $5,755,030
Liabilities (amount owed): $4,875,419
Revenue (income): $4,415,050

Source: IRS (2003).

FINANCIAL INFORMATION

The most recent information filed by NCTE indicates that the organization has over $23 million in assets, $5.7 million in expenses, $4.8 million in liabilities, and $4.4 million in revenue for the 2002 calendar year (IRS 2003). The actual amounts for assets, expenses, liabilities, and revenue are shown in Figure 31.5. In general, revenues are derived from direct public support through membership dues and assessments, program service revenue including government fees and contracts, interest on savings and securities, and rental income.

NCTE receives a large part of its revenue from membership dues as well as both private and government grants. Individual membership dues are $40 annually, and students and seniors can become members by paying an annual fee of $20. Institutional fees are based on the number of journals ordered on an annual basis. Additional information can be obtained online at www.ncte.org or at the following address: NCTE, 1111 W. Kenyon Road, Urbana, IL 61801–1096.

NATIONAL COUNCIL OF TEACHERS OF MATHEMATICS

The National Council of Teachers of Mathematics (NCTM) was established in 1920. With approximately 100,000 members, NCTM is one of the largest nonprofit subject-matter-based teacher organizations. As the organization states in its mission: "The National Council of Teachers of Mathematics is a public voice of mathematics education, providing vision, leadership, and professional development to support teachers in ensuring mathematics learning of the highest quality for all students." NCTM has six publications in circulation. These publications include four journals, which are grade band specific (*Journal for Research in Mathematics Education, Mathematics Teacher, Mathematics in the Middle School,* and *Teaching Children Mathematics*), one yearbook (*National Council of Teachers of Mathematics Yearbook*), and one newsletter (*NCTM News Bulletin*).

CONTRIBUTIONS TO EDUCATION

NCTM contributes to the field of education by disseminating information on the teaching, learning, and assessment of mathematics. The organization's journals are designed to make the teaching of mathematics accessible to professionals in the fields of general education and mathematics. Each journal targets a specific grade band (e.g., *Mathematics Teacher*, grades 9–12), and focuses on novel ideas that address issues and concerns in the teaching of mathematical concepts. The organization holds an annual conference around a specific theme such as "Embracing Mathematics Diversity." NCTM was one of the first organizations to develop national standards that have served as a model for other national organizations, states, and local authorities. These standards are used to guide the development of curricula, assessment, and instruction from preschool through college level mathematics. There are six principles and ten standards that guide methodological approaches in mathematical instruction. The principles suggest which components are necessary to achieve excellence in mathematics education. The organization presents the principles as guides and tools for making decisions with regard to the teaching, learning, and assessment of mathematics. The six NCTM Principles for School Mathematics (NCTM 2000, 11) are as follows:

The NCTM Principles

1. Equity. Excellence in mathematics education requires equity—high expectations and strong support for all students.
2. Curriculum. A curriculum is more than a collection of activities: it must be coherent, focused on important mathematics, and well articulated across the grades.
3. Teaching. Effective mathematics teaching requires understanding what students know and need to learn and then challenging and supporting them to learn it well.
4. Learning. Students must learn mathematics with understanding, actively building new knowledge from experience and prior knowledge.
5. Assessment. Assessment should support the learning of important mathematics and furnish useful information to both teachers and students.
6. Technology. Technology is essential in teaching and learning mathematics; it influences the mathematics that is taught and enhances students' learning.

NCTM Standards

The NCTM Standards address the mathematical concepts and processes that all students should learn and understand as they progress through school. There are five content standards and five process-skill or theme standards, for a total of ten standards. The standards remain the same and spiral through the grade levels. That is, each standard is addressed in the grade bands of Pre-K through grade 2, grades 3 through 5, grades 6 through 8, and grades 9 through 12. The ten NCTM content and process-skill standards (NCTM 2000, 11) are:

1. Content Standards

    • Number and Operations. The concept of number and the functions related to addition, subtraction, multiplication and division.
    • Algebra. Patterns and relationships with regard to sequences; manipulating equations,

and working with unknown quantities.
    • Geometry. The study of space and location.
    • Measurement. The comparison of magnitudes of objects.
    • Data Analysis and Probability. Making sense from gathered information, and the likelihood of obtaining a result.

2. Process-Skill Standards

    • Problem Solving. The process of developing and using a method to obtain a solution.
    • Reasoning and Proof. Supporting an answer with evidence.
    • Communication. The process of reporting and explaining through dialogue.
    • Connections. Finding relationships between different mathematical areas.
    • Representation. Developing unique interpretations and descriptions of mathematical ideas.

The principles and standards in mathematics were developed to change the way mathematics is taught, learned, and assessed by students and teachers.

FINANCIAL INFORMATION

The most recent information filed by NCTM indicates that the organization has over $21 million in assets, $18 million in expenses, $6.6 million in liabilities, and $14.6 million in revenue for the 2002 calendar year (IRS 2003). The actual amounts for assets, expenses, liabilities, and revenue are shown in Figure 31.6. In general, revenues are derived from direct public support through membership dues and assessments, program service revenue including government fees and contracts, interest on savings and securities, and rental income.

NCTM receives a large part of its revenue from membership dues. Annual dues for the individual receiving one school journal are $72 and individuals receiving one research journal are $94. Institutions pay $99 annually. Institution rates for one research journal are $154. Kindergarten through eighth grade institutional rates are $99 for one school journal. NCTM also accommodates students and senior citizens. Student rates are $36 and include online access to one school journal, Principles and Standards for School Mathematics, student math notes, and "ON-

Figure 31.6 **Financial Information for the National Council of Teachers of Mathematics, Fiscal Year Ending 2003**

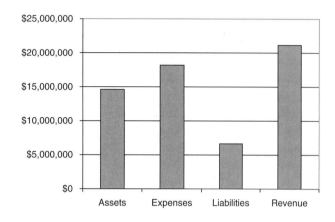

Assets (holdings): $14,614,381
Expenses (amount paid): $18,197,842
Liabilities (amount owed): $6,632,388
Revenue (income): $21,169,455

Source: IRS (2003).

Math." Dues for retired members are $25. Members receive the *NCTM News Bulletin*. Additional information can be obtained online at www.nctm.org or at the following address: NCTM, 1906 Association Drive, Reston, VA 20191–1502.

NATIONAL SCIENCE TEACHERS ASSOCIATION

The National Science Teachers Association (NSTA) serves teachers and students of all science-related branches. Founded in 1944, NSTA has a membership of approximately 53,000. The organization issues six publications—five journals and one newsletter. These publications include the *Journal of College Science Teaching* with a circulation of 5,600, *Science and Children* with a circulation of 24,000, *Science Scope* (for middle-school educators) with a circulation of 16,000, the *Science Teacher* (for high school educators) with a circulation of 30,000, *Quantum* with a circulation of 10,000, and the bimonthly newsletter *NSTA Reports* with a circulation of 53,000. NSTA also holds

one national meeting and three regional meetings per year.

CONTRIBUTIONS TO EDUCATION

NSTA contributes to the field of education by disseminating information on the teaching, learning, and assessment of science and its subdisciplines. The organization's journals are designed to make the teaching of science-related subjects accessible to professionals in the fields of general education, science, and technology. The NSTA journals target specific grade bands (e.g., *Science Scope*, grades 5–9), which focus on novel ideas that address issues and concerns related to instruction, curriculum, and assessment in science education. The organization holds an annual conference around a specific theme such as "Connecting Science to the World." NSTA's standards have served as a model for numerous state and local agencies. They are used to guide the development of curricula, assessment, and instruction from preschool through college level science. There are six overarching areas that address science teaching, professional development for teachers of science, standards for assessment in science education, standards for science content, standards for science education programs, and standards for science education systems. *The National Science Education Standards* represent a goal of what all students should achieve to be scientifically literate. Each of the six areas that the standards address are elaborated below (NSES 1996):

NSES Standards

1. The Science Teaching Standards

   - The planning of inquiry-based science programs
   - The ability to guide and facilitate student learning
   - The assessment of teaching and student learning
   - The development of environments conducive for learning science
   - The establishment of communities of science learners
   - The planning and development of the school science program

2. The Professional Development Standards

- The learning of science content through inquiry
- The integration of knowledge about science with knowledge about learning, pedagogy, and students
- The development of the understanding and ability of lifelong learning
- The coherence and integration of professional development programs

3. The Assessment Standards

- The consistency of assessments with the decisions they are designed to inform (the purpose of the assessment instrument, the use of the assessment instrument, and the interpretation of the results match the instrument's intended design)
- The assessment of both achievement and opportunity to learn science
- The match between the technical quality of the data collected and the consequences of the actions taken on the basis of those data
- The fairness of assessment practices
- The soundness of inferences made from assessments about student achievement and opportunity to learn

4. The Science Content Standards

- Unified Concepts and Processes in Science
- Learning Science as Inquiry
- Physical Science Related Content
- Life Science Related Content
- Earth and Space Science
- Science and Technology
- Science in Personal and Social Perspective
- History and Nature of Science

5. The Science Education Program Standards

- The consistency of the science program with the other standards across grade levels
- The inclusion of all content standards in a variety of curricula that are developmentally appropriate, interesting, relevant to students' lives, organized around inquiry, and connected with other school subjects
- The coordination of the science programs with mathematics education

- The provision of appropriate and sufficient resources to all students
- The provision of equitable opportunities for all students to learn the standards
- The development of communities that encourage, support, and sustain teachers

6. The Science Education System Standards

- The congruency of policies that influence science education with the teaching, professional development, assessment, content, and program standards
- The coordination of science education policies within and across agencies, institutions, and organizations
- The continuity of science education policies over time
- The provision of resources to support science education policies
- The equity embodied in science education policies
- The possible unanticipated effects of policies on science education
- The responsibility of individuals to achieve the new vision of science education portrayed in the standards
- The National Science Education Standards were developed to change the way science is taught, learned, and assessed by students and teachers.

Financial Information

The most recent information filed by NSTA indicates that the organization has over $19 million in assets, nearly $19 million in expenses, $14 million in liabilities, and $19 million in revenue for the 2002 calendar year (IRS 2003). The actual amounts for assets, expenses, liabilities, and revenue are shown in Figure 31.7. In general, revenues are derived from direct public support through membership dues and assessments, program service revenue including government fees and contracts, interest on savings and securities, and rental income.

NSTA receives a large part of its revenue from membership dues. Individual membership dues are $72 annually. Annual dues for new teachers, retir-

Figure 31.7   **Financial Information for the National Science Teachers Association, Fiscal Year Ending 2003**

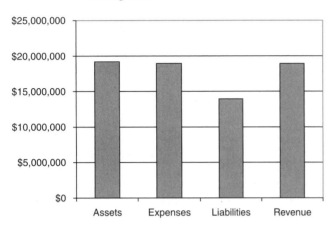

Assets (holdings): $19,182,245
Expenses (amount paid): $18,937,542
Liabilities (amount owed): $13,959,594
Revenue (income): $18,905,006

Source: IRS (2003).

ees, and students are $31. Institutional membership dues are $82 annually. Additional information can be obtained online at www.nsta.org or at the following address: NSTA, 1840 Wilson Boulevard, Arlington, VA 22201–3000.

Stephen J. Farenga and Daniel Ness

REFERENCES

American Council on the Teaching of Foreign Languages. (2005) "Home Page." Available at www.actfl.org/i4a/pages/index.cfm?pageid=1

Armbruster, Bonnie B., and Jean H. Osborn. (2001) *Reading Instruction and Assessment: Understanding the IRA Standards.* Boston: Allyn & Bacon.

Carroll, Jeri A., and Tonya L. Witherspoon. (2001) *Linking Technology and Curriculum: Integrating the ISTE NETS Standards into Teaching and Learning.* 2nd ed. Upper Saddle River, NJ: Prentice-Hall.

Internal Revenue Service (IRS). (2002) *Form 990.* Cincinnati, OH: Internal Revenue Service.

———. (2003) *Form 990.* Cincinnati, OH: Internal Revenue Service.

International Reading Association. (2004) "Standards for Reading Professionals." Available at www.reading.org/downloads/resources/545standards2003/.

National Council for the Social Studies (NCSS). (1994) *Expectations of Excellence: Curriculum Standards for Social Studies.* Silver Spring, MD: NCSS.

National Council of Teachers of Mathematics (NCTM). National Science Education Standards (NSES). (2000) *Principles and Standards of School Mathematics.* Reston, VA.

National Science Education Standards (NSES). (1996) *National Science Education Standards.* Washington, DC: National Research Council, National Academy Press.

Phillips, June K., and Robert M. Terry. (1998) *Foreign Language Standards: Linking Research, Theories, and Practices* (ACTFL Foreign Language Education Series). Lincolnwood, IL: National Textbook Company.

CHILD RELATED ORGANIZATIONS

Child related organizations include associations that foster and promote best practices for students in the field of teacher preparation. This entry includes four organizations. They are the National Association for the Education of Young Children (NAEYC), the Association for Childhood Education International (ACEI), the National Middle School Association (NMSA), and the Council for Exceptional Children (CEC). As indicated in the profiles below, these organizations vary in size, educational missions, contributions to the field, and financial status. A review of the broad standards for each of the organizations suggests the possible overlap in educational missions, student populations served, and teacher preparation.

NATIONAL ASSOCIATION FOR THE EDUCATION OF YOUNG CHILDREN

The National Association for the Education of Young Children (NAEYC) is the largest organization that supports teachers of a specific age or grade level. Founded in 1926, NAEYC is the largest organization in the world (with over 100,000 members) devoted to the education and development of young children. Moreover, as a nonprofit organization, it serves as a national network with approximately 450 local, state, and regional affiliates, and as an international partner with similar organizations in other world regions. NAEYC's mission "is to serve and act on behalf of the needs, rights and well-being of all young children with primary focus on the provision of educational and developmental services and resources." NAEYC publishes two journals (*Young Children* and the *Early Childhood Research Quarterly*) as well as other early childhood related media.

CONTRIBUTIONS TO EDUCATION

NAEYC contributes to the field of education by disseminating information on the teaching, learning, assessment, and the development of young children from birth through age eight. In addition, NAEYC influences the professional growth of teachers and others concerned with the development of young children. The organization's journals are designed to focus on trends in early childhood education. *Young Children* is a bimonthly practitioner-based journal that focuses on issues dealing with early childhood and development. The journal *Early Childhood Research Quarterly* deals with research, theory, practices, and critical issues in early childhood education. The organization holds an annual international conference to allow all interested parties in the field of early childhood to network and be exposed to the critical issues related to early childhood development. NAEYC's standards have served as a model for numerous state and local agencies. These standards are used to guide the development of curricula, assessment, and instruction in issues related to early childhood education. There are five broad standards that address the following: promoting child development and learning; building family and community relationships; observing, documenting, and assessing to support young children and families; teaching and learning; and becoming a professional. The NAEYC standards are designed to measure outcomes, professionalism, knowledge, skills or abilities, and dispositions (National Association for the Education of Young Children 1994). Each of the five domains and their descriptions are elaborated below:

NAEYC STANDARDS

1. Promoting child development and learning. Candidates use their understanding of young children's characteristics and needs, and of multiple interacting influences on children's development and learning, to create environments that are healthy, respectful, supportive, and challenging for all children.
2. Building family and community relationships. Candidates know about, understand, and value the importance and complex characteristics of children's families and communities. They use this understanding to create respectful, reciprocal relationships that support and empower families, and to involve all families in their children's development and learning.
3. Observing, documenting, and assessing to support young children and families. Candidates know about and understand the goals, benefits, and uses of assessment. They know about and use systematic observations, documentation, and other effective assessment strategies in a responsible way, in partnership with families and other professionals, to positively influence children's development and learning.
4. Teaching and Learning. Candidates integrate their understanding of and relationships with children and families; their understanding of developmentally effective approaches to teaching and learning; and their knowledge of academic disciplines to design, implement, and evaluate experiences that promote positive development and learning for all young children as follows:

   • Connecting with children and families. Candidates know, understand, and use positive relationships and supportive interactions as the foundation for their work with young children.
   • Using developmentally effective approaches. Candidates know, understand, and use a wide array of effective approaches, strategies, and tools to support young children's development and learning.
   • Understanding content knowledge in early education. Candidates understand the importance of each content area in young children's learning. They know the essential concepts, inquiry tools, and structure of content areas including academic subjects and can identify resources to deepen their understanding.
   • Building meaningful curriculum. Candidates use their own knowledge and other resources to design, implement, and evaluate meaningful, challenging curriculum that promotes comprehensive developmental and learning outcomes for all young children.

5. Becoming a professional. Candidates identify and conduct themselves as members of the early

Figure 31.8 **Financial Information for the National Association for the Education of Young Children, Fiscal Year Ending 2002**

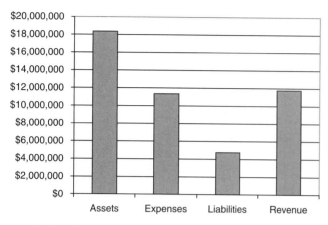

Assets (holdings): $18,367,852
Expenses (amount paid): $11,370,195
Liabilities (amount owed): $4,764,569
Revenue (income): $11,778,027

Source: IRS (2002).

childhood profession. They know and use ethical guidelines and other professional standards related to early childhood practice. They are continuous, collaborative learners who demonstrate knowledge, reflective, and critical perspectives on their work, making informed decisions that integrate knowledge from a variety of sources. They are informed advocates for sound educational practices and policies.

FINANCIAL INFORMATION

The most recent information filed by NAEYC indicates that the organization has over $18.3 million in assets, $11.3 million in expenses, $4.7 million in liabilities, and over $11.7 million in revenue for the 2001 calendar year (IRS 2002). The actual amounts for assets, expenses, liabilities, and revenue are shown in Figure 31.8. In general, revenues are derived from direct public support through membership dues and assessments, program service revenue including government fees and contracts, and interest on savings and securities.

NAEYC receives a large part of its revenue from membership dues. The organization has an extensive menu of membership options. Membership cat-

egories include comprehensive, regular, and student. Dues are dependent upon the county and state in which one lives. Additional information can be obtained online at www.naeyc.org or at the following address: NAEYC, 1509 16th Street NW, Washington, DC 20036.

ASSOCIATION FOR CHILDHOOD EDUCATION INTERNATIONAL

The Association for Childhood Education International (ACEI) was established in 1892. Originally established as the International Kindergarten Union, the ACEI is the oldest professional association having to do with age-based organizations in the United States. It is a nonprofit professional organization with approximately 11,000 members. ACEI's mission is "to promote and support in the global community the optimal education and development of children, from birth through early adolescence, and to influence the professional growth of educators and the efforts of others who are committed to the needs of children in a changing society." ACEI publishes two journals (*Childhood Education* and the *Journal of Research in Childhood Education*) as well as a series of Professional Focus newsletters in the fields of infancy, pre-kindergarten and kindergarten, elementary school, middle school, inclusive education, and teacher education.

CONTRIBUTIONS TO EDUCATION

ACEI contributes to the field of education by disseminating information on the teaching, learning, assessment, and the development of children from infancy through middle childhood. In addition, ACEI influences the professional growth of teachers and others concerned with the development of children. The organization's journals are designed to focus on trends in childhood education. Published since 1924 and with a circulation of six per year, the journal *Childhood Education* focuses on issues dealing with classroom practices, pedagogical techniques, child development, children and families, reviews of the current literature in childhood, and useful issues dealing with classroom practice. The journal *Research in Childhood Education* is published twice per year, and deals with research, theory, and practice in childhood education. The organization holds an annual international conference around a specific theme such as "The Future of Education: Government, Pedagogy, and Practice." ACEI's standards have served as a model for numerous state and local agencies. These standards are used to guide the development of curricula, assessment, and instruction in issues related to childhood education. There are five overarching standards that address development, learning, and motivation; curriculum; instruction; assessment; and professionalism. The ACEI standards are designed to measure the knowledge, skills or abilities, dispositions, and effect on student learning (See National Council for the Accreditation of Teacher Education 2000). Each of the five domains and their descriptions are elaborated below:

ACEI Standards

1. Development, Learning, and Motivation. Candidates know, understand, and use the major concepts, principles, theories, and research related to development of children and young adolescents to construct learning opportunities that support individual students' development, acquisition of knowledge, and motivation.

2. Curriculum

• English language arts. Candidates demonstrate a high level of competence in use of English language arts and they know, understand, and use concepts from reading, language, and child development to teach reading, writing, speaking, viewing, listening, and thinking skills, and to help students successfully apply their developing skills to many different situations, materials, and ideas.

• Science. Candidates know, understand, and use fundamental concepts in the subject matter of science—including physical, life, and earth and space sciences—as well as concepts in science and technology, science in personal and social perspectives, the history and nature of science, the unifying concepts of science, and the inquiry processes scientists use in the discovery of new knowledge to build a base for scientific and technological literacy.

• Mathematics. Candidates know, understand, and use the major concepts, procedures, and reasoning processes of mathematics that define number systems and number sense, geometry, measurement, statistics and probability, and algebra in order to foster student understanding and use of patterns, quantities, and spatial relationships that can represent phenomena, solve problems, and manage data.

• Social studies. Candidates know, understand, and use the major concepts and modes of inquiry from the social studies—the integrated study of history, geography, the social sciences, and other related areas—to promote elementary students' abilities to make informed decisions as citizens of a culturally diverse democratic society and interdependent world.

• The arts. Candidates know, understand, and use—as appropriate to their own knowledge and skills—the content, functions, and achievements of dance, music, theater, and the several visual arts as primary media for communication, inquiry, and insight among elementary students.

• Health education. Candidates know, understand, and use the major concepts in the subject matter of health education to create opportunities for student development and practice of skills that contribute to good health.

• Physical education. Candidates know, understand, and use—as appropriate to their own understanding and skills—human movement and physical activity as central elements to foster active, healthy lifestyles and enhanced quality of life for elementary students.

• Connections across the curriculum. Candidates know, understand, and use the connections among concepts, procedures, and applications from content areas to motivate elementary students, build understanding, and encourage the application of knowledge, skills, tools, and ideas to real world issues.

3. Instruction

• Integrating and applying knowledge for instruction. Candidates plan and implement instruction based on knowledge of students, learning theory, subject matter, curricular goals, and community.

• Adaptation to diverse students. Candidates understand how elementary students differ in their development and approaches to learning, and create instructional opportunities that are adapted to diverse students.

• Development of critical thinking, problem solving, and performance skills. Candidates understand and use a variety of teaching strategies that encourage elementary students' development of critical thinking, problem solving, and performance skills.

• Active engagement in learning. Candidates use their knowledge and understanding of individual and group motivation and behavior among students at the K–6 level to foster active engagement in learning, self-motivation, and positive social interaction and to create supportive learning environments.

• Communication to foster learning. Candidates use their knowledge and understanding of effective verbal, nonverbal, and media communication techniques to foster activity inquiry, collaboration, and supportive interaction in the elementary classroom.

4. Assessment. Candidates know, understand, and use formal and informal assessment strategies to plan, evaluate, and strengthen instruction that will promote continuous intellectual, social, emotional, and physical development of each elementary student.

5. Professionalism

• Practices and behaviors of developing career teachers. Candidates understand and apply practices and behaviors that are characteristic of developing career teachers.

• Reflection and evaluation. Candidates are aware of and reflect on their practice in light of research on teaching and resources available for professional learning; they continually evaluate the effects of their professional decisions and actions on students, parents, and other professionals in the learning community and actively seek out opportunities to grow professionally.

• Collaboration with families. Candidates know the importance of establishing and maintaining a positive collaborative relationship with families to promote the intellectual, social, emotional, and physical growth of children.

• Collaboration with colleagues and the community. Candidates foster relationships with school col-

Figure 31.9   **Financial Information for the Association for Childhood Education International, Fiscal Year Ending 2002**

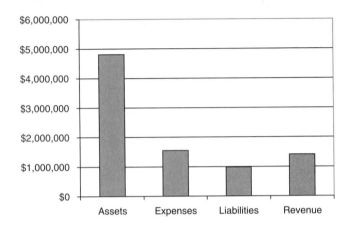

Assets (holdings): $4,814,235
Expenses (amount paid): $1,554,852
Liabilities (amount owed): $983,622
Revenue (income): $1,415,536

Source: IRS (2002).

leagues and agencies in the larger community to support students' learning and well-being.

FINANCIAL INFORMATION

The most recent information filed by ACEI indicates that the organization has over $4.8 million in assets, $1.5 million in expenses, nearly $1 million in liabilities, and over $1.4 million in revenue for the 2001 calendar year (IRS 2002). The actual amounts for assets, expenses, liabilities, and revenue are shown in Figure 31.9. In general, revenues are derived from direct public support through membership dues and assessments, program service revenue including government fees and contracts, and interest on savings and securities.

ACEI receives a large part of its revenue from membership dues. Individual membership dues are $45 annually for the professional. Institutional membership dues are $100 annually. Membership dues for students and retirees are $26 and $23, respectively. Additional information can be obtained online at www.acei.org or at the following address: ACEI, 17904 Georgia Avenue, Suite 215, Olney, MD 20832.

NATIONAL MIDDLE SCHOOL ASSOCIATION

The National Middle School Association (NMSA) was established in 1973. NMSA deals with issues related to middle level education, particularly the educational and developmental needs of young adolescents. It is a nonprofit professional organization with approximately 30,000 members. NMSA's mission is "dedicated to improving the educational experiences of young adolescents by providing vision, knowledge, and resources to all who serve them in order to develop healthy, productive, and ethical citizens." NMSA publishes three journals, two hardcopy (*Middle Ground* and *Middle School Journal*) and one online (*Research in Middle Level Education*), as well as three newsletters (Classroom Connections, Middle E-Connections, and NMSA in Action).

CONTRIBUTIONS TO EDUCATION

NMSA contributes to the field of education by advocating for the development and advancement of the middle level philosophy as a distinct entity in the educational system. In addition, NMSA influences the professional growth of teachers and others concerned with the development of young adolescents. The organization's journals are designed to focus on trends in middle level education. The journal *Middle Ground* is designed to give practitioner-based experiential knowledge to those concerned with middle level issues. *Middle School Journal* reports on research and trends in middle level education having to do with academics, discipline, social equity, and developmentally appropriate practice. The online journal, *Research in Middle Level Education*, publishes articles based on research syntheses, reviews, meta-analyses, case studies, action-research, and both qualitative and quantitative studies. The organization holds an annual conference around a specific theme such as "The Future of Education: Government, Pedagogy, and Practice." NMSA's standards have served as a model for numerous state and local agencies for middle level education. These standards are used to guide the development of curricula, assessment, and instruction in issues related to developmentally responsive middle level education. There are two groups of standards, one that examines the capacity of the institution and the other for candidate preparation. The

NMSA standards are designed to measure the capacity of the institution and to foster the candidate's development as a middle level educator. Candidates are expected to demonstrate knowledge, skills or abilities, dispositions, and their influence on adolescent students (National Middle School Association 2004). The standards are elaborated below:

NMSA Standards

1. National Middle School Association: Programmatic Standards for Initial Middle Level Teacher Preparation

• Middle Level Courses and Experiences. Institutions preparing middle level teachers have courses and field experiences that specifically and directly address middle level education.
• Qualified Middle Level Faculty. Institutions preparing middle level teachers employ faculty members who have middle level experience and expertise.

2. National Middle School Association: Performance-Based Standards for Initial Middle Level Teacher Preparation

• Young Adolescent Development. Middle level teacher candidates understand the major concepts, principles, theories, and research related to young adolescent development, and they provide opportunities that support student development and learning.
• Middle Level Philosophy and School Organization. Middle level teacher candidates understand the major concepts, principles, theories, and research underlying the philosophical foundations of developmentally responsive middle level programs and schools, and they work successfully within these organizational components.
• Middle Level Curriculum and Assessment. Middle level teacher candidates understand the major concepts, principles, theories, standards, and research related to middle level curriculum and assessment, and they use this knowledge in their practice.
• Middle Level Teaching Fields. Middle level teacher candidates understand and use the central concepts, tools of inquiry, standards, and structures of content in their chosen teaching fields, and they create meaningful learning experiences that develop

all young adolescents' competence in subject matter and skills.

• Middle Level Instruction and Assessment. Middle level teacher candidates understand and use the major concepts, principles, theories, and research related to effective instruction and assessment, and they employ a variety of strategies for a developmentally appropriate climate to meet the varying abilities and learning styles of all young adolescents.

• Family and Community Involvement. Middle level teacher candidates understand the major concepts, principles, theories, and research related to working collaboratively with family and community members, and they use that knowledge to maximize the learning of all young adolescents.

• Middle Level Professional Roles. Middle level teacher candidates understand the complexity of teaching young adolescents, and they engage in practices and behaviors that develop their competence as professionals.

FINANCIAL INFORMATION

The most recent information filed by NMSA indicates that the organization has over $2.8 million in assets, $4.8 million in expenses, $1.7 million in liabilities, and nearly $5 million in revenue for the 2001 calendar year (IRS 2002). The actual amounts for assets, expenses, liabilities, and revenue are shown in Figure 31.10. In general, revenues are derived from direct public support through membership dues and assessments, program service revenue including government fees and contracts, and interest on savings and securities.

NMSA receives a large part of its revenue from membership dues. There are four different types of membership available in the National Middle School Association: individual, institutional, institutional plus, and student/parent/retiree. All membership dues depend on residence within or outside of the United States. Individual annual membership dues are $59 for nationals and $74 for internationals. Institutional annual membership dues are $199 for national institutions and $234 for international institutions. Institutional Plus annual membership dues, which include double the number of subscriptions and double the number of voting members for NMSA posts, are $349 for national institutions and $384

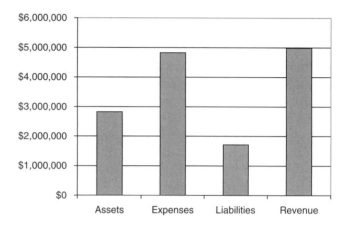

Figure 31.10 **Financial Information for the National Middle School Association, Fiscal Year Ending 2002**

Assets (holdings): $2,824,927
Expenses (amount paid): $4,827,220
Liabilities (amount owed): $1,713,029
Revenue (income): $4,989,959

Source: IRS (2002).

for international institutions. Membership dues for students and retirees are $40 for nationals and $55 for internationals. Additional information can be obtained online at www.nmsa.org or at the following address: NMSA, 4151 Executive Parkway, Suite 300, Westerville, OH 43081.

COUNCIL FOR EXCEPTIONAL CHILDREN

The Council for Exceptional Children (CEC) was established in 1922. CEC deals with issues related to the advocacy for the advancement of equitable educational opportunities of individuals with exceptionalities. In general, "exceptional" refers to individuals who have been identified with traits associated with disabilities or with giftedness. It is a nonprofit professional organization with approximately 50,000 members. CEC has developed a code of ethics for professionals in the field of special education. The organization's mission is "to improve educational outcomes for individuals with exceptionalities." CEC publishes two journals (*Teach-*

ing Exceptional Children and *Exceptional Children*) and one newsletter (CEC Today).

CONTRIBUTIONS TO EDUCATION

CEC contributes to the field of education by disseminating information on the teaching, learning, assessment, and the development of individuals with exceptionalities. In addition, CEC influences the professional growth of teachers and others concerned with the practices in special education. The organization's journals are designed to focus on trends and issues in educating individuals with exceptionalities. With a circulation of six editions per year, the journal *Teaching Exceptional Children* contains information about pedagogical practices, materials, and resources for working with students of a variety of ages and with a variety of special abilities. Further educational support is provided by the online companion to *Teaching Exceptional Children*. The journal *Exceptional Children* is a quarterly publication oriented toward research in the field of special education. The organization holds an annual international conference. CEC's standards have served as a model for numerous state and local agencies. These standards are used to guide the development of curricula, assessment, and instruction in issues related to the development of professionals in the field of special education. There are ten standards to help foster the development of future teachers of students with exceptionalities (Council for Exceptional Children 2004). They are as follows:

CEC Standards

1. Foundations. Special educators understand the field as an evolving and changing discipline based on philosophies, evidence-based principles and theories, relevant laws and policies, diverse and historical points of view, and human issues that have historically influenced and continue to influence the field of special education and the education and treatment of individuals with exceptional needs both in school and society.

2. Development and Characteristics of Learners. Special educators understand the similarities and differences in human development and the char-

acteristics between and among individuals with and without exceptional learning needs.

3. Individual Learning Differences. Special educators understand the effects that an exceptional condition can have on an individual's learning in school and throughout life. Special educators understand that the beliefs, traditions, and values across and within cultures can affect relationships among and between students, their families, and the school community.

4. Instructional Strategies. Special educators possess a repertoire of evidence-based instructional strategies to individualize instruction for individuals with special learning needs. Special educators select, adapt, and use these instructional strategies to promote challenging learning results in general and special curricula and to appropriately modify learning environments for individuals with special learning needs.

5. Learning Environments and Social Interactions. Special educators actively create learning environments for individuals with exceptional learning needs (ELN) that foster cultural understanding, safety and emotional well being, positive social interactions, and active engagement of individuals.

6. Language. Special educators understand typical and atypical language development and the ways in which exceptional conditions can interact with an individual's experience with and use of language.

7. Instructional Planning. Individualized decisionmaking and instruction is at the center of special education practice. Special educators develop long-range individualized instructional plans anchored in both general and special curricula.

8. Assessment. Assessment is integral to the decisionmaking and teaching of special educators and special educators use multiple types of assessment information for a variety of educational decisions. Special educators use the results of assessments to help identify exceptional learn-

ing needs and to develop and implement individualized instructional programs, as well as to adjust instruction in response to ongoing learning progress.

9. Professional and Ethical Practice. Special educators are guided by the profession's ethical and professional practice standards. Special educators practice in multiple roles and complex situations across wide age and developmental ranges.

10. Collaboration. Special educators routinely and effectively collaborate with families, other educators, related service providers, and personnel from community agencies in culturally responsive ways.

FINANCIAL INFORMATION

The most recent information filed by CEC indicates that the organization has nearly $6 million in assets, over $13 million in expenses, $5 million in liabilities, and $13.2 million in revenue for the 2001 calendar year (IRS 2002). The actual amounts for assets, expenses, liabilities, and revenue are shown in Figure 31.11. In general, revenues are derived from direct public support through membership dues and assessments, program service revenue including government fees and contracts, and interest on savings and securities.

CEC receives a large part of its revenue from membership dues. Membership categories include professional, student, associate (parents or family members of exceptional students), and premiere (individual non-specialized professionals). Membership dues for the professional are dependent upon the state in which one lives. Dues for students, associates, and premieres are $46, $51, and $159, respectively. Additional information can be obtained online at www.cec.sped.org or at the following address: CEC, 1110 North Glebe Road, Suite 300, Arlington, VA 22201.

Stephen J. Farenga and Daniel Ness

REFERENCES

Council for Exceptional Children (CEC). (2004) *About the Council of Exceptional Children.* Arlington, VA: CEC. Website: www.cec.sped.org.
Internal Revenue Service (IRS). (2002) *Form 990.* Cincinnati, OH: Internal Revenue Service.

Figure 31.11 **Financial Information for the Council for Exceptional Children, Fiscal Year Ending 2002**

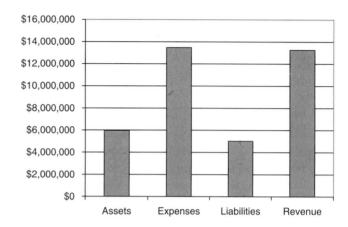

Assets: $5,963,966
Expenses: $13,484,947
Liabilities: $5,011,104
Revenue: $13,239,319

Source: IRS (2002).

National Association for the Education of Young Children (NAEYC). (1994) *Initial and Advanced Programs in Early Childhood Education.* Washington, DC: NAEYC. Website: www.naeyc.org.
National Council for the Accreditation of Teacher Education (NCATE). (2000). *Program Standards for Elementary Teacher Preparation.* Washington, DC: NCATE. Website: www.ncate.org.
National Middle School Association (NMSA). (2004) *About the National Middle School Association.* Westerville, OH: NMSA. Website: www.nmsa.org.

TEACHER RELATED ORGANIZATIONS

The National Education Association (NEA) and the American Federation of Teachers (AFT) are two of the largest and most influential organizations involved in representing the teaching profession at all levels of education. By December 2000, both the NEA and AFT agreed to collaborate on joint initiatives to benefit the membership of each organization. The National Education Association–American Federation of Teachers (NEAFT) partnership is committed to establishing equality in society through education. Nevertheless, both organizations are mutually exclusive entities, which sometimes differ on the methods and means of achieving their individual goals. The critical mass of both organizations totals an estimated 4 million individuals. In the past, each association was actively involved in improving its members' working conditions through public relations, contract negotiations, and collective bargaining. However, more recently, both NEA and AFT have increased their control over the profession to become active players in educational reform and the restructuring of schools. The NEA and the AFT are involved in the development of teaching as a profession at the initial and advanced levels of training. This common interest for each organization supports an agenda of greater independence and self-governance of the teaching profession. The literature is replete with contributions from both organizations that support recommendations for educational change at local, state, and national levels. In addition to the NEA and AFT, this entry includes a third Association, the American Educational Research Association (AERA), which provides research-related resources for both teacher practitioners and researchers.

NATIONAL EDUCATION ASSOCIATION

The National Education Association (NEA) is the largest professional employee organization devoted to the teaching profession in the United States. The organization's roots go back to 1857 when Robert Campbell, an African American educator, founded the National Teacher's Association—a forerunner of the NEA—at a convention in Philadelphia, Pennsylvania. Booker T. Washington was the keynote speaker at the 1884 NEA convention. Since then, NEA has served as an important medium for educators nationwide, and was deeply involved in a number of national movements both within (e.g., equal educational opportunity) and outside (e.g., women's suffrage, professional rights and human relations, legislation, and political action) the field of education. Moreover, NEA has made a number of inroads with other organizations in education; they are a powerful voice in the areas of professionalization and accreditation in teacher education. Recently, NEA has exceeded 2.7 million members who work in all levels of educational practice. In

addition, they have more than 14,000 affiliated organizations in all fifty states.

NEA is steadfast in its conviction that all students, regardless of race, ethnicity, or sexual orientation, deserve a quality education. As they state in their mission, NEA seeks "to fulfill the promise of a democratic society, the National Education Association shall promote the cause of quality public education and advance the profession of education; expand the rights and further the interest of educational employees; and advocate human, civil, and economic rights for all" (NEA 2004).

The NEA possesses a vast organizational structure. The NEA is composed of units such as divisions, committees, and commissions. Many of the specific subject area organizations, such as the National Council for the Social Studies, the National Science Teachers Association, and the National Council of Teachers of Mathematics, began as NEA units that were responsible for specific curriculum areas (e.g., civics/history, science, mathematics). Along with the standing committees of the Representative Assembly, NEA has established a committees on Budget, Planning and Organizational Development, Professional Negotiation, and Special Services, as well as the NEA DuShane Emergency Fund Advisory Committee.

CONTRIBUTIONS TO EDUCATION

NEA's contributions to education are numerous and can be traced back to its inception. NEA has developed basic policies that establish professional rights and responsibilities for all individuals who are involved in education. NEA has developed the Center for Human Relations, which has worked to address issues of the civil and human rights of students and teachers. In the same venue, NEA has worked on international relationships with organizations such as the United Nations Educational, Scientific, and Cultural Organization (UNESCO) to improve education in other countries throughout the world. The center supports conferences, workshops, and publications highlighting social issues that need to be addressed in an equitable manner. NEA has a long history in the struggle to improve the economic status of teachers. They have provided assistance in helping local teacher associations to negotiate salary schedules and educational policies dealing with administrative and instructional issues. NEA is active in helping to formulate national legislative policies in education, and serves as an organization that represents the teaching profession before the United States Congress.

NEA is very adept at promoting issues related to teachers, students, and administrators at all levels of education. NEA provides a large number of journals, newsletters, magazines, and other forms of media to address a variety of issues, such as providing basic education statistics, school law, salaries, school programs, school finance, and educational equity, among other issues. Among its large number of publications, NEA's flagship journal, *NEA Today*, is published eight times per year. Having a circulation of nearly 3 million, *NEA Today* brings readers up-to-date information on the nation's most pressing educational issues. Other NEA publications include *Higher Education Advocate* (newsletter on general trends in higher education), *Thought & Action* (theoretical and practical issues in higher education), *The NEA Almanac of Higher Education* (for the latest employment figures in higher education), *Tomorrow's Teachers* (for students of education), *This Active Life* (for retired teachers and educational professionals), *Education Statistics*, as well as advertising and multimedia.

A major policy statement that reflects the concerns and values of the NEA can be found in the organization's Preamble and Code of Ethics. The Code of Ethics was first adopted in 1929, and highlights the organization's concern and responsibility for ensuring the quality of education and the character of all parties involved in the teaching profession. The NEA Code of Ethics appear below:

NEA Code of Ethics of the Education Profession

Preamble

The educator, believing in the worth and dignity of each human being, recognizes the supreme importance of the pursuit of truth, devotion to excellence, and the nurture of the democratic principles. Essential to these goals is the protection of freedom to learn and to teach and the guarantee of equal educational opportunity for all. The educator accepts the responsibility to adhere to the highest ethical standards.

The educator recognizes the magnitude of the responsibility inherent in the teaching process. The desire for the respect and confidence of one's colleagues, of students, of parents, and of the members of the community provides the incentive to attain and maintain the highest possible degree of ethical conduct. The Code of Ethics of the Education Profession indicates the aspiration of all educators and provides standards by which to judge conduct.

The remedies specified by the NEA and/or its affiliates for the violation of any provision of this Code shall be exclusive and no such provision shall be enforceable in any form other than the one specifically designated by the NEA or its affiliates.

PRINCIPLE I

Commitment to the Student

The educator strives to help each student realize his or her potential as a worthy and effective member of society. The educator therefore works to stimulate the spirit of inquiry, the acquisition of knowledge and understanding, and the thoughtful formulation of worthy goals.

In fulfillment of the obligation to the student, the educator:

1. Shall not unreasonably restrain the student from independent action in the pursuit of learning.
2. Shall not unreasonably deny the student's access to varying points of view.
3. Shall not deliberately suppress or distort subject matter relevant to the student's progress.
4. Shall make reasonable effort to protect the student from conditions harmful to learning or to health and safety.
5. Shall not intentionally expose the student to embarrassment or disparagement.
6. Shall not on the basis of race, color, creed, sex, national origin, marital status, political or religious beliefs, family, social or cultural background, or sexual orientation, unfairly—
   a. Exclude any student from participation in any program.
   b. Deny benefits to any student.
   c. Grant any advantage to any student.
7. Shall not use professional relationships with students for private advantage.

8. Shall not disclose information about students obtained in the course of professional service unless disclosure serves a compelling professional purpose or is required by law.

PRINCIPLE II

Commitment to the Profession

The education profession is vested by the public with a trust and responsibility requiring the highest ideals of professional service.

In the belief that the quality of the services of the education profession directly influences the nation and its citizens, the educator shall exert every effort to raise professional standards, to promote a climate that encourages the exercise of professional judgment, to achieve conditions that attract persons worthy of the trust to careers in education, and to assist in preventing the practice of the profession by unqualified persons.

In fulfillment of the obligation to the profession, the educator:

1. Shall not in an application for a professional position deliberately make a false statement or fail to disclose a material fact related to competency and qualifications.
2. Shall not misrepresent his/her professional qualifications.
3. Shall not assist any entry into the profession of a person known to be unqualified in respect to character, education, or other relevant attribute.
4. Shall not knowingly make a false statement concerning the qualifications of a candidate for a professional position.
5. Shall not assist a noneducator in the unauthorized practice of teaching.
6. Shall not disclose information about colleagues obtained in the course of professional service unless disclosure serves a compelling professional purpose or is required by law.
7. Shall not knowingly make false or malicious statements about a colleague.
8. Shall not accept any gratuity, gift, or favor that might impair or appear to influence professional decisions or action.

Adopted by the NEA 1975 Representative Assembly (NEA 2004).

Figure 31.12 **Financial Information for the National Education Association, Fiscal Year Ending 2003**

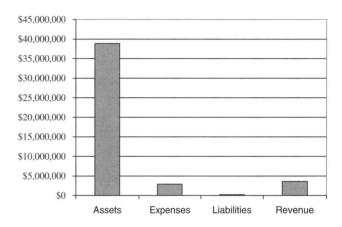

Assets (holdings): $38,854,345
Expenses (amount paid): $2,909,465
Liabilities (amount owed): $226,680
Revenue (income): $3,625,485

Source: IRS (2003).

FINANCIAL INFORMATION

The most recent information filed by NEA indicates that the organization has over $38 million in assets, nearly $3 million in expenses, over $226 thousand in liabilities, and $3.6 million in revenue for the 2002 calendar year (IRS 2003). The actual amounts for assets, expenses, liabilities, and revenue are shown in Figure 31.12. In general, revenues are derived from direct public support through membership dues, program service revenue that includes government fees and contracts, interest on savings and securities, and rental income.

NEA receives a large part of its revenue from membership dues, grants, and the sale of media. In order to obtain membership in the NEA, an individual will become a member at the local, state, and national levels. NEA affiliate organizations are present in over 13,000 local communities in all fifty states. There are three different categories of membership. These include active, student, and retired membership. Membership dues in any of these three categories depend upon the state in which one resides. Therefore, prospective members must contact the NEA state affiliate. Additional information can be obtained online at www.nea.org or at the following address:

NEA, 1201 16th Street NW, Washington, DC 20036–3290.

AMERICAN FEDERATION OF TEACHERS

The American Federation of Teachers (AFT) is the fastest growing affiliate of the American Federation of Labor and Congress of Industrial Organizations (AFL-CIO). The AFT was established in 1916 in Chicago, Illinois, by teacher groups from Chicago, Gary (Indiana), New York, Scranton (Pennsylvania), and Washington, D.C. Since its association with the AFL-CIO, the AFT has been seen as a member of organized labor and clearly linked with the American labor movement. The AFT has approximately 1.3 million members who work in all levels of educational practice. The AFT has more than 3,000 local affiliates nationwide in addition to forty-three state affiliates. The AFT is committed to the field of education and all parties concerned with educational practice in society such as teachers, students, and their families. The AFT mission statement reflects this commitment: "The mission of the American Federation of Teachers, AFL-CIO, is to improve the lives of our members and their families, to give voice to their legitimate professional, economic and social aspirations, to strengthen the institutions in which we work, to improve the quality of the services we provide, to bring together all members to assist and support one another and to promote democracy, human rights and freedom in our union, in our nation and throughout the world" (from the Futures II report adopted at the AFT Convention, July 5, 2000, AFT 2004).

The AFT's organizational structure consists of five divisions: teachers; paraprofessionals and school-related personnel (PSRP); local, state, and federal employees; higher education faculty and staff; and nurses and other healthcare professionals. Along with these divisions, The AFT works on establishing a strong partnership between schools and parents.

CONTRIBUTIONS TO EDUCATION

The AFT was an early supporter of equal rights in education. After its inception, the organization sup-ported the women's suffrage movement, disassociated itself from locals that refused to desegregate, was active in the civil rights movement, and supported democratic principles through its participation in voter registration drives. The AFT also aggressively supported equality in education by fighting against tuition increases in publicly funded institutions, supported increased funding of urban schools, rallied against tuition tax credits, and established criteria for safe working environments (Eaton 1975).

The AFT has worked diligently on the early issues of tenure and academic freedom. Like the NEA, the AFT has served as an important vehicle for educators nationwide, and is deeply involved in a number of national movements both within (e.g., academic freedom, fight against tuition tax credits, equitable funding for urban schools) and outside (e.g., civil rights, the organization's steadfast support for desegregation) the field of education. The AFT was also known for its teacher militancy in supporting walkouts and teacher strikes. These actions sometimes earned the AFT the reputation of a more radical organization than its NEA counterpart. It is also noteworthy that the AFT affiliates supported the first major strike by university professors to take place in the United States. Since that time, the AFT has been extremely active in educational reform. Like the NEA, the AFT also has made several inroads with other organizations by representing healthcare professionals and state and local employees. The organization is actively involved in fostering professional development and hosts numerous conventions for all its members in its five divisions. The AFT has become a powerful voice in the areas of professionalization and accreditation in teacher education. The AFT has been active in promoting academic achievement and excellence as evidenced by its publication "Making Standards Matter" (AFT 2001). This publication identified the progress that states were making in establishing benchmarks for what students should know and be able to do. The AFT was most concerned with having the states establish clear standards and aligning those standards with high-stakes tests.

The AFT sponsors conferences, workshops, and publications that highlight social issues involving educational innovations, healthcare, human rights, the promotion of democracy, and academic standards.

The AFT has been aggressive in the struggle to improve the economic status of teachers. They have been involved in directly supporting their affiliates by providing assistance in helping local teacher associations to negotiate salary schedules, collective bargaining, and establishing educational policies. The AFT is also actively involved in formulating national, state, and local legislative policies in education. One way that this is accomplished is through voluntary member contributions that support the Committee on Political Education (COPE). COPE supports candidates for public office and provides lobbyists to work in state capitals to urge legislation that will improve the lives of AFT members.

The AFT publishes a large number of journals, newsletters, magazines, and other forms of media to address a variety of issues, such as providing basic education statistics, school law, salaries, school programs, school finance, and educational equity, among others. The AFT publishes a quarterly magazine, *American Educator*. With a circulation of nearly 1.3 million, *American Educator* informs readers on current research in the field of education, best practices, assessment, career related matters, and societal issues in education. Other AFT publications include two newspapers: *The American Teacher* (a newspaper on general trends in Pre-Kindergarten through Grade 12); and *AFT On-Campus* (a newspaper having to do with issues in higher education). All three AFT publications address educational issues of interest from both national and international perspectives.

FINANCIAL INFORMATION

The most recent information filed by the AFT indicates that the organization has over $1.8 million in assets, $1.3 million in expenses, over $848 thousand in liabilities, and $1.5 million in revenue for the 2002 calendar year (IRS 2003). The actual amounts for assets, expenses, liabilities, and revenue are shown in Figure 31.13. In general, revenues are derived from direct public support through membership dues, interest on savings and securities, and rental income.

AFT receives a large part of its revenue from membership dues, grants, and the sale of media. In order to obtain membership with the AFT, an individual will become a member at the local level,

Figure 31.13 **Financial Information for the American Federation of Teachers, Fiscal Year Ending 2003**

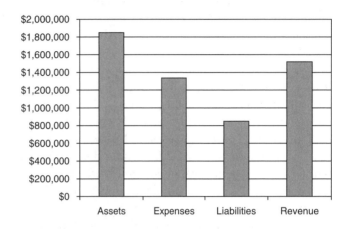

Assets (holdings): $1,849,649
Expenses (amount paid): $1,335,832
Liabilities (amount owed): $848,833
Revenue (income): $1,519,688

Source: IRS (2003).

which will be affiliated with the state and national levels. As stated above, there are forty-three state affiliated organizations and over 3,000 local AFT affiliate organizations. Membership dues will vary depending on the affiliates and the local unions to which members belong. Additional information can be obtained online at www.aft.org or at the following address: AFT, 555 New Jersey Avenue NW, Washington, DC 20001.

AMERICAN EDUCATIONAL RESEARCH ASSOCIATION

The American Educational Research Association (AERA) is the largest educational organization devoted to the research in the field of education in the United States. The AERA was originally formed by eight directors of educational research of urban schools in Cincinnati, Ohio. The organization was established in 1916 in an effort to identify best teaching practices in urban school settings (Owens 1991). However, its current charge is vastly different. As stated in its mission, the AERA "strives to improve the educational process by encouraging scholarly inquiry related to education. AERA offers a comprehensive program of scholarly publications, training, fellowships, and meetings to advance educational research, to disseminate knowledge, and to improve the capacity of the profession to enhance the public good" (AERA 2004). Past presidents of the AERA have included distinguished figures in education such as Benjamin Bloom, Maxine Greene, and Alan Schoenfeld. Recently, AERA reached a membership of 22,000 individuals, most of whom are college faculty in education and the social and behavioral sciences, administrators, educational researchers, and graduate students.

The AERA possesses a vast organizational structure. Its legislative branch, called the Association Council, includes the AERA president, the president-elect, the immediate past president, three members-at-large, the vice presidents of each of the twelve divisions of the organization (see "Contributions to Education"), the chair of the Special Interest Group (SIG) Executive Committee, and a graduate student representative. All members of the Association Council are elected officials.

CONTRIBUTIONS TO EDUCATION

The AERA has promoted issues related to research in all areas of education. The organization consists of twelve divisions, each of which emphasizes a general area in the education field. These divisions cover a broad range of areas: Division A: *Administration*; Division B: *Curriculum Studies*; Division C: *Learning and Instruction*; Division D: *Measurement and Research Methodology*; Division E: *Counseling and Human Development*; Division F: *History and Historiography*; Division G: *Social Context of Education*; Division H: *School Evaluation and Program Development*; Division I: *Education in the Professions*; Division J: *Postsecondary Education*; Division K: *Teaching and Teacher Education*; and Division L: *Educational Policy and Politics*. In addition to these divisions, AERA is comprised of 148 Special Interest Groups (SIGs), which provide opportunities for individual AERA members to meet others with similar interests of study. The AERA accommodates the SIGs at all AERA events, including the annual meeting, and allocates funds for publicity, scheduling of events,

and support staff. The AERA hosts annual meetings that are based on particular educational themes, such as "Demography and Democracy in the Era of Accountability."

The AERA publishes six peer-reviewed journals. Moreover, each of the divisions and SIGs provides numerous newsletters, magazines, and other forms of media to address specific issues of educational research. Among its large number of publications, AERA's flagship journal, *Educational Researcher*, is published nine times per year. The other AERA journals include the *American Educational Research Journal*, *Educational Evaluation and Policy Analysis*, the *Journal of Educational and Behavioral Statistics*, the *Review of Educational Research*, and the *Review of Research in Education*.

FINANCIAL INFORMATION

The most recent information filed by AERA indicates that the organization has over $15.4 million in assets, nearly $6.7 million in expenses, over $1.7 million in liabilities, and $6.4 million in revenue for the 2002 calendar year (IRS 2003). The actual amounts for assets, expenses, liabilities, and revenue are shown in Figure 31.14. In general, revenues are derived from direct public support through membership dues, program service revenue that includes government fees and contracts, interest on savings and securities, and rental income.

AERA receives most of its revenue from membership dues, grants, and the sale of media. In order to obtain membership in the AERA, an individual will become a member at the national level, at which point the individual may wish to join a special interest group (SIG). Memberships are divided into two types: voting members and nonvoting members. Voting member dues are $110 annually and include the *Educational Researcher*, a subscription to one of the five other journals, and a newsletter from one of the twelve divisions. Voting members must demonstrate the equivalent of a master's degree or higher in an educationally related field. Other voting members include individuals who have been dues-paying members for twenty consecutive years. These individuals, referred to as "emeritus" members, pay nothing. Nonvoting members include associates, who do not demonstrate the equivalent of a master's degree in an educa-

Figure 31.14 **Financial Information for the American Educational Research Association, Fiscal Year Ending 2003**

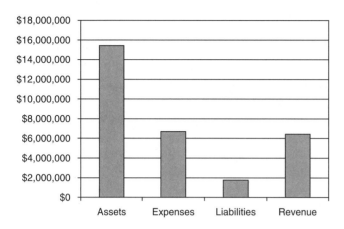

Assets (holdings): $15,444,130
Expenses (amount paid): $6,696,560
Liabilities (amount owed): $1,766,299
Revenue (income): $6,432,144

Source: IRS (2003).

tionally related field, or who have professional status in a non–educationally related field. Associate's dues are also $110 annually. Other non-voting AERA members include graduate students, who pay annual dues of $25 (not to exceed five years), and foreign members, who pay annual dues of $90. Additional information can be obtained online at www.aera.net or at the following address: AERA, 1230 17th Street NW, Washington, DC 20036.

Stephen J. Farenga and Daniel Ness

REFERENCES

American Educational Research Association (AERA). (2004) "AERA 2004–2005 SIG Membership Dues." Available at www.aera .net/uploadedFiles/SIGs/SIGForm.pdf.

American Federation of Teachers (AFT). (2001) *Making Standards Matter: A Fifty State Report on Efforts to Implement a Standards-Based System.* Washington, DC: AFT. Available at www.aft.org/pubs-reports/downloads/teachers/msm2001.pdf.

———. (2004) From the Futures II report adopted at the AFT Convention, July 5, 2000. Available at www.aft.org.

Eaton, William Edward. (1975) *The American Federation of Teachers, 1916–1961: A History of the Movement.* Carbondale, IL: University of Southern Illinois Press.

Internal Revenue Service (IRS). (2003). *Form 990.* Cincinnati, OH: Internal Revenue Service.

National Education Association (NEA). (2004) *About the National Education Association.* Washington, DC: NEA. Available at www.nea.org.

Owens, Hon. Major R. (1991) "American Educational Research Association Celebrates Its 75th Anniversary." *Extension Remarks: Hon. Major R. Owens in the House of Representatives* (March 22). Available at http://thomas.loc.gov/cgi-bin/query/z?r102:E22MR1–645.

EDUCATIONAL TESTING ORGANIZATIONS

Educational testing organizations include associations that are in the business of test creation, development, and assessment. This entry includes two of the largest organizations in the field. They are the College Entrance Examination Board (the College Board) and the Educational Testing Service (ETS). These organizations vary in size, contributions to the field of test development, and financial status. Both the College Board and ETS are perhaps best known for the development, distribution, administration, and assessment of well-known high-stakes tests, for example, the Scholastic Achievement (formerly "Aptitude") Test (SAT) and the Graduate Record Examination (GRE), which are given throughout the world, as well as numerous subject specific tests.

COLLEGE ENTRANCE EXAMINATION BOARD

The College Entrance Examination Board (College Board) is a national nonprofit membership association founded in 1900. The membership includes more than 4,700 schools, colleges, universities, and other educational organizations. It also serves more than 3.5 million students, over 23,000 high schools, and 3,500 colleges and universities. The College Board functions as a placement organization for prospective freshman who wish to attend college. The organization owns a number of selective educational programs designed to measure the achievement of students. The College Board's mission is "to connect students to college success and opportunity." The College Board suggests that its placement tests provide a reciprocal relationship between the college applicant and the colleges to which the applicant applies. It does so in the following ways: "as a way to compare yourself with students already attending the colleges you're considering; another way to show what you have achieved throughout your academic life; a way to compare you with others applying for admission and with their currently enrolled students; a fair, standardized way for admission staff to make important decisions about the likelihood of your being a successful, contributing member of their freshman class" (College Board 2001, 8).

CONTRIBUTIONS TO EDUCATION

The early contributions to education from the College Board were done in collaboration with the Educational Testing Service (ETS). ETS developed the test questions and managed the scoring for the College Board SAT examinations. Recently, the College Board contracted with the publishing firm Pearson NCS to grade the new writing sample that was part of the new SAT in the spring of 2005. In addition to its widely known reputation in administering college entrance examinations, the College Board sponsors a variety of workshops for curricular development, professional programs for teacher development, guidance counselors, and financial aid officers.

The College Board is best known for creating and designing pre-college and college entrance examinations. The most well-known tests that the College Board has created are the Advanced Placement (AP) Program®, the Scholastic Achievement Test (SAT)®, and the Preliminary Scholastic Assessment Test/National Merit Scholarship Qualifying Test (PSAT/NMSQT)®. The College Board publications include information on a wide variety of college related information from financial aid to guidance and admission requirements of select colleges. Other publications are designed to prepare applicants with sample questions that would be found in their selected examination. Students may also find a great deal of information on its website. A selection of College Board publications include *Campus Visits and College Interviews,* the *College Handbook,* the *College Board Guide to High Schools, College Cost and Financial Aid,* the *International Student Handbook, 10 Real SATs, SAT II: Subject Tests,* and *Index of Majors and Graduate Degrees.*

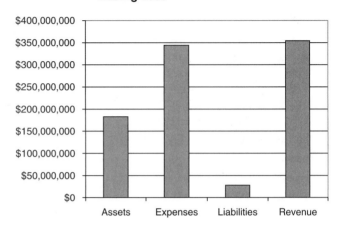

Figure 31.15 **Financial Information for the College Entrance Examination Board, Fiscal Year Ending 2003**

Assets (holdings): $182,933,721
Expenses (amount paid): $344,033,000
Liabilities (amount owed): $28,423,752
Revenue (income): $354,434,560

Source: IRS (2003).

FINANCIAL INFORMATION

The most recent information filed by the College Board indicates that the organization has nearly $183 million in assets, over $344 million in expenses, $28.4 million in liabilities, and $354 million in revenue for the 2002 calendar year (IRS 2003). The actual amounts for assets, expenses, liabilities, and revenue are shown in Figure 31.15. In general, revenues are derived from test applicant registration fees, test development fees, consulting fees, and test processing fees.

Additional information can be obtained online at www.collegeboard.com or at the following address: College Board, 45 Columbus Avenue, New York, NY 10023.

EDUCATIONAL TESTING SERVICE

The Educational Testing Service (ETS) is the largest producer and administrator of standardized tests in the world. During the 1940s, the well-known Harvard University president, James Bryant Conant, was responsible for creating the rationale for an autonomous and research based testing organization like ETS. Founded in 1947, ETS was formed by three organizations—American Council on Education, the Carnegie Foundation for the Advancement of Teaching, and the College Entrance Examination Board—that identified what they believed to be their most effective testing tools and equipment. The primary architect of the present-day ETS was Henry Chauncey, who had originally designed tests for the purpose of easing the transition of soldiers into civilian roles. These three organizations also contributed a good deal of their assets and a number of employees to create ETS.

CONTRIBUTIONS TO EDUCATION

ETS, as well as other educational organizations, often associate educational quality with test-taking performance. This observation is clear in the organization's mission statement and vision statement. ETS's mission is to "advance quality and equity in learning worldwide" and their vision is to expand their mission to a worldwide level. In fact, in their vision statement, ETS wishes to become a "global leader" in the areas of testing and research in education and related issues.

ETS has developed a wide variety of assessments used by states for teacher certification and licensure. The organization administers 144 different tests in this area alone (ETS 1999; National Research Council 2001). ETS offers paper and pencil and computer-based versions of its basic skills tests. They provide 126 different subject-matter tests covering over fifty different subject areas.

ETS has a large stake in the testing of teachers. Its examinations are widely used at the initial and professional levels of teacher licensing. The initial level tests are designed to identify candidates with the appropriate knowledge and skills that are required for effective performance prior to entering the profession. As part of the teaching and licensing of beginning teachers, basic skills, general knowledge, subject matter knowledge, pedagogical knowledge, and subject specific pedagogical knowledge have been developed by ETS, and may be required on an individual basis, depending on the state in which one resides.

These professional assessments are designed to measure the abilities of initial and professional levels of knowledge and skills of teachers. The Praxis series contains three components: Praxis I includes

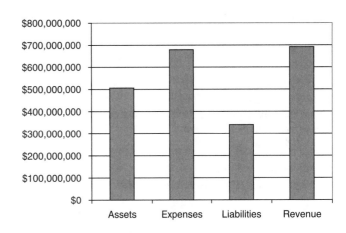

Figure 31.16 **Financial Information for the Educational Testing Service, Fiscal Year Ending 2003**

Assets (holdings): $506,134,835
Expenses (amount paid): $678,910,634
Liabilities (amount owed): $340,048,993
Revenue (income): $691,882,210

Source: IRS (2003).

Academic Skills Assessments; Praxis II includes Subject Assessments in a specialty area, Professional Knowledge, and Core Battery tests, the Principles of Learning and Teaching (PPLT), and the Multiple Subject Assessment for Teachers (MSAT); Praxis III includes Classroom Performance Assessment.

FINANCIAL INFORMATION

The most recent information filed by ETS indicates that the organization has over $506 million in assets, $678 million in expenses, $340 million in liabilities, and nearly $700 million in revenue for the 2002 calendar year (IRS 2003). The actual amounts for assets, expenses, liabilities, and revenue are shown in figure 31.16. In general, revenues are derived from test applicant registration fees, test development fees, consulting fees, and test processing fees.

Additional information can be obtained online at www.ets.org or at the following address: Educational Testing Service, Rosedale Road, Princeton, NJ 08541.

Stephen J. Farenga and Daniel Ness

REFERENCES

College Board. (2001) *College Handbook*, 38th Edition. New York: College Board.

———. (2004) *College Board: Connect to College Success.* New York: College Entrance Examination Board. Available at www.collegeboard.com.

Educational Testing Service (ETS). (1999) *Validity for Licensing Tests.* Brochure. Princeton, NJ: ETS, Teaching and Learning Division.

——— . (2004) *About the Educational Testing Service.* Princeton, NJ: ETS. Available at www.ets.org.

Internal Revenue Service. (2003) *Form 990.* Cincinnati, OH: Internal Revenue Service.

Lewin, Tamar. (2004) "An Evolving Relationship, Kept Together for the Sake of the Students." *New York Times* (March 3), B8.

National Research Council. (2001) *Testing Teacher Candidates: The Role of Licensure Tests in Improving Teacher Quality.* Washington, DC: National Academy Press.

NATIONAL CERTIFICATION AND ACCREDITATION ORGANIZATIONS

The role of accreditation in teacher education in the early days (c. 1940s–1950s) did not have as strong an impact on the training of teachers and educational professionals as it does today. Prior to 1954, the year that the National Council for Accreditation of Teacher Education (NCATE) was established, institutions of higher education that solely trained teachers (also known as normal schools) were, for the most part, accredited by legislative agencies that dealt primarily with the training of teachers. By the end of the Second World War, legislative organizations agreed to include any liberal arts and science college or university with programs or schools of education. NCATE, formed by five organizations associated with college and university teaching, quickly rose to be the eminent national organization to accredit teacher training programs in institutions of higher education.

By the early 1960s, NCATE maintained a stronghold in this position, and remained the leading accreditor for nearly forty years. By the late 1990s, other organizations had formed—the most prominent of them being the Teacher Education Accreditation Council (TEAC). In addition to the accrediting agencies, other related organizations, particularly associated with the development of standards in education, were formed as a result of the highly controversial publication of *A Nation at Risk* (NCEE 1983). In addition to NCATE and TEAC,

we discuss the origin and development of the National Board for Professional Teaching Standards (NBPTS).

NATIONAL COUNCIL FOR ACCREDITATION OF TEACHER EDUCATION

The National Council for Accreditation of Teacher Education (NCATE) was established in 1954 as a voluntary nonprofit organization in an effort to accredit college and university programs of teacher education in the United States. In its inception, NCATE was recognized as the sole accrediting agency for teacher education institutions. At present, despite its role as the largest accreditor of teacher education preparation, NCATE is one of several accrediting agencies in the United States.

CONTRIBUTIONS TO EDUCATION

Established on November 14, 1952, the founders of NCATE were affiliated with five organizations: the American Association of Colleges for Teacher Education, the Council of Chief State School Officers, the National Association of State Directors of Teacher Education and Certification, the National Education Association, and the National School Boards Association. By 1957, the NCATE structure consisted of a council of nineteen representatives from these organizations (seven from AACTE, one from CCSSO, one from NASDTEC, six from the NEA, and one from NSBA) including three who were appointed by the National Commission on Accrediting. When NCATE assumed its responsibilities of accrediting teacher education institutions on July 1, 1954, it had accepted 275 out of the 284 institutions that were already members of AACTE. By 1961, almost one decade after its inception, NCATE accredited 150 institutions of which 82 were previously denied accreditation and 68 that were granted accreditation. After six years, NCATE accredited 343 institutions in total.

Prior to 2000, NCATE attempted to overhaul its accreditation process. The publication of *A Nation at Risk* (1983) resulted in the formation of standards by nearly all educational organizations, particularly those having to do with subject matter knowledge. NCATE has developed six standards to evaluate the effectiveness of teacher preparation institutions. They are as follows:

NCATE TEACHER PREPARATION STANDARDS

1. Candidate Knowledge, Skills, and Dispositions: This standard refers to the qualities, attributes, and characteristics of the teacher. This includes all matters related to the teacher candidates' professional and pedagogical knowledge of human development and the ability to facilitate learning for all students.

2. Assessment System and Unit Evaluation: This standard refers to the teacher candidates' ability to accurately assess and analyze student learning. From the data gathered, the teacher candidate is expected to make appropriate modifications to instruction, further assessment, and evaluation.

3. Field Experiences and Clinical Practice: This standard refers to the teacher candidates' experience in the field with students. It evaluates teacher candidates on their ability to demonstrate knowledge, skills, and dispositions that are necessary to help all students learn.

4. Diversity: This standard refers to the unit's (educational program's) capacity to provide teacher candidates with the opportunities to work with diverse school faculty, other diverse candidates, and diverse students from preschool to grade 12 schools.

5. Faculty Qualifications: This standard refers to the unit's capacity to provide qualified faculty who can model best professional practices in scholarship, service to the community, and teaching.

6. Unit Governance and Resources: This standard refers to the unit's autonomy in budget, personnel, and leadership. In addition, the unit must provide the appropriate resources and facilities to prepare teacher candidates.

NCATE has established partnerships with forty-eight states, the District of Columbia, and Puerto Rico. The only states that have not established partnerships with the organization are New Hampshire and Vermont.

In the June 2003 "A List of Professionally Accredited Schools, Colleges, and Departments of Education," one of the numerous pages on its website, NCATE lists a total of 552 colleges and universities in the United States and Puerto Rico (NCATE 2003). Most recently, NCATE is seeking to certify international institutions of higher education for their teacher education programs. In 2004, the same list showed an increase of 26 higher education institutions, for a total of 578 institutions accredited by NCATE. This is an approximately 4.7 percent increase in the twelve-month period from June 2003 to May 2004. Of these 26 newly accredited institutions, 7 were from New York, 3 were from Illinois, 2 from both Maryland and Oklahoma, and 1 from Alabama, California, Connecticut, Georgia, Kansas, Louisiana, Missouri, Ohio, South Carolina, Texas, Utah, and Virginia.

FINANCIAL INFORMATION

The most recent information filed by NCATE indicates that the organization has over $1.4 million in assets, $3.6 million in expenses, $760 thousand in liabilities, and over $3.5 million in revenue for the 2002 calendar year (IRS 2003). The actual amounts for assets, expenses, liabilities, and revenue are shown in Figure 31.17. In general, revenues are derived from direct public support through membership dues and assessments, program service revenue including government fees and contracts, interest on savings and securities, and rental income.

In addition to the information supplied by the IRS 990 form, the following are figures that demonstrate how NCATE obtains its financial support (Vergari and Hess 2002). NCATE uses a sliding scale with regard to each institution's annual dues. Depending on the financial status, an accredited department in a college or university pays an annual accreditation fee of somewhere between $1,615 and $3,095. Institutions that are not AACTE members must pay an additional fee of $745 to $1,245 to be a sustaining member of NCATE. NCATE also charges from $3,000 to $8,000 for each five-year visit required for each accredited department to sustain accreditation.

NCATE also charges annual dues from its thirty-

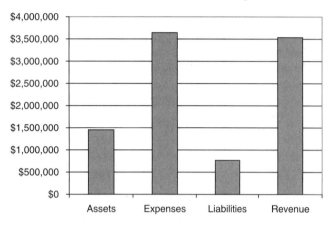

Figure 31.17   **Financial Information for the National Council for the Accreditation of Teacher Education, Fiscal Year Ending 2003**

Assets (holdings): $1,451,126
Expenses (amount paid): $3,646,596
Liabilities (amount owed): $769,085
Revenue (income): $3,536,676

Source: IRS (2003).

three member organizations, also known as specialized professional associations (SPAs). Annual NCATE dues can range from $12,000 for smaller organizations to as much as $250,000 for larger organizations like the National Education Association (NEA). According to Vergari and Hess (2002), NCATE has made an agreement with its member organizations to allow them to play a role in the development and implementation of the NCATE standards.

Additional information can be obtained online at www.ncate.org or at the following address: NCATE, 2010 Massachusetts Avenue NW, Suite 500, Washington, DC 20036–1023.

TEACHER EDUCATION ACCREDITATION COUNCIL

The Teacher Education Accreditation Council (TEAC) is a nonprofit organization that was established in 1997 at the University of Delaware. The organization, however, has two locations—one in Newark, Delaware, and the other in Washington,

DC. TEAC was developed in response to the National Council for the Accreditation of Teacher Education (NCATE) to provide schools of education with an alternative means for obtaining national accreditation. The major philosophical difference between the two accreditation agencies, at the inception of TEAC, was the accreditation of the individual programs (TEAC) as opposed to the accreditation of the unit that houses the educational programs (NCATE).

CONTRIBUTIONS TO EDUCATION

TEAC distinguishes itself from NCATE in a number of ways. First, unlike NCATE, TEAC accredits individual programs and NCATE accredits the units that house the programs and the capacity of each unit to support the program. TEAC has the option of using either national standards or institutionally developed standards. For TEAC accreditation, the individual institution of higher education itself has the autonomy to identify the necessary components and features of what constitutes a satisfactory program. The administrators of TEAC developed three quality principles and a set of standards to assist colleges and universities with educational programs in upholding these principles. The three quality principles are the following:

TEAC Principles and Standards

1. Evidence of student learning: The core of TEAC accreditation is the quality of the evidence the program faculty members provide in support of their claims about their students' learning and understanding of the teacher education curriculum.

2. Valid Assessment of Student Learning: TEAC expects program faculty to provide (1) a rationale justifying its claims that the assessment techniques it uses are reasonable and credible, and (2) evidence documenting the reliability and validity of the assessments.

3. Institutional Learning: TEAC expects that a faculty's decisions about its programs are based on evidence, and that the program has a quality control system that (1) yields reliable evidence

about the program's practices and results, and (2) influences policies and decisionmaking.

The TEAC Standards provide benchmarks that help programs demonstrate that they have met the quality principles. According to TEAC, a "quality program" is "one that has credible evidence that it satisfies the three quality principles" (TEAC 2002). However, TEAC also requires the program faculty to provide evidence that it has the capacity—curriculum, faculty, resources, facilities, publications, student support services, and policies—to support student learning and program quality. This evidence should be independent of student learning and based on some traditional input features of capacity.

The program faculty can make the case that it has a sufficient capacity for quality in any way that meets scholarly standards of evidence; however, TEAC requires that the faculty cover the following basic points in making its case.

1. Quality Control: The faculty must show that it monitors systematically the quality of the program and that the faculty is disposed to act to continuously improve program quality.

2. Evidence of Commitment: The faculty must also provide evidence that the institution is committed to the program. Commitment is most conveniently seen in the evidence of parity of the program within the institution.

3. Unique Capacity: The faculty must also address whatever unique capacity is needed for program quality in professional education. Teacher education programs, for example, have unique features, such as student teaching and clinical courses. The institution and program must provide resources, administrative direction, and facilities for these unique and distinctive features. The program faculty must make a case that overall it has the capacity to offer a quality program.

A program needs to demonstrate that it has the capacity to produce qualified candidates. The standards that measure capacity are included in the following components: Curriculum; Faculty; Facilities, Equip-

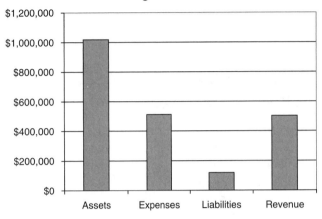

Figure 31.18 **Financial Information for the Teacher Education Accreditation Council, Fiscal Year Ending 2003**

Assets (holdings): $1,018,720
Expenses (amount paid): $513,261
Liabilities (amount owed): $120,080
Revenue (income): $503,346

Source: IRS (2003).

ment, and Supplies; Fiscal and Administrative Services; Student Support Services; Recruiting and Admissions Practices; Academic Calendars, Catalogs, Publications; and Student Feedback.

FINANCIAL INFORMATION

The most recent information filed by TEAC indicates that the organization has over $1 million in assets, $513 thousand in expenses, $120 thousand in liabilities, and over $500 thousand in revenue for the 2002 calendar year (IRS 2003). The actual amounts for assets, expenses, liabilities, and revenue are shown in figure 31.18. In general, revenues are derived from direct public support through membership dues and assessments, program service revenue including government fees and contracts, interest on savings and securities, and rental income.

TEAC receives a large part of its revenue from membership dues and from the periodic review process of institutions of higher education. Individual membership dues are $65 annually. Institutional membership dues are $100 annually. Additional information can be obtained online at www.teac.org

or at the following address: TEAC, One Dupont Circle, Suite 320, Washington, DC 20036–0110.

NATIONAL BOARD FOR PROFESSIONAL TEACHING STANDARDS

The National Board for Professional Teaching Standards (NBPTS) is a nonprofit organization that was established in 1987. The organization was established by both the Carnegie Forum on Education and the Economy's Task Force on Teaching as a Profession as an answer to the government's controversial diatribe *A Nation at Risk* (NCEE 1983), which derided public education in the United States. As stated in the organization's mission, NBPTS seeks "to advance the quality of teaching and learning by: (1) maintaining high and rigorous standards for what accomplished teachers should know and be able to do; (2) providing a national voluntary system certifying teachers who meet these standards; and (3) advocating related education reforms to integrate National Board Certification in American education and to capitalize on the expertise of National Board Certified Teachers" (NBPTS 2004). Professionals who are successful in meeting these demands are nationally certified and believed to represent and reflect the best practices in the field of education.

CONTRIBUTIONS TO EDUCATION

NBPTS's major contribution to education is that it is an organization that has been developed by teachers and for teachers in order to raise the status of teaching to a recognized profession analogous to the status of physicians, attorneys, and certified public accountants. The organization is the first to certify nationally recognized teachers. As stated previously, NBPTS's goal is to identify and recognize teachers who demonstrate knowledge, skills, and dispositions that reflect the five propositions listed below.

NBPTS TEACHER'S PROPOSITION STANDARDS

1. Teachers are Committed to Students and Their Learning.

- Teachers Recognize Individual Differences in Their Students and Adjust Their Practice Accordingly: To respond effectively to individual differences, teachers must know many things about the particular students they teach.
- Teachers Have an Understanding of How Students Develop and Learn: In addition to particular knowledge of their students, teachers use their understanding of individual and social learning theory, and of child and adolescent development theory, to form their decisions about how to teach.
- Teachers Treat Students Equitably: Accomplished teachers are vigilant in ensuring that all pupils receive their fair share of attention, and that biases based on real or perceived ability differences, handicaps or disabilities, social or cultural background, language, race, religion, or gender do not distort relationships between themselves and their students.
- Teachers' Mission Extends Beyond Developing the Cognitive Capacity of Their Students: Teachers are concerned with their students' self-concept, with their motivation, with the effects of learning on peer relationships, and with the development of character, aspiration, and civic virtues.

2. Teachers Know the Subjects They Teach and How to Teach Those Subjects to Students.

- Teachers Appreciate How Knowledge in Their Subjects is Created, Organized and Linked to Other Disciplines: Teachers in command of their subject understand its substance—factual information as well as its central organizing concepts—and the ways in which new knowledge is created, including the forms of creative investigation that characterize the work of scholars and artists.
- Teachers Command Specialized Knowledge of How to Convey a Subject to Students: Accomplished teachers possess "pedagogical content knowledge." Such understanding is the joint product of wisdom about teaching, learning, students, and content.
- Teachers Generate Multiple Paths to Knowledge:

Knowledgeable teachers are aware there is value in both structured and inductive learning.

3. Teachers are Responsible for Managing and Monitoring Student Learning.

- Teachers Call on Multiple Methods to Meet Their Goals: Accomplished teachers know and can employ a variety of generic instructional skills—how to conduct Socratic dialogues, how to lecture, how to oversee small cooperative learning groups.
- Teachers Orchestrate Learning in Group Settings: Teachers know how to manage groups of students. They are responsible for setting forth the social norms by which students and teachers act and interact, helping students learn to adopt appropriate roles and responsibilities for their own learning and that of their peers.
- Teachers Place a Premium on Student Engagement: The National Board Certified teacher understands the ways in which students can be motivated and has strategies to monitor student engagement.
- Teachers Regularly Assess Student Progress: Proficient teachers . . . can judge the relative success of the activities they design. They can track what students are learning (or not learning), as well as what they, as teachers, are learning.
- Teachers Are Mindful of Their Principal Objectives: Teachers know about planning instruction—identifying and elaborating educational objectives, developing activities to help them meet their goals, and drawing upon resources that will serve their purposes.

4. Teachers Think Systematically About Their Practice and Learn from Experience.

- Teachers Are Continually Making Difficult Choices That Test Their Judgment: The demands of teaching often present stiff challenges that do not lend themselves to simple solutions.
- Teachers Seek the Advice of Others and Draw on Education Research and Scholarship to Improve Their Practice: Aware that experience is not always a good teacher, proficient teachers search out other opportunities that will serve to cultivate their own learning.

5. Teachers are Members of Learning Communities.

- Teachers Contribute to School Effectiveness by Collaborating with Other Professionals: The National Board advocates a more proactive and creative role for teachers: engaging them in the analysis and construction of curriculum, in the coordination of instruction, in the professional development of staff and in many other school-site policy decisions fundamental to the creation of highly productive learning communities.
- Teachers Work Collaboratively with Parents: Teachers share with parents the education of the young. They communicate regularly with parents and guardians, listening to their concerns and respecting their perspective, enlisting their support in fostering learning and good habits, informing them of their child's accomplishments and successes, and educating them about school programs.
- Teachers Take Advantage of Community Resources: Professional teachers cultivate knowledge of their school's community as a powerful resource for learning.

FINANCIAL INFORMATION

The most recent information filed by NBPTS indicates that the organization has over $32 million in assets, $59.6 million in expenses, $32.3 million in liabilities, and over $54.8 million in revenue for the 2002 calendar year (IRS 2003). The actual amounts for assets, expenses, liabilities, and revenue are shown in Figure 31.19. In general, revenues are derived from direct public support through membership dues and assessments, program service revenue including government fees and contracts, interest on savings and securities, and rental income.

NBPTS is governed by a board of directors, most of whom are practitioners in the education field. A segment of the organization's income is derived from candidates' applications for national certification, grants from private and government organizations, and sponsorship from other professional organizations.

Figure 31.19 **Financial Information for the National Board for Professional Teaching Standards, Fiscal Year Ending 2002**

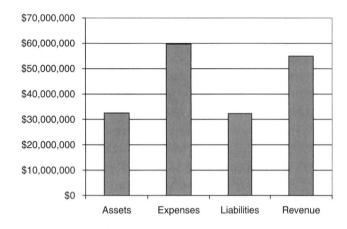

Assets (holdings): $32,485,380
Expenses (amount paid): $59,642,344
Liabilities (amount owed): $32,300,367
Revenue (income): $54,874,883

Source: IRS (2003).

Additional information can be obtained online at www.nbpts.org or at the following address: NBPTS, 1525 Wilson Boulevard, Arlington, VA 22209.

Stephen J. Farenga and Daniel Ness

REFERENCES

Internal Revenue Service (IRS). (2003) *Form 990.* Cincinnati, OH: Internal Revenue Service.

National Commission on Excellence in Education (NCEE). (1983) *A Nation at Risk: The Imperative for Educational Reform.* Washington, DC: NCEE.

National Board for Professional Teaching Standards (NBPTS). (2004) *About NBPTS.* Available at www.nbpts.org/about/index.cfm.

National Council for the Accreditation of Teacher Education (NCATE). (2003) "A List of Professionally Accredited Schools, Colleges, and Departments of Education." Washington, DC: NCATE.

Teacher Education Accreditation Council (TEAC). (2002) *About TEAC.* Available at www.teac.org/educaleadership/index.asp.

Vergari, Sandra, and Frederick M. Hess. (2002) The accreditation game. *Education Next* (Fall): 48–57.

INDEX